"All you've got to do is decide to go and the hardest part is over.

So go!"

TONY WHEELER, COFOUNDER – LONELY PLANET

THIS EDITION WRITTEN AND RESEARCHED BY

Alison Bing,
John A Vlahides, Sara Benson

Contents

Plan Your Trip 4

Explore San Francisco 42

Understand San Francisco 243

Survival Guide 271

San Francisco Maps 296

MITCHELL FUNK / GETTY IMAGES ©

THOMAS WINZ / GETTY IMAGES ©

(left) Ferry Building (p73)

(above) Haight St (p183)

(right) Parrot at Telegraph Hill (p112)

MICHAEL FILIPPOFF / 500PX©

The Marina, Fisherman's Wharf & the Piers
p46

North Beach & Chinatown
p110

Nob Hill, Russian Hill & Fillmore
p129

Downtown, Civic Center & SoMa
p71

The Haight, NoPa & Hayes Valley
p181

Golden Gate Park & the Avenues
p197

The Mission & Potrero Hill
p146

The Castro & Noe Valley
p170

Welcome to San Francisco

Grab your coat and a handful of glitter, and enter the land of fog and fabulousness. So long, inhibitions; hello, San Francisco.

Natural Highs

If California is one grand, sweeping gesture, a long arm cradling the Pacific, then San Francisco, that seven-by-seven-mile peninsula, is a forefinger pointing upwards. Take this as a hint to look up: you'll notice San Francisco's crooked Victorian rooflines, wind-sculpted treetops and fog tumbling over the Golden Gate Bridge. Heads are perpetually in the clouds atop San Francisco's 43 hills. Cable cars provide easy access to Russian and Nob Hills, and splendid panoramas reward the slog up to Coit Tower – but the most exhilarating highs are earned on Telegraph Hill's garden-lined stairway walks and windswept hikes around Land's End.

Food & Drink

Every available Bay Area–invented technology is needed to make dinner decisions in this city, which has the most restaurants and farmers markets per capita in North America, supplied by pioneering local organic farms. San Francisco set the gold standard for Wild West saloons, but drinking was driven underground in the 1930s with Prohibition. Today San Francisco celebrates its speakeasies and vintage saloons – and with Wine Country and local distillers providing a steady supply of America's finest hooch, the West remains wild.

Neighborhood Microclimates

Microclimates add magic realism to San Francisco days: when it's drizzling in the outer reaches of Golden Gate Park, it may be sunny in the Mission. A few degrees' difference between neighborhoods grants permission for salted caramel ice cream in Dolores Park, or a hasty retreat to tropical heat inside California Academy of Sciences' rainforest dome. This town will give you goose bumps one minute, and warm you to the core the next.

Outlandish Notions

Consider permission permanently granted to be outlandish: other towns may surprise you, but in San Francisco you will surprise yourself. Good times and social revolutions tend to start here, from manic gold rushes to blissful hippie be-ins. If there's a skateboard move yet to be busted, a technology still unimagined, a poem left unspoken or a green scheme untested, chances are it's about to happen here. Yes, right now. This town has lost almost everything in earthquakes and dot-com gambles, but never its nerve.

Why I Love San Francisco

By Alison Bing, Author

On my way from Hong Kong to New York, I stopped in San Francisco for a day. I walked from the Geary St art galleries up Grant Ave to Waverly Place, just as temple services were starting. The fog was scented with incense and roast duck. In the basement of City Lights bookstore, near the Muckraking section, I noticed a sign painted by a 1920s cult: 'I am the door.' It's true. San Francisco is the threshold between East and West, body and soul, fact and fiction. That was 20 years ago. I'm still here. You have been warned.

For more about our authors, see p328.

Above: Haight St (p183)

San Francisco's Top 10

1

Golden Gate Bridge *(p55)*

1 Other suspension bridges impress with engineering, but none can touch the Golden Gate Bridge for showmanship. On sunny days it transfixes crowds with its radiant glow – thanks to 25 daredevil painters, who reapply 1000 gallons of International Orange paint weekly. When afternoon fog rolls in, the bridge performs its disappearing act: now you see it, now you don't and, abracadabra, it's sawn in half. Return tomorrow for its dramatic unveiling, just in time for the morning commute.

The Marina, Fisherman's Wharf & the Piers

Golden Gate Park *(p199)*

2 You may have heard that San Francisco has a wild streak a mile wide, but it also happens to be 4.5 miles long. Golden Gate Park lets San Franciscans do what comes naturally: roller-discoing, drum-circling, petting starfish, sniffing orchids and racing bison toward the Pacific. It's hard to believe these 1017 acres of lush terrain were once just scrubby sand dunes, and that San Franciscans have successfully preserved this stretch of green since 1866, ousting casinos and resorts. Today, everything San Francisco really needs is here: inspiration, nature and microbrewed beer at the Beach Chalet. BELOW: JAPANESE TEA GARDEN (P201)

Golden Gate Park & the Avenues

PRAKASH BRAGGS / EYEEM / GETTY IMAGES ©

HSING-WEN HSU / GETTY IMAGES ©

3

4

Soup
chickpea and lentil
soup
meat/poultry larder
pork tenderloin marinated in nettles and basil
marrow bones
pork meatloaf
duck legs with dried cherries figs and apricots
harvested seafood
sardines
assorted sweets
lemon meringue tart
cherry clafoutis
all cake slices are 5 each
almond cake
pluot gateau basque
cardamom rose cake
caramel and sea salt tartlet
frais de bois tartlet
crispy meringues
canele de bordeaux
basil panna cotta
saturdays only, after 10am
english muffins
anson mills cornbread
savory kugelhopf

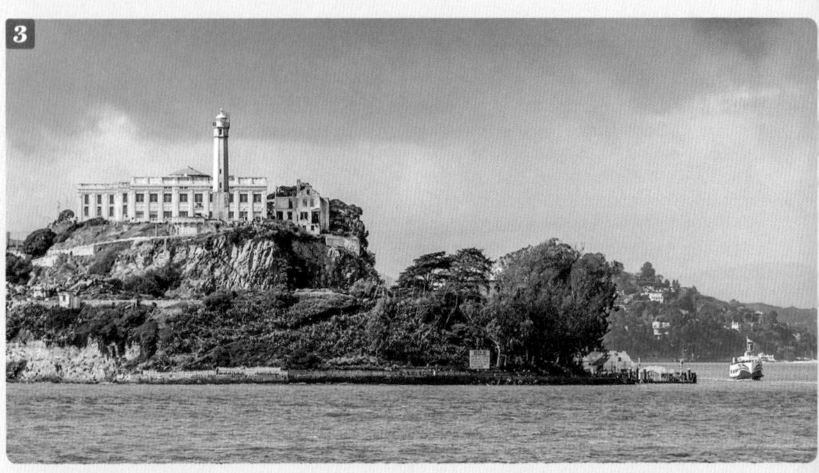

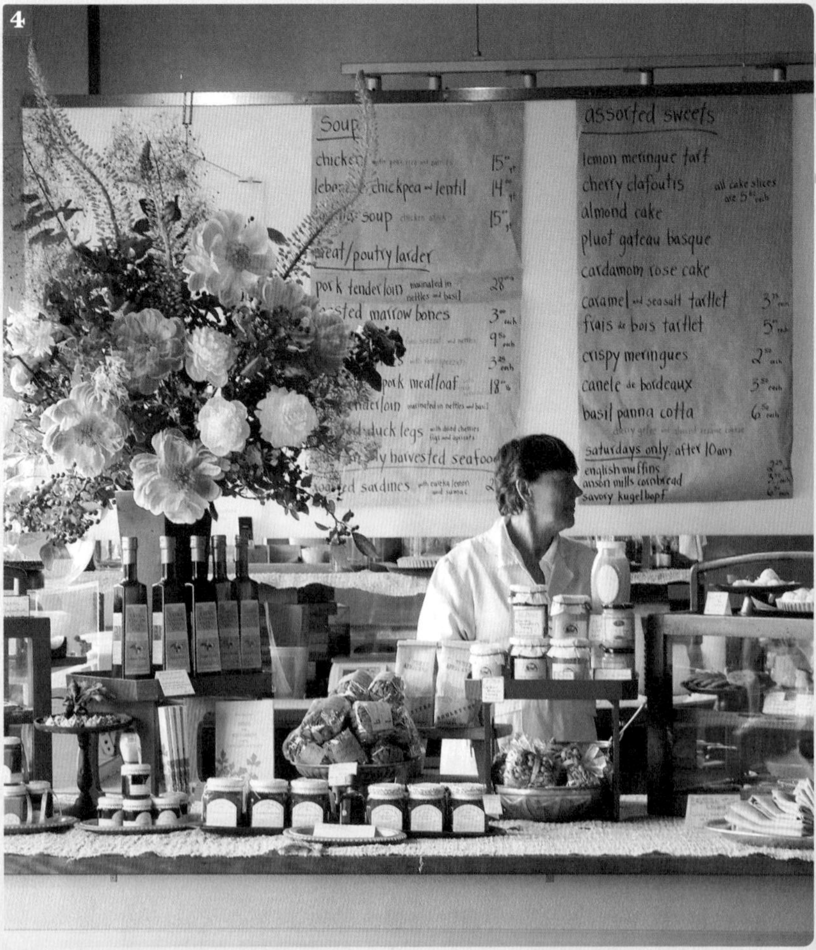

Alcatraz *(p48)*

3 From its 19th-century founding (to hold Civil War deserters and Native American dissidents) to its closure by Bobby Kennedy in 1963, Alcatraz was America's most notorious jail. No prisoner is known to have escaped alive – but after entering D-Block solitary and hearing carefree city life humming across the bay, the 1.25-mile swim through riptides seems worth a shot. For maximum chill factor, book the spooky twilight jailhouse tour. On the return ferry to San Francisco, freedom never felt so good.

The Marina, Fisherman's Wharf & the Piers

Ferry Building *(p73)*

4 Global food trends start in San Francisco and to see what's next on the menu, head to the Ferry Building, the city's monument to local, sustainable food. Don't miss Saturday farmers markets here, when star chefs trawl stalls for rare heirloom varietals and foodie babies blissfully teethe on organic California peaches. Picnic on Pier 2 with food-truck finds, feet dangling over the sparkling bay – and let lunch and life exceed expectations. LEFT: BOULETTE'S LARDER (P92)

Downtown, Civic Center & SoMa

Mission Murals *(p150)*

5 When modern-art power couple Diego Rivera and Frida Kahlo rekindled their romance in San Francisco during the 1930s, an inspired Rivera created some mural masterpieces. San Franciscans have been captivated by the Mexican artist's bold colors and fearless social commentary ever since, and today the Mission district is an urban-art showstopper, featuring more than 400 murals. Balmy Alley has some of the oldest, while 24th Street and the landmark San Francisco Women's Building are covered with glorious portrayals of community pride and political dissent. ABOVE: JOEL BERGNER'S 2004 *UN PASADO QUE AÚN VIVE* IN BALMY ALLEY (P148)

The Mission & Potrero

The History-Making Castro *(p170)*

6 Somewhere over the rainbow crosswalk, you'll realize you've officially arrived in the Castro district. For more than 50 years this has been the most out and proud neighborhood on the planet, as you'll discover walking Castro Street's LGBT walk of fame on the way to showtime at the historic Castro Theatre. Learn more at America's first LGBT History Museum, and join in every June at San Francisco's month-long, million-strong Pride celebrations. BELOW: CASTRO THEATRE (P172)

The Castro & Noe Valley

Cable Cars *(p86)*

7 Carnival rides can't compare to cable cars, San Francisco's vintage public transit. Novices slide into strangers' laps (cable cars were invented in 1873, long before seatbelts), but regulars just grip the leather hand-straps, lean back and ride downhill slides like pro surfers. Follow their lead and you'll soon master the San Francisco stance and conquer the city's hills without breaking a sweat.

Downtown, Civic Center & SoMa

6

Showtime in Civic Center *(p101)*

8 Jazz, classical, opera, Broadway – no matter what you call entertainment, you'll be shouting 'encore' around San Francisco City Hall. The cool kid on the block is SFJAZZ Center, America's biggest jazz venue and global talent magnet. Grammy-award-winning San Francisco Symphony performs edge-of-your-seat classical concerts, while divas at San Francisco Opera belt out arias, like they have since the Gold Rush. American Conservatory Theater has expanded its repertoire to Civic Center's Strand Theater, so you can count on San Francisco to bring the drama. LEFT: ESPERANZA SPALDING PERFORMANCE AT SFJAZZ CENTER (P192)

☆ ***Downtown, Civic Center & SoMa***

Barbary Coast Nights *(p125)*

9 In the mid-19th century, you could start a San Francisco bar crawl with smiles and 10¢ whiskey and end up two days later involuntarily working on a vessel bound for Patagonia. Now that double-crossing barkeep Shanghai Kelly is happily no longer a danger to drinkers, revelers can relax at North Beach's once-notorious Barbary Coast saloons. These days you can pick your own poison: historically correct cocktails, cult California wines and/or enough micro-brewed beer and pizza to keep you snoring to Patagonia and back.

North Beach & Chinatown

10

Coit Tower *(p112)*

10 Wild parrots might mock your progress up Telegraph Hill, but they can't expect to keep scenery like this to themselves. Filbert St Steps pass cliffside cottage gardens to reach SF's monument to independent thinking: Coit Tower. Fire-fighting heiress Lillie Hitchcock Coit commissioned this deco monument honoring fire-fighters, and muralists captured 1930s San Francisco in freshly restored lobby frescoes. Coit Tower's paintings and panoramic viewing platform show San Francisco at its best: a city of broad perspectives, outlandish and inspiring.

North Beach & Chinatown

What's New

SFMOMA Extension

San Francisco's horizons just got broader – doors open to a half-billion-dollar expansion in 2016 at San Francisco Museum of Modern Art (SFMOMA; p79), showcasing a new collection of 1100 modern masterworks.

24th St Paper Trail

Even Silicon Valley techies unplug and go analog in the Mission on 24th St, with member-supported book collectives and galleries showcasing works on paper.

Dogpatch Creative Corridor

Hop on the T streetcar to 22nd St to discover arts workshops, local designers, wineries, the Museum of Craft & Design (p155) and (oh yes) chocolate factories.

Dragstravaganzas

San Francisco has entertained in drag since the Gold Rush, and Jose Sarria ran for city government in drag back in 1961 – now SF does drag night and day at Oasis shows (p103), Castro Theatre (p178) movie spoofs and historical Drag Me Along Tours (p127).

Maker/hackerspaces

The ultimate SF souvenir is a freshly acquired DIY skill, whether that's leather tooling at Workshop (p196), app-making at Mission hackerspaces or taxidermy at Paxton Gate (p167).

Comedy Comeback

Comic geniuses like Woody Allen and Lenny Bruce emerged from North Beach's underground in the '60s, and Punch Line (p102) and Cobb's Comedy Club (p127) launched talents like Ellen Degeneres and Chris Rock. Now bars citywide are hosting comedy nights, and new clubs like Doc's Lab (p127) and Oasis are doing their bit to keep San Francisco outrageous (p103).

Potrero Flats Galleries

Potrero's Design District is branching out from sofas into art, with some of SF's best contemporary art galleries taking up residence around nonprofit arts hubs SOMArts (p149) and SF Center for the Book (p169).

Local food hubs

If you're traveling with a pack of picky eaters, never fear – there's something for everyone at local-food hubs SoMa StrEat Food Park (p93), Twitter HQ's new ground-floor Marketplace (p87), The Hall (p91), and the mother of all local, sustainable food halls: SF's Ferry Building (p73).

Green Rules

America's greenest city already has mandatory composting and recycling citywide, and now bags will cost you 10¢ at stores and restaurants – a fine excuse to score a souvenir tote-bag.

49ers at Levi's Stadium

Technically San Francisco's NFL team isn't in SF anymore – but the '49ers (p168) have definitely raised their game with their new high-tech, low-impact stadium 38 miles south of the city.

For more recommendations and reviews, see **lonelyplanet.com/usa/san-francisco**

Need to Know

For more information, see Survival Guide (p271)

Currency
US dollar ($)

Language
English

Visas
The US Visa Waiver program allows nationals of 38 countries to enter the US without a visa.

Money
ATMs widely available; credit cards accepted at most hotels, stores and restaurants. Many farmers market stalls and food trucks and some bars are cash-only.

Cell Phones
Most US cell phones (apart from the iPhone) operate on CDMA, not the European standard GSM; check compatibility with your phone service provider.

Time
Pacific Standard Time (GMT/UTC minus eight hours)

Tourist Information
SF Visitor Information Center (Map p304; ☎415-391-2000; www.sanfrancisco.travel; lower level, Hallidie Plaza, Market & Powell Sts; ⏰9am-5pm Mon-Fri, to 3pm Sat & Sun; Powell-Mason, Powell-Hyde, M Powell St, B Powell St) Muni Passports, activities deals, culture and event calendars.

Daily Costs

Budget: up to $150
- Dorm bed: $30–$50
- Burrito: $6–$9
- Food-truck dishes: $5–$10
- Mission & Coit Tower murals: free
- Live music or comedy in a Mission or North Beach club: free–$15
- Castro Theatre show: $11

Midrange: $150–$350
- Motel, downtown hotel or home-share: $125–$180
- Ferry Building meal: $15–$40
- Mission share-plates meal: $20–$50
- Thursday Exploratorium After Dark/Academy of Sciences NightLife: $15/12
- Symphony rush tickets: $20
- Muni Passport: $17

Top End: more than $350
- Boutique hotel: $180–$380
- Chef's tasting menu: $60–$228
- City Pass (Muni, cable cars plus four attractions): $94
- Alcatraz night tour: $37
- Opera orchestra seats: $90–$135

Advance Planning

Two months before Book your reservations at Coi, Chez Panisse or French Laundry; start walking to build stamina for Coit Tower climbs and Mission bar crawls.

Three weeks before Book Alcatraz tour, Chinatown History Tour or Precita Eyes Mission Mural Tour.

One week before Search for tickets to American Conservatory Theater, SF Symphony or SF Opera – and find out what else is on next weekend.

Useful Websites

SFGate (www.sfgate.com) *San Francisco Chronicle* news and event listings.

7x7 (www.7x7.com) Trend-spotting SF restaurants, bars and style.

Craigslist (http://sfbay.craigslist.org) SF-based source for jobs, dates and free junk.

Lonely Planet (www.lonelyplanet.com/san-francisco) Destination information, hotel bookings and a traveler forum.

WHEN TO GO

June and July bring fog and chilly 55°F (13°C) weather to SF; August, September and October are best for warm weather, street fairs and harvest cuisine.

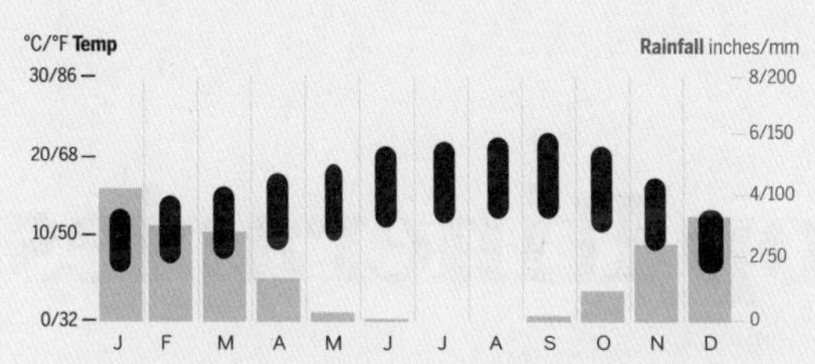

Arriving in San Francisco

San Francisco Airport (SFO) Fast rides to downtown SF on BART cost $8.65; door-to-door shuttle vans cost $17 to $20; express bus fare to Temporary Transbay Terminal is $5; taxis cost $40 to $55.

Oakland International Airport (OAK) Catch BART from the airport to downtown SF ($10.05); take a shared van to downtown SF for $30 to $40; or pay $60 to $75 for a taxi to SF destinations.

Temporary Transbay Terminal Greyhound buses arrive/depart downtown SF's temporary depot (until 2017) at Howard and Main Sts.

Emeryville Amtrak station (EMY) Located outside Oakland, this depot serves west coast and nationwide train routes; Amtrak runs free shuttles to/from San Francisco's Ferry Building, Caltrain, Civic Center and Fisherman's Wharf.

For much more on **arrival** see p272.

Getting Around

For Bay Area transit options, departures and arrivals, call ☎511 or check www.511.org. A detailed Muni Street & Transit Map is available free online.

- **Cable cars** Frequent, slow and scenic, from 6am to 1am daily. Single rides cost $7; for frequent use, get a Muni Passport ($17 per day).
- **Muni streetcar and bus** Reasonably fast but schedules vary wildly by line; infrequent after 9pm. Fares cost $2.25.
- **BART** High-speed transit to East Bay, Mission St, SFO and Millbrae, where it connects with Caltrain.
- **Taxi** Fares cost about $2.75 per mile; meters start at $3.50.

For much more on **getting around** see p273.

Sleeping

San Francisco offers stylish rooms at a price: $150 to $350 midrange, plus 16.25% downtown hotel tax (hostels exempt) and $35 to $50 for overnight parking. Some downtown hotels cost less, but proceed with caution: west of Mason is the sketchy, depressing Tenderloin. Motels are better options for parking, and hostels offer value for solo travelers but no privacy.

Useful Websites

- **B&B San Francisco** (www.bbsf.com) Personable, privately owned B&Bs and neighborhood inns.
- **Hotel Tonight** (www.hoteltonight.com) SF-based hotel search app offering discount last-minute bookings.
- **Airbnb** (www.airbnb.com) SF-based app offering short-term home-sharing and vacation rentals.
- **Lonely Planet** (www.lonelyplanet.com/usa/san-francisco/hotels) Expert author reviews, user feedback and a booking engine.

For much more on **sleeping** see p232.

Top Itineraries

Day One

Telegraph Hill & Waterfront (p110 & p46)

Grab a leather strap on the **Powell-Mason cable car** and hold on: you're in for hills and thrills. Hop off at **Washington Square Park**, where parrots squawk encouragement for your hike up to **Coit Tower** for WPA murals and giddy, 360-degree panoramas. Take scenic **Filbert Street Steps** to the **Embarcadero** and wander across Fog Bridge to explore the freaky Tactile Dome at the **Exploratorium**.

Lunch Try local oysters and Dungeness crab at the Ferry Building (p73).

Alcatraz & North Beach (p48 & p110)

Catch your pre-booked ferry to **Alcatraz**, where D-block solitary raises goose bumps and library books were censored for romance and curse-words. Make your island prison break, taking in **Golden Gate Bridge** views on the ferry ride back. Take the Powell-Mason cable car to North Beach, where you can read freely at free-speech landmark **City Lights** and mingle with San Francisco's freest spirits at the **Beat Museum**.

Dinner Reserve ahead for North Beach's best pasta at Cotogna (p88).

North Beach (p110)

Since you just escaped prison, you're tough enough to handle too-close-for-comfort comics at **Cobb's Comedy Club**, or razor-sharp satire at **Beach Blanket Babylon**. Toast the wildest night in the west with potent Pisco sours at **Comstock Saloon** or spiked cappuccinos at **Tosca**.

Day Two

Chinatown (p110)

Take the **California cable car** to pagoda-topped Grant St for an eye-opening **Red Blossom** tea tasting, then a jaw-dropping history of Chinatown at **Chinese Historical Society of America**. Wander temple-lined **Waverly Place** and notorious **Ross Alley** to find your fortune at **Golden Gate Fortune Cookie Company**.

Lunch Hail dim sum carts for dumplings at City View (p124).

Fisherman's Wharf (p46)

To cover the waterfront, take the **Powell-Hyde cable car** past zigzagging **Lombard St** to **Maritime National Historical Park**, where you can see what it was like to stow away on a schooner. Save the world from Space Invaders at **Musée Mécanique**, or enter underwater stealth mode inside a real WWII submarine: **USS Pampanito**. Watch sea lions cavort as the sun fades over **Pier 39**, then hop onto the vintage **F-line streetcar**.

Dinner Inspired NorCal fare at Rich Table (p187) satisfies and surprises.

Hayes Valley (p181)

Trawl Hayes Valley boutiques before your concert at **San Francisco Symphony** or **SFJAZZ Center**, and toast your good fortune at **Hotel Biron**.

The Embarcadero and the Bay Bridge

Day Three

Golden Gate Park (p197)

Hop the N Judah to Golden Gate Park to see carnivorous plants enjoying insect breakfasts at the **Conservatory of Flowers** and dahlias wet with dew in the **Dahlia Garden**. Follow Andy Goldsworthy's artful sidewalk fault lines to find Oceanic masks and faultless tower-top views inside the **MH de Young Museum**, then take a walk on the wild side in the rainforest dome of the **California Academy of Sciences**. Enjoy a moment of Zen with green tea at the **Japanese Tea Garden** and bliss out in the secret redwood grove at the **San Francisco Botanical Garden**.

Lunch Visit Outerlands (p207) for artisan grilled cheese and organic soup.

The Richmond (p197)

Beachcomb **Ocean Beach** up to the **Beach Chalet** to glimpse 1930s WPA murals celebrating Golden Gate Park. Follow the **Coastal Trail** past **Sutro Baths** and **Land's End** for **Golden Gate Bridge** vistas and priceless paper artworks at **Legion of Honor**.

Dinner Organic Cal-Moroccan feasts satisfy cravings at Aziza (p205).

Japantown (p129)

Psychedelic posters and top acts make for rock-legendary nights at the **Fillmore**.

Day Four

The Mission (p146)

Wander 24th St past mural-covered bodegas to **Balmy Alley**, where the Mission muralist movement began in the 1970s. Stop for a 'secret breakfast' (bourbon and cornflakes) ice cream sundae at **Humphry Slocombe**, then head up Valencia to **Ritual Coffee Roasters**. Pause for pirate supplies and Fish Theater at **826 Valencia** and duck into **Clarion Alley**, the Mission's outdoor graffiti-art gallery. See San Francisco's first building, Spanish adobe **Mission Dolores**, and visit the memorial to native Ohlone who built it.

Lunch Get La Taqueria (p155) burritos to go and enjoy in Dolores Park.

The Haight (p181)

Spot Victorian 'Painted Ladies' around **Alamo Sq** and browse **NoPa boutiques**. Stroll the green Panhandle park to Stanyan, then window-shop your way down hippie-historic **Haight St** past record stores, vintage emporiums, drag designers and **Bound Together Anarchist Book Collective**.

Dinner Early walk-ins may score sensational small plates at Frances (p176).

The Castro (p170)

Sing along to show tunes pounded out on the Mighty Wurlitzer organ before shows at deco-fabulous **Castro Theatre**. Party boys cruise over to **440 Castro**, while straight-friendly crowds clink glasses at **Blackbird**.

If You Like...

Museums

SFMOMA Expand horizons with expanded contemporary collections in SF's supersized art museum. (p79)

Exploratorium Totally trippy hands-on exhibits test scientific theories and blow minds at Pier 15. (p58)

MH de Young Museum Global arts and craft masterworks, with provocative ideas and enviable hand–eye coordination. (p200)

Asian Art Museum Sightsee halfway across the globe in an hour, from romantic Persian miniatures to daring Chinese installation art. (p75)

Legion of Honor Iconic impressionist paintings, 90,000 graphic artworks, and weekend organ recitals amid Rodin sculptures. (p202)

Vista Points

Coit Tower Up Greenwich St stairs, atop Telegraph Hill, inside the 1930s tower and on the viewing platform: 360-degree panoramas. (p112)

Land's End Shipwrecks, Golden Gate Bridge views and windblown Monterey pines line the scenic hike from Sutro Baths to Legion of Honor. (p202)

Sterling Park Poetic views of the Golden Gate Bridge from atop Russian Hill are worth jumping off the Powell-Hyde cable car to find. (p132)

Corona Heights Park Rocky outcropping with views over the Haight, Castro and Mission to the silvery bay beyond. (p172)

JAY PASACHOFF / GETTY IMAGES ©

Roof of the California Academy of Sciences (p200)

Local Hangouts

Dolores Park Athletes, radical politicos, performance artists and toddlers: on sunny days, they all converge on this grassy hillside. (p148)

Japantown The unofficial living room of film festival freaks, Lolita Goths, anime aficionados and grandmas who fought for civil rights. (p136)

Adobe Books & Backroom Gallery Meet backroom artists-in-residence and talk books with strangers in this community-supported bookshop. (p164)

Coffee to the People The quadruple-shot Freak Out with hemp milk could wake the Grateful Dead at this radical Haight coffeehouse. (p191)

Washington Square Mellow out with poets and tai chi masters, while wild parrots eye your foccacia from the trees. (p114)

Cafe Flore Castro corner venue that serves coffee with a side of local eye candy. (p177)

Movie Locations

Nob Hill What a ride: Steve McQueen's muscle car goes flying over the summit in *Bullitt* and somehow lands in SoMa. (p45)

Ocean Beach The windswept beach sets the scene for turbulent romance in Woody Allen's *Blue Jasmine*. (p203)

Sutro Baths San Francisco's splendid ruin made a suitable setting for the May–December romance in *Harold and Maude*. (p202)

Human Rights Campaign Action Center & Store Harvey Milk's camera shop in the movie *Milk* was the real-life Castro location, now home to the GLBT civil rights organization. (p179)

Bay Bridge Oops: when Dustin Hoffman sets out for Berkeley in *The Graduate*, he is heading the wrong way across the bridge.

Alcatraz Even America's highest-security prison can't contain Clint Eastwood, who plots to escape with a spoon and razor-sharp wits in *Escape from Alcatraz*. (p48)

Fort Point Hitchcock was right: swirling noir-movie fog and giddy Golden Gate views make for a thrilling case of *Vertigo*. (p57)

Avant-Garde Architecture

California Academy of Sciences Renzo Piano's LEED-certified green landmark, capped with a 'living roof' of California wildflowers. (p200)

MH de Young Museum Pritzker Prize–winning Swiss architects Herzog & de Meuron clad the museum in copper, which is slowly oxidizing green to match park scenery. (p200)

Contemporary Jewish Museum Daniel Libeskind's repurposed SF power station makes a powerful statement with a blue steel addition to form the Hebrew word for life. (p82)

I Magnin Building Timothy Pflueger's 1948 white-marble plinth stands stark-naked amid Union Square clothing stores. (p77)

Historic Sites

Mission Dolores The first building in San Francisco was this Spanish adobe mission, built by conscripted Ohlone and Miwok labor. (p149)

Alcatraz 'The Rock' was a Civil War jail, an A-list gangster penitentiary, and contested territory between Native Americans and the FBI. (p48)

City Lights Publishing poetry got City Lights founder Lawrence Ferlinghetti arrested – and won a landmark case for free speech. (p113)

Chinese Historical Society of America California's first licensed woman architect Julia Morgan built the tile-roofed brick Chinese YWCA, which now highlights turning points in Asian-American history. (p115)

City Hall History keeps getting made under this rotunda – the first 1960s sit-in, the first publicly gay elected official, the first city-wide composting law. (p84)

Portsmouth Square The Gold Rush, kangaroo trials and burlesque shows in City Hall all happened around here. (p115)

Beaches

Baker Beach This cove was once an army base, but now it's packed with families, fishers and, at the north end, nudists. (p57)

Ocean Beach Beachcombing and bonfires are the preferred activities at SF's 4-mile Pacific Ocean beach, where riptides limit swimming. (p203)

Crissy Field Windsurfing, fishing and casual paddling are much easier in this Bay cove than at blustery Ocean Beach. (p56)

Año Nuevo State Reserve Elephant seals come here to mate in the dunes, or mope on 'Losers Beach.' (p231)

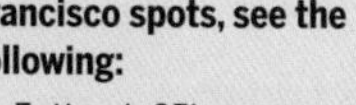

For more top San Francisco spots, see the following:

- ➡ Eating (p25)
- ➡ Drinking & Nightlife (p29)
- ➡ Entertainment (p32)
- ➡ GLBT (p35)
- ➡ Shopping (p37)
- ➡ Sports & Activities (p40)

Month by Month

TOP EVENTS

Pride Parade, June

Lunar New Year Parade, February

San Francisco International Film Festival, April

Bay to Breakers, May

Outside Lands, August

Hardly Strictly Bluegrass, October

February

Lion-dancing, freakishly warm days and alt-rock shows provide sudden relief from February drizzle.

Noise Pop

Winter blues, be gone: discover your new favorite indie band and catch rockumentary premieres and rockin' pop-up gallery openings during the Noise Pop festival (www.noisepop.com); last week of February.

Lunar New Year Parade

Chase the 200ft dragon, lion dancers and frozen-smile runners-up for the Miss Chinatown title during Lunar New Year celebrations (www.chineseparade.com).

April

Reasonable room rates and weekends crammed with cultural events will put some spring in your step in San Francisco.

Perpetual Indulgence in Dolores Park

Easter Sunday is an all-day event with the Sisters of Perpetual Indulgence (www.thesisters.org) in Dolores Park, from a morning Easter egg hunt to the Hunky Jesus Contest – for those who prefer their messiahs muscle-bound.

Cherry Blossom Festival

Japantown blooms and booms in April when this festival (www.nccbf.org) arrives with *taiko* drums and homegrown hip-hop, *yakitori* stalls and Lolita Goth costumes.

San Francisco International Film Festival

The nation's oldest film festival is still looking stellar, with 325 films, 200 directors and star-studded premieres; held end of April to early May at Sundance Kabuki Cinema.

May

As inland California warms up, fog settles over the Bay Area – but goose bumps haven't stopped the naked joggers and conga lines yet.

Bay to Breakers

Run costumed or naked from Embarcadero to Ocean Beach for Bay to Breakers, while joggers dressed as salmon run upstream. Race registration costs $64 and up; held third Sunday in May.

Carnaval San Francisco

Brazilian or just faking it with a wax and a tan? Shake your tail feathers in the Mission and conga through the inevitable fog during Carnaval (www.carnavalsf.com); last weekend of May.

June

Since 1970, Pride has grown into a month-long extravaganza, with movie premieres and street parties culminating in the million-strong Pride Parade.

(Top) Children's band, Lunar New Year Parade

(Bottom) Elvis impersonators taking part in Bay to Breakers

ROBERTO SONCIN GEROMETTA / GETTY IMAGES ©

EZRA SHAW / GETTY IMAGES ©

Haight Ashbury St Fair

Free music, tie-dye galore and herbal brownies surreptitiously for sale – the Summer of Love stages a comeback in the Haight every mid-June since 1978, when Harvey Milk helped make the first Haight Ashbury Street Fair happen.

San Francisco International LGBT Film Festival

Here, queer and ready for a premiere for three decades, this is the oldest, biggest lesbian/gay/bisexual/transgender/queer film fest anywhere. Binge-watch up to 300 films from 30 countries over two weeks in late June (www.frameline.org).

Dyke March & Pink Saturday

Starting with a roar from Dykes on Bikes motorcycle contingent, the 100K-strong, all-women Dyke March heads from Dolores Park gaily onward to the Castro's Pink Party. Castro St and upper Market St are closed to traffic, and dancing in the street continues until sunset.

Pride Parade

Come out wherever you are: SF goes wild for LGBT pride on the last Sunday of June, with 1.2+ million people, seven stages, tons of glitter and ounces of thongs at the Pride Parade. Join crowds cheering for civil rights pioneers, gays in uniform and proud families.

July

Wintry summer days make bundling up advisable, but don't miss July barbecues and

outdoor events, including hikes, free concerts and fireworks.

Independence Day

July 4 explodes with Fisherman's Wharf fireworks, celebrating San Francisco's dedication to life, liberty and the pursuit of happiness no matter the climate – economic, political or meteorological.

AIDS Walk San Francisco

Until AIDS takes a hike, you can: the 10km fundraising AIDS Walk through Golden Gate Park benefits 43 AIDS organizations. Over three decades, $84 million has been raised to fight the pandemic, and support those living with HIV; third Sunday in July.

Stern Grove Festival

Music for free among the redwood and eucalyptus trees, every summer since 1938. Stern Grove Festival's free concerts include hip-hop, world music and jazz, but the biggest events are performances by SF Ballet, SF Symphony, and SF Opera; 2pm Sundays July and August.

August

Finally San Francisco fog rolls back and permits sunset views on Ocean Beach, just in time for one last glorious summer fling in Golden Gate Park.

Outside Lands

Golden Gate Park hosts Outside Lands' major marquee acts and gleeful debauchery at Wine Lands, Beer Lands and star-chef food trucks. One of America's top music and comedy festivals; tickets sell out months in advance (per day/three days $135/325).

September

Warm weather arrives at last and SF celebrates with more outrageous antics than usual.

Folsom Street Fair

Bondage enthusiasts emerge from dungeons worldwide for San Francisco's wildest street party on Folsom St. Enjoy leather, beer, and public spankings for local charities the last Sunday of September.

SF Shakespeare Festival

The play's the thing in the Presidio, outdoors and free of charge on sunny September weekends during the Shakespeare Festival. Kids' summer workshops are also held, culminating in performances throughout the Bay Area.

October

Expect golden sunshine and events for all kinds of aficionados.

Hardly Strictly Bluegrass Festival

The West goes wild for free bluegrass at Golden Gate Park, with three days of concerts and seven stages; held early October.

Litquake

Stranger-than-fiction literary events take place the second week of October during SF's literary festival, with authors leading lunchtime story sessions and spilling trade secrets over drinks at the Lit Crawl.

Alternative Press Expo

Rebel little sister to San Diego's Comic-Con, SF's indie Alternative Press Expo brings a punk-rock DIY spirit to Fort Mason. Rising-star comic artists shyly sign hand-stapled comics, fans score original art, and workshops feature major talents. It takes place mid-October.

November

Party to wake the dead and save the planet as San Francisco celebrates its Mexican history and green future.

Día de los Muertos

Zombie brides and Aztec dancers in feather regalia party like there's no tomorrow on Día de los Muertos, paying respects to the dead along the 24th St parade route on November 2.

Green Festival

Energy-saving spotlights are turned on green cuisine, technology and fashion during the three-day, mid-November Green Festival.

December

Twinkling lights and belly laughs can get you through anything – even downtown holiday shopping.

Kung Pao Kosher

A San Francisco holiday tradition to rival SF Ballet's *The Nutcracker,* Kung Pao Kosher is a Jewish comedy marathon held in a Chinese restaurant on Christmas.

With Kids

San Francisco has the fewest kids per capita of any US city and, according to SPCA data, about 20,000 more dogs than children live here. Yet many locals make a living entertaining kids – from Pixar animators to video game designers – and this town is full of attractions for young people.

LONELY PLANET / GETTY IMAGES ©

Bicycling on the trail to Golden Gate Bridge (p55)

Alcatraz & the Piers

Prison tours of Alcatraz (p48) fascinate kids and keep them on their best behavior for hours. Afterwards, hit the Exploratorium's (p58) award-winning, hands-on exhibits to explore the science of skateboarding and glow-in-the-dark animals. Free the world from Space Invaders at Musée Mechanique (p53), then trawl the waterfront for fish-wiches. Don't be shy: bark back at the **sea lions at Pier 39** (Map p298, D1; 415-981-1280; www.pier39.com; Beach St & the Embarcadero, Pier 39; Jan-Jul & whenever else they feel like it; 15, 37, 49, F), and ride a purple pony on the vintage San Francisco carousel at Pier 39.

Freebies

See SF history at the free Cable Car Museum (p132), and take free mechanical pony rides and peeks inside vintage stagecoaches at the Wells Fargo History Museum (p76). Cool kids will want to head to 24th St to see Balmy Alley murals and skaters at Potrero del Sol Skatepark (p169). The free Randall Junior Museum (p172) introduces kids to urban wildlife, earth science and, on Saturdays, the fascinating Golden Gate model railroad. Daredevils can conquer the concrete **Seward Street Slides** (Seward St at Douglass St; daylight; ; 33, Castro) in the Castro and the Winfield Street slides in Bernal Heights. Lunchtime concerts are free at Old St Mary's (p118) and, in summer, at Yerba Buena Gardens (p83) and Justin Herman Plaza (p76). Kids can graze free samples at the Ferry Building (p73), and score free toys in exchange for a bartered song, drawing or poem at 826 Valencia (p148).

The Wild Side

Penguins, buffalo and white alligators call Golden Gate Park (p199) home. Chase butterflies through the rainforest dome, pet starfish in the petting zoo and squeal in the Eel Forest at the California Academy of Sciences (p200). Get a whiff of insect breath from carnivorous flowers at Conservatory of Flowers (p201) – pee-eeww! – and brave the shark tunnel at Aquarium of

NEED TO KNOW

- **Change facilities** Best public facilities are at Westfield San Francisco Centre (p106) and San Francisco Main Library (p280).
- **Emergency care** San Francisco General Hospital (p279).
- **Babysitting** Available at high-end hotels or American Child Care (www.americanchildcare.com/san_francisco.htm).
- **Strollers and car seats** Bring your own or hire from a rental agency like **Travel BaBees** (☎877-922-2337; www.travelbabees.com).
- **Diapers and formula** Available citywide at Walgreens.
- **Kiddie menus** Mostly in cafés and downtown diners; call ahead about dietary restrictions.

the Bay (p54). San Francisco Zoo (p204) is out of the way but worth the trip for monkeys, lemurs and giraffes.

Museums & Interactive

San Francisco Children's Creativity Museum (p83) allows future tech moguls to design their own video games and animations, while the Exploratorium's (p58) interactive displays let kids send fog signals and figure out optical illusions for themselves. Kids are strongly encouraged to explore art in San Francisco, with free admission to kids aged 12 and under at Asian Art Museum (p75), Legion of Honor (p202), MH de Young Museum (p200), Museum of the African Diaspora (p82) and Contemporary Jewish Museum (p82). To make your own hands-on fun, hit Paxton Gate kids' store (p167) for shadow puppets and organic play-dough.

Cable Cars & Boats

When junior gearheads demand to know how cable cars work, the Cable Car Museum (p132) lets them glimpse the inner workings for themselves. Take a joyride on the Powell-Hyde cable car to Fisherman's Wharf, where you can enter submarine stealth mode aboard the USS Pampanito (p54) and climb aboard schooners and steamships at the Maritime National Historical Park (p53). Future sea captains will enjoy model-ship regattas on weekends at Spreckels Lake in Golden Gate Park (p199).

Warm Days

On sunny Sundays when Golden Gate Park is mostly closed to traffic, rent paddleboats at Stow Lake (p201) or strap on some rentals at Golden Gate Park Bike & Skate (p210). Crissy Field (p56) is a better bet for kid-friendly beaches than Ocean Beach, where fog and strong currents swiftly end sand-castle-building sessions. Hit Chinatown for teen-led Chinatown Alleyways Tours (p278), and cookies at Golden Gate Fortune Cookie Company (p128).

Top 5 Playgrounds

Golden Gate Park (p199) Swings, monkey bars, play castles with slides, hillside slides and a vintage carousel.

Dolores Park (p148) Jungle gym, Mayan pyramid and picnic tables.

Yerba Buena Gardens (p83) Grassy Downtown playground surrounded by museums, cinemas and kid-friendly dining.

Portsmouth Square (p115) Chinatown's outdoor play-room.

Old St Mary's Square (p118) Skateboarders and play equipment.

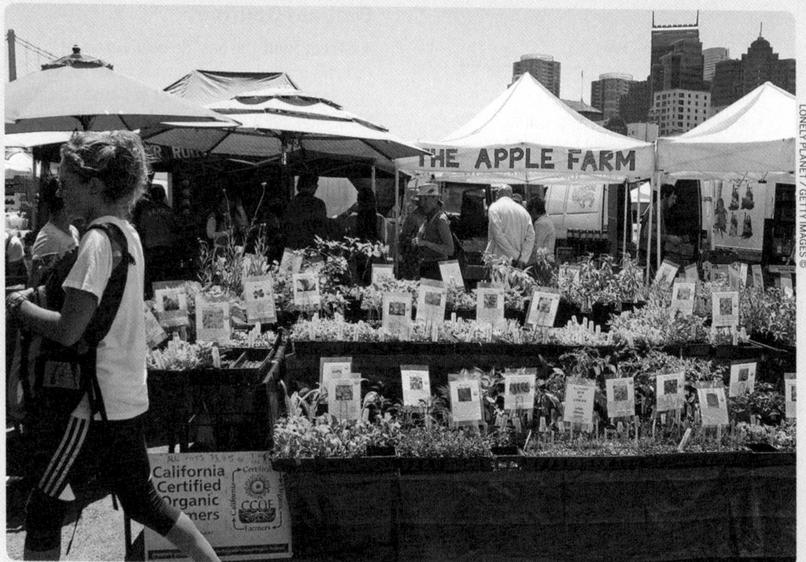

LONELY PLANET / GETTY IMAGES ©

Ferry Plaza Farmers Market (p73)

Eating

Other US cities boast bigger monuments, but San Francisco packs more flavor. Chef Alice Waters set the Bay Area standard for organic, sustainable, seasonal food back in 1971 at Chez Panisse, and today you'll find California's pasture-raised meats and organic produce proudly featured on the Bay Area's cross-cultural menus. Congratulations: you couldn't have chosen a better time or place for dinner.

Fine Dining

➡ **Reservations** Most SF restaurants have online reservations through their websites or **OpenTable** (www.opentable.com), but if the system shows no availability, call the restaurant directly – some seats may be held for phone reservations and early-evening walk-ins, and there may be last-minute cancellations or room at the bar. Landmark restaurants like French Laundry (p227) and Chez Panisse (p215) and small, celebrated SF bistros like Rich Table (p187), State Bird Provisions (p140) and Frances (p176) offer limited seating, so call a month ahead and take what's available.

➡ **Walk-ins** Best bets are restaurant-dense areas like the Mission, Japantown, the Avenues or North Beach.

➡ **Local and sustainable** If you don't see sourcing footnotes or mentions of sustainable, organic ingredients on the menu, ask – it's an SF server's job to know where and how your food was sourced.

➡ **Dietary restrictions** Mention any dietary limitations when reserving, and you'll be cheerfully accommodated.

➡ **California casual** Nice jeans are acceptable and personable interactions appreciated. Service is well informed, friendly and never snooty.

NEED TO KNOW

Price Ranges

The following price ranges apply for a main course, exclusive of drink, tax and tip:

$ less than $15

$$ $15–$25

$$$ more than $25

Tipping

Together, tax and tip add 25% to 35% to the bill. SF follows the US tipping standard: 20% to 25% is generous, 15% minimum, unless something went horribly wrong with service. Many restaurants add 18% service charge for parties of six or more, and some include service in prix-fixe rates.

Surcharges

Some restaurants tack on a 4% surcharge to cover the cost of providing health care to restaurant employees, as required by SF law. If you don't appreciate restaurants passing on their business costs to customers, say so in an online restaurant review.

Just don't blame your server, who may not actually be benefiting. In a 2013 scandal, the city found 50 restaurants were pocketing surcharge fees earmarked for employee health care – 12 pocketed more than $100K each. The city published the list at www.sfgate.com and fined the restaurants heavily.

Opening Hours

Many restaurants are open seven days a week, though some close Sunday and/or Monday night. Breakfast is served 8am to 11am; lunch is usually noon to 3pm; dinner starts around 5:30pm with last service 9pm to 9:30pm weekdays or 10pm weekends. Brunch on weekends is from 10am to 2pm. Exceptions are noted in reviews.

Feedback

Get local opinions and share your own experience at **Chowhound** (www.chowhound.chow.com/boards/1) and SF-based **Foodspotting** (www.foodspotting.com), **Instagram** (http://instagram.com/), **Twitter** (www.twitter.com) and **Yelp** (www.yelp.com).

Bargain Gourmet

➡ **Street food** The best street eats are at farmers market stalls, citywide food trucks and downtown food halls. For in-house street food, hit mom-and-pop eateries in the Avenues, Mission and the gritty, gourmet Tenderloin.

➡ **Gourmet for less** At many upscale SF restaurants, you'll find affordable bar menus and midweek deals.

➡ **Corkage** Restaurants without liquor licenses typically offer free corkage, but otherwise it's usually $15 to $25 – a bargain when you consider wine mark-up is three to five times wholesale costs.

➡ **Deals** Look out for deals at top SF restaurants at **Blackboard Eats** (www.blackboardeats.com/san-francisco) and during SF Restaurant Week (http://www.sfrestaurantweek.com/) in January.

Nontraditional Dining

POP-UP RESTAURANTS

To test out possible restaurant ventures or trial new culinary concepts, guest chefs occasionally commandeer SF bars, cafés and restaurants with creative pop-up menus. At theLab (p154), experimental meals are prepared by SF star chocolatier Michael Recchiuti and guest food artisans; reserve ahead online. Educational community food nonprofit 18 Reasons (p168) hosts pop-ups where chefs share cooking tips with diners.

Look for announcements on **EaterSF** (http://sf.eater.com), **Grub Street San Francisco** (http://sanfrancisco.grubstreet.com) and **Inside Scoop** (http://insidescoopsf.sfgate.com) for upcoming pop-ups. Bring cash and arrive early: most pop-ups don't accept credit cards, and popular dishes run out fast.

DESTINATION DINING

Outstanding in the Field (www.outstandinginthefield.com/) Dinners with guest star chefs like Alice Waters and this Bay Area–based crew pop up in the unlikeliest places – strawberry fields, sea caves, sand bars – to bring diners to the source of their food.

ForageSF (www.foragesf.com) Wild Kitchen events gather adventurous eaters for communal summer meals made with locally foraged ingredients in unexpected Bay Area settings, ranging from a Mission rooftop garden to a Sausalito houseboat.

FOOD TRUCKS & CARTS

Look for prominently displayed permits as guarantee of proper food preparation, refrigeration and regulated working conditions.

SF's largest gathering of gourmet trucks is Off the Grid (p64), which hosts several events weekly. Sundays bring OTG picnics to the Presidio (p64), on Fridays 30-plus food trucks circle their wagons in Fort Mason (p64), and Thursdays are food-truck hootenannies in the Haight (p187) with live music. Trucks and carts are mostly cash-only businesses, and lines for popular trucks can take 10 to 20 minutes.

An excellent pre-party option before hitting SoMa clubs is SoMa StrEat Food Park (p93), a permanent food-truck parking lot with over a dozen trucks, picnic tables, beer and DJs.

For the best gourmet to go, try empanadas from **El Sur** (http://www.elsursf.com/), clamshell buns stuffed with duck and mango from **Chairman** (www.thechairmantruck.com), free-range herbed roast chicken from **Roli Roti** (www.roliroti.com), and dessert from Kara's Cupcakes (p63) and the **Créme Bruleé Cart** (www.twitter.com/cremebruleecart).

You can track food trucks at **Roaming Hunger** (www.roaminghunger.com/sf/vendors) or on **Twitter** (@MobileCravings/sf-food-trucks, @streetfoodsf). Start getting hungry now for August's **SF Street Food Festival** (www.sfstreetfoodfest.com), featuring hundreds of mom-and-pop food vendors – proceeds provide training and kitchens for low-income culinary entrepreneurs.

FARMERS MARKETS & DIY DINING

For California-fresh ingredients, you can't beat SF farmers markets, Rainbow Grocery (p159) and Bi-Rite. (p159) Downtown are several handy **Whole Foods** (www.wholefoodsmarket.com) and **Trader Joes** (www.traderjoes.com) stores.

NorCal idealists who headed back to the land in the 1970s started the nation's organic farming movement. Today the local bounty can be sampled across SF, the US city with the most farmers markets per capita. Top picks:

Ferry Plaza Farmers Market (p73) Star chefs, heirloom ingredients, and food trucks on weekends.

Mission Community Market (p159) Nonprofit, neighborhood-run market with 30 local vendors, offering farm-fresh ingredients and artisan food meals.

Heart of the City Farmers Market (p91) Low-cost, farmer-run market brings healthy, fresh food to the inner city, including California-grown produce and mom-and-pop food trucks.

Alemany Farmers Market (http://sfgsa.org; ⌚Sat dawn-dusk) California's first farmers market, offering bargain California-grown produce and ready-to-eat artisan food since 1943.

Castro Farmers Market (Map p320; www.pcfma.com; Market St at Noe St; ⌚4-8pm Wed Mar-Dec) Local produce and artisan foods at moderate prices, plus charmingly offbeat folk music groups.

HANDS-ON COOKING EVENTS

Excellent hands-on cooking events are held at 18 Reasons (p168) – spots fill quickly so book early.

Eating by Neighborhood

- **The Marina, Fisherman's Wharf & the Piers** Fusion fare in the Marina; seafood and fast food on Fisherman's Wharf; food trucks in Fort Mason.
- **Downtown, Civic Center & SoMa** Vietnamese and tandoori in the Tenderloin; bar bites, tasting menus and sandwiches in SoMa; business lunches and date-night dinners downtown.
- **North Beach & Chinatown** Pizza, pasta and experimental Californian in North Beach.
- **The Mission & Potrero Hill** Tacos, innovative Californian, vegetarian, and Asian soul food.
- **The Castro & Noe Valley** Bistros and burgers in the Castro.
- **The Haight, NoPa & Hayes Valley** Market menus, Japanese *izakaya* (bar snacks) and dessert in Hayes Valley.
- **Golden Gate Park & the Avenues** Dim sum, surfer cuisine and international desserts in the Avenues.

Lonely Planet's Top Choices

Coi (p121) Wild tasting menus featuring foraged morels, wildflowers and Pacific seafood are like licking the California coastline.

Benu (p94) Fine dining meets DJ styling in ingenious remixes of Eastern classics and the best ingredients in the West.

La Taqueria (p155) Serving some of SF's most memorable meals, wrapped in foil and under $9.

Rich Table (p187) Tasty, inventive California fare with French fine-dining finesse makes you feel clever by association.

Al's Place (p158) California dreams are shared here, with imaginative plates of pristine seafood and seasonal specialties.

Best for NorCal Cuisine

Coi (p121) See Top Choices.

Rich Table (p187) See Top Choices.

Al's Place (p158) See Top Choices.

Chez Panisse (p215) Alice Waters' Berkeley bistro has championed local, sustainable, fabulous food since 1971.

Outstanding in the Field (p26) California roots cuisine served by star chefs at pioneering organic farms.

French Laundry (p227) Napa's finest multicourse feasts celebrate the good life and bounty of California.

Jardinière (p190) Mood-altering, luxuriant meals cater to California's decadent appetites.

Outerlands (p207) Organic surfer fare with hearty flavor to take on big waves.

Best Meals under $15

La Taqueria (p155) See Top Choices.

Off the Grid (p64) First course: empanadas; next course: pork-belly bun; cupcakes for dessert.

Cinderella Russian Bakery (p204) Piroshki pastry and dumplings brings SF's Russian community to Cinderella's sociable parklet.

Craftsman & Wolves (p155) Not baked goods, but baked greats – try Thai coconut curry scones and the ingenious Rebel Within.

Greens (p64) At the to-go counter, get black bean chili and portobello panini to enjoy with bayfront Golden Gate Bridge views.

Liguria Bakery (p119) Foccacia hot from the 100-year-old oven.

La Palma Mexicatessen (p159) Beyond tacos: Salvadoran *pupusas* and stuffed *huaraches* handmade with organic masa.

Best Cal-Fusion

Benu (p94) See Top Choices.

Acquerello (p138) Spaghetti western fine dining, with creative handmade pastas and California quail salads.

Aziza (p205) Sunny Moroccan flavors and organic Californian ingredients heat up foggy SF date nights.

Brenda's Meat & Three (p186) Cal-Creole brunches bring Southern comfort north of SF's Pandhandle.

Ichi Sushi (p158) Sustainable Pacific seafood dressed to impress – no soy sauce necessary.

Namu Gaji (p158) Organic Korean surfer soul food at communal tables.

Best Al Fresco Frisco

Boulette's Larder (p92) Sunny market-inspired lunches at the Ferry Building waterfront.

Greens (p64) Sitting on the dock of the bay, with chili that will distract you from the Golden Gate Bridge.

Beach Chalet (p207) Toast the bison with bubbly over brunches in Golden Gate Park's heated backyard.

Mission Cheese (p156) Gloat over your California goat cheese selections and trend-spot Mission street fashion.

Warming Hut (p65) Let's Be Frank hot dogs and sustainable tuna sandwiches under the Golden Gate Bridge.

Cafe Flore (p177) Brunch on the glassed-in patio at the center of the gay universe.

Best Gourmet Gifts

Heath Ceramics (p164) Top SF chefs' tableware of choice, handmade in Sausalito.

Bi-Rite (p159) SF's best-curated selection of local artisan chocolates, cured meats and small-production wines.

Rainbow Grocery (p159) Vast selection of NorCal's finest coffees, cheeses and organic airplane snacks.

Poco Dolce (p154) Award-winning savory chocolates destined to convert dessert non-believers.

Fatted Calf (p196) Heirloom beans, organic chutneys, sustainable cured meats and other California gourmet essentials.

Omnivore (p180) Rare vintage cookbooks and author events with star chefs.

Drinking & Nightlife

No matter what you're having, SF bars, cafés and clubs are here to oblige. But why stick to your usual, when there are California wines, Bay spirits, microbrews and local roasts to try? Adventurous drinking is abetted by local bartenders, who've been making good on Gold Rush saloon history. SF baristas take their cappuccino-foam-drawings seriously, and, around here, DJs invent their own software.

Cocktails

Tonight you're gonna party like it's 1899. Gone are the mad scientist's mixology beakers of five years ago: today SF drink historians are judged by their Old Tom gin selections and displays of swizzle sticks from defunct ocean liners. All that authenticity-tripping over cocktails may sound self-conscious, but after enjoying strong pours at vintage saloons and speakeasies, consciousness is hardly an issue.

➡ **Cost** Happy-hour specials or well drinks run $5 to $8 and gourmet choices with premium hooch run $9 to $15.

➡ **Local spirits** Top-shelf SF Bay liquor includes St George gin, 1512 Barbershop white rye, Anchor Old Tom gin, Hangar 1 vodka, Workhorse rye, Spirit Works sloe gin, Old Potrero whiskey and Emperor Norton Absinthe.

➡ **Tip** With $1 to $2 per drink, bartenders return the favor with heavy pours next round – that's why it's called getting tip-sy.

Wine

To get the good stuff, you don't need to commit to a bottle or escape to Wine Country. San Francisco restaurants, wine bars and urban wineries are increasingly offering top-notch, small-production California wines *alla spina* (on tap). Organically grown, sustainable and even biodynamic wines feature on most SF restaurant lists.

➡ **Wine Country deals** Plan your trip to Napa or Sonoma for late fall, when you can taste new releases and score harvest specials.

➡ **SF's warehouse wineries** Toast city living at Bluxome Street Winery (p98) and Sutton Cellars (p154), where San Francisco's best vintages are made in industrial warehouses.

➡ **Food-truck pairings** Consult the bar's Twitter feed or Facebook page – or see what trucks are around at www.roaminghunger.com/sf/vendors or @MobileCravings/sf-food-trucks on Twitter.

➡ **Cult wine retailers** Bi-Rite (p159), Ferry Plaza Wine Merchant (p100), Dig (p154) and California Wine Merchant (p66) sell hard-to-find wines at reasonable prices.

Beer

SF's first brewery (1849) was built before the city was, and beer has been a staple ever since.

➡ **Cost** Budget $4 to $7 a pint for draft microbrews, $2 to $3 for Pabst Blue Ribbon (PBR) – plus $1 tip.

➡ **Beer gardens** Drink in the great outdoors at Biergarten (p190), Zeitgeist (p160), Beach Chalet (p207) and Wild Side West (p166).

➡ **House brews** Doesn't get more local than beer brewed on-site at Anchor Brewing Company (p168), 21st Amendment Brewery (p94), Magnolia Brewpub (p186) and Social (p208).

➡ **Brew it yourself** Attend meet-ups with local brewers at the **SF Brewers' Guild** (www.sfbrewersguild.org); pick up trade secrets at City Beer Store & Tasting Room (p99); or take a Workshop (p196) brewing class.

NEED TO KNOW

Smoking

Not legal indoors. Some bars have smoking patios, including Rye (p96), Bar Agricole (p97) and Irish Bank (p96), or backyards such as El Rio (p160), Wild Side West (p166) and Zeitgeist (p160) – otherwise, you'll be puffing on the sidewalk.

Opening Hours

Downtown and SoMa bars draw happy-hour crowds from 4pm to 7pm; otherwise, bars are hopping by 9pm, with last call 10:30pm to 11:30pm weekdays and 1:30am weekends. Clubs kick in around 10pm and many close at 2am.

Websites

To find out what's up where this weekend, check **SF Weekly** (www.sfweekly.com) and **Funcheap SF** (http://sf.funcheap.com/), and skim calendars at **SF Station** (www.sfstation.com/), **UrbanDaddy** (www.urbandaddy.com/home/sfo) and **Thrillist** (www.thrillist.com).

Café Scene

When San Francisco couples break up, the thorniest issue is: who gets the café? San Franciscans are fiercely loyal to specific roasts and baristas – especially in the Mission, Hayes Valley and North Beach – and the majority of first internet dates meet on neutral coffee grounds. When using free café wi-fi, remember: order something every hour, deal with interruptions graciously and don't leave laptops unattended.

➡ **Cost** Budget $2 to $3 for American coffee and $3 to $5 for espresso drinks.

➡ **Tip** Leave a buck in the tip jar for espresso drinks, especially when staying a while.

➡ **Cell phones** Texting is fine, but phone calls are many baristas' pet peeve.

Clubbing

DJs set the tone at clubs in SF, where the right groove gets everyone on the dance floor – gay, straight and a glorious swath of whatever. You'll usually only wait 10 minutes to get in anywhere, unless you're stumbling drunk.

➡ **Cost** Most clubs charge $10 to $25 at the door. For discounted admission, show up before 10pm or sign up on the club's online guest list (look for a VIP or RSVP link). Seating may be reserved for bottle service at high-end clubs.

➡ **Dress code** SF is pretty casual, though club bouncers do turn away people wearing flip-flops, shorts or T-shirts (unless they're spiffy), especially at swing and salsa clubs.

➡ **Late night** Last call at many clubs is around 11:30pm weekdays and 1:30am on weekends. Many clubs close around 2am, though a few after-hours clubs like EndUp (p98) rage till dawn.

Drinking by Neighborhood

➡ **The Marina, Fisherman's Wharf & the Piers** Straight bars in the Marina.

➡ **Downtown, Civic Center & SoMa** Dives, chichi lounges, old-school gay bars in Civic Center and the Tenderloin; art lounges, wine bars, men's cruising bars and clubs in SoMa.

➡ **North Beach & Chinatown** Barbary Coast saloons, eccentric bars, Italian cafés and deco lounges in North Beach.

➡ **The Mission & Potrero Hill** Coffee roasters, hipster saloons, friendly wine bars, salsa clubs, and women's and trans bars in the Mission.

➡ **The Castro & Noe Valley** Gay bars in the Castro.

➡ **The Haight, NoPa & Hayes Valley** Cheap whiskey, serious beer and boho lounges in the Haight; wine bars and coffee kiosks in Hayes Valley.

➡ **Golden Gate Park & the Avenues** Irish and tiki bars in the Richmond; coffee in the Sunset.

Lonely Planet's Top Choices

Comstock Saloon (p125) Vintage wild west saloon with potent, period-perfect concoctions and dainty bar bites.

Bar Agricole (p97) Drink your way to a history degree with well-researched cocktails – anything with hellfire bitters earns honors.

Toronado (p190) Beer for every season and any reason – summer ales, holiday barley-wines and Oktoberfest wheats.

Local Edition (p95) Extra, extra – read all about specialty cocktails in the Hearst newspaper building speakeasy.

Smuggler's Cove (p192) Roll with the rum punches at this Barbary Coast shipwreck bar.

Best Cocktails

Bar Agricole (p97) See Top Choices.

Comstock Saloon (p125) See Top Choices.

Smuggler's Cove (p192) See Top Choices.

Local Edition (p95) See Top Choices.

Rickhouse (p95) Impeccable bourbon drinks in shotgun-shack atmosphere.

Trick Dog (p160) Every six months the cocktail menu reflects a new SF obsession – landmark buildings, say, or Chinese diners.

Bourbon & Branch (p96) Not since Prohibition have secret passwords and gin knowledge been this handy.

Best Wine Bars

Hôtel Biron (p192) Walk-in closet wine bar with small, standout selection.

20 Spot (p161) Expect the unexpected: unusual wines and double-deviled eggs in a former punk-record storefront.

Terroir Natural Wine Merchant (p98) Red, white and green: sustainably produced wines from cult winemakers.

St. Vincent Tavern (p161) Smart pairings and adventurous tastings around sociable communal tables.

Bluxome Street Winery (p98) Sample the latest SF vintages at this SoMa warehouse winery's tasting bar.

Best for Beer

Toronado (p190) See Top Choices.

Zeitgeist (p160) Surly lady bartenders tap 40 microbrews to guzzle in the beer garden.

City Beer Store & Tasting Room (p99) Beer sommeliers earn the title here with expert-led tastings, brewing and pairing tips.

Specs Museum Cafe (p125) Blow off steam with Anchor Steam by the pitcher in this nautical back-alley bar.

Biergarten (p190) A shipping-container bar keeps this beer garden well watered.

Irish Bank (p96) Downtown's secret Emerald Isle getaway offers properly poured Guinness and fish and chips in cozy snugs.

Best Dance Clubs

Endup (p98) Offers epic 24-hour dance sessions in an urban-legendary SoMa gay club that's been going since 1973.

DNA Lounge (p102) Known for booty-shaking mash-ups, burlesque, Goth, and roof-raising live acts like Prince.

Cat Club (p97) Something for everyone: '80s one-hit wonders, '90s mega-pop and go-go bondage.

El Rio (p160) Get down and funky in the Mission and flirt internationally in the backyard.

BeatBox (p100) Mixed-gender warehouse club where the gays come out to play.

Rickshaw Stop (p97) Beats won't quit at this all-ages, all-orientations, all-fabulous shoebox club.

Best Cafés

Caffe Trieste (p125) Legendary North Beach café, fueling epic Beat poetry and weekend accordion jams since the '50s.

Ritual Coffee Roasters (p160) Heady roasts, local art and sociable seating in a cult roastery-café.

Réveille (p126) Sunny flatiron café with stellar espresso drinks, decadent pastries and sidewalk people-watching.

Sightglass Coffee (p97) This SoMa roastery looks industrial but serves small-batch roasts from family farms.

Blue Bottle Coffee Company (p192) The back-alley garage that kicked off the Third Wave coffee roastery craze.

ANTHONY PIDGEON / GETTY IMAGES ©

Revelers at Hardly Strictly Bluegrass Festival (p22)

Entertainment

SF is one of the top five US cities for the number of creative types per square mile – and when all those characters take the stage, look out. Though the city has a world-famous orchestra, opera, jazz center, film festival, theater and ballet, the SF scene isn't all about marquee names: you can see cutting-edge dance, comedy and music for the price of an IMAX movie.

Comedy & Spoken Word

For laughs, try drag comedy at Oasis (p103), Marsh (p162) monologues, upstart comics at Doc's Lab (p127), campy Beach Blanket Babylon (p126), or TV comedians at Cobb's Comedy Club (p127) and the Punch Line (p102) – or get onstage with BATS Improv (p67) comedy workshops.

Literary types should check out SF's annual Litquake (p22), San Francisco Main Library (p85) and Booksmith (p193) author events. For raucous readings, check out Writers with Drinks at Make-Out Room (p163), Porchlight storytelling at Verdi Club (p164) and Mortified's teen diary excerpts at DNA Lounge (p102).

Dance

SF supports the longest-running US ballet company, San Francisco Ballet (p101), and multiple independent troupes at Yerba Buena Center for the Arts (p103). Experimental styles are championed at Oberlin Dance Collective (p162) and **Joe Goode** (Map p312; ☎415-561-6565; www.joegoode.org; 499 Alabama St; 🚌22, 33), and you can invent your own style at Dance Mission (p169). **Dancers' Group** (www.dancersgroup.org) keeps a comprehensive calendar.

Film

Cinemaniacs adore SF's vintage movie palaces, including the Roxie (p162), Castro (p178) and Balboa (p208). For major releases and film-festival favorites in a certified-green cinema, head to Sundance Kabuki Cinema (p142). Foreign films and award contenders show at Embarcadero Center Cinema (p102), while IMAX blockbusters screen at AMC Loews Metreon 16 (p104).

➡ **Festivals** Beyond SF International Film Festival (p20), SF hosts LGBT (p21) and Jewish and Arab Film Festivals.

➡ **Tickets** Most tickets run $10 to $15, with weekday matinees around $8.

Live Music

Eclectic SF clubs host funk, reggae, bluegrass and punk; check online calendars.

➡ **Bluegrass** Hear the original music of SF's Gold Rush at Hardly Strictly Bluegrass festival (p22), at Berkeley's Freight & Salvage Coffeehouse (p215) and on SF public radio's Bluegrass Signal (91.7FM; www.kalw.org).

➡ **Funk & Hip-Hop** Oakland has tougher rap and faster beats, but SF plays it loose and funky at Mezzanine (p103) and Independent (p193).

➡ **Jazz** Major jazz talents are in residence year-round at SFJAZZ Center (p192), and jazz ensembles regularly play Revolution Cafe (p163), The Chapel (p162), Café Royale (p103), Club Deluxe (p193) and Doc's Lab (p127).

➡ **Punk** Punk's not dead at SUB-Mission (p163), Edinburgh Castle (p97), Hemlock Tavern (p102) and Slim's (p103).

➡ **Rock** Psychedelic rock legends played at the Fillmore (p141), but alt-rock takes the stage at Outside Lands (p22), Warfield (p102) and the Great American Music Hall (p102).

Opera & Classical Music

Between San Francisco Opera (p101) seasons, hear opera by the Grammy-winning, 12-man chorus **Chanticleer** (www.chanticleer.org; ⏲dates vary) and SF's **Pocket Opera Company** (www.pocketopera.org; ⏲Feb-Jun).

Michael Tilson Thomas conducts the Grammy-winning San Francisco Symphony (p101), and **San Francisco Performances** (www.performances.org) hosts world-class classical performances at Herbst Theater.

➡ **Free music** SF Opera and SF Symphony perform gratis at Stern Grove Festival (p22). Stop by Old St Mary's (p118) for regular Tuesday noon concerts, and check http://noontimeconcerts.org for other donation-requested concerts.

➡ **Bargain tickets** SF Opera offers America's least expensive opera tickets (starting from $10); SF Symphony offers rush tickets and open rehearsal tickets ($20 to $25).

NEED TO KNOW

Arts Calendar

Check **KQED's The Do List** (http://ww2.kqed.org/arts/programs/the-do-list/) for an excellent selection of upcoming performing arts events.

Discounts

Sign up at **Gold Star Events** (www.goldstarevents.com) for discounts on comedy, theater, concerts and opera, or stop by **Tix Bay Area's** (Map p304; www.tixbayarea.org; 350 Powell St) Union Square ticket booth for cheap tickets for same-day or next-day shows.

Theater

Before winning Tonys and a Pulitzer Prize, *Angels in America* got its wings at the American Conservatory Theater (p101) – and you can see the next theatrical breakthrough in progress at ACT's new Strand Theater. In summer the **San Francisco Mime Troupe** (www.sfmt.org) performs free political-comedy satire in Dolores Park, while the SF Shakespeare Festival (p22) is held gratis in the Presidio.

Theatre Bay Area (www.theatrebayarea.org) is a comprehensive calendar of 100 Bay Area theater companies.

➡ **Broadway shows** See listings at www.shnsf.com.

➡ **Tickets** Marquee shows run $35 to $150, but same-day, half-price tickets are often available. Indie theater runs $10 to $40.

Entertainment by Neighborhood

➡ **Downtown, Civic Center & SoMa** Symphony, opera, theater, punk, jazz, rock and comedy.

➡ **North Beach & Chinatown** Comedy, jazz, folk, blues and spoken word.

➡ **The Mission & Potrero Hill** Dance, alt-bands, punk, bluegrass, experimental theater and spoken word.

➡ **Golden Gate Park & the Avenues** Festivals and free concerts.

Lonely Planet's Top Choices

San Francisco Symphony (p101) Sets the tempo for modern classical, with guests like Jessye Norman, Metallica and Rufus Wainwright.

SFJAZZ Center (p192) Top talents reinvent standards and create new works inspired by mariachis, skateboarders, Hunter S Thompson and Joni Mitchell.

San Francisco Opera (p101) Divas like Renée Fleming bring down the house with classics and contemporary works including Stephen King's *Dolores Claiborne*.

American Conservatory Theater (p101) Daring theater – from operas by Tom Waits and William S Burroughs to controversial David Mamet plays – plus experimental works at the Strand Theater.

Castro Theatre (p178) Organ overtures and cult classics with enthusiastic audience participation raise the roof at this art-deco movie palace.

Best Live Music Venues

San Francisco Symphony (p101) See Top Choices.

SFJAZZ Center (p192) See Top Choices.

San Francisco Opera (p101) See Top Choices.

Fillmore Auditorium (p141) Rock-legendary since the '60s, with the psychedelic posters to prove it.

Great American Music Hall (p102) Marquee acts in a historic, intimate venue that was once a bordello.

Slim's (p103) Big names play this smallish club, from punk legends to surprise shows by the likes of Prince.

Best for Theater & Dance

American Conservatory Theater (p101) See Top Choices.

San Francisco Ballet (p101) Elegant lines and gorgeous original staging from America's oldest ballet company.

Oberlin Dance Collective (p162) Style and substance in balance, with muscular, meaningful, original choreography.

Yerba Buena Center for the Arts (p103) Modern dance troupes throw down and represent SF's cutting edge.

Magic Theatre (p67) Original works by major playwrights, performed in a converted army base.

Best for Movies

Castro Theatre (p178) See Top Choices.

SF International Film Festival (p20) Breakthrough indies and stealth Oscar favorites premiere here, with directors from Afghanistan to Uganda and movie-star Q&As.

Sundance Kabuki Cinema (p142) Balcony bars, reserved seating and zero ads make great films better.

Roxie Cinema (p162) Offers cult classics, documentary premieres and indie films not yet distributed in a vintage cinema.

Balboa Theatre (p208) Art-deco cinema features first-run and art-house films, plus family matinees.

Best Free Entertainment

Hardly Strictly Bluegrass Festival (p22) See bluegrass greats like Alison Krauss jam alongside Elvis Costello, Patti Smith and Dwight Yoakam – for free.

Stern Grove Festival (p22) SFJAZZ legends and symphony soloists perform in the great outdoors.

San Francisco Mime Troupe (p33) Social satire, Kabuki and musical comedy make scenes in Dolores Park.

SF Shakespeare Festival (p22) Audiences warm to *The Winter's Tale* at foggy Presidio performances.

Amoeba Music (p193) Free in-store concerts by rock and alt-pop radio favorites, plus oddballs and cult bands.

Best for Laughs

Cobb's Comedy Club (p127) Comics from the streets to Comedy Central test risky new material.

Oasis (p103) Drag comedy variety acts so outrageously funny, you'll laugh until you cough up glitter.

Beach Blanket Babylon (p126) Laugh your wig off with San Francisco's over-the-top Disney-drag cabaret.

Punch Line (p102) Breakthrough comedians like Ellen Degeneres, Chris Rock and Margaret Cho started here.

Marsh (p162) Monologues range from uproarious to heartbreaking, sometimes in the same act.

GLBT

Doesn't matter where you're from, who you love or who's your daddy: if you're here and queer, welcome home. San Francisco is America's pinkest city, and though New York Marys may call it the retirement home of the young – the sidewalks roll up early here – there's nowhere better to be out and proud.

Gay/Lesbian/Bi/Trans Scene

In San Francisco, you don't need to trawl the urban underworld for a gay scene. The intersection of 18th and Castro is the historic center of the gay world, but dancing queens head to SoMa for thump-thump clubs.

So where are all the ladies? They're busy sunning on the patio at Wild Side West (p166) or El Rio (p160), screening documentaries at the Roxie Cinema (p162), inventing new technologies at SF hackerspaces, working it out on the dance floor at Rickshaw Stop (p97) or BeatBox, (p100) and/or raising kids in Noe Valley and Bernal Heights. The Mission remains the preferred 'hood of alt-chicks, dykes, trans female-to-males (FTMs) and flirty femmes.

Gender need not apply in SF, where the DMV officially acknowledges trans-queer identities. Drag shows happen nightly in SF, though you'll never need a professional reason to blur gender lines here – next to baseball, gender-bending is SF's favorite sport.

Party Planning

On Sundays in the 1950s, SF bars held gay old times euphemistically called 'tea dances' – and Sundays remain the most happening nights in town.

Cockblock (www.cockblocksf.com) Women-centric 'homolicious' dance party mayhem breaks out at Rickshaw Stop (p97).

Juanita MORE! (www.juanitamore.com) This drag superstar throws fierce fundraising parties, especially for Pride – plus monthly fetish-drag Beat Pig parties at Powerhouse (p100).

Honey Soundsystem Map p308 (http://hnysndsystm.tumblr.com/) Kick-ass roving dance party is a mash-up of queer folk and queerer music, from obscure disco B-sides to German techno. Regular venues include Mighty (p163), BeatBox (p100) and The EndUp (p98).

Comfort & Joy (http://playajoy.org) The queer 'radical faerie' Burning Man collective lists happening dance parties and creative community events.

Go Bang! (www.facebook.com/GoBANGSF) Atomic-scale disco inferno tears through SF, including regular monthly appearances at Stud (p100).

GLBT by Neighborhood

➡ **Downtown, Civic Center & SoMa** Raging dance clubs, leather bars, drag shows and men's sex clubs in SoMa; bars, trans venues and queer cabaret in the Tenderloin.

➡ **The Mission & Potrero Hill** Women's and trans-queer bars, arts venues and community spaces in the Mission.

➡ **The Castro & Noe Valley** Gay history, activism and men's cruising bars in the Castro; LGBT family scene in Noe Valley.

NEED TO KNOW

News & Events

San Francisco Bay Times (www.sfbaytimes.com) focuses on LGBT perspectives and events; *Bay Area Reporter* (www.ebar.com) circulates community news and listings; and *Gloss Magazine* (www.glossmagazine.net) does nightlife.

Women's Community Venues

Women's Building (p284) for organizations; Lyon-Martin Women's Health Services (p280) for health and support; and Brava Theater (p162) for arts.

Support & Activism

LYRIC (www.lyric.org) for queer youth; Human Rights Campaign Action Center & Store (p179) for political organizing; GLBT History Museum (p172) for context; **Transgender Law Center** (http://transgenderlawcenter.org) for civil rights activism and support; and **Homobiles** (www.homobiles.org) for a nonprofit LGBT taxi service.

Lonely Planet's Top Choices

Pride (p21) The most extravagant celebration on the planet culminates in the Dyke March, Pink Party and an exhilarating 1.2-million-strong Pride Parade.

Human Rights Campaign Action Center & Store (p179) Been there, signed the petition, bought the T-shirt supporting civil rights at Harvey Milk's camera storefront.

Castro Theatre (p178) San Francisco International LGBT Film Festival premieres here as well as audience-participatory cult classics.

Oasis (p103) SF's dedicated drag venue, hostessed by drag icons Heklinka and D'Arcy Drollinger.

GLBT History Museum (p172) Proud moments and historic challenges, captured for posterity.

Best for Gay Old Times with Straight Friends

Pride (p21) See Top Choices.

GLBT History Museum (p172) See Top Choices.

Castro Theatre (p178) See Top Choices.

AsiaSF (p104) Waitresses serve drink and sass with a secret: they're in drag.

San Francisco International LGBT Film Festival (p21) Worldwide queer premieres, from Argentina to Vietnam.

Best for Women

Wild Side West (p166) Cheers to queers and beers in the herstory-making sculpture garden.

El Rio (p160) Mix it up with world music, free oysters and SF's flirtiest patio.

Rickshaw Stop (p97) All-ages parties and all-out estrogen at Cockblock.

Women's Building (p284) Glorious murals crown this community institution.

Brava Theater (p162) Original shows by, for and about lesbians and transwomen.

BeatBox (p100) Women bring it all to the dance floor at UHaul.

Best for Men

Aunt Charlie's Lounge (p96) Knock-down, drag-out winner for gender-bending shows and dance-floor freakiness.

Eagle Tavern (p100) Landmark SoMa leather rocker bar, as friendly/sleazy as you wanna be.

Stud (p100) Low visibility and the tantalizing aroma of bourbon and testosterone: guaranteed good times.

BeatBox (p100) Dare to bear at Bearracuda or get Served.

EndUp (p98) Hit your groove Saturday night and work it until Monday.

HiTops (p177) Sports on the TV and guys ready to play in the Castro.

Best Daytime Scene

Dolores Park (p148) Sun and cityscapes on hillside 'Gay Beach,' plus protests and Hunky Jesus Contests.

Baker Beach (p57) Only Baker Beach regulars knew you could get goose bumps there.

Cafe Flore (p177) The best people-watching on the gay planet: blind dates, parents showing support for GLBT kids, and dogs in drag.

El Rio (p160) Sunday's Daytime Realness brings back-patio drag fabulousness.

Eagle Tavern (p100) At Sunday afternoon beer bashes, leather daddies mix with local politicians.

LONELY PLANET / GETTY IMAGES ©

Dema (p166)

Shopping

All those tricked-out dens, well-stocked spice racks and fabulous ensembles don't just pull themselves together – San Franciscans scour their city for them. Eclectic originality is San Francisco's signature style, and that's not one-stop shopping. But consider the thrill of the hunt: while shopping in SF, you can watch fish theater, make necklaces from zippers and trade fashion tips with drag queens.

Shopping Hubs

➡ **Union Square** Ringed by department stores and megabrands, including Neiman Marcus, Macy's, Saks and Apple.

➡ **Valencia St** Made in San Francisco gifts, West Coast style and scents, and pirate supplies.

➡ **Hayes Valley** Local designers, gourmet treats and home decor.

➡ **Powell St** Lined with flagship stores and bargains: Gap, Uniqlo, H&M and Urban Outfitters.

Unconventional Retail

Indie designers and vintage shops supply original style on SF's most boutique-studded streets: Haight, Valencia, Hayes, upper Grant, Fillmore, Union and Polk. For further adventures in retail, don't miss these shopping events:

Art Market San Francisco (http://artmarketsf.com/; ⏱last weekend Apr) At Fort Mason, San Francisco's signature art fair attracts curators with major museum pieces, but also sells affordable original works for as little as $80. For further art

NEED TO KNOW

Business Hours

Most stores are open daily from 10am to 6pm or 7pm, though hours often run 11am to 8pm Saturdays and 11am to 6pm Sundays. Stores in the Mission and the Haight tend to open later and keep erratic hours; many downtown stores stay open until 8pm.

Sales Tax

Combined SF city and CA state sales taxes tack 8.75% onto the price of your purchase. This tax is not refundable.

Returns

Try before you buy and ask about return policies. Many stores offer returns for store credit only, so when in doubt, consider a gift certificate. In California, they never expire and you can often use them online.

Websites

Check **Urban Daddy** (www.urbandaddy.com) for store openings and pop-ups; **Thrillist** (www.thrillist.com) for gear and gadgets; and **Refinery 29** (www.refinery29.com) for sales and trends.

action, look for renegade satellite fairs in Fort Mason's parking lot and nearby motels.

West Coast Craft (http://westcoastcraft.com/; ⏲mid-Jun & mid-Nov) That laid-back, homespun California look takes handiwork – or you can leave it to the pros at West Coast Craft, featuring 100+ indie makers. Held at Fort Mason.

Monster Drawing Rally (www.soex.org; ⏲Jul) Artists scribble furiously and audience members snap up their work while still wet.

Litquake (www.litquake.org; ⏲2nd week Oct) Stranger-than-fiction literary events take place during SF's literary festival, with authors leading lunchtime story sessions and spilling trade secrets over drinks at the legendary Lit Crawl.

Alternative Press Expo (www.comic-con.org/ape; ⏲mid-Oct) Rebel little sister to San Diego's Comic-Con, SF's indie Alternative Press Expo brings a punk-rock DIY spirit to Fort Mason with fantastic undiscovered talents shyly signing hand-stapled comics, scrappy crafts and workshops with rising-star comic artists.

Celebration of Craftswomen (www.womensbuilding.org; ⏲last weekend Nov) The nation's largest juried showcase for crafty women kicks off the holiday season, with proceeds supporting the Women's Building. Held at Fort Mason.

Shopping by Neighborhood

➡ **The Marina, Fisherman's Wharf & the Piers** Date outfits, girly accessories, wine and design in the Marina.

➡ **Downtown & Civic Center** Department stores, global megabrands, discount retail and Apple's flagship store.

➡ **The Hills & Japantown** Home design, stationery, toys, accessories and anime in Japantown; designer clothes, jewelry and decor in Pacific Heights and Russian Hill.

➡ **The Mission & Potrero Hill** Local makers, bookstores, art galleries, artisan foods, dandy style, vintage whatever.

➡ **The Haight, NoPa & Hayes Valley** Design boutiques, decor, food and coffee in Hayes Valley; quirky gifts and accessories in NoPa; head shops, music, vintage and skate gear in the Haight.

Lonely Planet's Top Choices

City Lights (p113) If you can't find nirvana in the Poetry Chair upstairs, try Lost Continents in the basement.

826 Valencia (p148) Your friendly neighborhood pirate supply store and publishing house; proceeds support on-site youth writing programs.

Gravel & Gold (p164) Get good Californian vibrations from G&G's SF-made, feel-good clothing and beach-shack housewares.

Little Paper Planes (p165) Original gifts by indie makers, gallery-ready clothing and works on paper from LPP's artist's residency program.

Heath Ceramics (p164) The local, handmade tableware of choice for SF's star chefs, in essential modern shapes and appetizing earthy colors.

Workshop Residence (p154) SF artists are paired with local fabricators to produce artistically inspired, limited-edition fashion, decor and more.

Best SF Fashion Designers

Gravel & Gold (p164) See Top Choices.

Aggregate Supply (p165) Pop-art windbreakers and tees from Turk+Taylor.

Nooworks (p165) Eighties new-wave designs reinvented with edgy art-schooled graphics.

Dema (p166) Flattering vintage silhouettes in African-print cottons and psychedelic paisley silks.

Harputs (p105) Striking sculptural styles good to go from Potrero galleries to SoMa clubs.

Paloma (p195) Leather bags handmade in-store and historical SF T-shirts.

Community Thrift (p166) Vintage scores and local designer seconds, with proceeds benefiting local charities.

Best for Eclectic SF Decor

Heath Ceramics (p164) See Top Choices.

Workshop Residence (p154) See Top Choices.

Electric Works (p107) A cabinet of wonders: art prints of philosophical poodles, North Korean wind-up toys and Klein bottles.

Viracocha (p163) Typewriters, driftwood lamps, bottled messages and other decor for incorrigible romantics.

Accident & Artifact (p167) Homespun indigo, altered topographical maps, SF-themed aromatherapy: decor beyond design magazines.

Adobe Books & Backroom Gallery (p164) Art freshly made on-site by the artist in residence, out-of-print books and 'zines galore.

Best for the Person Who Has Everything

826 Valencia (p148) See Top Choices.

Good Vibrations (p166) Adult toys, with informed staff and zero judgment.

New People (p143) Ninja shoes, Lolita Goth petticoats and the latest in wooden speakers at this Japantown showcase.

Foggy Notion (p208) Presidio hiking-trail scents, un-washing powder for Ocean Beachy hair and other SF beauty secrets.

Piedmont Boutique (p194) Drag like you mean it, honey: boas, fake-fur bootie shorts and airplane earrings.

Loved to Death (p194) Goth jewelry, macabre Victoriana and taxidermied everything.

Sports & Activities

San Franciscans love the outdoors, and their historic conservation efforts have protected acres of parks, beaches and woodlands for all to enjoy. This city lives for sunny days spent biking, skating, surfing and drifting on the Bay. Foggy days are spent making art projects, but nights are for dancing and Giants games.

Spectator Sports

See the Giants play baseball on their home turf at AT&T Park (p109). You might be able catch some Giants action for free at the Embarcadero waterfront boardwalk. Golden State Warriors (p216) play NBA basketball to win in Oakland, as they did in 2015 – but they're moving back to SF in 2018. To see the 49ers (p168) play, you'll need to drive an hour south of SF to Santa Clara, where they now play in Levi's Stadium.

➡ **Tickets** Book through team websites or try **Ticketmaster** (www.ticketmaster.com). If games are sold out, search the 'Tickets' category on www.craigslist.org.

➡ **Sports coverage** *San Francisco Chronicle* (www.sfgate.com) offers complete coverage, but *The Examiner* (www.sfexaminer.com) also has sports stats and predictions.

Outdoor Activities

On sunny weekends, SF is out kite-flying, surfing or biking. Even on foggy days, don't neglect sunscreen: UV rays penetrate SF's thin cloud cover.

BICYCLING

Every weekend thousands of cyclists cross Golden Gate Bridge (p55) to explore the Marin Headlands and Mt Tamalpais. Since the 1970s, 'Mt Tam' has remained the Bay Area's ultimate mountain-biking challenge.

Many SF streets have bicycle lanes and major parks have bike paths. The safest places to cycle in SF are Golden Gate Park (car-free on Sundays), the Embarcadero and wooded Presidio. SF bikers' favorite street-biking route is the green-painted, flat bike lane connecting Market St and Golden Gate Park called the **Wiggle** (www.sfbike.org/our-work/street-campaigns/the-wiggle/).

➡ **City biking maps** The San Francisco Bicycle Coalition (p277) produces *San Francisco Bike Map & Walking Guide*, which outlines the Wiggle route and shows how to avoid traffic and hills.

➡ **Route planning** Put your smart phone to work finding the perfect route using the **San Francisco Bike Route Planner** (http://amarpai.com/bikemap).

➡ **Critical Mass** To claim bicyclists' right of way on city streets, join the **Critical Mass** (www.sfcriticalmass.org/) protest parade on the last Friday of the month. Use caution around motorists, who may be unsympathetic with this interruption in rush-hour traffic, and always yield to pedestrians.

➡ **Riding naked** In early June the **World Naked Bike Ride** (www.sfbikeride.org) protests the US dependence on fossil fuels.

GOLF

Tee up and enjoy mild weather, clipped greens and gorgeous views on SF's top public courses: Lincoln Park Golf Course (p210) and Golden Gate Municipal Golf Course (p211).

RUNNING

Crissy Field (p56) has a 2.5-mile jogging track, and trails run 3 miles through Golden Gate Park (p199) from the Panhandle to Ocean Beach. The Presidio (p60) offers ocean breezes through eucalyptus trees. SF's major races, including Bay to Breakers (p20), are festive – bring a costume, or at least a feather boa.

SKATING & SKATEBOARDING

SF is the home of roller disco and the skateboard magazine *Thrasher*. Inline skaters skate the Embarcadero Friday nights and disco-skate in Golden Gate Park (p199) on Sundays. Golden Gate Park Bike & Skate (p210) rents inline and four-wheeled roller skates in good weather.

Potrero del Sol/La Raza Skatepark (p169) has ramps for kids and bowls for pros. Haight St is urban skating at its obstacle-course best, especially the downhill slide from Baker to Pierce.

For signature SF skateboards and skate gear, hit Mission Skateboards (p167) and FTC Skateboarding (p194); for skate fashion and street graphics, check out Upper Playground (p194).

Water Sports & Activities

SAILING

Sailing is best April through August, and classes and rentals are available from Spinnaker Sailing (p109) or City Kayak (p109). Newbies may feel more comfortable on a catamaran with Adventure Cat (p70) or a booze cruise with Red & White Fleet (p70).

Whale-watching season peaks mid-October through December, when the mighty mammals are easy to spot from Point Reyes. Book whale-watching tours through Oceanic Society Expeditions (p70).

SURFING & WINDSURFING

About a 90-minute drive south of SF, Santa Cruz is NorCal's top surf destination for kooks (newbies) and pros alike. SF's Ocean Beach (p203) is surfed by locals at daybreak in winter, but these Pacific swells are not for beginners. **Mavericks** (http://titansofmavericks.com/) big-wave surfing competition is held each February in Half Moon Bay (30 minutes south of SF), and is strictly for pros.

A safer bet is bay windsurfing and bodysurfing off the beach at Crissy Field (p56). Hit up Mollusk (p209) for specialty boards and Aqua Surf Shop (p209) for rental gear. Check the **surf report** (☎415-273-1618) before you suit up.

SWIMMING

Ocean Beach (p203) is best for walking – the Pacific undertow is dangerous. Hardy swimmers brave chilly Bay waters at Aquatic Park (p53) or Baker Beach (p57; nude around the northern end).

➡ **Local pools** Embarcadero YMCA (p109) has a well-kept pool; city pool schedules are listed at www.parks.sfgov.org.

NEED TO KNOW

Free Outdoor Activities

Lawn bowling, lindy-hopping, disc golf: try something new gratis at Golden Gate Park (p199).

Gear

From mountaineering to diving, gear up at Sports Basement (p68).

Group Activities

Join groups kayaking, surfing and camping through www.meetup.com or **University of California San Francisco's Outdoors Programs** (☎415-476-2078; www.outdoors.ucsf.edu).

Rainy Day Adventures

Head to the Marina to Planet Granite rock-climbing gym (p70) and House of Air trampoline park (p70), start a new arts project at Mission Cultural Center for Latino Arts, (p168) discover hidden talents at Workshop (p196) or hit Yerba Buena Center Ice Skating & Bowling (p109).

➡ **Alcatraz Sharkfest Swim** Swim 1.5 miles from Alcatraz to Aquatic Park. Entry is $175; check **Envirosports** (www.envirosports.com) for info.

Dance

Learn to lindy-hop (p211) at Golden Gate Park, tango at Mission Cultural Center for Latino Arts (p168) and vogue at Dance Mission (p169). Some music venues offer dance classes before the evening's entertainment, including Bimbo's 356 Club (p126) and Verdi Club (p164).

Sports & Activities by Neighborhood

➡ **The Marina, Fisherman's Wharf & the Piers** Running, biking, windsurfing, kayaking, skating and yoga in the Marina.

➡ **The Mission & Potrero Hill** Arts, dance, skateboarding and yoga in the Mission.

➡ **Downtown, Civic Center & SoMa** Swimming, kayaking and sailing in SoMa.

➡ **Golden Gate Park & the Avenues** Surfing, biking, archery, golf, disc golf and lawn bowling in the Avenues.

CHRIS BOSWELL / GETTY IMAGES ©

Explore San Francisco

SAN FRANCISCO'S **TOP SIGHTS**

Neighborhoods at a Glance

❶ The Marina, Fisherman's Wharf & the Piers p46

Since the Gold Rush, this waterfront has been the point of entry for new arrivals – and it remains a major attraction for sea lion antics and getaways to and from Alcatraz. To the west, the Marina has chic boutiques in a former cow pasture and organic dining along the waterfront. At the adjoining Presidio, you'll encounter Shakespeare on the loose and public nudity on a former army base.

❷ Downtown, Civic Center & SoMa p71

Downtown has all the urban amenities: art galleries, swanky hotels, first-run theaters, a mall and XXX cinemas. Civic Center is a zoning conundrum, with great performances

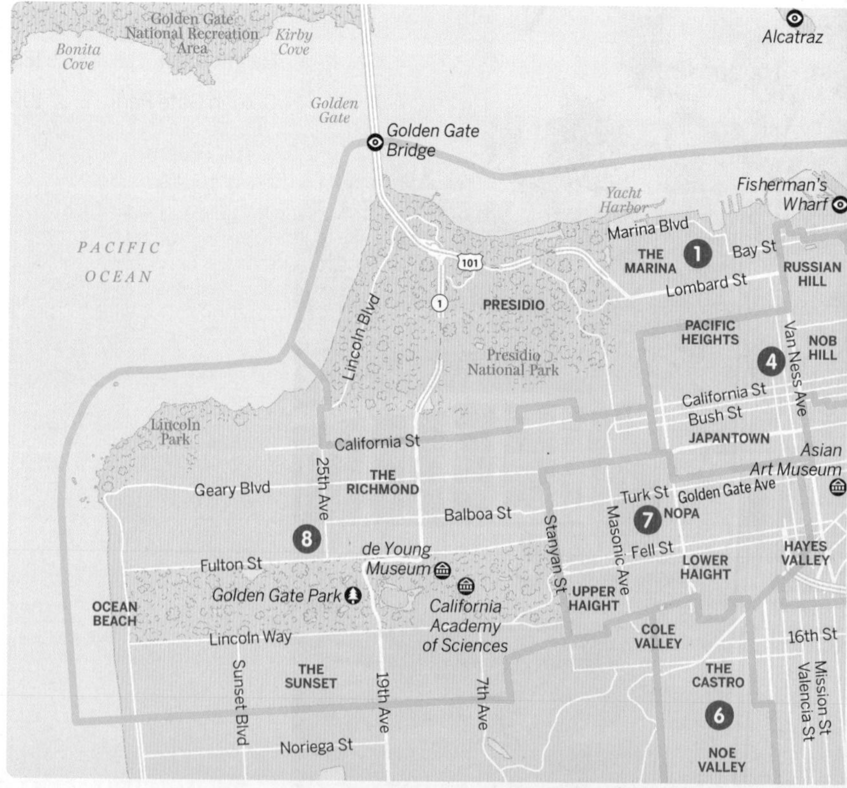

and Asian art treasures on one side of City Hall and dive bars and soup kitchens on the other. Some are drawn to South of Market (SoMa) for high technology, others for high art, but everyone gets down and dirty on the dance floor.

❸ North Beach & Chinatown p110

In North Beach, wild parrots circle over Italian cafés and bohemian bars. On the main streets of Chinatown, dumplings and rare teas are served under pagoda roofs, but its historic back alleys are filled with temple incense, mah jong tile clatter and distant echoes of revolution.

❹ Nob Hill, Russian Hill & Fillmore p129

Russian and Nob Hills are the stomping grounds of millionaires and urban hikers, with cable cars delivering customers to hill-top bars and high-fashion boutiques. When you see sushi picnics, anime-inspired fashion and the legendary Fillmore, you'll know you've arrived in Japantown.

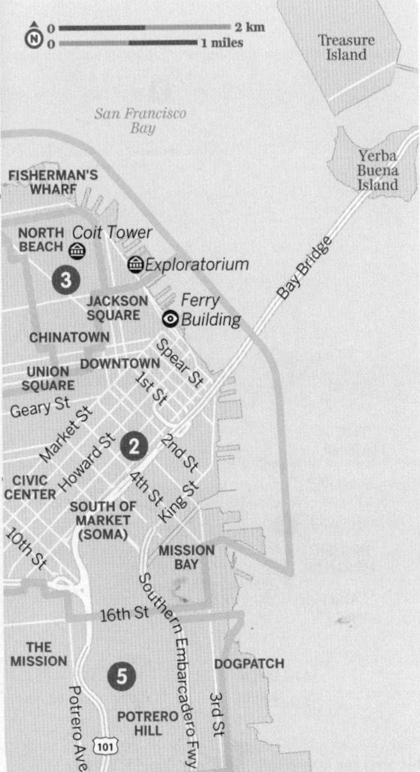

❺ The Mission & Potrero Hill p146

The best way to enjoy the Mission is with a book in one hand and a burrito in the other, amid murals, sunshine and the usual crowd of documentary filmmakers and novelists. Largely Latin American 24th St also attracts Southeast Asians, lesbians and dandies. Silicon Valley refugees take to Potrero Hill, while barflies and artists lurk in the valleys below.

❻ The Castro & Noe Valley p170

Rainbow flags wave their welcome to party boys, career activists and leather daddies in the Castro, while over the hill in Noe Valley megastrollers brake for bakeries and boutiques, as parents load up on sleek shoes and strong coffee.

❼ The Haight, NoPa & Hayes Valley p181

Hippies reminisce in the Haight, land of flower-power souvenirs, anarchist comic books and skateboards. Eat at trendy NoPa bistros and try on local designs in Hayes Valley, where Zen monks and jazz legends drift down the sidewalks.

❽ Golden Gate Park & the Avenues p197

Around Golden Gate Park, hardcore surfers and gourmet adventurers find a home where the buffalo roam, with the MH de Young's tower rising above it all. The foggy Avenues offer authentic Irish bars, organic Cali-Moroccan cuisine and Japanese convenience stores.

The Marina, Fisherman's Wharf & the Piers

THE MARINA | COW HOLLOW | FISHERMAN'S WHARF | THE PIERS | PRESIDIO

Neighborhood Top Five

❶ Strolling across the **Golden Gate Bridge** (p55) just as the fog clears, revealing magnificent views of downtown San Francisco with sailboats plying the waves below.

❷ Feeling cold winds blow through **Alcatraz** (p48) and imagining the misery of prison life.

❸ Giggling at the shenanigans of braying and barking sea lions at **Pier 39** (p52).

❹ Poking into hidden courtyards and finding indie boutiques along **Union St** (p67).

❺ Marveling at 19th-century arcade games at the **Musée Mécanique** (p53).

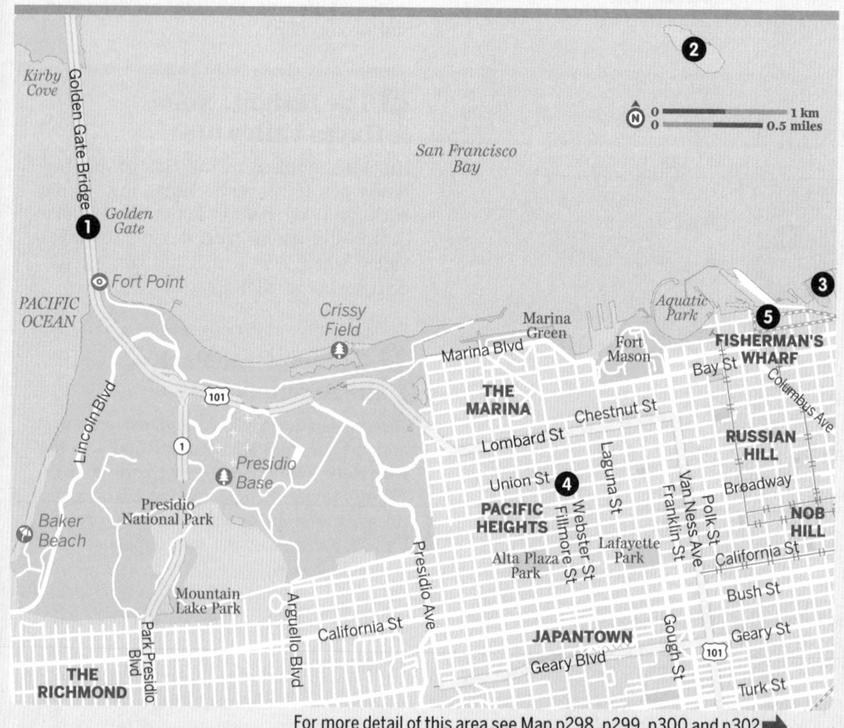

For more detail of this area see Map p298, p299, p300 and p302

Explore the Marina, Fisherman's Wharf & the Piers

Fisherman's Wharf is the epicenter of tourism in San Francisco; the few remaining fishermen moor their boats around Pier 45. Locals don't usually visit the Wharf because it's entirely geared to tourists. Budget two hours to a half-day maximum. Weekends it gets packed by early afternoon: come first thing in the morning to avoid crowds. Summertime fog usually clears by midday (if it clears at all), so visit the Golden Gate Bridge during early afternoon – but be forewarned that afternoon fog blows in around 4pm. Carry a jacket and don't wear shorts, unless you're here during the rare heat wave (locals spot the tourists by their short pants). Most people walk further than they anticipate: wear comfortable shoes and sunscreen. Cow Hollow and the Marina have good boutique-shopping strips, bars and restaurants. Explore them later in the day, after working hours but while shops are still open, when the busy sidewalks provide a glimpse of the fancy-pants Marina crowd.

Local Life

➜ **Nature walks** San Franciscans love the outdoors – joggers and dog walkers flock to the waterfront trails at Crissy Field, and head for the hills of the Presidio for wooded trails and site-specific art installations.

➜ **Barhopping** The Marina District bars on Fillmore St, from Union St to Chestnut St, are ground zero for party-girl sorority sisters and the varsity jocks who love them. Not all locals approve.

➜ **City views** For dramatic views of Fisherman's Wharf and the San Francisco skyline – and a break from the crowds – hop on a ferry at Pier 41.

Getting There & Away

➜ **Streetcar** Historic F Market streetcars run along Market St, then up the Embarcadero waterfront to Fisherman's Wharf.

➜ **Cable car** The Powell-Hyde and Powell-Mason lines run up Powell St to the Wharf; the Mason line is quicker but the hills are better on the Hyde line.

➜ **Bus** Major routes to the Wharf and/or the Marina from downtown include the 19, 30, 47 and 49.

➜ **Parking** At the Wharf, there are garages at Pier 39 and Ghiradelli Square (enter on Beach St, between Larkin and Polk Sts). At the Marina, there's parking at Crissy Field and Fort Mason. The Presidio is the only place where it's easy to park – and free.

Lonely Planet's Top Tip

To escape the crowds, head west of Ghiradelli Square. Make your way on foot or bike to Aquatic Park, then cut west along the waterfront path, through Fort Mason to the Marina Green. Aim for the bobbing masts of the yacht club, along Marina Blvd, stopping to explore the piers but keeping your eye on the prize: the Golden Gate Bridge.

Best Places to Eat

- ➜ Gary Danko (p63)
- ➜ A16 (p65)
- ➜ Betelnut (p65)
- ➜ Off the Grid (p64)
- ➜ Greens (p64)

For reviews, see p61 

Best Places to Drink

- ➜ Interval Bar & Cafe (p66)
- ➜ Buena Vista Cafe (p66)
- ➜ Gold Dust Lounge (p66)
- ➜ Pier 23 (p67)
- ➜ West Coast Wine & Cheese (p66)

For reviews, see p66 

Best for Waterfront Vistas

- ➜ Golden Gate Bridge (p55)
- ➜ Warming Hut (p65)
- ➜ Crissy Field (p56)
- ➜ Municipal pier at Aquatic Park (p53)
- ➜ Sea lions at Pier 39 (p52)

For reviews, see p52 

TOP SIGHT
ALCATRAZ

DAVID CLAPP / GETTY IMAGES ©

Alcatraz: for over 150 years, the name has given the innocent chills and the guilty cold sweats. Over the decades, it's been the nation's first military prison, a forbidding maximum-security penitentiary and disputed territory between Native American activists and the FBI. So it's no surprise that the first step you take off the ferry and onto 'the Rock' seems to cue ominous music: dunh-dunh-dunnnnh!

Early History

It all started innocently enough back in 1775, when Spanish lieutenant Juan Manuel de Ayala sailed the *San Carlos* past the 22-acre island that he called Isla de Alcatraces (Isle of the Pelicans). In 1859 a new post on Alcatraz became the first US West Coast fort and it soon proved handy as a holding pen for Civil War deserters, insubordinates and the court-martialed. Among the prisoners were Native American scouts and 'unfriendlies,' including 19 Hopis who refused to send their children to government boarding schools, where speaking Hopi and practicing their religion were punishable by beatings. By 1902 the four cell blocks of wooden cages were rotting, unsanitary and ill-equipped for the influx of US soldiers convicted of war crimes in the Philippines. The army began building a new concrete military prison in 1909, but upkeep was expensive and the US soon had other things to worry about: WWI, financial ruin and flappers.

DON'T MISS...

- Introductory films and self-guided audio tour
- Solitary-confinement cells on D-block
- Any site-specific temporary art installations
- Waterfront vistas along (seasonal) Agave Trail

PRACTICALITIES

- Map p218, H4
- ☎Alcatraz Cruises 415-981-7625
- www.alcatraz cruises.com
- day tours adult/child/family $30/18/90, night tours adult/child $37/22
- ⏲call center 8am-7pm, ferries depart Pier 33 half-hourly 8:45am-3:50pm, night tours 5:55pm & 6:30pm

Prison Life

In 1922, when the 18th Amendment to the Constitution declared selling liquor a crime, rebellious Jazz Agers weren't prepared to give up their tipple – and gangsters kept the booze coming. Authorities were determined to make a public example of criminal ringleaders and in 1934 the Federal Bureau of Prisons took over Alcatraz as a prominent showcase for its crime-fighting efforts. The Rock averaged only 264 inmates, but its roster read like a list of America's Most Wanted. A-list criminals doing time on Alcatraz included Chicago crime boss Al 'Scarface' Capone, dapper kidnapper George 'Machine Gun' Kelly, hot-headed Harlem mafioso and sometime-poet 'Bumpy' Johnson and Morton Sobell, the military contractor found guilty of Soviet espionage along with Julius and Ethel Rosenberg.

Today, first-person accounts of daily life in the Alcatraz lockup are included on the excellent self-guided audio tour. But take your headphones off for just a moment and you'll notice the sound of carefree city life traveling from across the water: this is the torment that made perilous escapes into riptides worth the risk. Although Alcatraz was considered escape-proof, in 1962 the Anglin brothers and Frank Morris stuffed their beds with dummies, floated away on a makeshift raft and were never seen again. Security and upkeep proved prohibitively expensive and finally the island prison was abandoned to the birds in 1963.

Indian Occupation

Native Americans claimed sovereignty over the island in the '60s, noting that Alcatraz had long been used by the Ohlone people as a spiritual retreat. But federal authorities refused their proposal to turn Alcatraz into a Native American study center. Then on the eve of Thanksgiving 1969, 79 Native American activists swam to the island and took it over. During the next 19 months, some 5600 Native Americans would visit the occupied island. Public support eventually pressured President Richard Nixon in 1970 to restore Native territory and strengthen self-rule for Native nations.

Each Thanksgiving Day since 1975, an 'Un-Thanksgiving' ceremony has been held at dawn on Alcatraz, with Native leaders and supporters showing their determination to reverse the course of colonial history. After the government regained control of the island, it became a national park and by 1973 it had already become a major tourist draw. Today the cell blocks' 'Home of the free Indian land' water-tower graffiti and rare wildlife are all part of the attraction.

NEED TO KNOW

Book well ahead: a month for self-guided daytime visits, and two to three months for popular ranger-led nighttime tours. When visiting by day, to avoid crowds book the day's first or last boat. You need only reserve the outbound boat, not the return, so take your time.

Weather changes fast and it's often windy and much colder on Alcatraz, so wear extra layers, long pants and a cap.

Find out if there's a site-specific art installation during your visit. They're included in your ticket price, but may have limited hours.

Visiting Alcatraz means walking – a lot. The ferry drops you off at the bottom of a 130ft-high hill, which you'll have to ascend to reach the cell block. The ¼-mile path is paved, but if you're out of shape you'll be panting by the top. For people with mobility impairment, there's a twice-hourly tram from dock to cell house. Wear sturdy shoes, as you may want to explore some of the unpaved bird-watching trails.

Note: eating is allowed only at the ferry dock. There's no food on the island, only bottled water, coffee and nuts.

Alcatraz

Book a ferry from Pier 33 and ride 1.5 miles across the bay to explore America's most notorious former prison. The trip itself is worth the money, providing stunning views of the city skyline. Once you've landed at the **Ferry Dock & Pier** 1, you begin the 580-yard walk to the top of the island and prison; if you're out of shape, there's a twice-hourly tram.

As you climb toward the **Guardhouse** 2, notice the island's steep slope; before it was a prison, Alcatraz was a fort. In the 1850s, the military quarried the rocky shores into near-vertical cliffs. Ships could then only dock at a single port, separated from the main buildings by a sally port (a drawbridge and moat in what became the guardhouse). Inside, peer through floor grates to see Alcatraz' original prison.

Volunteers tend the brilliant **Officer's Row Gardens** 3 – an orderly counterpoint to the overgrown rose bushes surrounding the burned-out shell of the **Warden's House** 4. At the top of the hill, by the front door of the **Main Cellhouse** 5, beautiful shots unfurl all around, including a **view of the Golden Gate Bridge** 6. Above the main door of the administration building, notice the **historic signs & graffiti** 7, before you step inside the dank, cold prison to find the **Frank Morris cell** 8, former home to Alcatraz' most notorious jail-breaker.

TOP TIPS

- Book at least one month prior for self-guided daytime visits, longer for ranger-led night tours. For info on garden tours, see www.alcatrazgardens.org.
- Be prepared to hike; a steep path ascends from the ferry landing to the cell block. Most people spend two to three hours on the island. You need only reserve for the outbound ferry; take any ferry back.
- There's no food (just water) but you can bring your own; picnicking is allowed at the ferry dock only. Dress in layers as weather changes fast and it's usually windy.

Historic Signs & Graffiti

During their 1969–71 occupation, Native Americans graffitied the water tower: 'Home of the Free Indian Land.' Above the cellhouse door, examine the eagle-and-flag crest to see how the red-and-white stripes were changed to spell 'Free.'

Warden's House

Fires destroyed the warden's house and other structures during the Indian Occupation. The government blamed the Native Americans; the Native Americans blamed agents provocateurs acting on behalf of the Nixon Administration to undermine public sympathy.

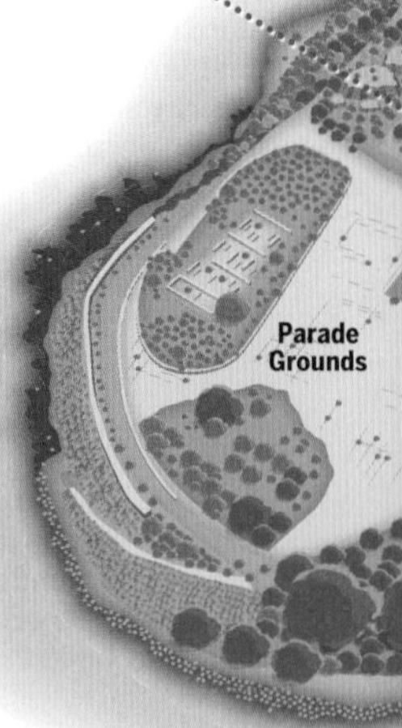

Ferry Dock & Pier

A giant wall map helps you get your bearings. Inside nearby Bldg 64, short films and exhibits provide historical perspective on the prison and details about the Indian Occupation.

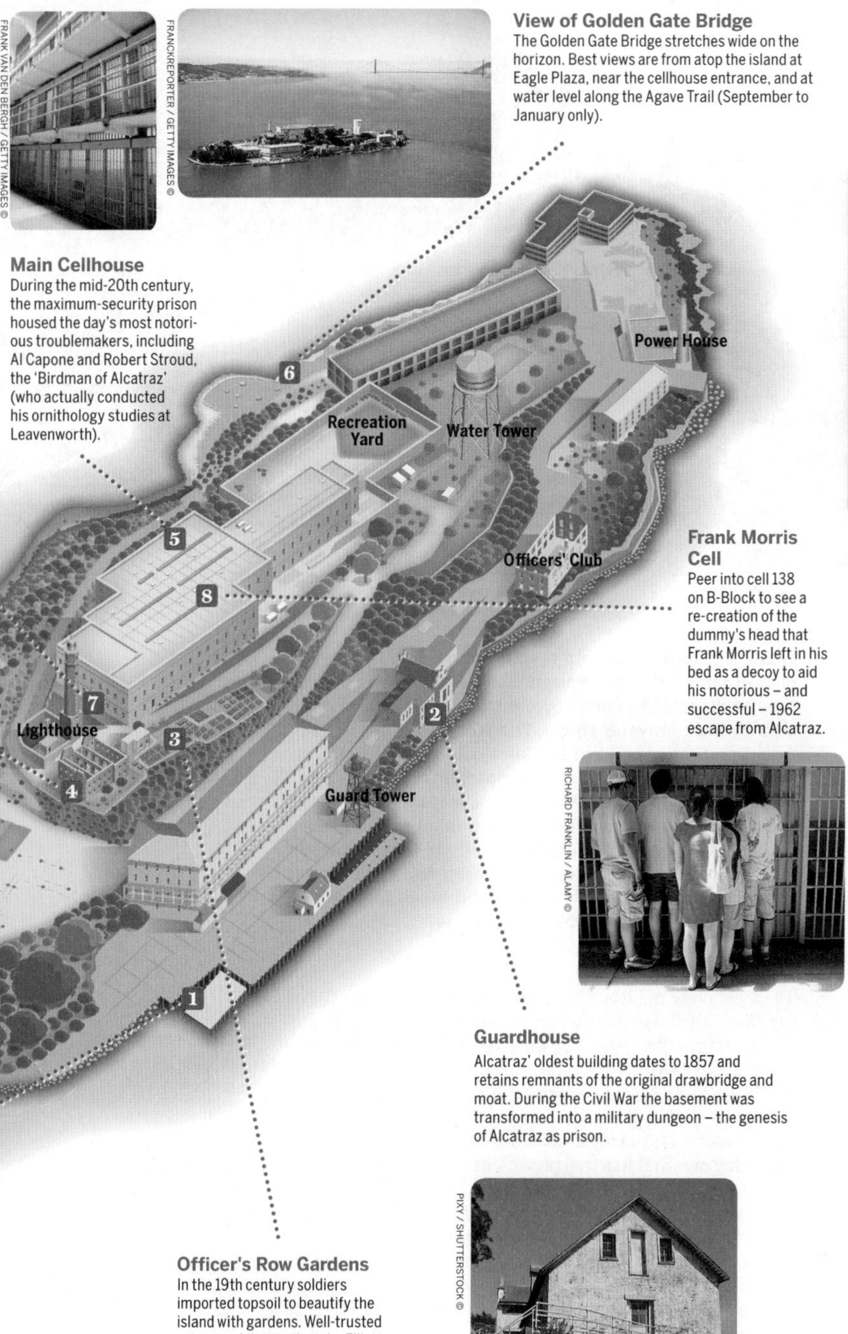

FRANK VAN DEN BERGH / GETTY IMAGES ©

FRANCKREPORTER / GETTY IMAGES ©

View of Golden Gate Bridge
The Golden Gate Bridge stretches wide on the horizon. Best views are from atop the island at Eagle Plaza, near the cellhouse entrance, and at water level along the Agave Trail (September to January only).

Main Cellhouse
During the mid-20th century, the maximum-security prison housed the day's most notorious troublemakers, including Al Capone and Robert Stroud, the 'Birdman of Alcatraz' (who actually conducted his ornithology studies at Leavenworth).

Frank Morris Cell
Peer into cell 138 on B-Block to see a re-creation of the dummy's head that Frank Morris left in his bed as a decoy to aid his notorious – and successful – 1962 escape from Alcatraz.

RICHARD FRANKLIN / ALAMY ©

Guardhouse
Alcatraz' oldest building dates to 1857 and retains remnants of the original drawbridge and moat. During the Civil War the basement was transformed into a military dungeon – the genesis of Alcatraz as prison.

PIXY / SHUTTERSTOCK ©

Officer's Row Gardens
In the 19th century soldiers imported topsoil to beautify the island with gardens. Well-trusted prisoners later gardened – Elliott Michener said it kept him sane. Historians, ornithologists and archaeologists choose today's plants.

TOP SIGHT
FISHERMAN'S WHARF

FRED BAHURLET / EYEEM / GETTY IMAGES ©

Truth be told, you won't find many fishermen at Fisherman's Wharf. Though some still moor here, they're difficult to spot beyond the blinking neon and side-by-side souvenir shops. The Wharf may not be the 'real San Francisco,' but it's always lively and holds a few surprises. Stick near the waterfront, where sea lions bray, street performers scare unsuspecting passersby, and an aquarium and carousel entice wide-eyed kids. Once you've explored tall ships, consulted mechanical fortune tellers and eaten the obligatory clam chowder in a sourdough-bread bowl, hightail it away to more authentic neighborhoods.

Pier 39

The focal point of Fisherman's Wharf isn't the waning fishing fleet but the carousel, carnival-like attractions, shops and restaurants of **Pier 39** (www.pier39.com; Beach St & the Embarcadero; P 👪; 🚌47, 🚋Powell-Mason, MF). Developed in the 1970s to revitalize tourism, the pier draws thousands of tourists daily but it's really just a big outdoor shopping mall. On the plus side, its visitors center rents strollers, stores luggage and has free phone-charging stations.

By far the best reason to walk the pier is to spot the famous sea lions, who took over this coveted waterfront real estate in 1989. These unkempt squatters have been making a public display ever since and now they're San Francisco's favorite mascots. The valuable boat slips accommodate as many as 1300 sea lions that 'haul out' onto the docks between January and July. Follow signs along the pier's western edge – you can't miss 'em.

DON'T MISS...

- Sea lions at Pier 39
- Musée Mécanique
- San Francisco Maritime National Historical Park
- Aquatic Park

PRACTICALITIES

- Map p298, C2
- www.fishermanswharf.org
- Embarcadero & Jefferson St waterfront, from Pier 29 to Van Ness Ave
- admission free
- 🚌19, 30, 47, 49, 🚋Powell-Mason, Powell-Hyde, MF

San Francisco Maritime National Historical Park

Four historic Bay Area ships are floating museums at the **Maritime National Historical Park** (www.nps.gov/safr; 499 Jefferson St, Hyde St Pier; 7-day ticket adult/child $5/free; 9:30am-5pm Oct-May, to 5:30pm Jun-Sep; ; 19, 30, 47, Powell-Hyde, F), the Wharf's most authentic attraction. Moored along the Hyde St Pier, standouts include the elegant 1891 schooner *Alma* and the large 1890 steamboat *Eureka*. For more mariner action, check out the paddle-wheel tugboat *Eppleton Hall* and the iron-hulled *Balclutha*, which brought coal to San Francisco and took grain back to Europe via dreaded Cape Horn. It's free to walk out along the pier; pay only to board ships.

National Parks Visitors Center

San Francisco grew from its docks. This 10,000 sq ft **visitors center** (415-447-5000; www.nps.gov/safr; 499 Jefferson St; 9:30am-5:30pm; ; 19, 30, 47, Powell-Hyde) FREE for the nearby maritime national historical park details how it happened, in a permanent exhibit that re-creates the 19th-century waterfront. Also on display is a rich collection of maritime artifacts, from a giant 1850s first-order lighthouse lens to scale models of 19th-century schooners. Kids love running around the vast space. Rangers provide maps and information about the surrounding area's trails and walks, as well as all national parks and monuments of the American West, including Yosemite.

Musée Mécanique

A flashback to penny arcades, the **Musée Mécanique** (415-346-2000; www.museemechanique.org; Pier 45, Shed A; 10am-7pm Mon-Fri, to 8pm Sat & Sun; ; 47, Powell-Mason, Powell-Hyde, F) houses a mind-blowing collection of vintage mechanical amusements. Sinister, freckle-faced Laughing Sal has creeped out kids for over a century, but don't let this manic mannequin deter you from the best arcade west of Coney Island. A quarter lets you start brawls in Wild West saloons, peep at belly dancers through a vintage Mutoscope and even learn a cautionary tale about smoking opium.

Aquatic Park

Fisherman's Wharf eccentricity is mostly staged, but at **Aquatic Park** (northern end of Van Ness Ave; ; 19, 30, 47, Powell-Hyde) FREE it's the real deal: extreme swimmers dive into the bone-chilling waters of the bay in winter, while oblivious old men cast fishing lines and listen to AM-radio sport. Aside from being

FISHERMEN AT PIER 47

A few third- and fourth-generation fishermen remain in the bay, but to survive the drop in salmon and other local stocks some now use their boats for tours, surviving off the city's new lifeblood: tourism. Find the remaining fleet around Pier 47.

It's hard to resist waterfront restaurants and their breathtaking views, but you really should – unless only for drinks and appetizers. Aside from places we recommend, Wharf restaurants are way overpriced and the food can't compare to what's available in nearby neighborhoods. Go simple – maybe a cup of chowder or some crab Louis from the fish stands at the foot of Taylor St.

the city's principal swimming beach (bathrooms but no lifeguard), the park is ideal for people-watching and sandcastle-building. For perspective on the Wharf, wander out along the enormous pier at the foot of Van Ness Ave.

Maritime Museum (Aquatic Park Bathhouse)

The **Maritime Museum** (Aquatic Park Bathhouse; www.maritime.org; 900 Beach St; 10am-4pm; ; 19, 30, 47, Powell-Hyde) FREE was built as a casino and public bathhouse in 1939 by the Depression-era Works Projects Administration (WPA). Beautifully restored murals depict the mythical lands of Atlantis and Mu and the handful of exhibits include maritime ephemera and dioramas. Note the entryway slate carvings by celebrated African American artist Sargent Johnson and the back veranda's sculptures by Beniamino Bufano.

USS Pampanito

The **USS Pampanito** (415-775-1943, tickets 855-384-6410; www.maritime.org/pamphome.htm; Pier 45; adult/child $12/6, plus $3 audio tour; 9am-8pm Thu-Tue, to 6pm Wed; ; 19, 30, 47, Powell-Hyde, F), a WWII-era US navy submarine, completed six wartime patrols, sank six Japanese ships, battled three others and lived to tell the tale. Submariners' stories of tense moments in underwater stealth mode will have you holding your breath, and all those cool brass knobs and mysterious hydraulic valves make 21st-century technology seem overrated.

SS Jeremiah O'Brien

It's hard to believe the historic 10,000-ton **SS Jeremiah O'Brien** (415-554-0100; www.ssjeremiahobrien.org; Pier 45; adult/child $12/6; 9am-4pm; ; 19, 30, 47, Powell-Hyde, F) was turned out by San Francisco's ship builders in under eight weeks. It's harder still to imagine how it dodged U-boats on a mission delivering supplies to Allied forces on D-Day. Of the 2710 Liberty ships launched during WWII, only this one is still fully operational. Check the website for upcoming four-hour cruises.

Aquarium of the Bay

Sharks circle overhead, manta rays sweep by and seaweed sways all around at **Aquarium of the Bay** (www.aquariumofthebay.org; Pier 39; adult/child/family $21.95/12.95/64; 9am-8pm late May-early Sep, shorter off-season hours; ; 49, Powell-Mason, F), where you wander through glass tubes surrounded by sea life from San Francisco Bay. Not for the claustrophobic, perhaps, but the thrilling fish-eye view leaves kids and parents wide-eyed. Kids love the critters and touch-pools upstairs.

San Francisco Carousel

A chariot awaits to whisk you and the kiddies past the Golden Gate Bridge, Alcatraz and other SF landmarks hand-painted onto this Italian **carousel** (www.pier39.com; Pier 39; admission $3; 11am-7pm; ; 47, Powell-Mason, F), twinkling with 1800 lights, at the bayside end of Pier 39.

Ghirardelli Square

Willy Wonka would tip his hat to Domingo Ghirardelli, whose business became the West's largest chocolate factory in 1893. After the company moved to the East Bay, developers reinvented the factory as a mall and ice-cream parlor in 1964. Today, **Ghirardelli Square** (www.ghirardellisq.com; 900 North Point St; 10am-9pm; 19, 30, 47, Powell-Hyde) has entered its third incarnation as a boutique timeshare/spa complex with wine-tasting rooms. The square looks quite spiffy with local boutiques, Kara's Cupcakes and, of course, Ghirardelli Ice Cream (p63).

TOP SIGHT

GOLDEN GATE BRIDGE, THE MARINA & PRESIDIO

The city's most spectacular icon towers 80 stories above the roiling waters of the Golden Gate, the narrow entrance to San Francisco Bay. It's hard to believe SF's northern gateway lands not into a tangle of city streets but into the Presidio, a former army base turned national park, where forested paths and grassy promenades look largely as they have since the 19th century.

Golden Gate Bridge

San Francisco's famous suspension bridge, painted a signature shade called International Orange, was almost nixed by the navy in favor of concrete pylons and yellow stripes. Joseph B Strauss rightly receives praise as the engineering mastermind behind this iconic marvel, but without the aesthetic intervention of architects Gertrude and Irving Murrow and incredibly quick work by daredevil workers, this 1937 landmark might have been just another traffic bottleneck.

How It Came to Be

Nobody thought it could happen. Not until the early 1920s did the City of San Francisco seriously investigate building a bridge over the treacherous, windblown strait. The War Department owned the land on both sides and didn't want to take chances with ships: safety and solidity were its goals. But the green light was given to the counterproposal by Strauss and the Murrows for a subtler suspension span, economic in form, that harmonized with the natural environment. Before the War Department could insist on

DON'T MISS...

- Fort Point
- Cross-section of suspension cable, behind Bridge Pavilion visitors center
- Midday summer fog clearing; bridge towers emerging through clouds
- Municipal pier behind the Warming Hut

PRACTICALITIES

- Map p302, B1
- www.goldengatebridge.org/visitors
- off Lincoln Blvd
- northbound free, southbound toll $6, billed electronically to vehicle's license plate; for details, see www.goldengate.org/tolls
- 🚌28, all Golden Gate Transit buses

BEST PLACES TO SEE IT

Hitchcock had it right: seen from below at Fort Point, the bridge induces a thrilling case of *Vertigo*. For wider vistas, explore the headlands just southwest of the toll plaza, atop high bluffs dotted with wildflowers. Fog aficionados prefer the lookout at Vista Point, in Marin, on the bridge's sunnier northern side, to watch gusting clouds rush through the bridge cables. Better still, find your way up the Marin Headlands to look down upon the span. Crissy Field reveals the span's entirety, with windsurfers and kite-fliers adding action to snapshots. Unlike the Bay Bridge, the Golden Gate allows pedestrians and cyclists to cross.

On the foggiest days, up to one million gallons of water, in the form of fog, blow through the Golden Gate hourly.

City Guides (p278) offers free, twice-weekly tours of the bridge, departing Sunday and Thursday at 11am, from the statue of Joseph Strauss by the visitors center on the bridge's SF side; plan to tip $5 per person.

an eyesore, laborers dove into the treacherous riptides of the bay and got the bridge underway in 1933. Just four years later workers balanced atop swaying cables to complete what was then the world's longest suspension bridge – nearly 2 miles long, with 746ft suspension towers, higher than any construction west of New York.

Crossing the Bridge

For on-site information, stop into the **Bridge Pavilion Visitors Center** (Map p302; ☎415-426-5220; www.ggnpc.org; Golden Gate Bridge toll plaza; ⏰9am-7pm Jun-Aug, to 6pm Sep-May).

Pedestrians take the eastern sidewalk. Dress warmly! From the parking area and bus stop (off Lincoln Blvd), a pathway leads past the toll plaza, then it's 1.7 miles across. If a 3.4-mile round-trip seems too much, bus to the north side via Golden Gate Transit, then walk back (for exact instructions, see www.goldengatebridge.org/visitors). Note: pedestrian access is open summer 5am to 9pm, winter 5am to 6:30pm.

By bicycle, from the toll plaza parking area, ride toward the Roundhouse then follow signs to the western sidewalk, reserved for bikes only. (Caution: locals pedal fast; avoid collisions.) Bicycles cross 24 hours but travel the eastern sidewalk certain hours; see www.goldengatebridge.org.

From the toll plaza, it's 4.5 miles to Sausalito; ferry back to SF via **Golden Gate Ferry** (☎415-455-2000, 511; http://goldengateferry.org) (to downtown) or Blue & Gold Fleet (p70) (to Fisherman's Wharf). Bikes are allowed on ferries.

Muni bus 28 runs west from Fort Mason (Marina Blvd and Laguna St) to the bridge parking lot, then cuts south down 19th Ave, intersecting with the N-Judah metro line at Judah St. Marin County-bound Golden Gate Transit buses (routes 10, 70/71 and 101; $4.50 one way) are the fastest, most comfortable way from downtown; alert the driver and disembark at the toll plaza *just before* the bridge. On Sundays only, Muni bus 76 travels from downtown, crosses the bridge and loops through the spectacular Marin Headlands.

Parking at the toll plaza is extremely limited. Find additional parking west along Lincoln Blvd.

Crissy Field

War is for the birds at **Crissy Field** (Map p302; www.crissyfield.org; 1199 East Beach; P; 30, PresidioGo Shuttle), a military airstrip turned waterfront nature preserve with knockout Golden Gate views. Where military aircraft once zoomed in for landings, birdwatchers now huddle in the silent rushes of a reclaimed tidal marsh. Joggers pound beachside trails and the only security alerts are raised by puppies suspiciously sniffing surfers. On foggy days, stop by the certified-green Warming Hut (p65) to browse regional-nature books and warm up with fair-trade coffee.

Baker Beach

Picnic amid wind-sculpted pines, fish from craggy rocks or frolic nude at mile-long **Baker Beach** (Map p302; ⏲sunrise-sunset; P; 29, PresidiGo Shuttle), with spectacular views of the bridge. Crowds come weekends, especially on fog-free days; arrive early. For nude sunbathing (mostly straight girls and gay boys), head to the north end. Families in clothing stick to the south end, nearer the parking lot. Mind the currents and the c-c-cold water.

Presidio Base

What began in 1776 as a Spanish fort, built by conscripted Ohlone people, is now a treasure trove of surprises, set in an urban national park, Presidio of San Francisco (p60).

Begin at the Main Post parade grounds to gather maps and shuttle schedules at the **visitors center** (Map p302; www.presidio.gov; Bldg 105, Montgomery St & Lincoln Blvd; ⏲10am-4pm Thu-Sun; PresidiGo Shuttle), then explore the free **Officers' Club** (Map p302; 415-561-4165; www.presidioofficersclub.com; 50 Moraga Ave; ⏲10am-6pm Tue-Sun; ; PresidGo Shuttle) FREE. Here you can learn the Presidio's checkered history, and warm up on fireside sofas, cozy on foggy days. Mickey Mouse fans head to Walt Disney Family Museum (p60), while fans of the macabre hike to the **Pet Cemetery**, off Crissy Field Ave, where handmade tombstones mark final resting places of hamsters and kitties. East of the parade grounds, towards the Palace of Fine Arts, lies the **Letterman Campus**, home to nonprofits and *Star Wars* creator George Lucas's Lucas Arts (now owned by Disney) – offices are closed to visitors but you can pay respects to the Yoda statue outside. Thursday evenings and Sunday afternoons, Off the Grid (p64) sets up food trucks on the parade grounds.

There's excellent hiking, too. To find exciting site-specific sculptures by environmental artist Andy Goldsworthy, consult **Presidio Trust** (Map p302; 415-561-5300; www.presidio.gov; Bldg 103, Montgomery St at Lincoln Blvd; ⏲information 8am-5pm Mon-Fri, gallery 11am-5pm Wed-Sun; PresidiGo Shuttle), which publishes good maps to scenic overlooks and is open days the adjacent visitors center is closed.

Free **PresidiGo** (415-561-2739; www.presidio.gov/shuttle) buses loop the park, via two routes, from the **Presidio Transit Center** (Map p302; 215 Lincoln Blvd). Service runs every 30 minutes, 6:30am to 7:30pm weekdays, 11am to 6:30pm weekends. There's weekday-only service to downtown, free to the public 9:30am to 4pm and 7:30pm to 8pm. Download maps and schedules from the PresidiGo website.

Fort Point

Fort Point (Map p302; 415-556-1693; www.nps.gov/fopo; Marine Dr; admission free; ⏲10am-5pm Fri-Sun; P; 28) FREE – a triple-decker, brick-walled US military fortress – was completed in 1861, with 126 cannons, just in time to protect the bay against certain invasion during the Civil War…or not, as it turned out. Without a single shot having been fired, Fort Point was abandoned 1900. When the bridge was built overhead, engineers added an extra span to preserve it. Alfred Hitchcock saw deadly potential in Fort Point, and shot the trademark scene from *Vertigo* of Kim Novak leaping from the lookout to certain death into the bay…or not, as it turned out. Fort Point has since given up all pretense of deadliness, and now showcases Civil War displays and knockout panoramic viewing decks. Saturdays once monthly March through October, staff demonstrate crabbing from the pier; November to February, inquire about spooky candlelight night tours. Reservations required for both.

TOP SIGHT
THE EXPLORATORIUM

Is there a science to skateboarding? Do toilets really flush counterclockwise in Australia? Find answers to questions you wish you'd learned in school at San Francisco's dazzling hands-on science museum. Combining science with art, the Exploratorium nudges you to question how you know what you know. As thrilling as the exhibits is the setting: a 9-acre, glass-walled pier jutting over San Francisco Bay, with vast outdoor portions you can explore for free, 24 hours a day.

Covering a whopping 330,000 sq ft of indoor-outdoor space, the 600-plus exhibits have buttons to push, cranks to ratchet and dials to adjust, all tinkered together by artists and scientists at the in-house building shop. Try on a punk hairdo, courtesy of the static-electricity station. Turn your body into the gnomon of a sundial. Slide, climb and feel your way – in total darkness – through the labyrinth of the thrilling **Tactile Dome** (☎415-528-4444; www.exploratorium.edu; $15, reservations & separate ticket required; ⏰10am-5pm Tue-Sun, 6pm-10pm Thu adults only).

In 2013 the Exploratorium moved from the Marina to Pier 15, a purpose-built solar-powered space, constructed in concert with scientific agencies, including NOAA, which hard-wired the entire pier with sensors delivering real-time data on weather, wind, tides and the bay. See the data flow in at your final stop, the glass-enclosed Observatory Gallery. Frank Oppenheimer founded the Exploratorium in 1969. He'd been a physicist on the atom bomb, was blackballed during the McCarthy era, then later re-emerged as a high-school teacher, eschewing secret scientific study in favor of public education. The Exploratorium is his lasting legacy, with the mission to incorporate technology with human values.

DON'T MISS

- Tactile Dome (reservations required)
- 'Visualizing the Bay' exhibit
- Tinkering Studio
- Plankton exhibit
- Everyone is You and Me (mirror)

PRACTICALITIES

- Map p299, A5
- ☎415-528-4444
- www.exploratorium.edu
- Pier 15
- adult/child $29/19, 6-10pm Thu $15
- ⏰10am-5pm Tue-Sun, over 18yr only Thu 6-10pm
- P 🚻
- M F

SIGHTS

The Marina & Cow Hollow

The Marina generally refers to everything north of busy Lombard St, west of Van Ness Ave, and east of the Presidio; Cow Hollow refers to the area around Union St, just south of Lombard, on the slope below Pacific Heights.

FORT MASON CENTER CULTURAL PRECINCT
Map p300 (415-345-7500; www.fortmason.org; cnr Marina Blvd & Laguna St; P; 22, 28, 30) San Francisco takes subversive glee in turning military installations into venues for nature, fine dining and out-there experimental art. Evidence: Fort Mason, once a former shipyard and embarkation point for WWII troops, now a vast cultural center and gathering place for events, drinking and eating. Wander the waterfront, keeping eyes peeled for fascinating outdoor art-and-science installations designed by the Exploratorium.

The mess halls are replaced by vegan-friendly Greens (p64), a Zen-community-run restaurant; and also the **Long Now Foundation** (Map p300; http://longnow.org; Bldg A, Fort Mason; 10:30am-5pm Mon-Fri, 11am-6pm Sat-Sun; Marina Blvd), whose compelling exhibits reconsider extinction and the future of time. Warehouses now contain cutting-edge theater at the Magic (p67), home base of Pulitzer Prize–winning playwright Sam Shepard, and improvised comedy workshops at BATS Improv (p67). The Herbst Pavilion counts major arts events and fashion shows among its arsenal – see the website for upcoming events. Hidden art exhibits include 'Tasting the Tides' water fountain, which lets you taste, with the touch of a button, the varying salinity of the bay – it's next to the firehouse, with glorious water views.

WAVE ORGAN MONUMENT
Map p300 (www.exploratorium.edu/visit/wave-organ; Marina Small Craft Harbor jetty; daylight hours; ; 22, 30) FREE A project of the Exploratorium (p58), the Wave Organ is a sonic sculpture of PVC tubes and concrete pipes capped with found marble from San Francisco's old cemetery, built into the tip of the yacht-harbor jetty. Depending on the waves, winds and tide, the tones emitted sound like nervous humming from a dinnertime line-chef or spooky heavy breathing over the phone in a slasher film.

CHURCH OF ST MARY THE VIRGIN CHURCH
Map p300 (415-921-3665; www.smvsf.org; 2325 Union St; 9am-5pm Tue-Thu; occasionally Mon & Fri; 22, 41, 45) You'd expect to see this rustic arts-and-crafts-style building on the slopes of Tahoe, not Pacific Heights, but this Episcopal church is full of surprises. The structure dates from 1891 but the church has kept pace with its progressive-minded parish, with homeless-community outreach, adult forums and exceptional music programs during Sunday services.

VEDANTA SOCIETY TEMPLE
Map p300 (415-922-2323; www.sfvedanta.org; 2963 Webster St; closed to public; 22, 41, 45) Meandering the Marina, you'll pass Mexican-inspired art deco, Victorian mansions, generic bay-windowed boxes – and, hello, what's this? A riotous 1905 mishmash of architectural styles, with red turrets representing major world religions and the Hindu-inspired Vedanta Society's organizing principle: 'the oneness of existence.' The society founded a new temple in 1959 but its original architectural conundrum remains.

OCTAGON HOUSE HISTORIC BUILDING
Map p300 (415-441-7512; 2645 Gough St; admission by donation $3; noon-3pm 2nd & 4th Thu & 2nd Sun of month, closed Jan; 41, 45) Crafty architects are always trying to cut corners on clients and here architect William C McElroy succeeded. This is among the last examples of a brief San Franciscan vogue for octagonal houses in the 1860s, when some believed that catching direct sunlight from eight angles was healthful. Three afternoons monthly, you can peruse collections of colonial antiques and peek inside a time capsule that McElroy hid under the stairs.

Fisherman's Wharf & the Piers

FISHERMAN'S WHARF LANDMARK
See p52.

EXPLORATORIUM MUSEUM
See p58.

FISHERMAN'S WHARF PROMENADES

What's beautiful at Fisherman's Wharf are the bay views. When walking west of Pier 39, avoid the inland streets; instead hug the shoreline, and stride broad promenades and docks jutting over the bay. Plunk down at benches to picnic (beware seagulls!). Near Pier 41, with sea lions in view, locate the huge topographical model of the entire Bay Area to wrap your head around this gorgeous vast geography.

Presidio

ALCATRAZ HISTORIC SITE

See p48.

GOLDEN GATE BRIDGE BRIDGE

See p55.

PRESIDIO OF SAN FRANCISCO PARK

Map p302 (415-561-4323; www.nps.gov/prsf; dawn-dusk; P; 28, 43) Explore that splotch of green on the map between Baker Beach and Crissy Field, and you'll find a parade grounds, Yoda, a centuries-old adobe wall and some thrilling site-specific art installations. What started out as a Spanish fort built by conscripted Ohlone in 1776 is now a treasure hunt of surprises.

Begin at the Main Post to get trail maps at the visitors center (p57) and inquire about site-specific art installations by Andy Goldsworthy. Brush up on your history at the Spanish-Moorish Officers' Club (p57), which dates from the late 1700s, and now hosts a small museum of local history, plus a lovely club lounge and restaurant. Fans of Mickey Mouse head to the Disney Museum; while fans of the macabre hike directly to the Pet Cemetery (p57). Head east of the parade grounds towards the Palace of Fine Arts and you'll come across the Letterman Campus (p57). On Thursday evenings and Sunday midday, spring through fall, Off the Grid (p64) sets up food trucks at the Main Post, creating a giant party on the grass.

PALACE OF FINE ARTS MONUMENT

Map p302 (www.lovethepalace.org; Palace Dr; 28, 30, 43) FREE Like a fossilized party favor, this romantic, ersatz Greco-Roman ruin is the city's memento from the 1915 Panama-Pacific International Exposition. The original was built of wood, burlap and plaster, designed by celebrated Berkeley architect Bernard Maybeck, then later reinforced. By the 1960s it was crumbling. The structure was recast in concrete, so future generations could gaze up at the rotunda relief to glimpse 'Art under attack by materialists, with idealists leaping to her rescue.'

Early 21st-century renovations permanently restored the palace to its initial glory. Pose for pictures by the swan lagoon.

SWEDENBORGIAN CHURCH CHURCH

Map p302 (415-346-6466; www.sfswedenborgian.org; 2107 Lyon St; hours vary; 3, 43) Radical ideals in the form of distinctive buildings make beloved SF landmarks; this standout 1894 example is the collaborative effort of 19th-century Bay Area progressive thinkers, such as naturalist John Muir, California arts-and-crafts leader Bernard Maybeck and architect Arthur Page Brown. Inside, nature is everywhere – in hewn-maple chairs, mighty madrone trees supporting the roof and in scenes of Northern California that took muralist William Keith 40 years to complete.

Church founder Emanuel Swedenborg was an 18th-century Swedish theologian, scientist and occasional conversationalist with angels; he believed humans are spirits in a material world unified by nature, love and luminous intelligence. Enter the church through a modest brick archway and pass into a garden sheltered by trees from around the world.

WALT DISNEY FAMILY MUSEUM MUSEUM

Map p302 (415-345-6800; www.waltdisney.org; 104 Montgomery St, Presidio; adult/student/child $20/15/12; Wed-Mon 10am-6pm, last entry 5pm; P; 43, PresidiGo Shuttle) An 1890s military barracks houses 10 galleries that chronologically tell the exhaustively long story of Walt Disney's life. Opened 2009, the museum gets high marks for design, integrating 20,000 sq ft of contemporary glass-and-steel exhibition space with the original 19th-century brick building, but it's definitely geared toward grown-ups and will bore kids after an hour (too much reading).

In typical Disney style, exhibits are impeccably presented, with lavish detail in a variety of media, including a jaw-dropping scale model of Disneyland that will delight die-hard Mouseketeers, but budgeteers may prefer to save their $20 toward a trip to Anaheim. Discount coupons often available; check online.

EATING

The fishing fleet unloads its catch at Fisherman's Wharf; mid-November to June, the specialty is Dungeness crab. Wharf restaurants are generally mediocre and expensive. If you're a serious foodie, explore the Wharf before lunch, from west to east (if you're arriving by cable car, ride the Powell-Hyde line); then go to the Ferry Building, either on foot (1-mile/20-minute walk) or F-Market streetcar, which goes directly there. In the Marina, good restaurants line Chestnut St, from Fillmore to Divisadero Sts, and Union St, between Fillmore St and Van Ness Ave. There's also good-priced ethnic fare on Lombard St, if you're willing to hunt. Greens (p64) gives reason to trek to Fort Mason.

Fisherman's Wharf

FISHERMAN'S WHARF CRAB STANDS — SEAFOOD $

Map p298 (Foot of Taylor St; mains $5-15; MF) Brawny-armed men stir steaming cauldrons of Dungeness crab at several side-by-side take-away crab stands at the foot of Taylor St, the epicenter of Fisherman's Wharf. Crab season typically runs winter through spring, but you'll find shrimp and other seafood year-round. Instead of dining on the giant, noisy, crowded plaza, either head east along the waterfront to the Pier 43 Promenade to find benches where you can sit; or if you don't mind standing to eat, look behind the crab stalls, between 8 and 9 Fisherman's Wharf, for swinging glass doors marked 'Passageway to the Boats' and amble out the docks to eat in view of the boats that hauled in your lunch.

FISHERMAN'S WHARF FOOD TRUCKS — FOOD TRUCKS $

Map p298 (2850 Jones St; 47, Powell-Mason, MF) Three side-by-side food trucks provide perfect alternatives to the Wharf's overpriced restaurants. **Carmel Pizza** (Map p298; 415-676-1185; www.carmelpizzaco.com; 2826 Jones St; pizzas $11-18; 11:30am-3:30pm & 5-8pm Mon, Tue & Thu, noon-8pm Fri & Sat, to 6pm Sun; 47, Powell-Mason, MF) bakes gooey-delicious single-serving pizza in a wood-fired oven. **Codmother** (Map p298; 415-606-9349; 2824 Jones St; mains $5-10; 11:30am-7pm; 47, Powell-Mason, MF) serves note-perfect fish and chips, plus Baja-style fish tacos. **Tanguito** (Map p298; 415-577-4223; 2850 Jones St; dishes $4-13; 11:30am-8pm Tue-Sun; 47, Powell-Mason, MF) makes its own Argentinian-style empanadas with chicken or steak, stellar saffron rice and even paella (if you can wait 45 minutes). Note early close times and outdoor-only seating.

BOUDIN BAKERY — BAKERY $

Map p298 (www.boudinbakery.com; 160 Jefferson St; items $7-15; 11am-9:30pm; 47, MF) Dating from 1849, Boudin was one of the first five businesses in San Francisco and still uses the same yeast starter in its sourdough bread. Though you can definitely find better bread elsewhere, Boudin's cafeteria-style fast-food court remains a Wharf staple for clam chowder in a hollowed-out bread bowl. The best reason to come is the remarkably well-curated **bread-baking museum**, which chronicles SF's role in the Gold Rush and the city's long love affair with sourdough. Though there's usually a $3 museum admission charge, employees tell us you're welcome to peek inside for free if nobody's staffing the door.

PAT'S CAFE — AMERICAN $

Map p318 (415-776-8735; patscafesf.com; 2330 Taylor St; mains $8-12; 7:30am-2:30pm; ; 30, Powell-Mason) Just beyond the tourist hubbub, this cute little storefront diner serves classic-American food – scrambles, pancakes and waffles for breakfast; hot pastrami, patty melts and club sandwiches for lunch – to locals and out-of-towners who appreciate no-fuss cooking, cheerful service and the easy location between the Wharf and North Beach.

IN-N-OUT BURGER — BURGERS $

Map p298 (800-786-1000; www.in-n-out.com; 333 Jefferson St; meals under $10; 10:30am-1am Sun-Thu, to 1:30am Fri & Sat; ; 30, 47, Powell-Hyde) Gourmet burgers have taken SF by storm, but In-N-Out has had a good

> **FINDING WATERFRONT ADDRESSES**
>
> When searching for waterfront addresses, note that even-numbered piers lie *south* of the Ferry Building, and odd-numbered piers are *north* of the Ferry Building. All even-numbered piers are south of Market St.

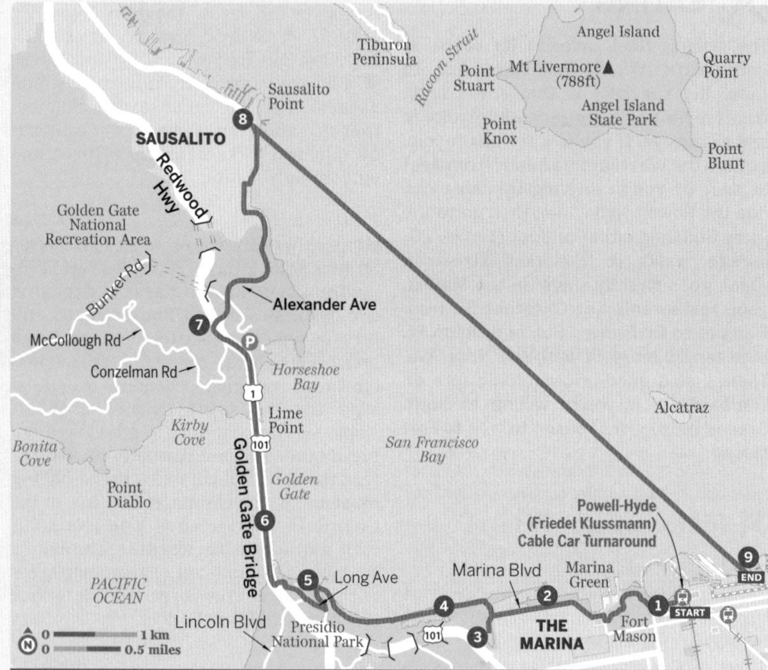

City Ride
Freewheeling Over the Bridge

START MARITIME MUSEUM
FINISH PIER 41
LENGTH EIGHT MILES; TWO TO FOUR HOURS

Built in Streamline Moderne style, the 1939 ❶ **Maritime Museum** (p54) resembles an art-deco ocean liner. Head behind the building to the sandy shore along Aquatic Park and dip your toes into the icy bay.

Joggers, Frisbee-throwers and kite-fliers congregate at ❷ **Marina Green**. A right turn bisects two boat marinas; at the end is the curious Wave Organ. Flash back to the 1915 Panama–Pacific International Expo at the ❸ **Palace of Fine Arts** (p60). Hear how your voice echoes inside. Watch kids chase swans, while you pose for photos beside gorgeous Greco-Roman arches.

Head to ❹ **Crissy Field** (p56) to watch windsurfers and kiteboarders attempt one of SF's windiest beaches. Take the Golden Gate Promenade, a foot-and-bike path skirting the field, toward Fort Point. Fuel up on organic sandwiches and coffee at ❺ **Warming Hut** (p65). Afterwards, backtrack to Long Ave and hang a sharp right up super-steep Lincoln Blvd toward the bridge.

With everyone craning their necks, it's no surprise bicycles sometimes collide on the ❻ **Golden Gate Bridge** (p55); keep your eyes peeled. Before crossing, stop at the visitors center and see the exhibits. You'll be grateful you brought a hat and windbreaker if the fog suddenly blows in.

Just across the bridge, turn left onto Conzelman Rd and ascend the ❼ **Marin Headlands** to look down on the bridge from a former WWII bunker, Battery Spencer – pedal up the giant hill or walk your bike. Or just enjoy the views and pedal past. Swanky ❽ **Sausalito**, with bayside vistas and galleries aplenty, is ideal for a stroll, but first get the ferry schedule at the dock to coordinate your timing.

Ferry from Sausalito back to ❾ **Pier 41** at Fisherman's Wharf or, if you're headed downtown, board a boat to the Ferry Building.

thing going for 60 years: prime chuck beef processed on-site, plus fries and shakes made with ingredients you can pronounce, all served by employees paid a living wage. Consider ordering yours off the menu 'animal style,' cooked in mustard with grilled onions.

GHIRARDELLI ICE CREAM ICE CREAM $

Map p298 (☎415-771-4903; www.ghirardelli.com; 900 North Point St, Ghirardelli Square; ice creams $4-10; ⏰10am-11pm Sun-Thu, to midnight Fri & Sat; 👪; 🚌19, 30, 47, 🚋Powell-Hyde) Mr Ghirardelli sure makes a swell sundae. The legendary Cable Car comes with Rocky Road ice cream, marshmallow topping and enough hot fudge to satisfy a jonesing chocoholic.

KARA'S CUPCAKES BAKERY, DESSERT $

Map p298 (☎415-563-2253; www.karascupcakes.com; 900 North Point St; cupcakes $2-3.75; ⏰10am-8pm Sun-Thu, to 10pm Fri & Sat; 🚌28, 30, 49, 🚋Powell-Hyde, Powell-Mason) 🌿 Proustian nostalgia washes over fully grown adults as they bite into cupcakes that recall childhood magician-led birthday parties. Varieties range from yummy chocolate marshmallow to classic carrot cake with cream-cheese frosting, all meticulously calculated for maximum glee – there's even gluten-free.

EAGLE CAFE AMERICAN $$

Map p298 (☎415-433-3689; www.eaglecafe.com; Pier 39, 2nd fl, Ste 103; mains $10-20; ⏰7:30am-9pm; 👪; 🚌47, 🚋Powell-Mason, Ⓜ F) Good for breakfast or a no-fuss lunch at Pier 39, the Eagle's straightforward fare includes pancakes and omelets, crab-salad sandwiches and burgers. Views are good, the prices right for families and it takes reservations, which you should make on weekends to spare yourself (long) waits.

★ **GARY DANKO** CALIFORNIAN $$$

Map p298 (☎415-749-2060; www.garydanko.com; 800 North Point St; 3-/5-course menu $81/117; ⏰5:30-10pm; 🚌19, 30, 47, 🚋Powell-Hyde) Gary Danko wins James Beard Awards for his impeccable haute California cuisine. Smoked-glass windows prevent passersby from tripping over their tongues at the exquisite presentations – roasted lobster with trumpet mushrooms, blushing duck breast and rhubarb compote, lavish cheeses and trios of crèmes brûlées. Reservations a must. Best to order the chef's three- to five-course menu – and why not start with champagne? From the first bite of oysters and caviar to the gift-wrapped tiny chocolates handed you on leaving, this is one meal to remember.

HOW TO KNOW IF IT'S FOGGY AT THE COAST

San Francisco is famous for summertime microclimates. Downtown may be sunny and hot while the Golden Gate is fogged-in and 20°F (10°C) colder. Thanks to satellite imagery, you can view the fog line over the California coast (during daylight hours) and immediately know if clouds are hugging the shoreline and – most importantly – how warmly to dress before trekking to the Golden Gate Bridge. Go to the **National Oceanic & Atmospheric Administration** (NOAA; www.wrh.noaa.gov/mtr) website for San Francisco, navigate to 'Satellite' and click on '1km visible satellite' for Monterey, California. SF is the thumb-shaped peninsula, surrounded by bays to its right. For on-the-ground views, search for 'Golden Gate Bridge cams' – note that conditions change fast.

FORBES ISLAND GRILL $$$

Map p298 (☎415-951-4900; www.forbesisland.com; Pier 41; 4-course menu $75; ⏰5pm-late; 👪; 🚌47, Ⓜ F) No man is an island, except for an eccentric millionaire named Forbes Thor Kiddoo. A miniature lighthouse, thatched hut, waterfall, sandy beach and swaying palms transformed his moored houseboat into the Hearst Castle of the bay. Today this bizarre domicile is a gently rocking romantic restaurant, strong on grilled meats and atmosphere – consider the lamb lollipops. Reservations essential. Take the putt-putt boat taxi from the west side of Pier 39; landlubbers dining below deck should bring motion-sickness meds.

SCOMA'S SEAFOOD $$$

Map p298 (☎415-771-4383; www.scomas.com; Pier 47; mains $28-42; ⏰11:30am-10pm; 🅿; 🚋Powell-Hyde, Ⓜ F) Flash back to the 1960s, with waiters in white dinner jackets, pine-paneled walls decorated with signed photographs of forgotten celebrities, and plate-glass windows overlooking the docks – Scoma's is the Wharf's long-standing staple for seafood. Little changes except prices. Expect classics like cioppino and lobster

WEEKEND FOOD TRUCKS

April through October, the most happening Friday-night food scene is at **Off the Grid** (Map p300; www.offthegridsf.com; items $5-12; ⏲Fort Mason Center 5-9pm Thurs Apr-Oct, Presidio 5-9pm Thu & 11am-4pm Sun Apr-Oct; 👪; 🚌22, 28). SF's largest mobile-gourmet hootenanny, with 40 Bay Area food trucks assembled in the parking lot of Fort Mason Center. Arrive before 6:30pm or expect 20-minute waits for the Chairman's clamshell buns stuffed with duck and mango, Roli Roti's free-range herbed roast chicken, and dessert from the Crème Brûlée man. The scene repeats on the Presidio Post's Main lawn Sunday midday (11am to 4pm) for **Picnic at the Presidio** and Thursday evenings (5pm to 9pm) for **Twilight at the Presidio**. Live music, DJs, beer, wine and cocktails keep crowds lingering. Cash only for all events. For the full list, see offthegridsf.com, but these three are the major events.

Thermidor – never groundbreaking, always good – that taste better when someone else buys. The restaurant accepts limited reservations but always accommodates walk-ins and has a retro-cool cocktail lounge where you can wait for your table.

✗ The Marina

PLUTO'S FRESH FOOD AMERICAN $

Map p300 (☎415-775-8867; www.plutosfreshfood.com; 3258 Scott St; mains $6-12; ⏲11am-10pm; 🖉👪; 🚌28, 30, 43) When you're hungry for a wholesome meal but don't want to fuss, Pluto's serves good food fast, with build-your-own salads, stick-to-your-ribs mac 'n' cheese, and carved-to-order roast beef and turkey with all the fixings. Order at the counter, then snag a seat. Kids' meals cost just $4.95.

ROAM ARTISAN BURGER BURGERS $

Map p300 (☎415-440-7626; www.roamburgers.com; 1785 Union St; burgers $8-10; ⏲11:30am-10pm; 👪; 🚌41, 45) 🍃 Obsessive about ingredients, Roam serves burgers of beef, bison and turkey, all locally grown and sustainably farmed. For classics, stick to juicy grass-fed beef served on a fresh-baked bun with housemade pickles. Don't ask for Coke: Roam makes its own organic sodas, plus stellar milkshakes with ice cream from Sonoma. There's also a branch on **Fillmore** (Map p315; www.roamburgers.com; 1923 Fillmore St; ⏲11:30am-10pm; 🚌1, 3, 22).

REAL FOOD DELI $

Map p300 (☎415-567-6900; www.realfoodco.com; 3060 Fillmore St; ⏲8am-9pm; 🖉; 🚌22, 41, 45) 🍃 This organic grocery's deli is packed with housemade foods, including respectable sushi, roasted-eggplant-and-tomato salad, free-range herb-turkey sandwiches and organic gingerbread. On sunny days, grab a patio seat.

LITE BITE CAFE, NEW AMERICAN $

Map p300 (☎415-931-5483; www.litebite.com; 1796 Union St; items $5-10; ⏲8:30am-8:30pm Mon-Thu, 8am-7pm Fri, 9am-7pm Sat & Sun; 🖉; 🚌41, 45, 47, 49) 🍃 Just because you're traveling doesn't mean you have to give up your diet. Lite Bite keeps you in check with quality fast food, made with organic ingredients. Expect dishes like whole-wheat turkey lasagna and shepherd's pie, with minimal fat, sugar and salt – plus fresh green drinks, cold-pressed juices and prepared foods to go.

LUCCA DELICATESSEN DELI $

Map p300 (☎415-921-7873; www.luccadeli.com; 2120 Chestnut St; sandwiches $8-10; ⏲9am-6:30pm Mon-Fri, to 6pm Fri & Sat; 🚌28, 30, 43) Open since 1929, this classic Italian deli is an ideal spot to assemble picnics for Marina Green. Besides perfect prosciutto and salami, nutty cheeses and fruity Chiantis, expect made-to-order sandwiches on fresh-baked Acme bread. There's hot homemade soup from 11am to 3pm.

SEED AND SALT VEGAN $

Map p300 (☎415-872-9173; seedandsalt.com; 2240 Chestnut St; items $7-14; ⏲8am-8pm Mon-Sat, 10am-8pm Sun; 🖉; 🚌30, 43) 🍃 Vegans, rejoice! This tiny café, with just two shared tables, exclusively serves organic, vegan, gluten-free foods, including great collard-green wraps, scratch-made veggie burgers, homemade pastries, and fresh-pressed green drinks and smoothies.

★GREENS VEGETARIAN, CALIFORNIAN $$

Map p300 (☎415-771-6222; www.greensrestaurant.com; Bldg A, Fort Mason Center, cnr Marina Blvd & Laguna St; lunch $15-18, dinner $18-25; ⏲11:45am-2:30pm & 5:30-9pm Tue-Fri, from 11am Sat, 10:30am-2pm & 5:30-9pm Sun, 5:30-9pm Mon;

; 28) Career carnivores won't realize there's zero meat in the hearty black-bean chili, or in the other flavor-packed vegetarian dishes, made using ingredients from a Zen farm in Marin. And oh!, what views – the Golden Gate rises just outside the window-lined dining room. The on-site café serves to-go lunches. For sit-down meals, including Sunday brunch, reservations are essential.

★BETELNUT ASIAN $$

Map p300 (415-929-8855; www.betelnutrestaurant.com; 2030 Union St; mains $8-14; 11:30am-10pm Sun-Thu, to 11pm Fri & Sat; 22, 41, 45) Palm-frond ceiling fans whirl overhead at high-energy Betelnut, a Marina District spin on the Chinese beer house, where fiery pan-Asian street foods are designed to pair with house-label brews and fresh-fruit cocktails. Standouts: Szechuan string beans, Cecilia's lettuce cups and succulent glazed pork ribs. Plan to share. Up-tempo beats set a party mood, perfect before a night out. Make reservations.

BLUE BARN GOURMET SANDWICHES, SALADS $$

Map p300 (415-441-3232; www.bluebarngourmet.com; 2105 Chestnut St; salads & sandwiches $10-14; 11am-8:30pm Mon-Thu, to 8pm Fri-Sun; ; 22, 28, 30, 43) Toss aside ordinary salads. For $11.75, build a mighty mound of organic produce, topped with six fixings: artisan cheeses, caramelized onions, heirloom tomatoes, candied pecans, pomegranate seeds, even Meyer grilled sirloin. For something hot, try toasted panini oozing with manchego cheese, fig jam and salami.

MAMACITA MEXICAN $$

Map p300 (415-346-8494; www.mamacitasf.com; 2317 Chestnut St; items $10-18; 5:30pm-late Mon-Thu, 5pm-late Fri-Sun; 30) One of the city's best for sit-down Mexican, Mamacita makes everything from scratch – tortillas, tamales and two dozen fresh-daily sauces for wide-ranging dishes, from spit-roasted goat to duck *carnitas*. The knock-out cocktail menu lists 60 tequilas, which explains the room's deafening roar. Make reservations.

BELGA BELGIAN $$

Map p300 (415-872-7350; http://belgasf.com; 2000 Union St; mains $15-29; 5-10pm Sun-Thu, to 11pm Fri & Sat; 22, 41, 45) Happening and swanky, Belga resembles a European brasserie, with side-by-side tables flanking red-leather banquettes – fitting for northern French and Belgian specialties, like mussels and fries, wood-fired roasts and sausages, spaetzle and cabbage, gratins and carbonnade (beef stew in beer), all made with a lighter, California sensibility. Reservations essential.

BRAZEN HEAD PUB $$

Map p300 (415-921-7600; www.brazenheadsf.com; 3166 Buchanan St; mains $19-28; 5pm-1am; 22, 28, 30) You have to know where you're going to find the Brazen Head, a tiny pub with low lighting and cozy nooks, reliably good onion soup and steaks, and the added bonus that the kitchen stays open till 1am – rarity in early-to-bed SF.

ROSE'S CAFÉ ITALIAN, CALIFORNIAN $$

Map p300 (415-775-2200; www.rosescafesf.com; 2298 Union St; mains lunch $10-17, dinner $17-28; 8am-10pm; ; 22, 41, 45) Follow your salads and housemade soups with rich organic polenta with gorgonzola and thyme, or a simple grass-fed beef burger, then linger over espresso or tea. Shop if you must, but return to this sunny corner café from 4pm to 6pm for half-price wine by the glass. Great breakfasts, too.

★A16 ITALIAN $$$

Map p300 (415-771-2216; www.a16sf.com; 2355 Chestnut St; pizza $13-19, mains $21-36; 11:30am-2:30pm Wed-Fri, 5:30-10pm Mon-Thu, to 11pm Fri, 5-11pm Sat, to 10pm Sun; 28, 30, 43) Even before A16 won a James Beard Award, it was hard to book, but persevere: the housemade mozzarella *burrata*, blister-crusted pizzas from the wood-burning oven, and 12-page Italian wine list make it worth your while. Skip the spotty desserts and instead double up on adventurous appetizers, including house-cured *salumi* platters and delectable marinated tuna.

Presidio

WARMING HUT CAFE, SANDWICHES $

Map p302 (415-561-3040; 983 Marine Dr; items $4-6; 9am-5pm; P; PresidiGo Shuttle) Wetsuited windsurfers and Crissy Field kite-fliers recharge with fair-trade coffee, organic pastries and hot dogs at the Warming Hut, while browsing field guides and sampling honey from Presidio bees. Ingeniously insulated with recycled denim, this eco-shack below the Golden Gate Bridge evolved from a heartwarming concept: all purchases fund Crissy Field's ongoing conversion from US army airstrip to wildlife preserve.

ARGUELLO MEXICAN $$
Map p302 (415-561-3650; www.arguellosf.com; 50 Moraga Ave; mains $12-18; 11am-9pm Wed-Sat, brunch to 4pm Sun; ; 43, PresidiGo Shuttle) Inside the Presidio Officers' Club, this Mexican restaurant, by James Beard Award–winner Traci des Jardins, features small dishes good for sharing, plus several mains, including standout caramelized pork shoulder. The bar makes great margaritas.

DRINKING & NIGHTLIFE

Fisherman's Wharf bars cater almost entirely to tourists but can be good fun, if pricey. If you're at a Wharf hotel but prefer a local scene, head a mile up Polk St. Clustered around Fillmore and Greenwich Sts, Marina District watering holes – which author Armistead Maupin called 'breeder bars' – cater to frat boys and bottle blonds.

★BUENA VISTA CAFE BAR
Map p298 (415-474-5044; www.thebuenavista.com; 2765 Hyde St; 9am-2am Mon-Fri, 8am-2am Sat & Sun; ; 19, 47, Powell-Hyde) Warm your cockles with a little goblet of bitter-creamy Irish coffee, introduced to America at this destination bar that once served sailors and cannery workers. The creaky Victorian floor manages to hold up carousers and families alike, served community-style at round tables overlooking the cable-car turnaround at Victoria Park.

★INTERVAL BAR & CAFE BAR
Map p300 (www.theinterval.org; Bldg A, Fort Mason Center, 2 Marina Blvd; 10am-midnight; 28, 30) Designed to stimulate discussion of philosophy and art, the Interval is our favorite spot in the Marina for cocktails and conversation. It's inside the Long Now Foundation, with floor-to-ceiling bookshelves, which contain the canon of Western lit, rising above a glorious 10,000-year clock – fitting backdrop for aged Tom Collins, daiquiris and gimlets, or single-origin coffee, tea and snacks.

GOLD DUST LOUNGE BAR
Map p298 (415-397-1695; www.golddustsf.com; 165 Jefferson St; 9am-2am; 47, Powell-Mason, MF) The Gold Dust is so beloved by San Franciscans that when it lost its lease on the Union Square building it had occupied since the 1930s, then reopened in 2013 at the Wharf – with the same precarious Victorian brass chandeliers and twangy rockabilly band – the mayor declared it 'Gold Dust Lounge Day.' This is likely the only Wharf bar where you may spot an actual local; come for a dose of red-velvet nostalgia.

WEST COAST WINE & CHEESE WINE BAR
Map p300 (www.westcoastsf.com; 2165 Union St; dishes $9-21; 4-10pm Mon-Fri, 11am-10pm Sat & Sun; 22, 41, 45) A rack of 720 bottles frames the wall at this austerely elegant storefront wine bar, which exclusively pours wines from California, Oregon and Washington, 26 by the glass. All pair with delectable small bites, including octopus a la plancha, charcuterie and cheese plates. Weekends (11am to 2:30pm) there's excellent brunch.

CALIFORNIA WINE MERCHANT WINE BAR
Map p300 (www.californiawinemerchant.com; 2113 Chestnut St; 11am-midnight Mon-Wed, to 1:30am Thu-Sat, to 11pm Sun; 22, 30, 43) Part wine store, part wine bar, this small shop on busy Chestnut St caters to neighborhood wine aficionados, with a daily-changing list of 50 wines by the glass, available in half pours. Arrive early to score a seat, or stand and gab with the locals.

LIGHTNING TAVERN BAR
Map p300 (415-704-1875; 1875 Union St; 4pm-2am Mon-Fri, 10am-2am Sat & Sun; 41, 45) Edison-bulb chandeliers and laboratory equipment lend a mad-scientist backdrop for bartenders, who serve good beers and cocktails, also available by the pitcher (think messy night out). Good pub grub – including 'totchos,' tater-tot nachos – keep your buzz in check.

MATRIXFILLMORE LOUNGE
Map p300 (www.matrixfillmore.com; 3138 Fillmore St; 8pm-2am Wed-Mon; 22, 28, 30, 43) The neighborhood's most notorious upmarket pick-up joint provides a fascinating glimpse into the lives of single Marina swankers. Treat it as a comic sociological study, while enjoying stellar cocktails, a blazing fireplace and sexy lounge beats – if, that is, you can get past the door. Bring your credit card.

BUS STOP BAR
Map p300 (415-567-6905; 1901 Union St; 10am-2am; 41, 45) Bus Stop has 18 flickering TV screens, two pool tables and a manly crowd that roars when their team scores. If your girlfriend wants to shop but you must watch the game, wait here as she trawls surrounding Union St boutiques.

ENTERTAINMENT

PIER 23 LIVE MUSIC

Map p299 (☎415-362-5125; www.pier23cafe.com; Pier 23; admission free-$10; ⏰shows 5-7pm Tue, 6-8pm Wed, 7-10pm Thu, 8pm-midnight Fri & Sat, 4-8pm Sun; MF) It resembles a surf shack, but this old waterfront restaurant on Pier 23 regularly features R&B, reggae, Latin bands, mellow rock and the occasional jazz pianist. Wander out to the bayside patio to soak in views. The dinner menu features pier-worthy options like whole roasted crab.

MAGIC THEATRE THEATER

Map p300 (☎415-441-8822; www.magicthea tre.org; 3rd fl, Bldg D, Fort Mason Center, cnr Marina Blvd & Laguna St; tickets $30-60; 🚌28) The Magic is known for taking risks and staging provocative plays by playwrights such as Bill Pullman, Terrence McNally, Edna O'Brien, David Mamet and longtime playwright-in-residence Sam Shepard. If you're interested in seeing new theatrical works and getting under the skin of the Bay Area theater scene, the Magic is an excellent starting point. Check the calendar.

BATS IMPROV THEATER

Map p300 (☎415-474-8935; www.improv.org; 3rd fl, Bldg B, Fort Mason Center, cnr Marina Blvd & Laguna St; admission $17-20; ⏰shows 8pm Fri & Sat; 🚌28) Bay Area Theater Sports explores all things improv, from audience-inspired themes to whacked-out musicals at completely improvised weekend shows. Or take center stage yourself at an improv-comedy workshop (held on weekday nights and weekend afternoons). Classes fill quickly.

LOU'S FISH SHACK LIVE MUSIC

Map p298 (☎415-771-5687; www.lousfishshack.com; 300 Jefferson St; admission free; ⏰shows 8:30pm-midnight Fri & Sat, 4-8pm Sun; 👪; 🚌30, 47, 🚋Powell-Mason, MF) Lou's presents live blues on Friday and Saturday nights and Sunday afternoons. Primarily a restaurant, it also has a few bar tables near the bandstand and tiny dance floor. And unlike bona fide blues bars, Lou's welcomes kids.

SHOPPING

Wharf shopping yields 'I Escaped Alcatraz' T-shirts, Golden Gate Bridge fridge magnets and miniature cable cars. The latter are perfect only-in-SF souvenirs; the best are of wood or metal. However, unless you're hunting for Christmas ornaments in July, there's (far) better shopping nearby on Polk St (Russian Hill) and in the Marina. First choice for Marina shopping is Cow Hollow – Union St between Gough and Fillmore Sts – where you'll find indie boutiques and upmarket chains; watch for shops hidden in courtyards. Second choice is Chestnut St, between Fillmore and Divisadero Sts, where chains like Apple, Gap and Pottery Barn sit beside boutiques catering almost exclusively to wealthy stay-at-home moms.

Fisherman's Wharf & the Piers

ELIZABETHW PERFUME

Map p298 (www.elizabethw.com; 900 North Point St; ⏰10am-9pm Mon-Sat, to 8pm Sun; 🚌19, 30, 47, 🚋Powell-Hyde) Local scent-maker elizabethW supplies the tantalizing aromas of changing seasons without the sweaty brows or frozen toes. 'Sweet Tea' smells like a Georgia porch in summertime; 'Vetiver' like autumn in Maine. For a true SF fragrance, 'Leaves' is as audaciously green as Golden Gate Park in January.

EXPLORATORIUM STORE GIFTS, TOYS

Map p299 (☎415-528-4390; www.exploratorium.edu/visit/store; Pier 17; ⏰10am-5:30pm Fri-Wed, to 10:30pm Thu; 👪; MF) Bring home gifts for the kids that you won't find anywhere else. The shop at the Exploratorium – the city's famous art and science museum – carries unique novelties, games, books and artworks, many made in San Francisco, all designed to inspire imagination.

HELPERS BAZAAR VINTAGE, FASHION

(☎415-441-0779; Plaza Bldg, Ghiradelli Square; ⏰10am-9pm Mon-Sat, to 6pm Sun; 🚌19, 30, 47, 49, 🚋Powell-Hyde) Socialite and philanthropist Joy Venturini Bianchi operates this 100%-for-charity boutique, where, if you dig, you may find Chanel. If not, there's always costume jewelry and Christmas ornaments. For high-end fashions at second-hand prices, book an appointment at **Helpers House of Couture** (Map p326; ☎415-609-0658, 415-387-3031; 2626 Fulton St; ⏰by appointment, open house one Sunday per month; 🚌5), near GG Park, an entire house packed with top-end couture donated by SF's elite.

The Marina & Presidio

★ATYS HOUSEWARES, GIFTS

Map p300 (www.atysdesign.com; 2149b Union St; 11am-6:30pm Mon-Sat, noon-6pm Sun; 22, 41, 45) Tucked in a courtyard, this design showcase is like a museum store for exceptional, artistic household items – to wit, a rechargeable flashlight that turns a wineglass into a lamp, and a zero-emissions, solar-powered toy airplane. Expect sleek, modern designs of superior quality that you won't find anywhere else. Of all the shops on Union St, this one's our favorite.

★SUI GENERIS ILLA FASHION

Map p300 (415-800-4584; www.suigenerisconsignment.com; 2147 Union St; 11am-7pm Mon-Sat, to 5pm Sun; 22, 41, 45) *Sui generis* is latin for one of a kind – which is what you'll find at this high-end designer consignment shop that features recent seasons' looks, one-of-a-kind gowns and a few archival pieces by key couturiers from decades past. No jeans, no pants – unless they're leather or super-glam. Yes, it's pricey, but far cheaper than you'd pay shopping retail.

MY ROOMMATE'S CLOSET FASHION

Map p300 (www.shopmrc.com; 3044 Fillmore St; 11am-7pm Mon-Sat, noon-5:30pm Sun; 22, 41, 45) All the half-off bargains and none of the clawing dangers of a sample sale. Stocks constantly change but have included cloud-like Catherine Malandrino chiffon party dresses, executive Diane Von Fürstenberg wrap dresses, and designer denim at prices approaching reality.

Y AND I BOUTIQUE FASHION

Map p300 (www.shopyandi.com; 2101 Chestnut St; 10:30am-8pm Mon-Fri, 10am-7pm Sat, to 6pm Sun; 22, 30, 43) When Marina girls need an outfit that won't break the bank, they shop Y and I for their cute dresses, priced at $50 to $200, by brands including Everly and Yumi Kim, plus fun sandals and shoes under $100, and big selection of all-handmade jewelry starting at just $20.

AMBIANCE ACCESSORIES, FASHION

Map p300 (www.ambiancesf.com; 1858 Union St; 11am-8pm Mon-Fri, 10am-8pm Sat, 11am-7pm Sun; 41, 45) The Union St outpost of this three-store SF-based chain showcases mid-range designers, with a good mix of trendy and classic cuts in jeans, dresses, shirts, shoes and locally made jewelry. Half the store is devoted to sale items, at least 20% below retail, sometimes yielding great bargains.

ITOYA TOP DRAWER GIFTS

Map p300 (http://itoyatopdrawer.tumblr.com; 1840 Union St; 11am-7pm Tue-Sat, to 6pm Sun-Mon; 41, 45) The first boutique outside Japan of Japanese brand Itoya showcases ingenious gadgets for travel you never knew you needed, including pocket-sized hotel-room humidifiers, collapsible bottles, travel alarms and portable bento boxes, plus pouches and totes to carry them home.

PLUMPJACK WINES WINE

Map p300 (www.plumpjackwines.com; 3201 Fillmore St; 11am-8pm Mon-Sat, to 6pm Sun; 22, 28, 30, 43) Discover a new favorite California vintage for under $25 at the distinctive wine boutique that won partial-owner and former mayor Gavin Newsom respect from even Green Party gourmets. A more knowledgeable staff is hard to find anywhere in SF and they'll set you up with the right bottles to cross party lines. Also in Noe Valley (p180).

DRESS WOMEN'S CLOTHING

Map p300 (415-440-3737; www.dresssanfrancisco.com; 2271 Chestnut St; 10:30am-6:30pm Mon-Sat, noon-5pm Sun; 28, 30, 43) A tiny shop for girly-girls with big clothing allowances, Dress draws from leading contemporary designers, such as Diane von Fürstenberg and Rag & Bone, to piece together an eclectic inventory that ranges from casual weekend wear to fancy cocktail dresses, rendered prettier with the good selection of locally designed jewelry.

TOSS DESIGNS ACCESSORIES, GIFTS

Map p300 (415-440-8677; www.tossdesigns.com; 2185 Chestnut St; 10am-7pm Mon-Sat, 10:30am-6:30pm Sun) If you've bought too much and need an extra bag, but can't bear schlepping an ugly disposable carry-on, Toss has you covered with a good selection of reasonably priced day-bags, all colorfully patterned in bold stripes or prints, some with matching hip flasks so you can tipple while you tote. Cashmere, candles and Waspy hostess gifts complete the collection.

SPORTS BASEMENT OUTDOOR GEAR

Map p302 (415-437-0100; www.sportsbasement.com; 610 Old Mason St; 9am-9pm Mon-Fri, 8am-8pm Sat & Sun; 30, 43, PresidiGo Shuttle - Crissy Field Route) Specializing in odd lots of sporting goods at close-out prices, this 80,000-sq-ft sports-and-camping emporium is also the best place to rent wetsuits for

THE BAY BY BOAT

Some of the best views of San Francisco are from the water – if the weather is fair, we highly recommend you take a boat ride. Here's a list of tour boats and ferry rides that will get you out on the bay and provide some stellar photo opps too. Be forewarned: it's always at least 10 degrees cooler on the bay's chilly waters. Bring a jacket.

Bay cruises The quickest way to familiarize yourself with the view from the bay is aboard a narrated one-hour cruise that loops beneath the Golden Gate Bridge. Red & White Fleet (p70) operates multiple trips from Pier 43½; Blue & Gold Fleet (p70) operates from Pier 41 and also offers 30-minute trips aboard its high-speed Rocketboat. (Note: Blue & Gold's Alcatraz-themed cruise only sails *around* the island, not to it.)

Sailboat tours If you prefer sailboats to ferries, hit the bay aboard the Adventure Cat (p70) – a catamaran with trampoline between hulls – for a 90-minute bay cruise or sunset sail. Or charter a private sailboat, with or without skipper, from Spinnaker Sailing (p109).

Paddle tours Explore the bay's calm eastern shoreline in canoe or kayak from City Kayak (p109), which guides tours, including full-moon paddles, and rents boats to experienced paddlers.

Whale-watching tours To go beyond the Golden Gate and onto the open ocean, we most recommend the excellent trips operated by the Oceanic Society (p70).

Guided tours Various companies offer tours for niche audiences. Ride the Ducks (p70) uses amphibious vehicles – thrilling for little kids.

Alcatraz trips Only one ferry operator (p277) is licensed to sail to Alcatraz and you'll need advance reservations, but other ferries sail nearby, providing a fleeting glimpse of the notorious island.

Sausalito & Tiburon trips It's a quick, inexpensive ferry ride to these neighboring waterside villages across the bay from SF. **Golden Gate Ferry** (415-455-2000; www.goldengateferry.org; adult/child $9.75/4.75; 6am-9:30pm Mon-Fri, 10am-6pm Sat & Sun) and Blue & Gold Fleet (p70) operate services.

Angel Island trips Spend the day hiking and picnicking at this state park in the middle of the bay. From San Francisco, take Blue & Gold Fleet (p70).

Oakland trips Ferries land at Jack London Square, where you can eat bayside and have a beer at historic Heinold's First & Last Chance Saloon, whose sloping bar has been operating since 1883. Take **San Francisco Bay Ferry** (415-705-8291; sanfranciscobayferry.com; adult/child $6.25/3.10).

Alameda trips Ferry to Oakland's small-town neighbor (via San Francisco Bay Ferry) and go wine-and-spirits tasting. Rosenblum Cellars is adjacent to the ferry landing. Or bring a bike and pedal to wineries and distilleries that lie a little further afield.

swims at Aquatic Park, gear for last-minute trips to Yosemite, or bikes to cross the nearby GG bridge – and free parking makes it easy to trade your rental car for a bike.

JACK'S MEN'S CLOTHING

Map p300 (415-409-6114; www.jackssf.com; 2260 Chestnut St; 10:30am-6:30pm; 28, 30, 43) Jack's dresses Marina dudes in sexy denim by Hudson, Agave and J Brand. But we most like the screen-print T-shirts, emblazoned with logos of Bay Area sports teams, present and past, from the A's to the Seals – not cheap at $40 but perfect souvenirs for fans.

SPORTS & ACTIVITIES

Fisherman's Wharf

BLAZING SADDLES CYCLING

Map p298 (415-202-8888; www.blazingsaddles.com/san-francisco; 2715 Hyde St; bicycle rental per hour $8-15, per day $32-88, electric bikes per day $48-88; 8am-8pm; Powell-Hyde) Blazing Saddles is tailored to visitors, with a main shop on Hyde St and six rental stands around Fisherman's Wharf, convenient for biking the Embarcadero or to the Golden Gate Bridge. It also rents electric bikes and offers 24-hour return service. Reserve online for a 10% discount; rental includes all extras (bungee cords, packs etc). Also has a **Downtown location** (Map p304; ☎415-202-8888; 433 Mason St; ⏰8am-8pm).

BASICALLY FREE BIKE RENTALS BICYCLE RENTAL
(☎415-741-1196; http://basicallyfree.com; 1196 Columbus Ave; half-/full-day bike rentals from $24/32, kids $15/20; ⏰8am-8pm; 👪; 🚌F, 30, 47, 🚋Powell-Mason, Powell-Hyde) This quality bike-rental shop cleverly gives you the choice of paying for your rental, or taking the cost as credit for purchases (valid 72 hours) at sporting-goods store Sports Basement (p68), in the Presidio, en route to the Golden Gate. If you buy too much to carry, they'll mount paniers or mail your stuff home.

OCEANIC SOCIETY EXPEDITIONS TOUR
Map p300 (☎415 256 9604; www.oceanicsociety.org; 3950 Scott St; whale-watching trips per person $120-128; ⏰office: 9am-5pm Mon-Fri, to 2pm Sat; 🚌30) Runs top-notch, naturalist-led weekend boat trips – sometimes to the Farallon Islands – during both whale-migration seasons. Cruises depart from the yacht harbor and last all day. Kids must be 10 years or older. Reservations required.

ADVENTURE CAT SAILING
Map p298 (☎415-777-1630; www.adventurecat.com; Pier 39; adult/child $40/20, sunset cruise $55; 👪; 🚌47, MF) There's no better view of San Francisco than from the water, especially at twilight on a fogless evening aboard a sunset cruise. Adventure Cat uses catamarans, with indoor cabins for grandmums and a trampoline between hulls for kids. Three daily cruises depart March through October; weekends-only in November.

RED & WHITE FLEET BAY CRUISE
Map p298 (☎415-673-2900; www.redandwhite.com; Pier 43½; adult/child $30/20; 👪; 🚌47, MF) A one-hour bay cruise with Red & White lets you see the Golden Gate Bridge from water level. Brave the wind and sit on the outdoor upper deck. Audio tours in multiple languages provide a narrative.

BLUE & GOLD FLEET BOAT TOUR
Map p298 (☎415-705-8200; www.blueandgoldfleet.com; Pier 41; adult/child 60min ferry tour $30/20, 30min Rocketboat ride $26/18; 👪) See the bay up close aboard a one-hour round-trip cruise to the Golden Gate Bridge or on a 30-minute high-speed thrill ride aboard the fleet's Rocketboat (May to October only). Blue & Gold also operates regularly scheduled ferry services to Sausalito, Tiburon and Angel Island, departing from Pier 41 at Fisherman's Wharf and (some) from the Ferry Building.

RIDE THE DUCKS BOAT TOUR
Map p298 (☎415-922-2425, 877-887-8225; http://sanfrancisco.rideth educks.com; 2766 Taylor St, cnr Jefferson St; adult $35-39, child $22-25) The Ducks' 90-minute tour covers the Wharf, North Beach, Chinatown and eastern waterfront. What's special is the conveyance: amphibious vehicle – bus to boat – that launches for a loop south of the Bay Bridge. Bring ear plugs: passengers get kazoo-like, noisy 'quackers' and blow them often.

Presidio

HOUSE OF AIR TRAMPOLINING
Map p302 (☎415-345-9675; www.houseofairsf.com; 926 Old Mason St, Crissy Field; $17; ⏰10am-9pm Mon-Thu, to 10pm Fri & Sat, to 8pm Sun; 👪; 🚌28) If you resented your gym teacher for not letting you jump like you wanted on the trampoline, you can finally have your way at this incredible trampoline park, with multiple jumping areas where you can literally bounce off the walls on 42 attached trampolines. Kids get dedicated play areas. Reservations strongly recommended – book three days ahead, especially weekends.

PLANET GRANITE ROCK CLIMBING
Map p302 (☎415-692-3434; www.planetgranite.com; 924 Old Mason St, Crissy Field; day use adult/child $17-20/14; ⏰6am-11pm Mon-Fri, 8am-8pm Sat, to 6pm Sun; 🚌28) Take in spectacular bay views as you ascend false-rock structures inside this 25,000-sq-ft glass-walled climbing center. Master top ropes of 45ft or test your strength ascending giant boulders and vertical-crack climbing walls; finish in the full gym or stretch in a yoga session. Check website for schedules.

PRESIDIO GOLF COURSE GOLF
Map p302 (☎415-561-4661; www.presidiogolf.com; Arguello Blvd & Finley Rd; 18 holes SF resident $65-85, non-resident $125-145; ⏰sunrise-sunset; 🚌33) Whack balls with military-style precision on the course once reserved exclusively for US forces. The course overlooks the bay and is considered one of the country's best. Book up to 30 days in advance on the website, which sometimes lists specials too. Rates include cart.

Downtown, Civic Center & SoMa

FINANCIAL DISTRICT | JACKSON SQUARE | UNION SQUARE | SOMA | CIVIC CENTER | THE TENDERLOIN

Neighborhood Top Five

❶ Taking a bite out of the Northern California food scene at the **Ferry Building** (p73) – showcase for the Bay Area's food purveyors and organic farmers – with incredible bay views.

❷ Squealing with glee aboard the **cable cars**, and congratulating yourself for not wearing shorts and shivering the whole way.

❸ Seeing all the way across the Pacific and glimpsing priceless treasures inside the **Asian Art Museum** (p75).

❹ Watching impresario Michael Tilson Thomas conduct Beethoven from the tips of his toes at the Grammy-winning **San Francisco Symphony** (p101).

❺ Wandering south along the Embarcadero for daytime people-watching, sneak peeks at Giants Games and dazzling nighttime views of the **Bay Bridge Lights** (p74).

For more detail of this area see Map p303, p304, p306 and p308

Lonely Planet's Top Tip

Most tourists begin their trips at Powell St but often get stuck waiting in the long lines at the Powell St cable-car turnaround at Market St – and subjected to panhandlers and bad street performers. Either queue up for the Powell St cable car before noon, or get your fix on the lesser-traveled California St line.

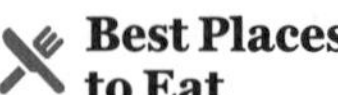

Best Places to Eat

- Ferry Building (p73)
- Benu (p94)
- Kusakabe (p89)
- Cotogna (p88)
- Tout Sweet (p89)

For reviews, see p87

Best Places to Drink

- Bar Agricole (p97)
- Local Edition (p95)
- Eagle Tavern (p100)
- Wilson & Wilson Detective Agency at Bourbon & Branch (p96)
- Sightglass Coffee (p97)

For reviews, see p95

Best Live Performances

- San Francisco Symphony (p101)
- San Francisco Opera (p101)
- American Conservatory Theater (p101)
- Yerba Buena Center for the Arts (p103)
- Oasis (p103)

For reviews, see p101

Explore Downtown

The cluster of public buildings around City Hall is called Civic Center. Start your day at Asian Art Museum, then graze local food stalls at Heart of the City Farmers Market, The Hall, or Twitter building marketplace. A word of warning: seedy Tenderloin streets west of Powell, east of Van Ness and south of Geary to Mission St are best avoided, except for groundbreaking nonprofit art galleries along Market St between 8th and 6th. Hop the F line to Powell St for Union Square shopping, or to Montgomery to admire Financial District architecture. Come nightfall, SoMa clubs and drag cabarets encourage outrageousness – and SF Symphony and SF Opera offer glimpses of greatness.

Local Life

- **Markets** Ferry Building farmers market days are local foodie magnets with heirloom produce, local artisan foods and free samples galore.
- **Arts revival** Blighted blocks of SoMa and Market St west of Powell may not be much to look at outside, but inside they're full of ideas as arts nonprofits stage provocative shows in formerly derelict dives.
- **Happy hours** Whether your drink of choice is wine, beer or a craft cocktail, you're spoiled for choice downtown – and weekday drink specials beckon.

Getting There & Away

- **Streetcar** Historic F-Market streetcars run above Market St, between the Castro and Fisherman's Wharf.
- **Cable car** Powell-Hyde and Powell-Mason lines link downtown with the Wharf (Mason is shorter, Hyde more scenic); the California St line runs perpendicular, over Nob Hill.
- **Bus** Market St–bound Muni lines serve downtown: 2, 5, 6, 7,14, 21, 30, 31, 38, 41, 45. In SoMa the 30 and 45 run down 4th St from the Marina and Union Square, and the 14 runs through SoMa to the Mission along Mission St. The 27 runs from the Mission to Nob Hill via SoMa; the 47 runs along Harrison St through SoMa, up Van Ness to Fisherman's Wharf; and the 19 runs up 8th and Polk Sts to the Wharf.
- **Metro** J, K/T, L, M and N metro lines run under Market St. The N continues to the Caltrain station, connecting SoMa to the Haight and Golden Gate Park. The T runs from downtown, via SoMa, stopping along 3rd St.
- **BART** Downtown stations are Embarcadero, Montgomery and Powell.

TOP SIGHT
FERRY BUILDING & SURROUNDS

Other towns have gourmet ghettos, but San Francisco puts its love of food front and center at the Ferry Building. The once-grand port was overshadowed by a 1950s elevated freeway – until the overpass collapsed in 1989's Loma Prieta earthquake. The Ferry Building survived and became a symbol of San Francisco's reinvention, marking your arrival onto America's most-happening food scene.

Ferry Building

Like a grand salute, the Ferry Building's trademark 240ft tower greeted dozens of ferries daily after its 1898 inauguration. But with the opening of the Bay Bridge and Golden Gate, ferry traffic subsided in the 1930s. An overhead freeway was built, obscuring the building's stately facade and turning it black with exhaust. Only after the 1989 earthquake did city planners realize what they'd been missing: with its grand halls and bay views, this was the perfect place for a new public commons.

Even before building renovations were completed in 2003, the **Ferry Plaza Farmers Market** (☎415-291-3276; www.cuesa.org; Market St & the Embarcadero; ⏲10am-2pm Tue & Thu, 8am-2pm Sat; Ⓜ Embarcadero) began operating out front on the sidewalk. While some complained the prices were higher than at other markets, there was no denying this one offered seasonal, sustainable gourmet treats and local specialty foods not found elsewhere, which soon captured the imagination of SF's professional chefs and semiprofessional eaters. Today the local gourmet action continues indoors, where select local stalls sell artisanal cheese, wild-harvested mushrooms,

DON'T MISS...

- Ferry Building farmers markets
- Food stalls in the Ferry Building's grand arrivals hall
- Bay Bridge views along the Embarcadero waterfront promenade
- Wild parrots and weird scenes at Justin Herman Plaza

PRACTICALITIES

- Map p303, D2
- ☎415-983-8030
- www.ferrybuilding marketplace.com
- Market St & the Embarcadero
- ⏲10am-6pm Mon-Fri, 9am-6pm Sat, 11am-5pm Sun
- P 🚻
- 🚌2, 6, 9, 14, 21, 31, Ⓜ Embarcadero, Ⓑ Embarcadero

NEED TO KNOW

You can still catch ferries at the Ferry Building, and on sunny days, crossing the sparkling bay is a great escape. Otherwise, follow the Embarcadero waterfront promenade south from the Ferry Building to Giants Stadium for San Francisco's favorite leisurely stroll.

Saturday morning's farmers market (p73) presents the best people-watching – it's not uncommon to spot an occasional celebrity – but arrive early if you're shopping, before star chefs snap up the best finds.

locally roasted espresso, and organic ice cream in foodie-freak flavors like barley wine and *foie gras*. People-watching wine bars and award-winning restaurants provide enticing reasons to miss your ferry.

Justin Herman Plaza

The plaza (p76) across the Embarcadero from the Ferry Building is a crowd-pleaser, and its central **Vaillancourt Fountain** is SF's favorite eyesore. San Franciscans love to debate what it looks like – concrete intestines? plumbing by angry ogres? unwinnable Atari video game? – but it was originally designed to mirror the freeway overpass that once roared above. Join the scene already in progress here among wild parrots, local craft-makers, lunchtime concertgoers, Critical Mass bike protesters, Friday-night roller skaters, wintertime ice-skaters and Valentine's Day pillow fighters.

Bay Bridge Views

The Bay Bridge looms large on the horizon south of the Ferry Building, and even larger in the minds of San Franciscans. Fear of crossing the bridge is invoked by San Franciscans as a legitimate excuse for skipping social engagements in Berkeley and Oakland – and when you watch Friday-night bridge traffic crawl as you stroll the Embarcadero, you'll concede the point. Some San Franciscans are still shaken by the 1989 Loma Prieta Earthquake, which collapsed the Bay Bridge's eastern span – it cost taxpayers $6.4 billion and took 12 years to fix. But the Bay Bridge is finally winning the admiration of San Franciscans, thanks to one local artist's bright idea. In 2013 Leo Villareal strung 25,000 LED lights onto the vertical suspension cable of the Bay Bridge's western span, transforming it into a 1.8-mile-long nightly light show. The **Bridge Lights** blink in never-repeating patterns – one second the bridge looks like bubbly champagne, then a lava-lamp forest, then Vegas-style fountains spraying 50 stories high. The installation was meant to be temporary, but thanks to local donors, it will be permanently installed in 2016.

Bay Bridge boosters and detractors agree on this much: the Bay Bridge was the inspiration of a certifiable madman. Joshua Norton arrived in San Francisco in 1849, made and lost a fortune, then disappeared – only to reappear in SF a decade later in a gold-braided jacket, declaring himself 'Emperor of the United States and Protector of Mexico.' SF newspapers gamely published the Emperor's decrees punishing use of the term 'Frisco' with a $25 fine (payable to His Highness) and – even wackier – ordering the construction of a trans-bay bridge in 1872. Petitions periodically circulate to rename the span **The Emperor Norton Bay Bridge** – though no one can agree if it's a compliment or an insult.

TOP SIGHT
ASIAN ART MUSEUM

One of the largest, most comprehensive collections of Asian art outside Asia covers 6000 years and thousands of miles of terrain. A trip through the galleries is a treasure-hunting expedition, from priceless Persian carpets and modern minimalist Japanese sculpture to the jewel-box gallery of lustrous Chinese jade – just don't bump into those priceless Ming vases.

The Asian Art Museum's distinguished collection of 18,000 Asian treasures does San Francisco proud, reflecting the city's 150-year history as the gateway to Asia. The museum's curators have performed diplomatic wonders under this roof, bringing Taiwan, China and Tibet together, uniting Pakistan and India, and striking harmonious balance between Japan, Korea and China. Granted, the Chinese collection takes up two wings and South Asia only one – but that healthy cultural competition has encouraged donations of South Asian artifacts lately.

The Asian Museum's curatorial concept is to follow the evolution of Asian art from West to East toward San Francisco, along Buddhist pilgrimage trails and trade routes. If you're tight on time, you might head directly to ground-floor special exhibitions, or follow the mapped trail of masterworks. Parents can pick up Explorer Cards for kids to find favorite animals and characters in the galleries.

Start your tour on the 3rd floor with a treasure trove of Indian miniatures and jewels. Detour through dizzying Iranian geometric tiles and Javanese shadow puppets, and turn a corner to find Tibetan prayer wheels. Ahead are Chinese jades and snuff bottles, and downstairs on the 2nd floor are Chinese calligraphy, Korean celadon bowls and an entire Japanese tea ceremony room. Look for artworks by contemporary artists responding to pieces in the collection, and don't miss artist's demonstrations in Samsung Hall before you return to ground-floor special exhibits.

Italian architect Gae Aulenti's clever repurposing of the old San Francisco Main Library left intact the much-beloved building's Beaux Arts exterior, and the entryway's travertine arches and polished stone grand staircase. She also added two ground-floor indoor courts for oversize installations and events, leaving plenty of room for educational activities. Hands-on workshops for kids, frequent evening lectures and occasional free yoga classes are major draws for pan-generational crowds. Make a day of it with lunch at ground-floor **Cafe Asia** (www.asianart.org/visit/cafe-asia; 200 Larkin St; mains $5-14; ⏲10am-4:30pm Tue-Sun, to 8:30pm Thu Feb-Oct; 👪; 🚌5,6,7,21, Ⓜ Civic Center), where sunny days mean sipping tea on the balcony terrace.

On Thursday evenings from 5pm to 9pm February through September, hipsters flock to the Asian for $5 entry with free evening events hosted by leading artists. Lineups vary, but recently included an interactive tour of China's digital culture, Korean quilting, protest art from both sides of the Pacific, Asian American jazz poetry and demonstrations from Olympian martial artists.

DON'T MISS...

- South Asian and Persian miniatures
- Japanese tea-house artifacts
- 3000-year-old Chinese bronze rhinoceros wine vessel with a twinkle in its eye
- Breakthrough contemporary Asian art
- Thursday night live artist-led events

PRACTICALITIES

- Map p306, B5
- ☎415-581-3500
- www.asianart.org
- 200 Larkin St
- adult/student/child $15/10/free, 1st Sun of month free
- ⏲10am-5pm Tue-Sun, to 9pm Thu
- Ⓜ Civic Center, Ⓑ Civic Center

SIGHTS

The Financial District centers on Montgomery St – the 'Wall St of the West' – and stretches to Jackson Square, the city's oldest neighborhood, with low-slung brick buildings and high-end antiquarians. Union Square refers to the square proper *and* the surrounding neighborhood; it's the principal retail-shopping and hotel district. South of Market (SoMa) was formerly the warehouse district, but massive construction projects are transforming the Mission Bay area around the ballpark into a new downtown. Museums and galleries cluster around 3rd and Mission, but most of SoMa's long, industrial blocks lack sights and are tedious to walk. Civic Center refers to the cluster of public buildings around City Hall. To the north, the gritty Tenderloin area is best avoided without a specific destination and a carefully mapped route.

Financial District & Jackson Square

FERRY BUILDING — LANDMARK

See p73.

TRANSAMERICA PYRAMID & REDWOOD PARK — NOTABLE BUILDING

Map p303 (www.thepyramidcenter.com; 600 Montgomery St; ⌚9am-6pm Mon-Fri; Ⓜ Embarcadero, Ⓑ Embarcadero) The defining feature of San Francisco's skyline is this 1972 pyramid, built atop the wreck of a whaling ship abandoned in the Gold Rush. A half-acre redwood grove sprouted out front, on the site of Mark Twain's favorite saloon and the newspaper office where Sun Yat-sen drafted his Proclamation of the Republic of China. Although these transplanted redwoods have shallow roots, their intertwined root network allows them to reach dizzying heights. Mark Twain couldn't have scripted a more perfect metaphor for San Francisco.

Architect William Pereira's triangular structure allows light to reach the trees and narrow streets beneath the Pyramid. But at first, critics claimed Pereira's Hollywood special-effects background was too obvious in his 853ft rocket-ship design. Today San Francisco would be unthinkable without the Pyramid – Godzilla respectfully left it intact in the 2014 remake of the Japanese sci-fi classic. Free entry to the lobby visitors center is possible weekdays, but only employees can use the elevators. Since September 11, the top-floor viewing deck has been closed for 'security reasons.'

JACKSON SQUARE — NEIGHBORHOOD

(www.jacksonsquaresf.com; around Jackson & Montgomery Sts; Ⓜ Embarcadero, Ⓑ Embarcadero) Today upscale Jackson Square is framed by Washington, Columbus, Pacific and Sansome Sts – but before the Gold Rush filled in the area with abandoned ships, this was a notorious waterfront dock area. Behind the iron shutters of these Italianate brick buildings, whiskey dealers, loan sharks, madams, lawyers and other hustlers plied their trades. Current tenants are ad agencies, antiques dealers and interior designers – all of them much more subtle about wheedling money from unsuspecting consumers than Jackson Square's original occupants. Notorious Gold Rush saloon owner Shanghai Kelly and madam Miss Piggot made an almost literal killing, conking new arrivals on the head and delivering them to ships in need of crew.

JUSTIN HERMAN PLAZA — PLAZA

Map p303 (http://sfrecpark.org; Market St & the Embarcadero; 🚌2, 6, 7, 9, 14, 21, 31, 32, Ⓑ Embarcadero, Ⓜ Embarcadero) The plaza across from the Ferry Building may not be much to look at – Vaillancourt Fountain was built to mirror the ugliness of the now-gone elevated freeway – but for years Justin Herman has been popular with lunchtime concertgoers, Critical Mass protesters, ice-skaters on the wintertime rink, and internet daters screening their dates from behind the fountain's wall of water.

WELLS FARGO HISTORY MUSEUM — MUSEUM

Map p303 (☎415-396-2619; www.wellsfargohistory.com/museums; 420 Montgomery St; ⌚9am-5pm Mon-Fri; 👪; Ⓜ Montgomery, Ⓑ Montgomery) **FREE** Gold miners needed somewhere to stash and send cash, so Wells Fargo opened in this location in 1852. Today this storefront museum covers Gold Rush–era innovations, including the Pony Express, transcontinental telegrams and statewide stagecoaches. Wells Fargo was the world's largest stagecoach operator circa 1866, and you can climb aboard a preserved stagecoach to hear pioneer-trail stories while kids ride a free mechanical pony. Notwithstanding blatant PR for Wells Fargo, the exhibits are well researched, fascinating and free.

TIMOTHY PFLUEGER'S JAWDROPPING SKYSCRAPERS

When a downtown skyscraper makes you stop, stare and crane your neck, it's probably Timothy Pflueger's fault. San Francisco's prolifically fanciful architect was responsible for downtown's most jawdropping buildings from 1925 to 1948, in styles ranging from opulent art deco to monumental minimalism. Movie buffs and architecture aficionados will want to hop the F line to catch a movie in Pflueger's 1922 palatial Mexican baroque Castro Theatre (p178), then take BART to Oakland to see how his 1931 glittering mosaic deco Paramount Theatre (p216) inspired *Wizard of Oz* Emerald City sets. But first, stop and stare at these Pflueger masterpieces downtown.

Pacific Telephone & Telegraph Company Building (1925; 140 New Montgomery St) Recently renovated and gilt to the hilt indoors, this building made Pflueger's reputation with its black marble deco lobby and soaring, streamlined shape. Winston Churchill made his first transatlantic telephone call here in 1929, but ironically the tower now seems to interfere with cell-phone coverage. Notice the cable-like lines running right up the building, past stylized telegraph insulators to fierce stone eagles. Today it's the headquarters for review site Yelp, as well as Morocco-moderne Mourad (p94) restaurant.

450 Sutter St (1929) A 26-story deco dental building fit for the gods, this Mayan Revival stone skyscraper has a lobby covered floor to ceiling with cast bronze snakes representing healing, grimacing figures apparently in need of dentistry, and panels covered with mystifying glyphs – early insurance forms, perhaps? With glowing inverted-pyramid lights, this landmark makes getting a cavity filled seem like a spiritual experience.

I Magnin Store (1948; Stockton & Geary Sts) When Pflueger's radical design was revealed on Union Square, San Francisco society was shocked: San Francisco's flagship clothing store appeared completely naked. Stripped of deco adornment, Pflueger's avant-garde white marble plinth caused consternation – until Christian Dior himself pronounced it 'magnifique.' Today it's a Macy's with new interiors – only the original 6th-floor women's bathroom remains intact. Pflueger's daring minimalist building remains Union Square's most timeless fashion statement, and was his final work before his untimely death of a heart attack at 54. His legacy includes a dozen other Bay Area landmarks, including the Bay Bridge, plus the arts institution he co-founded: San Francisco Museum of Modern Art (p79).

AP HOTALING WAREHOUSE — HISTORIC BUILDING

Map p303 (451-55 Jackson St; MEmbarcadero, BEmbarcadero) 'If, as they say, God spanked the town/For being over-frisky/Why did He burn His churches down/And spare Hotaling's whiskey?' The snappiest comeback in SF history was this saloon-goers' retort after Hotaling's 1866 whiskey warehouse survived the 1906 earthquake and fire. A bronze plaque with this ditty graces the resilient Italianate building.

⊙ Union Square

UNION SQUARE — SQUARE

Map p304 (intersection of Geary, Powell, Post & Stockton Sts; Powell-Mason, Powell-Hyde, MPowell, BPowell) High-end stores ring Union Square now, but this people-watching plaza was once a hotbed of protest – it's named for pro-Union Civil War rallies held here. Atop the central pillar is the Goddess of Victory, who's apparently having a wardrobe malfunction. This bare-breasted deity is modeled after Big Alma Spreckles, who volunteered her nude-modeling services when she heard sugar-baron Adolph Spreckels was heading the monument committee. Spreckles became her 'sugar daddy,' and Alma donated her fortune to build the Legion of Honor.

POWELL ST CABLE CAR TURNAROUND — LANDMARK

Map p304 (cnr Powell & Market Sts; Powell-Mason, Mason-Hyde, MPowell, BPowell) Stand awhile at Powell and Market Sts and spot arriving cable-car operators leaping out, gripping the trolleys' chassis and slooowly turning the car atop a revolving wooden platform. Cable cars can't go in reverse, so they need to be turned around by hand here at the terminus of Powell St lines. Riders queue up mid-morning to early evening

LOCAL KNOWLEDGE

DIEGO RIVERA'S ALLEGORY OF SAN FRANCISCO FRESCO

Hidden in a downtown skyscraper is a San Francisco art treasure: Diego Rivera's 1930–31 **Allegory of California fresco** (Map p304; 155 Sansome St, stairwell btwn 10th & 11th floors; ⏲mural access 3-5pm Mon-Fri; Ⓑ Montgomery, Ⓜ Montgomery). Take the elevator to the 10th floor and walk upstairs to see Rivera's depiction of California as a golden goddess offering farm-fresh produce, while beneath her gold miners toil and oil refineries loom large on the horizon. Rivera's Depression-era fresco is glorious but cautionary – while Californian workers, inventors and dreamers go about their business, the pressure gauge in the left-hand corner is entering the red zone.

Today it might seem strange that architect Timothy Pflueger would invite such an outspoken critic of capitalism as Diego Rivera to paint the staircase entry to San Francisco's Stock Exchange Lunch Club (now the City Club) – but after the 1929 US stock market crash, Rivera wasn't the only skeptic of unregulated markets. *The Allegory of California* was his first US fresco commission, and it would be a couple years yet before his Rockefeller Center mural in New York would be denounced as communist and scrapped. But in San Francisco, Rivera and his young bride – the groundbreaking surrealist artist Frida Kahlo – were the toast of the town, and started a mural movement that continues here today.

here to secure a seat, with raucous street performers and doomsday preachers on the sidelines as entertainment.

If you're not sure how long the wait will be, count heads and do the math: cable cars hold 60 people (29 seated, 31 standing), but depart carrying fewer to leave room for passengers to board en route. Cable cars depart every five to 10 minutes at peak times. Powell-Mason cars are quickest to the Wharf, but Powell-Hyde cars traverse more terrain and hills.

RUTH ASAWA'S SAN FRANCISCO FOUNTAIN — FOUNTAIN

Map p304 (Hyatt on Union Square Fountain; www.ruthasawa.com/art/pub7.html; Post & Stockton Sts; 🚋Powell-Mason, Mason-Hyde, Ⓜ Powell, Ⓑ Powell) Covered in local landmarks and colorful SF characters, Ruth Asawa's 1973 San Francisco Fountain captures the city's spirit. Sculptor Asawa used unconventional techniques: she collected favorite images of San Francisco from 250 people – famous artists to schoolchildren – sculpted them in bread dough, then cast them in bronze. Apple Inc. designed its flagship store for this spot, but there was a public outcry defending the fountain – so Apple eventually redesigned its building around it and restored the fountain.

49 GEARY — ART GALLERY

Map p304 (www.sfada.com; 49 Geary St; ⏲10:30am-5:30pm Tue-Fri, 11am-5pm Sat; 🚌5, 6, 7, 9, 21, 31, 38, Ⓜ Powell, Ⓑ Powell) FREE Pity the collectors silently nibbling endive in austere Chelsea galleries – at 49 Geary, openings mean unexpected art, goldfish-shaped crackers and outspoken crowds. Four floors of galleries feature standout international and local works, from 19th to 21st century photography at Fraenkel Gallery to Andy Goldsworthy installation art at Haines Gallery and sculptor Seth Koen's minimalist pieces at Gregory Lind. For quieter contemplation, visit weekdays.

LOTTA'S FOUNTAIN — MONUMENT

Map p304 (intersection of Market & Kearny Sts; 🚌5, 6, 7, 9, 21, 31, Ⓜ Montgomery, Ⓑ Montgomery) Lotta Crabtree made a fortune as San Francisco's diminutive opera diva, and never forgot the city that paid for her trademark cigars. In 1875 she donated this cast-metal spigot fountain (thrice her size) to San Francisco. Her gift came in mighty handy during the April 18, 1906 earthquake and fire, when it became downtown's sole water source – corrupt officials had pocketed funds to hook up fire hydrants. Descendants of 1906 earthquake survivors meet here each April 18 at 5:12am for rousing sing-a-longs.

PALACE HOTEL — HISTORIC BUILDING

Map p304 (☎415-512-1111; www.sfpalace.com; 2 New Montgomery St; Ⓜ Montgomery, Ⓑ Montgomery) A true San Francisco survivor, the Palace opened in 1875, but was gutted during the 1906 earthquake. Opera star Enrico Caruso was jolted from his Palace bed by the quake and fled town, never to return to San Francisco. But the Palace reopened by

1909, and Woodrow Wilson gave his League of Nations speech here 10 years later. Visit by day to see the Garden Court stained-glass ceiling, then peek into **Pied Piper Bar** to see Maxfield Parrish's *Pied Piper* mural.

Recently Palace management removed the Parrish mural with the intention of auctioning it off – but San Franciscans rallied, and insisted on the Piper's return to his rightful place. Toast San Franciscan resilience under the *Pied Piper*, and if you're feeling brave, head to the House of Shields (p99) for another at the opulent mahogany back bar. This ornate bar was originally intended to frame Parrish's mural, but maybe the woodworker had one too many – it was too small to fit the Pied Piper.

FRANK LLOYD WRIGHT BUILDING NOTABLE BUILDING

Map p304 (VC Morris Store; 140 Maiden Lane; 38, Powell, Powell) Shrink the Guggenheim, plop it inside a yellow-brick box with a round Romanesque entryway and put it where you'd least expect it: on a shady San Francisco alley that was once a backstreet brothel. Groundbreaking American architect Frank Lloyd Wright designed this as the VC Morris Gift Store in 1948, and it's his only San Francisco building. It's changed hands since, and at this writing, the building is for sale. If it's open, duck inside to see Wright's signature nautilus-shell atrium ramp.

BOHEMIAN CLUB HISTORIC BUILDING

Map p304 (624 Taylor St; 2, 3, 38, Powell-Mason, Powell-Hyde) San Francisco's most infamous, secretive men's club was originally founded by bonafide bohemians – but they couldn't afford the upkeep, so they allowed the ultra-rich to join. Today's member roster lists an odd mix of power elite and artists: apparently both George W Bush and Greatful Dead frontman Bob Weir are current members. On the Post St side of the ivy-covered club, look for the plaque honoring Gold Rush–era author Bret Harte, which depicts characters from his works.

On the plaque's extreme right is 'The Heathen Chinee.' It's not a racist attack, but a reference to the eponymous 1870 satirical poem Harte wrote mocking anti-Chinese sentiment in Northern California. Ironically, the poem had the opposite effect, and became a rallying cry against Chinese immigration.

JAMES FLOOD BUILDING HISTORIC BUILDING

Map p304 (cnr Market & Powell Sts; Powell, Powell) This 1904 stone building survived the 1906 earthquake and retains its original character, notwithstanding the Gap downstairs. Upstairs, labyrinthine marble hallways are lined with frosted-glass doors, just like a noir movie set. No coincidence: in 1921 the SF office of infamous Pinkerton Detective Agency hired a young investiga tor named Dashiell Hammett, author of the 1930 noir classic *The Maltese Falcon*.

SoMa

SAN FRANCISCO MUSEUM OF MODERN ART MUSEUM

Map p308 (SFMOMA; 415-357-4000; www.sfmoma.org; 151 3rd St; 5, 6, 7, 14, 19, 21, 31, 38, Montgomery, Montgomery) SFMOMA was destined from its start in 1935 to defy convention, investing early in photography, installations, video and other then-experimental media. Once the collection moved into architect Mario Botta's light-filled brick box in 1995, SFMOMA showed its backside to New York and leaned full-tilt toward the western horizon, pushing the art world to embrace new media, new artists and new ideas. Currently undergoing a

KIOSK MUSEUM

Ever since the web was invented in the Bay Area, San Francisco has been circulating news online – rendering newspaper kiosks on downtown street corners largely obsolete. Community Arts International is working with the city to upcycle them into mini-museums, turning long waits for traffic lights into opportunities to illuminate and delight passersby. The **Kiosk Museum** (www.kioskmuseum.com) started with two kiosks, one at Post and Stockton and the second at Maiden Lane and Grant Ave. Theatrical scenes are created in kiosk windows, where newspaper sellers once announced the day's headlines. In the recent *Creatures of the Sea* exhibit, a Oaxacan wooden mermaid greeted passing shoppers, while a Japanese porcelain baby shyly hugged her giant goldfish. An instant hit with passersby and critics alike, the upstart museum is expanding its reach – check the website map for current locations and shows.

1

ANDRIA PATINO / DESIGN PICS / GETTY IMAGES ©

GETTY IMAGES ©

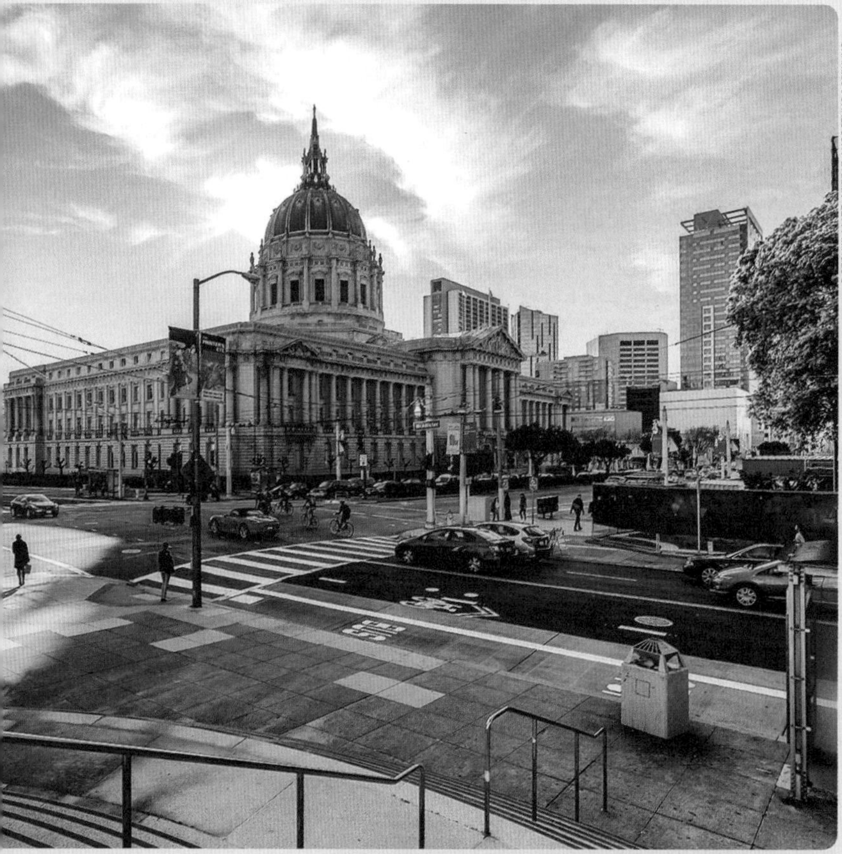

1. Yerba Buena Gardens (p83)
A welcome green oasis in the concrete heart of SoMa.

2. City Hall (p84)
Designed in 1915, the City Hall's mighty beaux arts dome has been retrofitted with technology that allows it to swing on its base during earthquakes.

3. Bay Bridge (p74)
Nighttime views of the Bay Bridge are sure to dazzle, with 25,000 LED lights strung over 1.8 miles of the brigde's western span.

4. Bar Agricole (p97)
A James Beard Award–winner, this bar is at the forefront of San Francisco's cocktail scene: stop by for a well-researched drink and some bar bites.

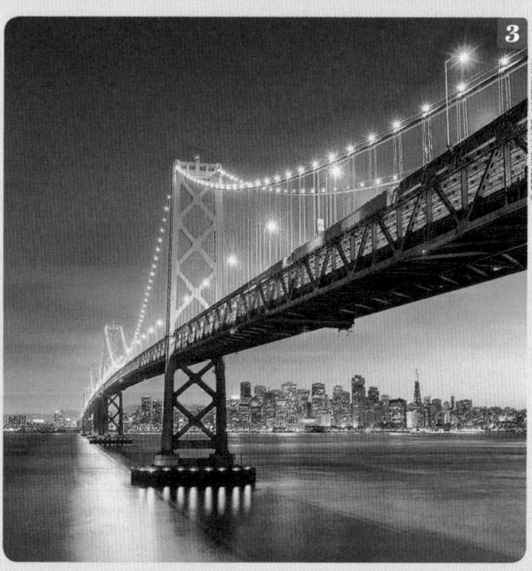
3

LOCAL KNOWLEDGE

CUPID'S SPAN

You may wonder: what's that giant yellow bow and red arrow doing buried in a patch of grass along the Embarcadero? Many San Franciscans wonder the same thing – 'Cupid's Span' is the most divisive public artwork in San Francisco. Sculptors Claes Oldenburg and Coosje van Bruggen planted this one on San Francisco as a romantic gesture, but the kitschy five-story-high sculpture is a bit too much for some – just because some jokers left their in art in San Francisco doesn't mean locals want to keep it. The optical effects are intriguing, though: up close it looks like a shipwreck, but from afar, its lines mirror Bay Bridge cables. Signs warn passersby not to touch the sculpture, but that hasn't stopped people from climbing, skateboarding and taking selfies on it. Love or hate it, San Franciscans can't keep their hands off Cupid's Span.

half-billion-dollar, 235,000-sq-ft expansion to house extended collections, the museum is closed until summer 2016.

SAN FRANCISCO MURALS AT RINCON ANNEX POST OFFICE — BUILDING

Map p308 (101 Spear St; 2, 6, 7, 14, 21, 31, M Embarcadero, B Embarcadero) FREE Only in San Francisco could a post office be so controversial. This art-deco landmark is lined with vibrant Works Project Administration murals of San Francisco history, begun by Russian-born painter Anton Refregier in 1941 – but WWII and political squabbles over differing versions of San Francisco history caused delays. After 92 changes to satisfy censors, Refregier finally concluded the mural cycle in 1948 with *War & Peace,* pointedly contrasting scenes of Nazi book-burning and postwar promises of 'freedom from fear/want/of worship/speech.'

Initially denounced as 'communist' by McCarthyists, Refregier's masterpiece is now protected as a National Landmark.

CONTEMPORARY JEWISH MUSEUM — MUSEUM

Map p308 (415-344-8800; www.thecjm.org/; 736 Mission St; adult/child $12/free, after 5pm Thu $5, 1st Tue of month free; 11am-5pm Mon-Tue & Fri-Sun, to 8pm Thu; ; 14, 30, 45, M Montgomery, B Montgomery) That upended brushed-steel box miraculously balancing on one corner isn't a sculpture but the entry to the Contemporary Jewish Museum – and inside this building, any preconceived ideas about religion and art are also upended. Exhibits are compelling, provocative explorations of Jewish culture and ideals featuring artists as diverse as Andy Warhol and Amy Winehouse, Gertrude Stein and Harry Houdini. The affectionately nicknamed 'Jewseum' invites theological and artistic debate over respectable pastrami, served on-site from 11am to 2pm by SF's Wise Sons Jewish Deli.

The 2008 Jewish Museum building merges the new steel structure with the original 1907 brick facade of the Jesse St power substation, an early industrial structure whimsically decorated with cherubs and garlands. Before designing New York's controversial September 11 memorial, architect Daniel Liebskind planned San Francisco's 'Jewseum' to be both rational and mystical. Its blue-steel cladding forms the Hebrew word *l'chaim* (to life) – an intriguing idea, though perhaps best appreciated from a helicopter. But the museum and plaza he designed are a welcome pause for reflection in the heart of San Francisco, and a fitting tribute to the Bay Area's diverse Jewish community.

MUSEUM OF THE AFRICAN DIASPORA — MUSEUM

Map p308 (MoAD; 415-358-7200; www.moadsf.org; 685 Mission St; adult/student/child $10/5/free; 11am-6pm Wed-Sat, noon-5pm Sun; P ; 14, 30, 45, M Montgomery, B Montgomery) MoAD assembles an international cast of characters to tell the epic story of diaspora, including a moving video of slave narratives told by Maya Angelou. Standouts among quarterly changing exhibits have included contemporary Afro-Cuban art, postcolonial Nigerian fashion statements and radical '60s graphics by African American printmaker and social activist Elizabeth Catlett. Public dialogues put art in context, with lively discussions on such current topics as African American archetypes in Hollywood, African masculinity and the Black Lives Matter movement.

CALIFORNIA HISTORICAL SOCIETY MUSEUM — MUSEUM

Map p308 (415-357-1848; www.californiahistoricalsociety.org; 678 Mission St; adult/child

$5/free; ⏰gallery & store 11am-8pm Tue, to 5pm Wed-Sun, library noon-5pm Wed-Fri; 👪; Ⓜ Montgomery, Ⓑ Montgomery) Enter a Golden State of enlightenment at this Californiana treasure trove, featuring themed exhibitions drawn from the museum's million-plus California photographs, paintings and ephemera. Recent exhibits have unearthed 19th-century photographs of pioneers gleefully climbing trees in Yosemite, scrapped designs for a futuristic Ferry Building, and the epic life story of fiercely independent Californian businesswoman Juana Briones, whose 1837 farmstead is now SF's North Beach neighborhood.

California Historical Society events are rare opportunities to discuss San Francisco poetry, what it was like to be gay in 1940s San Francisco, or what was on the menu at Gold Rush saloons (short answer: whiskey, opium and tamales). If there's a Californian topic you'd like to pursue, call the **research library** ahead so that librarians can pull related materials from vaults full of rare manuscripts and ephemera.

CHILDREN'S CREATIVITY MUSEUM — MUSEUM

Map p308 (☎415-820-3320; http://creativity.org/; 221 4th St; admission $12; ⏰10am-4pm Tue-Sun; 👪; 🚌14, Ⓜ Powell, Ⓑ Powell) No velvet ropes or hands-off signs here: kids rule, with high-tech displays double-daring them to make music videos, claymation movies and soundtracks. Jump into live-action video games and sign up for workshops with Bay Area superstar animators, techno whizzes and robot builders. For low-tech fun, take a spin on the vintage-1906 **Loof Carousel** outside, operating 10am to 5pm daily; one $4 ticket covers two rides (you get $1 off with museum admission).

YERBA BUENA GARDENS — PARK

Map p308 (☎415-820-3550; www.yerbabuenagardens.com; 3rd & Mission Sts; ⏰sunrise-10pm; 👪; Ⓜ Montgomery, Ⓑ Montgomery) Breathe a sigh of relief: you've found the best stretch of green in the concrete heart of SoMa, between Yerba Buena Center for the Arts and Metreon shopping mall. This is a prime spot to picnic, hear free noontime summer concerts (see website) or duck behind the fountain for a smooch. Martin Luther King Jr Memorial Fountain is a wall of water that runs over the Reverend's immortal words: '...until justice rolls down like water and righteousness like a mighty stream.'

CROWN POINT PRESS — GALLERY

Map p308 (☎415-974-6273; www.crownpoint.com; 20 Hawthorne St; ⏰10am-5pm Mon, to 6pm Tue-Sat; 🚌14, Ⓑ Montgomery, Ⓜ Montgomery) FREE Bet you didn't think anyone could capture Chuck Close's giant portraits, Robert Bechtle's hyperrealistic street scenes or Chris Ofili's glitter-and-elephant-dung paintings on paper – yet here they are. Crown Point Press printmakers work with international artists to turn singular visions into large-scale, limited edition woodblocks and etchings. When master printmakers are at work, you're often invited to watch – and if you're inspired to make your own, you can pick up how-to books and tools here.

ALTER SPACE — GALLERY

Map p308 (☎415-735-1158; http://alterspace.co/; 1158 Howard St; ⏰1-6pm Thu-Sat; 🚌12, 14, 19, Ⓑ Civic Center, Ⓜ Civic Center) In a SoMa warehouse storefront that was once Stormy Leather bondage shop, Alter Space arts collective hosts boundary-pushing gallery shows on themes ranging from obsession to Jello. Stop by to see the latest show and you might also glimpse works in progress by the current artist in residence, who has the distinct honor of working in the basement dungeon.

SPUR URBAN CENTER GALLERY — CULTURAL CENTER

Map p308 (☎415-781-8726; www.spur.org; 654 Mission St; ⏰11am-5pm Tue-Fri; 🚌12, 14, Ⓑ Montgomery, Ⓜ Montgomery) FREE Cities are what you make of them, and urban planning nonprofit SPUR invites you to reimagine San Francisco (and your own hometown) with gallery shows that explore urban living, from smells to stories told on street corners. Exhibitions are free, thought-provoking and visually appealing, featuring local and international artists. For the ultimate SF treasure hunt, check out SPUR's interactive map to hidden downtown 'privately owned public spaces' (POPOs), which are actually open to the public (www.spur.org/blog/2012-08-27/get-spurs-guide-public-spaces-your-smart-phone).

FEDERAL BUILDING — NOTABLE BUILDING

Map p308 (90 7th St; Ⓜ Civic Center, Ⓑ Civic Center) The groundbreaking green design of this government-office building by 2005 Pritzker Architecture Prize–winner Thom Mayne means major savings in energy – and taxpayer dollars. Open layouts eliminate internal political battles over corner

SOUTH PARK OR BUST

'Dot-com' entered the global vernacular via San Francisco in the mid-'90s, when venture capitalists and techies first plotted website launches in cafés ringing **South Park** (Map p308; S Park St; Ⓜ4th St). But when online ice-cream delivery services failed to deliver profits, South Park became a dot-com ghost town, adding yet another bust to its checkered history.

Speculation is nothing new to South Park, originally planned by an 1850s real-estate developer as a bucolic gated community. A party celebrating a Crimean War victory was thrown here in 1855 to attract some of San Francisco's Gold Rush millionaires – but it degenerated into a cake-throwing food fight and the development flopped. But this turf remained fertile ground for wild ideas: as a plaque around the corner indicates, 601 3rd St was the **birthplace of Jack London**, best-selling author of *The Call of the Wild, White Fang* and other Wild West adventure stories.

After WWII, Filipino American war veterans formed a quiet community here – at least until dot-com HQs suddenly moved in and abruptly out of the neighborhood. South Park offices weren't vacant for long before social-media speculators moved in, including a scrappy start-up with an outlandish notion of communicating in online haiku. Twitter has since moved its operations (and 302 million active users) to Market St.

offices, providing direct sunlight, natural ventilation and views for 90% of work stations. Critics call it a fortress and employees call it chilly, but it adds green distinction to the otherwise bland industrial skyline of SoMa warehouses.

Civic Center & the Tenderloin

ASIAN ART MUSEUM MUSEUM

See p75.

★LUGGAGE STORE GALLERY GALLERY

Map p306 (☎415-255-5971; www.luggagestoregallery.org; 1007 Market St; ⊙noon-5pm Wed-Sat; 🚌5, 6, 7, 21, 31, ⓂCivic Center, ⒷCivic Center) Like a dandelion pushing through sidewalk cracks, this plucky nonprofit gallery has brought signs of life to one of the Tenderloin's toughest blocks for two decades. By giving SF street artists a gallery platform, the Luggage Store helped launch graffiti-art star Barry McGee, muralist Rigo and urban folklorist Clare Rojas. Find the graffitied door and climb to the 2nd-floor gallery, which rises above the street without losing sight of it.

Two Luggage Store regulars you might recognize around town are Rigo and Brazilian duo Ogemeos. Rigo did the 'One Tree' mural that looks like a one-way sign by the 101 Fwy on-ramp in SoMa. Ogemeos created the mural of a daredevil graffiti artist leaping off the side of the Luggage Store building. With such poignant streetwise works and regular community arts events, this place puts the tender in the Tenderloin.

CITY HALL HISTORIC BUILDING

Map p306 (☎art exhibit line 415-554-6080, tour info 415-554-6139; http://sfgsa.org/index.aspx?page=1085; 400 Van Ness Ave; ⊙8am-8pm Mon-Fri, tours 10am, noon & 2pm; 👪; ⓂCivic Center, ⒷCivic Center) FREE Rising from the ashes of the 1906 earthquake, this beaux arts landmark echoes with history. Singing protesters determined to end red-scare McCarthy hearings were blasted with firehoses here in 1960 – yet America's first sit-in worked. America's first openly gay official Supervisor Harvey Milk was assassinated here in 1978, along with Mayor George Moscone – but in 2004, 4037 same-sex couples were legally wed here for the first time. Lately City Hall has approved pioneering green initiatives, making SF the nation's environmental leader.

The dome's gilded exterior is a cringe-worthy reminder of 1990s dot-com excess, when the city squandered a short-lived windfall on gold leafing – but at least its foundations are solid now. Designed in 1915 to outdo Paris for flair and outsize the capitol in Washington, DC, the world's fifth-largest dome was unsteady until its retrofit after the 1989 earthquake, when ingenious technology enabled it to swing on its base without raising alarm. Don't miss public art exhibitions, which range from portraits of iconic LGBT performers to photographs of fog banks hovering inside San Francisco buildings.

Free docent-led tours meet at the tour kiosk near the Van Ness Ave entrance, but City Hall is best seen in action. For insight into how San Francisco government works – or doesn't – the Board of Supervisors meets Tuesdays at 2pm in City Hall; check the agenda and minutes online. Theoretically, visitors may be removed for 'boisterous' behavior, but this being San Francisco, democracy in action can get pretty rowdy without fazing security guards.

SAN FRANCISCO MAIN LIBRARY NOTABLE BUILDING

Map p306 (☎415-557-4400; www.sfpl.org; 100 Larkin St; ⏰10am-6pm Mon & Sat, 9am-8pm Tue-Thu, noon-6pm Fri, noon-5pm Sun; 📶👪; 🚌5, 6, 7, 19, 21, 31, Ⓜ Civic Center, Ⓑ Civic Center) A grand lightwell illuminates San Francisco's favorite subjects: graphic novels in the Teen Center, poetry in the Robert Frost Collection, civil rights in the Hormel Gay & Lesbian Center and comic relief in the Schmulowitz Wit and Humor Collection. Check out the 2nd-floor wallpaper made from the old card catalog – artists Ann Chamberlain and Ann Hamilton invited 200 San Franciscans to add multilingual commentary to 50,000 cards. The library quietly hosts high-profile basement lectures, plus enlightening Skylight Gallery ephemera exhibits.

GLIDE MEMORIAL UNITED METHODIST CHURCH CHURCH

Map p306 (☎415-674-6090; www.glide.org; 330 Ellis St; ⏰celebrations 9am & 11am Sun; 👪; 🚌38, Ⓜ Powell, Ⓑ Powell) The rainbow-robed Glide gospel choir enters singing their hearts out, and the 2000-plus congregation stomps and dances along. Raucous Sunday Glide celebrations capture San Francisco at its most diverse and welcoming, embracing all ethnicities, abilities and income brackets, the entire GLBT spectrum and many who'd lost all faith in faith. After the celebration ends, the congregation keeps the inspiration coming, serving a million free meals a year and providing housing for 52 formerly homeless families – and yes, Glide welcomes volunteers.

SF CAMERAWORK GALLERY

Map p306 (☎415-487-1011; www.sfcamerawork.org; 2nd fl, 1011 Market St; ⏰noon-6pm Tue-Sat; 🚌6, 7, 9, 21, Ⓑ Civic Center, Ⓜ Civic Center) FREE Since 1974, this nonprofit art organization has explored and encouraged experimental photo-based imagery beyond classic B&W prints and casual digital snapshots. Since moving into this spacious new Market St gallery, Camerawork's far-reaching exhibitions have shed new light on contemporary photography in Mexico City, encouraged visitors to shove around Chris Fraser's interactive light installations, and provided room for reflection on Kerry Mansfield's powerful self-portraits chronicling her breast-cancer treatment.

ROOT DIVISION GALLERY

Map p306 (☎415-863-7668; www.rootdivision.org; 1059 Market St; donations welcome; ⏰gallery 2-6pm Wed-Sat; 👪; 🚌Powell St, Ⓑ Powell St) FREE Everyone's a winner at this arts

DOWNTOWN ROOFTOP GARDENS

Above the busy sidewalks, there's a serene world of unmarked public rooftop gardens that grant perspective on downtown's skyscraper-canyons. They're called 'privately owned public-open spaces' (POPOs). Local public-advocacy urbanist group SPUR (p83) publishes a complete list; its downloadable map lists them all. Here's a short list of favorites:

One Montgomery Terrace (Map p304; 50 Post St/1 Montgomery St; ⏰10am-6pm Mon-Sat; Ⓜ Montgomery, Ⓑ Montgomery) Great Market St views of old and new SF. Enter through Crocker Galleria, take the elevator to the top, then ascend stairs; or enter Wells Fargo at One Montgomery and take the elevator to 'R.'

Sun Terrace (Map p303; 343 Sansome St; ⏰10am-6pm Mon-Fri; Ⓜ Embarcadero, Ⓑ Embarcadero) Knockout vistas of the Financial District and Transamerica Pyramid from atop a slender art-deco skyscraper. Take the elevator to floor 15.

Fairmont San Francisco (Map p316; 950 Mason St; ⏰24hr; 🚌1, 🚋California St, Powell-Hyde, Powell-Mason) Traverse the lobby toward the Pavilion Room, then out glass doors to a deliciously kitsch rooftop courtyard and edible garden. Hearst Castle architect Julia Morgan was brought in to fix the Fairmont after the devastating 1906 earthquake, and her pioneering use of reinforced concrete has stood the test of time here.

Cable Cars: SF's Ultimate Joyride

Roller-coaster rides can't compare to the death-defying thrills of riding a 15,000-pound cable car down San Francisco hills, careening toward oncoming traffic. But Andrew Hallidie's 1873 contraptions have held up miraculously well on these giddy slopes, and groaning brakes and clanging brass bells add to the carnival-ride thrills.

This vintage Victorian transport does have drawbacks. Cable cars can't move in reverse, and require burly gripmen – and one buff gripwoman – to hand-operate brakes to keep them from losing control downhill. San Francisco receives many applicants for this job, but 80% fail the strenuous tests of upper-body strength and hand-eye coordination.

To see what it takes to turn around a cable car, head to the Powell St Cable Car Turnaround (p77) or the Powell-Hyde Cable Car Turnaround at Fisherman's Wharf. This turnaround is named after Friedel Klussman, who rallied her ladies' gardening club in 1947 against the mayor's scheme to replace cable cars with buses. In a public vote, the mayor lost to 'The Cable Car Lady' by a landslide.

Powell-Mason cars (with yellow signs) are quickest to reach Fisherman's Wharf, but **Powell-Hyde** cars (red signs) are more scenic, and the **California line** is least crowded; see www.sfmuni.com for maps. Other need-to-know info:

➡ Cable car lines operate from around 6am to 1am daily, with scheduled departures every three to 12 minutes; for schedules, see http://transit.511.org.

➡ If you're planning to stop en route, get a Muni Passport (per day $17). One-way tickets cost $7, with no on-and-off privileges.

➡ This 19th-century transport is not child-proof – you won't find car seats or seat belts on these wooden benches. Kids love open-air seating in front, but holding small children securely inside the car is safer.

➡ Cable cars are not accessible for people with disabilities.

➡ On hillside runs, cable cars make rolling stops. To board on hills, act fast: leap onto the baseboard and grab the closest leather hand-strap.

nonprofit, which hosts curated shows on such themes as endangered languages and art stunts. Root Division keeps the inspiration coming, offering artists subsidized studio space in exchange for providing low-cost community art classes from painting to electronics – see the class schedule for youth and adult classes from weaving to watercolors. Don't miss events like the annual Misfit Toy Factory, where artists create works live for sale.

TWITTER HEADQUARTERS LANDMARK

Map p306 (Western Furniture Exchange & Merchandise Mart; https://about.twitter.com/company; 1355 Market St; 6, 7, 21, M Civic Center, B Civic Center) Market St's traffic-stopping 1937 Mayan deco landmark was built to accommodate 300 wholesale furniture design showrooms – but a decade ago, fewer than 30 remained. The city offered tax breaks to Twitter to move here from its South Park (p84) headquarters, and after a $1.2 million LEED-certified green makeover, including a rooftop farm, Twitter nested here. Only employees can access Twitter's free video arcade and Birdfeeder cafeteria, but ground-floor public **Marketplace** offers 22,000 sq ft of local gourmet fare.

The upscale oyster bar overlooking a gritty street corner is a definite clunker, but the Four Barrell coffee kiosk, multi-culti food stalls and central wine bar are hits with techie lunch crowds. Tweeting about your meal here seems uniquely appropriate, but consider what the emergency sign says upstairs: 'In case of fire: exit building before tweeting about it.'

UNITED NATIONS PLAZA SQUARE

Map p306 (Market St, btwn Hyde & Leavenworth Sts; 6am-6pm; 5, 6, 7, 9, 21, M Civic Center, B Civic Center) This brick-paved triangle with an often-dry fountain awkwardly commemorates the signing of the UN charter in San Francisco. At best in broad daylight, UN Plaza offers clear views of City Hall, skateboarders attempting fountain flips, Scientologists drumming up converts and the odd drug deal in progress. The wonderful Heart of the City Farmers Market (p91) provides a fresher perspective on the Tenderloin, and Pride, Tet (Vietnamese lunar new year) and other community celebrations bring signs of life to grim UN Plaza.

TENDERLOIN NATIONAL FOREST PARK

Map p306 (http://www.luggagestoregallery.org/tnf/; Ellis St btwn Leavenworth & Hyde Sts; noon-5pm; 27, 31, 38, B Powell, M Powell) FREE Urban blight is interrupted by bucolic splendor on one of the Tenderloin's grittiest blocks. Once littered with hypodermic needles and garbage, dead-end Cohen Alley has been transformed by a nonprofit artists' collective. A grove of trees is taking root, concrete walls are covered with bright murals, and asphalt has been replaced with mosaic pathways and coi ponds. If you feel so inspired – and really, who wouldn't? – garden tools are available to help maintain SF's scrappiest natural wonder.

This forest is a project of the nonprofit Luggage Store Gallery (p84) in cooperation with the city of San Francisco, which allows the nonprofit to lease the alley for $1 a year. See the Luggage Store's website for upcoming events in the Tenderloin National Forest, including free clothes mending by artist Michael Swain on the 15th of each month (weather permitting) and occasional community pizza-making in the garden patio pizza oven.

EATING

Make reservations whenever possible for downtown restaurants. Downtown and South of Market (SoMa) are best known for high-end restaurants, but lunchtime eateries in the neighborhood cater to office workers, with meals around $10 to $20. The Financial District is dead at night, when only midrange and top-end joints stay open. The Tenderloin (west of Powell St, south of Geary St and north of Market St) feels sketchy and rough, but as always in San Francisco, bargain eats reward the adventurous. Some cheap eats in the 'Loin close earlier than their posted hours.

Financial District & Jackson Square

MIXT GREENS SALADS $

Map p303 (415-296-8009; www.mixtgreens.com; 120 Sansome St; salads $9-14; 10:30am-3pm Mon-Fri; ; California, M Montgomery, B Montgomery) Stockbrokers and Paleo dieters line up out the door for generous organic salads with zingy dressings – don't worry, the line moves fast. Sustainable sushi-grade tuna and grass-fed steak are pricey but tasty additions. Grab a stool for a

SAN FRANCISCO'S HOMELESS: WHAT'S THE DEAL?

It's inevitable: panhandlers *will* ask you for spare change during your visit to San Francisco, especially around Union Square and downtown tourist attractions.

If it seems like more people are homeless in San Francisco than other cities, you're not wrong. Homelessness exists across America, but police crackdowns and a lack of appropriate social services in cities nationwide have created a 'weed and seed' effect: homeless populations forced out of other cities come to San Francisco for its milder climate, history of tolerance and safety-net services. San Francisco's homeless population is now estimated to exceed 10,000 – the highest per capita in the US – despite the city's limited shelter capacity of around 3000 beds.

Some historians date San Francisco's challenges with homelessness to the 1940s, when shell-shocked WWII Pacific Theater veterans were discharged here without sufficient support. Local homeless advocates say the real crisis in California started in the 1960s, when then-governor Ronald Reagan slashed funding to mental hospitals, drug-rehab programs and low-income housing programs – policies he continued as president in the 1980s.

San Francisco City Hall schemes to address homelessness have had minimal success. Former mayor Willie Brown proposed seizing homeless people's shopping carts – a notorious failure. Ex-mayor Gavin Newsom's controversial 2002 'Care Not Cash' policy replaced cash payments with social services, which left some San Franciscans unable to pay rent. The equally controversial 2010 'Sit/Lie Ordinance' made daytime sidewalk loitering punishable by fines, which has been disproportionately enforced with vulnerable homeless teens in the Haight. Current mayor Ed Lee seems to be skirting the problem; he discontinued the City Hall position of 'Homeless Czar,' focusing instead on downtown business development. But given San Francisco's growing income inequality, the city can't ignore homelessness.

So you may well sympathize with homeless San Franciscans who ask you to share food or spare change. Whether you choose to or not, know that there are also other ways you can make an immediate difference. You can volunteer or make a donation with an SF homeless services organization like Glide (p85), or you could offer your services to an organization back home. Homelessness isn't a uniquely San Franciscan problem – it's a global human tragedy.

quick nosh before seeing Diego Rivera murals next door, or get take-out to enjoy in the Transamerica Pyramid redwood grove.

THE GOLDEN WEST SANDWICHES, SALADS **$**

Map p304 (☎415-216-6443; http://theauwest.com/; 8 Trinity Place; lunch $9-12; ⏰8am-2pm Mon-Fri; 🚌3, 8, 30, 45, Ⓑ Montgomery, Ⓜ Montgomery) Eureka! Wedged between brokerage firms under the glowing sign that says Au (periodic table symbol for gold) is an elusive FiDi find: a memorable lunch with top-notch California-grown ingredients that won't break the bank. Menu items are seasonal, but look for short-rib sandwiches with caramelized onions and housemade mayo, or spicy chicken salads with mango, organic greens and pumpkin seeds.

★COTOGNA ITALIAN **$$**

Map p303 (☎415-775-8508; www.cotognasf.com; 490 Pacific Ave; mains $17-38; ⏰11:30am-10:30pm Mon-Thu, to 11pm Fri & Sat, 5-9:30pm Sun; 🖉; 🚌10, 12) Chef-owner Michael Tusk is racking up James Beard Awards for best chef, and you'll discover why: he balances a few pristine flavors in rustic pastas, woodfired pizzas and authentic Florentine steak. Reserve ahead or plan to eat late (2pm to 5pm) to score the bargain $28 prix-fixe lunch. On the excellent wine list all bottles cost $50, including hard-to-find Italian cult wines.

TRESTLE CALIFORNIAN **$$**

Map p318 (☎415-772-0922; http://trestlesf.com/; 531 Jackson St; 3-course meal $35; ⏰5:30-10:30pm Mon-Thu, to 11pm Fri & Sat, to 10pm Sun; 🚌8, 10, 12, 30, 45) Whether your fortunes are up or down in SF, you're in luck here: $35 brings three courses of tasty rustic comfort food. You get two options per course – typically soup or salad, meat or seafood, and fruity or chocolatey dessert – so you and your date can taste the entire menu. Get the bonus handmade pasta course ($10). Seating is tight but friendly.

BOCADILLOS BASQUE **$$**

Map p303 (415-982-2622; www.bocasf.com; 710 Montgomery St; mains $8-17; 11am-10pm Mon-Fri, 5-10pm Sat; 8, 10, 12, 41) Forget multipage menus and giant portions: for lunch, choose two small sandwiches on toasted rolls with salad for $12 at this little bistro with mighty Mediterranean flavors. For dinner, juicy lamb burgers, snapper ceviche and Catalan sausages are just-right Basque bites, enhanced with good wine by the glass. Anticipate deafening noise at peak times.

★**KUSAKABE** SUSHI, JAPANESE **$$$**

Map p303 (415-757-0155; http://kusakabe-sf.com/; 584 Washington St; prix-fixe $95; 5-10pm, last seating 8:30pm; 8, 10, 12, 41) Trust chef Mitsunori Kusakabe's *omakase* (tasting menu). Soy sauce isn't provided, nor missed. Sit at the counter while chef adds an herbal hint to fatty tuna with the *inside* of a shiso leaf. After you devour the menu – mostly with your hands, 'to release flavors' – you can special-order Hokkaido sea urchin, which chef perfumes with the *outside* of the shiso leaf. Brilliant.

KOKKARI GREEK **$$$**

Map p303 (415-981-0983; www.kokkari.com; 200 Jackson St; mains $18-49; 11:30am-2:30pm Mon-Fri, 5:30-10pm Mon-Thu, 5:30-11pm Fri, 5-11pm Sat, 5-10pm Sun; ; 8, 10, 12, 41) This is one Greek restaurant where you'll want to lick your plate instead of break it, with starters like grilled octopus with a zing of lemon and oregano, and a signature lamb, eggplant and yogurt moussaka as rich as the Pacific Stock Exchange. Reserve ahead to avoid waits, or make a meal of hearty Mediterranean appetizers at the happening bar.

WAYFARE TAVERN AMERICAN **$$$**

Map p303 (415-772-9060; www.wayfaretavern.com; 558 Sacramento St; lunch mains $18-28, dinner mains $18-39; 11am-11pm Mon-Fri, 11:30am-11pm Sat, 11:30am-10pm Sun; 1, 8, 10, California St, Montgomery) All signs say San Francisco: barkeeps wear white jackets over their tats, couples canoodle around a fireplace salvaged from the 1906 earthquake, and lunch crowds toast to venture capital. Here American classics get the California treatment – flank steak comes with California chanterelles, strawberry cobbler is served with fennel ice cream, and organic fried chicken is laced with mysteriously addicting woodland herbs.

Union Square

★**TOUT SWEET** BAKERY **$**

Map p304 (415-385-1679; www.toutsweetsf.com; Macy's, 3rd fl, Geary & Stockton Sts; baked goods $2-8; 10am-8pm Mon-Wed, to 9pm Thu-Sat, 11am-7pm Sun; ; 2, 38, Powell-Mason, Powell-Hyde, Powell St) Sour cherry and bourbon, or peanut butter and jelly? Choosing your new favorite French macaron flavor isn't easy at Tout Sweet, where *Top Desserts* champion Yigit Pura keeps outdoing his own inventions – he's like the lovechild of Julia Child and Steve Jobs. Chef Pura's sweet retreat on the 3rd floor of Macy's also offers unbeatable views of Union Square, excellent teas and free wi-fi.

SUSHIRRITO JAPANESE, FUSION **$**

Map p304 (415-544-9868; www.sushirrito.com/; 226 Kearny St; dishes $9-13; 11am-4pm Mon-Thu, to 7pm Fri, noon-4pm Sat; ; 30, 45, Montgomery, Montgomery) Ever get a sushi craving, but you're hungry enough for a burrito? Join the crowd at Sushirrito, where fresh Latin and Asian ingredients are rolled in rice and nori seaweed, then conveniently wrapped in foil. Pan-Pacific Rim flavors shine in Geisha's Kiss, with line-caught yellowfin tuna and piquillo peppers, and the vegetarian Buddha Belly, with spicy Japanese eggplant, kale and avocado.

BOXED FOODS SANDWICHES, SALADS **$**

Map p304 (415-981-9377; www.boxedfoodscompany.com; 245 Kearny St; sandwiches & salads $10-11; 10:30am-3pm Mon-Sat; ; 8, 30, 45, Montgomery, Montgomery) Local, seasonal, sustainable ingredients make outrageously flavorful lunches, whether you choose the free-range flank-steak salad with feta, tomatoes and mint, or the BLTA, with crunchy applewood smoked bacon, lettuce, heirloom tomato and avocado spread. Get yours to go to the Transamerica Pyramid redwood grove or grab a table out back.

SWEET WOODRUFF CALIFORNIAN **$**

Map p316 (415-292-9090; www.sweetwoodruffsf.com; 798 Sutter St; mains $8-14; 8am-9:30pm Mon-Fri, 9:30am-9:30pm Sat & Sun; ; 2, 3, California) Little sister to groundbreaking, Michelin-starred Sons & Daughters, this storefront gourmet hot spot uses ingredients grown on the restaurant's own farm in its abbreviated, affordable small-plates menu. There's limited service and a tiny kitchen, yet somehow it turns out sourdough pancakes, homemade soups, impeccable bone-marrow deviled eggs and inspired vegetarian options like beet burgers.

GALETTE 88 CREPES $

Map p304 (www.galettesf.com; 88 Hardie Pl; crepes $8-12.50; ⌚11am-2:30pm Mon-Fri; ; 8, 30, 45, MMontgomery, BMontgomery) Hidden in an alley, this minimalist storefront creperie lures lunchtime crowds with authentic, Brittany-style savory buckwheat gallettes. Fillings range from classic emmental cheese with caramelized onions to gourmet chicken with leeks, spinach and crème fraîche. Wash it down with spiked French cider or Belgian ale, and leave room for dessert crepes, including salted caramel with roasted apples.

MURACCI'S CURRY JAPANESE $

Map p304 (415-773-1101; www.muraccis.com; 307 Kearny St; curry dishes $8-10; ⌚11am-7pm Mon-Thu, to 6pm Fri, to 4pm Sat; ; 8, 30, 45, MMontgomery, BMontgomery) Warm up foggy days with steaming curry-topped *katsu* (pork cutlet), grilled chicken rice plate or classic Japanese comfort-food curry – neither spicy nor sharp but gently tingling, faintly sweet and powerfully savory. Order at the counter and wait for your name to be called. If no stools are free, take lunch to the Transamerica Pyramid redwood grove.

BIO CAFÉ, SANDWICHES $

Map p304 (415-362-0255; www.biologiquesf.com; 75 O'Farrell St; dishes $5-10; ⌚8am-6pm; ; MPowell, BPowell) Dietary constraints are no barrier to tasty, fast French fare here. Quiches and cookies are gluten-free, split pea soup is vegetarian, salads are organic and vegan, and coffee is fair trade. If you're juicing, try a cayenne-lavendar kombucha cleanse – but you're going to want that baguette with prosciutto, goat cheese and housemade jam. No seating; picnic at Union Square.

BREAD & COCOA CAFÉ, SANDWICHES $

Map p304 (www.breadandcocoa.com; 199 Sutter St; dishes $8-12.50; ⌚6:30am-5pm Mon-Fri, 8am-5pm Sat & Sun; ; MMontgomery, BMontgomery) Local, artisanal ingredients add zing to sandwiches, such as roast-chicken panini with pesto, and tangy Humboldt Fog cheese with prosciutto, organic tomato and arugula. For $8 to $12.50 they're not huge, but their flavor sure is. For decadence, try the dark chocolate chai.

CAFE CLAUDE FRENCH $$

Map p304 (415-392-3505; www.cafeclaude.com; 7 Claude Lane; mains $15-26; ⌚11:30am-10:30pm Mon-Sat, 5:30pm-10:30pm Sun; 30, 45, MMontgomery, BMontgomery) Escape down an SF alleyway to the perfect French café, with zinc bar, umbrella tables outside and staff chattering *en français*. Lunch is served till a civilized 4:30pm and jazz combos play Thursday to Saturday dinnertimes. Expect classics like *coq au vin* and steak tartare, always good, if not great – but wine and romance make it memorable.

FARMERBROWN NEW AMERICAN $$

Map p304 (415-409-3276; www.farmerbrownsf.com; 25 Mason St; mains $13-26; ⌚9:30am-2:30pm & 5-9pm Mon-Wed, to 10pm Thu-Fri, 10am-2:30pm Sat, 9:30am-2:30pm Sun; 8, 27, 31, 45, MPowell, BPowell) This rebel from the wrong side of the block dishes up ribs that will stick to yours, coleslaw with a kick that'll leave your lips buzzing, and 16oz Mason jars of spiked farmhouse lemonade. Chef-owner Jay Foster works with local organic and African American farmers to provide food with actual soul. Buffet brunches ($25) include fried chicken and waffles and live music.

HAKKASAN DIM SUM, CHINESE $$$

Map p304 (415-829-8148; http://hakkasan.com/; 1 Kearny St; mains $20-38; ⌚11:30am-2:30pm & 5:30-11pm Tue-Sat, to 10pm Mon; MMontgomery, BMontgomery) Bootstrapping start-ups and venture capitalists alike hit Hakkasan for the three-course lunch special ($35), with elegant dim sum (get the XO

NO RESERVATIONS? NO PROBLEM HERE

For maximum choice without prior reservations, try food marketplaces like The Hall, the Twitter Headquarters (p87) ground-floor Marketplace, or the Ferry Building (p73). The best-curated selection is at the **Ferry Building**, with chef-operated lunch counters, high-end take-out, and food trucks at the farmers market (10am to 2pm Tuesday and Thursday and 8am to 2pm Saturday). For SF's best round-up of food trucks, hit SoMa StrEat Food Park (p93) or Off the Grid Thursdays in the Haight (p187), Fridays at Fort Mason (p64), and Sundays in the Presidio (p64).

brandy scallop and prawn and chive dumplings), decadent mains like claypot pork belly, and sensational greens. Small dishes and big bartender pours make this a prime spot for business deals. For dinner, count on two to three dishes per person; $15 parking available.

GITANE MEDITERRANEAN $$$

Map p304 (☎415-788-6686; www.gitanerestaurant.com; 6 Claude Lane; mains $24-30; ⏰5:30-11pm Mon-Thu, to midnight Fri & Sat; 🍷; 🚌30, 45, Ⓜ Montgomery, Ⓑ Montgomery) Slip out of the Financial District and into something more comfortable at this sultry Mediterranean bistro, where the decor is cushioned, tufted, tasseled and decadently dateworthy. Andalucian-accented menu standouts include local Petrale sole with preserved Meyer lemon, and the duo of lamb with *merguez* sausage and *fava pistou*. Dress sharp and mingle over craft cocktails; reserve ahead for dinner dates.

ALFRESCO DINING ON WARM NIGHTS

During the odd heat wave in SF, when it's too hot to stay indoors without air-con (which nobody in SF has) and warm enough to eat outside, two downtown streets become go-to destinations for dining alfresco: **Belden Place** (www.belden-place.com) and **Claude Lane**. Both are pedestrian alleyways lined with European-style restaurants and convivial sidewalk seating. The food is marginally better on Claude Lane, notably at Gitane and Cafe Claude. Belden is sunnier and more colorful – the restaurants here make up for average Francophone fare with big smiles and generous wine pours.

Civic Center & the Tenderloin

THE HALL FAST FOOD $

Map p306 (www.thehallsf.com; 1028 Market St; mains $5-14; ⏰11am-8pm Mon-Fri; 🚌6, 7, 9, 21, Ⓑ Civic Center, Ⓜ Civic Center) Life is too short to debate lunch – everyone wins at The Hall, lined with tempting options from local food purveyors. Check daily menus online – standouts include Little Green Cyclo's organic sirloin *pho* (Vietnamese noodle soup), Fine & Rare's crab Louie salad, Raj & Singh's chickpea samosas, Cassia's coconut-milk braised pork and The Whole Beast's local lamb gyros. Worth braving a sketchy block.

HEART OF THE CITY FARMERS MARKET MARKET $

Map p306 (www.hotcfarmersmarket.org; United Nations Plaza; ⏰7am-5:30pm Wed, to 5pm Sun; 🚌6, 7, 9, 21, Ⓜ Civic Center, Ⓑ Civic Center) Bringing farm freshness to the city center since 1981, this nonprofit, farmer-operated market is on a mission to provide local, affordable, healthy food to low-income inner-city communities. Seasonal scores include organic Yrena Farms berries, De Santis farm Buddha's hand citrus and Ortiz Brothers pesticide-free salad greens. Prepared food vendors include RoliRoti free-range rotisserie chicken and All-Star Tamales. Bargain prices.

FARM:TABLE AMERICAN $

Map p306 (☎415-292-7089; www.farmtablesf.com; 754 Post St; dishes $6-9; ⏰7:30am-2pm Tue-Fri, 8am-3pm Sat & Sun; 🚌2, 3, 27, 38) 🌿 A ray of sunshine in the concrete heart of the city, this plucky little storefront uses seasonal, regional organics in just-baked breakfasts and farmstead-fresh lunches. Check the daily menu on Twitter (@farmtable) for the savory tart of the day and ever-popular themed pop-ups. Great coffee. Cash only.

LERS ROS THAI $

Map p306 (☎415-931-6917; www.lersros.com/larkin; 730 Larkin St; mains $10-15; ⏰11am-midnight; 🚌19, 31, 38, 47, 49) Most Thai eateries stick to familiar favorites, but Lers Ros imports regional Thai cooking with bold spicing and wild ingredients – house specialties include garlic frog legs, salt and pepper rabbit, and boar with on-the-vine green peppercorns. Good wine and late hours make this a magnet after the movies or symphony, never mind the sketchy neighborhood.

CAFE ZITOUNA MOROCCAN $

Map p306 (☎415-673-2622; www.sfcafezitouna.com; 1201 Sutter St; mains $8-15; ⏰11:30am-9pm Tue-Thu & Sat & Sun, 2-9pm Fri; 🚌2, 3, 19, 47, 49) Hearty couscous platters, lamb stew, kebabs and shawarma are family recipes at Cafe Zitouna, a spotlessly clean window-lined café serving big plates of savory home-style Moroccan cooking. The kindly chef-owner hails from Tunisia, his wife from Morocco – and everything, *merguez* (lamb sausage)

TOP EATS AT THE FERRY BUILDING

Hog Island Oyster Company (Map p303; ☎415-391-7117; www.hogislandoysters.com; 1 Ferry Bldg; 4 oysters $13; ⏰11am-9pm; Ⓜ Embarcadero, Ⓑ Embarcadero) Slurp the bounty of the North Bay with East Bay views, at this local, sustainable oyster bar. Get them raw with caper *beurre blanc* or oysters Rockefeller (grilled with local spinach, Pernod and cream). Monday to Thursday 5pm to 7pm are happy hours indeed, with half-price oysters and $4 pints. Stop by the Hog Island farmers market stall 8am to 2pm Saturday for $2 oysters.

Boulette's Larder & Boulibar (Map p303; ☎415-399-1155; www.bouletteslarder.com; 1 Ferry Bldg; mains $18-24; ⏰Larder 8am-10:30am & 11:30am-3pm Tue-Sat, 10am-2:30pm Sun, Boulibar 11:30am-9:30pm Tue-Fri, 11am-8pm Sat; Ⓜ Embarcadero, Ⓑ Embarcadero) Dinner theater doesn't get better than brunch at Boulette's communal table, strategically placed inside a working kitchen amid a swirl of chefs with views of the Bay Bridge. At the adjoining Boulibar, get tangy Mideastern mezze platters, beautifully blistered wood-fired pizzas and flatbreads at indoor picnic-style tables perfect for Ferry Building people-watching. Find spices and mixes at their pantry shop.

El Porteño Empanadas (Map p303; ☎415-513-4529; www.elportenosf.com/; 1 Ferry Bldg; empanadas $4.50; ⏰9am-7pm Mon-Sat, 10am-5pm Sun; Ⓑ Embarcadero, Ⓜ Embarcadero) Pocket change left over from farmers market shopping will score you an Argentine pocket pastry packed with local flavor at El Porteño. Vegetarian versions like *acelga* (organic swiss chard and Gruyère) and *humita* (Brentwood sweet corn and caramelized onions) are just as mouthwatering as classic *jamon y queso* (prosciutto and fontina). Save room for *dulce de leche alfajores*, cookies with gooey caramel centers.

Slanted Door (Map p303; ☎415-861-8032; www.slanteddoor.com; 1 Ferry Bldg; mains $18-42; ⏰11am-4:30pm & 5:30-10pm Mon-Sat, 11:30am-4:30pm & 5:30-10pm Sun; Ⓜ Embarcadero, Ⓑ Embarcadero) Live the dream at this bayfront bistro, where California-fresh, Vietnamese-inspired dishes are served with sparkling waterfront views. Chinatown-raised chef-owner Charles Phan is a James Beard Award winner and local hero for championing California-grown ingredients in signature dishes like garlicky grass-fed 'shaking beef' and Dungeness crab heaped atop cellophane noodles. Book weeks ahead, or settle for *banh mi* (sandwich) take-out.

Mijita (Map p303; ☎415-399-0814; www.mijitasf.com; 1 Ferry Bldg; dishes $4-10; ⏰10am-7pm Mon-Thu, to 8pm Fri, 9am-8pm Sat, 9am-3pm Sun; 🌶 👪; Ⓜ Embarcadero, Ⓑ Embarcadero) Jealous seagulls circle above your outdoor bayside table, eying your sustainable fish tacos and tangy jicama and grapefruit salad. James Beard Award–winning Traci Des Jardins adapts her Mexican grandmother's cooking at this sunny taqueria with authentic flavors – the Mexico City–style quesadilla is laced with *epazote* (sacred Mayan herb), and *agua fresca* (fruit punch) is made from just-squeezed juice.

Il Cane Rosso (Map p303; ☎415-391-7599; www.canerossosf.com; 1 Ferry Bldg; mains breakfast $5-12.50, lunch & dinner $10-15; ⏰9am-8pm; Ⓜ Embarcadero, Ⓑ Embarcadero) Farmstead fare served at a former ferry ticket counter: only in San Francisco. Expect soul-satisfying meals that make the most of Ferry Building farmers market produce: organic housemade yogurt with seasonal fruit compote for breakfast, Petaluma Farms warm egg-salad sandwich lunches, and roast chicken with Rancho Gordo quinoa dinner. Check daily menus online, and snag an outdoor bayside table.

to mint tea, is homemade. They sometimes close early: call ahead. Great value.

SAIGON SANDWICH SHOP — VIETNAMESE $

Map p306 (☎415-474-5698; www.saigon-sandwich.com; 560 Larkin St; sandwiches $3.75-4.25; ⏰7am-5pm; 🚌19, 31) Order your bargain *banh mi* (Vietnamese sandwich) when the ladies of the Saigon call you, or you'll get skipped. Act fast and be rewarded with a baguette piled high with your choice of roast pork, chicken, pâté, meatballs and/or tofu, plus pickled carrots, cilantro, jalapeño and thinly sliced onion.

LITTLE GRIDDLE — AMERICAN $

Map p306 (☎415-864-4292; www.littlegriddlesf.com/; 1400 Market St; mains $10-15; ⏰7:30am-

5pm Mon-Tue, to 9pm Wed-Sat, to 3pm Sun; 6, 7, 9, 21, M Van Ness) Start the day with a Morning Cliche (eggs, hash browns, toast, bacon/sausage) or get clever with the A-Plus Student Omelet packed with vegetables and avocado (aka California brain food). Service is leisurely even when there's no line – Twitter HQ employees across the street keep popping in to pick up orders – but the coffee's strong and there's sunny storefront seating.

SAI JAI THAI THAI $

Map p306 (415-673-5774; www.saijaithairestaurant.com; 771 O'Farrell St; mains $7-11; 11am-10:30pm; ; 19, 38, 47, 49) Mom and the cooks shout at each other in Thai, hardly anyone speaks English and the room is grungy, but the classic cooking's spot on. Try the pork-shoulder fried rice, and when they ask how hot, say, 'Spicy like for Thai people!' Alas, no beer and cash only. Free delivery to downtown hotels.

SHALIMAR SOUTH ASIAN $

Map p306 (415-928-0333; www.shalimarsf.com; 532 Jones St; dishes $5-10; noon-3pm & 5-11:30pm; ; 27, 38) Follow your nose to tandoori chicken straight off the skewer and naan bread still bubbling from the oven at this fluorescent-lit, linoleum-floored downtown Pakistani tandoori diner. Watch and learn as foodies who demand five-star service elsewhere meekly fetch their own water pitchers and tamarind sauce from the fridge.

BRENDA'S FRENCH SOUL FOOD CREOLE, SOUTHERN $$

Map p306 (415-345-8100; www.frenchsoulfood.com; 652 Polk St; mains lunch $9-13, dinner $12-17; 8am-3pm Mon & Tue, to 10pm Wed-Sat, to 8pm Sun; 19, 31, 38, 47, 49) Chef-owner Brenda Buenviaje blends New Orleans–style Creole cooking with French technique into 'French soul food.' Expect updated classics like beignets, serious biscuits and grits, impeccable Hangtown Fry (eggs with bacon and fried oysters), and fried chicken with collard greens and hot-pepper jelly. Long waits on sketchy sidewalks are unavoidable – but Brenda serves takeaway sandwiches two doors down.

SoMa

SENTINEL SANDWICHES $

Map p308 (415-284-9960; www.thesentinelsf.com; 37 New Montgomery St; sandwiches $9-10.50; 7:30am-2:30pm Mon-Fri; 12, 14, M Montgomery, B Montgomery) Rebel SF chef Dennis Leary is out to revolutionize lunchtime take-out with top-notch seasonal ingredients. Tuna salad gets radical with chipotle mayo and artichokes, and corned beef crosses borders with Swiss cheese and housemade Russian dressing. Check website for daily menus and call in your order, or expect a 10-minute wait – sandwiches are made to order. Enjoy in the Crocker Galleria rooftop garden.

SOMA STREAT FOOD PARK FOOD TRUCKS $

Map p308 (http://somastreatfoodpark.com/; 428 11th St; dishes $5-12; 11am-3pm & 5-9pm Mon-Fri, 11am-10pm Sat, to 5pm Sun; 9, 27, 47) Your posse is hungry, but one of you is vegan, another wants burritos with beer, and another only likes burritos made with Korean barbecue beef. So what do you do? First: recognize that you and your friends belong in San Francisco. Second: head to this SoMa parking lot where the food trucks can satisfy your every whim. The area gets sketchy – mind your wallet.

DOTTIE'S TRUE BLUE CAFÉ AMERICAN, BREAKFAST $

Map p308 (415-885-2767; 28 6th St; mains $7-13; 7:30am-3pm Thu-Mon; B Powell, M Powell) Consider yourself lucky if you queue up less than half an hour and get hit up for change only once – but fresh baked goods come to those who wait at Dottie's. Cinnamon pancakes, grilled cornbread, scrambles with whiskey fennel sausage and anything else off the griddle are tried and true blue.

BUTLER & THE CHEF FRENCH $

Map p308 (415-896-2075; http://butlerandthechef.com/; 155a S Park St; mains $9-13; 8am-3pm Tue-Sat, 10am-3pm Sun; 10, 30, 45, M N,T) Find authentic French-café classics among the SoMa warehouses at this lunch-only South Park favorite. Tables are tiny: mind your elbows or they'll wind up in your French onion soup, made properly with rich beef stock and a real crouton topped with melting Gruyère.

TIN VIETNAMESE VIETNAMESE $

Map p308 (415-882-7188; www.tinsf.com; 937 Howard St; mains $7.50-11; 11:30am-3pm & 5:30-10pm Mon-Sat; 14, 27) Two blocks from the convention center's overpriced tourist restaurants, hole-in-the-wall Tin caters to SoMa locals with consistently good *pho,* rice plates and rice-noodle bowls topped with lemongrass chicken, shrimp-and-pork fried spring rolls and other fragrant Vietnamese classics. There's beer and wine, too, however limited.

1601 BAR & KITCHEN CALIFORNIAN, FUSION **$$**

Map p308 (☎415-552-1601; http://1601sf.com/; 1601 Howard St; mains $12-22; ⏰6-10pm Tue-Thu, to 11pm Fri & Sat; 🚌9, 12, 47, Ⓜ Van Ness) Rising star-chef alert: Brian Fernando is turning Sri Lankan inspirations into Californian cravings. Velvety halibut ceviche in coconut milk is an instant obsession, Marin Sun Farms goat stew with red basmati rice for two is dateworthy, and you'll want the pork belly and fenugreeek-vinegar home fries again for breakfast. Ingenuity without pretension, at half the cost of most downtown tasting menus ($76 here).

TROPISUEÑO MEXICAN **$$**

Map p308 (☎415-243-0299; www.tropisueno.com; 75 Yerba Buena Lane; mains lunch $7-12, dinner $14-18; ⏰11am-10:30pm; 🚌8, 14, 30, 45, Ⓜ Powell, Ⓑ Powell) Last time you enjoyed casual Mexican dining this much, there were probably balmy ocean breezes and hammocks involved. Instead, you're steps away from SoMa's museums, savoring *al pastor* (marinated pork) burritos with mesquite salsa and grilled pineapple, while sipping margaritas with chili-salted rims. The rustic-organic decor is definitely downtown, but prices are down to earth.

BASIL THAI CANTEEN THAI **$$**

Map p308 (☎415-552-3963; www.basilcanteen.com; 1489 Folsom St; mains $10-16; ⏰11:30am-2:30pm & 5-10pm Mon-Fri, 5-10pm Sat & Sun; 🍸; 🚌9, 12, 47) Inside a brick-walled former brewery, Basil Canteen is a smart stop before a night at SoMa's bars and clubs, with fresh-fruit cocktails and reasonably priced, brightly spiced Thai cooking. Happy hours (5pm to 7pm weekdays) bring a variety of $5 snack plates ideal for sharing, including skewers, rolls and savory tapioca dumplings. Reservations advised.

21ST AMENDMENT BREWERY AMERICAN **$$**

Map p308 (☎415-369-0900; http://21st-amendment.com; 563 2nd St; mains $10-20; ⏰kitchen 11:30am-10pm Mon-Sat, 10am-10pm Sun, bar till midnight; 👪; 🚌10, Ⓜ N,T) Perfectly placed before Giants games, 21st Amendment brews stellar IPA and Hell or High Watermelon wheat beer. The respectable bar-and-grill menu – burgers, pizza, chops, sandwiches, salads – checks your buzz, but the cavernous space is so loud, nobody'll notice you're shouting. Kids get ice-cream floats made with homemade root beer. Ground zero for techies who lunch.

★**BENU** CALIFORNIAN, FUSION **$$$**

Map p308 (☎415-685-4860; www.benusf.com; 22 Hawthorne St; tasting menu $228; ⏰5:30-8:30pm seatings Tue-Sat; 🚌10, 12, 14, 30, 45) SF has set fusion cuisine standards for 150 years, but chef-owner Corey Lee remixes California ingredients and Pacific Rim inspiration with a superstar DJ's finesse. Dungeness crab and truffle custard bring such outsize flavor to Lee's faux-shark's fin soup, you'll swear there's Jaws in there. The prix-fixe menu is pricey (plus 20% service), but don't miss star-sommelier Yoon Ha's ingenious pairings ($160).

BOULEVARD CALIFORNIAN **$$$**

Map p308 (☎415-543-6084; www.boulevardrestaurant.com; 1 Mission St; mains lunch $18-31, dinner $29-48; ⏰11:30am-2:15pm & 5:30-10pm Mon-Thu, to 10:30pm Fri & Sat, 5:30-10pm Sun; Ⓜ Embarcadero, Ⓑ Embarcadero) The 1889 belle epoque Audiffred Building was once the Coast Seamen's Union, but for the last 20-plus years James Beard Award–winning chef Nancy Oakes has made culinary history with Boulevard. Reliably tasty, effortlessly elegant menu signatures include juicy oven-roasted Kurobuta pork chops, crisp California quail and dumplings, and grilled Pacific salmon with wild morel mushrooms – plus sticky toffee pudding with black-pepper ice cream.

MOURAD MOROCCAN, MEDITERRANEAN **$$$**

Map p308 (☎415-660-2500; http://mouradsf.com/; 140 New Montgomery St; mains $18-48, family-style platters $75-160; ⏰4-10pm Mon-Fri, from 5pm Sat & Sun; 🚌12, 14, Ⓑ Montgomery, Ⓜ Montgomery) In the historic Pacific Telephone & Telegraph building, *Iron Chef* Mourad Lahlou creates conversation-starting dishes like lamb with pistachio charmoula and duck-liver pâté with blueberries. Family-style platters serve two to six, accompanied by several sides – a taste/texture sensation, if you can agree on a protein (go duck). Trust your sommelier's pairings, and star pastry chef Melissa Chou to work magic with honey and almonds.

SALT HOUSE CALIFORNIAN **$$$**

Map p308 (☎415-543-8900; www.salthousesf.com; 545 Mission St; mains lunch $15-25, dinner $24-36; ⏰lunch & dinner Mon-Sat, to midnight Fri & Sat; 🚌6, 7, 10, 14, 21, 31, 71, F, J, K, L, M, N,

Montgomery) For a business lunch that feels more like a spa getaway, take your choice of light fare such as satiny yuzu-avocado tuna tartare or shrimp salad with a jalapeno kick. Forget the ice tea, and unwind with wine by the glass or cucumber-lime rickeys until happy hour (2pm to 6pm). Service is leisurely, so order that caramel-apple crisp with bacon brittle now.

DRINKING & NIGHTLIFE

Most nightclubs are in SoMa, but they're spread across a large area – don't get stuck walking in heels. The highest concentration of bars and clubs is around 11th and Folsom Sts. The SoMa scene pops weekends, and shrivels weekdays. Financial District bars pack Wednesdays through Fridays, from 5pm to 8pm, empty suddenly, and close by midnight. A downside to downtown drinking is the scene: too-loud dudes in suits and after-hours office drama between co-workers, and it gets sloppy on Fridays. For cheaper drinks on the wild side, brave the Tenderloin and swill with hipsters, free spirits and career drinkers. Drink prices rise as you move toward the Financial District, exceeding $10 east of Powell St.

Financial District & Jackson Square

GASPAR BRASSERIE & COGNAC ROOM BAR

Map p304 (415-576-8800; http://gasparbrasserie.com; 185 Sutter St; bar 3-10:30pm; Montgomery, Montgomery) When Gold Rush prospectors struck it rich, they upgraded from rotgut rye to fine French cognac – and history repeats itself nightly at Gaspar's Cognac Room. SF's biggest, best selection of cocktails made with cognac features the drop-dead-delicious Corpse Reviver #1 (cognac, calvados, vermouth and orange). Come boom or bust, don't miss weekday 4pm to 6pm happy hours for $1 oysters and deviled eggs.

TAVERNA AVENTINE BAR

Map p303 (415-981-1500; www.aventinesf.com; 582 Washington St; 11:30am-10pm Mon-Tue, to 11pm Wed, to midnight Thu, to 2am Fri, 7pm-midnight Sat; 1, 8, 10, 12, 41) Back in SF's wild Barbary Coast days, the Aventine's 150-year-old building fronted the bay – you can still see salt-water marks on brick walls downstairs. Now bartenders hit a high-water mark during happy hours (3pm to 7pm Monday to Friday), mixing bourbon and Scotch cocktails fit for a sailor.

BIX BAR

Map p303 (415-433-6300; www.bixrestaurant.com; 56 Gold St; bar 4:30pm-midnight; 1, 8, 10, 12, 41) Head down a Jackson Square alleyway and back in time at Bix, a 1930s-style supper club with white-jacketed barmen shaking martinis at the mahogany bar. The restaurant's good – order the tuna tartare – but the bar is great, with nightly live piano and jazz combos. Look sharp and swagger.

Union Square

★**LOCAL EDITION** BAR

Map p304 (415-795-1375; www.localeditionsf.com; 691 Market St; 5pm-2am Mon-Fri, from 7pm Sat; Montgomery, Montgomery) Get the scoop on the SF cocktail scene at this new speakeasy in the basement of the historic Hearst newspaper building. Lighting is so dim you might bump into typewriters, but all is forgiven when you get The Pulitzer – a scotch-sherry cocktail that goes straight to your head.

★**RICKHOUSE** BAR

Map p304 (415-398-2827; www.rickhousebar.com; 246 Kearny St; 5pm-2am Mon, 3pm-2am Tue-Fri, 6pm-2am Sat; 8, 30, 45, Montgomery, Montgomery) Like a shotgun shack plunked downtown, Rickhouse is lined floor-to-ceiling with repurposed whiskey casks imported from Kentucky and back-bar shelving from an Ozark Mountains nunnery that once secretly brewed hooch. The emphasis is (naturally) on whiskey, specifically hard-to-find bourbons – but the cocktails are sublime. Round up a posse to help finish that garage-sale punchbowl of Pisco Punch.

CANTINA BAR

Map p316 (415-398-0195; www.cantinasf.com; 580 Sutter St; 5pm-2am Mon-Sat, 2pm-2am Sun; 2, 3, 8, 30, 38, 45, Powell-Mason, Powell-Hyde) All the Latin-inspired cocktails (think tequila, cachaça and mezcal) are made with fresh juice at this mixologist's dream bar – there's not even a soda gun behind the bar. The local crowd includes off-duty bartenders

LOCAL KNOWLEDGE

HUSH-HUSH HOOCH

Psst...keep a secret? Some of the best cocktails you'll have in San Francisco (or anywhere) are hiding in plain sight under a deliberately misleading Anti-Saloon League sign. **Bourbon & Branch** (Map p306; ☎415-346-1735; www.bourbonandbranch.com; 501 Jones St; ⏰6pm-2am; 🚌27,38) is an authentic recreation of a Prohibition-era speakeasy, complete with secret exits and basement bullet holes from its Prohibition-era heyday – only now the locally crafted spirits aren't made in a bathtub. For historically researched, highly original top-shelf gin and bourbon cocktails, give the bouncer the password ('books') and you'll be led through a bookcase secret passage to the most liquored-up library in America. 'Don't even think of asking for a cosmo' reads one of many posted House Rules here. Instead, you're encouraged to order the Scofflaw (whiskey, vermouth, grenadine and housemade bitters). Reservations are required for front-room booths, and for **Wilson & Wilson Detective Agency**, the noir-themed speakeasy-within-a-speakeasy (password supplied with reservations). Shhhh...keep it under your hat.

sipping Cantina's definitive pisco sour with equal parts awe and envy. Mellow enough for conversation most weeknights; DJs get the joint thumping on weekends.

BURRITT ROOM — LOUNGE

Map p304 (☎415-400-0561; www.mystichotel.com; 417 Stockton St; ⏰5pm-midnight Sun-Thu, to 2am Fri & Sat; 🚌2, 3, 8, 30, 38, Ⓜ Montgomery, Ⓑ Montgomery) Upstairs at the Mystic Hotel, enter a decadent Victorian parlor bar with century-old tile floors, red-velvet sofas and gaudy chandeliers – as though Gold Rush burlesque troupes might arrive any moment, demanding champagne cocktails and punchbowls of Pimm's Cup. Celebrity chef-owner Charlie Palmer expanded the place with a tavern and meat-heavy menu, but the bar remains the star attraction.

IRISH BANK — PUB

Map p304 (☎415-788-7152; www.theirishbank.com; 10 Mark Lane; ⏰11:30am-2am; 🚌2, 3, 30, 45, Ⓜ Montgomery, Ⓑ Montgomery) Perfectly pulled pints and thick-cut fries with malt vinegar, plus juicy burgers, brats and anything else you could possibly want with lashings of mustard are staples at this cozy Irish pub. There are tables beneath a big awning in the alley out front, ideal for smokers – even on a rainy night.

TUNNEL TOP — BAR

Map p304 (☎415-722-6620; 601 Bush St; ⏰5pm-2am Mon-Sat, noon-2am Sun; 🚌2, 3, 8, 30, 45, Ⓜ Montgomery, Ⓑ Montgomery) You can't tell who's local and who's not in this happening hilltop bar with exposed beams, beer-bottle chandelier and a rickety mezzanine where you can spy on the crowd. Head up the Stockton St staircase to find the place, and you'll be rewarded with craft beer on tap and bargain $6 to $8 cocktails. Cash only, but there's an ATM on-site.

JOHN'S GRILL — BAR

Map p304 (www.johnsgrill.com; 63 Ellis St; ⏰11am-10pm; 🚋Powell-Mason, Powell-Hyde, Ⓜ Powell, Ⓑ Powell) 'She was a real gone gal, until she double-crossed me...' Tough-guy martinis at Dashiell Hammett's favorite bar will get you talking like a noir-movie villain, telling tales of lost love and true crimes while chewing toothpicks. Cocktails are strictly classic and the food greasy-spoon – nothing fancy here, except for the golden *Maltese Falcon* movie prop statuette upstairs.

Civic Center & the Tenderloin

RYE — LOUNGE

Map p306 (☎415-474-4448; www.ryesf.com; 688 Geary St; ⏰5:30pm-2am Mon-Fri, from 6pm Sat, from 7pm Sun; 🚌2, 3, 27, 38) Swagger into this sleek sunken lounge for cocktails that look sharp and pack more heat than Steve McQueen in *Bullet*. The soundtrack is '70s soul and the drinks strictly old-school – whiskey sours are stiff with egg whites and drizzled with housemade bitters. Come early to sip at your leisure on leather couches, and leave before the smokers' cage overflows.

AUNT CHARLIE'S LOUNGE — GAY, CLUB

Map p306 (☎415-441-2922; www.auntcharlieslounge.com; 133 Turk St; admission free-$5; ⏰noon-2am Mon-Fri, from 10am Sat, 10am-midnight Sun; 🚌27, 31, Ⓜ Powell, Ⓑ Powell) Vintage pulp-fiction covers come to life when the Hot Boxxx Girls take the stage at Aunt Charlie's on Friday and Saturday nights at 10pm ($5; call for reservations). Thursday is Tubesteak Connection ($5, free before 10pm), when bathhouse anthems and '80s disco draw throngs of art-school gays. Other nights bring minor mayhem, seedy glamour guaranteed.

EDINBURGH CASTLE PUB

Map p306 (☎415-885-4074; www.thecastlesf.com/; 950 Geary St; ⊙5pm-2am; 🚌19, 38, 47, 49) Bagpiper murals on the walls, the *Trainspotting* soundtrack on the jukebox, ale on tap, and a service delivering vinegary fish and chips provide all the Scottish authenticity you could ask for, short of haggis. This flag-waving bastion of drink comes fully equipped with dartboard, pool tables, and alternating pop-punk and hip-hop DJs on Saturdays.

RICKSHAW STOP CLUB

Map p306 (☎415-861-2011; www.rickshawstop.com; 155 Fell St; admission $5-35; ⊙hours variable, check website; 🚌21, 47, 49, Ⓜ Van Ness) Welcome to the high-school prom you always wanted – theme parties here have been known to bring burlesque trapeze, Brazilian dancers, gypsy brass bands and crowds dressed in drag as dead celebrities. Regular events include Friday night's all-ages (18 plus), Popscene indie bands, monthly Nerd Nite lecture mixers and monthly Cockblock lesbian '90s dance parties.

LUSH LOUNGE GAY, BAR

Map p306 (☎415-771-2022; www.lushloungesf.com/; 1221 Polk St; ⊙3pm-2am Mon-Fri, 1pm-2am Sat & Sun; 🚌2, 3, 19, 38, 47, 49) Snag a wooden table by the steel-front fireplace and order anything in stemware – here the lemon drops, cosmos and other girly drinks kick burly men's asses. Lush Lounge marks the line on Polk where grit ends and hip begins, and sexual orientations blur. At its generous happy hours (weekdays 3pm to 7pm, weekends 1pm to 7pm), everyone becomes a lush.

WHISKEY THIEVES BAR

Map p306 (☎415-506-8331; 839 Geary St; ⊙1pm-2am; 🚌19, 27, 38) The scene outside this Tenderloin dive makes whiskey seem like a comparatively harmless drug of choice, and this joint has it all, from rare rye to aged single malts. The backbar is subdivided by category – Irish, Scotch, Bourbon and Rye – and $7 buys a bartender's choice shot plus a PBR. Feed the jukebox between rounds of pool. Cash only.

RUBY SKYE CLUB

Map p304 (☎415-693-0777; www.rubyskye.com; 420 Mason St; admission $10-40; ⊙9pm-late Thu-Sat; 🚋Powell-Mason, Powell-Hyde, Ⓜ Powell, Ⓑ Powell) Spaceship laser effects in an 1890s Victorian theater bring the drama to club nights. The boozy mainstream crowd gets messy – hence the gruff security – but when the international roster of EDM DJs get the state-of-the-art sound system booming, everyone works it out on the dance floor. Check online calendar for occasional live acts like English Beat and Lauryn Hill.

SoMa

★BAR AGRICOLE BAR

Map p308 (☎415-355-9400; www.baragricole.com; 355 11th St; ⊙6-10pm Sun-Thu, 5:30-11pm Fri & Sat; 🚌9, 12, 27, 47) 🌿 Drink your way to a history degree with well-researched cocktails: Bellamy Scotch Sour with house bitters and egg whites passes the test, but El Presidente with white rum, farmhouse curaçao and California pomegranate grenadine takes top honors. This overachiever racks up James Beard Award nods for its spirits and eco-savvy design, and pairs decadent drink with local oysters and excellent California cheeses.

SIGHTGLASS COFFEE CAFÉ

Map p308 (☎415–861–1313; www.sightglasscoffee.com; 270 7th St; ⊙7am-7pm; 🚌12, 14, 19, Ⓑ Civic Center, Ⓜ Civic Center) Follow the aroma of cult coffee into this sunny SoMa warehouse, where family-grown, high-end bourbon-shrub coffee is roasted daily. Aficionados sip signature Owl's Howl Espresso around the downstairs bar – but for the ultimate pick-me-up, head to the mezzanine Affogato Bar for a scoop of creamy gelato in your coffee. Caffeinated socializing is encouraged; no wi-fi or outlets.

CAT CLUB CLUB

Map p308 (www.sfcatclub.com; 1190 Folsom St; admission free-$10 after 10pm; ⊙9pm-3am Tue-Sat; 🚌12, 19, 27, 47, Ⓜ Civic Center, Ⓑ Civic Center) You never really know your friends till you've seen them belt out A-ha's 'Take on Me' at Class of '84, Cat Club's Thursday-night retro dance party, where the euphoric

LOCAL KNOWLEDGE

TIPS FROM A TOP-FLIGHT SOMMELIER

Drinking in the Bay Area Scenery

Even though I worked in Napa, I still find the tasting rooms along Silverado Trail full of surprises, including some exceptional white wines. Everyone knows about the well-researched wine list at RN74 (p101), but have you had its cocktails? Rye (p96) is also on top of its mixology and Bar Agricole (p97) doesn't serve beginner cocktails – they're strong enough that you have to respect them with little sips and know they're going to take three times as long to finish.

Pop-up Pairings

All the food trucks and pop-up restaurants in San Francisco let you play around with the pairing possibilities, without a big investment. Look for Sonoma's versatile coastal Pinot Noirs and cool-climate Chardonnays that aren't over-oaked, so they're better at the table.

How Wine Pairing is Like Air Traffic Control

Finding room on the palate for wine is like landing a plane: it works better if you have a wide airstrip. Benu chef Corey Lee has me taste menu items early on and asks what four flavors come to the forefront. Once all those flavors are perfectly aligned, that creates a solid platform for wine – it just takes aim.

Becoming a Wine Aficionado

I was raised in a non-wine culture, in Seoul, Korea. Growing up, we never had wine at the table. I had to learn everything, but I worked hard and enjoyed it. Nothing is innate. Just keep drinking.

Yoon Ha is Head Sommelier at Benu (p94).

bi/straight/gay/undefinable scene is like some sweaty, surreal John Hughes movie. Tuesdays it's free karaoke, Wednesdays Bondage-a-Go-Go, Fridays Goth and Saturdays '80s-'90s power pop – RSVP online for $3 off entry.

ENDUP GAY, CLUB

Map p308 (☎415-646-0999; www.theendup.com; 401 6th St; admission $5-20; ⏰10pm Thu-4am Fri, 11pm Fri-11am Sat, 10pm Sat-4am Mon, 10pm Mon-4am Tue; 🚌12, 19, 27, 47) Forget the Golden Gate Bridge: once you EndUp watching the sunrise over the 101 freeway ramp, you've officially arrived in SF. Dance sessions are marathons fueled by EndUp's 24-hour license, so Saturday nights have a way of turning into Monday mornings. Straight people sometimes EndUp here – but gay Sunday tea dances are legendary, in full force since 1973.

TERROIR NATURAL WINE MERCHANT WINE BAR

Map p308 (☎415-558-9946; terroirsf.com; 1116 Folsom St; ⏰3pm-midnight Mon-Thu, 2pm-2am Fri & Sat, 4-9pm Sun; 🚌12, 19, 27, 47, Ⓑ Civic Center) 🌿 Whether red or white, your wine is green here – Terroir specializes in natural-process, organic and biodynamic wines, with impressive lists from key French and Italian producers. Relax in the loft or pull up a stool at a reclaimed wood bar, and explore lesser-known cult wines with assists from laid-back but knowledgeable sommeliers.

BLOODHOUND BAR

Map p308 (☎415-863-2840; www.bloodhoundsf.com; 1145 Folsom St; ⏰4pm-2am; 🚌12, 14, 19, 27, 47) The murder of crows painted on the ceiling is an omen: nights at Bloodhound often assume mythic proportions. Vikings would feel at home amid these antler chandeliers, while bootleggers would appreciate barnwood walls and top-shelf hooch served in Mason jars. Shoot pool or chill on leather couches until your jam comes on the jukebox.

BLUXOME STREET WINERY WINE BAR

Map p308 (☎415-543-5353; www.bluxomewinery.com; 53 Bluxome St; ⏰noon-7pm Tue-Sun; Ⓜ N, T) Rolling vineyards seem overrated once you've visited SoMA's finest back-alley winery. Grab a barrel-top stool and watch winemakers at work in the adjoining warehouse while you sip Syrah rosé. Food trucks park out front; trust your pourer to provide the perfect Russian River Pinot Noir for that pork-belly taco. Call ahead, or you might accidentally crash a start-up launch.

CITY BEER STORE & TASTING ROOM
BAR

Map p308 (☎415-503-1033; www.citybeerstore.com; 1168 Folsom St; ⊙noon-10pm; 🚌12, 14, 19) Sample exceptional local and Belgian microbrews in 6oz-to-20oz pours at SF's top beer store. Mix and match your own six-pack of stouts or ales to go, or join the crowd enjoying featured craft brews of the day on draft. Think beyond cheese-and-cracker pairings with bar bites like grass-fed beef jerky and bacon caramel corn. Check online for brewery-hosted sipping sessions.

MONARCH
BAR, CLUB

Map p308 (www.monarchsf.com; 101 6th St; admission varies; ⊙5:30pm-2am Mon-Fri, 8pm-2am Sat & Sun; 🚌6, 7, 9, 14, BPowell, MPowell) A boom-town club on a busted SoMa block, Monarch has a plush parlor bar and cozy library bar on the main floor, and downstairs a black-box dance hall ($10 to $25 admission, cash only), killer sound system and party-ready DJs. Upgrade from merely happy to 'amazing hours' weekdays 5:30pm to 8:30pm, when contortionist comedians and circus burlesque acts often perform over the bar.

CLUB OMG
CLUB, GAY

Map p308 (☎415-896-6473; www.clubomgsf.com; 43 6th St; admission free-$10; ⊙5pm-2am Mon-Fri, 7pm-2am Sat & Sun; MPowell, BPowell) Tiny OMG draws a mostly gay, mostly 20s-40ish crowd to the heart of San Francisco's Skid Row with its mesmerizing turquoise Lucite bar and fabulous dancefloor with trippy LED light shows on the overhead planetarium dome. Saturday Bollywood nights are epic at Indian-American-owned OMG, and Tuesday to Friday happy hours get the party started with double-drink deals 5pm to 8pm.

WATERBAR
BAR

Map p308 (☎415-284-9922; www.waterbarsf.com; 399 The Embarcadero; ⊙11:30am-9:30pm Sun-Mon, to 10pm Tue-Sat; BEmbarcadero, MN, T) Waterbar's massive glass-column aquariums and picture-window vistas of the Bay Bridge lights are SF's surest way to impress a date over drinks. Leave the dining room to Silicon Valley start-up founders trying to impress investors and make a beeline for the oval oyster bar, where seating is closer, plates and prices smaller, and oysters are $1.05 during happy hour.

111 MINNA
BAR, CLUB

Map p308 (☎415-974-1719; www.111minnagallery.com; 111 Minna St; admission free-$15; ⊙7:30-9pm Mon-Fri, to 2am Fri, 10pm-2am Sat; MMontgomery, BMontgomery) Minna St is named after a notorious Gold Rush–era harlot, and today 111 Minna works three jobs on this street corner: urban art gallery-café by day (7:30am to 5pm Monday to Friday), transforming into a weekday happy-hour scene (5pm to 9pm) and thumping club on weekends. At monthly Sketch Tuesdays artists create works for sale ($5 to $30) to the audience.

HOUSE OF SHIELDS
BAR

Map p308 (www.thehouseofshields.com; 39 New Montgomery St; ⊙2pm-2am Mon-Fri, from 3pm Sat & Sun; MMontgomery, BMontgomery) Flash back 100 years at this gloriously restored mahogany bar with original 1907 chandeliers and old-fashioned cocktails without the frippery. You won't find any TVs or clocks, so it's easy to lose all track of time here. This is one bar Nob Hill socialites and downtown bike messengers can agree on – especially after a few $5 cocktails in dimly lit corners.

BUTTER
BAR

Map p308 (☎415-863-5964; www.smoothasbutter.com; 354 11th St; ⊙6pm-2am Wed-Sat, from 8pm Sun; 🚌9, 12, 27, 47) Lowbrow and loving it: everyone's glugging Tang cocktails and wailing to rock anthems here. For a cheap date, you can't beat a Shotgun Wedding (shot and PBR) with Butter's standout selection of 'trailer treats' – including Tater Tots, corn dogs and deep-fried PB&J. Check the website for raucous events, including retro FUBAR Fridays and genuinely sloppy Sunday karaoke.

83 PROOF
BAR

Map p308 (☎415-296-8383; www.83proof.com; 83 1st St; ⊙2pm-midnight Mon & Tue, to 2am Wed-Thu, noon-2am Fri, 8pm-2am Sat; 🚌14, MMontgomery, BMontgomery) On average weeknights when the rest of downtown is dead, you may have to shout to be heard over 83's flirtatious, buzzing crowd. High ceilings make room for five shelves of top-shelf spirits behind the bar – including 200 plus whiskeys – so trust your bartender to make a basil gimlet that won't hurt at work tomorrow. Arrive early for loft seating.

SOMA GAY BARS

Sailors have cruised Polk St and Tenderloin gay/trans dives since the 1940s, Castro bars boomed in the 1970s and women into women have been hitting Mission dives since the '60s – but SoMa warehouses have been the biggest weekend gay scene for decades. From leather bars and drag cabarets to full-time LBGT clubs, SoMa has it all. True, internet cruising has thinned the herd, many women still prefer the Mission, and some nights are slow starters – but the following fixtures on the gay drinking scene pack on weekends.

BeatBox (Map p308; ☎415-500-2675; http://beatboxsf.com; 314 11th St; admission free-$30; ⏲10pm-2am; 🚌9, 12, 27, 47) The warehouse dance club at the end of the rainbow, where the wooden floors, beers and men can take a pounding. Most nights are mixed-gender queer – check out who's smoking/hot on the sidewalk before you enter. Women rule at UHaul, Red Hots Burlesque bring circus-freak fabulousness, men totally get Served and Bearracuda is America's biggest, barest bear party.

Eagle Tavern (Map p308; www.sf-eagle.com; 398 12th St; admission $5-10; ⏲2pm-2am Mon-Fri, from noon Sat & Sun; 🚌9, 12, 27, 47) Sunday afternoons, all roads in the gay underground lead to the Eagle, and the crowd gets hammered on all-you-can-drink beer ($10) from 3pm to 6pm. Wear leather – or flirt shamelessly – and blend right in; arrive before 3pm to beat long lines. Thursdays bring mixed crowds for rockin' bands; Fridays and Saturdays range from bondage to drag. Check online.

Stud (Map p308; www.studsf.com; 399 9th St; admission $5-8; ⏲noon-2am Tue, 5pm-3am Thu-Sat, 5pm-midnight Sun; 🚌12, 19, 27, 47) The Stud has rocked the gay scene since 1966. Anything goes at Meow Mix Tuesday drag variety shows; Thursdays bring raunchy comedy and karaoke. But Friday's the thing, when the freaky 'Some-thing' party brings bizarre midnight art-drag, pool-table crafts and dance-ready beats. Saturdays, various DJs spin – kick-ass GoBang is among the best. Check the online calendar.

Powerhouse (Map p308; www.powerhouse-sf.com; 1347 Folsom St; ⏲4pm-2am; 🚌9, 12, 27, 47) Thursdays through Sundays are best at Powerhouse, a sweaty SoMa bar for leathermen, shirtless gym queens and the occasional porn star. Draft beer is cheap and specials keep the crowd loose, and dance erupts around the pool table on weekends. Smokers grope on the (too-smoky) back patio, while oddballs lurk in the corners.

Lone Star Saloon (Map p308; ☎415-863-9999; http://lonestarsf.com/; 1354 Harrison St; ⏲2pm-2am Mon-Fri, from noon Sat & Sun; 🚌9, 12, 27, 47) Like bears to a honeycomb, big guys with bushy beards fill the Lone Star. There's a huge back patio and competitive pool table, but no women-specific bathroom – this is a guys' scene. Busiest Thursday through Sunday; drinks are $2.50 to $3 during weekday 2pm to 8pm happy hours.

Hole in the Wall (Map p308; www.holeinthewallsaloon.com; 1369 Folsom St; ⏲noon-2am; 🚌9, 12, 47) Filthy bikers and loudmouth punks proudly call this Hole their home. The tangle of neon and bike parts hanging over the bar sets the mood amid walls plastered with vintage party handbills and erotica. Tattooed regulars give the pool table a workout. Check online for beer busts and Thursday drink specials for shirtless men.

FERRY PLAZA WINE MERCHANT — WINE BAR

Map p303 (☎415-391-9400; www.fpwm.com; 1 Ferry Bldg; ⏲11am-8pm Mon, 10am-8pm Tue, 10am-9pm Wed-Fri, 8am-8pm Sat, 10am-7pm Sun; Ⓜ Embarcadero, Ⓑ Embarcadero) Are you feeling flinty or flirty? With 25 wines available to try by 2oz taste or 5oz pour, you're bound to find a flavor profile that suits you with some help from Ferry Plaza Wine Merchant's well-informed staff. The bar is jammed Saturdays, but otherwise staff take time to introduce exciting new California releases.

DADA — BAR

Map p308 (☎415-357-1367; www.dadasf.com; 86 2nd St; ⏲3pm-2am Mon, from 2pm Tue-Fri, from 7pm Sat; 🚌14, Ⓜ Montgomery, Ⓑ Montgomery) Happy-hour flavored martinis for $5 to $7 until 9pm and rotating local art shows take the commercial edge off downtown and restore the art-freak factor to SoMa. The high ceilings can make the scene loud when the DJ hits a groove, but that doesn't stop impassioned art-school debates about the future of photography.

1015 FOLSOM CLUB

Map p308 (www.1015.com; 1015 Folsom St; admission $10-20; ⏲10pm-2am Thu-Sat; 🚌12, 27) Among the city's biggest clubs, 'Ten-Fifteen' packs for weekend DJ headliners. Five dance floors and bars mean you'll lose your posse if you're entranced by videos projected onto the 400ft water wall. Prepare for entry pat-downs; there's a serious no-drugs (or weapons) policy. For a smaller, more laid-back scene, try little-sister club 103 Harriet next door. Sketchy block, but pricey drinks.

RN74 BAR

Map p308 (☎415-543-7474; www.michaelmina.net; 301 Mission St; ⏲11:30am-1am Mon-Fri, 5pm-1am Sat, 5-11pm Sun; 🚌14, Ⓜ Embarcadero, Ⓑ Embarcadero) Wine collectors pore over (or is that pour over?) the wine menu at RN74 developed by award-winning sommelier Rajat Parr, covering obscure Italian and Austrian entries, long-lost French vintages and *négociant* wines co-created by Parr with select wineries. Relax on leather couches for the duration of your worldwide wine adventure, and don't miss bar-menu dessert pairings by star chef Michael Mina.

HARLOT CLUB

Map p308 (www.harlotsf.com; 46 Minna St; admission free-$20; ⏲5pm-2am Wed-Fri, from 9pm Sat, sometimes Sun from 4pm; 🚌14, Ⓜ Montgomery, Ⓑ Montgomery) Back when SoMa was the stomping ground of sailors, alleys were named for working girls – and Harlot pays them homage. Vampire bordello is the vibe in this 1907 tabloid-press building, with intense red lighting, tufted love seats and table centerfolds of nudes with boa constrictors. After 9pm the sound system pumps EDM; bouncers enforce no jeans/T-shirts rule.

☆ ENTERTAINMENT

☆ Financial District, Union Square & Civic Center

★SAN FRANCISCO SYMPHONY CLASSICAL MUSIC

Map p306 (☎box office 415-864-6000; www.sfsymphony.org; Grove St, btwn Franklin St & Van Ness Ave; tickets $20-150; 🚌21, 45, 47, Ⓜ Van Ness, Ⓑ Civic Center) The moment conductor Michael Tilson Thomas bounces up on his toes and raises his baton, the audience is on the edge of their seats for another thunderous performance by the Grammy-winning SF Symphony. Don't miss signature concerts of Beethoven and Mahler, live Symphony performances with such films as *Star Trek,* and creative collaborations with artists from LeAnn Rimes to Metallica.

★SAN FRANCISCO OPERA OPERA

Map p306 (☎415-864-3330; www.sfopera.com; War Memorial Opera House, 301 Van Ness Ave; tickets $10-350; 🚌21, 45, 47, Ⓑ Civic Center, Ⓜ Van Ness) Opera was SF's Gold Rush soundtrack – and today SF rivals the Met with world premieres of original works covering WWII Italy *(Two Women,* or *La Ciociara),* Stephen King thrillers *(Dolores Claiborne),* and Qing Dynasty Chinese courtesans *(Dream of the Red Chamber).* Don't miss Tuscany-born musical director Nicola Liusotti's signature Verdi operas. Score $10 same-day standing-room tickets at 10am and two hours before curtain.

★AMERICAN CONSERVATORY THEATER THEATER

Map p304 (ACT; ☎415-749-2228; www.act-sf.org; 415 Geary St; ⏲box office noon-6pm Mon, to curtain Tue-Sun; 🚌8, 30, 38, 45, 🚋Powell-Mason, Powell-Hyde, Ⓑ Powell, Ⓜ Powell) Breakthrough shows launch at this turn-of-the-20th-century landmark, which has hosted ACT's landmark productions of Tony Kushner's *Angels in America* and Robert Wilson's *Black Rider,* with William S Burroughs' libretto and music by Tom Waits. Major playwrights like Tom Stoppard, David Mamet and Sam Shepard premiere work here, while experimental works are staged at ACT's new **Strand Theater** (Map p306; 1127 Market St).

SAN FRANCISCO BALLET DANCE

Map p306 (☎tickets 415-865-2000; www.sfballet.org; War Memorial Opera House, 301 Van Ness Ave; tickets $15-160; ⏲ticket sales 10am-4pm Mon-Fri; 🚌5, 21, 47, 49, Ⓜ Van Ness, Ⓑ Civic Center) America's oldest ballet company is looking sharp in more than 100 shows annually, from the *Nutcracker* (the US premiere was here) to modern Mark Morris originals. It performs mostly at War Memorial Opera House January to May, with occasional performances at Yerba Buena Center for the Arts. Score $15 to $20 same-day standing-room tickets at

SYMPHONY TICKET DEALS

Call the **San Francisco Symphony rush-ticket hotline** (☎415-503-5577) after 6:30pm to find out whether the box office has released $20 next-day tickets, which you must pick up in person on the day of performance. Choose side terrace seats where you can see the conductor's expressions over the front orchestra – you're 10ft from the strings in the front orchestra, but the sound is uneven. The best sound is in the cheap seats in the center terrace, but the loge is most comfortable and glamorous and has the best sight lines. If you're on a budget, sit in the front section of AA, BB, HH or JJ or behind the stage in the center terrace – for some shows, center terrace tickets are available for just $15. The sound doesn't blend evenly here, but you get the musicians' perspective and can look into the conductor's eyes.

the box office (noon Tuesday to Friday, 10am weekends).

GREAT AMERICAN MUSIC HALL LIVE MUSIC

Map p306 (☎415-885-0750; www.gamh.com; 859 O'Farrell St; shows $16-26; ⏲box office 10:30am-6pm Mon-Fri & on show nights; 🚌19, 38, 47, 49) Everyone busts out their best sets at this opulent 1907 former bordello – The Dead occasionally show up, Tuvan throat-singing supergroup Huun Huur Tu throws down and John Waters throws Christmas extravaganzas here. Pay $25 extra for dinner with priority admission and prime balcony seating where you can watch shows comfortably, or enter the standing-room scrum downstairs and rock out on the floor.

WARFIELD LIVE MUSIC

Map p306 (☎888-929-7849; www.thewarfieldtheatre.com; 982 Market St; tickets vary; ⏲box office 10am-4pm Sun & 90min before shows; Ⓜ Powell, Ⓑ Powell) Big acts with international followings play this former vaudeville theater. Marquee names like Wu Tang Clan, Paramore and Nick Cave explain the line down this seedy Tenderloin block and packed, pot-smoky balconies. Beer costs $9 to $10 and water $4, so you might as well get cocktails. Street parking isn't advisable – try the 5th & Mission garage.

HEMLOCK TAVERN LIVE MUSIC

Map p306 (☎415-923-0923; www.hemlocktavern.com; 1131 Polk St; admission free-$10; ⏲4pm-2am; 🚌2, 3, 19, 47, 49) When you wake up tomorrow with peanut shells in your hair (weren't they on the floor?) and a stiff neck from rocking too hard to Parachute on Fire (weren't they insane?), you'll know it was another successful, near-lethal night at the Hemlock. Blame it on cheap drink at the oval bar, pogo-worthy punk and sociable smoker's room (yes, in California).

DNA LOUNGE CLUB

Map p308 (☎415-626-1409; www.dnalounge.com; 375 11th St; admission $9-35; ⏲9pm-5am; 🚌9, 12, 27, 47) SF's reigning mega-club hosts bands, literary slams and big-name DJs, with two floors of late-night dance action just seedy enough to be interesting. Saturdays bring Bootie, the original mash-up party (now franchised worldwide); Fridays Mortified writers read from their teenage diaries; Goth/industrial bands play Sunday's 18-and-over Death Guild; and Mondays mean Hubba Hubba burlesque revues. Check calendar; early arrivals may hear crickets.

PUNCH LINE COMEDY

Map p303 (☎415-397-7573; www.punchlinecomedyclub.com; 444 Battery St; admission $15-25, plus 2-drink minimum; ⏲shows 8pm Tue-Thu & Sun, 8pm & 10pm Fri, 7:30pm & 9:30pm Sat; Ⓜ Embarcadero, Ⓑ Embarcadero) Known for launching big talent – including Robin Williams, Chris Rock, Ellen DeGeneres and David Cross – this historic stand-up venue is small enough for you to hear sighs of relief backstage when jokes kill, and teeth grind when they bomb. Strong drinks loosen up the crowd, but be warned: you might not be laughing tomorrow.

EMBARCADERO CENTER CINEMA CINEMA

Map p303 (☎415-267-4893; www.landmarktheatres.com; 1 Embarcadero Center, Promenade Level; adult/child $10.50/8.25; Ⓜ Embarcadero, Ⓑ Embarcadero) Forget blockbusters – here locals line up to claim stadium seating for the latest art-house flick or whatever won best foreign film at the Oscars. The snack bar caters to discerning tastes with good local coffee, fair-trade chocolate and freshly popped kettle corn – and don't miss the new wine bar.

CAFÉ ROYALE LOUNGE

Map p306 (☎415-441-4099; www.caferoyale-sf.com; 800 Post St; ⌚4pm-midnight Sun-Wed, to 2am Thu-Sat; 🚌2, 3, 27, 38) The pool table and TV are mostly ignored at this artsy Parisian style café-bar, where the local crowd roars for free live jazz, stand-up comedy, author readings, art openings and Beatles karaoke with live musical accompaniment. Craft cocktails are priced to move ($6 to $10), there's local beer on tap, and food is served until 10pm.

BISCUITS & BLUES LIVE MUSIC

Map p304 (☎415-292-2583; www.biscuitsandblues.com; 401 Mason St; admission $15-30; ⌚shows 7:30pm & 9:30pm Tue-Thu, 7:30pm & 10pm Fri & Sat, 7pm & 9pm Sun, restaurant 5:30-10:30pm; 🚌8, 30, 38, 45, 🚋Powell-Mason, Powell-Hyde, BPowell) With a steady lineup of top-notch blues and jazz talent like John Primer, Paula Harris and Guitar Shorty, Biscuits & Blues has earned its reputation as one of America's top blues clubs. The name isn't a gimmick – the joint serves biscuits, California catfish and Southern fried chicken ($15 minimum food purchase at weekend 8pm shows). Check calendar and reserve online.

STARLIGHT ROOM LIVE MUSIC, DANCING

Map p304 (☎415-395-8595; www.starlightroomsf.com; 450 Powell St, 21st fl; admission varies; ⌚5pm-midnight Tue-Thu, to 2am Fri & Sat, 10:30am-3:30pm Sun; 🚋Powell-Mason, Powell-Hyde, MPowell, BPowell) Views are mesmerizing from the 21st floor of the Sir Francis Drake Hotel, where tourists and couples on date night cut loose and dance to live bands (weekends) or DJs (weekdays). Sundays, there's a kooky drag-show brunch (make reservations). Dress for fun, not work.

COMMONWEALTH CLUB LECTURES

Map p304 (☎415-597-6700; www.commonwealthclub.org; 595 Market St; admission $15-30; ⌚events vary; MMontgomery St, BMontgomery St) For ideas too big to squeeze into a 10-minute TED talk, count on the Commonwealth Club. America's most influential public-affairs forum hosts 400 annual events, where intellectual luminaries cover current issues in politics, the arts, security and the environment – every US president since Teddy Roosevelt has spoken here. Many programs are broadcast on public radio, including local KQED-FM (88.5).

☆ SoMa

★OASIS CABARET, LGBT

Map p308 (☎415-795-3180; www.sfoasis.com/; 298 11th St; tickets $10-30; 🚌9, 12, 14, 47, MVan Ness) Forget what you've learned about drag from TV – at this dedicated dragstravaganza venue, SF drag is so fearless, freaky-deaky and funny you'll laugh until it stops hurting. SF drag icons Heklina and D'Arcy Drollinger host variety acts, put on original shows like '70s-'ploitation *Sh*t & Champagne,* and perform drag versions of *Sex in the City* (makes 393% more sense in drag).

★SLIM'S LIVE MUSIC

Map p308 (☎415-255-0333; www.slimspresents.com; 333 11th St; tickets $12-30; ⌚box office 10:30am-6pm Mon-Fri & on show nights; 🚌9, 12, 27, 47) Guaranteed good times by Gogol Bordello, Stiff Little Fingers, Veruca Salt and Killer Queen (an all-female Queen tribute band) fit the bill at this midsized club, owned by R&B star Boz Scaggs. Shows are all-ages, though shorties may have a hard time seeing once the floor starts bouncing. Reserve dinner for an additional $25 and score seats on the small balcony.

YERBA BUENA CENTER FOR THE ARTS LIVE MUSIC

Map p308 (YBCA; ☎415-978-2700; www.ybca.org; 700 Howard St; tickets free-$35; ⌚box office noon-6pm Sun & Tue-Wed, to 8pm Thu-Sat, galleries closed Mon-Tue; 👪; 🚌14, MPowell, BPowell) Rock stars would be jealous of art stars at YBCA openings, which draw overflow crowds of art-school groupies to see shows ranging from live hip-hop by Mos Def, to modern Chinese opera, to creepy Cronenberg film festivals. Most touring dance and jazz companies perform at YBCA's main theater (across the sidewalk from the gallery).

MEZZANINE LIVE MUSIC

Map p308 (☎415-625-8880; www.mezzaninesf.com; 444 Jessie St; admission $10-40; MPowell, BPowell) Big nights come with bragging rights at the Mezzanine, with one of the city's best sound systems and crowds hyped for breakthrough shows by hip-hop greats like Wyclef Jean and Quest Love, EDM powerhouses like Knife Party, mash-up artists like Lido (think Bill Withers meets Disclosure), plus Throwback Thursdays featuring

MODERN DANCE AT YERBA BUENA CENTER FOR THE ARTS

The biggest, boldest moves in town are made at the theater main stage at Yerba Buena Center for the Arts (p103), home of the annual **Ethnic Dance Festival** (www.sfethnicdancefestival.org). You never have to wait long for an encore here, because three major SF modern dance companies regularly perform on this stage.

Alonzo King's Lines Ballet (Map p308; ☎415-863-3040; www.linesballet.org; Yerba Buena Center for the Arts; 🚌14, Ⓑ Montgomery, Ⓜ Montgomery) Long, lean dancers perform complicated, angular movements that showcase impeccable technical skills. Original works include dance set to the sounds of tropical tree frogs, and collaborations with architect Christopher Haas and Grateful Dead drummer Mickey Hart. King also offers classes and workshops.

Liss Fain Dance (Map p308; ☎415-380-9433; www.lissfaindance.org; Yerba Buena Center for the Arts; 🚌14, Ⓑ Montgomery, Ⓜ Montgomery) Holding your breath is instinctual as you watch this modern-dance troupe with solid classical training throw themselves into original choreography, finding new ways to crack the mold. Their movement is precise yet muscular – very western American. Their home season is hosted by Yerba Buena Center for the Arts; see website for additional performances and venues.

Smuin Ballet (Map p308; ☎415-912-1899; www.smuinballet.org; Yerba Buena Center for the Arts; ⊙box office phone line 1-5pm Tue-Fri; 🚌14, Ⓑ Montgomery, Ⓜ Montgomery) Not your grandma's ballet, Smuin debuts original balletic works inspired by Tom & Jerry cartoons, Soviet jazz and modern cello prodigies. Performances are witty and poignant, with mass appeal – ideal for those who find ballet too stiff but interpretive dance too precious. Also performs at Palace of Fine Arts; see website for dates and venues.

power-pop legends like Howard Jones. No in/out privileges.

HOTEL UTAH SALOON — LIVE MUSIC

Map p308 (☎415-546-6300; www.hotelutah.com; 500 4th St; admission free-$10; ⊙11:30am-2am; 🚌30, 47, Ⓜ N, T) This Victorian saloon ruled SF's '70s underground scene, when upstarts Whoopi Goldberg and Robin Williams took the stage – and fresh talents regularly surface here on Monday Night Open Mics, indie-label debuts and twangy weekend showcases. Back in the '50s, the bartender graciously served Beats and drifters, but snipped off businessmen's ties; now you can wear whatever, but there's a $20 credit-card minimum.

ASIASF — DRAG, CABARET

Map p308 (☎415-255-2742; www.asiasf.com; 201 9th St; admisson from $38; ⊙7:15-11pm Wed, Thu & Sun, 7:15pm-2am Fri, 5pm-2am Sat; 🚌12, 14, 19, Ⓜ Civic Center, Ⓑ Civic Center) First ladies of the world, look out: these dazzling Asian ladies can out-hostess you in half the time and half the clothes. Cocktails and Asian-inspired dishes are served with sass and a secret: your servers are drag stars. Hostesses rock the bar/runway hourly, and on weekends everyone hits the downstairs dance floor. Three-course dinner runs $38 to $58 – and honey, those tips are well earned.

PUBLIC WORKS — LIVE MUSIC

Map p308 (☎415-496-6738; http://publicsf.com; 161 Erie St; tickets vary; 🚌14, 49, Ⓑ 16th St) Go Public for story-slam nights with NPR's The Moth, afterparties with EDM pioneers The Chemical Brothers, and DJ sets that range from euphoric *bhangra* nights to toga parties where everyone dances like Rome is burning. The on-site **Roll Up Gallery** encourages SF obsessions with art shows dedicated to Bill Murray, sci-fi and urban flora.

BRAINWASH — LIVE MUSIC, LAUNDRY

Map p308 (☎415-861-3663; www.brainwash.com; 1122 Folsom St; ⊙7am-10pm Mon-Thu, to 11pm Fri & Sat, 8am-10pm Sun; 📶; 🚌12, 19, Ⓜ Civic Center, Ⓑ Civic Center) The barfly's eternal dilemma between going out or doing laundry is finally solved at this bar-café with live music most nights and open mic showcases Sundays and Thursdays. Last wash is at 8:30pm and the kitchen closes an hour before the bar, so plan your presoaking and order of Wash Load Nachos accordingly.

AMC LOEWS METREON 16 — CINEMA

Map p308 (☎415-369-6201; www.amctheatres.com; 101 4th St; adult/child $12.99/10.29; 🚌14, Ⓜ Powell, Ⓑ Powell) Sprawling across the top floor of the Metreon mall complex, the 16-screen Metreon cinema has comfortable stadium seats with clear views of digital projection screens, plus 3D screenings ($4 extra per ticket) and a 3D IMAX theater ($7 3D screenings). To grab dinner before showtime, there's a passable ground-floor food court.

SHOPPING

Union Square is the city's principal shopping district, with flagship stores and department stores, including international chains. The shopping area's borders are (roughly) Powell St (west), Sutter St (north), Kearny St (east) and Market St (south); the epicenter of the Union Square shopping area is along Post St, near Grant Ave. Stockton St crosses Market St and becomes 4th St, ringed by flagship stores.

Union Square

★HARPUTS — CLOTHING, ACCESSORIES

Map p304 (415-392-2222; www.harputs.com/; 2nd fl, 109 Geary St; 11am-7pm Mon-Sat; 6, 7, 38, B Montgomery, M Montgomery) Superheroes have to squeeze into phone booths and tights to make their transformations, but you can just duck into Harputs to summon your SF alter ego with a ninja romper, fog-stopping swacket (sweater jacket) or peace-making dress (straps form a peace sign on your shoulders). Designs involve clever wraps and flattering folds that show off your shape, smarts and wit.

★BRITEX FABRICS — FABRIC

Map p304 (415-392-2910; www.britexfabrics.com; 146 Geary St; 10am-6pm Mon-Sat; 38, Powell-Mason, Powell-Hyde, M Powell, B Powell) Runway shows can't compete with Britex's fashion drama. First floor: designers bicker over dibs on caution-orange chiffon. Second floor: glam rockers dig through velvet goldmines. Third floor: Hollywood costumers make vampire movie magic with jet buttons and silk ribbon. Top floor: fake fur flies and remnants roll as costumers prepare for Burning Man, Halloween and your average SF weekend.

LEVI'S FLAGSHIP STORE — CLOTHING

Map p304 (415-501-0100; www.us.levi.com; 815 Market St; 9am-9pm Mon-Sat, 10am-8pm Sun; Powell-Mason, Powell-Hyde, M Powell, B Powell) The flagship store in Levi Strauss' hometown sells classic jeans that fit without fail, plus limited-edition Japanese selvage pairs and remakes of Levi's original copper-riveted miner's dungarees. Scour the impressive discount racks for limited-edition Levi's Made & Crafted shirts (30% to 60% off) but don't count on sales – rare lines like 1950s prison-model denim jackets sell fast. Hemming costs $10.

MARGARET O'LEARY — CLOTHING, ACCESSORIES

Map p304 (415-391-1010; www.margaretoleary.com; 1 Claude Lane; 10am-5pm Tue-Sat; 8, 30, 45, M Montgomery, B Montgomery) Ignorance of the fog is no excuse in San Francisco, but should you confuse SF for LA (the horror!) and neglect to pack the obligatory sweater, Margaret O'Leary will sheathe you in knitwear, no questions asked. The SF designer's specialties are warm, whisper-light cardigans in Scottish cashmere, cotton and silk.

MACY'S — DEPARTMENT STORE

Map p304 (www.macys.com; 170 O'Farrell St; 10am-9pm Mon-Sat, 11am-8pm Sun; Powell-Mason, Powell-Hyde, M Powell, B Powell) Five floors of name brands fill two historic buildings with charming old-school amenities – especially 3rd-floor Tout Sweet (p89) patisserie and the basement post office. The men's department across Stockton St is easy to navigate, but women will have to brave the perfume police and slightly insulting free-makeover offers to reach shoe sales (totally worth it).

JOHN VARVATOS — CLOTHING

Map p304 (415-986-0138; www.johnvarvatos.com; 152 Geary St; 11am-7pm Mon-Sat, noon-6pm Sun; 38, B Powell, M Powell) America's most wanted men's look is classic California outlaw – and nobody does it better than designer John Varvatos. Western jackets, waxed jeans and brushed canvas waistcoats make any dude seem destined to rob a bank, and steal a few hearts along the way. Cuts are slim, prices steep and colors dark, but you're in the right place to live and dress dangerously.

UNIQLO — CLOTHING

Map p304 (www.uniqlo.com; 111 Powell St; 10am-9pm Mon-Sat, 11am-8pm Sun; M Powell, B Powell) Ever since Japanese retailer Uniqlo landed on the West Coast here, SF has been rocking pop-art tees, cashmere in rainbow colors and down jackets that scrunch to the size of a coffee mug. Uniqlo's wardrobe basics may not be built to last, but the color, price and fit are on point.

BARNEYS DEPARTMENT STORE

Map p304 (☎415-268-3500; www.barneys.com; 77 O'Farrell St; ⊙10am-7pm Mon-Sat, noon-7pm Sun; Powell-Mason, Powell-Hyde, M Powell, B Powell) The high-end New York fashion staple known for inspired window displays and up-to-70%-off sales has hit the West Coast. Barneys showcases emerging designers, plus well-priced, well-fitted sportswear on its Co-op label and its own affordable Green Label, focusing on clean lines with a clean conscience.

GUMP'S JEWELRY, HOMEWARES

Map p304 (☎415-982-1616; www.gumps.com; 135 Post St; ⊙10am-6pm Mon-Sat, noon-5pm Sun; M Montgomery, B Montgomery) San Francisco's original department store opened in 1861, importing luxury items from the Far East. Today it's famous for jade, silk, rugs, porcelain and homewares – if you're a guest in a San Franciscan home and want to express your gratitude with a high-end host gift, something from Gump's will always impress.

H&M CLOTHING, ACCESSORIES

Map p304 (www.hm.com; 150 Powell St; ⊙9:30am-10pm Mon-Sat, to 9pm Sun; Powell-Mason, Powell-Hyde, M Powell, B Powell) What IKEA is to home furnishing, H&M is to fashion: suspiciously affordable, perpetually crowded, not really made for the long haul and perfect for parties. Its limited-edition runs and special collections minimize the chance that you'll bump into someone wearing the same thing. SF has several H&Ms, but Powell St is biggest, with a vast men's section and killer sales.

WESTFIELD SAN FRANCISCO CENTRE DEPARTMENT STORE

Map p304 (www.westfield.com/sanfrancisco; 865 Market St; ⊙10am-8:30pm Mon-Sat, 11am-7pm Sun; ; Powell-Mason, Powell-Hyde, M Powell, B Powell) Wait, is this suburbia? Sure looks it inside this nine-level chain-store city, with Bloomingdale's and Nordstrom, plus 400 retailers and multiplex theater. Supposedly the mall has a 'distinctive boutique' concept, which translates to same stuff, smaller stores. Best reasons to brave this behemoth: post-holiday sales, touchups at SF's BareMinerals makeup bar, bathrooms (including lounges with baby-changing tables) and respectable food court.

Financial District

★RECCHIUTI CHOCOLATES FOOD & DRINK

Map p303 (☎415-834-9494; www.recchiuticonfections.com; 1 Ferry Bldg; ⊙10am-7pm Mon-Fri, 8am-6pm Sat, 10am-5pm Sun; M Embarcadero, B Embarcadero) No San Franciscan can resist Recchiuti: Pacific Heights parts with old money for its *fleur de sel* caramels; Noe Valley's foodie kids prefer S'more Bites to the campground variety; North Beach toasts to the red-wine-pairing chocolate box; and the Mission approves SF landmark chocolates designed by developmentally disabled artists from Creativity Explored – part of the proceeds benefit the nonprofit gallery.

ARTIST & CRAFTSMAN SUPPLY ARTS, CRAFTS

Map p318 (☎415-931-1900; www.artistcraftsman.com; 555 Pacific Ave; ⊙8:30am-7pm Mon-Fri, from 10am Sat, 11am-6pm Sun; ; 8, 10, 12, 41) Ditch your day job and take up painting at this employee-owned art supply store, housed in the former Hippodrome burlesque theater. This Barbary Coast hot spot later became The Gay Nineties club – check out the figures cavorting in entry reliefs and peek into the original speakeasy tunnel downstairs. Two floors of supplies anticipate every SF inspiration and rainy-day kids' project.

JAPONESQUE HOMEWARES

Map p303 (☎415-391-8860; http://japonesquegallery.com/; 824 Montgomery St; ⊙10:30am-5:30pm Tue-Fri, 11am-5pm Sat; 10, 12, 41) Wabi-sabi is not something you smear on sushi, but the fine appreciation for imperfect, organic forms and materials exemplified at Japonesque. Owner Koichi Hara stocks antique Japanese bamboo baskets and contemporary ceramics alongside Kaname Higa's postapocalyptic ballpoint-pen landscapes and Hiromichi Iwashita's graphite-coated, chiseled-wood panels that look like bonfire embers.

T-WE TEA FOOD & DRINK

Map p304 (www.t-wetea.com/; Crocker Galleria, 50 Post St, Level 1; ⊙10am-6pm Mon-Fri; B Montgomery, M Montgomery) Start days the SF way with T-We tea to match your attitude: sprawl in Dolores Park with Hipsters in Wonderland (green tea, jasmine, carrot chips), huddle like Sunset surfers over Foggy Morning Brekkie (four-tea blend with vanilla bean), or recover from SoMa clubs with Bad Bromance (nettle-ginger afterparty tisane). T-We blends teas in SF with sass and local flavor, with nothing artificial.

FOG CITY NEWS BOOKS, CHOCOLATE

Map p303 (☎415-543-7400; www.fogcitynews.com; 455 Market St; ⊙10am-6pm Mon-Fri, noon-5pm Sat; MEmbarcadero, BEmbarcadero) The perfect stopover before a long flight, Fog City stocks a vast variety of domestic magazines and newspapers, as well as 700 international titles from 25 countries – plus one of the city's most diverse selections of chocolates, including 200-plus candy bars. Historic photos of SF line the walls between the old wooden racks.

WINGTIP CLOTHING, ACCESSORIES

Map p304 (☎415-765-0993; http://wingtip.com/; 550 Montgomery St; ⊙10am-6:30pm Mon-Fri, to 6pm Sat; BMontgomery, MMontgomery) Get the look of an outdoorsy professor who invested early in Apple at this old-school men's store in the handsome 1908 Bank of Italy building. Visiting power brokers will find FiDi wardrobe basics and accessories from cigars to Venetian shoe cream, and score perks: commit to spend $1200 in-store or online, and gain access to a swanky top-floor clubhouse.

EDEN & EDEN

Detour from reality at **Eden & Eden** (Map p318; www.edenandeden.com; 560 Jackson St; ⊙10am-7pm Mon-Fri, 10am-6pm Sat; 🚌8,10,12,41), a Dadaist design boutique, where anchors float on silk dresses, clouds rain on pillows, architectural blueprints serve as placemats and Ozzy Osbourne has been transformed into a stuffed mouse wearing batwings. Prices are surprisingly down to earth for far-out, limited-edition finds from local and international designers.

Civic Center & the Tenderloin

★ELECTRIC WORKS ARTS, BOOKS

Map p306 (☎415-626-5496; www.sfelectricworks.com; 1360 Mission St; ⊙11am-6pm Tue-Fri, to 5pm Sat; 👪; 🚌14, MVan Ness) Everything a museum store aspires to be, with a fascinating collection of arty must-haves – beeswax crayons, East German ice-cream spoons, Klein bottles, vintage wind-up toys – plus limited-edition prints and artists' books by David Byrne, Enrique Chagoya and other contemporary artists. Sales of many artworks printed on-site benefit nonprofits – including Dave Eggers' panda drawing, tragicomically titled *Doomed by Charm.*

★KAYO BOOKS BOOKS

Map p306 (☎415-749-0554; www.kayobooks.com; 814 Post St; ⊙11am-6pm Thu-Sat; 🚌2, 3, 27, 38) Juvenile delinquents will find an entire section dedicated to their life stories at Kayo, where vintage pulp, true crime and erotica titles ending in exclamation points (such as the succinct *Wench!*) earn John Waters' personal endorsement. Look here for first-edition Dashiell Hammett gumshoe capers, totally trippy tales filed under Hippies & Drugs or *Women's Medical Problems* in the Bizarre Nonfiction section.

SAN FRANCYCLE CLOTHING, ACCESSORIES

Map p306 (☎415-872-5014; www.wearesfc.com/; 702 Larkin St; ⊙11am-5pm Mon-Sat, 11am-4pm Sun; 🚌19, 31, 38, 47, 49) Keep those muscles warm and show your cyclist pride as you whip through downtown streets wearing San Francycle's California-bear-on-a-bicycle tee and SF bike district hoodie (Mission is represented by fixies, Castro by exercise bikes). Designer/owner/cyclist Tommy Pham prints his designs here in SF, so your souvenir tee has neighborhood street cred that wins nods from bike messengers.

GYPSY ROSALIE'S FASHION

Map p306 (☎415-771-8814; 1222 Sutter St; ⊙10am-6pm Mon-Sat; 🚌2, 3, 19, 38, 47, 49) Costuming is a competitive sport in SF, and Rosalie's will help you find a head-to-toe ensemble that will have the whole city gagging on your glamour. Choose from SF's most fabulous wig selection and try out over-the-top looks, from slinky Marilyn Monroe numbers to Marie Antoinette velvet frock coats that will make heads roll.

THE MAGAZINE MAGAZINES

Map p306 (www.themagazinesf.com; 920 Larkin St; ⊙noon-7pm Mon-Sat; 🚌19, 38, 47, 49) The motherlode of magazines since 1973. The Magazine's old wooden shelves barely contain all the 1940s pinup mags, 1950s *Vogue,* 1960s Beatles fan mags, 1970s *Tiger Beat* and timeless pulp classics like *Aliens Ate My Baby* – plus a back room packed with early issues of Playboy and other vintage smut. Many titles run 35¢, and few are over $10.

SoMa

SAN FRANCISCO RAILWAY MUSEUM GIFT SHOP GIFTS

Map p308 (415-974-1948; www.streetcar.org/museum; 77 Steuart St; 10am-6pm Tue-Sun; Embarcadero, Embarcadero) The next best thing to taking an SF cable car home with you is getting a scale model streetcar from this tiny free Municipal Railway museum showcasing SF public transit. Earn instant SF street cred with baseball caps and T-shirts emblazoned with Muni slogans, including everyone's favorite: 'Information gladly given, but safety requires avoiding unnecessary conversation.'

MADAME S & MR S LEATHER CLOTHING, ACCESSORIES

Map p308 (415-863-7764; www.mr-s-leather.com; 385 8th St; 11am-8pm; 12, 19, 27, 47) Only in San Francisco would you find an S&M superstore, with such musts as suspension stirrups, latex hoods and, for that special someone, a chrome-plated codpiece. If you've been a very bad puppy, there's an entire doghouse department catering to you here, and gluttons for punishment will find home-decor inspiration in Dungeon Furniture.

GENERAL BEAD JEWELRY, GIFTS

Map p308 (www.generalbead.net; 637 Minna St; noon-6pm; 14, 19, Civic Center, Civic Center) Blind beading ambition may seize you among the racks of bagged bulk beads, where visions of DIY holiday gifts for the entire family appear like mirages: multi-tiered necklaces, sequined seascapes, mosaic frames, even fringed lampshades. To practice restraint, order smaller quantities downstairs from the bead-bedecked staff behind the counter, who will ring up your sale on bejeweled calculators.

MAKE YOUR OWN KILLER APP

Few San Francisco visitors realize that most of the personal technology they use every day was invented within 50 miles of where they're standing – all those handy search engines, websites and apps, plus the smartphones, glasses and watches they run on. But even fewer people realize how many of the most widely used apps were invented within the half-sq-mile area of SoMa district – including Instagram, Twitter, Pinterest and Airbnb.

Is there something in the water in SoMa? No, but there may be something in the beer. By joining techies for downtime in SoMa start-up hubs, you can get a sneak preview of the next big technology in the making. Several of Silicon Valley's most important start-up incubator spaces are in SoMa, including **RocketSpace** (http://rocketspace.com/), **PARISOMA** (www.parisoma.com/) and **Impact Hub** (https://bayarea.impacthub.net/). Check their websites for happy hours, meet ups and pitch nights, where you can hear technology ideas and beta-test the next big tech launch and/or flop.

When you are seized with your own technology breakthrough – yep, it happens to everyone in SF eventually – you're in the right place to make it happen. San Francisco has several hackerspaces where you can socialize over circuitry with people who could probably break into your bank account, but who instead graciously share pointers. Three hackerspaces that host events open to nonmembers are the FiDi's business-minded **RockIT CoLabs** (http://rockitcolabs.com/; $18 day passes available), the Mission's nonprofit women's maker/hackerspace **Double Union** (https://www.doubleunion.org/; check online for open-house hack sessions & workshops), and anarchically creative nonprofit Mission hackerspace **Noisebridge** (https://www.noisebridge.net/; donations welcome).

Don't be discouraged if your invention doesn't turn out as planned. As the Silicon Valley saying goes: if at first you don't succeed, fail better. Most technologies become obsolete eventually – some just do it faster than others. On Friday afternoons, you can pay your respects to bygone blogs and glimpse the inner workings of the Wayback Machine at the Internet Archive (p202), housed in a converted 1927 neoclassical temple in the Richmond District.

So what else is left to invent in San Francisco? Time machines, for starters. Drink to the future at the Interval (p66), the **Long Now Foundation** (http://longnow.org/) bar where you can participate in ongoing experiments in 4D engineering directed by artist Brian Eno and internet pioneer Stewart Brand.

SPORTS & ACTIVITIES

★GIANTS STADIUM
BASEBALL

Map p308 (AT&T Park; ☎415-972-2000, tour 415-972-2400; http://sanfrancisco.giants.mlb.com; AT&T Park; tickets $14-280, tour tickets adult/senior/child $22/17/12; ⏲tour 10:30am & 2:30pm; 👪; Ⓜ N, T) Hometown crowds go wild April to October at the San Francisco Giants' 81 home games. As any orange-blooded San Franciscan will remind you, the Giants were three-time World Series champions in 2010, 2012 and 2014 – and you'll know the Giants are on another winning streak when you see superstitious San Franciscans sporting team colors (orange and black) and bushy beards (the Giants rallying cry is 'Fear the Beard!). On non-game days, tours cover the clubhouse, dugout, solar-powered scoreboard and the world's largest baseball glove.

SPINNAKER SAILING
BOATING

Map p308 (☎415-543-7333; www.spinnaker-sailing.com; Pier 40, South Beach Harbor; skippered charters from $445, lessons from $425; ⏲10am-5pm; 🚌30, 45, Ⓜ N, T) Do 'luff,' 'cringle' and 'helms-a-lee' mean anything to you? If yes, captain a boat from Spinnaker and sail into the sunset. If not, charter a skippered vessel or take classes and learn to talk like a sailor – in a good way.

CITY KAYAK
KAYAKING

Map p308 (☎415-294-1050; www.citykayak.com; Pier 40, South Beach Harbor; kayak rentals per hour $35-65, 3hr lesson & rental $59, tours $58-98; ⏲rentals 11am-3pm, return by 5pm Thu-Mon; 🚌30, 45, Ⓜ N, T) You haven't seen San Francisco until you've seen it from the water. Newbies to kayaking can take lessons and paddle calm waters near the Bay Bridge, alone or escorted; experienced paddlers can brave choppy Bay currents near the Golden Gate (conditions permitting; get advice first). Sporty romantics: calm-water moonlight tours are ideal for proposals. Check website for details.

EMBARCADERO YMCA
HEALTH & FITNESS

Map p308 (☎415-957-9622; www.ymcasf.org/embarcadero; 169 Steuart St; day pass $20; ⏲5:30am-9:45pm Mon-Fri, 8am-7:45pm Sat, 9am-5:45pm Sun; 👪; Ⓜ Embarcadero, Ⓑ Embarcadero) The Embarcadero YMCA gym has knockout bay views with zero distractions – no TVs, amplified music or cell phones here. The full-service facility includes 25m pool, co-ed hot tub, basketball courts, extensive gym equipment, and separate men's and women's sauna and steam. Towels included. Bring a lock or use free small lockers outside the locker rooms.

YERBA BUENA ICE SKATING & BOWLING CENTER
ICE SKATING, BOWLING

Map p308 (☎415-820-3532; www.skatebowl.com; 750 Folsom St; skating adult/child $10/8, skate rental $4, bowling per game $5.50-7, shoe rental $4; ⏲10am-10pm Sun-Thu, to midnight Fri & Sat; 👪; 🚌14, Ⓜ Powell, Ⓑ Powell) While businesspeople are working Moscone Convention Center, upstairs you can skate figure eights or throw strikes at this rooftop family-fun center. Book bowling lanes ahead – especially for glow-in-the-dark Ultra Bowling. Check website or call for availability and deals, including Family Bowling specials (Sunday to Monday), and adults-only Coffee Club skating sessions (free coffee and donuts).

ℹ GIANTS GAME TICKETS

The downside of the Giants' winning streak is that Giants games often sell out, even though this is among America's most expensive ballparks – the average cost for a family of four, including food and beer, is $239.50. Don't despair: season-ticket holders sell unwanted tickets through the team's Double Play Ticket Window on the website (http://sanfrancisco.giants.mlb.com)

If you can't find tickets, head to the park's east side along the waterfront, where you may be able to stand at the archways and watch innings for free. You'll need to show up hours early with die-hard local fans for a decent view – or be prepared to just glimpse the game and enjoy the party instead.

North Beach & Chinatown

Neighborhood Top Five

❶ Wandering **Chinatown alleyways** (p118) to hear mah jong tiles, temple gongs and Chinese orchestras.

❷ Climbing Filbert St Steps past heckling parrots and fragrant gardens to panoramic **Coit Tower** (p112).

❸ Reflecting in the Poet's Chair and celebrating free speech at **City Lights** (p113).

❹ Time-traveling through the old Chinatown at the **Chinese Historical Society of America** (p115) in the historic Julia Morgan–designed Chinatown YWCA.

❺ Picking up where Jack Kerouac left off at historic Beat hangouts: **Li Po** (p126), **Vesuvio** (p126) and **Caffe Trieste** (p125).

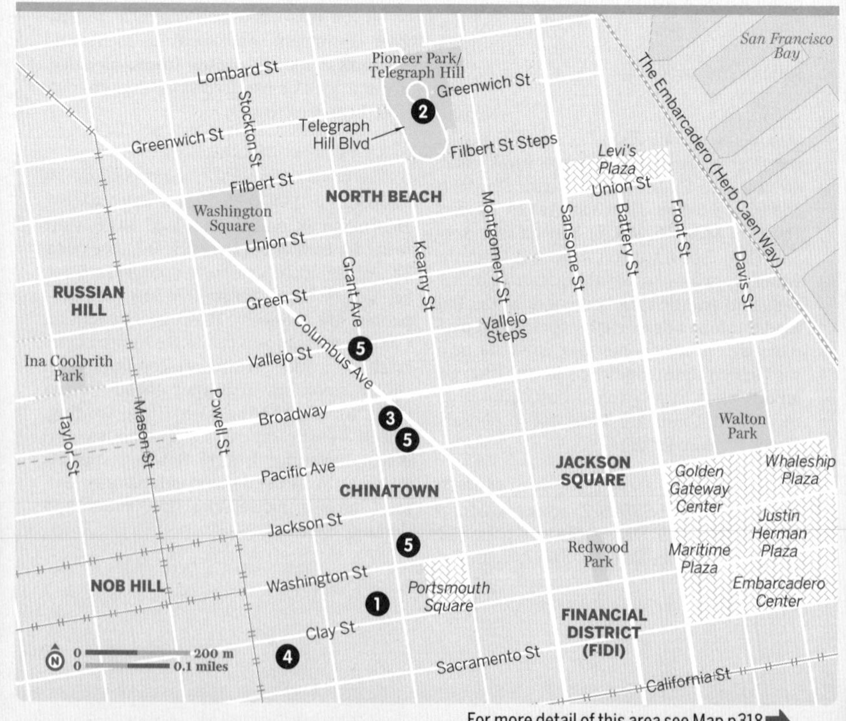

For more detail of this area see Map p318

Explore North Beach & Chinatown

From downtown, enter Dragon's Gate onto Chinatown's main tourist drag, Grant Ave. Hard to believe this pagoda-topped, souvenir-shopping strip was once notorious brothel-lined Dupont St – at least until you see the fascinating displays at the Chinese Historical Society of America. Duck into Chinatown's historic alleyways to glimpse a neighborhood that's survived against daunting odds, and detour for dim sum at City View. Cross into North Beach via Jack Kerouac Alley and City Lights, birthplace of Beat literature. Fuel up with espresso at Caffe Trieste for your North Beach Beat walking tour, and hike garden-lined Filbert St Steps to giddy panoramas and daring murals at Coit Tower. Descend for a bar crawl or dinner at Coi.

Local Life

➡ **Hangouts** Join regular crowds of writers at Caffe Trieste (p125), martial arts masters at Washington Square (p114) and skaters at Old St Mary's Square (p118).

➡ **Foodie discoveries** Even been-there, tried-that San Franciscans find new taste sensations at Coi (p121), Z & Y (p124), Red Blossom Tea Company (p128) and Naked Lunch (p121).

➡ **Local celebrity sightings** Keep an eye out for Sean Penn at Tosca Cafe (p125), Francis Ford Coppola at Columbus Tower (p114), Tom Waits and Carlos Santana at 101 Music (p127), and Countess Lola Montez reincarnated at Drag Me Along Tours (p127).

➡ **Five-buck bargains** Fly a butterfly kite from Chinatown Kite Shop (p128), carbo-load at Liguria Bakery (p119), and catch a show at Doc's Lab (p127).

Getting There & Away

➡ **Bus** Key routes passing through Chinatown and North Beach are 1, 10, 12, 30, 39, 41 and 45.

➡ **Cable car** From Downtown or the Wharf, take the Powell-Mason and Powell-Hyde lines through Chinatown and North Beach. The California St cable car passes through the southern end of Chinatown.

Lonely Planet's Top Tip

Wild hawks and parrots circle above North Beach as though looking for a parking spot. The weekend parking situation is so dire that locals avoid North Beach and Chinatown – forgetting there's public parking underneath Portsmouth Square and at Good Luck Parking Garage, where spots are stenciled with fortune-cookie wisdom: 'You are not a has-been.'

Best Places to Eat

➡ Coi (p121)
➡ Z & Y (p124)
➡ Liguria Bakery (p119)
➡ Ristorante Ideale (p121)
➡ City View (p124)

For reviews, see p119 ➡

Best Places to Drink

➡ Specs Museum Cafe (p125)
➡ Caffe Trieste (p125)
➡ Comstock Saloon (p125)
➡ Tosca Cafe (p125)
➡ 15 Romolo (p125)

For reviews, see p125 ➡

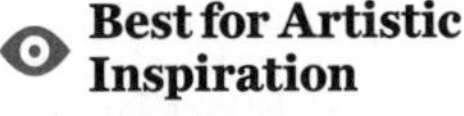

Best for Artistic Inspiration

➡ City Lights (p113)
➡ Coit Tower (p112)
➡ Chinese Culture Center (p115)
➡ Bob Kaufman Alley (p113)
➡ Jack Kerouac Alley (p114)

For reviews, see p112 

JEJIM / GETTY IMAGES ©

TOP SIGHT
COIT TOWER & TELEGRAPH HILL

The exclamation point on San Francisco's skyline is Coit Tower, the stark white deco building that eccentric heiress Lillie Hancock Coit left a fortune to build as a monument to San Francisco firefighters. The tower has been a lightning rod for controversy for its 1930s Works Project Administration (WPA) murals – but there's no debating the panorama from the viewing platform.

WPA Murals & Viewing Platform

The lobby murals show city life during the Great Depresssion: people lining up at soup kitchens, organizing dock-workers' unions, partying despite Prohibition, and reading books in Chinese, Italian and English – including Marx manifestos.

When completed in 1934, these federally funded artworks were politically controversial. Authorities denounced the 26 artists that painted them as communists, and demanded that radical elements be removed. The artists refused, and park employees were tasked with painting over one hammer and sickle symbol. San Franciscans, however, embraced the murals as symbols of the city's openness to all perspectives, and in 2012 voters passed a measure to preserve these cherished landmarks.

To glimpse seven recently restored murals up a hidden stairwell on the second floor, join the free tour at 11am Wednesdays and Saturdays. For a wild parrot's view of San Francisco 210ft above the city, take the elevator to the open-air platform.

Filbert Street Steps

In the 19th century, a ruthless entrepreneur began quarrying and blasting away roads here, and this garden-lined cliffside boardwalk became the main uphill route. City Hall eventually stopped the quarrying of **Telegraph Hill**, but the view of the bay from **Filbert St steps** is still (wait for it) dynamite. The steep climb leads past hidden cottages along **Napier Lane**, sweeping **Bay Bridge** vistas and colorful **wild parrot flocks**.

DON'T MISS...

- WPA murals
- 360-degree viewing platform panorama

PRACTICALITIES

- Map p318, D2
- 415-249-0995
- http://sfrecpark.org/destination/telegraph-hill-pioneer-park/coit-tower
- Telegraph Hill Blvd
- elevator entry (nonresident) adult/child $8/5
- 10am-6pm May-Oct, 9am-5pm Nov-Apr
- 39

SIGHTS

Standing atop the Filbert St Steps, you can understand what Italian fishermen, Beat poets and wild parrots saw in North Beach: more sky than ground, civilized but never entirely tamed. Coit Tower punctuates the scenery, lifting North Beach out of the fog of everyday life. Across Columbus Ave is Chinatown, survivor of gold booms and busts, anti-Chinese riots and bootlegging wars, trials by fire and earthquake. Yet Chinatown repeatedly made history, providing labor for America's first cross-country railroad, rebuilding San Francisco and leading the charge for China's revolution and US civil rights.

North Beach

COIT TOWER
HISTORIC BUILDING, ART

See p112.

★CITY LIGHTS
CULTURAL CENTER, LANDMARK

Map p318 (415-362-8193; www.citylights.com; 261 Columbus Ave; 10am-midnight; ; 8, 10, 12, 30, 41, 45, Powell-Mason, Powell-Hyde) Free speech and free spirits have flourished at City Lights since 1957, when founder and poet Lawrence Ferlinghetti and manager Shigeyoshi Murao won a landmark ruling defending their right to publish Allen Ginsberg's magnificent epic poem 'Howl.' Celebrate your right to read freely in the sunny upstairs Poetry Room, with its piles of freshly published verse and designated Poet's Chair.

Idle browsing is highly encouraged too – Ferlinghetti's hand-lettered sign describes City Lights as 'A Kind of Library Where Books Are Sold.' On the main floor, City Lights publications include titles by Angela Davis, Charles Bukowski, Diane di Prima and Noam Chomsky, proving the point on another of Ferlinghetti's signs: 'Printer's Ink is the Greater Explosive.' The nonfiction cellar is unconventionally organized by book buyer Paul Yamazaki according to counter-cultural themes like Stolen Continents, Muckraking and Commodity Aesthetics. This cellar was once the lair of the paper dragon used in Chinatown's lunar new year celebrations, and enigmatic slogans on the walls like 'I am the door' are left behind by a cult that worshipped here in the 1930s – and for readers, City Lights is a cause for celebration and a source of continuing revelation.

BEAT MUSEUM
MUSEUM

Map p318 (1-800-537-6822; www.kerouac.com; 540 Broadway; adult/student $8/5; walking tours $25; museum 10am-7pm; walking tours 2-4pm Mon, Wed & Sat; 8, 10, 12, 30, 41, 45, Powell-Mason) The closest you can get to the complete Beat experience without breaking a law. The 1000+ artifacts in this museum's literary ephemera collection include the sublime (the banned edition of Ginsberg's *Howl*) and the ridiculous (those Kerouac bobble-head dolls are definite head-shakers). Downstairs, watch Beat-era films in ramshackle theater seats redolent with the odors of literary giants, pets and pot. Upstairs, pay respects at shrines to individual Beat writers. Guided two-hour walking tours cover the museum, Beat history and literary alleys.

WORTH A DETOUR

BOB KAUFMAN ALLEY

What, you mean your hometown doesn't have a street named after an African American Catholic-Jewish-voodoo anarchist street poet who refused to speak for 12 years? The man revered in France as the 'American Rimbaud' was a major Beat poet who helped found the legendary *Beatitudes* magazine in 1959, and a spoken-word bebop jazz artist who was never at a loss for words. Yet he felt compelled to take a Buddhist vow of silence after John F Kennedy's assassination that he kept until the end of the Vietnam War.

Kaufman's life was hardly pure poetry: he was a teenage runaway, periodically found himself homeless, was occasionally jailed for mocking police in rhyme, battled methamphetamine addiction with varying success and once claimed his goal was to be forgotten. Yet like the man himself, hidden **Bob Kaufman Alley** (Map p318; off Grant Ave near Filbert St; 8,30, 41, 45, Powell-Mason) named in his honor is offbeat and surprisingly silent – a prime spot for a profound moment of reflection.

LOCAL KNOWLEDGE

COGSWELL MONUMENT

Washington Square's 1897 statue of Benjamin Franklin seems misplaced – um, wrong founding father – and the taps below his feet falsely advertise mineral water from Vichy, France. This puzzling public artwork was donated by temperance crusader Henry D Cogswell, who made his fortune fitting miners with gold fillings and advocated drinking water to prevent alcoholism. Apparently the monument was originally topped by a statue of Cogswell himself, but self-appointed art critics mocked the dentist's statue as ugly in the press, and finally knocked him off his pedestal in 1894. Ben Franklin was raised in the dentist's stead – and though undeniably squatty, the founding father stood his ground here.

Cogswell buried a time capsule under this monument in 1879, and in accordance with his instructions, a century later it was opened to reveal an early women's liberation manifesto, a San Francisco Chinese-language newspaper and sundry dental tools. Another time capsule was buried in its stead in 1979, to be opened in 2079. Spoiler alert: it contains a Lawrence Ferlinghetti poem, Levi's jeans and local wine (sorry, Henry).

You enter the museum through a turnstile in the adjoining museum store, where you can buy poetry chapbooks and obscure Beat titles you won't find elsewhere. Entry to the store is free, and so are readings held here (check website). You'll notice there's a dusty old car parked downstairs: that's a 1949 Hudson roadster, and it's covered with dust accumulated over 4000 miles of driving coast-to-coast for the filming of 2012's *On the Road* movie.

JACK KEROUAC ALLEY — STREET

Map p318 (btwn Grant & Columbus Aves; 8, 10, 12, 30, 41, 45, Powell-Mason) 'The air was soft, the stars so fine, the promise of every cobbled alley so great...' This ode by the *On the Road* and *Dharma Bums* author is embedded in his namesake alley, a fittingly poetic and slightly seedy shortcut between Chinatown and North Beach via Kerouac haunts City Lights and Vesuvio – Kerouac took literature, Buddhism and beer seriously.

COLUMBUS TOWER — HISTORIC BUILDING

Map p318 (Sentinel Building; 916 Kearny St; 8, 10, 12, 30, 41, 45, California St) If these copper-clad walls could talk, they'd name-drop shamelessly. Its original occupant was political boss Abe Rueff, ousted in 1907 and sent to San Quentin for bribing city supervisors. Grammy-winning folk group The Kingston Trio bought the tower in the 1960s, and the Grateful Dead recorded in the basement. Since 1972 it's been owned by *The Godfather* director Francis Ford Coppola, who occasionally shares office space with *The Joy Luck Club* director Wayne Wang and Academy Award-winning actor/director Sean Penn.

During Prohibition, Columbus Tower housed a speakeasy – now you can sip Coppola wines in plain sight, around the heated sidewalk tables of ground-floor **Cafe Zoetrope** (Map p318; 415-291-1700; http://www.cafecoppola.com/cafezoetrope/; Columbus Tower, 916 Kearny St; 11:30am-10pm Tue-Fri, noon-10pm Sat, noon-9pm Sun; 8, 10, 12, 30, 41, 45).

WASHINGTON SQUARE — PARK

Map p318 (http://sfrecpark.org/destination/washington-square/; Columbus Ave & Union St; 8, 30, 39, 41, 45, Powell-Mason) Wild parrots, tai chi masters and nonagenarian churchgoing *nonnas* (grandmothers) are the company you'll keep on this lively patch of lawn. This was the city's earliest official park, built in 1850 on the ranchland of pioneering businesswoman Juana Briones – there's a bench dedicated to her. The parrots keep their distance in the treetops, but like anyone else in North Beach, they can probably be bribed into friendship with a focaccia from Liguria Bakery (p119) on the square's northeast corner.

SAINTS PETER & PAUL CHURCH — CHURCH

Map p318 (415-421-0809; www.sspeterpaulsf.org/church/; 666 Filbert St; 7:30am-12:30pm Mon-Fri, to 5pm Sat & Sun; 8, 30, 39, 41, 45, Powell-Mason) Wedding-cake cravings are inspired by this frosted white, triple-decker 1924 cathedral. The church holds Catholic masses in Italian, Chinese, Latin and English and pulls triple wedding shifts on Saturdays – Joe DiMaggio and Marilyn Monroe took wedding photos here, but they weren't permitted to marry in the church, as both had been divorced (they got hitched at City Hall). The mosaic Dante quote over the entryway evokes Beat poets and Beatles: 'The glory of Him who moves all things/Penetrates and glows throughout the universe.'

⊙ Chinatown

CHINESE HISTORICAL SOCIETY OF AMERICA MUSEUM

Map p318 (CHSA; ☎415-391-1188; www.chsa.org; 965 Clay St; ⊙noon-5pm Tue-Fri, 11am-4pm Sat; 🚌1, 8, 30, 45, 🚋California St, Powell-Mason, Mason-Hyde) FREE Picture what it was like to be Chinese in America during the Gold Rush, transcontinental railroad construction or Beat heyday in this 1932 landmark, built as Chinatown's YWCA by Julia Morgan (chief architect of Hearst Castle). CHSA historians unearth fascinating artifacts, such as 1920s silk *qipao* dresses worn by socialites from Shanghai to San Francisco. Exhibits reveal once-popular views of Chinatown, including the sensationalist opium den exhibit at San Francisco's 1915 Panama-Pacific International Expo, inviting fair-goers to 'Go Slumming' in Chinatown.

Rotating exhibits are held in this graceful red-brick, green-tile-roofed landmark building; check CHSA's website for current shows, openings and events.

CHINESE CULTURE CENTER ART GALLERY

Map p318 (☎415-986-1822; www.c-c-c.org; 3rd fl, Hilton Hotel, 750 Kearny St; suggested donation $5; ⊙during exhibitions 10am-4pm Tue-Sat; 👪; 🚌1, 8, 10, 12, 30, 41, 45, 🚋California St, Powell-Mason, Powell-Hyde) You can see all the way to China from the Hilton's 3rd floor inside this cultural center, which hosts exhibits ranging from showcases of China's leading ink-brush painters to XianRui ('fresharp') cutting-edge installations, recently including videos exploring generation gaps. In odd-numbered years, don't miss Present Tense Biennial, where 30-plus Bay Area artists present personal takes on Chinese culture. Check the center's online schedule for upcoming concerts, hands-on arts workshops for adults and children, Mandarin classes and genealogy services.

PORTSMOUTH SQUARE PARK

Map p318 (http://sfrecpark.org/destination/portsmouth-square; Washington St & Walter Lum Place; P 👪; 🚌1, 8, 10, 12, 30, 41, 45, 🚋California St, Powell-Hyde, Powell-Mason) Chinatown's unofficial living room is named after John B

LOCAL KNOWLEDGE

CHINATOWN'S CLINKER BRICK ARCHITECTURE

As you walk through Chinatown, take a close look at the brick buildings around you. Some of the bricks are blackened, twisted and bubbled. You might notice bricks jutting out from the wall at odd angles, because they're not flat enough to be laid flush. You've spotted clinker bricks, warped and discolored by fire over a century ago.

Clinker bricks are part of Chinatown's extraordinary survival story. Chinatown was originally largely built by non-Chinese landlords in cheap, unreinforced brick – and when the great 1906 earthquake hit, those buildings toppled. Fire swept Chinatown at such high temperatures that the bricks began to melt and turn glassy, becoming clinker bricks. Many residents returned to find they had lost everything – their homes, workplaces, social centers, churches and temples were reduced to rubble. The streets were choked with clinker bricks.

Bricklayers typically toss out over-fired clinker bricks as defective, because they're hard to lay straight and don't insulate well – but Chinatown couldn't wait for better materials to start rebuilding. Ruthless developers like Abe Ruef – of Columbus Tower fame – were conspiring to relocate Chinatown outside of San Francisco, with the backing of City Hall. When Chinatown residents caught wind of the plan, they marched back into their still-smoking neighborhood, cleared the streets, and started rebuilding Chinatown, brick by brick. They made ingenious use of warped bricks others would consider useless, turning them on their ends to create decorative patterns.

Chinatown not only stood its ground – it made an architectural statement. Architect Julia Morgan incorporated clinker bricks as a poignant decorative motif for Chinatown's 1908 Donaldina Cameron House (920 Sacramento St), a refuge for women and children escaping indentured servitude. Chinatown's architecture of survival soon became a signature of California's 1920s arts-and-crafts movement, and today clinker bricks can be seen on religious buildings and family homes across the state.

Chinatown Alleyways

Forty-one historic alleyways packed into Chinatown's 22 blocks have seen it all since 1849: gold rushes and revolution, incense and opium, fire and icy receptions. These narrow backstreets are lined with towering buildings because there was nowhere to go but up in Chinatown after 1870, when laws limited Chinese immigration, employment and housing.

Waverly Place

Off Sacramento St are the flag-festooned balconies of Chinatown's historic temples, where services have been held since 1852 – even in 1906, while the altar was still smoldering at Tin How Temple (p118). Downstairs are noodle shops, laundries and traditional Chinese apothecaries.

Ross Alley

Ross Alley was known as Mexico, Spanish and Manila St after the women who staffed its notorious back-parlor brothels. Colorful characters now fill alleyway murals, and anyone can make a fortune the easy way at Golden Gate Fortune Cookie Company (p128). You may luck into a concert at Jun Yu's barbershop at 32 Ross Alley, where the octogenarian barber often plays the *erhu* (Chinese lap violin) between customers on weekends.

Spofford Alley

As sunset falls on sociable Spofford Alley, you'll hear clicking mah jong tiles and a Chinese orchestra warming up. But generations ago, you might have overheard Sun Yat-sen and his conspirators at number 36 plotting the 1911 overthrow of China's last dynasty.

Commercial Street

Across Portsmouth Square from San Francisco's City Hall, this euphemistically named hot spot caught fire in 1906. The city banned the 25¢ Chinese brothels of Commercial St in favor of 'parlor houses,' where basic services were raised to $3 and watching cost $10.

1

3

2

ROBERTO SONCIN GEROMETTA / GETTY IMAGES ©

1. Production at Golden Gate Fortune Cookie Company (p128)
2. Dragon's Gate (p119) 3. Tin How Temple (p118) 4. Waverly Place

SABRINA DALBESIO / GETTY IMAGES ©

CHINATOWN WALKING TOURS

On two-hour **Chinatown Alleyway Tours** (Map p318; ☎415-984-1478; www.chinatownalleywaytours.org/; tours depart Portsmouth Square, near Washington & Kearny Sts; adults/students $26/16; ⏰tours 11am Mon, Tue & Sat, 3pm Thu & Fri; 👪; 🚌1, 8, 10, 12, 30, 41, 45, 🚋California St, Powell-Mason, Powell-Hyde), teenage Chinatown residents guide you through backstreets that have seen it all: Sun Yat-sen plotting China's revolution, forty-niners squandering fortunes on opium, services held in temple ruins after the 1906 earthquake. Your presence here helps the community remember its history and shape its future – Chinatown Alleyway Tours are a nonprofit youth-led program of the Chinatown Community Development Center. Credit cards are accepted for advance online reservations only; drop-ins must pay with exact change.

Local-led, kid-friendly **Chinatown Heritage Walking Tours** (Map p318; ☎415-986-1822; www.c-c-c.org; tours depart Chinese Cultural Center, 3rd fl, Hilton Hotel, 750 Kearny St; group walking tour adult $25-30, student $15-20, private walking tour (1-4 people) $60; ⏰tours 10am, noon & 2pm Tue-Sat; 🚌1, 8, 10, 12, 30, 41, 45, 🚋California St, Powell-Mason, Powell-Hyde) winding through backstreets to key historic sights, including Golden Gate Fortune Cookie Factory, Tin How Temple and Portsmouth Square. Tours follow one of two themes: The Tale of Two Chinatowns, covering Chinatown's daily life and cultural influence, or From Dynasty to Democracy, exploring Chinatown's role in the US civil rights and international human rights movements. Proceeds support nonprofit Chinese Culture Center (p115); make bookings online or by phone three days in advance.

Montgomery's sloop, which staked the US claim on San Francisco in 1846. San Francisco's first city hall moved into Portsmouth Square's burlesque Jenny Lind Theater in 1852, and today the square is graced by the Goddess of Democracy, a bronze replica of the statue Tiananmen Square protesters made in 1989. Tai chi practitioners greet the dawn, toddlers rush the playground at noon, and chess marathons continue well into the night.

OLD ST MARY'S CATHEDRAL & SQUARE — CHURCH

Map p318 (☎415-288-3800; www.oldsaintmarys.org; 660 California St; ⏰cathedral 11am-6pm Mon & Tue, to 7pm Wed-Fri, 9am-6:30pm Sat, 9am-4:30pm Sun; 🚌1, 30, 45, 🚋California St) California's first cathedral was started in 1854 by an Irish entrepreneur determined to give wayward San Francisco some religion – despite its location on brothel-lined Dupont St. The 1906 earthquake miraculously spared the church's brick walls but destroyed a bordello across the street, making room for St Mary's Square. Today, skateboarders do tricks of a different sort in the park, under the watchful eye of Beniamino Bufano's 1929 pink-granite-and-steel statue of Chinese revolutionary Sun Yat-sen.

Eventually the archdiocese abandoned attempts to convert Dupont St and handed the church over to America's first Chinese community mission, run by the activism-oriented Paulists. During WWII, Old St Mary's served 450,000 members of the US armed forces as a cafeteria and recreation center. The church still holds regular Tuesday noontime concerts (suggested donation $5).

CHINESE TELEPHONE EXCHANGE — HISTORIC BUILDING

Map p318 (743 Washington St; 🚌1, 30, 45, 🚋California St, Powell-Hyde, Powell-Mason) California's earliest adopters of advanced technology weren't Silicon Valley programmers but Chinatown switchboard operators. This triple-decker tiled pagoda revolutionized communication in 1894. To connect callers, switchboard operators spoke fluent English and five Chinese dialects and memorized at least 1500 Chinatown residents by name, residence and occupation. Managers lived on-site and kept the switchboard operating 365 days a year. The exchange operated until 1949 and the landmark was bought and restored by Bank of Canton in 1960.

Since anyone born in China was prohibited by US law from visiting San Francisco throughout the 1882–1943 Chinese Exclusion era, this switchboard was the main means of contact with family and business partners in China for 60 years.

TIN HOW TEMPLE — TEMPLE

Map p318 (Tien Hau Temple; 125 Waverly Place; donation customary; ⏰10am-4pm, except holidays; 🚌1, 8, 30, 45, 🚋California St, Powell-Mason, Powell-Hyde) There was no place to go but up in Chinatown in the 19th century, when laws restricted where Chinese San Franciscans could live and work. Atop barber shops, laundries and diners lining Waverly Place, you'll spot lantern-festooned temple balconies. Tin How Temple was built in 1852; its altar miraculously survived the 1906 earthquake. To pay your respects, follow sandalwood incense aromas up three flights of stairs. Entry is free, but offerings customary for temple upkeep. No photography is allowed inside.

DRAGON'S GATE MONUMENT

Map p318 (intersection of Grant Ave & Bush St; 1, 8, 30, 45, California St) Enter the Dragon archway donated by Taiwan in 1970, and you'll find yourself on the street formerly known as Dupont in its notorious red-light heyday. The pagoda-topped 'Chinatown Deco' architecture beyond this gate was innovated by Chinatown merchants led by Look Tin Ely in the 1920s – a pioneering initiative to lure tourists with a distinctive modern look. It worked: dragon streetlights chased away the shady ladies, and now light the way to bargain souvenirs and tea shops.

GOOD LUCK PARKING GARAGE LANDMARK

Map p318 (735 Vallejo St; 10, 12, 30, 41, 45, Powell-Mason) Each parking spot at this garage comes with fortune-cookie wisdom stenciled onto the asphalt: 'The time is right to make new friends' or 'Stop searching forever: happiness is just next to you.' These omens are supplied by artists Harrell Fletcher and Jon Rubin, who also gathered local residents' photographs of Chinese and Italian ancestors that grace the parking-lot entry like heraldic emblems. Parking costs $3 per hour.

EATING

North Beach

★LIGURIA BAKERY BAKERY $

Map p318 (415-421-3786; 1700 Stockton St; focaccia $4-5; 8am-1pm Tue-Fri, from 7am Sat; 8, 30, 39, 41, 45, Powell-Mason) Bleary-eyed art students and Italian grandmothers are in line by 8am for cinnamon-raisin focaccia hot out of the 100-year-old oven, leaving 9am dawdlers a choice of tomato or classic rosemary/garlic and 11am stragglers out of luck. Take yours in wax paper or boxed for picnics – but don't kid yourself that you're going to save some for later. Cash only.

GOLDEN BOY PIZZA $

Map p318 (415-982-9738; www.goldenboypizza.com/; 542 Green St; slice $2.75-3.75; 11:30am-11:30pm Sun-Thu, to 2:30am Fri & Sat; 8, 30, 39, 41, 45, Powell-Mason) Looking for the ultimate slice post-bar-crawl and morning-after brunch? Here you're golden. Second-generation Sodini family pizza-slingers make theirs Genovese-style with focaccia crust, hitting that mystical mean between chewy and crunchy with the ideal amount of olive oil. Go for Genovese toppings like clam/garlic or pesto, and bliss out with hot slices and draft beer at the tin-shed counter.

MARIO'S BOHEMIAN CIGAR STORE CAFE CAFE $

Map p318 (415-362-0536; 566 Columbus Ave; sandwiches $6.50-13; 10am-11pm; 8, 30, 39, 41, 45, Powell-Mason) A boho North Beach holdout on Washington Square Park, Mario's gave up smoking in the 1970s and turned to piping-hot panini. By now, generations of artistic movements have been fueled by Mario's oven-baked onion focaccia sandwiches. It's also a prime corner for people-watching, glugging wine by the carafe or pints of Anchor Steam served by art-schooled wait staff.

MAMA'S BRUNCH $

Map p318 (415-362-6421; www.mamas-sf.com; 1701 Stockton St; brunch mains $8.95-13.75; 8am-3pm Tue-Sun; 8, 30, 39, 41, 45, Powell-Mason) Generations of North Beachers have entrusted the most important meal of the day to Mama and Papa Sanchez, whose sunny Victorian storefront diner has offered definitive cures for barbaric Barbary Coast hangovers for 50 years. Local farm-egg omelettes and *kugelhopf* (house-baked brioche) French toast are cure-alls, but weekend specials like Dungeness-crab eggs benedict make waits down the block worthwhile.

MARA'S ITALIAN PASTRY PASTRY $

Map p318 (415-397-9435; 503 Columbus Ave; pastries $2-6; 7am-10:30pm Sun-Thu, to midnight Fri & Sat; 8, 30, 39, 41, 45, Powell-Mason) Join early risers for shots of Illy espresso and *crostata* (jam tart), or wander in at night between bars and *Beach Blanket Babylon* for *torta di mandorla* (almond-meal tart with layer of jam) and chocolate-chip-ricotta cannoli. Twice-baked, extra-crunchy biscotti are an acquired taste for non-Italians

City Walk North Beach Beat

START CITY LIGHTS BOOKSTORE
END LI PO
LENGTH 1.5 MILES; TWO HOURS

At ❶ **City Lights bookstore** (p113), home of Beat poetry and free speech, pick up something to inspire your journey into literary North Beach – Ferlinghetti's *San Francisco Poems* and Ginsberg's *Howl* are excellent choices.

Head to ❷ **Caffe Trieste** (p125) for potent espresso and opera on the jukebox in the back booth, where Francis Ford Coppola allegedly drafted *The Godfather* screenplay.

At ❸ **Washington Square** (p114), you'll spot parrots in the treetops and octogenarians in tai chi tiger stances on the lawn: pure poetry in motion. At the corner, ❹ **Liguria Bakery** (p119) will give you something to write home about: focaccia hot from a 100-year-old oven.

Quiet ❺ **Bob Kaufman Alley** (p113) was named for the legendary street-corner poet, who broke a 12-year vow of silence when he walked into a North Beach café and recited his poem *All Those Ships That Never Sailed:* 'Today I bring them back/Huge and transitory/And let them sail/Forever.'

Dylan jam sessions erupt in the bookshop, Allen Ginsberg gyrates nude in backroom documentary screenings, and onlookers grin beatifically at it all. Welcome to the ❻ **Beat Museum** (p113), where visitors are all (to quote Ginsberg's *Howl*) 'angelheaded hipsters burning for the ancient heavenly connection.'

Begin your literary bar crawl at ❼ **Specs** (p125) amid merchant-marine memorabilia, tall tales and pitchers of Anchor Steam.

On the Road author Jack Kerouac once blew off Henry Miller to go on a bender at ❽ **Vesuvio** (p126), until bartenders ejected him into the street now named for him: ❾ **Jack Kerouac Alley** (p114). Note the words of Chinese poet Li Po embedded in the alley: 'In the company of friends, there is never enough wine.'

Follow the lead of Kerouac and Ginsberg and end your night under the laughing Buddha at ❿ **Li Po** (p126) – there many not be enough wine, but there's plenty of beer.

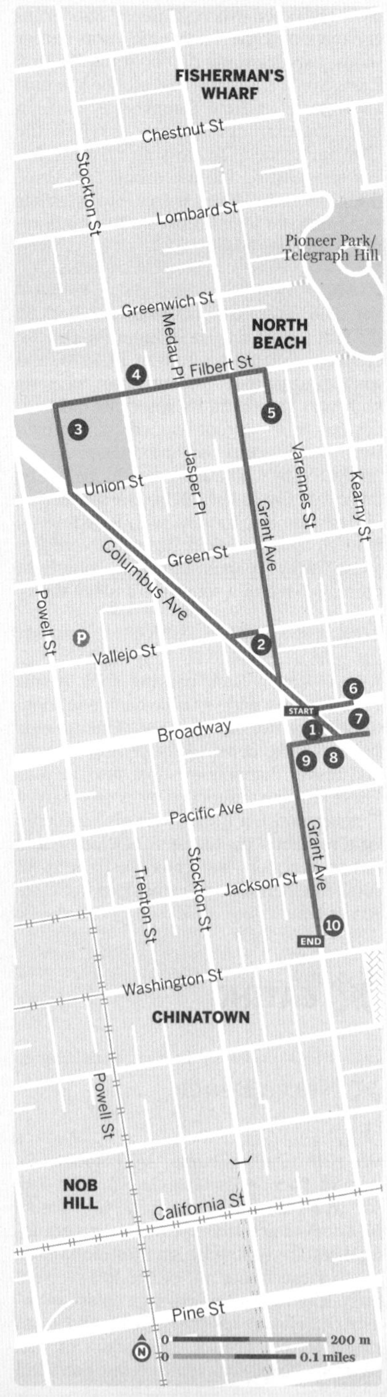

(try dunking them in *vin santo*), but pine-nut-studded chewy *pignoli* cookies are cross-cultural crowd-pleasers.

TONY'S COAL-FIRED PIZZA & SLICE HOUSE PIZZA $

Map p318 (☎415-835-9888; http://tonyscoalfired.com/; 1556 Stockton St; slices $4.50-6; ⏰11:30-11pm Wed-Sun, to 10pm Mon, to 8pm Tue; 🚌8, 30, 39, 41, 45, 🚋Powell-Mason) Fuggedaboudit, New York pizza loyalists: in San Francisco, you can grab a cheesy, thin-crust slice from nine-times world champion pizza-slinger Tony Gemignani. What, you were expecting Kosher salt shakers and bottled Coke from a vintage machine? Done. Difference is, here you can take that slice to sunny Washington Square, and watch tai chi practice and wild parrots year-round. Sorry, Manhattan – whaddayagonnado?

MOLINARI DELI $$

Map p318 (☎415-421-2337; www.molinarisalame.com; 373 Columbus Ave; sandwiches $10-12.50; ⏰9am-6pm Mon-Fri, to 5:30pm Sat, 10am-4pm Sun; 🚌8, 10, 12, 30, 39, 41, 45, 🚋Powell-Mason) Grab a number and a crusty roll, and when your number rolls around, wise-cracking deli staff in paper hats will stuff it with translucent sheets of *prosciutto di Parma,* milky buffalo mozzarella, tender marinated artichokes or slabs of the legendary house-cured salami. Enjoy yours hot from the panini press at sidewalk tables or in Washington Square.

CINECITTÀ PIZZA $$

Map p318 (☎415-291-8830; www.cinecittarestaurant.com; 663 Union St; pizza $12-15; ⏰noon-10pm Sun-Thu, to 11pm Fri & Sat; 🍷👶; 🚌8X, 30, 39, 41, 45, 🚋Powell-Mason) Follow tantalizing aromas into this tiny hot spot for thin-crust Roman pizza, made from scratch and served with sass by Roman owner Romina. Local loyalties are divided between the Roman Travestere (fresh mozzarella, arugula and prosciutto) and Neapolitan O Sole Mio (capers, olives, mozzarella and anchovies). Local brews are on tap, house wine is $5 from 4pm to 7pm, and Romina's tiramisu is San Francisco's best.

NAKED LUNCH SANDWICHES $$

Map p318 (☎415-577-4951; www.nakedlunchsf.com; 504 Broadway; sandwiches $10-18; ⏰11:30am-2pm Tue-Sat; 🐾; 🚌8, 10, 12, 30, 41, 🚋Powell-Mason) Unpredictable, utterly decadent cravings worthy of a William S Burroughs novel are satisfied by this patio pub tucked between XXX entertainment venues. For pure indulgence, try the free-range fried chicken sandwich, followed by foie gras ice cream with sea salt and lavender. Sunny days call for house margaritas, Southern cinnamon iced tea and/or $4 happy hour draft beer (4:30pm to 7pm).

RISTORANTE IDEALE ITALIAN $$

Map p318 (☎415-391-4129; www.idealerestaurant.com; 1309 Grant Ave; pasta $16-20; ⏰5:30-10:30pm Mon-Thu, to 11pm Fri & Sat, 5-10pm Sun; 🚌8, 10, 12, 30, 41, 45, 🚋Powell-Mason) Other North Beach restaurants fake Italian accents, but this trattoria has Italians in the kitchen, on the floor and at the table. Roman chef/owner Maurizio Bruschi serves authentic, al dente *bucatini ammatriciana* (tube pasta with tomato-pecorino sauce and house-cured pancetta) and ravioli and gnocchi handmade in-house ('of course!'). Ask Tuscan staff to recommend well-priced wine and everyone goes home happy.

E' TUTTO QUA ITALIAN $$

Map p318 (☎415-989-1002; www.etuttoqua.com/; 270 Columbus Ave; mains $16-29; ⏰5pm-midnight; 🚌8, 10, 12, 30, 41, 45, 🚋Powell-Mason) The Colosseum is 6000 miles from the corner of Columbus and Broadway, but you'll eat like a gladiator at E' Tutto Qua (translation: It's All Here). Boisterous Roman service and over-the-top decor create a party atmosphere – but they're serious about homemade pasta, grilled meats, and top-flight Italian wines. Order the lamb chops and truffled paccheri (tube pasta) and emerge victorious.

★COI CALIFORNIAN $$$

Map p303 (☎415-393-9000; www.coirestaurant.com; 373 Broadway; set menu $195; ⏰5:30-10pm Tue-Sat; 🅿; 🚌8, 10, 12, 30, 41, 45, 🚋Powell-Mason) 🌿 Chef Daniel Patterson's restlessly imaginative 12-course tasting menu is like licking the California coastline: satiny Meyer-lemon gelee melts onto oysters, nutty wild morels hug blush-pink trout, California sturgeon caviar crowns velvety smoked farm-egg yolk. Bright, only-in-California flavors deserve adventurous wine pairings ($105; generous enough for two). Book your 'ticket' online, or chance a walk-in ($20 more per person); 20% service and tax added.

CAFE JACQUELINE FRENCH $$$

Map p318 (☎415-981-5565; 1454 Grant Ave; soufflés per person $15-30; ⏰5:30-11pm Wed-Sun; 🚌8, 30, 39, 41, 45, 🚋Powell-Mason) The secret terror of top chefs is the classic French soufflé, but Chef Jacqueline's perfectly puffy

1. Chinese Historical Society of America (p115)
The Julia Morgan–designed Chinatown YWCA now highlights turning points in Asian American history.

2. City Lights (p113)
One of the world's most famous bookstores, this North Beach institution was at the center of the Beat movement.

3. Filbert St Steps (p133)
Parrots squawk as pedestrians ascend Telegraph Hill, passing hidden cottages and gardens to reach Coit Tower.

2

DIANA MAYFIELD / GETTY IMAGES ©

3

LONELY PLANET / GETTY IMAGES ©

HOW TO TELL ITALIAN IMPOSTERS

When choosing an Italian restaurant in North Beach, use this rule of thumb: if a host has to lure you inside with a 'Ciao, bella!', keep walking. Ditto for any restaurant with a gimmicky or too-obvious name – Stinking Rose and Mona Lisa are every bit as touristy as you'd expect. Try smaller neighborhood restaurants on side streets off Grant Ave and Washington St, where staff gossip in Italian.

creations float across the tongue like fog over the Golden Gate Bridge. With the right person across the tiny wooden table to share that seafood soufflé, dinner could hardly get more romantic – until you order the chocolate or seasonal berry version for dessert.

PARK TAVERN CALIFORNIAN **$$$**

Map p318 (415-989-7300; www.parktavernsf.com; 1652 Stockton St; mains dinner $25-36, brunch $12-16; 5:30-10pm Sun-Thu, 11:30am-2:30pm & 5:30-11pm Fri, 10am-2:30pm & 5:30-11pm Sat, 10am-2:30pm Sun; 8, 30, 39, 41, 45, Powell-Mason) An instant Washington Square institution, this women-run, Kiwi-founded bistro cheekily updates continental classics with California ingredients: Dungeness crab toast, venison carpaccio with bone marrow and capers, truffled fries to dip in soft-cooked egg and caviar. Brunch brings oatmeal-raisin pancakes with grilled apricots and grapefruit mimosas. Never mind the noise; have a Negroni and some Brussels-sprout chips and join the happy din.

Chinatown

CITY VIEW CHINESE **$**

Map p318 (415-398-2838; http://cityviewdimsum.com; 662 Commercial St; dishes $3-8; 11am-2:30pm Mon-Fri, from 10am Sat & Sun; ; 1, 8, 10, 12, 30, 45, California St) Take your seat in the sunny dining room and your pick from carts loaded with delicate shrimp and leek dumplings, garlicky Chinese broccoli, tangy spare ribs, coconut-dusted custard tarts and other tantalizing dim sum. Arrive before the midday lunch rush, so you can nab seats in the sunny upstairs room and get first dibs from passing carts.

★Z & Y CHINESE **$$**

Map p318 (415-981-8988; www.zandyrestaurant.com; 655 Jackson St; mains $9-20; 11am-10pm Mon-Thu, to 11pm Fri-Sun; 8, 10, 12, 30, 45, Powell-Mason, Powell-Hyde) Graduate from ho-hum sweet-and-sour and middling *mu-shu* to sensational Szechuan dishes that go down in a blaze of glory. Warm up with spicy pork dumplings and heat-blistered string beans, take on the house-made *tantan* noodles with peanut-chili sauce, and leave lips buzzing with fish poached in flaming chili oil and buried under red Szechuan chili-peppers. Go early; it's worth the wait.

GREAT EASTERN RESTAURANT CHINESE, DIM SUM **$$**

Map p318 (415-986-2500; http://greateasternrestaurant.net; 649 Jackson St; mains $8-20; 10am-11pm Mon-Fri, from 9am Sat & Sun; ; 8, 10, 12, 30, 45, Powell-Mason, Powell-Hyde) Eat your way across China, from northern Peking duck to southern pan-fried shrimp and Cantonese chive dumplings. President Obama stopped by Great Eastern for take-out and weekend dim sum throngs around noon may make you wish for your own secret-service escort – call ahead for reservations or come around 1pm as dim sum brunch crowds stagger out satisfied.

LAI HONG LOUNGE DIM SUM **$$**

Map p318 (415-397-2290; www.lhklounge.com/; 1416 Powell St; dim sum $3.50-12; 10am-2:30pm & 5:30-8:30pm Mon-Fri, from 9am Sat & Sun; 8, 10, 12, 30, 41, 45, Powell-Hyde) Like a greatest-hits album, Lai Hong's menu features remastered dim sum classics: properly plump shrimp dumplings, crisp Peking duck, baked barbecue pork buns with the right ratio of savory-sweet pork to meltaway bun. Choose from the menu – no carts – and bide your time while food is cooked to order with Californian Au Bon Climat Chardonnay. Expect a wait outdoors.

HOUSE OF NANKING CHINESE **$$**

Map p318 (415-421-1429; http://houseofnanking.net; 919 Kearny St; mains $9-15; 11am-2pm & 5-9pm Mon-Fri, noon-10pm Sat & Sun; 8X, 10, 12, 30, 45, Powell-Mason) Meekly suggest an interest in seafood, nothing deep-fried, perhaps some greens and your server nods, grabs the menu and returns laden with Shanghai specialties: fragrant gingery greens with poached scallops, garlicky noodles and black-bean-glazed eggplant. Expect bossy service and a wait for a shared table – but also bright, fresh flavors at reasonable prices.

YUET LEE CHINESE, SEAFOOD $$

Map p318 (☎415-982-6020; 1300 Stockton St; mains $9-20; ⊙11am-3am Wed-Sat & Mon, 9am-midnight Sun; 🚌8, 10, 12, 30, 41, 45, 🚋Powell-Mason) With a radioactive-green paint job and merciless fluorescent lighting, this Chinese seafood diner isn't for first dates, but is perfect for drinking buddies and committed couples who have nothing to hide and are willing to share batter-fried, salt-and-pepper calamari and tender roast duck.

DRINKING & NIGHTLIFE

North Beach

★SPECS MUSEUM CAFE BAR

Map p318 (☎415-421-4112; 12 William Saroyan Pl; ⊙5pm-2am; 🚌8, 10, 12, 30, 41, 45, 🚋Powell-Mason) What do you do with a drunken sailor? Here's your answer. The walls are plastered with merchant-marine mementos, and you'll be plastered too if you try to keep up with the salty old-timers holding court in back. Surrounded by nautical memorabilia, your order is obvious: pitcher of Anchor Steam, coming right up.

★COMSTOCK SALOON BAR

Map p318 (☎415-617-0071; www.comstocksaloon.com; 155 Columbus Ave; ⊙noon-2am Mon-Fri, 4pm-2am Sat, 4pm-midnight Sun; 🚌8, 10, 12, 30, 45, 🚋Powell-Mason) Relieving yourself in the marble trough below the bar is no longer advisable, but otherwise this 1907 Victorian saloon revives the Barbary Coast's glory days. Get the authentic Pisco Punch or martini-precursor Martinez (gin, vermouth, bitters, maraschino liqueur). Reserve booths or back-parlor seating, so you can hear dates when ragtime-jazz bands play. Call it dinner with pot pie and buckets of shrimp.

★CAFFE TRIESTE CAFE

Map p318 (☎415-392-6739; www.caffetrieste.com; 601 Vallejo St; ⊙6:30am-10pm Sun-Thu, to 11pm Fri & Sat; 📶; 🚌8, 10, 12, 30, 41, 45) Poetry on bathroom walls, opera on the jukebox, live accordion jams and sightings of Beat poet laureate Lawrence Ferlinghetti: this is North Beach at its best, since the 1950s. Linger over legendary espresso and scribble your screenplay under the Sardinian fishing mural just as young Francis Ford Coppola did. Perhaps you've heard of the movie: *The Godfather*. Cash only.

15 ROMOLO BAR

Map p318 (☎415-398-1359; www.15romolo.com; 15 Romolo Pl; ⊙5pm-2am Mon-Fri, from 11:30am Sat & Sun; 🚌8, 10, 12, 30, 41, 45, 🚋Powell-Mason) Strap on your spurs: it's gonna be a wild western night at this back-alley Basque saloon squeezed between burlesque joints. The strong survive the Suckerpunch, a knockout potion of bourbon, sherry, hibiscus, lemon and Basque bitters – but everyone falls for Frida Kahlo, with mezcal, chartreuse, lavender and lemon. Bask in $7 Basque Picon punch at 5pm to 7:30pm happy hours.

TOSCA CAFE BAR

Map p318 (☎415-986-9651; www.toscacafesf.com; 242 Columbus Ave; ⊙5pm-2am; 🚌8, 10, 12, 30, 41, 45, 🚋Powell-Mason) When this historic North Beach speakeasy was nearly evicted in 2012, devotees like Sean Penn, Bobby DeNiro and Johnny Depp rallied, and New York star-chef April Bloomfield took over. Now 1930s murals and red leather banquettes are restored, and the revived kitchen serves rustic Italian fare (get the meatballs). Jukebox opera and spiked house cappuccino here deserve SF landmark status. Reservations essential.

THE DEVIL'S ACRE BAR

Map p318 (☎415-766-4363; www.thedevilsacre.com; 256 Columbus; ⊙5pm-2am Tue, from 3pm Wed-Sat, 3pm-midnight Sun; 🚌8, 10, 12, 30, 41, 45, 🚋Powell-Mason) Magic potions and quack cures are proudly served by this apothecary-style Barbary Coast saloon. Tartly quaffable Lauchlan's Antiscorbutic (lime, sea salt, and two kinds of gin) is a surefire cure for scurvy and/or sobriety, and for a boost of luck, get the Clover Leaf (Genever, Carpano Bianco, lemon and foamy egg white). No food here – take your medicine.

SALOON BAR

Map p318 (☎415-989-7666; www.sfblues.net/Saloon.html; 1232 Grant Ave; cover free-$5; ⊙noon-2am; 🚌8, 10, 12, 30, 41, 45, 🚋Powell-Mason) Blues in a red saloon that's been jumping since 1861: what more do you need on a North Beach night out? Local legend has it that when the rest of San Francisco burned in 1906, loyal patrons saved the Saloon by dousing it with buckets of hooch. Today it's the oldest bar in SF, and blues and rock bands perform nightly plus weekend afternoons. Cash only.

TONY NIK'S LOUNGE

Map p318 (☎415-693-0990; www.tonyniks.com/; 1534 Stockton St; ⏲4pm-2am Mon-Fri, from 2pm Sat & Sun; 🚌8, 30, 39, 41, 45, 🚋Powell-Mason) Vintage neon points the way to Tony Nik's, keeping North Beach nicely naughty since 1933. This tiny cocktail lounge is co-owned by the original Tony 'Nik' Nicco's grandson, who has preserved the original glass-brick entry, Deco wood paneling and Rat Pack-worthy martini recipe. Aim for the vintage banquettes in back, or hang with neighborhood characters at the mosaic bar.

VESUVIO BAR

Map p318 (☎415-362-3370; www.vesuvio.com; 255 Columbus Ave; ⏲6am-2am; 🚌8, 10, 12, 30, 41, 45, 🚋Powell-Mason) Guy walks into a bar, roars and leaves. Without missing a beat, the bartender says to the next customer, 'Welcome to Vesuvio, honey – what can I get you?' Jack Kerouac blew off Henry Miller to go on a bender here, and after joining neighborhood characters on the stained-glass mezzanine for microbrews or Kerouacs (rum, tequila and OJ), you'll get why.

Chinatown

LI PO BAR

Map p318 (☎415-982-0072; www.lipolounge.com; 916 Grant Ave; ⏲2pm-2am; 🚌8, 30, 45, 🚋Powell-Mason, Powell-Hyde) Beat a hasty retreat to red vinyl booths where Allen Ginsberg and Jack Kerouac debated the meaning of life under a golden Buddha. Enter the 1937 faux-grotto doorway and dodge red lanterns to place your order: Tsing Tao beer or sweet, sneaky-strong Chinese mai tai made with *baijiu* (rice liquor). Bathrooms and random DJ appearances are in the basement. Cash only.

RÉVEILLE CAFE

Map p318 (☎415-789-6258; http://reveillecoffee.com; 200 Columbus Ave; ⏲7am-6pm Mon-Fri, from 8am Sat, 8am-5pm Sun; 🚌8, 10, 12, 30, 41, 45, 🚋Powell-Mason) If this sunny flatiron storefront doesn't instantly lighten your mood, cappuccino with a foam-art heart will. Réveille's coffee is like San Francisco on a good day: nutty and uplifting, without a trace of bitterness. Check the circular marble counter for just-baked chocolate-chip cookies and sticky buns. No wi-fi makes for easy conversation and sidewalk-facing counters offer some of SF's best people-watching.

PLENTEA TEAHOUSE

Map p304 (☎415-757-0223; www.plenteasf.com/; 341 Kearny St; ⏲11am-11pm; 🚌1, 8, 30, 45, 🚋California) Chinatown's latest, greatest import is Taiwanese bubble tea, milky iced tea polka-dotted with *boba* (chewy, gently sweet tapioca pearls). PlenTea fills vintage milk bottles with just-brewed bubble tea in your choice of flavors: green, black, oolong, Thai, or any of the above plus fresh mango, peach or strawberry. For only-in-SF flavor, try extra-rich crema tea with oolong and sea-salt cream.

BUDDHA LOUNGE BAR

Map p318 (☎415-362-1792; 901 Grant Ave; ⏲1pm-2am Mon-Sat; 🚌8, 30, 45, 🚋Powell-Mason, Powell-Hyde) Vintage red neon promises evenings worthy of WWII sailors on shore leave. Drink in the atmosphere, but stick to basic well drinks and beer straight from a laughing Buddha bottle. Cue selections on the eclectic jukebox (Dylan, Outkast, The Clash), ask the bartender for dice and you're in for the duration. Bathrooms are in the former opium-den basement. Cash only.

☆ ENTERTAINMENT

BEACH BLANKET BABYLON CABARET

Map p318 (BBB; ☎415-421-4222; www.beachblanketbabylon.com; 678 Green St; admission $25-100; ⏲shows 8pm Wed, Thu & Fri, 6:30pm & 9:30pm Sat, 2pm & 5pm Sun; 🚌8, 30, 39, 41, 45, 🚋Powell-Mason) Snow White searches for Prince Charming in San Francisco: what could possibly go wrong? The Disney-spoof musical-comedy cabaret has been running since 1974, but topical jokes keep it outrageous and wigs big as parade floats are gasp-worthy. Spectators must be over 21 to handle racy humor, except at cleverly sanitized Sunday matinees. Reservations essential; arrive one hour early for best seats.

BIMBO'S 365 CLUB LIVE MUSIC

Map p318 (☎415-474-0365; www.bimbos365club.com; 1025 Columbus Ave; tickets from $20; ⏲box office 10am-4pm, showtimes vary; 🚌8, 30, 39, 41, 45, 🚋Powell-Mason) Get your kicks at this vintage speakeasy with stiff drinks, bawdy 1951 bar murals, parquet dance floor for high-stepping like Rita Hayworth (she was in the chorus line here), and intimate live shows by the likes of Beck, Pinback,

WORTH A DETOUR

DRAG ME ALONG BARBARY COAST TOUR

Explore San Francisco's bawdy Barbary Coast with a bonafide legend: Gold Rush burlesque star Countess Lola Montez, reincarnated in drag by San Francisco historian Rick Shelton. Her Highness leads **Drag Me Along Tours** (Map p318; www.dragmealongtours.com; tour begins in Portsmouth Square; $20 ; tours usually 11am-1pm Sun; 1, 8, 10, 12, 30, 41, 45, California St, Powell-Mason, Powell-Hyde) through Chinatown alleyways where Victorian ladies made and lost reputations, to Jackson Square saloons where sailors were shanghaied – introducing the Barbary Coast characters who gambled big, loved hard and lived large. Adults only – true Barbary Coast history is not for the faint of heart, or children. Reservations required; cash only.

English Beat and Bebel Gilberto. Bring change to tip the ladies' powder room attendant – this is a classy joint. Two-drink minimum; cash only.

COBB'S COMEDY CLUB COMEDY

Map p318 (415-928-4320; www.cobbscomedyclub.com; 915 Columbus Ave; admission $13-45, plus 2-drink minimum; showtimes vary; 8, 30, 39, 41, 45, Powell-Mason) There's no room to be shy at Cobb's, where bumper-to-bumper shared tables make an intimate (and vulnerable) audience. The venue is known for launching local talent and giving big-name acts from Louis CK to Kevin Smith a place to try risky new material. Check the website for shows and showcases like Really Funny Comedians (Who Happen to Be Women).

DOC'S LAB LIVE MUSIC, COMEDY

Map p318 (415-649-6191; www.docslabsf.com; 124 Columbus Ave; admission free-$20; showtimes vary; see website; 8, 10, 12, 30, 41, 45, Powell-Mason) Social experiments begin in this subterranean venue, where potent drinks are concocted with mad-scientist beakers and the daring bill upholds North Beach traditions of experimental jazz, out-there comedy, boom-boom burlesque and anything-goes Americana. Doc's Lab occupies the space left by the Purple Onion, home of breakout performances from Maya Angelou to Zach Galifianakis – and fills the void.

SHOPPING

North Beach

ARIA ANTIQUES, COLLECTIBLES

Map p318 (415-433-0219; 1522 Grant Ave; 11am-6pm Mon-Sat; 8, 30, 39, 41, 45, Powell-Mason) Find inspiration for your own North Beach epic poem on Aria's weathered wood counters, piled with anatomical drawings of starfish, castle keys lost in gutters a century ago, rusty numbers pried from French village walls and 19th-century letters still in their wax-sealed envelopes. Hours are erratic whenever owner/chief scavenger Bill Haskell is treasure-hunting abroad, so call ahead.

101 MUSIC MUSIC

Map p318 (415-392-6369; 1414 Grant Ave; 10am-8pm Mon-Sat, from noon Sun; 8, 30, 39, 41, 45, Powell-Mason) You'll have to bend over those bins to let DJs and hardcore collectors pass (and, hey, wasn't that Tom Waits?!), but among the $8 to $25 discs are obscure releases *(Songs for Greek Lovers)* and original recordings by Nina Simone, Janis Joplin and San Francisco's own anthem-rockers, Journey. At the **sister shop** (513 Green St), don't bonk your head on vintage Les Pauls.

AL'S ATTIRE CLOTHING, ACCESSORIES

Map p318 (415-693-9900; www.alsattire.com; 1300 Grant Ave; 11am-7pm Mon-Sat, noon-6pm Sun; 8, 10, 12, 30, 41, 45, Powell-Mason) Hepcats and slick chicks get their handmade threads at Al's, where vintage styles are reinvented in noir-novel twill, dandy high-sheen cotton and midcentury flecked tweeds. Prices aren't exactly bohemian for these bespoke originals, but turquoise wing-tips are custom-made to fit your feet and svelte hand-stitched jackets have silver-screen star quality. Ask about custom orders for weddings and other shindigs.

LYLE TUTTLE TATTOO ART MUSEUM & SHOP BEAUTY

Map p318 (415-255-2473; 841 Columbus Ave; noon-7pm; 8, 30, 39, 41, 45, Powell-Mason) Tattooed ladies are the life's work of ink icon Lyle Tuttle, who inked women across seven continents, including Janis Joplin,

LOCAL KNOWLEDGE

TEA TASTING

Several Grant Ave tea importers let you sample tea free, but the hard sell may begin before you finish sipping. For a more relaxed, enlightening teatime experience, Red Blossom Tea Company offers half-hour tea immersion classes with tastings and tips on preparing tea for maximum flavor ($30 for up to four participants). Drop-in classes may be available weekdays but call ahead on weekends; seating is limited.

Cher and Joan Baez. Since his retirement, his shop's been a working museum, with inking done to Tuttle standards by Madeline Bluebird. Tuttle worked with SF's Health Department to set industry standards for safe, sanitary practices, so you're in good hands.

SAN FRANCISCO ROCK POSTERS & COLLECTIBLES — ANTIQUES, COLLECTIBLES

Map p318 (☎415-956-6749; www.rockposters.com; 1851 Powell St; ⏲10am-6pm Mon-Sat; 🚌8, 30, 39, 41, 45, 🚋Powell-Mason) Are you ready to rock? Enter this trippy temple to classic rock gods – but leave your lighters at home, because these concert posters are valuable. Expect to pay hundreds for first-run psychedelic Fillmore concert posters featuring the Grateful Dead – but you can score bargain handbills for San Francisco acts like Santana, Dead Kennedys, and Sly and the Family Stone.

Chinatown

RED BLOSSOM TEA COMPANY — TEA

Map p318 (☎415-395-0868; www.redblossomtea.com; 831 Grant Ave; ⏲10am-6:30pm Mon-Sat, to 6pm Sun; 🚌1, 10, 12, 30, 35, 41, 🚋Powell-Mason, Powell-Hyde, California St) Crook your pinky: it's always teatime at Red Blossom, featuring 100+ specialty teas imported by second-generation, brother-sister tea merchants Alice and Peter Luong. Sniff shiny canisters lining wooden shelves, ask about seasonal offerings and try premium blends before you buy. For gourmet gifts, go with namesake blossoms – tightly wound balls of tea that unfurl into flowers in hot water.

GOLDEN GATE FORTUNE COOKIE COMPANY — FOOD & DRINK

Map p318 (☎415-781-3956; 56 Ross Alley; ⏲8am-6pm; 🚌8, 30, 45, 🚋Powell-Mason, Powell-Hyde) Make a fortune in San Francisco at this bakery, where cookies are stamped from vintage presses and folded while hot – much as they were in 1909, when fortune cookies were invented for San Francisco's Japanese Tea Garden (p201). Write your own wise words for custom cookies (50¢ each) or get bags of regular or risqué cookies. Cash only; 50¢ tip per photo.

CLARION MUSIC CENTER — MUSIC

Map p318 (☎415-391-1317; www.clarionmusic.com; 816 Sacramento St; ⏲11am-6pm Mon-Fri, 9am-5pm Sat; 🚌1, 30, 45, 🚋California St) Minor chords played on *erhu* (Chinese two-stringed instrument) pluck at your heartstrings as you walk through Chinatown's alleyways; here you can try your hand at the bow on a rosewood student model. With impressive ranges of congas, gongs and hand-carved drums, you could become your own multi-culti, one-man band. Check the website for concerts, workshops and demonstrations by masters.

CHINATOWN KITE SHOP — GIFTS

Map p318 (☎415-989-5182; www.chinatownkite.com; 717 Grant Ave; ⏲10am-8pm; 👪; 🚌1, 10, 12, 30, 35, 41, 🚋Powell-Hyde, Powell-Mason, California St) Be the star of Crissy Field and wow any kids in your life with a fierce 9ft-long flying dragon, a pirate-worthy wild parrot (SF's city bird), surreal floating legs or a flying panda that looks understandably stunned. Pick up a two-person, papier-mâché lion dance costume and invite a date to bust ferocious moves with you next lunar new year.

FAR EAST FLEA MARKET — GIFTS

Map p318 (☎415-989-8588; 729 Grant Ave; ⏲10am-9:30pm; 🚌1, 10, 12, 30, 35, 41, 🚋Powell-Mason, Powell-Hyde, California St) The shopping equivalent of crack, this bottomless store is dangerously cheap and certain to make you giddy and delusional. Of course you can get that $8.99 samurai sword through airport security! There's no such thing as too many bath toys, bobble-heads and Chia Pets! Step away from the $1 Golden Gate Bridge snow globes while there's still time…

Nob Hill, Russian Hill & Fillmore

NOB HILL | RUSSIAN HILL | JAPANTOWN | PACIFIC HEIGHTS

Neighborhood Top Five

❶ Stepping off the Powell-Hyde cable car atop twisty **Lombard Street** (p131) and thrilling to spectacular hilltop vistas, before descending the hill's famous switchbacks.

❷ Marveling at afternoon fog blowing through the Golden Gate, from atop **George Sterling Park** (p132) – a lovely spot for a picnic.

❸ Soaking naked in silence in communal Japanese baths at **Kabuki Springs & Spa** (p145), a cozy hideaway on a cold, foggy day.

❹ Exploring hidden stairway walks (p133) – through gardens, past mansions and up impossibly high hills – to see the city unfurl at your feet.

❺ Shopping for Japanime and kooky ephemera at the vintage-'60s **Japan Center** (p143), then slurping on a bowl of hot noodles.

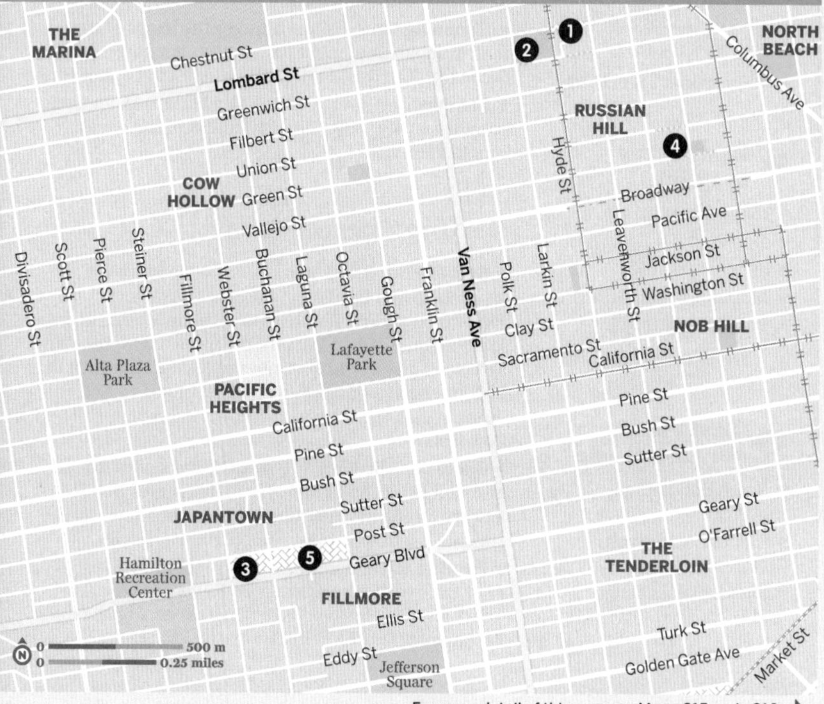

For more detail of this area see Map p315 and p316

Lonely Planet's Top Tip

Cable cars serve Russian and Nob Hills, but the Powell St lines have notoriously long waits at their terminuses. Alternatively take the California St line, which rarely has queues. Ride west from the foot of Market St to Van Ness Ave, then walk to Pacific Heights and Japantown. Instead of taking busy California St west of Van Ness, walk along pretty Sacramento St (one block north of California), detouring through Lafayette Park.

Best Places to Eat

- Acquerello (p138)
- Swan Oyster Depot (p137)
- State Bird Provisions (p140)
- Cocotte (p138)
- Leopold's (p138)

For reviews, see p137

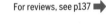

Best Places to Drink

- Tonga Room (p140)
- Amélie (p141)
- Hi-Lo Club (p140)
- 1300 on Fillmore (p141)
- Social Study (p141)

For reviews, see p140

Best Places for Live Music

- Boom Boom Room (p142)
- Fillmore Auditorium (p141)
- Sheba Piano Lounge (p142)

For reviews, see p141

Explore the Hills & Japantown

Tackle Japantown and Pacific Heights together – they're adjacent, connected via Fillmore St. Start at Geary Blvd and Fillmore St, wander east through Japantown, then go north on Fillmore to window-shop spiffy boutiques. Continue uphill till the street becomes residential, around Jackson St, then walk west to Alta Plaza Park for knockout hilltop city-view picnics – there's a fantastic playground, too. Russian and Nob Hills are likewise adjacent, but their ultra-steep gradients render them harder to explore on foot if you're out of shape. Fortunately they're accessible via cable car. Nob Hill stands between downtown and Chinatown; Russian Hill abuts Fisherman's Wharf and North Beach. Consider exploring the hills with these other neighborhoods. Polk St is the happening shopping and nightlife strip near Russian Hill; Fillmore St, in Pacific Heights, is swankier by day, quieter by night.

Local Life

- **Music** Several live-music venues lie near Geary and Fillmore Sts – the famous Fillmore Auditorium, plus a couple of intimate jazz clubs.
- **Cinema** Locals come to Japantown for dinner and a movie at Sundance Kabuki Cinema, which serves food and wine in its main theater.
- **Shopping** Most visitors only see the inside of the mall at Japan Center but there's also shopping *outside* the mall, along Post St, from Webster St to Laguna St.
- **Canines** Dog lovers flock to Alta Plaza Park for a pug parade – awww! – on the first Sunday of the month, 1pm to 4pm.

Getting There & Away

- **Bus** The 1, 2, 3 and 38 connect Downtown with Japantown and Pacific Heights; the 22 connects Japantown and Pacific Heights with the Marina and the Mission. Buses 10 and 12 link Downtown with Russian and Nob Hills; the 10 continues to Pacific Heights. The 27 connects Mission, SoMa and Downtown to Nob Hill. Buses 41 and 45 connect downtown to Russian Hill and Cow Hollow.
- **Cable car** The Powell-Hyde cable car serves Russian and Nob Hills; the Powell-Mason line serves Nob Hill; and the California line runs between downtown, Nob Hill and the easternmost edge of Pacific Heights.
- **Parking** Street parking is difficult but possible. Find garages at Japan Center on Fillmore St (between Geary and Post Sts) and Post St (between Webster and Buchanan Sts).

TOP SIGHT
LOMBARD STREET

You've seen its eight switchbacks in 1000 photographs and maybe a few movies, commercials and TV shows, too. Hitchcock used it in *Vertigo*, MTV shot episodes of *The Real World* here and Barbra Streisand and Ryan O'Neal came flying down the twisty street in the classic-cinema car chase in *What's Up, Doc?* Everyone knows Lombard St as the 'world's crookedest street,' but is it really true?

Russian Hill, as it descends Lombard St, has a natural 27% grade – too steep in the 1920s for automobiles to ascend. Lombard St property owners decided to install a series of curves. The result is what you see today: a red-brick street with eight sweeping turns, divided by lovingly tended flower beds and 250 steps rising on either side.

Once the street appeared on postcards in the 1950s, the tourist board dubbed it the 'world's crookedest street,' which is factually incorrect. Vermont St, on Potrero Hill, between 20th and 22nd Sts, deserves this cred but don't bother trekking across town: Lombard St is (way) prettier. To avoid throngs of tourists, come early morning, but chances are it'll be foggy; for sun-lit pictures, time your visit for late morning (the hill faces east).

Don't try anything funny. The recent clampdown on renegade skaters means that the Lombard St thrills featured in the *Tony Hawk's Pro Skater* video game will remain strictly virtual, at least until the cops get slack. Until 2008, every Easter Sunday for seven years adults had arrived at the crest of Lombard St toting plastic toy tricycles for the annual Bring Your Own Big Wheel Race. But after vehement complaints from kill-joy residents, the art-prankster organizers moved their toy-joyride to – where else? – Vermont St. Check http://bringyourownbigwheel.com for the latest.

DON'T MISS...

- Snapping pictures from the bottom of the hill, looking up
- Arriving via the Powell-Hyde cable car
- Seeing Lombard St from Coit Tower, the next hill over

PRACTICALITIES

- Map p316, B1
- 900 block of Lombard St
- Powell-Hyde

SIGHTS

Nob & Russian Hills

LOMBARD STREET STREET

See p131.

★CABLE CAR MUSEUM HISTORIC SITE

Map p316 (☎415-474-1887; www.cablecarmuseum.org; 1201 Mason St; donations appreciated; ⏰10am-6pm Apr-Sep, to 5pm Oct-Mar; 👪; 🚋Powell-Mason, Powell-Hyde) FREE Hear that whirring beneath the cable-car tracks? That's the sound of the cables that pull the cars, and they all connect inside the city's long-functioning cable-car barn. Grips, engines, braking mechanisms…if these warm your gearhead heart, you'll be besotted by the Cable Car Museum. See three original 1870s cable cars and watch cables whir over massive bull wheels – as awesome a feat of physics now as when Andrew Hallidie invented it in 1873.

GRACE CATHEDRAL CHURCH

Map p316 (☎415-749-6300; www.gracecathedral.org; 1100 California St; suggested donation adult/child $3/2, Sun services free; ⏰8am-6pm Mon-Sat, to 7pm Sun, services 8:30am, 11am & 6pm Sun; 🚌1, 🚋California St) The city's Episcopal cathedral has been rebuilt three times since the Gold Rush; the current French-inspired, reinforced concrete cathedral took 40 years to complete. The spectacular stained-glass windows include a series dedicated to human endeavor, including Albert Einstein uplifted in swirling nuclear particles. Check website for events on the indoor and outdoor labyrinths, including candlelight meditation services and yoga, plus inclusive weekly spiritual events, such as Thursday Evensong.

Grace's commitment to pressing social issues is embodied in its AIDS Memorial Chapel, with a bronze altarpiece by artist-activist Keith Haring, his signature figures angels taking flight – especially powerful since this was his last work before his 1990 death from AIDS. Day and night, spot yogis walking the outdoor, inlaid stone labyrinth, meant to guide restless souls through three spiritual stages: releasing, receiving and returning.

HUNTINGTON PARK PARK

Map p316 (California St, btwn Mason & Taylor Sts; 👪; 🚌1, 🚋California St) San Francisco's poshest park, Huntington's 1.3 acres mark the crest of Nob Hill. At the center rises the 'Fountain of the Tortoises,' a century-old recreation of a 400-year-old limestone fountain in Rome. If you're staying down the hill and don't have a lot of time to explore, the park makes a perfect picnic destination – especially with kids, who love the big playground.

MACONDRAY LANE STREET

Map p316 (btwn Jones & Leavenworth Sts; 🚌41, 45, 🚋Powell-Mason, Powell-Hyde) The scenic route down from Ina Coolbrith Park – via steep stairs, past gravity-defying wooden cottages – is so charming, it looks like something from a novel. And so it is: Armistead Maupin used this as the model for Barbary Lane in his *Tales of the City* series.

GEORGE STERLING PARK PARK

Map p316 (www.rhn.org/pointofinterestparks.html; Greenwich & Hyde Sts; 👪; 🚋Powell-Hyde) 'Homeward into the sunset/Still unwearied we go/Till the northern hills are misty/With the amber of afterglow.' Poet George Sterling's *City by the Sea* is almost maudlin – that is, until you watch the sunset over the Golden Gate Bridge from his namesake hilltop park – the perfect vantage point over the 'cool, grey city of love.'

Sterling was a great romancer of all San Francisco offered – nature, idealism, free love and opium – and was frequently broke. But as toast of the secretive, elite Bohemian Club, San Francisco's high society indulged the poet in his eccentricities, which included carrying a lethal dose of cyanide as a reminder of life's transience. Broken by his ex-wife's suicide and loss of his best friend, novelist Jack London, the 'King of Bohemia' apparently took this bitter dose in 1926 inside his apartment at the club. Afterward, his influential friends named this park – with zigzagging paths and stirring, Sterling views – for him.

If you're not breathless from these hilltop vistas, play tennis on the adjacent public court named after San Francisco's Alice Marble, the 1930s tennis champ who recovered from tuberculosis to win Wimbledon and serve during WWII as a US secret agent among Nazis. Sure puts a little post-tennis panting into perspective, doesn't it?

DIEGO RIVERA GALLERY GALLERY

Map p316 (☎415-771-7020; www.sfai.edu; 800 Chestnut St; ⏰9am-7pm; 🚌30, 🚋Powell-Mason) FREE Diego Rivera's 1931 *The Making of a*

Fresco Showing the Building of a City is a *trompe l'oeil* fresco within a fresco, showing the artist himself, pausing to admire his work, as well as the work in progress that is San Francisco. The fresco covers an entire wall in the Diego Rivera Gallery at the San Francisco Art Institute. For a memorable San Francisco aspect, head to the terrace café for espresso and panoramic bay views.

INA COOLBRITH PARK — PARK

Map p316 (Vallejo & Taylor Sts; 🚌10, 12, 🚋Powell-Mason) On San Francisco's literary scene, all roads eventually lead to Ina Coolbrith, California's first poet laureate; colleague of Mark Twain and Ansel Adams; mentor to Jack London, Isadora Duncan, George Sterling and Charlotte Perkins Gilman; and lapsed Mormon (she kept secret that her uncle was Mormon-prophet Joseph Smith). The tiny park is a fitting honor – long on romance and exclamation-inspiring vistas. Climb past gardens, decks and flower-framed apartments, and when fog blows, listen for the whooshing in the treetops.

JACK KEROUAC'S LOVE SHACK — HISTORIC SITE

Map p316 (29 Russell St; 🚌41, 45, 🚋Powell-Hyde) This modest house on a quiet alley was the source of major literature *and* drama from 1951 to 1952, when Jack Kerouac shacked up with Neal and Carolyn Cassady and their baby daughter to pound out his 120ft-long scroll draft of *On the Road.*

Jack and Carolyn became lovers at her husband Neal's suggestion, but Carolyn frequently kicked them both out – though Neal was allowed to move back for the birth of their son John Allen Cassady (named for Jack, and Allen Ginsberg).

STAIRWAY WALKS

To appreciate San Francisco's brilliant vistas means ascending her hills. Sure, you could ride a cable car, but you'd miss all those marvelous staircases hidden behind hedgerows and backyard gardens cascading with fragrant flowers. Better to walk.

Here's a short list of our favorite staircases. Add some to your itinerary and be rewarded with knockout views – and strong thighs. Take care on damp days, when wet leaves render some routes slippery. And keep your eyes peeled for the famous wild parrots zipping between hilltops – you'll hear them before you see them.

Filbert Street Steps, Telegraph Hill (Map p318; 🚌39) Famous wooden staircase through backyard gardens, with brilliant East Bay vistas. Start at Coit Tower and find the route through the bushes. Be careful not to confuse it with adjacent Greenwich St steps – also beautiful but concrete. Tired afterward? Board the F-Market Streetcar at Greenwich and the Embarcadero.

Francisco Street Steps (Map p318) The high route from the Wharf to North Beach. Between 150 and 155 Francisco St, traverse the courtyard, ascend to Grant Ave, then turn left to Jack Early Park and climb higher for Golden Gate-to-Bay Bridge panoramas. Descend via Grant Ave to North Beach.

Lyon Street Steps (Map p302) Two blocks, between Broadway and Green St, flanked by forests and glamorous mansions – including Senator Dianne Feinstein's. Jaw-dropping bay and Marina views. Popular with stair-runners and coffee klatches. Connects Cow Hollow with Pacific Heights.

Baker Street Steps (Map p300) Quiet alternative to adjacent Lyon St's social and fitness scene. Two hundred steep, narrow steps between Broadway and Vallejo St, dense with greenery flanking the Getty mansions. Note: no handrail.

Vallejo Street Steps (Map p316) Connects North Beach with Russian Hill. Ideal for working off a pasta dinner. Ascend Vallejo toward Mason St; stairs rise toward Jones St, passing Ina Coolbrith Park. Sit at the top for brilliant views of the Bay Bridge lights, then continue west to Polk St for nightlife.

16th Avenue Steps (Map p326) Well off the beaten path on the western side of Twin Peaks but famous for its brilliant tile mosaics. See www.tiledsteps.org. To appreciate the artwork, ascend. Start at 1700 16th Ave, at Moraga St. Most easily reached by car.

HERMAN AU PHOTOGRAPHY / GETTY IMAGES ©

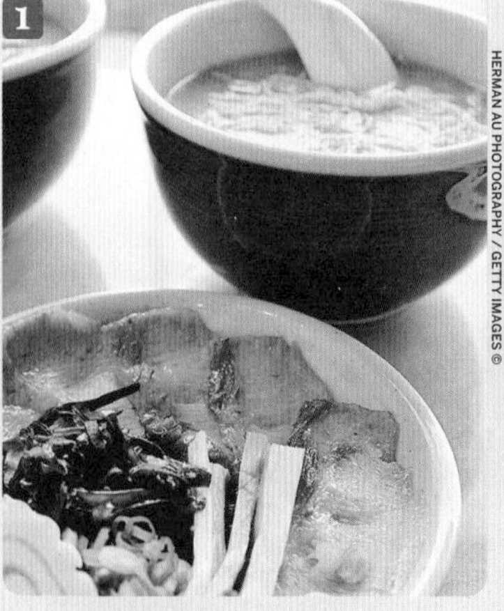

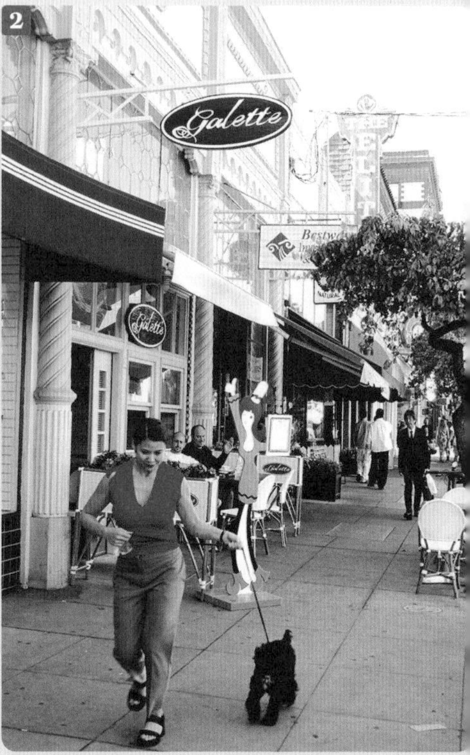

1. Dining in Japantown (p139)
Slurp ramen in one of this neighborhood's many Japanese eateries.

2. Fillmore St (p130)
This thoroughfare in Pacific Heights plays host to some of the neighborhood's best boutiques and cafes.

3. View from Nob Hill (p132)
Pound the pavement or ride a cable car up to knockout city and bay vistas.

4. San Francisco cable cars
Experience the ultimate urban joyride on vintage Victorian-era transport.

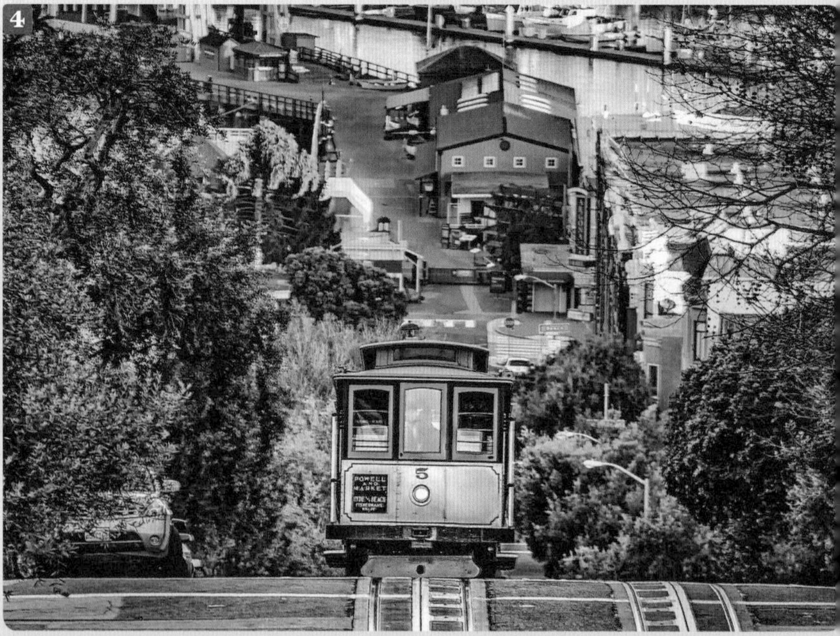

3

JEAN-PIERRE LESCOURRET / GETTY IMAGES ©

MASONIC AUDITORIUM AND TEMPLE BUILDING

Map p316 (☎415-292-9137; www.masonicheritage.org (museum); 1111 California St; ⊙Lobby 9am-5pm Mon-Fri, Museum 10am-3pm Mon-Thu & by appointment; 🚌1, 🚋California St) FREE Conspiracy theorists, rock aficionados and anyone exploring immigrant roots must know the Masonic Auditorium. Built as a temple to freemasonry in 1958 in mid-century modern style, and remodeled in 2014, the building hosts headline acts and, every other Tuesday, mass US-citizenship swearing-in ceremonies. Peak inside the lobby to see the window mosaics. The on-site museum focuses on California's Masonic history.

If you're looking for confirmation that California is run by a secret club, here you have it: many of the nation's founding fathers were Freemasons, including George Washington, and the same can be said about California's. It's all captured in the modernist stained-glass windows, which depict founders of freemasonry in California and their accomplishments – if you can decipher the enigmatic symbols and snippets of fabric embedded in the glass. The frieze below the windows has soil and gravel samples from all 58 California counties, plus Hawaii for some reason known only to those in on the secret handshake. Downstairs reveals some of the society's intriguing secrets.

PACIFIC-UNION CLUB HISTORIC BUILDING

Map p316 (1000 California St; 🚋California St) The only Nob Hill mansion to survive the 1906 earthquake and fire is this neoclassical brownstone, which despite its grandeur lacks architectural imagination. Today it's a private men's club. The exclusive roster lists newspaper magnates, both Hewlett and Packard of Hewlett-Packard, several US secretaries of defense and government contractors (insert conspiracy theory here).

Democrats, people of color and anyone under 45 are scarce on the published list, but little else is known about the 800-odd membership: members can be expelled for leaking information. Cheeky cross-dressing protesters have pointed out there's no specific ban on transgender or transvestite visitors supping in its main dining room or walking through the front door – privileges denied women.

⊙ Japantown & Pacific Heights

PEACE PAGODA MONUMENT

Map p315 (Peace Plaza, Japan Center; Ⓟ; 🚌22, 38) When in 1968 San Francisco's sister city of Osaka, Japan, made a gift of Yoshiro Taniguchi's five-tiered concrete stupa, the city seemed stupefied about what to do with the minimalist monument, clustering boxed shrubs around its stark nakedness. But with well-placed cherry trees and low, hewn-rock benches in the plaza, the pagoda is finally in its element, *au naturel.*

RUTH ASAWA FOUNTAINS MONUMENT

Map p315 (Buchanan St Pedestrian Mall, at Post St; 🚌2, 3, 38) During drought years you'll have to imagine how they look with water flowing, but even without, they're a sight to behold. Celebrated sculptor and former WWII internee Ruth Asawa designed these fountains to be lived in, not observed from polite distance. Bronze origami dandelions sprout from polished-pebble pools, with built-in benches for bento-box picnics; never mind the breeze along this wind-tunnel pedestrian block.

IKENOBO IKEBANA SOCIETY GALLERY

Map p315 (☎415-567-1011; www.ikenoboamerica.com; Suite 150 Kinokuniya Bldg, Japan Center, 1581 Webster St; ⊙9:30am-5:30pm Tue-Sat; 🚌2, 3, 22, 38) FREE The largest, oldest society outside Japan for *ikebana* (the Japanese art of flower-arranging) has the window displays to prove it: a curly willow tickling a narcissus in an abstract *jiyubana* (free-style) arrangement, or traditional seven-part *rikka* landscape featuring pine and iris. Even shoppers hell-bent on iron teapots and *maneki neko* (waving kitty) figurines can't resist looking.

COTTAGE ROW STREET

Map p315 (off Bush St btwn Webster & Fillmore Sts; 🚌2, 3, 22, 38) Detour to days of yore, when San Francisco was a sleepy seaside fishing village, before houses got all uptight, upright and Victorian. Easygoing 19th-century California clapboard cottages hang back along a brick-paved pedestrian promenade, where plum trees and bonsai take center stage. Homes are private but the mini-park is public, good for sushi picnics.

KONKO CHURCH CHURCH

Map p315 (415-931-0453; www.konkofaith.org; 1909 Bush St; 8:30am-6pm Mon-Sat, to 1pm Sun; 1, 2, 3) Inside this low-roofed, high-modernist church, you'll find a handsome blond-wood sanctuary with lofty beamed ceiling, vintage photographs of Konko events dating back 80 years, and friendly Reverend Joanne Tolosa, who'll answer questions about spirituality, the church or its Shinto-inspired beliefs, then leave you to contemplation. On New Year's Day, visitors jot down an appreciation, apology and request on a slip of paper, affix it to a tree and receive blessings with sacred rice wine.

HAAS-LILIENTHAL HOUSE HISTORIC BUILDING

(415-441-3000; www.sfheritage.org/haas-lilienthal-house; 2007 Franklin St; adult/child $8/5; noon-3pm Wed & Sat, 11am-4pm Sun; ; 1, 10, 12, 19, 27, 47, 49) A grand Queen Anne–style Victorian, its original 1886 splendor intact, this family mansion looks like a Clue game come to life – Colonel Mustard could certainly have committed murder with a rope in the dark-wood ballroom, or Miss Scarlet with a candlestick in the red-velvet parlor. One-hour tours are led by docents devoted to Victoriana. Kids get to play with Victorian toys and a vintage toy train. Sundays the society leads neighborhood **walking tours** (415-441-3000; www.sfheritage.org/walking-tours/; adult/child $8/5; 12:30pm Sun).

AUDIUM SOUND SCULPTURE

Map p315 (415-771-1616; www.audium.org; 1616 Bush St; admission $20; performances 8:30pm Fri & Sat, arrive by 8:15pm; 2, 3, 19, 38, 47, 49, California St) Sit in total darkness as Stan Shaff plays his compositions of sounds emitted by his sound chamber, which sometimes degenerate into 1970s sci-fi sound effects before resolving into oddly endearing Moog synthesizer wheezes. The Audium was specifically sculpted in 1962 to produce bizarre acoustic effects and eerie soundscapes that only a true stoner could enjoy for two solid hours.

EATING

Japan Center is packed with satisfactory Japanese restaurants; noodle shops line the Buchanan St Mall (outdoors), north of Post St. Upper Fillmore St has diverse, quality restaurants north of Sutter St. Along Hyde St, on Russian Hill, climb to prime picnic spots and neighborhood bistros, but if walking afterward seems anticlimactic, hop a cable car.

Nob & Russian Hills

CHEESE PLUS DELI $

Map p316 (www.cheeseplus.com; 2001 Polk St; sandwiches $9; 10am-7pm; 10, 12, 19, 27, 47, 49) Foodies, rejoice: here's one deli where they won't blink if you request aged, drunken chèvre instead of provolone on your sandwich. The specialty is classic grilled cheese, made with artisan *fromage du jour,* but for $9 get a salad loaded with oven-roasted turkey and sustainable Niman Ranch bacon.

ZA PIZZA $

Map p316 (415-771-3100; www.zapizzasf.com; 1919 Hyde St; pizza slice $4-5; noon-10pm Sun-Wed, to 11pm Thu-Sat; 41, 45, Powell-Hyde) You don't get gourmet, cornmeal-dusted, thin-crust slices like this every day. Pizza lovers brave uphill climbs for pizza piled with fresh toppings, a pint of Anchor Steam and a cozy bar setting – all for under $10.

SWENSEN'S ICE CREAM $

Map p316 (www.swensensicecream.com; 1999 Hyde St; ice-cream cones from $3.75; noon-10pm Tue-Thu & Sun, to 11pm Fri & Sat; 41, 45, Powell-Hyde) Bite into your ice-cream cone, and get an instant brain-freeze and hit of nostalgia besides. Oooh-ouch, that peppermint stick really takes you back, doesn't it? The 16oz root-beer floats are the 1950s version of Prozac, but the classic hot fudge sundae is pure serotonin with sprinkles on top.

★SWAN OYSTER DEPOT SEAFOOD $$

Map p316 (415-673-1101; www.sfswanoysterdepot.com/; 1517 Polk St; dishes $8-24; 10:30am-5:30pm Mon-Sat; 1, 19, 47, 49, California St) Superior flavor without the superior attitude of typical seafood restaurants – Swan's downside is an inevitable wait for the few stools at the vintage lunch counter, but the upside of high turnover is incredibly fresh seafood.

Sunny days, place your order to go, browse Polk St boutiques, then breeze past the line to pick up crab salad with Louie dressing and the obligatory top-grade

RESTAURANTS ON THE CABLE CAR LINE

For a romantic, only-in-SF night on the town, book a table at one of several cozy neighborhood restaurants along the cable-car lines on Nob or Russian Hill. Make reservations and leave plenty of time for transport – cable-car service can be erratic – and if running late, taxi there, cable home. Just make sure you board the correct line, going in the right direction.

Cocotte (Map p316; ☎415-292-4415; www.cocottesf.com; 1521 Hyde St; dinner mains $21-32; ⏰5:30-9:30pm Tue-Sat; 🚌10, 12, 🚋Powell-Hyde) This tiny French bistro on Russian Hill has an open kitchen, lined with copper pots, where the French-born chef-owner creates fabulous lobster salad, hearty coq au vin, and the house-specialty rotisserie chicken, served with dipping sauces, including an outstanding mushroom-cream demi-glace that merits an extra serving of bread to mop up the plate.

Stone's Throw (Map p316; ☎415-796-2901; stonesthrowsf.com; 1896 Hyde St; brunch mains $13-19, dinner $22-29; ⏰5:30-10:30pm Tue-Thu, to 11pm Fri & Sat, brunch Sun 11am-2pm, dinner 5:30-10pm; 🍷; 🚌41, 45, 🚋Powell-Hyde) This New American storefront bistro has great service – staff are alums of some of SF's top houses – and gets busiest for brunch – yum, those mimosas and lavender-glazed doughnuts! – but we also love it at dinner, when dishes include standout duck-liver paté with warm pretzels, and squid-ink pasta.

Seven Hills (Map p316; ☎415-775-1550; www.sevenhillssf.com; 1550 Hyde St; mains $19-31; ⏰5:30-9:30pm Sun-Thu, to 10pm Fri & Sat; 🚌10, 12, 🚋Powell-Hyde) Chef Anthony Florian studied in California with some of the state's great chefs, and in Italy too. His market-driven menu showcases the best of both, with elegantly simple dishes, made with all-California olive oils. The housemade pastas are outstanding, notably ravioli uovo and spaghetti with homemade pancetta.

Zarzuela (Map p316; ☎415-346-0800; 2000 Hyde St; mains $16-24; ⏰5:30-10pm Tue-Thu, to 10:30pm Fri & Sat; 🚌41, 45, 🚋Powell-Hyde) One of Russian Hill's bright stars, Zarzuela's real Spanish tapas include terrific paella and garlic-prawns, plus unusual dishes such as braised quail and Madrid-style tripe. Ocher-washed walls and terracotta tile set a simple backdrop for the dynamic cooking. Alas, no reservations: come early or expect 30- to 45-minute waits at peak times.

Venticello (Map p316; ☎415-922-2545; venticello.com; 1257 Taylor St; mains $19-33; ⏰5:30-10pm; 🚌1, 🚋Powell-Hyde) To enter Venticello's two-story-high dining room, you descend via staircase – which may be why so many of the Nob Hill regulars dress up for this otherwise casual neighborhood Italian bistro: everyone sees you arrive. Standouts include spaghetti carbonara, risotto and anything from the wood-fired oven, especially pizzas.

oysters with mignonette sauce. Hike or bus up to George Sterling Park (p132) for superlative seafood with ocean views.

LEOPOLD'S — GERMAN $$

Map p316 (www.leopoldssf.com; 2400 Polk St; mains $18-22; ⏰dinner 5:30-10pm Sun-Thu, to 10:30pm Fri & Sat, brunch 11am-2:30pm Sat & Sun; 🚌19, 41, 45, 47, 49) Polk St was traditionally called Polkstrasse by German immigrants. Leopold's pays homage with lip-schmacking Austrian-German Alpine cooking, served beer-hall style at pinewood booths. The 20-something crowd gets deafeningly loud, but after a boot full of beer you'll hardly notice. Hearty specialties include chicken soup with dumplings, goulash, schnitzel, flatbread and housemade salumi – *lecker!* No reservations; expect waits.

★ACQUERELLO — CALIFORNIAN, ITALIAN $$$

Map p316 (☎415-567-5432; www.acquerello.com; 1722 Sacramento St; 3-/5-course menu $82/110; ⏰5:30-9:30pm Tue-Sat; 🚌1, 19, 47, 49, 🚋California St) A converted chapel is a fitting location for a meal that'll turn Italian culinary purists into true believers in Cal-Italian cuisine. Chef Suzette Gresham's generous pastas and ingenious seasonal meat dishes include heavenly quail salad, devilish lobster *panzerotti* and venison loin chops. Suave maitre d'hotel Giancarlo Paternini indulges every whim, even providing black-linen napkins if you're worried about lint.

An anteroom where brides once steadied nerves is now lined with limited-production Italian vintages.

Japantown & Pacific Heights

CROWN & CRUMPET — CAFÉ $

Map p315 (415-771-4252; www.crownandcrumpet.com; 1746 Post St; dishes $9-12, afternoon tea $28; 11am-5pm daily; 2, 3, 22, 38) In this café inside New People (p143), designer style and rosy cheer usher tea time into the 21st century: girlfriends rehash hot dates over scones with strawberries and tea, and dads and daughters clink porcelain cups after choosing from 24 kinds of tea. Weekend reservations recommended.

NIJIYA SUPERMARKET — JAPANESE $

Map p315 (415-563-1901; www.nijiya.com; 1737 Post St; 10am-8pm daily; 2, 3, 22, 38) Picnic under the Peace Pagoda with sushi or teriyaki bento boxes fresh from the deli counter, swig Berkeley-brewed Takara Sierra Cold sake from the drinks aisle and have change from a $20 for mango-ice-cream-filled *mochi* (chewy Japanese cakes with savory or sweet fillings). Tip: by the door, there's a microwave for customers' use.

BUN MEE — VIETNAMESE, SANDWICHES $

Map p315 (415-800-7698; www.bunmee.co; 2015 Fillmore St; sandwiches $7-12; 11am-9pm daily; 1, 3, 22) Lines out the door are evidence of Bun Mee's delicious, if tiny, Vietnamese sandwiches: order two. Five-spice chicken is the classic, but the pork belly is sublime. Rice bowls and salads present alternatives. The tiny storefront packs; consider picnicking at nearby Alta Plaza Park.

GROVE — AMERICAN $

Map p315 (415-474-1419; www.thegrovesf.com; 2016 Fillmore St; dishes $9-13; 7am-11pm; 1, 3, 22) Rough-hewn recycled wood, bric-a-brac in the rafters and a stone fireplace lend a ski-lodge aesthetic to this Fillmore St café, where Pacific Heights locals recover from hangovers with made-to-order breakfasts, hunch over laptops with salads and sandwiches, and gab fireside with warm-from-the-oven cookies and hot cocoa. There's another branch in the **Marina** (Map p300; 415-474-4843; www.thegrovesf.com; 2250 Chestnut St; 7am-11pm Mon-Fri, 8am-11pm Sat & Sun).

BENKYODO — JAPANESE $

Map p315 (415-922-1244; www.benkyodocompany.com; 1747 Buchanan St; mochi $1.50; 8am-5pm Mon-Sat; 2, 3, 22, 38) The perfect retro lunch counter cheerfully serves an old-school egg-salad sandwich or pastrami for $5, but the real draw is the $1.15 *mochi* made in-house daily – come early for popular varieties of green tea and chocolate-filled strawberry. Cash only.

SIFT DESSERT BAR — BAKERY $

Map p315 (siftdessertbar.com; 2411 California St; cupcakes $3.50; 10am-10pm; 1, 22) Heavy with buttercream frosting, the fabulous cupcakes here come in exotic combinations – no surprise, since Sift won the second season of Food Network's *Cupcake Wars*.

UDON MUGIZO — JAPANESE $$

Map p315 (415-931-3118; Suite 215, 1581 Webster St; mains $10-15; 11:30am-2pm & 5:30-9:30pm Mon-Fri, 11:30am-3pm & 5-9:30pm Sat; 11:30am-3pm & 5:30-9pm Sun; 22, 38) A change from the usual ramen, Mugizo serves only udon noodles – all homemade – in unexpected combinations such as sea urchin in cream sauce, plus copious donburi rice plates. The unusual flavors are more inventive than at traditional Japantown noodle joints, but the small kitchen means limited sushi.

TATAKI — JAPANESE $$

(415-931-1182; www.tatakisushibar.com; 2815 California St; dishes $12-20; 11:30am-2pm & 5:30-9:45pm Mon-Thu, 11:30am-2pm & 5:30-10:30pm Fri, 5-10:30pm Sat, 5-9:30pm Sun; 1, 24) Pioneering sushi chefs Kin Lui and Raymond Ho rescue the oceans with sustainable delicacies: silky Arctic char drizzled with yuzu-citrus replaces at-risk wild salmon; the Golden State Roll is a local hero, featuring spicy, line-caught scallop, Pacific tuna, organic-apple slivers and edible 24-karat gold. It's tiny, off-the-beaten-path, and accepts no reservations, but the quality is better than in Japantown.

PIZZERIA DELFINA — PIZZA $$

Map p315 (415-440-1189; www.pizzeriadelfina.com; 2406 California St; pizzas $12-17; 11:30am-10pm Sun, Mon, Wed & Thu, 5-10pm

Tue, 11:30am-11pm Fri & Sat; ; 1, 3, 22) Pizzeria Delfina derives success from simplicity: fresh-from-the-farm ingredients in copious salads and house-cured meats on tender-to-the-tooth, thin-crusted pizzas – this is one place you actually *want* anchovies on your pizza. Inside gets loud; sit on the sidewalk. Expect waits at peak times.

IZAKAYA KOU SUSHI, IZAKAYA **$$**

Map p315 (415-441-9294; www.izakayakou.com; 1560 Fillmore St; dishes $6-12; 5:30-11pm Tue-Thu, to midnight Sat, to 10pm Sun; 22, 38) Finding good sushi means leaving Japan Center mall. This is our favorite for its lively bar and artful presentations of sushi, small plates and rice bowls, which integrate Western ingredients, like bacon and parsley, for deliciously different spins on classic beer-hall food.

WOODHOUSE FISH CO SEAFOOD **$$**

Map p315 (www.woodhousefish.com; 1914 Fillmore St; mains $16-32; 11:30am-10pm; 2, 3, 22) If being near the ocean makes you crave fish but you (rightly) don't want to eat at the Wharf, Woodhouse's New England–style seafood provides an alternative, with no-fuss meals of crab and lobster rolls, fried clams, fish and chips and traditional SF-style *cioppino* (seafood stew). It has $1 oysters on Tuesdays. No reservations. There's another branch in the **Castro** (Map p312; www.woodhousefish.com; 2073 Market St; 11:30am-9:30pm).

★**STATE BIRD PROVISIONS** CALIFORNIAN **$$$**

Map p315 (415-795-1272; statebirdsf.com; 1529 Fillmore St; dishes $9-26; 5:30-10pm Sun-Thu, to 11pm Fri & Sat; 22, 38) Even before winning back-to-back James Beard Awards, State Bird attracted lines for 5:30pm seatings not seen since the Dead played neighboring Fillmore Auditorium. The draw is a thrilling play on dim sum, wildly inventive with seasonal-regional ingredients and esoteric flavors, like fennel pollen or garum. Plan to order multiple dishes. Book exactly 60 days ahead.

Also consider a table at **The Progress** (Map p315; 415-673-1294; theprogress-sf.com; 1525 Fillmore St; 6-course meal $65; 5:30-10pm Sun-Thu, to 11pm Fri & Sat; 22, 38), the adjacent family-style banquet restaurant by the same team, where you order six courses to share. It too won a James Beard Award (Best Restaurant West, 2015), and is equally sublime – and hard to book. As of this writing, they accepted reservations 30 days ahead, but were considering extending bookings further out: check the website for current details.

OUT THE DOOR VIETNAMESE **$$$**

Map p315 (415-923 9575; www.outthedoors.com; 2232 Bush St; mains lunch $10-20, dinner $18-36; 11am-4:30pm Mon-Fri, 9am-3pm Sat & Sun, 5:30-10pm Mon-Sat, 5:30-9:30pm Sun; 2, 3, 22) Offshoot of the famous Slanted Door (p92), this casual outpost jump-starts early shopping with stellar French beignets and Vietnamese coffee, or salty-sweet Dungeness crab frittatas. Lunchtime's rice plates and noodles are replaced at dinner with savory clay-pot meats and fish. Make reservations.

DRINKING & NIGHTLIFE

Nob & Russian Hills

★**TONGA ROOM** LOUNGE

Map p316 (reservations 415-772-5278; www.tongaroom.com; Fairmont San Francisco, 950 Mason St; cover $5-7; 5:30-11:30pm Sun, Wed & Thu, 5pm-12:30am Fri & Sat; 1, California St, Powell-Mason, Powell-Hyde) Tonight's San Francisco weather: 100% chance of tropical rainstorms every 20 minutes, but only around the top-40 band playing on the island in the middle of the indoor pool – you're safe in your grass hut. For a more powerful hurricane, order one in a plastic coconut. Come before 8pm to beat the cover charge.

THE BIG 4 BAR

Map p316 (www.big4restaurant.com; 1075 California St; bar 11:30am-midnight; ; 1, California St) A classic address for swank cocktails, the Big 4 is named for the railroad barons who once dominated Nob Hill society, and its decor pays tribute with opulence – oak-paneled walls, studded green leather and a big mahogany bar that makes great martinis. The attached restaurant is also lovely – if pricy.

HI-LO CLUB BAR

Map p316 (http://hilosf.com; 1423 Polk St; 4pm-2am Mon-Sat; 1, 19, 47, 49, California St) A must-visit on any Polk St pub crawl, the Hi-Lo plays trashy-fancy, with peeling paint, tarnished-tin ceilings and distressed-wood floors that make it resemble a candlelit squat. The classic cocktails showcase lesser-known craft spirits, never brand names – don't ask for Absolut! – and the soundtrack is vintage soul, rock and punk. Come early; otherwise it's packed – and loud.

AMÉLIE BAR

Map p316 (☎415-292-6916; www.ameliesf.com; 1754 Polk St; ⊙5pm-2am; 🚌1, 10, 12, 19, 27, 47, 49, 🚋Powell-Hyde, California St) This *très* cool neighborhood wine bar, with sexy lipstick-red counters, serves well-priced vintages – happy-hour (5pm to 7pm) flights of three cost just $10 – and delish cheese and charcuterie plates. Weekends get too crowded (make reservations); weekdays it's an ideal spot to cozy up with your sweetheart.

HARPER & RYE COCKTAIL BAR

Map p316 (web.harperandrye.com; 1695 Polk St; ⊙4pm-2am; 🚌1, 19, 47, 49, 🚋California St) Small batch rye, craft cocktails and artisinal beers are the specialties at this Polk St bar, styled out with floor-to-ceiling weathered wood and exposed steel. The upstairs mezzanine provides a stellar vantage point over an often shoulder-to-shoulder crowd of well-heeled 20- and 30-somethings. We recommend the punch jars, but careful! – they serve four, not one.

TOP OF THE MARK BAR

Map p316 (www.topofthemark.com; 999 California St; cover $10-15; ⊙4:30-11.30pm Sun-Thu, 4.30pm-12.30am Fri & Sat; 🚌1, 🚋California St) So what if it's touristy? Nothing beats twirling in the clouds in your best cocktail dress on the city's highest dance floor. Fridays are best, when a full jazz orchestra plays, but there's music other nights, too: call ahead to make sure. Expect $15 drinks.

CINCH GAY BAR

Map p316 (http://cinchsf.com; 1723 Polk St; ⊙9am-2am Mon-Fri, from 6am Sat & Sun; 🚌1, 19, 27, 47, 49, 🚋California St) The last of the old-guard Polk St gay bars still has an old-timey saloon vibe, with pool, pinball, free popcorn and a big smokers patio where you get yelled at if you spark a joint (but people do it anyway).

Japantown & Pacific Heights

SOCIAL STUDY CAFÉ, BAR

Map p315 (www.socialstudysf.com; 1795 Geary Blvd; ⊙5-11pm Mon, from 10am Tue-Sun; 📶; 🚌22, 38) Part café, part bar, Social Study draws an upbeat collegiate crowd for strong coffee and good beer, wi-fi and board games. An alternative to booze bars, it's ideal for a post-movie tête-à-tête or catch-up time with friends.

JANE CAFÉ

Map p315 (www.itsjane.com; 2123 Fillmore St; ⊙7am-6pm; 📶; 🚌1, 3, 22) Pac Heights girlfriends gab at side-by-side tables, over fair-trade coffee, housemade pastries and gorgeous salads, while freelance workers hunch over their laptops at this upbeat and happening café, a great spot for a quick nosh before shopping surrounding boutiques.

1300 ON FILLMORE LOUNGE

Map p315 (www.1300fillmore.com; 1300 Fillmore St; ⊙4:30-10pm Sun-Thu, to midnight Fri & Sat; 🚌22, 31, 38) Reviving swank south of Geary, 1300 on Fillmore's enormous heavy doors open into a double-high living-room space, with Oriental rugs, tufted-leather sofas and floor-to-ceiling, black-and-white portraits of jazz luminaries. On Fridays, jazz plays at 8:30pm. There's good Southern-inspired food, and on Sundays gospel brunch (reservations required) – big with the after-church crowd.

HARRY'S BAR BAR

Map p315 (www.harrysbarsf.com; 2020 Fillmore St; ⊙4pm-2am Mon-Fri, from 11am Sat & Sun; 🚌1, 3, 22) Cap off a shopping trip at Harry's mahogany bar with freshly muddled *mojitos* or Bloody Marys made properly with horseradish. A Pacific Heights mainstay, Harry's appeals to aging debutantes who love getting politely hammered.

☆ ENTERTAINMENT

FILLMORE AUDITORIUM LIVE MUSIC

Map p315 (☎415-346-6000; http://thefillmore.com; 1805 Geary Blvd; admission $20-50; ⊙box office 10am-3pm Sun, plus 30min before doors open on show nights until 10pm; 🚌22, 38) Jimi Hendrix, Janis Joplin, the Doors – they all played the Fillmore. Now you might catch the Indigo Girls, Duran Duran or Tracy Chapman in the historic 1250-capacity, standing-room theater (if you're polite and lead with the hip, you might squeeze up to the stage). Don't miss the priceless collection of psychedelic posters in the upstairs gallery.

SHEBA PIANO LOUNGE JAZZ

Map p315 (☎415-440-7414; www.shebapianolounge.com; 1419 Fillmore St; ⏰5pm-midnight, later on weekends) One of the last remaining jazz clubs on Fillmore, Sheba doubles as a good Ethiopian restaurant, but it's the bar we most like, where combos perform nightly from 8pm. Arrive early to score the little table by the fireplace.

BOOM BOOM ROOM LIVE MUSIC, DANCING

Map p315 (☎415-673-8000; www.boomboomblues.com; 1601 Fillmore St; cover varies; ⏰4pm-2am Tue-Sun; 🚌22, 38) Jumping since the '30s, Boom Boom is a relic from the Fillmore's heyday – dig the old photos lining the walls. The black-box room ain't fancy – just a bar, stage, tables and dance floor – but rocks six nights a week with blues, soul and New Orleans funk by top touring talent. Shows start 'round 9pm.

SUNDANCE KABUKI CINEMA CINEMA

Map p315 (☎415-346-3243; www.sundancecinemas.com; 1881 Post St; adult $10.50-15, child $9.75-13; 🚌2, 3, 22, 38) 🍃 Cinema-going at its best. Reserve a stadium seat, belly up to the bar, and order wine and surprisingly good food to enjoy during the film. A multiplex initiative by Robert Redford's Sundance Institute, Kabuki features big-name flicks and festivals – and it's green, with recycled-fiber seating, reclaimed-wood decor and local chocolates and booze. Validated parking available. Note: expect a $1.50 to $3 surcharge to see a movie not preceded by commercials.

ENCORE KARAOKE LOUNGE KARAOKE LOUNGE

Map p316 (☎415-775-0442; www.encorekaraokesf.com; 2nd fl, 1550 California St; ⏰3pm-2am, karaoke from 8pm Mon-Thu, from 5pm Fri-Sun; 🚌1, 19, 27, 47, 49, 🚋California St) What a dump. Still, it's hard to resist this throwback-to-1970s rumpus room, crammed with low-slung, swiveling stitched-Naugahyde chairs and a happy-tipsy crowd of raucous karaoke-philes who cheer when you nail it but talk when you suck.

SHOPPING

Near Russian Hill, Polk St (from California St to Broadway) is great for browsing indie boutiques. Japantown is packed with kitschy-fun gift shops and authentic Japanese wares. Fillmore St, in Pacific Heights, caters to an upmarket demographic (hence its nickname, Specific Whites); there's fab shopping between Bush and Jackson Sts – continue to Broadway for brilliant bay views. For more high-end indie boutiques, head to Presidio Heights – Sacramento St, west of Presidio Ave.

Russian Hill

★PICNIC CLOTHING, HOMEWARES

Map p316 (www.picnicsf.com; 1806-8 Polk St; ⏰11am-8pm Tue-Sat, noon-6pm Sun-Mon; 🚌19, 27, 47, 49, 🚋Powell-Hyde) The kind of boutique young moms hope to find when they're out for a girly-girl afternoon, Picnic caters to women of childbearing age, who say c-u-u-u-t-e! to the pretty tops, smart skirts, baby clothes, children's toys, hand-crafted jewelry, cozy home decor, stationery, handcrafted woodwork and SF-specific gifts emblazoned with images of the GG Bridge.

STUDIO GIFTS, ARTS & CRAFTS

Map p316 (☎415-931-3130; www.studiogallerysf.com; 1641 Pacific Ave; ⏰11am-7pm Mon, Thu & Fri, to 6pm Sat & Sun, by appointment Tue & Wed; 🚌1, 19, 47, 49, 🚋California St) Spiff up your pad with locally made art at great prices. For a visual remembrance of your visit to SF, Studio is the place, with a mix of prints and fine art of local haunts by Elizabeth Ashcroft and architectural etchings by Alice Gibbons, plus paintings of local land- and city-scapes. Monthly receptions are open to the public.

VELVET DA VINCI JEWELRY

Map p316 (www.velvetdavinci.com; 2015 Polk St; ⏰11am-6pm Tue-Sat, to 4pm Sun; 🚌10, 12, 19, 27, 47, 49, 🚋Powell-Hyde) At this jewelry and sculpture gallery, you can see the ideas behind the handiwork: Lynn Christiansen puts food obsession into a purse resembling whipped cream, and Tom Hill makes evident his fascination with birds in wire sculptures (note the fire escape outside). Eight annual shows bring an ever-changing collection of contemporary-art jewelry from around the world.

MOLTE COSE CLOTHING, ACCESSORIES

Map p316 (www.moltecose.com; 2036 Polk St; ⌚11am-6:30pm Mon-Fri, 11am-6pm Sat, noon-5pm Sun; 🚌10, 12, 19, 47, 49) Thrilling for browsers, Molte Cose's imaginative, unpredictable collection of vintage bric-a-brac ranges from French stemware to Royal typewriters that double as set decoration for displays of pretty-frilly dresses, elegant accessories, cufflinks, shaving kits, hip flasks, super-cute kids' gear, plus locally made candles by ElizabethW.

CRIS CLOTHING, ACCESSORIES

Map p316 (☎415-474-1191; 2056 Polk St; ⌚11am-6pm Mon-Sat, from noon Sun; 🚌10, 12, 19, 47, 49, 🚋Powell-Hyde) The sharpest windows on Polk St are consistently at Cris, a consignment shop specializing in contemporary high-end fashion by big-name designers like Balenciaga, Lanvin, Marni, Alexander Wang and Chloé, all in beautiful condition and at amazing prices, carefully curated by an elegant Frenchwoman with an eagle's eye and duchess' taste. Also great for handbags by Prada, Dolce & Gabbana, yada-yada-yada...

RELOVE VINTAGE

Map p316 (shoprelove.com; 1815 Polk St; ⌚11am-7pm Tue-Sat, to 6pm Sun, noon-6pm Mon; 🚌1, 10, 12, 19, 27, 47, 49, 🚋California St) Find a snappy new outfit at this fab vintage store, noteworthy for its colorful, eccentric collection. Expect fur, spiked leather, silk kimonos, vintage Ts, formal party dresses – looks that spice yours, without ruining your economy.

JOHNSON LEATHERS LEATHER

Map p316 (www.johnsonleather.com; 1833 Polk St; ⌚11am-6pm Tue-Sat; 🚌10, 12, 19, 27, 47, 49) If you've been looking for a new leather jacket – the ideal garment in chilly SF – Johnson custom-tailors classic cuts, built to last. Their materials and craftsmanship are so reliable, so durable, they outfit both the SFPD's motorcycle patrolmen *and* the Hell's Angels.

GOOD VIBRATIONS ADULT TOYS

Map p316 (www.goodvibes.com; 1620 Polk St; ⌚shop 10am-9pm Sun-Thu, to 10pm Fri & Sat, museum 12:30-6:30pm daily; 🚌1, 19, 47, 49, 🚋California St) Good Vibrations made history as the first women-owned sex-shop chain. This branch is special for its broad selection (no pun) of shame-free sex toys, and on-site vibrator museum (free), where famous local sexologist Dr Carol Queen leads tours third Sundays of the month. Check the website for workshops and events.

Japantown & Pacific Heights

★NEW PEOPLE CLOTHING, GIFTS

Map p315 (www.newpeopleworld.com; 1746 Post St; ⌚noon-7pm Mon-Sat, to 6pm Sun; 🚌2, 3, 22, 38) A three-story emporium devoted to Japanese pop culture, New People carries Japantown's most interesting clothing. At **Maruq**, you'll find Japanese streetwear from Tokyo's Shibuya and Harajuku districts (locale of independent-designer boutiques), plus Rilakkuma bear toys. Try on Lolita fashions (imagine *Alice in Wonderland*) at 2nd-floor **Baby the Stars Shine Bright** and traditional Japanese footwear emblazoned with contemporary graphics at **Sou-Sou**.

Afterward, recharge over tea at Crown & Crumpet (p139).

JAPAN CENTER MALL

Map p315 (www.sfjapantown.org; 1625 Post St; ⌚10am-midnight; 🚌2, 3, 22, 38) Entering this oddly charming mall is like walking onto a 1960s Japanese movie set – the fake-rock waterfall, indoor wooden pedestrian bridges, rock gardens and curtained wooden restaurant entryways have hardly aged since 1968. The mall covers three square blocks but you'll also find Japantown shops outside, along Buchanan and Post Sts.

NEST HOUSEWARES, GIFTS

Map p315 (www.nestsf.com; 2300 Fillmore St; ⌚10:30am-6pm Mon-Sat, from 11am Sun; 🚌1, 3, 10, 22, 24) Make your nest cozier with one-of-a-kind accessories from this well-curated collection, including Provençal quilts, beaded jewelry, craft kits and papier-mâché trophy heads for the kids' room, and mesmerizing century-old bric-a-brac and toys.

BENEFIT BEAUTY PRODUCTS

Map p315 (www.benefitcosmetics.com; 2117 Fillmore St; ⌚9am-7pm Mon-Fri, 10am-6:30pm Sat, to 6pm Sun; 🚌1, 3, 22) Get cheeky with BeneTint, dab-on liquid blush from roses, or raise eyebrows with Brow Zings tinted wax – two of Benefit's signature products invented in San Francisco by the twin-sister team. Surgery is so LA: in SF, overnight Angelinas swear by LipPlump and dark-eye-circles are cured with Ooh-La Lift. There's another in the **Marina** (Map p300; ☎415-567-1173; www.benefitcosmetics.com; 2219 Chestnut St; ⏰10am-7pm Sun-Tue, to 8pm Wed-Fri, 9am-7pm Sat; 🚌28, 30, 43).

BROOKLYN CIRCUS MEN'S CLOTHING, SHOES

Map p315 (thebkcircus.com; 1521 Fillmore St; ⏰noon-7pm Tue-Sat, to 6pm Sun; 🚌22, 38) Stylish men who skew casual appreciate Brooklyn Circus' classic American aesthetic. Find wool-and-leather varsity-letter jackets, snappy shirts and hats and quality US-made shoes, including high-top leather PF Flyers and Red Wing boots.

ALICE & OLIVIA WOMEN'S CLOTHING

Map p315 (www.aliceandolivia.com; 2259 Fillmore St; ⏰11am-7pm Mon-Fri, 10am-6pm Sat, 11am-6pm Sun; 🚌1, 3, 10, 22, 24) NYC-based designer Stacey Bendet makes perfect party dresses and gorgeous hand-beaded gowns for pretty girls prepping for the ball. Racks display only size 2; larger sizes are kept hidden in back like Cinderella.

MARGARET O'LEARY CLOTHING, ACCESSORIES

Map p315 (☎415-771-9982; www.margaretoleary.com; 2400 Fillmore St; ⏰10am-6pm Mon-Sat, 11am-6pm Sun; 🚌1, 3, 10, 22, 24) At her flagship store, San Francisco local Margaret O'Leary showcases whisper-light cardigans of cashmere, organic cotton or eco-minded bamboo yarn.

MUDPIE CHILDREN

Map p315 (www.mudpie-sf.com; 2185 Fillmore St; ⏰11am-5:30pm Mon-Fri, to 6pm Sat & Sun; 👪; 🚌1, 3, 22) Outfit your kids like those in nearby mansions with cute-as-a-button clothing, teddy bears, tea-party sets, matchbox cars and SF-centric books, including the 1962 illustrated classic *This Is San Francisco* – a must-read for curious kids wondering where you've been.

KINOKUNIYA BOOKS & STATIONERY BOOKS

Map p315 (☎415-567-7625; www.kinokuniya.com/us; Japan Center, 1581 Webster St; ⏰10:30am-8pm daily; 🚌22, 38) Like warriors in a showdown, the bookstore, stationery and manga divisions of Kinokuniya compete for your attention. Only you can decide where your loyalties lie: with stunning photography books and Harajuku fashion mags upstairs, vampire comics downstairs or the stationery department's *washi* paper, supersmooth Sakura gel pens and pig notebooks with the motto 'what lovely friends, they will bring happy.'

SANKO COOKING SUPPLY CERAMICS, HOUSEWARES

Map p315 (www.shop.sankosf.com; 1758 Buchanan St; ⏰9:30am-5:30pm Mon-Sat, 11:30am-5pm Sun; 🚌2, 3, 22, 38) The elegant owner serves you tea while you browse aisle upon aisle of Japanese ceramics, teapots, sake sets, tableware and cookware at this extraordinary Japantown shop. Where else, we ask, can you find restaurant-grade plastic sushi suitable for display?

SOKO HARDWARE HOUSEWARES

Map p315 (☎415-931-5510; 1698 Post St; ⏰9am-5:30pm Mon-Sat; 🚌2, 3, 22, 38) *Ikebana,* bonsai, tea ceremony and Zen rock-garden supplies are all here at fair prices.

KATSURA GARDEN BONSAI

Map p315 (☎415-931-6209; 1825 Post St, Japan Center; ⏰10am-5:30pm Mon-Sat, 11am-5pm Sun; 🚌2, 3, 22, 38) For a special gift, consider a bonsai. Katsura Garden will set you up with a miniature juniper that looks like it grew on a windswept molehill, or a stunted maple that next autumn will shed five tiny, perfect red leaves.

ICHIBAN KAN GIFTS

Map p315 (☎415-409-0472; www.ichibankanusa.com; Suite 540, 22 Peace Plaza, Japan Center; ⏰10am-8pm; 🚌2, 3, 22, 38) It's a wonder you got this far in life without penguin soy-sauce dispensers, 'Men's Pocky' chocolate-covered pretzels, extra-spiky Japanese hair wax, soap dishes with feet and the ultimate in gay gag gifts, the handy 'Closet Case' – all for under $5.

KOHSHI GIFTS

Map p315 (www.kohshisf.com; Suite 355, Japan Center, West Mall, 1737 Post St; ⏰11am-7pm Wed-Mon; 🚌2, 3, 22, 38) Fragrant Japanese incense for every purpose, from long-burning sandalwood for meditation to cinnamon-tinged Gentle Smile to atone for laundry left too long, plus lovely gift ideas: gentle charcoal soap, cups that look like crumpled paper, and purple Daruma figurines for making wishes.

JONATHAN ADLER HOUSEWARES

Map p315 (www.jonathanadler.com; 2133 Fillmore St; 10am-6pm Mon-Sat, noon-5pm Sun; 1, 3, 22) Vases with handlebar mustaches and cookie jars labeled 'Quaaludes' may seem like holdovers from a Big Sur bachelor pad c 1974, but they're snappy interior inspirations from California pop potter (and *Top Design* judge) Jonathan Adler. Don't worry whether that leather pig foot-stool matches your midcentury couch – as Adler says, 'Minimalism is a bummer.'

ZINC DETAILS HOUSEWARES

Map p315 (www.zincdetails.com; 1905 Fillmore St; 10am-6pm Tue-Sat, noon-6pm Sun; 2, 3, 22) Pacific Heights chic meets Japantown mod at Zinc Details, with items like orange lacquerware salad-tossers, a sake dispenser that looks like a Zen garden boulder and bird-shaped soy dispensers, all noteworthy for their smart designs and artful presentations.

CROSSROADS CLOTHING, ACCESSORIES

Map p315 (www.crossroadstrading.com; 1901 Fillmore St; 11am-8pm Mon-Sat, to 7pm Sun; 2, 3, 22, 38) Pssst, fashionistas: you know those designers you see lining Fillmore St? Many of their creations wind up at Crossroads for a fraction of retail, thanks to Pacific Heights clotheshorses who ditch last season's wardrobe here. That's why this Crossroads is better than others in the city. For better deals, trade in your old clothes for credit.

SPORTS & ACTIVITIES

★KABUKI SPRINGS & SPA SPA

Map p315 (415-922-6000; www.kabukisprings.com; 1750 Geary Blvd; admission $25; 10am-9:45pm, co-ed Tue, women-only Wed, Fri & Sun, men-only Mon, Thu & Sat; 22, 38) Our favorite urban retreat recreates communal, clothing-optional Japanese baths. Salt-scrub in the steam room, soak in the hot pool, then cold plunge, and reheat in the sauna. Rinse and repeat. Silence is mandatory, fostering a meditative mood – if you hear the gong, it means Shhhh! Men and women alternate days, except co-ed Tuesdays (bathing suits required Tuesdays).

The look befits the location – slightly dated Japanese modern, with vaulted lacquered-wood ceilings, tile mosaics and low lighting. Plan two hours' minimum, plus a 30- to 60-minute wait at peak times (add your name to the waitlist, then go next door to slurp noodles or shop). Communal bathing discounted with massage appointments; book ahead and come on the gender-appropriate day.

REAL ESCAPE GAME GAME

Map p315 (realescapegame.com; 1746 Post St; tickets $28-33; by reservation; ; 2, 3, 22, 38) Gamers put down their screens for this real-life puzzle, developed in Japan, imported to SF. You and your teammates get locked in a room, portal to a mysterious somewhere – maybe a time-travel laboratory or cursed forest – and you've an hour to find hidden clues to discover the key to escape. Few succeed. Will you?

The Mission & Potrero Hill

Neighborhood Top Five

❶ Seeing garage doors, billboards and storefronts transformed into canvases with over 400 **Mission murals** (p150).

❷ Watching puffer fish completely immersed in a role inside the Fish Theater at **826 Valencia** (p148).

❸ Playing, tanning, picnicking and protesting entire days away in **Dolores Park** (p148).

❹ Getting a handle on California history at San Francisco's oldest building, **Mission Dolores** (p149).

❺ Joining local design, wine and chocolate already in progress in **Dogpatch's Creative Corridor** (p154).

For more detail of this area see Map p312 and p314

Explore the Mission & Potrero Hill

Get to know San Francisco from the inside out, from pirate stores to mural-covered Mission alleys. Score new looks and old books at Mission stores, and book ahead at local venues for the ultimate SF souvenir: a new talent, discovered at a hands-on cooking class, arts workshop, dancing or rock-climbing lesson. Combine epic bar crawls with taco tastings and end up salsa dancing with suave strangers at Mission clubs.

Local Life

➡ **Learn something new** Upcycle office supplies into art at SCRAP (p167), concoct edible perfumes at 18 Reasons (p168), skate the bowl at Potrero del Sol/La Raza Skatepark (p169) and tell likely stories at 826 Valencia (p148).

➡ **Do dessert** After another lap of Mission murals, you're ready for Mission Pie (p157), boozy ice cream at Humphry Slocombe (p156), tea cakes from Tartine (p157) and salted caramel eclairs from Craftsman & Wolves (p155).

➡ **Look the part** Define your own streetwise Mission style with local designers at Gravel & Gold (p164), Betabrand (p167), Nooworks (p165), Dema (p166) and Aggregate Supply (p165).

Getting There & Away

➡ **Bus** The 14 runs from Downtown to the Mission District along Mission St. The 22 runs from Mission to the Marina. Bus 49 follows Mission St and Van Ness Ave to the wharf, while the 33 links Potrero and the Mission to the Castro, the Haight and Golden Gate Park.

➡ **Streetcar** The J streetcar heads from Downtown through the Mission. The T Muni line from Downtown via SoMa stops along 3rd St between 16th and 22nd, in Potrero's Dogpatch district.

➡ **BART** Stations at 16th and 24th Sts serve the Mission.

Lonely Planet's Top Tip

The Mission is packed with bars, boutiques, galleries and clubs, and although you should be fine in the daytime, it's not always the safest area to walk alone in at night. Recruit a friend and be alert in the Mission east of Valencia, in Potrero Hill below 18th St and around deserted Dogpatch warehouses. Don't bring the bling, and don't leave belongings unattended.

Best Places to Eat

- La Taqueria (p155)
- Craftsman & Wolves (p155)
- Ichi Sushi (p158)
- Al's Place (p158)
- La Palma Mexicatessen (p159)

For reviews, see p155 ➡

Best Places to Shop

- Gravel & Gold (p164)
- Adobe Books & Backroom Gallery (p164)
- Heath Ceramics (p164)
- Needles & Pens (p164)
- Aggregate Supply (p165)

For reviews, see p164 ➡

Best Places to Drink

- %ABV (p160)
- Dalva & Hideout (p160)
- El Rio (p160)
- Elixir (p160)
- Trick Dog (p160)

For reviews, see p160 ➡

SIGHTS

The Mission is a crossroads of contradictions and at its heart is Mission St, San Francisco's faded 'miracle mile' of deco cinemas now occupied by 99¢ stores and shady characters, surrounded by colorful murals and trend-setting restaurants. West of Mission St, Valencia St has quirky boutiques, reasonable restaurants and seven-figure condos. Further east, Potrero Hill has become a bedroom community for Silicon Valley tech execs, with art and culinary schools taking over warehouses downhill in Potrero Gulch and in waterfront Dogpatch.

★BALMY ALLEY — MURALS

Map p312 (415-285-2287; www.precitaeyes.org; btwn 24th & 25th Sts; 10, 12, 14, 27, 48, B24th St Mission) Inspired by Diego Rivera's 1930s San Francisco murals and outraged by US foreign policy in Central America, 1970s Mission *muralistas* (muralists) set out to transform the political landscape, one mural-covered garage door at a time. Today, Balmy Alley murals span three decades, from an early memorial for El Salvador activist Archbishop Óscar Romero to an homage to Frida Kahlo, Georgia O'Keeffe and other trailblazing women modern artists.

The earliest works in Balmy Alley by Mujeres Muralistas (Women Muralists) and Placa ('mark-making') transformed back-alley fences into a united artistic front. Now nonprofit Precita Eyes restores these murals, commissions new ones by San Francisco artists and runs muralist-led tours that cover more than 50 Mission murals within an eight-block radius of Balmy Alley. On November 1, the annual Mission parade Día de los Muertos (Day of the Dead) begins in this alley.

★826 VALENCIA — CULTURAL SITE

Map p312 (415-642-5905; www.826valencia.org; 826 Valencia St; noon-6pm; ; 14, 33, 49, B16th St Mission, MJ) Avast, ye scurvy scalawags! If ye be shipwrecked without yer eye patch or McSweeney's literary anthology, lay down ye dubloons and claim yer booty at this here nonprofit Pirate Store. Below decks, kids be writing tall tales for dark nights a'sea, and ye can study making video games and magazines and suchlike, if that be yer dastardly inclination. Arrrr!

This eccentric pirate supply store selling eye patches, spyglasses and McSweeney's literary magazines fronts a nonprofit offering free writing workshops and tutoring for youth. 'No buccaneers! No geriatrics!' warns the sign above the vat of sand where kids rummage for buried pirates' booty. Found treasure is theirs to keep, in exchange for barter at the front counter – a drawing, maybe, or a knock-knock joke. Yank open wooden drawers organized according to pirate logic: a drawer marked 'illumination' holds candles, 'thump' is full of mallets. But leave the tub o' lard well enough alone, or you might get mopped – a pirate hazing ritual that involves a trapdoor, a mop and the element of surprise.

Before you leave, step behind the velvet curtain into the Fish Theater, where a blue-eyed and smirking (yes, smirking) puffer fish is immersed in Method acting. The ichthyoid antics may not be quite up to Sean Penn standards, but as the sign says, 'Please don't judge the fish.' Check the calendar for evening writing workshops ranging from perfume-inspired fiction to neighborhood oral history projects.

★CREATIVITY EXPLORED — ART GALLERY

Map p312 (415-863-2108; www.creativityexplored.org; 3245 16th St; donations welcome; 10am-3pm Mon-Fri, to 7pm Thu, noon-5pm Sat & Sun; ; 14, 22, 33, 49, B16th St Mission, MJ) Brave new worlds are captured in celebrated artworks destined for museum retrospectives, international shows, and even Marc Jacobs handbags and CB2 pillowcases – all by the local developmentally disabled artists who create at this nonprofit center. Intriguing themes range from monsters to Morse code, and openings are joyous celebrations with the artists, their families and rock-star fan base.

DOLORES PARK — PARK

Map p312 (http://sfrecpark.org/destination/mission-dolores-park/; Dolores St, btwn 18th & 20th Sts; ; 14, 33, 49, B16th St Mission, MJ) Semiprofessional tanning, taco picnics and a Hunky Jesus Contest at Easter: welcome to San Francisco's sunny side. Dolores Park has something for everyone, from street ball and tennis to the Mayan pyramid playground (sorry kids: no blood sacrifice allowed). Political protests and other favorite local sports happen year-round, and there are free movie nights and Mime Troupe performances in summer. Climb to the upper southwest corner for the best views of downtown, framed by palm trees.

Dolores Park was built on the site of a former Jewish cemetery used as a staging ground by Barnum and Bailey Circus, sold to the city in 1905. San Francisco's 1906 earthquake and fire violently interrupted park planning, and it remained bumpy, squishy and poorly drained until its 2015 regrading. At the corner of 20th and Church, note the fire hydrant painted gold: this little fireplug was the Mission's main water source during the 1906 earthquake and fire, and stopped the fire from spreading south of 20th St. Flat patches further down are generally reserved for soccer games, cultural festivals, candlelight vigils and ultimate Frisbee. Fair warning: secondhand highs copped near the refurbished bathroom may have you chasing the *helados* (ice-cream) cart.

MISSION DOLORES CHURCH

Map p312 (Misión San Francisco de Asís; ☎415-621-8203; www.missiondolores.org; 3321 16th St; adult/child $5/3; ⊙9am-4pm Nov-Apr, to 4:30pm May-Oct; 🚌22, 33, B16th St Mission, MJ) The city's oldest building and its namesake, whitewashed adobe Misión San Francisco de Asís was founded in 1776 and rebuilt in 1782 with conscripted Ohlone and Miwok labor – a graveyard memorial hut commemorates 5000 Ohlone and Miwok laborers who died in mission measles epidemics in 1814 and 1826. Today the modest adobe mission is overshadowed by the ornate adjoining 1913 basilica, featuring stained-glass windows of California's 21 missions.

The building's nickname, Mission Dolores (Mission of the Sorrows), was taken from a nearby lake – but it turned out to be tragically apt for native conscripts exposed

WORTH A DETOUR

ARTISTICALLY INCLINED POTRERO FLATS

San Francisco's Design District has found its edge with the arrival of avant-garde galleries, showing art that easily upstages beige sofas. Between SoMa and Potrero Hill is a gulch dotted with warehouse design-trade showrooms long overlooked, unless you were in the business of selecting window treatments. But ever since **California College of the Arts** (Wattis Institute for Contemporary Arts; Map p314; ☎Wattis Institute 415-355-9670; www.cca.edu; 360 Kansas St; ⊙during school sessions 11am-7pm Tue & Thu, to 6pm Wed, Fri & Sat; 🚌10, 19, 22, 33) FREE creatively repurposed the neighborhood's old bus depot for its campus, the emerging Potrero Flats district (also called 'SoMissPo,' for SoMa, Mission and Potrero) is becoming an eye-catcher. Stop inside CCA to discover fresh provocations in student-curated PLAySPACE and the Wattis Institute of Contemporary Arts, which recently featured Brazilian artist Cinthia Marcelle's sketches created while watching art lectures.

Head under the highway overpass to discover **SOMArts** (☎415-863-1414; www.somarts.org; 934 Brannan St; ⊙gallery noon-7pm Tue-Fri, to 5pm Sat; 🚌8, 9, 10, 19, 27, 47), a nonprofit community hub for creative thinking that hosts shows featuring edible murals, cave paintings of internet memes, and live-action Samoan tattooing performances. Just down the street, **San Francisco Center for the Book** (p169) features shows of handmade pop-up books and matchbook-sized 'zines.

The magnetic creative pull of Potrero Flats is irresistible now that several of San Francisco's leading galleries have moved to the neighborhood. **Catharine Clark Gallery** (Map p312; ☎415-399-1439; www.cclarkgallery.com; 248 Utah St; ⊙11am-6pm Tue-Sat; 🚌9, 10, 19, 22, 27, 33) FREE instigates art revolutions with Masami Teraoka's monumental paintings of geisha superheroines fending off wayward priests, while **Hosfelt Gallery** (Map p312; ☎415-495-5454; 260 Utah St; ⊙10am-6pm Tue-Sat; 🚌9, 10, 22, 27, 33) mesmerizes visitors with Emil Lukas' drawings made by thousands of fly larvae dragging ink across paper. Meanwhile, collage artists at **Jack Fischer Gallery** bring mesmerizing interior worlds to life inside a warehouse space off Hwy 101. Friendly art debates continue around the corner at **Thee Parkside** (Map p314; ☎415-252-1330; www.theeparkside.com; 1600 17th St; ⊙2pm-2am; 🚌10, 19, 22), where bikers and art students converge for cheap drinks, parking-lot BBQs, and vintage photo-booth photo-ops. Once bluegrass or punk bands play, artistic differences are set aside, and dancing mayhem begins.

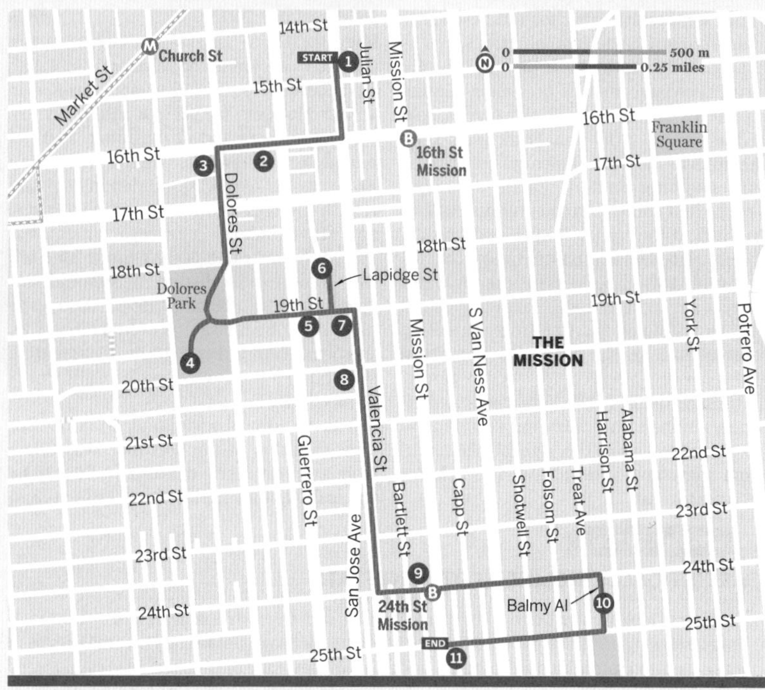

City Walk
The Mission's Most Colorful Characters

START FOUR BARREL
END MISSION PIE
LENGTH 2.7 MILES; THREE HOURS

Begin by fueling up with house roast in the parklet at **1 Four Barrel** (p161) and buzz right past boutiques to **2 Creativity Explored** (p148), where the window showcases works by developmentally disabled artists. Ahead is the city's first building: adobe **3 Mission Dolores** (p149), built by some 5000 native Ohlone and Miwok. You can glimpse the Miwok memorial hut through the mission fence on Chola Lane.

To see how San Francisco has evolved, climb to the upper southwest corner of **4 Dolores Park** (p148) for panoramic views – and pay respects to the **5 golden fire hydrant** that saved much of the Mission from the 1906 fire. Walking down 19th St, you'll pass Daniel Doherty's impressionist-inspired 2009 mural **6 Dejeuner Dolores**, showing Dolores Park's regular cast of characters including frolicking pugs, handlebar-mustachoied men in matching Speedos and families in their Sunday best. Swing left on Lapidge to spot Georgia O'Keeffe and goddesses galore in **7 Women's Building** (p151) murals.

Back on Valencia, you'll see the Chris Ware mural and storefront art installation of **8 826 Valencia** (p148), where you can duck inside for pirate supplies. Down the street, pause to pay respects to bygone celebrities at **9 Dog-Eared Books** (p167) – the front window features hand-drawn obituary cartoons of luminaries from Liz Taylor to Susan Sontag. Window-shop down Valencia, and hang a left onto 24th St. Here you'll pass **10 Campfire Gallery** (p155), which features imaginary ancestors and beastly businessmen invented by SF artists.

Swing down **11 Balmy Alley** (p148), where you may recognize recently beatified activist Archbishop Romero and surrealist painter Frida Kahlo among the colorful characters illuminating garage doors in this mural-covered backstreet. After this slice of Mission life, join locals for a slice of strawberry-rhubarb pie at Mission Pie (p157).

to harsh living conditions and with little resistance to introduced diseases. Their work survives them in the original adobe mission. The ceiling is patterned after Native baskets, and recent restorations revealed a hidden Ohlone mural behind the altar of a sacred heart, pierced by a sword and dripping with blood.

Surrounding the Ohlone memorial in the mission graveyard, you'll notice graves dating from the Gold Rush. Alongside mission founders are buried Don Luis Antonio Arguello, the first governor of Alta California under Mexican rule, and Don Francisco de Haro, the first mayor of San Francisco. Hitchcock fans looking for the grave of Carlotta Valdes will be disappointed: the tomb was only a prop for the film *Vertigo*.

Next door to the modest adobe mission is a grand churrigueresque basilica, built after an 1876 brick Gothic cathedral collapsed in the 1906 earthquake. The front doors are usually only open during services, so you'll need to pass through the original adobe mission structure and cross a courtyard to enter the basilica's side door.

Your eyes may take a moment to adjust once you're inside, because most of the light is filtered through the basilica's splendid stained-glass windows. The choir windows show St Francis beaming beatifically against an orange background. Lower windows along the nave feature 21 California missions from Santa Cruz to San Diego, plus mission builders Father Junípero Serra and Father Francisco Palou. True to Mission Dolores' name, seven panels depict the Seven Sorrows of Mary: one above the main door and three on each of the side balconies.

CLARION ALLEY MURALS

Map p312 (btwn 17th & 18th Sts, off Valencia St; 14, 22, 33, B 16th St Mission, M J) FREE Most graffiti artists shun broad daylight – but not in Clarion Alley, San Francisco's open-air street-art showcase. You'll spot artists touching up pieces and making new ones, with full consent of neighbors and Clarion Alley Collective's curators. Few pieces survive for years, such as Megan Wilson's daisy-covered *Tax the Rich* or Jet Martinez' glimpse of Clarion Alley inside a forest spirit. Incontinent art critics often take over Clarion Alley's east end – pee-eew – so topical murals usually go up on the west end.

WOMEN'S BUILDING NOTABLE BUILDING, MURALS

Map p312 (415-431-1180; www.womensbuilding.org; 3543 18th St; ; 14, 22, 33, 49, B 16th St Mission, M J) The nation's first women-owned-and-operated community center has quietly done good work with 170 women's organizations since 1979, but the 1994 addition of the *Maestrapeace* mural showed the Women's Building for the landmark it truly is. An all-star team of *muralistas* covered the building with images of cross-cultural goddesses and women trailblazers, including Nobel Prize winner Rigoberta Menchú, poet Audre Lorde, artist Georgia O'Keeffe and former US Surgeon General Dr Joycelyn Elders.

GALERÍA DE LA RAZA ART GALLERY

Map p312 (415-826-8009; www.galeriadelaraza.org; 2857 24th St; donations welcome; during exhibitions noon-6pm Wed-Sat, 1-5pm Tue; ; 10, 14, 33, 48, 49, B 24th St Mission) Art never forgets its roots at this nonprofit that has showcased Latino art since 1970. Culture and community are constantly being redefined here, from contemporary Mexican photography and group shows exploring Latin gay culture to performances capturing community responses to Mission gentrification. Outside is the Digital Mural Project, a billboard featuring slogans like '*¡Mujeres Divinas y Poderosas!*/Divine Strong Women!' instead of the usual cigarette advertisements.

SOUTHERN EXPOSURE ART GALLERY

Map p312 (415-863-2141; www.soex.org; 3030 20th St; donations welcome; noon-6pm Thu-Sat; 12, 22, 27, 33, B 16th St Mission) Art really ties the room together at nonprofit arts center Southern Exposure, where works are carefully crafted not just with paint and canvas but a sense of community. Recent projects include Bernie Lubell's wooden flying machine invented on-site with community input, and 24 artists making artworks according to other artists' instructions. Don't miss SoEx's annual Monster Drawing Rally, where major Bay Area artists draw live and the audience snaps up works for $75 while the ink's still wet.

ELEANOR HARWOOD GALLERY ART GALLERY

Map p312 (415-867-7770; www.eleanorharwood.com; 1295 Alabama St; 1-5pm Wed-Thu, 11am-6pm Fri & Sat; 10, 27, 33, 48, B 24th St Mission) FREE On a sleepy Mission street,

1

FOTOVOYAGER / GETTY IMAGES ©

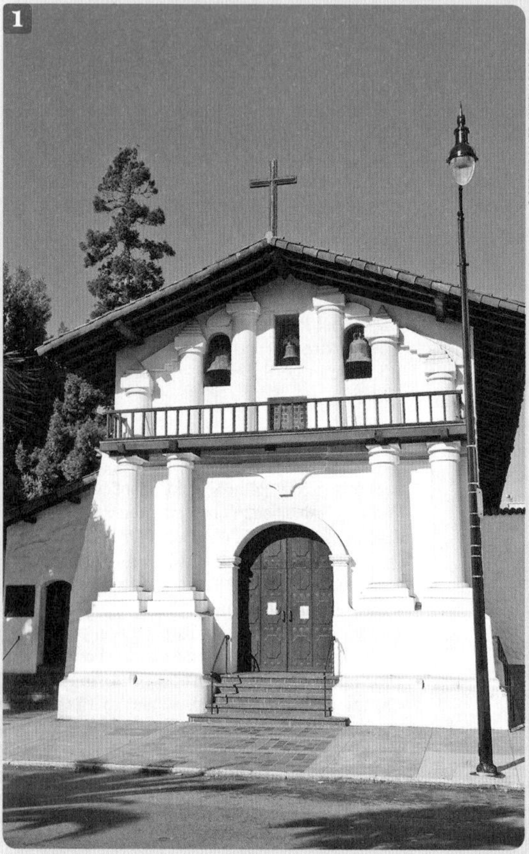

2

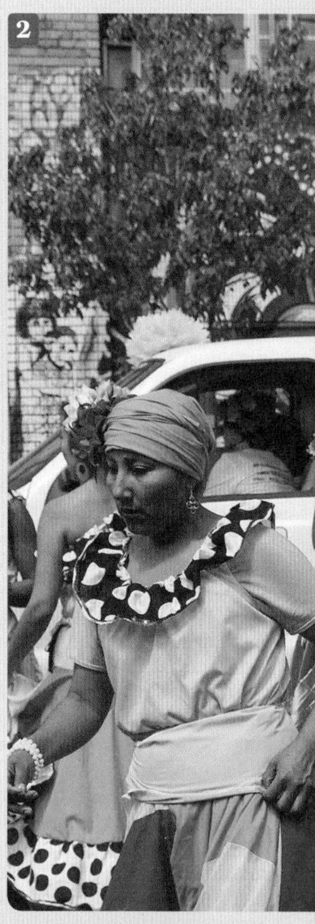

4

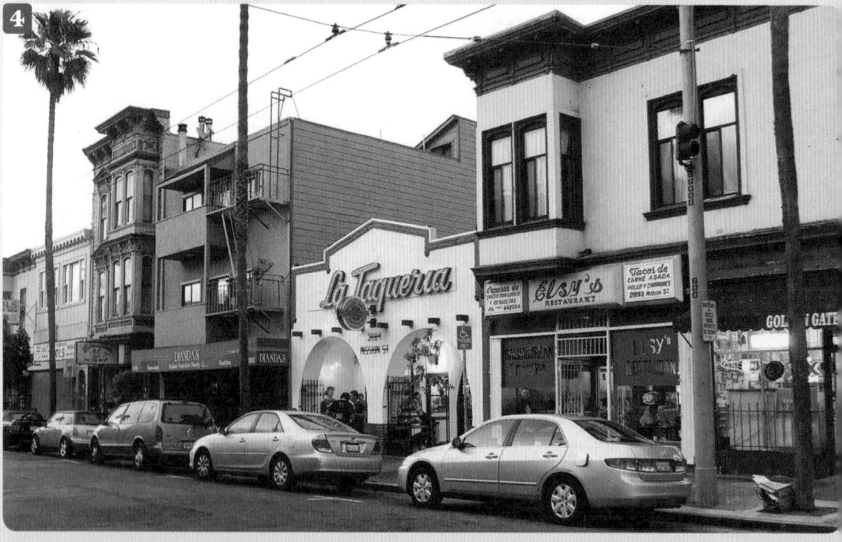

JUDY BELLAH / GETTY IMAGES ©

1. Mission Dolores (p149)
The city's first building, this Spanish adobe mission was built by conscripted Ohlone and Miwok labor.

2. Carnaval San Francisco (p20)
The Mission bursts with color on the last weekend of May, as crowds fill the streets for this vibrant celebration of Latin American and Caribbean music and culture.

3. Dolores Park (p148)
This gathering point in the Mission plays host to protests, taco picnics, sports, movies, mime peformances and everything in between.

4. La Taqueria (p155)
Head here for some of the best burritos and tacos in town; choice ingredients such as spicy pickles and *crema* (Mexican sour cream) have made this a local institution.

JEJIM / GETTY IMAGES ©

WORTH A DETOUR

DOGPATCH CREATIVE CORRIDOR

Potrero Hill's convenient location off Hwy 101 has made it a Silicon Valley bedroom community, but upstart creatives have the run of waterfront warehouses downhill around 22nd and 3rd St. After the shipping business moved to Oakland in the 1950s, this neighborhood was left in dry-dock for decades – even waterfront dive bars like Tom's Dry Dock closed (though the sign remains). But sprawling brick shipping warehouses proved ideal for **San Francisco Art Institute's** MFA graduate student studios, and now that Muni's T line has made the area accessible from downtown, the Museum of Craft & Design (p155) has moved in down the block. Creativity is also fostered at the **Minnesota Street Project** (www.minnesotastreetproject.com), an arts complex funded by Deborah and Andy Rappaport, arts patrons and tech entrepreneurs who recognized the need for low-cost studio and gallery space for SF artists and nonprofits. Watch this space at 1295 Minnesota St for shows, open studios and workshops.

Dogpatch's dock-workers' neighborhood has some of San Francisco's oldest Victorians and brick buildings, miraculously standing their ground through quakes and development schemes. One prime example is the 1859 **Yellow Building**, whose latest incarnation includes a sister branch for Hayes Valley's MAC (p195) clothing store. Cottage industry is alive and creating at **Workshop Residence** (Map p314; ☎415-285-2050; http://workshopresidence.com/; 833 22nd St; ⏲10am-6pm Tue-Sat; 🚌22, 48, Ⓜ T), where artists and designers collaborate with fabricators to produce limited-edition designs – Osgut mats made of recycled firehose, Stephanie Sjuyco's dresses printed with a battleship water-dazzle pattern, Lauren Dicioccio's nylon bags embroidered with the slogan 'Thank you – have a nice day.' Check the blog for upcoming artist talks and hands-on workshops. Around the corner, **Triple Aught Design** (Map p314; ☎415-318-8252; www.tripleaughtdesign.com; 660 22nd St; ⏲11am-7pm Tue-Sun; 🚌22, 48, Ⓜ T) produces thoughtfully designed, multi-functional menswear worthy of James Bond, with sleek Stealth Hoodies and trousers with reinforced knees perfect for parties or parkour.

This industrial waterfront may not look much like Napa Valley, but urban wineries and wine bars are making Dogpatch the toast of SF. **Sutton Cellars** (Map p314; ☎707-874-9466; www.suttoncellars.com; 601 22nd St; tastings $10; ⏲5-8pm Thu & Fri, noon-5pm Sat & Sun; 🚌22, 48, Ⓜ T) offers $10 tastings that range from organic rosé of Carignane to botanical vermouth that's too tasty to mix into martinis. Across the street, **Yield** (Map p314; ☎415-401-8984; www.yieldsf.com; 2490 3rd St; ⏲3pm-midnight Mon-Sat; 🚌22, 48, Ⓜ T) 🌿 wine bar specializes in organic wine pairings with seasonal small plates, while around the corner, **Dig** (Map p314; ☎415-648-6133; http://digwinesf.com; 1005 Minnesota St; ⏲noon-7pm Tue-Sat; 🚌22, 48, Ⓜ T) wine merchant features a well-curated collection of wines from small producers in Italy, France and Austria.

Hungry yet? **Serpentine** (Map p314; ☎415-252-2000; www.serpentinesf.com; 2495 3rd St; mains $10-26; ⏲11:30am-2:30pm & 6-10pm Mon-Thu, to 11pm Fri, 10am-2:30pm & 6-11pm Sat, 10am-2:30pm Sun; 🚌22, Ⓜ T) has brunch down to a science, thanks to med-schooled chef Deepak Kaul's restorative Dungeness Benedict. For no-fuss brews and burgers on a sunny dock, head down to the **Ramp** (Map p314; ☎415-621-2378; www.theramprestaurant.com; 855 Terry Francois St; mains $10-15; ⏲lunch 11am-3:30pm Mon-Fri, 9:30am-4pm Sat-Sun, bar 11am-9pm; 🚌22, Ⓜ T).

Dogpatch is always ready for dessert – this stretch of waterfront has become San Francisco's sweet spot. The Mr & Mrs Miscellaneous (p156) factory-outlet ice-cream parlor does a brisk business in bourbon caramel ice cream, while Recchiuti Chocolate concocts experimental candy and chocolate tasting menus at **theLab** (Map p314; ☎415-489-2881; http://chocolatelabsf.com; 801 22nd St; ⏲event times vary; 🚌22, 48, Ⓜ T) in Dogpatch before launching them at the Ferry Building (p106). Even people who swear they're not into dessert go wild for **Poco Dolce** (Map p314; ☎415-255-1443; http://pocodolce.com; 2419 3rd St; ⏲11am-5pm Mon-Fri, to 4pm Sat; 🚌22,48, Ⓜ T) 🌿, San Francisco's savory, sustainably sourced chocolate confections with a touch of gray sea salt. Poco Dolce chocolatier Kathy Wiley has created Aztec chili bittersweet chocolate tiles ideal with Dogpatch wine tastings – but her silky California olive oil chocolate bar may just be the reason you leave your heart in San Francisco.

this eye-opening gallery showcases Bay Area talents. Works showcased here are entrancing and meticulous – recent shows have featured Francesca Pastine's totem masks made of intricately folded and carved issues of *Artforum* magazine, and William Swanson's 4D topographical paintings mapping a single location over centuries.

MUSEUM OF CRAFT & DESIGN — MUSEUM

Map p314 (415-773-0303; www.sfmcd.org; 2569 3rd St; adult/student $8/6; 11am-6pm Tue-Sat, noon-5pm Sun; ; 22, 48, MT) Corporate fighter jets, woven metal jellyfish, porcelain maps: dazzling, experimental designs not meant for mass production reignite wonder at the Museum of Craft & Design. Check the online schedule for Etsy Craft Lab nights and workshops where accomplished artisans lead hands-on projects related to museum shows, from miniature wire chairs to upcycled festival jewelry.

INCLINE GALLERY — ART GALLERY

Map p312 (www.inclinegallerysf.com; 766 Valencia St; during shows 6-9pm Thu & Fri, 11am-6pm Sat & Sun; 14, 22, 33, 49, B16th St Mission, MJ) FREE Ramp up your art collection at Incline, a sloping gallery in the rear of an ex-mortuary where bodies were once transported for embalming. Today this is where SF's emerging talents begin upward career trajectories, with shows hung along the sloping, skylit stairwell on themes ranging from displacement to mythological birds. Wall installations add discoveries around every corner, while prices remain surprisingly down to earth. Don't miss interactive art in the project room.

RATIO 3 — ART GALLERY

Map p312 (415-821-3371; www.ratio3.org; 2831a Mission St; 11am-6pm Tue-Sat; 12, 14, 48, 49, B16th St Mission) Art-fair buzz begins at this trippy gallery that's all-black outside, and stark-white inside for maximum art impact. While some gallery artists are recognizable from frequent *Artforum* and Miami Basel appearances, gallerist Chris Perez also showcases artworks that remain inexplicably less known – such as Mitzi Pederson's diaphanous tulle dipped in glitter and housepaint, or urban folklore paintings by pioneering SF street artist Margaret Kilgallen.

CAMPFIRE GALLERY — ART GALLERY

Map p312 (415-800-7319; www.campfiregallery.com; 3344 24th St; 11am-7pm Mon & Wed-Sat, noon-5pm Sun) Slick pop-art graphics and rough-hewn wood objects give Campfire Gallery an urban Mission edge over downtown galleries. Driftwood lamps and cast-brass amulets share space here with mixed-media cultural mash-ups by emerging artists. Cindy Steiler's hand-sewn Victorian ancestor portraits speak to San Francisco's past, while Colin Frangicetto's buffalo-headed flower-child businessman represents its freaky future.

EATING

★LA TAQUERIA — MEXICAN $

Map p312 (415-285-7117; 2889 Mission St; burritos $6-8; 11am-9pm Mon-Sat, to 8pm Sun; ; 12, 14, 48, 49, B24th St Mission) SF's definitive burrito has no debatable saffron rice, spinach tortilla or mango salsa – just perfectly grilled meats, slow-cooked beans and classic tomatillo or mesquite salsa wrapped in a flour tortilla. They're purists at La Taqueria – you'll pay extra without beans, because they pack in more meat – but spicy pickles and *crema* (Mexican sour cream) bring complete burrito bliss.

★CRAFTSMAN & WOLVES — BAKERY, CALIFORNIAN $

Map p312 (415-913-7713; http://craftsman-wolves.com; 746 Valencia St; pastries $3-7; 7am-7pm Mon-Thu, to 8pm Fri, 8am-8pm Sat, to 7pm Sun; 14, 22, 33, 49, B16th St Mission, MJ) Conventional breakfasts can't compare to the Rebel Within: savory sausage-spiked Asiago cheese muffin with a silken soft-boiled egg baked inside. SF's surest pick-me-up is Highwire macchiato and matcha (green tea) snickerdoodle cookies, and Thai coconut curry scone, chilled pea soup, and Provence rose makes a sublime lunch. Exquisite hazelnut and *horchata* (cinnamon-rice) cube cakes are ideal for celebrating SF half-birthdays, foggy days and imaginary holidays.

UDUPI PALACE — INDIAN $

Map p312 (415-970-8000; www.udupipalaceca.com; 1007 Valencia St; mains $8-12; 11:30am-10pm Sun-Thu, to 10:30pm Fri & Sat; ; 12, 14, 33, 49, B24th St Mission) Tandoori in the Tenderloin is for novices – SF foodies queue for the bright, clean flavors of Udupi's South Indian *dosa* (light, crispy lentil-flour pancake) dipped in *sambar* (vegetable

SF À LA MODE: BEST LOCAL ICE CREAM

Humphry Slocombe (Map p312; ☎415-550-6971; www.humphryslocombe.com; 2790 Harrison St; ice cream $4-6; ⊙noon-9pm Mon-Thu, to 10pm Fri-Sun; 👪; 🚌12, 14, 49, Ⓑ24th St Mission) Indie-rock organic ice cream may permanently spoil you for Top 40 flavors. Once Thai Curry Peanut Butter and Magnolia Brewery Stout have rocked your taste buds, cookie dough seems so obvious, and ordinary sundaes can't compare to Secret Breakfast (bourbon and corn flakes) and Vietnamese Coffee drizzled with hot fudge, olive oil and sea salt.

Bi-Rite Creamery (Map p312; ☎415-626-5600; www.biritecreamery.com; 3692 18th St; ice cream $3.50-7; ⊙11am-10pm Sun-Thu, to 11pm Fri & Sat; 👪; 🚌33, Ⓑ16th St Mission, ⓂJ) Velvet ropes at clubs seem pretentious in laid-back San Francisco, but at organic Bi-Rite Creamery they make perfect sense: once temperatures pass 70 degrees, the line wraps around the corner for organic salted caramel ice cream with housemade hot fudge, or Sonoma honey-lavender ice cream packed into organic waffle cones. For a quicker fix, get balsamic strawberry soft-serve at the window (1pm to 9pm).

Mitchell's Ice Cream (☎415-648-2300; www.mitchellsicecream.com; 688 San Jose Ave; ice cream $3.50-6; ⊙11am-11pm; 👪; 🚌14, 49, Ⓑ24th St Mission, ⓂJ) An otherwise mellow Mission block is thronged with grinning grown-ups and kids doing happy dances as they make their Mitchell's selections: classic Kahlua mocha cream or exotic tropical *macapuno* (young coconut)? The avocado and *ube* (purple yam) are acquired tastes, but they've been local favorites for generations – Mitchell's has kept San Francisco coming back for seconds since 1953.

Mr & Mrs Miscellaneous (Map p314; ☎415-970-0750; 699 22nd St; ice cream $4-8; ⊙11:30am-6pm Wed-Sat, to 5pm Sun; 🚌22, 48, ⓂT) Chicory coffee, toasted black sesame, and salted mango are among the many savory, seasonal, Miscellaneous flavors that make this ice creamery worth the trek to Dogpatch. Popular flavors sell out fast, so consider this your excuse to eat dessert first.

stew) and coconut chutney. Marathoners may need help finishing two-foot-long paper *dosa* – save room for pea and onion *utthappam* (lentil-flour pancake) or *bagala bhath* (yogurt rice with nutty toasted mustard seeds).

TACOLICIOUS — CAL-MEX $

Map p312 (☎415-626-1344; http://tacolicious.com/; 741 Valencia St; tacos $4 each; ⊙11:30am-midnight; 🍸; 🚌14, 22, 33, 49, Ⓑ16th St Mission, ⓂJ) Never mind the name: once you get a mouthful of *carnitas* (slow-roasted pork) tacos and passionfruit-habanero margaritas, you're in no position to argue authenticity or grammar, or say anything besides *uno mas, por favor* (another, please). Choose four tacos for $14, including seasonal vegetarian options. No reservations, but while you wait you can work through the 100-tequila menu at the bar.

MISSION CHEESE — CHEESE $

Map p312 (☎415-553-8667; www.missioncheese.net; 736 Valencia St; ⊙11am-9pm Tue-Thu & Sun, to 10pm Fri & Sat; 🍸; 🚌14, 22, 33, 49, 🚋J, Ⓑ16th St Mission) 🌿 Smile and say wine at this cheese bar, serving up sublime pairings with expert advice and zero pretension. The all-domestic cheese menu ranges from triple-creamy to extra-stinky, raw cow's milk to sheep's milk, and California wines reign supreme. When in dairy doubt, try the 'mongers choice' surprise-cheese platters with pickles, nuts and dried fruit. Order at the bar; note early closing.

CHINO — CALIFORNIAN, CHINESE $

Map p312 (☎415-552-5771; http://chinosf.com/; 3198 16th St; share plates $9-14; ⊙5-11pm Mon-Thu, to midnight Fri, 11:30am-midnight Sat, 11:30am-11pm Sun; 🚌14, 22, 49, Ⓑ16th St, ⓂJ) San Francisco has been inventing new pseudo-Asian dishes since the Gold Rush – chop suey, anyone? – but Chino's menu is a gold mine of dastardly clever, cheerfully inauthentic Asian soul food. Spicy lamb dumplings get your lips buzzing with Sichuan peppercorns, 'dope-ass Japan-o-Mission wings' with lime hot-and-sour sauce will convert authenticity-trippers, and spiked *boba* (tapioca-pearl) cocktails are pure evil genius.

GALAJEE
SEAFOOD, INDIAN $

Map p312 (☎415-552-9000; 525 Valencia St; mains $9-13; ⊙11:30am-10pm Sun-Thu, to 10:30pm Fri & Sat; 🚌14, 22, 33, 49, Ⓑ16th St) Laid-back West Coast seafood with a twist: these dishes originate from India's southwest coast. Malvani fish curry from the beaches of Goa is deeply savory and rich with roasted coconut, and Galajee does it right. For lighter but equally flavorful fare, go with fish *pollichathu,* marinated and slow-cooked in a banana leaf, or *ambat tikhat kolambhi,* tangy-hot shrimp with mango.

PANCHO VILLA
MEXICAN $

Map p312 (☎415-864-8840; www.sfpanchovilla.com; 3071 16th St; burritos $5-10; ⊙10am-midnight; 🌿👪; 🚌14, 22, 33, 49, Ⓑ16th St Mission) The hero of the downtrodden and burrito-deprived, Pancho Villa supplies tin-foil-wrapped meals the girth of your forearm and lets you add ammunition at the fresh, heaping salsa bar. The line moves fast going in, and as you leave, the door is held open for you and your newly acquired Pancho's paunch. Stick around for serenades by roving mariachis.

OLD JERUSALEM
MIDDLE EASTERN $

Map p312 (☎415-642-5958; 2976 Mission St; mains $7-13; ⊙noon-10pm Mon-Sat, to 9pm Sun; 🌿; 🚌12, 14, 48, 49, Ⓑ24th St Mission) Foodies scouring the Mission for the ultimate taco shouldn't overlook this outpost of Middle Eastern authenticity, complete with Dome of the Rock poster and pristine hummus that doesn't overdo the tahini. Get the classic falafel, *shwarma* (marinated, roasted lamb) or *shish taouk* (marinated grilled chicken) with all the fixings: hummus, onion, eggplant, potato and tangy purple sumac, with optional hot-pepper paste.

TARTINE
BAKERY $

Map p312 (☎415-487-2600; www.tartinebakery.com; 600 Guerrero St; pastries $3-6, sandwiches $10-13; ⊙8am-7pm Mon, 7:30am-7pm Tue & Wed, to 8pm Thu & Fri, 8am-8pm Sat, 9am-8pm Sun; 🌿; 🚌14, 22, 33, 49, ⓂJ, Ⓑ16th St Mission) Riches beyond your wildest dreams: butter-golden *pain au chocolat,* cappuccino with ferns drawn in dense foam and *croque monsieurs* turbo-loaded with ham, two kinds of cheese and béchamel. Don't be dismayed by the inevitable line out the door – it moves fast – but be aware that lolling in Dolores Park is the only possible post-Tartine activity.

TORTAS LOS PICUDOS
MEXICAN $

Map p312 (☎415-824-4199; 2969 24th St; tortas $6-8; ⊙7am-8pm; 🚌14, 26, 33, 49, Ⓑ24th St Mission) Mexico City's signature street food gets reinvented to satisfy famished Potrero del Sol skateboarders. These sandwiches are stuffed with farm-fresh veggies and healthy poached chicken or tangy marinated pulled pork, with optional pickled jalapeños and slabs of avocado. Wash it down with a strawberry *agua fresca* (smoothie) or fresh-squeezed OJ, and you can skip dinner.

MISSION PIE
AMERICAN, BAKERY $

Map p312 (☎415-282-1500; http://missionpie.com/; 2901 Mission St; pie slice $3.50-5.50; ⊙7am-2pm Mon, to 10pm Tue-Fri, from 8am Sat, from 9am Sun; 📶🌿👪; 🚌12, 14, 48, 49, Ⓑ24th St Mission) 🍃 Like mom used to make, only better: hot-from-the oven pies at this certified-green bakery range from savory organic chicken pot pies ($7) to all-American heirloom apple ($5 per slice with free organic whipped cream). The sunny Victorian storefront doubles as a neighborhood hangout with board games, blocks for kiddies and a library of conscientious cookbooks to inspire your own food revolution.

RADISH
CALIFORNIAN CREOLE $

Map p312 (☎415-834-5441; www.radishsf.com; 3465 19th St; mains $8-16; ⊙10am-10pm Tue-Fri, 9am-10pm Sat, to 3pm Sun; 🌿; 🚌14, 22, 33,

TOP 5 MISSION TACOS

La Palma Mexicatessen (p159) *Carnitas* (slow-roasted pork) with pickled red onion on tortillas made fresh in-house with organic masa (corn-flour dough).

Pancho Villa *Pollo verde* (green-chili-stewed chicken) with *escabeche* (spicy pickled) carrots and *crema* (Mexican sour cream).

Namu Gaji (p158) Korean steak tacos, with grass-fed beef and spicy sauce rolled into a seaweed wrapper.

Tacolicious Seasonal vegetarian taco with roasted butternut squash, poblano peppers and *pepitas* (spiced pumpkin seeds).

La Taqueria (p155) *Lengua* (marinated beef tongue) with onions, cilantro and pickled jalapeño.

B 16th St Mission) Hedonists and picky eaters converge at Radish, where decadent Southern-inspired food is made with organic Californian produce, sustainable meats, and ample gluten-free options. Sensational salads cure Mission burrito overload, and catfish po'boy sandwiches piled with tangy slaw are flavor bombs. Mission barflies recover with Radish's brunch: homemade biscuits with eggs and house-cured bacon, plus bottomless mimosas.

★AL'S PLACE CALIFORNIAN $$

Map p312 (415-416-6136; www.alsplacesf.com; 1499 Valencia St; share plates $13-18; 5:30-10pm Wed-Sun; ; 12, 14, 49, B 24th St, M J) The Golden State dazzles on Al's plates, featuring homegrown heirloom ingredients, pristine Pacific seafood, and grass-fed meat on the side. Painstaking preparation yields sun-drenched flavors and exquisite textures: crispy-skin cod with frothy preserved-lime dip, creamy grits with goat-cheese curds and salsa verde. Dishes are half the size but thrice the flavor of mains elsewhere – get two or three, and you'll be California dreaming.

★ICHI SUSHI SUSHI $$

(415-525-4750; www.ichisushi.com; 3282 Mission St; sushi $4.50-8.50; 5:30-10pm Mon-Thu, to 11pm Fri & Sat; 14, 24, 49, B 24th St Mission, M J) Alluring on the plate and positively obscene on the tongue, Ichi Sushi is a sharp cut above other fish joints. Chef Tim Archuleta slices silky, sustainably sourced fish with a jeweler's precision, balances it atop well-packed rice, and tops it with tiny but powerfully tangy dabs of gelled yuzu and microscopically cut spring onion and chili daikon that make soy sauce unthinkable.

★NAMU GAJI KOREAN, CALIFORNIAN $$

Map p312 (415-431-6268; www.namusf.com; 499 Dolores St; small plates $10-22; 11:30am-3pm Wed-Fri, from 10:30am Sat & Sun, 5-10pm Tue-Thu & Sun, 5-11pm Fri & Sat; 14, 22, 33, 49, M J, B 16th St Mission) SF's unfair culinary advantages – organic local ingredients, Silicon Valley inventiveness and Pacific Rim roots – are showcased in Namu's Korean-inspired soul food. Menu standouts include ultra-savory shiitake mushroom dumplings, meltingly tender marinated beef tongue, and Namu's version of *bibimbap:* Marin Sun Farms grass-fed steak, organic vegetables, spicy *gojuchang* (savory-sweet Korean chili sauce) and Sonoma farm egg atop rice, served sizzling in a stone pot.

PIZZERIA DELFINA PIZZA $$

Map p312 (415-437-6800; www.delfinasf.com; 3621 18th St; pizzas $11-17; 11:30am-10pm Tue-Thu, to 11pm Fri, noon-11pm Sat & Sun, 5-10pm Mon; 14, 22, 33, 49, M J, B 16th St) One bite explains why SF is obsessed with pizza lately: Delfina's thin crust heroically supports the weight of fennel sausage and fresh mozzarella without drooping or cracking. On sauce-free white pizzas, chefs freestyle with California ingredients such as broccoli rabe, Maitake mushrooms and artisan cheese. No reservations; sign the chalkboard and wait with a glass of wine at next-door Delfina bar.

LOLO CEVICHERIA LATIN AMERICAN, SEAFOOD $$

Map p312 (415-913-7898; www.lolosf.com/lolo-cevicheria/; 3230 22nd St; tapas $10-15; 6-10pm Mon-Thu, 5:30-11:30pm Fri & Sat; 14, 49, B 24th St) Explore the Pacific Rim from the comfort of a Mission bar stool, cardamom-scented sangria in hand. Get the Californian catch of the day cured in Peruvian *leche de tigre* (lime marinade) and the seared tuna with homemade Japanese *unagi* (barbecued eel) sauce on fresh tortillas, but don't overlook meaty mains – the Yucatan pork *carnitas* slow-cooked in a banana leaf is sublime.

LOCANDA ITALIAN $$

Map p312 (415-863-6800; www.locandasf.com; 557 Valencia St; mains $14-27; 5:30-10pm Mon-Wed, to 11pm Thu-Sat, 5-10pm Sun; 14, 22, 33, 49, B 16th St Mission) Friends, Romans, San Franciscans – join the crowd for pizza bianca and prosciutto, scrumptious tripe melting into rich tomato-mint sauce, Roman fried artichokes and tender fried sweetbreads. Pasta dishes are less adventurous than mains and small plates invented with market-fresh organic ingredients, like the whole fish of the day (served head on) and minty spring lamb carpaccio.

MISSION CHINESE FUSION $$

Map p312 (Lung Shan; 415-863-2800; www.missionchinesefood.com; 2234 Mission St; mains $12-20; 11:30am-3pm & 5-10:30pm Thu-Mon, 5-10:30pm Tue & Wed; 14, 33, 49, B 16th St Mission) Extreme gourmets and Chinese takeout fans converge on Danny Bowien's

GOURMET SUPPLIES

Bi-Rite (Map p312; ☎415-241-9760; www.biritemarket.com; 3639 18th St; sandwiches $7-10; ⏰9am-9pm; 👪; 🚌14, 22, 33, 49, Ⓑ16th St Mission, ⓂJ) Diamond counters can't compare to the sheer foodie dazzle of Bi-Rite. Upbeat, knowledgeable staff will help you navigate the brilliant wall of local artisan chocolates, treasure-boxes of organic fruit, and expertly curated Californian wines and cheeses. Step up to the altar-like deli counter to order bespoke sandwiches for five-star Dolores Park picnics. The jaw-dropping, mouthwatering experience continues at Bi-Rite's second location (500 Divisadero).

La Palma Mexicatessen (Map p312; ☎415-647-1500; www.lapalmasf.com/; 2884 24th St; ⏰8am-6pm Mon-Sat, to 5pm Sun; 🌿 👪; 🚌12, 14, 27, 48, Ⓑ24th St Mission) Follow the applause: that's the sound of organic tortilla-making in progress at La Palma. You've found the Mission motherlode of handmade tamales, *pupusas* (tortilla-pockets) with potato and *chicharones* (pork crackling), *carnitas* (slow-roasted pork), *cotija* (Oaxacan cheese) and La Palma's own tangy tomatillo sauce. Get takeout, or bring a small army to finish that massive meal at sunny sidewalk tables.

Mission Community Market (Map p312; http://missioncommunitymarket.org/; Bartlett St btwn 21st & 22nd Sts; ⏰4-8pm Thu mid-Jan–mid-Dec; 🌿 👪 🐾; 🚌14, 48, 49, Ⓑ24th St Mission) Back-alley bounty brings ravenous crowds Thursdays to this nonprofit, neighborhood-run market, come rain or shine. More than 30 local farmers and food artisans offer pristine California produce and inspired SF street food – look for Coastside Farms' smoked albacore, Tomatero Farms' heirloom green zebra tomatoes, Flour Chylde pastries and Chaac Mool's Yucatan *cochinita pibil* (dry-rubbed slow-roasted pork).

Rainbow Grocery (Map p312; ☎415-863-0620; www.rainbow.coop/; 1745 Folsom St; ⏰9am-9pm; 🌿; 🚌9, 12, 33, 47) The legendary cooperative attracts masses to buy eco/organic/fair-trade products in bulk, sample the bounty of local cheeses and flirt in the artisan chocolate aisle. To answer your questions about where to find what in the Byzantine bulk section, ask a fellow shopper – staff can be elusive. Small though well-priced wine and craft beer selections; no meat products.

cult-food dive. Tiki pork belly with pickled pineapple and spicy lamb-face (sheep's cheek) noodles are big enough for two – though not for the salt-shy – and satisfy your conscience: 75¢ from each main is donated to San Francisco Food Bank. Wine corkage is $10; parties of eight or less.

EL TECHO DE LOLINDA — LATIN AMERICAN $$

Map p312 (Lolinda Rooftop; ☎415-550-6970; http://eltechosf.com; 2518 Mission St; small plates $8-13; ⏰4-11pm Mon-Thu, to 1am Fri, 11am-1am Sat, to 11pm Sun; 🚌14, 33, 49, Ⓑ24th St Mission) Come here for Latin street food six floors above Mission St, with views over cinema marquees, palm trees and low-riders all the way to downtown. Sunny days call for shrimp *ceviche*, the Chilcano (pisco, lime, ginger, passion fruit and bitters) and sunblock; foggy days require *empanadas*, La Avenida (rum, lemon and vermouth) and a windbreaker.

COMMONWEALTH — CALIFORNIAN $$$

Map p312 (☎415-355-1500; www.commonwealthsf.com; 2224 Mission St; small plates $13-18; ⏰5:30-10pm Sun-Thu, to 11pm Fri & Sat; 🌿; 🚌14, 22, 33, 49, Ⓑ16th St Mission) Wildly imaginative farm-to-table dining where you'd least expect it: in a converted cinderblock Mission dive. Chef Jason Fox serves adventurous, exquisitely Instagrammable compositions like *uni* (sea urchin) and popcorn atop cauliflower pudding, and foie gras in an oatmeal crust with tangy rhubarb. Dishes are dainty but pack wallops of earthy flavors. Savor the $75 *prix fixe*, knowing $10 is donated to charity.

FOREIGN CINEMA — CALIFORNIAN $$$

Map p312 (☎415-648-7600; www.foreigncinema.com; 2534 Mission St; mains $22-33; ⏰5:30-10pm Mon-Wed, to 11pm Thu-Sun, brunch 11am-2:30pm Sat & Sun; 🚌12, 14, 33, 48, 49, Ⓑ24th St Mission) 🍃 New Californian comfort food classics like velvety Pacific poke (marinated tuna) and crisp sesame fried chicken are the main attractions, but silver screen features by Luis Buñuel and François Truffaut provide an entertaining backdrop in the courtyard, with subtitles you can follow if conversation lags with first dates or in-laws. Get the red-carpet treatment with valet parking ($12) and well-stocked oyster bar.

DRINKING & NIGHTLIFE

★%ABV — BAR

Map p312 (415-400-4748; www.abvsf.com; 3174 16th St; 2pm-2am daily; 14, 22, B 16th St Mission, M J) As kindred spirits will deduce from the name (abbreviation for 'percent alcohol by volume'), this bar is backed by cocktail crafters who know their Rittenhouse rye from Traverse City whiskey. Here top-notch hooch is served promptly and without pretension, including historically inspired cocktails under $10. Try toe-warming whiskey concoctions or Lefty's Fizz: mezcal, tart grapefruit shrub, and foamy egg white.

★EL RIO — CLUB

Map p312 (415-282-3325; www.elriosf.com; 3158 Mission St; cover free-$8; 1pm-2am; 12, 14, 27, 49, B 24th St Mission) Work it all out on the dance floor with SF's most down and funky crowd – SF's full rainbow spectrum of colorful characters is here to party. Calendar highlights include Wednesday's aptly named Mayhem Karaoke, Thursday ping-pong marathons, free oysters Fridays at 5:30pm, and monthly drag-star Daytime Realness. Expect knockout margaritas and shameless flirting in the back garden. Cash only.

★DALVA & HIDEOUT — COCKTAIL BAR

Map p312 (415-252-7740; http://dalvasf.com/; 3121 16th St; 4pm-2am; 14, 22, 33, 49, B 24th St) SF's best bars are judged not only by their cocktails, but by the conversations they inspire – and by both measures, Dalva is top-shelf. Discuss Dolores Park doings over Dirty Pigeons (mezcal, lime, grapefruit, gentian-flower bitters), and dissect Roxie documentaries over whiskey cocktails (rye, maraschino, housemade bourbon bitters) in the secret back-room Hideout (from 7pm; cash only). Bargain happy hours last from 4pm to 7pm.

★ELIXIR — BAR

Map p312 (415-522-1633; www.elixirsf.com; 3200 16th St; 3pm-2am Mon-Fri, from noon Sat, from 10am Sun; 14, 22, 33, 49, B 16th St Mission, M J) Do the planet a favor and have another drink at SF's first certified-green bar, in an actual 1858 Wild West saloon. Elixir expertly blends farm-fresh seasonal mixers with small-batch, organic, even biodynamic spirits – dastardly tasty organic basil Negronis and kumquat caipirinhas will get you air-guitar-rocking to the killer jukebox. Drink-for-a-cause Wednesdays encourage imbibing, with proceeds supporting local charities.

ZEITGEIST — BAR

Map p312 (415-255-7505; www.zeitgeistsf.com/; 199 Valencia St; 9am-2am; 14, 22, 49, B 16th St Mission) You've got two seconds flat to order from tough-gal barkeeps used to putting macho bikers in their place – but with 48 beers on draft, you're spoiled for choice. Epic afternoons unfold in the graveled beer garden, hanging and smoking out at long picnic tables. SF's longest happy hour lasts 9am to 8pm weekdays. Cash only and no photos (read: no evidence).

TRICK DOG — BAR

Map p312 (415-471-2999; www.trickdogbar.com; 3010 20th St; 3pm-2am; 12, 14, 49) Drink adventurously with ingenious cocktails inspired by local obsessions: SF landmarks, Chinese diners, '70s hits, horoscope signs. Every six months, Trick Dog adopts a new theme, and the entire menu changes – proof that you can teach an old dog new tricks, and improve on classics like the Manhattan. Arrive early for bar stools or hit the mood-lit loft for high-concept bar bites.

RITUAL COFFEE ROASTERS — CAFÉ

Map p312 (415-641-1011; www.ritualroasters.com; 1026 Valencia St; 6am-8pm Mon-Thu, to 10pm Fri, 7am-10pm Sat, to 8pm Sun; 14, 49, B 24th St Mission) Cults wish they inspired the same devotion as Ritual, where regulars solemnly queue for house-roasted cappuccino with ferns drawn in foam and specialty drip coffees with highly distinctive flavor profiles – descriptions comparing roasts to grapefruit peel or hazelnut aren't exaggerating. Electrical outlets are limited to encourage conversation, so you can eavesdrop on dates, art debates and political protest plans.

20 SPOT

WINE BAR

Map p312 (☎415-624-3140; www.20spot.com; 3565 20th St; ⏰5pm-midnight Mon-Thu, to 1am Fri & Sat; 🚌14, 22, 33, Ⓑ16th St Mission) Find your California mellow at this midcentury neighborhood wine lounge. After decades as Force of Habit punk record shop – note the vintage sign – this corner joint has earned the right to unwind with a glass of Californian Gamay noir rosé and not get any guff. Caution: double-deviled eggs with trout roe could become a habit.

FOUR BARREL COFFEE

CAFÉ

Map p312 (☎415-896-4289; www.fourbarrelcoffee.com; 375 Valencia St; ⏰7am-8pm; 🚌14, 22, 🚉16th St Mission) Surprise: the hippest café in town is also the friendliest, with upbeat baristas and no outlets or wi-fi to hinder conversation. Drip roasts are complex and powerful; the fruity espresso is an acquired taste. The front-bar Slow Pour comes with coffee-geek explanations of growing, roasting and cupping methods. Caffeinating crowds mingle in a sunny parklet with bike parking and patio seating.

ROCK BAR

BAR

(☎415-550-6664; http://rockbarsf.com; 80 29th St; ⏰4pm-2am Mon-Sat, from 10am Sun; 🚌14, 24, 49, ⓂJ) Eureka! Inside these rock-veneer walls, you're golden with original concoctions made of craft spirits and priced to move ($9 to $12). Happy hours from 4pm to 7:30pm feature house-specialty cocktails like the Gold Digger (gin, champagne, peach, ginger, pear liqueur). Order fried chicken across the street at Front Porch and they'll deliver it to your stool. Cash only.

HOMESTEAD

BAR

Map p312 (☎415-282-4663; www.homesteadsf.com; 2301 Folsom St; ⏰2pm-2am; 🚌12, 14, 22, 33, 49, Ⓑ16th St Mission) Your friendly Victorian corner dive c 1893, complete with carved-wood bar, pressed-tin ceiling, salty roast peanuts in the shell, salty Mission characters and their sweet dogs. SF's creative contingent pack the place to celebrate art openings, dance shows and writing assignments with cheap draft beer – and when Iggy Pop or David Bowie hits the jukebox, stand back.

BORDERLANDS

CAFÉ

Map p312 (☎415-970-6998; www.borderlandscafe.com; 870 Valencia St; ⏰8am-8pm; 🚌14, 33, 49, Ⓑ16th St Mission) Mysterious yet sociable Borderlands has limited wi-fi (9am to 5pm weekdays) to keep conversation flowing and thoughtfully provided racks of paperback mysteries for browsing – or buying at the 1950s purchase price of 50¢. West Coast coffeehouse culture is staging a comeback at this membership-supported neighborhood institution, complete with hairless cats, creaky wood floors, top-notch hot chocolate and sofas encouraging offline conversation.

DOC'S CLOCK

BAR

Map p312 (☎415-824-3627; www.docsclock.com; 2575 Mission St; ⏰5pm-2am Mon-Thu, 4pm-2am Fri & Sat, 3pm-2am Sun; 🚌12, 14, 49, Ⓑ24th St Mission) 🌿 If it's after lunch in the Mission, it's Doc's o'clock – head to the Prescriptions Counter at this mellow, green-certified dive for 14 local craft brews, free shuffleboard, Barbie Mutilation Nights, tricky pinball and easy conversation. Dog-friendly happy hours run 9pm to 2am daily, with a percentage of proceeds supporting city dog rescues.

ST. VINCENT TAVERN

WINE BAR

Map p312 (☎415-285-1200; www.stvincentsf.com; 1270 Valencia St; ⏰6-10pm Mon-Thu, to 11pm Fri & Sat; 🚌12, 14, 48, 49, Ⓑ24th St Mission) Dive into the deep end of the list of 100 bottles under $100 compiled by sommelier/owner David Lynch, including Italian cult wines. For starters, try a glass of Napa's Massican Ribolla blend or Nebbiolo rosé (bet you'll want the rest of those bottles). Food isn't an afterthought: bone marrow with smoked Calabrian chili is meant for earthy red Aglianico.

MONK'S KETTLE

PUB

Map p312 (☎415-865-9523; www.monkskettle.com; 3141 16th St; ⏰noon-2am; 🚌14, 22, 33, 49, Ⓑ16th St Mission) Unlike trendy gastropubs, Monk's Kettle realizes you're here for beer – and delivers, with 29 cult draft brews ranging in hue from Portland's Allagash white ale to San Diego's strong dark Belgian Widow. Regulars waiting an hour for seats are probably here for 100+ Belgian-style saison ales, accompanied by food with enough mustard and salt to perk thirst for more beer.

LATIN AMERICAN CLUB

BAR

Map p312 (☎415-647-2732; 3286 22nd St; ⏰6pm-2am Mon-Fri, from 3pm Sat & Sun; 🚌12, 14, 49, ⒷMission St) Margaritas go the distance here – just don't stand up too fast. Ninja *piñatas* and *papel picado* (cut-paper banners) add a festive atmosphere, and rosy lighting and generous pours enable shameless flirting outside your age range. Cash only.

BISSAP BAOBAB CLUB

Map p312 (☎415-643-3558; www.bissapbaobab.com; 3372 19th St; free-$5; ⊙events vary, club 9/10pm-2am Thu-Sat; 🚌14, 22, 33, 49, B16th St) A Senegalese restaurant early in the evening, Baobab brings on the DJ or live act around 10pm – and before you can say 'tamarind margarita,' tables are shoved out of the way to make room on the dance floor. Midweek Cuban mambo, occasional flamenco and jazz shows, and Friday and Saturday Paris-Dakar Afrobeat get the Mission in a universal groove.

PHONE BOOTH BAR

Map p312 (1398 S Van Ness Ave; ⊙2pm-2am; 🚌14, 49, B24th St Mission) Classic SF dive celebrating defunct technology, with naked Barbie chandeliers and year-round Christmas lights. Sexually ambiguous art-school students mingle with sundry techies (oh hi, Mark Zuckerberg) over pool tables and make out in dark corners. Cheap beer, Jameson and Bloody Marys flow freely, and the jukebox is perpetually on fire.

☆ ENTERTAINMENT

★ROXIE CINEMA CINEMA

Map p312 (☎415-863-1087; www.roxie.com; 3117 16th St; regular screening/matinee $10/7.50; ⊙showtimes vary; 🚌14, 22, 33, 49, B16th St Mission) This little neighborhood nonprofit cinema earns international clout for distributing documentaries and showing controversial films banned elsewhere. Tickets to film festival premieres, rare revivals and raucous annual Oscars telecasts sell out – reserve tickets online – but if the main show is packed, check out documentaries in teensy next-door Little Roxy instead. No ads, plus personal introductions to every film.

★OBERLIN DANCE COLLECTIVE DANCE

Map p312 (ODC; ☎box office 415-863-9834, classes 415-549-8519; www.odctheater.org; 3153 17th St; drop-in class $15, shows $20-50; ⊙shows vary; 🚌12, 14, 22, 33, 49, B16th St Mission) For 45 years, ODC has been redefining dance with risky, raw performances and the sheer joy of movement. ODC's season runs September to December, but its stage presents year-round shows featuring local and international artists. ODC Dance Commons is a hub and hangout for the dance community offering 200 classes a week, from flamenco to vogue; all ages and levels welcome.

★THE CHAPEL LIVE MUSIC

Map p312 (☎415-551-5157; www.thechapelsf.com; 777 Valencia St; tickets $15-40; ⊙bar 7pm-2am, showtimes vary; 🚌14, 33, MJ, B16th St Mission) Musical prayers are answered in a 1914 California Craftsman landmark with heavenly acoustics. The 40ft roof is regularly raised by shows by New Orleans brass bands, legendary rockers like John Doe, folkYEAH! Americana groups, and AC/DShe, the hard-rocking all-female tribute band. Many shows are all-ages, except when comedians like W Kamau Bell test edgy material.

MARSH THEATER, COMEDY

Map p312 (☎415-282-3055; www.themarsh.org; 1062 Valencia St; tickets $15-35; ⊙box office 1-4pm Mon-Fri, showtimes vary; 🚌12, 14, 48, 49, B24th St Mission) Choose your seat wisely: you may spend the evening on the edge of it. One-acts and monologues here involve the audience in the creative process, from W Kamau Bell's riffs to live tapings of NPR's *Philosophy Talk*. The sliding-scale pricing structure allows everyone to participate, and a few reserved seats are sometimes available ($50 per ticket).

BRAVA THEATER THEATER

Map p312 (☎415-641-7657; www.brava.org; 2781 24th St; prices vary; 👪; 🚌12, 27, 33, 48) Brava's been producing women-run theater for 30 years, hosting acts from comedian Sandra Bernhardt to V-day monologist Eve Ensler, and it's the nation's only company with a commitment to producing original works by women of color and LGBT playwrights. Brava honors the Mission's Mexican heritage with folkloric music and dance celebrations, plus hand-painted show posters modeled after Mexican cinema billboards.

BRICK & MORTAR LIVE MUSIC

Map p312 (☎415-800-8782; http://brickandmortarmusic.com; 1710 Mission St; cover $10-20; ⊙showtimes vary; 🚌14, 49, B16th St) Some bands are too outlandish for regular radio – to hear them, you need San Francisco's Brick & Mortar. The bill here features national acts from brass band showcases to

US air-guitar championships, plus homegrown SF upstarts like Ramones-inspired sister duo Dog Party, surf-rockers Hot Flash Heat Wave, and psychedelically groovy Coyote Trickster.

AMNESIA LIVE MUSIC

Map p312 (☎415-970-0012; www.amnesiathebar.com; 853 Valencia St; admission free-$10; ⊙6pm-2am; 🚌14, 33, 49, Ⓑ16th St Mission) Forget everything you've heard about SF nightlife – this closet-sized Boho dive will make you lose your mind for Monday bluegrass jams, Tuesday comedy sessions, Wednesday gaucho jazz, random readings and breakout dance parties. Shows are cheap and often sliding-scale, so the crowd is pumped and the beer flows freely. Check the website or just go with the flow.

SUB-MISSION LIVE MUSIC

Map p312 (☎415-255-7227; www.submissionartspace.com/; 2183 Mission St; shows $5-13; ⊙8pm-midnight; 🚌14, 22, 33, Ⓑ24th St Mission) Punk comes roaring out from the underground at SUB-Mission, with local punk bands inflaming weeknights and weekend-visitor bands from LA to Argentina leaving anyone within earshot with a nasty itch for more. Everything you'd expect from an underground Mission punk club is here: anarchic sets, unlockable bathrooms, surly bartenders and cheap, tasty tacos to warm hardcore hearts.

REVOLUTION CAFE LIVE PERFORMANCE

Map p312 (☎415-642-0474; www.revolutioncafesf.com/; 3248 22nd St; suggested donation $5-20; ⊙9am-midnight Sun-Thu, to 2am Fri & Sat; 📶; 🚌12, 14, 49, Ⓑ24th St Mission) Musicians, you're among friends here: classically trained musicians and jazz artists jam here daily. Hot days call for iced coffee and live Latin jazz, and Mondays are redeemed with Belgian brews and Classical Revolution's rollicking chamber music. Arrive by 7pm to snag a table, or hang on the sidewalk with free wi-fi. Bring cash for drinks and musicians' tip jars.

VIRACOCHA LIVE MUSIC, SPOKEN WORD

Map p312 (☎415-374-7048; www.viracochasf.com; 998 Valencia St; ⊙noon-6pm Wed-Fri, to 7pm Sat & Sun; 🚌14, 33, 49, Ⓑ24th St Mission) Shotgun-shack Western home decor and vintage boutique by day, by night Viracocha hosts oddball songwriters, shy poets and occasional vampire musicals in its downstairs gallery and back-room library and vinyl stash. Bang away on the badly tuned piano if you like – it's that kind of place – but be gentle with 1920s typewriters and driftwood-sculpture lamps, since they're for sale.

WORTH A DETOUR

BOTTOM OF THE HILL

Quite literally at the bottom of Potrero Hill, **Bottom of the Hill** (Map p314; ☎415-621-4455; www.bottomofthehill.com; 1233 17th St; admission $5-20; ⊙shows 9/10pm Tue-Sat; 🚌10, 19, 22) is definitely out of the way but always top of the list for seeing fun local bands, from notable alt-rockers like Deerhoof to newcomers worth checking out for their names alone (Truckstop Honeymoon, Strawberry Smog, You Are Plural). The smokers' patio is ruled by a cat that enjoys music more than people – totally punk rock. Anchor Steam on tap but it's a cash-only bar; check the website for lineups.

MIGHTY CLUB

Map p312 (☎415-762-0151; www.mighty119.com; 119 Utah St; admission free-$25; ⊙9pm-4am Thu-Sat; 🚌8, 9, 22, 33, 47) A Potrero warehouse packs a Mighty wallop with a booming sound system, thumping dance music, graffiti-inspired art and cool local crowds who don't do dress codes. Weekend DJs veer toward deep house, electronica and throwback '90s hip-hop; on other nights, events vary wildly from geek-out tech meet-ups to indie band showcases (check website).

MAKE-OUT ROOM LIVE MUSIC, SPOKEN WORD

Map p312 (☎415-647-2888; www.makeoutroom.com; 3225 22nd St; cover free-$10; ⊙6pm-2am; 🚌12, 14, 49, Ⓑ24th St Mission) Velvet curtains and round booths invite you to settle in for the evening's entertainment, which ranges from punk-rock fiddle to '80s one-hit-wonder DJ mash-ups and painfully funny readings at Writers with Drinks. Booze is a bargain, especially during 6pm-to-8pm weeknight happy hours – but the bar is cash-only.

MISSION BOWLING CLUB BOWLING

Map p312 (☎415-863-2695; www.missionbowlingclub.com; 3176 17th St; ⊙3-11pm Mon-Wed, to midnight Thu-Fri, 11am-midnight Sat, 11am-11pm Sun; 🚌12, 22, 33, 49, Ⓑ16th St Mission) Don't mock until you try bowling Mission-style: six lanes in a mood-lit warehouse, where the bar pours mean tangerine sours and green-tea gimlets, and $1 of happy hour orders of beef-cheek fries gets donated to local nonprofits. Book lanes in advance online (yes, really) or bide your time for walk-in lanes at the bar. Under-21s allowed only on weekends before 7pm.

VERDI CLUB CLUB, SPOKEN WORD

Map p312 (415-861-9199; www.verdiclub.net; 2424 Mariposa St; cover free-$25; 22, 27, 33) Throwing swanky soirees since 1916, the Verdi Club hosts the Porchlight storytelling series, punk homecoming dances and swing-dancing lessons. Thursday-night tango at the Verdi features live *bandoneón* (free-reed, accordion-like instrument) players and sharply dressed dancers circling the floor. Check the website for events and bring cash for the velvet-swagged bar.

RITE SPOT CAFE LIVE MUSIC

Map p312 (415-552-6066; www.ritespotcafe.net; 2099 Folsom St; donation appreciated; showtimes 9pm; 12, 22, 33, 16th St Mission) The vintage dive-bar neon in the middle of warehouse nowhere-land is pointing you in the Rite direction for offbeat performances banged out on a tinkling house piano nightly. Check the online calender for enchantingly kooky acts like Reuben Rye playing post-punk piano, Misery Index comedy night or Beatles karaoke – or just follow a hunch and discover the next Tom Waits.

ROCCAPULCO SALSA CLUB

Map p312 (415-648-6611; www.roccapulco.com; 3140 Mission St; admission $10-20; 9pm-2am Thu-Sat; 12, 14, 27, 49, 24th St Mission) Get your salsa, rumba and *bachata* (Dominican dance) on at this high-ceilinged, stadium-sized Latin venue that books sensational international touring acts. Most nights it's a straight bar, ripe with cologne and hormones; women and gay newcomers to the scene may feel more comfortable in a group. Dress like you mean it.

SHOPPING

For prime boutique shopping, hit 16th St between Valencia and Dolores Sts, Valencia from 15th to 24th Sts, and 24th St west of Bryant St. Dogpatch has design boutiques around 22nd and Third Sts and Potrero Flats has upstart galleries wedged between design showrooms.

★GRAVEL & GOLD CLOTHING, LOCAL ARTISANS

Map p312 (415-552-0112; www.gravelandgold.com; 3266 21st St; noon-7pm Mon-Sat, to 5pm Sun; 12, 14, 49, 24th St Mission) Get back to the land and in touch with California's grassroots, without ever leaving sight of a Mission sidewalk. Gravel & Gold celebrates California's hippie homesteader movement with hand-printed smock-dresses, trippy totes and graphic throw pillows. Homestead California-style with hand-thrown stoneware mugs, silkscreened '60s Osborne/Woods ecology posters, and rare books on '70s beach-shack architecture – plus DIY maker workshops (see website).

★ADOBE BOOKS & BACKROOM GALLERY BOOKS, ART

Map p312 (415-864-3936; www.adobebookshop.com; 3130 24th St; noon-8pm Mon-Fri, from 11am Sat & Sun; 12, 14, 48, 49, 24th St Mission) Come here for every book you never knew you needed used and dirt-cheap, plus 'zine launch parties, comedy nights and art openings. Navigate the obstacle course of art books and German philosophy to visit Little Paper Planes (p165) artists in residence, and see breakthrough Backroom Gallery shows – artists who debut here often return to Adobe after showing at Whitney Biennials.

★HEATH CERAMICS HOUSEWARES, LOCAL ARTISAN

Map p312 (415-361-5552; www.heathceramics.com/; 2900 18th St; 10am-6pm Mon-Wed & Fri & Sat, to 7pm Thu, 11am-6pm Sun; 12, 22, 27, 33) Odds are your favorite SF meal was served on Heath Ceramics, Bay Area chefs' tableware of choice ever since chef Alice Waters started using Heath's modern, hand-thrown dishes at Chez Panisse. Heath's muted colors and streamlined, mid-century designs stay true to Edith Heath's originals c 1948. New Heath models and factory rejects are sold here; factory tours also available weekends at 11:30am.

★NEEDLES & PENS GIFTS, BOOKS

Map p312 (415-255-1534; www.needles-pens.com; 3253 16th St; noon-7pm; 14, 22, 33, 49, 16th St Mission) Do it yourself or DIY trying: this scrappy 'zine/how-to/art gallery/publisher delivers inspiration to create your own artworks, 'zines and repurposed fash-

24TH STREET'S GREAT PAPER TRAIL

San Francisco may be the global hub for all things digital, but an analog revolution is afoot on 24th Street. Once-struggling bookstores like Adobe Books have reinvented themselves as member-supported collectives, drawing the community into their fold with raucous readings and local art openings. Down the street from Adobe, **Modern Times Bookstore Collective** (Map p312; ☎415-282-9246; 2919 24th St; ⏰noon-8pm; 👪; 🚌12, 14, 48, 49, Ⓑ24th St) showcases SF's Latin American roots, progressive politics and local lit obsessions. The membership-supported, worker-run collective maintains an action-packed author event calendar, plus deep fiction and nonfiction shelves, vast Spanish-language sections and terrific kids' reading zones.

Alley Cat Books (Map p312; ☎415-824-1761; www.alleycatbookshop.com; 3036 24th St; ⏰10am-9pm Mon-Sat, to 8pm Sun; 👪; 🚌12, 14, 48, 49, Ⓑ24th St) is part bookstore, part community center, with books in the front, art shows in the middle, and a ping-pong table in back. This is not a hush-hush library, but an authentic San Francisco scene – after 5pm, don't be surprised to bump into an urban square dance troupe, free writers' workshop or queer film series in progress.

Press: Works on Paper (Map p312; ☎415-913-7156; http://pressworksonpaper.com/; 3108 24th St; ⏰10am-7pm Mon-Sat, 11am-6pm Sun; 🚌12, 14, 48, Ⓑ24th St) is further proof that paper hasn't lost its touch, featuring deckle-edge stationery and original artworks on vellum alongside small-press poetry chapbooks, out-of-print art books and vintage DIY manuals on subjects from macrame to sex. With such unexpected insights and enticing palimpsest to be found along 24th St's paper trail, e-readers seem overrated.

ion statements. Nab limited-edition printings of Xara Thustra's manifesto *Friendship Between Artists Is An Equation of Love and Survival* and H Finn Cunningham's *Mental Health Cookbook* – plus alphabet buttons to pin your own credo onto a handmade messenger bag.

★AGGREGATE SUPPLY CLOTHING, GIFTS

Map p312 (☎415-474-3190; www.AggregateSupplySF.com; 806 Valencia St; ⏰11am-7pm Mon-Sat, noon-6pm Sun; 🚌14, 33, 49, Ⓑ16th St Mission) Wild West modern is the look at Aggregate Supply, purveyors of West Coast cool fashion and home decor. Local designers and indie makers get pride of place, including vintage Heath stoneware mugs, Turk+Taylor's ombre plaid shirt-jackets, and ingeniously repurposed rodeo-saddle tassel necklaces. Souvenirs don't get more authentically local than Aggregate Supply's own Op-art California graphic tee and NorCal-forest-scented organic soaps.

★LITTLE PAPER PLANES LOCAL ARTISANS, ART

Map p312 (☎415-643-4616; http://littlepaperplanes.com; 855 Valencia St; ⏰noon-7pm Mon-Sat, to 6pm Sun; 🚌14, 33, 49, Ⓑ16th St Mission, ⓂJ) Consider fresh gift possibilities at this purveyor of essential SF oddities: ocean-printed hoodies, SFMOMA-inspired Carrara marble necklaces, eco-friendly glossy black nail polish made in California and self-published manifestos (eg 'Art as a Muscular Principle'). The place is tiny, but thinks big – LPP's artist's residency at Adobe Books (p164) yields original works like Hannah Carr's 3D prints, on sale here.

★NOOWORKS CLOTHING, LOCAL ARTISANS

Map p312 (☎415-829-7623; www.nooworks.com; 395 Valencia St; ⏰11am-7pm Tue-Sat, to 5pm Sun & Mon; 🚌14, 22, 33, 49, Ⓑ16th St Mission) Get a streetwise Mission edge with Nooworks' local-artist-designed fashions, most under $100. Nooworks' evil-eye-print dresses ward off Marina-frat-boy advances, and Muscle Beach maxidresses are Dolores Park-ready, with a psychedelic print of rainbows and flexing bodybuilders that look like California ex-governor Arnold Schwarzenegger. Men's tees featuring cat-headed professors and Ferris Plock's Victorian rowhouses are good to go to any Mission gallery opening.

★TIGERLILY PERFUMERY PERFUME, LOCAL MAKER

Map p312 (☎510-230-7975; www.tigerlilysf.com/; 973 Valencia St; ⏰noon-6pm Wed-Thu, 11am-7pm Fri & Sat, noon-5pm Sun; 🚌14, 33, 49, Ⓑ24th St) If you just want to bottle San

WORTH A DETOUR

BERNAL HEIGHTS

For a quick getaway from the Mission's urban grit, veer off Mission St south of 30th St onto colorful **Cortland Avenue**, lined with quirky Victorian storefront boutiques and laid-back local hangouts. Weekends start just over the hill at **Alemany Market** (www.facebook.com/pages/Alemany-Flea-Market/238369190114; 100 Alemany Blvd (off Hwy 101); flea market 6am-3pm Sun, farmers market dawn-dusk Sat), where California's first farmers market has been held on Saturdays since 1943 – and also the site of Sunday morning flea markets that unearth hidden treasures from Victorian attics.

Urban hikers summit Bernal Heights and go flying down the **Winfield Street double hillside slides** – adults and kids alike – to get good and hungry for brunches at **Bernal Star** (415-695-8777; www.thelibertycafe.com; 410 Cortland Ave; 10am-10pm Tue-Fri, from 9pm Sat, 9am-noon Sun, 10am-3pm Mon; ; 24). If it's home-cooking you're craving, head over to **331 Cortland**, a marketplace that houses local mom-and-pop food kiosks – get the salmon cream cheese piroshki at **Anda Piroshki** (415-574-7334; www.andapiroshki.com; 331 Cortland Ave; piroshki $4.75; 8am-5pm Wed-Mon; 24) or crispy rice-ball salad at **Mae Krua** (415-574-7334; 331 Cortland; 24). Legend has it that Janis Joplin got lucky on the pool table at landmark lesbian bar **Wild Side West** (415-647-3099; www.wildsidewest.com; 424 Cortland Ave; 2pm-2am; 24), but sunny days are ultra-mellow in the blooming sculpture garden.

Francisco and take it home with you, you've come to the right place. Tigerlily stocks an intoxicating variety of local perfumers who will transport you from beach days to Barbary Coast nights, from Yosh Han's California-sunbeam scent appropriately called U4EAHH! to Bruno Fazzolari's inky, sultry Lampblack. Check the calendar for in-person perfume events.

DEMA CLOTHING, ACCESSORIES

Map p312 (415-206-0500; www.godemago.com; 1038 Valencia St; 11am-7pm Mon-Fri, from noon Sat, noon-6pm Sun; 12, 14, 33, 49, B 24th St Mission) BART from Downtown lunches to Mission restaurants in vintage-inspired chic by San Francisco's own Dema Grim. House specialties are flattering bias-cut dresses and floaty silk blouses in original prints, with buttons that look like gumdrops. At this indie designer, you get what you pay for here in squealed compliments – but check bins and sales racks for 60% off scores.

AQUARIUS RECORDS MUSIC

Map p312 (415-647-2272; www.aquariusrecords.org; 1055 Valencia St; noon-8pm Mon-Fri, 11am-9pm Sat, to 7pm Sun; 14, 33, 48, B 16th St Mission) When pop seems played out, this is the dawning of the age of Aquarius Records, featuring Armenian blues, Oakland ravers and rare Japanese releases since 1970. Recent staff favorites include Finnish heavy metal compilations, Thai pop's greatest hits, California's stoner-sound-wizards Vetiver and SF's own POW!, enthusiastically described as 'blown out synth punk.' Street cred alert: the Dead Kennedys met through the Aquarius bulletin board.

COMMUNITY THRIFT CLOTHING, VINTAGE

Map p312 (415-861-4910; www.communitythriftsf.org; 623 Valencia St; 10am-6:30pm; 14, 22, 33, 49, B 16th St Mission) When local collectors and retailers have too much of a good thing, they donate it to Community Thrift, where proceeds go to 200 local nonprofits – all the more reason to gloat over your $5 totem-pole teacup, $10 vintage windbreaker and $14 disco-era glitter romper. Donate your castoffs (until 5pm daily) and show some love to the Community.

GOOD VIBRATIONS ADULT TOYS

Map p312 (415-503-9522; www.goodvibes.com; 603 Valencia St; 10am-10pm Sun-Thu, to 11pm Fri & Sat; 14, 22, 33, 49, B 16th St Mission) 'Wait, I'm supposed to put that where?' The understanding salespeople in this worker-owned cooperative are used to giving rather explicit instructions, so don't hesitate to ask. Margaret Cho is on the board here, so you know they're not shy. Check out the display of antique vibrators, including one that looks like a floor-waxer – thank goodness for modern technology.

ACCIDENT & ARTIFACT GIFTS, LOCAL ARTISANS

Map p312 (415-437-9700; www.accidentandartifact.com; 381 Valencia St; noon-7pm Wed-Sun; 14, 22, 49, 16th St Mission) A highly curious curiosity shop, even by Mission standards. Decorative dried fungi grace scavenged wood displays alongside vintage Okinawan indigo textiles and artfully redrawn topographical maps. Local makers showcased here include the Mission's own Holly Samuelson, who handcrafts envelope clutches in teal and red leather. A&A also makes its own signature SF-scented products, including soul-cleansing Mission Dolores soap.

BLACK & BLUE TATTOO BODY ART

Map p312 (415-626-0770; www.blackandbluetattoo.com; 381 Guerrero St; noon-7pm; 14, 22, 33, 49, 16th St Mission) This women-owned tattoo parlor gets it in ink with designs ranging from geodesic dome bicep emblems to shoulder-to-shoulder Golden Gate Bridge spans. Check out artists' work at the shop or online, then book a consultation. Once you've talked over the design, you can book your tattoo – you'll need to show up sober, well-fed, fragrance-free and clear-headed for your transformation.

MISSION SKATEBOARDS CLOTHING, ACCESSORIES

Map p312 (415-647-7888; www.missionsk8boards.com; 3045 24th St; 11am-7pm; ; 12, 14, 48, 49, 24th St Mission) Street cred comes easy with locally designed Mission decks, custom tees to kick-flip over and cult skate shoes at this shop owned by SF street-skate legend Scot Thompson. Cool deal: kids who show report cards with GPAs over 3.0 get discounts. This shop is handy to Potrero del Sol/La Raza Skatepark (p169), and for newbies too cool for kneepads, SF General.

SCRAP (SCROUNGERS' CENTER FOR RE-USABLE ART PARTS) ACCESSORIES

(415-647-1746; www.scrap-sf.org; 801 Toland St; 9am-5pm Mon-Thu & Sat, to 6pm Fri; ; 9, 15, 23, 24, 44) Renew, recycle and rediscover your creativity with postindustrial arts-and-crafts materials from SCRAP. Take a workshop at SCRAP for inspiration and make your own upcycled dollhouse, repurposed glass mosaic or recycled shag rug. DIY classes are held most Saturdays (see website for listings); the entrance to SCRAP is at the confluence of Hwy 101 and Hwy 280.

DOG-EARED BOOKS BOOKS

Map p312 (415-282-1901; www.dogearedbooks.com; 900 Valencia St; 10am-10pm Mon-Sat, to 9pm Sun; ; 12, 14, 22, 33, 49, 24th St Mission) Novels, remainders and graphic novels pack the shelves, but intriguing new stuff also gets its due with trusty staff picks featuring small presses and local lit, including Gary Kamiya's *Cool Grey City of Love* and Jordan Karnes' *It Hasn't Stopped Being California Here*. Don't miss hand-drawn obituaries to celebrities like Susan Sontag, James Brown and Edward Said displayed in the front window.

BETABRAND CLOTHING

Map p312 (800-694-9491; www.betabrand.com; 780 Valencia St; 11am-7pm Mon-Fri, to 8pm Sat, noon-6pm Sun; 14, 22, 33, 49, 16th St Mission) Crowdsource your fashion choices at Betabrand, where experimental designs are put to an online vote and winners are produced in limited editions. Recent approved designs include office-ready dress yoga pants, disco-ball windbreakers and sundresses with a smiling-poo-emoji print. Some styles are clunkers – including the 'suitsy,' business-suit onesie – but at these prices you can afford to take fashion risks.

PAXTON GATE GIFTS

Map p312 (415-824-1872; paxtongate.com; 824 Valencia St; 11am-7pm; 12, 14, 33, 49, 16th St Mission) Salvador Dalí probably would've shopped here for all his taxidermy and gardening needs. With animal-skull puppets, mad terrariums sprouting from lab beakers and teddy bear heads mounted like hunting trophies, this place is beyond surreal. The kids' shop down the street (766 Valencia St) maximizes playtime with volcano-making kits, shadow puppet-theaters and solar-powered dollhouses. Check DIY taxidermy and amulet-making workshop dates online.

VOYAGER CLOTHING, ACCESSORIES

Map p312 (415-779-2712; www.thevoyagershop.com; 365 Valencia St; 11am-7pm; 14, 22, 33, 49, 16th St Mission) Post-apocalyptic art-school surf-shack is the general vibe inside this curated storefront. The communal love-child of the Haight's Revolver and Austin, Texas-based Spartan plus sundry indie makers, items for sale range from cultish denim shirts and sculptural ninja pants to surfwear and art books in the geodesic submarine gallery. Pop-ups feature statement jewelry, minimalist dresses and artistically inclined office supplies by SF makers.

SPORTS & ACTIVITIES

★PRECITA EYES MISSION MURAL TOURS — TOUR

Map p312 (☎415-285-2287; www.precitaeyes.org; adult $15-20, child $3; ⊙see website calendar for tour dates; 👪; 🚌12, 14, 48, 49, Ⓑ24th St Mission) Muralists lead weekend walking tours covering 60 to 70 Mission murals in a six- to 10-block radius of mural-bedecked Balmy Alley. Tours last 90 minutes to two hours and 15 minutes for the more in-depth Classic Mural Walk. Proceeds fund mural upkeep at this community arts nonprofit.

★18 REASONS — COOKING

Map p312 (☎415-568-2710; www.18reasons.org; 3674 18th St; classes & events $3-65; ⊙varies by event; 👪; 🚌22, 33, ⓂJ) Go gourmet at this Bi-Rite–affiliated community food nonprofit, which offers deliciously educational events: wine tastings, knife-skills and cheesemaking workshops, and cross-cultural culinary classes. Mingle with fellow foodies at family-friendly, $10 Wednesday community suppers and $3 to $10 Thursday happy hours. Check the website for bargain guest chef pop-ups and low-cost classes with cookbook authors. Spots fill up quickly for the excellent hands-on cooking classes, so book early.

MISSION CULTURAL CENTER FOR LATINO ARTS — ARTS CLASSES

Map p312 (☎415-643-5001; www.missionculturalcenter.org; 2868 Mission St; ⊙5-10pm Mon, 10am-10pm Tue-Fri, to 5:30pm Sat; 👪; 🚌14, 49, Ⓑ24th St Mission) Join a class in tango, take up the congas, get crafty with your kids or create a protest poster at the printmaking studio at the Mission's legendary Latino arts hub. Teachers are friendly and participants range from *niños* (kids) to *abuelos* (grandparents). Check the online calendar for upcoming gallery openings; don't miss **Día de los Muertos** altar displays in November.

URBAN PUTT — MINIATURE GOLF

(☎415-341-1080; www.urbanputt.com/; 1096 S Van Ness; adult/child $12/8; ⊙4pm-midnight Mon-Thu, to 1am Fri, 11am-1am Sat, 11am-midnight Sun) Leave it to the town that brought you Burning Man and The Exploratorium to make an innocent mini-golf game into a total trip. Urban Putt's course looks like a Tim Burton hallucination, from tricky windmill Transamerica Pyramid Hole 5 to Dia de los Muertos–themed Hole 9. Enjoy big beers with wee snacks, including mini-corndogs, mini-cupcakes and tiny chicken and waffle stacks on sticks.

ANCHOR BREWING COMPANY — BREWERY TOUR

Map p314 (☎415-863-8350; www.anchorbrewing.com; 1705 Mariposa St; tour adults $15, kids free (no beer); ⊙reservations 9am-4pm Mon-Fri, tours 10am & 1pm Mon-Fri, 11am & 1pm Sat; 🚌10, 19, 22) Beer lovers, here's your best-ever excuse for day-drinking: Anchor Brewing Company shares steam-brewing secrets on weekday public tours with extensive beer

WORTH A DETOUR

SAN FRANCISCO 49ERS

The **49ers** (☎415-656-4900; www.sf49ers.com; Levi's Stadium, Santa Clara, CA; tickets $43-569 at www.ticketmaster.com; 🚆Caltrain Santa Clara Station) were National Football League's dream team from 1981–94, claiming five Superbowl championships. But after decades of chilly, fumbled games at foggy Candlestick Park, the 49ers moved to Santa Clara's brand-new Levi's Stadium in 2014. Some fans argue the team should be renamed, since Santa Clara's 38 miles from San Francisco. But it was a winning move: Levi's Stadium is hosting Superbowl 50 in 2016.

To reach the stadium, take CalTrain one hour south to Santa Clara station, then catch the game-day shuttle. Since the new stadium is in Silicon Valley, it's tricked out with technology, from the power-generating solar roof to wi-fi-enabled tickets and concessions. Maybe there's hope yet: in a superstitious effort to align the team with San Francisco Giants' bearded winning streak, the team's bread-loving mining mascot Sourdough Sam now sports a beard.

tastings. The 45-minute tour covers Anchor's 1937 Potrero Hill landmark building and shiny-copper equipment, followed by a 45-minute beer-tasting with several half-pints of Anchor brews (sorry kids: no beer for under-21s). Make reservations via the website a month in advance.

POTRERO DEL SOL/LA RAZA SKATEPARK — SKATING

Map p312 (25th & Utah Sts; 8am-9pm; 9, 10, 27, 33, 48, B 24th St Mission) Grab air with pro skaters blasting ollies off SF's best concrete bowls. Downsides: the bathroom is sketchy and graffiti on the concrete can make for a slippery ride. Wait for a clean area of the bowl to bust big moves and leave room for little skaters in kneepads. For gear, hit up nearby Mission Skateboards (p167).

DANCE MISSION — DANCE CLASSES

Map p312 (415-826-4441; www.dancemission.com; 3316 24th St; ; 12, 14, 48, 49, B 24th St Mission) Step out and find your niche at this nonprofit Mission dance hub, featuring contact improv, dance jams and classes in styles from Afro-Haitian to vogue – there's a class here for every interest and skill level. Check the website for dance showcases in the 140-seat theater, plus events and guest-artist workshops ranging from beginner taiko drumming to dancing in stilts.

SAN FRANCISCO CENTER FOR THE BOOK — ART CLASSES

Map p314 (415-565-0545; www.sfcb.org; 300 De Haro St; admission free; classes vary; gallery 10am-5:30pm Mon-Sun; 8, 10, 19, 22, 33) FREE Beautiful books are handmade daily at San Francisco's community press. Beyond traditional binding workshops, this nonprofit offers hands-on classes that teach you to make books that fit into matchboxes, pop up into theaters and turn digital works into analog wonders. SFCB also hosts September's **Roadworks Street Fair**, where artists use a three-ton construction steamroller to make prints on the street.

The Castro & Noe Valley

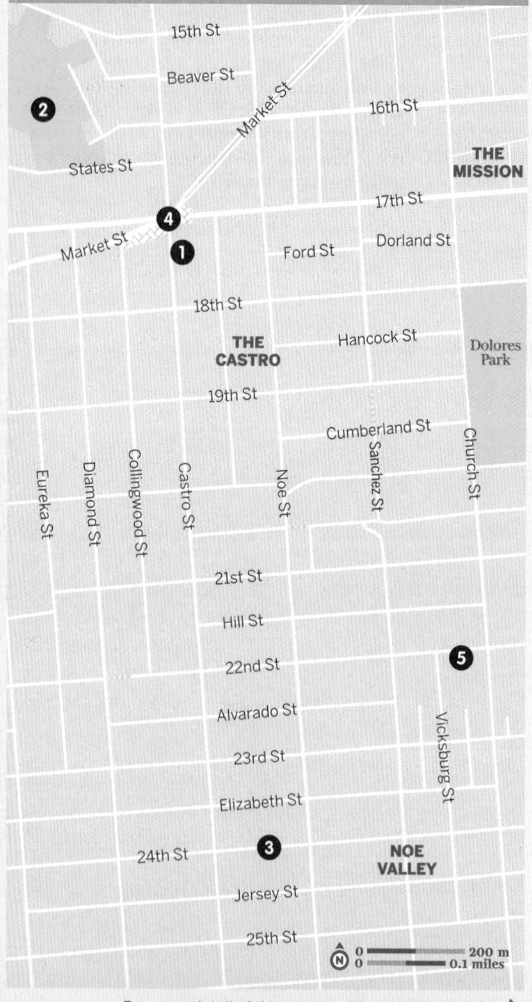

For more detail of this area see Map p320 and p321

Neighborhood Top Five

❶ Catching an evening film at the **Castro Theatre** (p178) and hearing the Mighty Wurlitzer's pipes roar before showtime.

❷ Climbing **Corona Heights** (p172) at sunset and watching Market St light up below.

❸ Dodging baby strollers on **24th St** as you window-shop indie stores.

❹ Watching for kooky naked dudes at **Jane Warner Plaza** (p172).

❺ Not going over the handlebars while biking down SF's steepest street, **22nd St** (p173).

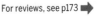

Explore the Castro & Noe Valley

The Castro's main crossroads is at the intersection of Market, 17th and Castro Sts. Noe Valley extends along 24th St, a scant mile down Castro, over the (gigantic) 21st St hill. You can explore both neighborhoods in a few hours.

Mornings are quiet. The Castro is busiest afternoons and evenings, especially weekends, when crowds come to people-watch, shop and drink; at night expect to see 20-somethings stumbling down Castro's wide sidewalks. Noe Valley is best midday and in the afternoon – there's not much open after 7pm, just some bars and restaurants.

If the 21st St Hill atop Castro St proves too daunting, bus 24-Divasadero connects the two neighborhoods but it's notorious for gaps in service: expect to wait or check www.nextmuni.com for real-time arrivals. In Noe Valley, shops on 24th St extend between Diamond and Church Sts; and on Church St, the restaurants and shops continue until the last stop on the J-Church line, around 29th St. Castro-area shops line Market St, between Church and Castro Sts, and Castro St itself, from Market to 19th Sts, with a few scattered along 18th St. Both neighborhoods are surrounded by residential streets, good for strolling, with many pretty Victorians.

Local Life

➡ **Hangouts** The Wednesday afternoon Castro Farmers Market (March through November) provides the best glimpse of locals, especially from sidewalk tables at Cafe Flore (p177).

➡ **Drinking** The Castro is packed with bars, but most don't get going till evening. For listings, pick up a copy of *BarTab* magazine – supplement to the local, gay *Bay Area Reporter* newspaper.

➡ **Paying homage** When a friend of the community dies, locals lay flowers and post pictures on the wall of the B of A building at 18th & Castro – always a touching sight.

➡ **What (not) to wear** You may be tempted to flaunt your gym-toned physique in the sexy Castro, but once afternoon fog blows, carry a jacket or shiver – locals spot tourists by their shorts and tank tops.

Getting There & Away

➡ **Metro** K, L and M trains run beneath Market St to Castro Station. J trains serve Noe Valley.

➡ **Streetcar** Vintage streetcars operate on the F-Market line, from Fisherman's Wharf to Castro St.

➡ **Bus** The 24 and 33 lines operate to the Castro but may have long waits between buses. The 24 and 48 lines serve Noe Valley.

Lonely Planet's Top Tip

Historic streetcars run like toy trains along the waterfront and up Market St, from Fisherman's Wharf to the Castro, via Downtown. Trouble is, trains sometimes get stuck in traffic and you can wait forever. Check arrival times at www.nextmuni.com, which uses GPS tracking; use the 'live map' to determine trains' exact locations. If the F-Market service is far away or running slow, take underground-metro K, L or M trains, which move (much) faster beneath Market St – same ticket, same price.

Best Places to Eat

➡ Frances (p176)
➡ Starbelly (p173)
➡ Anchor Oyster Bar (p173)
➡ Chow (p173)
➡ Dinosaurs (p176)

For reviews, see p173 

Best Places to Drink

➡ Cafe Flore (p177)
➡ Blackbird (p177)
➡ 440 Castro (p177)
➡ Moby Dick (p177)
➡ Twin Peaks Tavern (p177)

For reviews, see p177

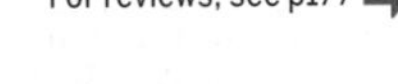

Best Places to Shop

➡ Sui Generis (p179)
➡ Unionmade (p179)
➡ The Podolls (p180)
➡ Omnivore (p180)
➡ Cliff's Variety (p179)

For reviews, see p179 

SIGHTS

★ **CASTRO THEATRE** THEATER

Map p320 (415-621-6120; www.castrotheatre.com; 429 Castro St; Tue-Sun; Castro) The city's grandest movie palace opened in 1922. The Spanish-Moorish exterior yields to mishmash styles inside, from Italianate to Oriental. Ask nicely and staff may let you peek, or come for the nightly cult or classic films, or one of the many film festivals here – check calendars online. For evening shows, arrive early to hear the organist play before the curtain rises. For the best photos of the blue-and-pink neon-lit marquis, shoot the downhill side from across the street.

GLBT HISTORY MUSEUM MUSEUM

Map p320 (415-621-1107; www.glbthistory.org/museum; 4127 18th St; admission $5, 1st Wed of month free; 11am-7pm Mon-Sat, noon-5pm Sun, closed Tue fall-spring; Castro) America's first gay-history museum cobbles ephemera from the community – Harvey Milk's campaign literature, matchbooks from long-gone bathhouses, and photographs of early activists – together with harder-hitting installations that focus on various aspects of queer history, incorporating electronic media to tell personal stories that illuminate the evolution of the struggle to gain rights and acceptance into the larger culture.

It's fascinating to see pieces of the gay collective past, and although the curatorial vision sometimes feels timid, it's well worth a look. You can also pick up great gay-SF souvenir T-shirts, including one of Milk, emblazoned with his famous inspirational quotation, 'You gotta give 'em hope.' Indeed.

HARVEY MILK & JANE WARNER PLAZAS SQUARE

Map p320 (Market & Castro Sts; Castro) A huge rainbow flag flaps above Castro and Market Sts, officially Harvey Milk Plaza. Look closer and spot a plaque honoring the man whose legacy is gay civic pride and political clout. Across Castro, by the F-train terminus, is Jane Warner Plaza, where rag-tag oddballs and kids too young for the bars congregate at public tables and chairs.

For more on Milk, wander down the Muni-metro stairs to see text and images of his life. Jane Warner was a much-loved lesbian police officer. Compared with loud-mouth Harvey, Jane was modest – which makes it doubly ironic that in 2012 her namesake plaza attracted international attention for public nudity. Several flagrant exhibitionists lollygagged here dawn till dusk, casually splaying their legs at oncoming traffic. Their passive-aggressive behavior incited such outcry that public nudity in SF was eventually dubbed illegal – but not a sex crime, just an infraction. Now it's legal to strip only at a handful of public events, like Folsom Street Fair. You can still often spot the 'naked guys' at the plaza, only now they wear socks on their penises, posing for pictures with tourists by F-Market trains.

RAINBOW HONOR WALK LANDMARK

(http://rainbowhonorwalk.org; Castro St, from 18th to 20th Sts; Castro) Castro Street got a major makeover in 2014, when the city doubled the width of the sidewalks, painted rainbow crosswalks at 18th St, and laid into the concrete 20 three-foot-square plaques honoring GLBT heroes – diverse as Oscar Wilde and Sylvester, Gertrude Stein and Keith Haring – whose portraits are acid-etched in bronze, captioned with illuminating text. They look particularly fab at night, when new LED lights, mounted on street-lamps above, cast changing colors onto the sidewalk. For the full roster of names, see the website.

CORONA HEIGHTS PARK PARK

Map p320 (btwn 16th St & Roosevelt Way; 37, Castro) Scramble up the rocky 520ft Corona Heights summit (aka Museum Hill or Red Rocks) for jaw-dropping, eastward 180-degree views. Come evening, the city unfurls below in a carpet of light. Take tiny Beaver St uphill to the steps through the bushes, then cut right of the tennis courts, up the trail. For an easier hike, enter via the Roosevelt Way side.

RANDALL JUNIOR MUSEUM CHILDREN'S MUSEUM

Map p320 (415-554-9600; www.randallmuseum.org; 199 Museum Way; admission free; 10am-5pm Tue-Sat; ; 24, 37, Castro) FREE Kids go cuckoo for live-animal exhibits of urban wildlife – racoons, owls, more racoons – and earth-science exhibits at this oh-so-cute nature museum near the summit of Corona Heights Park. Saturdays are best, when incredible **Golden Gate Model Railroad Club** (Map p320; www.ggmrc.org; admission free; 10am-4pm Sat) FREE opens its doors. Check website for wonder-inspiring hands-on workshops. Until autumn 2016, they're in temporary digs in the Mission while they redo the space; call ahead.

NOBBY CLARKE MANSION HISTORIC BUILDING

Map p320 (250 Douglass St, at Caselli Ave; ⓂCastro) Built in 1892 by an attorney who wanted sunnier weather than fashionable Nob Hill afforded, this gorgeous Queen Anne mansion went uninhabited after its construction: Snob Hill socialites dubbed the house 'Nobby Clarke's Folly' and his wife refused to move in. It served briefly as a hospital; now it's apartments.

22ND ST HILL STREET

Map p321 (22nd St, btwn Church & Vicksburg Sts; ⓂJ) The prize for the steepest street is shared between two SF streets: Filbert St (between Hyde and Leavenworth) and here. Both have 31.5% grades (17-degree slope), but there's barely any traffic on 22nd and nothing quite beats the thrill of cycling down it, grabbing two fistfuls of brakes, trying not to go over the bars – not for the faint of heart.

EATING

Most Castro restaurants lie on Market St, from Church to Castro Sts, and around the intersection of Castro and 18th Sts. In Noe Valley, find quick lunch spots along 24th St, between Church and Diamond Sts.

The Castro

CHILE PIES NEW MEXICAN $

Map p320 (http://greenchilekitchen.com; 314 Church St; dishes $5-9; ⏲noon-10pm; ⓂChurch) This tiny bakery and quick-lunch counter spins all-American classic pies with a Southwestern zip. Drawing inspiration from New Mexico, Chile Pies integrates not-hot green chilies into sweet and savory pastries, made with organic ingredients and flaky all-butter crusts. Standouts include sweet green chili-apple pie and savory chicken pot pies with green-chili stew.

STARBELLY CALIFORNIAN, PIZZA $$

Map p320 (☎415-252-7500; www.starbellysf.com; 3583 16th St; dishes $8-24; ⏲11:30am-11pm Mon-Thu, to midnight Fri, 10:30am-midnight Sat, 10:30am-11pm Sun; ⓂCastro) The seasonal small plates at always-busy Starbelly include standout *salumi,* market-fresh salads, scrumptious pâté, roasted mussels with housemade sausage and thin-crusted pizzas. The barnlike rooms get loud; sit on the heated patio for quieter conversation. If you can't score a table, consider its neighboring burger joint, **Super Duper Burger** (Map p320; www.superdupersf.com; 2304 Market St; ⏲11am-11pm; ⓂCastro) for all-natural burgers and milkshakes.

ANCHOR OYSTER BAR SEAFOOD $$

Map p320 (www.anchoroysterbar.com; 579 Castro St; mains $16-28; ⏲11:30am-10pm Mon-Sat, 4-9:30pm Sun; ⓂCastro) Since its founding in 1977, Anchor's formula has been simple: seafood classics, like local oysters, crab cakes, Boston clam chowder and copious salads. The nautical-themed room seats just 24 at stainless-steel tables; you can't make reservations, but for faster service sit at the marble-top bar. Or wait outside with vino on the bench until you're called.

CHOW AMERICAN $$

Map p312 (☎415-552-2469; www.chowfoodbar.com; 215 Church St; mains $11-20; ⏲11am-11pm; ; ⓂChurch) Chow's diverse menu appeals to all tastes, with everything from pizza to pork chops and Thai-style noodles to spaghetti and meatballs. The wood-floored room is big, loud and always busy. Avoid tables alongside the bar (you'll get jostled); request a table on the back patio for quiet(er) conversations. Call ahead for the 'no-wait' list.

HECHO MEXICAN $$

Map p320 (☎415-926-5630; www.hechoinsf.com; 2200 Market St; dinner mains $13-23, brunch $9-13; ⏲5-10pm Mon-Thu, 5-11pm Fri, 11am-11pm Sat, 11am-10pm Sun; ; ⓂChurch) Big, loud and fun, Hecho makes good sit-down Mexican food, including standout duck-mole tacos and short-rib quesadillas, good for sharing and served with bandanas as napkins. Its best asset may be the bar and the stellar selection of tequila and mezcal craft cocktails – including fabulous margaritas – perfect for a boozy weekend brunch.

LA MÉDITERRANÉE MIDDLE EASTERN $$

Map p320 (☎415-431-7210; www.lamediterranee.net; 288 Noe St; mains $12-18; ⏲11am-10pm Sun-Thu, to 10:30pm Fri & Sat; ; ⓂCastro) Zesty, lemon-laced Lebanese fare at friendly

LATITUDESTOCK - BILL BACHMANN / GETTY IMAGES ©

JUSTIN SULLIVAN / GETTY IMAGES ©

ALLARD SCHAGER / 500PX ©

LYNN Y / SHUTTERSTOCK ©

1. The Castro (p170)
Rainbow pride flags and buskers pepper the Castro and Market streetscapes.

2. GLBT History Museum (p172)
Proud moments and historic challenges are captured at the first gay-history museum in the USA.

3. F-Market Streetcar (p171)
Travel in retro style on the F-line trolley, which runs from Fisherman's Wharf to the Castro.

4. Castro Theatre (p172 & p178)
The city's grandest movie palace continues to draw crowds to its often-raucous screenings.

prices makes La Méd the Castro's meet-up spot. Chicken kebabs on rice pilaf are pleasingly plump; the *kibbe* harmoniously blends pine nuts, ground lamb and cracked wheat; and the smoky eggplant in the baba ghanoush was roasted for hours and isn't the least bit bitter about it.

There's a second branch in Pacific Heights.

★FRANCES CALIFORNIAN **$$$**

Map p320 (415-621-3870; www.frances-sf.com; 3870 17th St; mains $22-30; 5-10pm Sun-Thu, to 10:30pm Fri & Sat; MCastro) Chef/owner Melissa Perello earned a Michelin star for fine dining, then ditched downtown to start this market-inspired neighborhood bistro. Daily menus showcase bright, seasonal flavors and luxurious textures: cloudlike sheep's-milk ricotta gnocchi with crunchy breadcrumbs and broccolini, grilled calamari with preserved Meyer lemon, and artisan wine served by the ounce, directly from Wine Country.

L'ARDOISE FRENCH **$$$**

Map p320 (415-437-2600; www.ardoisesf.com; 151 Noe St; mains $19-34; 5:30-10pm Tue-Sat; MF, K, L, M, N) For date night with an all-local crowd, this storefront neighborhood charmer on a leafy side street is perfectly placed for some strolling hand-in-hand after dining on classic French-bistro fare, including perfect *steak-frites*. Dim lighting adds sex appeal but the room gets noisy – especially weekends – when the cheek-by-jowl tables fill. Make reservations.

Noe Valley

TATAKI SOUTH SUSHI **$$**

(415-282-1889; www.tatakisushibar.com; 1740 Church St; dishes $5-20; 5-10pm; MJ) Pioneering sushi chefs Kin Lui and Raymond Ho have high standards for sustainably sourced fish, paired with unusual ingredients for exceptional delicacies: silky Arctic char drizzled with yuzu-citrus (like a sour mandarin) replaces at-risk wild salmon; and the Golden State Roll is a local hero, featuring spicy, line-caught scallop, Pacific tuna, organic-apple slivers and yuzu-tobiko. It's right on the J-Church streetcar line.

LOVEJOY'S TEA ROOM BAKERY **$$**

Map p321 (415-648-5895; www.lovejoystearoom.com; 1351 Church St; high tea $15-25; 11am-5pm Wed-Sun; ; MJ) All the chintz you'd expect from an English tearoom but with a San Francisco crowd: curators talk video-installation art over Lapsang souchong, scones and clotted cream, while dual dads take their daughters and dolls out for 'wee tea' of tiny sandwiches, petits fours and hot chocolate. Make reservations.

DRINKING & NIGHTLIFE

Castro bars open earlier than in other neighborhoods; on weekends most open at noon.

CHEAP EATS: THE CASTRO & NOE VALLEY

Dinosaurs (Map p320; http://dinosaursrestaurant.com; 2275 Market St, lower level; sandwiches $7; 7am-10pm Tue-Fri, 10am-10pm Sat & Sun; MCastro) Stellar Vietnamese sandwiches on crusty French bread – our fave for quick eats.

Burgermeister (Map p320; www.burgermeistersf.com; 138 Church St; burgers $9-12; 11am-11pm; ; MChurch) All-natural burgers and fries.

Taqueria Zapata (Map p320; 4150 18th St; dishes $5-12; 11am-10pm Thu-Tue; ; MCastro) Castro's best burritos.

Mollie Stone's Market (Map p320; www.molliestones.com; 4201 18th St; 7am-11pm; MCastro) High-end grocery with prepared foods.

Noe Valley Bakery (Map p321; www.noevalleybakery.com; 4073 24th St; dishes $4-8; 7am-7pm Mon-Fri, to 6pm Sat & Sun; ; 24, 48) Sandwiches on house-baked bread, plus croissants and éclairs.

Barney's Burgers (Map p321; www.barneyshamburgers.com; 4138 24th St; burgers $8-12; 11am-9:30pm; ; 24, 48) All-natural burgers and big salads.

CAFE FLORE CAFE

Map p320 (☎415-621-8579; www.cafeflore.com; 2298 Market St; ⏰7am-1am Sun-Thu, to 2am Fri & Sat; 📶; Ⓜ Castro) You haven't done the Castro till you've idled on the sun-drenched patio at the Flore – everyone winds up here sooner or later. Weekdays present the best chance to meet neighborhood regulars, who colonize the tables outside. Weekends get packed. Great happy-hour drink specials, like two-for-one margaritas. The food's okay, too. Wi-fi weekdays only; no electrical outlets.

HEARTH COFFEE ROASTERS CAFE

Map p320 (www.hearthcoffee.com; 3985 17th St; ⏰7am-6pm Mon-Tue, 7am-8pm Wed-Fri, 8am-8pm Sat, 8am-6pm Sun; 📶; Ⓜ Castro) 🌿 At the F-Market terminus, Hearth is an ideal place to wait for the train on a foggy day, with a strong cup of single-origin house-roasted coffee or big glass of California wine. Mornings they make outstanding pastries, notably croissants, and at lunchtime there's a daily-changing menu of terrific soups, organic salads and sandwiches.

SAMOVAR TEA LOUNGE CAFE

Map p320 (☎415-626-4700; www.samovartea.com; 498 Sanchez St; ⏰10am-10pm; 📶; Ⓜ Castro) Zen-chic Samovar's sunny Castro location specializes in organic, fair-trade teas and provides a fresh alternative to the bars. Sandwiches and cheese plates, paired with tea, provide reason to linger. Make reservations for peak times.

BLACKBIRD GAY BAR

Map p320 (☎415-503-0630; www.blackbirdbar.com; 2124 Market St; ⏰3pm-2am Mon-Fri, from 2pm Sat & Sun; Ⓜ Church) Castro's first-choice lounge-bar draws an unpretentious mix of guys in tight T-shirts and their gal-pals for seasonally changing cocktails made with bitters and tinctures, good wine and craft beer by the glass, billiards and – everyone's favorite bar amenity – the photo booth. Ideal on a Castro pub crawl, but crowded on weekends.

440 CASTRO GAY BAR

Map p320 (☎415-621-8732; www.the440.com; 440 Castro St; ⏰noon-2am; Ⓜ Castro) The most happening bar on the street, 440 draws bearded, gym-fit 30- and 40-something dudes – especially for Thursday's 'CDXL', when go-go boys twirl – and an odd mix of Peter Pans for Monday's underwear night.

MOBY DICK GAY BAR

Map p320 (☎415-861-1199; www.mobydicksf.com; 4049 18th St; ⏰noon-2am; Ⓜ Castro) The name overpromises, but not regarding the giant fish tank behind the bar, which provides a focal point for shy boys who would otherwise look at their shoes. Weekdays it's a mellow spot for pool, pinball and meeting neighborhood 20-to-40-somethings.

TWIN PEAKS TAVERN GAY BAR

Map p320 (☎415-864-9470; www.twinpeakstavern.com; 401 Castro St; ⏰noon-2am Mon-Fri, from 8am Sat & Sun; Ⓜ Castro) Don't call it the glass coffin. Show some respect: Twin Peaks was the world's first gay bar with windows open to the street. The jovial crowd skews (way) over 40, but they're not chicken hawks (or they wouldn't hang here) and they love it when happy kids show up to join the party.

Ideal for a tête-à-tête after a film at the Castro, or for cards, Yahtzee or backgammon (BYO).

MIX GAY BAR

Map p320 (☎415-431-8616; www.sfmixbar.com; 4086 18th St; ⏰7am-2am Mon-Fri, from 6am Sat & Sun; Ⓜ Castro) The last Castro bar to open at 6am, Mix is a must on a pub crawl. We like the low-ceilinged pool and bar area but prefer the open-roofed smokers patio. Expect gal-next-door lesbians, 20-something gay boys, trans pals and the odd stumbling drag queen. Great drink specials keep everyone happy. On Mondays there's free pool.

HITOPS SPORTS BAR

Map p320 (http://hitopssf.com; 2247 Market St; ⏰4pm-midnight Mon-Wed, 4pm-2am Thu-Fri, 11am-2am Sat, noon-2am Sun; Ⓜ Castro) If you thought homosexuality and team sports were incompatible, you haven't spent Sunday at Castro's first gay sports bar, doing shots with softball leaguers, scarfing down fries and screaming at giant-screen TVs. Hard not to love its collegial pub vibe, full-length shuffleboard table, fat comfy bar stools and cutie-pie barkeeps – but damn, it's loud.

MIDNIGHT SUN GAY BAR

Map p320 (☎415-861-4186; www.midnightsunsf.com; 4067 18th St; ⏰2pm-2am; Ⓜ Castro) Midnight Sun got a makeover in 2014, and the once dark and gloomy video bar has become one of the Castro's A-list bars, especially for

Friday's always-packed bear happy hour, and on Monday evenings, when drag queen extraordinaire Honey Mahogany hosts her 10pm show. Other nights, it's a reliable spot for strong drinks and good videos.

LOOKOUT GAY BAR

Map p320 (☎415-431-0306; www.lookoutsf.com; 3600 16th St; ⏲3:30pm-2am Mon-Fri, from 12:30pm Sat & Sun; Ⓜ Castro) A favorite for its street-view balcony, Lookout packs in gym-fit 30-somethings. Monday's karaoke provides fun on Castro's quietest night; DJs spin other evenings. Hot rugby players come by on Sunday afternoons for Jock. No cat-calling from the balcony, please!

EDGE GAY BAR

Map p320 (http://qbarsf.com/EDGE/; 4149 18th St; ⏲noon-2am; Ⓜ Castro) When you're feeling kinda ratty and you're looking for a daddy, it's the Edge. And who says drag queens and leather men can't be friends? See how close they draw to one another on Musical Mondays, when everyone sings along to standards and show tunes.

BADLANDS GAY BAR

Map p320 (☎415-626-9320; www.badlands-sf.com; 4121 18th St; Ⓜ Castro) The Castro's longstanding dance bar gets packed with gay college boys, their screaming straight girlfriends and chicken hawks. If you're over 30, you'll feel old. Expect lines on weekends.

CAFE GAY NIGHTCLUB

Map p320 (www.cafesf.com; 2369 Market St; cover free to $5; ⏲5pm-2am Mon-Fri, from 3pm Sat & Sun; Ⓜ Castro) The Cafe draws a just-over-21 crowd – especially Fridays for Boy Bar – to its upstairs dance floor with kick-ass sound and high-tech lighting. Parties range from Latino to lesbian; check the calendar. If you're not dancing, cruise the open-air smokers lounge or shoot pool beneath trippy lights that make it hard to aim after your second cocktail.

TOAD HALL GAY BAR

Map p320 (☎415-621-2811; www.toadhallbar.com; 4146 18th St; ⏲3pm-2am; Ⓜ Castro) Posses of pals get their drink on fast with Toad Hall's 2-for-1 happy hour till 8:30pm. Dig the smokers patio and little dance floor. The name derives from Castro's original gay bar, forgotten until the film *Milk,* but this bears no resemblance.

BEAUX GAY & LESBIAN

Map p320 (www.beauxsf.com; 2344 Market St; cover free-$5; ⏲4pm-2am Mon-Fri, noon-2am Sat & Sun; Ⓜ Castro) Part lounge, part dance bar, Beaux has a changing lineup of live entertainment, theme nights and DJ parties, including Throwback Thursdays ('80s night), Manimal Fridays (plucked and primped go-go boys) and disco Saturdays (tip: find the mezzanine for best views over the floor). Arrive before 10pm to beat the cover.

QBAR GAY BAR

Map p320 (☎415-864-2877; www.qbarsf.com; 456 Castro St; ⏲4pm-2am Mon-Fri, from 2pm Sat & Sun; Ⓜ Castro) Barely 20-somethings pack shoulder-to-shoulder to shout over ear-splitting pop and dance on the tiny floor. Smokers fill the patio. Occasional go-go boys add spice but lately QBar's been going straight – except at Wednesday's staple, Booty Call.

ENTERTAINMENT

★CASTRO THEATRE CINEMA

Map p320 (☎415-621-6120; www.castrotheatre.com; 429 Castro St; adult/child $11/8.50; ⏲showtimes vary; Ⓜ Castro) The Mighty Wurlitzer organ rises from the orchestra pit before evening performances and the audience cheer for the Great American Songbook, ending with: 'San Francisco open your Golden Gate/You let no stranger wait outside your door...' If there's a cult classic on the bill, say, *Whatever Happened to Baby Jane?,* expect participation. Otherwise, crowds are well-behaved and rapt.

CAFE DU NORD/SWEDISH AMERICAN HALL LIVE MUSIC

Map p320 (☎415-471-2969; www.cafedunord.com; 2170 Market St; cover varies; ⏲5pm-2am; Ⓜ Church) Rockers, chanteuses and other musicians perform nightly at this former basement speakeasy with bar, restaurant and showroom, and the joint still looks like it did in the '30s. The hall upstairs, with balcony seating and Scandinavian woodwork, hosts bigger concerts. Check the online calendar.

SHOPPING

The Castro

★SUI GENERIS CLOTHING, ACCESSORIES

Map p320 (www.suigenerisconsignment.com; sportswear shop 2231 Market St, formal wear shop 2265 Market St; ⌚11am-7pm Mon-Sat, 11am-5pm Sun; Ⓜ Castro) Emerge with confidence from these designer boutiques – one for sportswear, one for formal wear – certain that nobody but you will be working your new look. The well-curated collection of contemporary and vintage clothing skews towards dressy – best for those with fat wallets who fit runway-model sizes.

★LOCAL TAKE GIFTS

Map p320 (localtakesf.com; 3979 B 17th St; ⌚11am-7pm; Ⓜ Castro) This marvelous little shop, next to the F-Market terminus, carries the perfect gifts to take home: SF-specific merchandise, all made locally. Our favorite items include a miniature scale model of Sutro Tower; T-shirts emblazoned with iconic SF locales; cable car and Golden Gate Bridge jewelry; woodcut city maps; knit caps; and snappy one-of-a-kind belt buckles.

CLIFF'S VARIETY HOUSEWARES

Map p320 (www.cliffsvariety.com; 479 Castro St; ⌚10am-8pm Mon-Sat, 10am-6pm Sun; Ⓜ Castro) None of the hardware maestros at Cliff's will raise an eyebrow if you express a dire need for a jar of rubber nuns, silver body paint and a case of cocktail toothpicks, though they might angle for an invitation. The window displays here, a community institution since 1936, are a local landmark.

UNIONMADE CLOTHING, SHOES

Map p320 (www.unionmadegoods.com; 493 Sanchez St; ⌚11am-7pm Mon-Sat, noon-6pm Sun; Ⓜ Castro) Upgrade your casual-Friday look with Unionmade's mix of classic quality labels – American-heritage brands like Pendleton and Levi's Vintage, plus European staples like Il Bisonte leather goods, and a fab selection of handmade shoes by Red Wing and Alden.

ALFIO MEN'S CLOTHING

Map p320 (☎415-241-9200; 2nd fl, 526 Castro St; ⌚11am-8pm Mon-Sat, to 7pm Sun; Ⓜ Castro) The line between Euro and gay blurs at this swanky upstairs boutique, specializing in clothing by lesser-known Italian designers, imported directly from Milan. Stellar shopping for those particular about cut and fit but expect to spend. Great for denim.

BOOKS INC BOOKS

Map p320 (www.booksinc.net; 2275 Market St; ⌚10am-9pm, to 10pm Fri & Sat; Ⓜ Castro) The Castro's indie bookstore carries new-release hardcovers, good fiction, extensive magazines and travel books. Check bulletin boards for readings and literary events.

HUMAN RIGHTS CAMPAIGN ACTION CENTER & STORE GIFTS, CLOTHING

Map p320 (http://shop.hrc.org; 575 Castro St; ⌚10am-8pm Mon-Sat, to 7pm Sun; Ⓜ Castro) Make more than a fashion statement in signature HRC tees designed by Marc Jacobs, Kenneth Cole and other fashion-forward thinkers, with proceeds supporting LGBT civil-rights initiatives. Hopeful romantics shop for sterling-silver rings, while activists scan the bulletin board and petitions.

If this storefront seems familiar, you're right: this was once Harvey Milk's camera shop and one of the locations used in the Academy Award–winning *Milk*.

KENNETH WINGARD HOUSEWARES

Map p320 (www.kennethwingard.com; 2319 Market St; ⌚noon-8pm Mon-Fri, 11am-7pm Sat & Sun; Ⓜ Castro) Upgrade from ho-hum IKEA to mod housewares that are positively scrumptious: glossy tangerine vases, vintage tiki-fabric cushions and mood-setting, ecofriendly, cork-shaded lamps, all priced for mass consumption.

WORN OUT WEST ACCESSORIES

Map p320 (http://worn-out-west-2nd-generation.myshopify.com; 582 Castro St; ⌚10am-midnight; Ⓜ Castro) Left your gear at home? Find leathers, original-cut Levi's 501s, cockrings and tanks at this old-school-Castro used-clothing store and dress like a slutty local. Good fetish wear at great prices. Not much for gals, alas.

Noe Valley

RABAT CLOTHING, SHOES

Map p321 (☎415-282-7861; www.rabatsshoes.com; 4001 24th St; ⌚10:30am-7pm Mon-Sat, 11am-6pm Sun; 🚌24, 48, Ⓜ J) With frenetic collections of high-end and local designers –

some of whom work in-store – Rabat offers style without sacrificing function, with Michael Stars tees and wrinkle-free Canadian brand Simply. The owner hits Europe's shows to personally select the bounce-in-your-step men's shoes and snazzy-but-flat women's shoes and boots.

THE PODOLLS CLOTHING, CHILDREN

Map p321 (http://shopthepodolls.com; 3985 24th St; ⏲11am-6pm Mon-Wed, 11am-7pm Thu-Fri, 10am-6pm Sat, 11am-5pm Sun; 🚌24, 48, ⓂJ) Husband-and-wife team Josh and Lauren Podoll design and manufacture in SF their own line of clothing – easy-to-wear tops, bottoms and dresses, with snappy prints on sand-washed silk and handwoven cotton, plus a fab line of kids' clothing – all sustainability manufactured. They also carry other eco-conscious local designers, plus jewelry, gifts and ceramics made in the Bay Area.

Alas, there's not much for men, but a fab little play house keeps kids content so moms can shop in peace.

AMBIANCE CLOTHING, ACCESSORIES

Map p321 (www.ambiancesf.com; 3979 24th St; ⏲11am-7pm; 🚌24, 48, ⓂJ) Expect to find some super-cute outfit requiring you hit the town. Dresses are particularly good, emphasizing girly-girl casual. For bargains, start next door at the shoe-and-sale store. Shop sister locations at 1458 Haight St for teen-appropriate prom dresses, and 1858 Union St in the Marina for cocktail attire.

OMNIVORE BOOKS

Map p321 (www.omnivorebooks.com; 3885a Cesar Chavez St; ⏲11am-6pm Mon-Sat, noon-5pm Sun; ⓂJ) Salivate over signed cookbooks by chef-legend Alice Waters, James Beard winner Charles Phan of Slanted Door, and signed copies of *The Omnivore's Dilemma* by Michael Pollan. Check the calendar for standing-room-only in-store events with star chefs. Don't miss the collection of vintage cookbooks and rarities, such as a Civil War–era recipe book, written longhand.

ISSO CLOTHING, ACCESSORIES

Map p321 (www.issosf.com; 3789 24th St; ⏲11am-7pm Mon-Fri, 10am-6pm Sat, noon-5pm Sun; 🚌48, ⓂJ) 'Made, found or designed in the Bay Area' is the motto of this purveyor of women's apparel that also designs its own line – expect updated classics with little zings, such as angle-pocket pencil skirts made of vintage fabric. Local designers round out the collection.

PLUMPJACK WINES WINE

Map p321 (☎415-282-3841; www.plumpjackwines.com; 4011 24th St; ⏲11am-8pm Mon-Thu, to 9pm Fri & Sat, to 6pm Sun; 🚌24, 28) A wine store since Prohibition, this Noe Valley sister to the excellent Marina district wine shop of the same name (owned in part by Lieutenant Governor Gavin Newsom) carries a distinctively different selection: in addition to California wines – many under $25 – you'll find excellent Burgundys, Champagne and great Italian vintages, plus beer and spirits, with an emphasis on whiskeys.

The Haight, NoPa & Hayes Valley

Neighborhood Top Five

❶ Bringing the Summer of Love back to **Haight Street** (p183): wear flowers, make a manifesto, sing freestyle folk songs on the corner of Haight and Ashbury Sts, or follow in the footsteps of psychedelic-rock gods.

❷ Toasting jazz giants between sets at **SFJAZZ** (p192) in front of Sandow Birk's tiled music history mural.

❸ Glimpsing San Francisco's towering achievements atop **Alamo Square** (p184), from Victorian mansions that housed hippie communes to City Hall's risen-from-the-ashes rotunda.

❹ Grazing your way around **Patricia's Green** (p190) in Hayes Valley.

❺ Picking up a new skill at **Workshop** (p196), from pizza-tossing to hair-teasing.

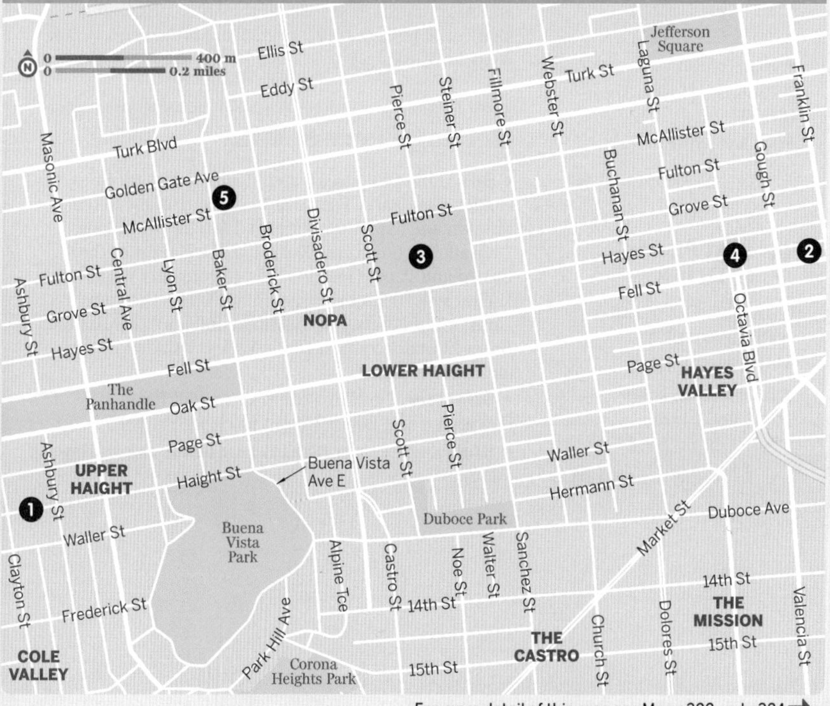

For more detail of this area see Map p322 and p324

Lonely Planet's Top Tip

Ever since the '60s, America's youth have headed to the Haight as a place to fit in, no questions asked. But in 2010 San Francisco passed the controversial Sit/Lie Ordinance, making 7am-to-11pm sidewalk loitering punishable by $50 to $100 fines. Critics note the law has been primarily enforced in the Haight, ticketing homeless teens – but with 1145 shelter beds to accommodate 6400 to 13,000 homeless citywide, many youth have no place else to go. Spare change is a short-term fix; consider donations to youth-service nonprofits instead.

Best Places to Eat

- Rich Table (p187)
- Jardinière (p190)
- Nojo (p187)
- Brenda's Meat & Three (p186)
- Souvla (p187)

For reviews, see p184

Best Places to Drink

- Smuggler's Cove (p192)
- Toronado (p190)
- Alembic (p191)
- Blue Bottle Coffee Company (p192)
- Hôtel Biron (p192)

For reviews, see p190

Explore the Haight, NoPa & Hayes Valley

Stroll Hayes Valley's trendsetting restaurants and local design boutiques, then discover its down-to-earth side on Patricia's Green. Pick up picnic fixings for lunch amid Victorians atop Alamo Square Park – or in case of fog, brunch in NoPa. Take a tour of hippie history in the upper Haight, then roll downhill for Rosamunde sausages and Toronado beer. Overcome powerful bar-stool inertia to brave karaoke at the Mint, show tunes at Martuni's or mosh pits at the Independent.

Local Life

- **Cheap eats and fancy drinks** Go high/low with Rosamunde sausages (p184) and Toronado Belgian ales (p190), oyster po' boy sliders and rare bourbon at Alembic (p191), Nojo's chicken yakatori skewers (p187) and agricole rum drinks at Smuggler's Cove (p192).
- **Hangouts** Aspiring flower children and original-issue hippies gather at Coffee to the People (p191), skaters hit Haight St's downhill slide to Lower Haight bars, and hipsters grab bites in NoPa before shows at the Independent (p193).
- **Musical stylings** Go acoustic on the corner of Haight and Ashbury Sts, belt it out at the Mint (p192), sing along at Martuni's (p192) or rock out at free concerts at Amoeba Music (p193).

Getting There & Away

- **Bus** Market St buses 6 and 71 run up Haight St to Golden Gate Park. The 22 links Lower Haight to the Mission and Japantown/Marina. Bus 24 runs along Divisadero, connecting NoPa and the Haight to the Castro and Pacific Heights. Bus 43 connects Upper Haight with the Marina, and bus 33 runs through Upper Haight between the Richmond and the Mission. Buses 21 and 5 connect Hayes Valley with downtown and Golden Gate Park.
- **Streetcar** The N line offers a shortcut from downtown and Lower Haight to Upper Haight.
- **BART** Civic Center BART is four blocks east of Hayes Valley.

TOP SIGHT
HAIGHT STREET

Was it the fall of 1966 or the winter of '67? As the Haight saying goes, if you can remember the Summer of Love, man, you probably weren't there. The fog was laced with pot, sandalwood incense and burning draft cards, entire days were spent contemplating Day-Glo Grateful Dead posters, and the corner of Haight and Ashbury Sts became the turning point of a generation.

Unlikely Landmarks

Flashbacks are a given in the Haight, which still has its swinging '60s tendencies. Only a very mysterious, very local illness could explain the number of neighborhood medical marijuana clubs, and tie-dyes and ideals have never entirely gone out of fashion here – hence the highly prized vintage rock tees on the wall at Wasteland (p194) and urban farming manuals in their umpteenth printing at Bound Together Anarchist Book Collective (p193). Some '60s memories are better left behind: habits were kicked in the neighborhood's many rehabs, and many an intimate itch has been mercifully treated gratis at the Haight-Ashbury Free Clinic (p280). To relive the highlights of the era, a short walking tour (p185) passes the former flophouses of the Haight's many legendary residents.

Lower & Upper Haight

Since the '60s, Haight St has divided into two major splinter factions, separated by a **Divisadero St** strip of indie boutiques, trendy bars and restaurants. The **Upper Haight** specializes in potent coffee, radical literature and retail therapy for rebels, while the **Lower Haight** has better beer selections and more economic and ethnic diversity – plus a pot-club mellow occasionally disrupted by gang activity northeast of Fillmore and Haight Sts.

DON'T MISS...

- ➡ Colorful Victorian town houses that made rock-n-roll history in the Upper Haight
- ➡ Mysterious 4:20 clock at Haight and Ashbury Sts
- ➡ *Anarchists of the Americas* mural at Bound Together Anarchist Book Collective
- ➡ Lower Haight bars

PRACTICALITIES

- ➡ Map p322, C4
- ➡ Haight St, btwn Fillmore & Stanyan Sts
- ➡ 7, 22, 33, 43, M N

SIGHTS

ALAMO SQUARE PARK PARK

Map p322 (www.sfparksalliance.org/our-parks/parks/alamo-square; Hayes & Scott Sts; sunrise-sunset; ; 5, 21, 22, 24) The pastel Painted Ladies of famed Postcard Row along the east side pale in comparison with the colorful characters along the northwest end of this 1857 Victorian hilltop park. Alamo Square's north side features Barbary Coast baroque mansions at their most bombastic, bedecked with fish-scale shingles and gingerbread trim dripping from peaked roofs.

BUENA VISTA PARK PARK

Map p322 (http://sfrecpark.org; Haight St, btwn Central Ave & Baker St; sunrise-sunset; 6, 7, 37, 43) True to its name, this park founded in 1867 offers splendid vistas over the city to Golden Gate Bridge as a reward for hiking up the steep hill ringed by stately century-old California oaks. Take Buena Vista Ave West downhill to spot Victorian mansions that survived the 1906 earthquake and fire. After-hours boozing or cruising is risky, given petty criminal activity.

GRATEFUL DEAD HOUSE NOTABLE BUILDING

Map p322 (710 Ashbury St; 6, 33, 37, 43, 71) Like surviving members of the Grateful Dead, this purple Victorian sports a touch of gray – but during the Summer of Love, this was where Jerry Garcia and bandmates blew minds, amps and brain cells. After their 1967 drug bust, the Dead held a press conference here arguing for decriminalization, claiming if everyone who smoked marijuana were arrested, San Francisco would be empty.

ZEN CENTER HISTORIC BUILDING

Map p324 (415-863-3136; www.sfzc.org; 300 Page St; 9:30am-12:30pm & 1:30-5pm Mon-Fri, 8:30am-noon Sat; 6, 7, 21, 22) With its sunny courtyard and soaring cased windows, this uplifting Italianate brick building is an interfaith landmark. Since 1969, it's been home to the largest Buddhist community outside Asia. Before she built Hearst Castle, California's first licensed woman architect Julia Morgan designed this Italianate brick structure in 1922 to house Emanu-El Sisterhood, a residence for low-income Jewish working women – note ironwork Stars of David on the 1st-floor loggia.

Today the Zen Center is open to the public for visits, meditation (see the website for schedule), introduction to Zen practice (8:45am Saturday mornings) and other Zen workshops, and also offers overnight stays by prior arrangement for intensive meditation retreats.

HUNTER S THOMPSON CRASH PAD NOTABLE BUILDING

Map p326 (318 Parnassus Ave; 6, MN) On the stuccoed bay-windowed facade, you might notice patched bullet holes – mementos of Hunter S Thompson's 1960s tenancy, when parties degenerated into Hell's Angels orgies and shoot-outs. Thompson narrowly survived to write *Hell's Angels: The Strange and Terrible Saga of the Outlaw Motorcycle Gang,* founding Gonzo journalism with this motto: 'When the going gets weird, the weird turn pro.'

EATING

The Haight

ROSAMUNDE SAUSAGE GRILL FAST FOOD $

Map p322 (415-437-6851; http://rosamundesausagegrill.com; 545 Haight St; sausages $7-7.50; 11:30am-10pm Sun-Wed, to 11pm Thu-Sat; 6, 7, 22, MN) Impress a dinner date on the cheap: load up classic Brats or duck-fig links with complimentary roasted peppers, grilled onions, whole-grain mustard and mango chutney, and enjoy with your choice of 45 seasonal draft brews at Toronado (p190) next door. To impress a local lunch date, call ahead or line up by 11:30am Tuesdays for massive $6 burgers.

THREE TWINS ICE CREAM ICE CREAM $

Map p322 (415-487-8946; www.threetwinsicecream.com; 254 Fillmore St; cones $2.75-5.50; 1-10pm Mon-Thu, noon-11pm Fri, 11am-11pm Sat, 11am-10pm Sun; 6, 7, 22, MN) For local flavor, join the motley crowd of Lower Haighters lining up for extra-creamy organic ice cream in local, seasonal flavors. To guess who gets what, here's a cheat sheet: Wiggle bikers brake for balsamic strawberry, foodie babies coo over lemon cookie, and stoned skaters freak for Mexican chocolate.

ESCAPE FROM NEW YORK PIZZA PIZZA $

Map p322 (415-668-5577; www.escapefromnewyorkpizza.com; 1737 Haight St; slices $5-6; 11am-midnight Sun-Wed, to 1am Thu, to 2am

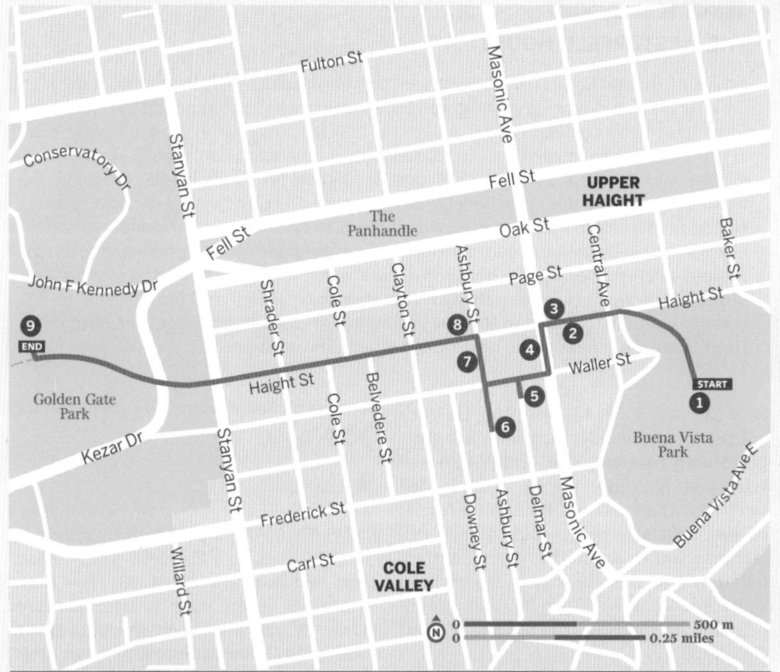

Neighborhood Walk
Haight Flashback

START BUENA VISTA PARK
END GOLDEN GATE PARK
LENGTH 1.3 MILES; 1 HOUR

Start your trip back in time in 1 **Buena Vista Park** (p184), with panoramic city views that moved surviving San Franciscans to tears after the 1906 earthquake.

Heading west up Haight St, you may recognize Emma Goldman and Sacco and Vanzetti in the *Anarchists of the Americas* mural at 2 **Bound Together Anarchist Book Collective** (p193) – if you don't, staff can provide you with some biographical comics by way of introduction. Continuing west, you can't miss 3 **Magnolia Brewpub** (p186), the corner microbrewery named after a Grateful Dead song.

Neighborhood old-timers recall that the Symbionese Liberation Army once used 4 **1235 Masonic Ave** as a safehouse to hold Patty Hearst, the kidnapped heiress turned revolutionary bank robber. To live here now, you'd have to rob a bank – one apartment here just sold for $1.5 million.

Turning right off Masonic Ave onto Waller St, you'll notice a narrow lane leading uphill. The stripped, shingled apartment at 5 **32 Delmar St** was the site of the Sid Vicious overdose that finally broke up the Sex Pistols in 1978. Pay your respects to the former flophouse of Jerry Garcia, Bob Weir and Pigpen at the 6 **Grateful Dead House** (p184) at 710 Ashbury St, site of a scandalous 1967 drug bust – and landmark press conference demanding the decriminalization of marijuana. Californian lawyers are still working on it.

Down the block, 7 **635 Ashbury St** is one of many known San Francisco addresses for Janis Joplin, who had a hard time hanging onto leases in the 1960s – but, as she sang, 'Freedom's just another word for nothin' left to lose.' At the corner of Haight and Ashbury, you'll notice that the 8 **clock** overhead always reads 4:20, better known in 'Hashbury' as International Bong Hit Time. Follow your bliss to the drum circle at 9 **Hippie Hill in Golden Gate Park**, where free spirits have gathered since the '60s to tune in, turn on, and flail to the beat.

LOCAL KNOWLEDGE

THE WESTERFELD HOUSE

On Alamo Square Park's (p184) northwest corner, you can't miss this extraordinary San Francisco survivor – a gilded green Stick Italianate Victorian capped by a spooky watchtower. This confectionary mansion was built by candy baron William Westerfeld in 1889, and miraculously survived subsequent incarnations as a czarist Russian speakeasy, Fillmore jazz musicians' flophouse, and the 50-strong hippie commune described in Tom Wolfe's psychedelic '60s chronicle *The Electric Kool-Aid Acid Test*. Filmed rituals held in the Westerfeld House tower by Church of Satan founder Anton LaVey were psychedelic indeed, and hard work – hundreds of candles needed to be lit without catching the house on fire, and a grumpy lion somehow coaxed up four flights of stairs. The Westerfeld House's legacy of reinvention continues – today it's painstakingly restored to Victorian glory by steampunk aficionado Jim Siegel, the former Haight teenage runaway who now owns Distractions on Haight St.

Fri & Sat; 6, 7, 33, 43, MN) The Haight's obligatory mid-bender stop for a hot slice. Pesto with roasted garlic and potato will send you blissfully off to carbo-loaded sleep, but the sundried tomato with goat cheese, artichoke hearts and spinach will recharge you to go another round. Art donated by fans includes signed rocker head shots (hello, Elvis Costello and Metallica) and cartoons by *The Simpsons*' Matt Groening.

AXUM CAFE ETHIOPIAN $

Map p322 (415-252-7912; www.axumcafe.com; 698 Haight St; mains $8-16; 5-10pm Mon-Sat; ; 6, 7, 22, 24, MN) Whether you've got a hot date with a vegan, the hunger of an athlete or the salary of an activist, Axum's vegetarian platter for two with spongy *injera* bread is handy. Dig in with your bare hands, try not to hog lip-tingling red lentils and mellow yellow chickpeas, and cool off with Anchor Steam brews by the pint or pitcher.

MAGNOLIA BREWPUB CALIFORNIAN, AMERICAN $$

Map p322 (415-864-7468; www.magnoliapub.com; 1398 Haight St; mains $14-26; 11am-midnight Mon-Thu, to 1am Fri, 10am-1am Sat, 10am-midnight Sun; 6, 7, 33, 43) Organic pub grub and homebrew samplers keep conversation flowing at communal tables, while grass-fed Prather Ranch burgers satisfy stoner appetites in booths – it's like the Summer of Love all over again, only with better food. Morning-after brunches of quinoa hash with brewer's yeast are plenty curative, but Cole Porter pints are powerful enough to revive the Grateful Dead.

NoPa

★BRENDA'S MEAT & THREE SOUTHERN AMERICAN $

(415-926-8657; http://brendasmeatandthree.com; 919 Divisadero St; mains $7-15; 8am-10pm Wed-Mon; 5, 21, 24, 38) The name means one meaty main course plus three sides – though only superheroes finish ham steak with Creole red-eye gravy and exemplary grits, let alone cream biscuits and eggs. Chef Brenda Buenviaje's portions are defiantly Southern, which explains brunch lines of marathoners and partiers who forgot to eat last night. Arrive early, share sweet potato pancakes, and pray for crawfish specials.

LITTLE CHIHUAHUA MEXICAN $

Map p322 (415-255-8225; www.thelittlechihuahua.com; 292 Divisadero St; tacos $4.50-5.50, burritos $8-12; 11am-11pm Mon-Fri, 10am-11pm Sat & Sun; ; 6, 7, 21, 24) Who says sustainable, organic food has to be expensive or French? Grass-fed meats and organic veggies and beans are packed into organic tortillas, all washed down with $4 draft beer. Burritos are a two-meal deal, especially the decadent *al pastor* (grilled pork with pineapple salsa and jack cheese) and garlic shrimp (sustainably sourced). Kids menu available.

BAR CRUDO SEAFOOD $$

Map p322 (415-409-0679; www.barcrudo.com; 655 Divisadero St; share plates $14-22; 5-10pm Tue-Thu & Sun, to 11pm Fri & Sat; 5, 6, 7, 21, 24) An international idea that's pure California: choice seafood served raw Italian-style, with pan-Asian condiments and East-West beers. Start with Japanese

Hitachino white ale with velvety avocado-*uni* (sea urchin) toast and graduate to potent Belgian Tripel ales with crudo platters featuring horseradish-spiked Arctic char. Don't miss happy hour (5pm to 6:30pm), when specials include $1 oysters, $6 chowder and $6 wine.

RAGAZZA PIZZA **$$**

Map p322 (415-255-1133; www.ragazzasf.com; 311 Divisadero St; pizza $14-19; 5-10pm Sun-Thu, to 10:30pm Fri & Sat; ; 6, 7, 21, 24) 'Girl' is what the name means, as in, 'Oooh, *girl*, did you try the wild nettle pizza?!' Artisan salumi is the star of many Ragazza pizzas, from the Amatriciana with pecorino, pancetta and egg to the Moto with Calabrian chili and sausage – best with carafes of Sardinian reds or weighty white Roero Arneis. Arrive early to nab garden patio tables.

Hayes Valley

SOUVLA GREEK **$**

Map p324 (415-400-5458; 517 Hayes St; sandwiches & salads $12-13; 11am-10pm; 5, 21, 47, 49, MVan Ness) Ancient Greek philosophers didn't think too hard about lunch, and neither should you at Souvla's. Get in line and make no-fail choices: pita or salad, wine or not. Instead of go-to gyros, try roast lamb atop kale with yogurt dressing, or tangy chicken salad with pickled onion and *mizithra* cheese. Go early/late for sky-lit communal seating, or order takeout for Patricia's Green.

DRAGONEATS VIETNAMESE **$**

Map p324 (415-795-1469; http://dragoneats.com/; 520 Gough St; sandwiches & bowls $6-7; 11am-4pm Mon-Fri, to 5pm Sat & Sun; 5, 21, 47, 49, MCivic Center) Velvety roast duck *banh mi* gives SF Opera stars something to sing about at this sunny Vietnamese deli, right around the corner from the symphony and opera. Divas order theirs with a shrimp roll side, while tenors in tight corsets opt for five-spice chicken 'fresh bowls' with vegetables and brown rice.

NOJO JAPANESE **$$**

Map p324 (415-896-4587; www.nojosf.com; 231 Franklin St; small plates $4-18; 5:30-9:30pm Mon, to 10pm Wed & Thu, to 10:30pm Fri, 11am-2:30pm & 5:30-10:30pm Sat, 11am-2:30pm & 5-9:30pm Sun; 5, 6, 7, 21, 47, 49, MVan Ness) Everything you could possibly want skewered and roasted at happy hour, except maybe your boss. Tasting-portion-size Japanese *izakaya* (bar snacks) specialties include grilled chicken *yakitori* (skewers), mushroom-trout surf and turf, and beef tongue slathered in ramp-miso sauce. Local, organic produce brightens every dish; trust staff on wine, beer and sake pairings.

CHEZ MAMAN WEST FRENCH **$$**

Map p324 (415-355-9067; www.chezmamansf.com; 401 Gough St; mains $10-21; 11:30am-11pm Mon-Fri, from 10:30am Sat & Sun; 5, 21, 47, 49, MVan Ness) Quit pretending you're considering the sensible Nicoise salad and go for the restorative brunch everyone needs mid-shopping spree: buckwheat crepes plumped with decadent fillings, like prosciutto with béchamel or chicken with creamy mustard sauce. Bubbly by the glass and cinnamon-laced berry *pain perdu* for dessert will leave you ready to take Hayes Valley sales racks by storm.

★**RICH TABLE** CALIFORNIAN **$$$**

Map p324 (415-355-9085; http://richtablesf.com; 199 Gough St; mains $12-30; 5:30-10pm Sun-Thu, to 10:30pm Fri & Sat; 5, 6, 7, 21, 47, 49, MVan Ness) Satisfy cravings for taste adventures at Rich Table, home of dried porcini doughnuts, octopus confit and totally trippy beet marshmallows. Married co-chefs/owners Sarah and Evan Rich riff on seasonal Californian fare like SFJAZZ masters, hitting their groove with exquisitely playful *amuse-bouches* such as the Dirty Hippie: silky goat-buttermilk panna cotta

OFF THE GRID THURSDAYS

Peace and love come easy in the Haight, but dinnertime can suddenly divide friends into warring factions – one party insists on Chinese, while a splinter group demands dessert. From 5pm to 9pm Thursdays, there's a diplomatic dinner solution at the corner of Stanyan and Waller: Off the Grid (p64). A dozen food trucks pull into the empty lot across from McDonald's – and for little more than a McMeal, you can go gourmet with pork-belly buns from Chairman (p27), empanadas from El Sur (p27) and mini-carrot-cakes from Kara's Cupcakes. Instead of debating dinner, you can have your cake and dance to live music too.

SEAN DAVEY / GETTY IMAGES ©

1. Haight & Ashbury Sts (p183)
This intersection – and the famous legs extending from Piedmont Boutique – mark the heart of Flower Power–era SF.

2. Victorian architecture (p267)
The Haight contains some of the city's finest Victorians, boasting vivid hues and eye-catching embellishments.

3. Shopping on Haight St (p193)
Browse retro fashions on this landmark shopping strip.

4. Around Alamo Square Park (p184)
Elegant, pastel-shaded row houses surround an 1857 hilltop park.

3

JEAN-PIERRE LESCOURRET / GETTY IMAGES ©

LOCAL KNOWLEDGE

SHIPPING-CONTAINER GOURMET SCENE

After the 1989 earthquake damaged freeway ramps around Fell and Octavia Sts, urban blight struck the neighborhood – until San Franciscan voters nixed the overpass and reinvented Octavia Blvd as a walkable, palm-tree-lined community hub. The social center is **Patricia's Green** (Map p324; http://sfrecpark.org; Octavia Blvd & Fell St; 5, 21), with a playground, picnic tables and rotating sculpture displays inspired by Burning Man. East of the green in two formerly vacant lots, SF's **PROXY** (http://proxysf.net/) project hosts food trucks, pop-up galleries and shipping-container shops. Don't miss the following three key gourmet attractions.

Biergarten (Map p324; http://biergartensf.com; 424 Octavia St; 3-9pm Wed-Sat, 1-7pm Sun; 5, 21) The faintest ray of sunshine brings lines down the block for beer and bratwurst at Biergarten – wear sunblock, order two rounds at once and get the pickled deviled eggs and pretzels to share with newfound friends at communal picnic tables.

Ritual Coffee (Map p324; www.ritualroasters.com; PROXY, 432b Octavia St; 7am-7pm Mon-Thu, to 8pm Fri-Sun; 5, 21) The Hayes Valley shipping-container outpost of the Mission roastery offers creamy espresso and powerful pour-overs to rival Blue Bottle around the corner...but beware, those are fighting words among SF's hardcore coffee loyalists.

Half-Hitch Goods (415-699-5697; www.halfhitchgoods.com; dates & locations vary) Gifts for gourmets are one-truck-stop shopping at this SF surfer van stocked with treats and handcrafted tableware. Stop by PROXY on sunny weekends (see website for dates and locations) to bring home a taste of California with Sqirl blueberry-rhubarb jam, Leaves & Flowers herbal tea, and SF-made Dandelion chocolates.

with hemp – a dish as offbeat and entrancing as Hippie Hill drum circles.

For maximum surprise factor, get the $85 chef's menu plus the optional $60 wine pairing (the best pairing deal in town). Book two to four weeks ahead online or call the restaurant directly – otherwise you'll need to arrive before 5:30pm to bide your time at the barn-wood bar, and hope for an opening before the California wine on tap runs dry.

★JARDINIÈRE CALIFORNIAN $$$

Map p324 (415-861-5555; www.jardiniere.com; 300 Grove St; mains $20-35; 5-9pm Sun-Thu, to 10pm Fri & Sat; 5, 21, 47, 49, M Van Ness) *Iron Chef, Top Chef* Master and James Beard Award winner Traci Des Jardins champions sustainable, salacious California cuisine. She has a way with California's organic produce, sustainable meats and seafood that's probably illegal in other states, slathering lamb with mole sauce and pairing velvety sea urchin with satiny lardo. On Monday, $49 scores three courses with wine pairings.

ZUNI CAFE AMERICAN $$$

Map p324 (415-552-2522; www.zunicafe.com; 1658 Market St; mains $12-29.50; 11:30am-11pm Tue-Thu, to midnight Fri & Sat, 11am-11pm Sun; 6, 71, 47, 49, M Van Ness) Gimmickry is for amateurs – Zuni has been turning basic menu items into gourmet staples since 1979. Reservations and fat wallets are handy for oyster-and-martini lunches, but the see-and-be-seen seating is a kick and simple signatures beyond reproach: Caesar salad with house-cured anchovies, brick-oven-roasted free-range chicken for two with Tuscan bread salad, and mesquite-grilled organic-beef burgers on focaccia (shoestring fries $6 extra).

DRINKING & NIGHTLIFE

The Haight

★TORONADO PUB

Map p322 (415-863-2276; www.toronado.com; 547 Haight St; 11:30am-2am; 6, 7, 22, M N) Glory hallelujah, beer lovers: your prayers have been answered. Be humbled before the chalkboard altar that lists 45-plus beers on tap and hundreds more bottled, including spectacular seasonal microbrews. Bring cash and order sausages from

Rosamunde (p184) next door to accompany ale made by Trappist monks. It may get too loud to hear your date talk, but you'll hear angels sing.

ALEMBIC BAR

Map p322 (415-666-0822; www.alembicbar.com; 1725 Haight St; 4pm-2am Mon-Fri, from noon Sat & Sun; 6, 7, 33, 37, 43, MN) The tin ceilings are hammered and floors well-stomped, but drinks expertly crafted from 250 specialty spirits aren't made for pounding – hence the 'No Red Bull/No Jägermeister' sign and dainty duck-heart bar snacks. The Southern Exposure (gin, mint, lime, celery juice) smooths over heated Haight arguments (Janis or Jimi?) but the Vow of Silence (rye, cherry liqueur, bitters) renders everyone speechless.

AUB ZAM ZAM BAR

Map p322 (415-861-2545; 1633 Haight St; 3pm-2am Mon-Fri, 1pm-2am Sat & Sun; 6, 7, 22, 33, 43, MN) Arabesque arches, an *Arabian Nights*-style mural, 1930s jazz on the jukebox and top-shelf cocktails at low-shelf prices have brought Bohemian bliss to Haight St since 1941. Legendary founder Bruno used to throw you out for ordering a vodka martini, but he was a softie in the end, bequeathing his beloved bar to regulars who had become friends. Cash only.

NOC NOC BAR

Map p322 (415-861-5811; www.nocnocs.com; 557 Haight St; 5pm-2am Mon-Thu, from 3:30pm Fri, from 3pm Sat & Sun; 6, 7, 22, 24, MN) Who's there? Nearsighted graffiti artists, anarchist hackers, electronica DJs practicing for Burning Man and other characters straight out of an R Crumb comic, that's who. Happy hour from 5pm to 7pm daily brings $3 local drafts, but mixing black-and-tans with sake will knock-knock you off your steampunk scavenged-metal stool.

COFFEE TO THE PEOPLE CAFÉ

Map p322 (415-626-2435; 1206 Masonic Ave; 6am-7:30pm Mon-Fri, 7am-8pm Sat & Sun; ; 6, 33, 37, 43, 71) The people united will never be decaffeinated at this radical coffee house – though dairy-free hemp milk and vegan cookies are optional. Grab seats at bumper-sticker-covered tables, admire hippie macramé on the walls and browse consciousness-raising books. But beware the quadruple-shot Freak Out, which has enough fair-trade espresso to revive the Sandinista movement. Free wi-fi.

UVA ENOTECA WINE BAR

Map p322 (415-829-2024; www.uvaenoteca.com; 568 Haight St; 5-10pm Mon, to 11pm Tue-Thu, to 11:30pm Fri, 11am-11:30pm Sat, 11am-10pm Sun; 6, 7, 22, 24, MN) Boys with shags and girls with bangs discover the joys of Bardolino and Barbera by the tasting glass. A staff of tattooed Lower Haight hotties suggest apt pairings for inventive local veggie plates and cheese and charcuterie boards. Daily happy hours (5pm to 6:30pm Monday to Thursday, 3pm to 6:30pm Saturday and Sunday) bring $6 house wine and a bargain bar menu.

NoPa

MADRONE ART BAR BAR

Map p322 (415-241-0202; www.madroneartbar.com; 500 Divisadero St; admission free-$5; 4pm-2am Tue-Sat, 3pm-1:30am Sun; 5, 6, 7, 21, 24) Expect the unexpected at this Victorian venue with the Burberry plaid Uzi over the bar, rotating art installations and Motown nights featuring the Ike Turner drink special: Hennessy served with a slap. But nothing beats jaw-dropping Purple Thriller mash-ups at the monthly Prince vs Michael Jackson party, when the tiny place packs. Cash only; acts range from punk-bluegrass to French rock.

VINYL COFFEE & WINE BAR CAFÉ, WINE BAR

Map p322 (415-621-4132; www.vinylsf.com; 359 Divisadero St; 7am-11pm Mon-Thu, 8am-midnight Fri & Sat, 8am-9pm Sun; 6, 21, 24, 71) Like a superhero in disguise, Vinyl by day is a slightly nerdy café serving Blue Bottle roasts to start-up founders – but once the lights are dimmed and happy hour kicks in with $6 wine (5:30pm to 7pm), this place gets action-packed. Check events listings for Brainstorm Trivia nights and Pizza Hacker pop-ups for margherita pizza baked in a modified Weber grill.

CANDYBAR BAR

Map p322 (415-673-7078; www.candybarsf.com; 1335 Fulton St; 6-10pm Tue-Thu & Sun, to midnight Fri & Sat; 5, 21, 24) Other bars mock froufrou drinks and inexpert dart players, but here you can shamelessly order a Strawberry Kiss (bubbly, frozen strawberries, ginger ale) and cheat at board games around candlelit tables. Turn Candyland into a drinking game: loser buys the next round of Drunken S'mores (Bailey's, chocolate sauce, toasted marshmallows).

Hayes Valley

★SMUGGLER'S COVE BAR

(☎415-869-1900; www.smugglerscovesf.com; 650 Gough St; ⏰5pm-1:15am; 🚌5, 21, 47, 49, Ⓜ Civic Center) Yo-ho-ho and a bottle of rum…or maybe a Dead Reckoning with Angostura bitters, Nicaraguan rum, tawny port and vanilla liqueur, unless someone will share the flaming Scorpion Bowl? Pirates are bedeviled by choice at this Barbary Coast shipwreck tiki bar, hidden behind a tinted-glass door. With 400-plus rums and 70 cocktails gleaned from rum-running around the world, you won't be dry-docked long.

BLUE BOTTLE COFFEE COMPANY CAFÉ

Map p324 (☎415-252-7535; www.bluebottlecoffee.net; 315 Linden St; ⏰7am-6pm; 🚌5, 21, 47, 49, Ⓜ Van Ness) Don't mock SF's coffee geekery until you've tried the elixir emerging from this back-alley garage-door kiosk. The Bay Area's Blue Bottle built its reputation with micro-roasted organic coffee – especially the Blue Bottle–invented, off-the-menu Gibraltar, the barista-favorite drink of foam and espresso poured together into the eponymous short glass. Expect a wait and seats outside on creatively repurposed traffic curbs.

HÔTEL BIRON WINE BAR

Map p324 (☎415-703-0403; www.hotelbiron.com; 45 Rose St; ⏰5pm-2am; 🚌6, 7, 21, 47, 49, Ⓜ Van Ness) Duck into the alley to find this walk-in wine closet, with standout Californian, Provençal and Tuscan vintages and a cork-studded ceiling. The vibe is French underground, with exposed-brick walls, surreal romantic art, a leather couch and just a few tables for two. Barkeeps let you keep tasting until you find what you like; pair with decadent cheese and salumi platters.

> **WORTH A DETOUR**
>
> **KARAOKE AT THE MINT**
>
> Die-hard singers pore over giant books of 30,000 tunes in every genre at mixed straight-gay karaoke bar the **Mint** (☎415-626-4726; www.themint.net; 1942 Market St; ⏰3pm-2am Mon-Fri, from 2pm Sat & Sun; Ⓜ F, J, K, L, M), where big voices rattle pennies in the basement of the US mint just uphill. Coinage won't get you far here, though: standard karaoke-jockey tip is $1 a song. Billy Idol is fair game for a goof, but only serious belters take on Barbra. Two-song maximum and two-drink minimum help keep American Idolatry from getting too serious.

KITTEA CAFÉ

Map p324 (www.kitteasf.com; 96 Gough St; ⏰11am-8pm; 🚌6, 7, 21, 47, 49, Ⓜ Van Ness) Craving green tea and a cuddle? Say hello, KitTea. San Francisco's first cat café serves Japanese tea amid feline cuteness for a good cause: all the cats you'll meet are being socialized for adoption in partnership with Give Me Shelter, a nonprofit cat rescue organization (volunteer signup online). Get *genmaicha* (toasted rice tea) for here and that tubby tabby to go.

MARTUNI'S GAY & LESBIAN, LOUNGE

Map p324 (☎415-241-0205; http://martunis.ypguides.net; 4 Valencia St; ⏰4pm-2am; 🚌6, 7, Ⓜ Van Ness) Slip behind the velvet curtains to see who's tickling the ivories at the city's best piano bar, where gay and straight, salt-and-pepper regulars seem to have committed the Great American Songbook to memory. You'll be singing too, after a couple of top-notch watermelon, lemon-drop or chocolate martinis under $10.

TWO SISTERS BAR & BOOKS BAR

Map p324 (☎415-863-3655; www.2sistersbarandbooks.com/; 579 Hayes St; ⏰4-11pm Tue-Thu, to midnight Fri, noon-midnight Sat, noon-10pm Sun; 🚌5, 21) Witty banter comes easily with well-priced wine and conversation-starting books in this cozy Victorian nook. Trade *Twilight* for *Fahrenheit 451* – there's a take-one, leave-one honor system – and settle in with a half-carafe of wine and truffled deviled eggs. Hit happy hour (4pm to 6pm weekdays, 1pm to 4pm weekends) for $5 cocktails and $3 beer.

ENTERTAINMENT

★SFJAZZ CENTER JAZZ

Map p324 (☎866-920-5299; www.sfjazz.org; 201 Franklin St; tickets $25-120; ⏰showtimes vary; 🚌5, 6, 7, 21, 47, 49, Ⓜ Van Ness) Jazz greats coast-to-coast and legends from Argentina to Yemen are showcased at America's newest, largest jazz center. Hear fresh takes on classic jazz albums like *Ah Um* and *Getz/Gilberto* downstairs in the Lab, or book ahead for extraordinary main-stage collaborations like Laurie Anderson with David Coulter playing the saw, or pianist Jason Moran's performance with skateboarders improvising moves on indoor ramps.

Jazz-themed cocktails are served on the balcony, and you can take them into the LEED-certified glass-and-concrete auditorium – even upper-tier cheap seats have drink holders and clear stage views. Upstairs, test your knowledge of jazz history with Sandow Birk's tile murals capturing the scene from coast to coast. Check the website for family matinees and master classes on subjects ranging from Afro-Peruvian rhythms to studio audio mixing.

INDEPENDENT LIVE MUSIC

Map p322 (☎415-771-1421; www.theindependentsf.com; 628 Divisadero St; tickets $12-45; ⏲box office 11am-6pm Mon-Fri, to 9:30pm show nights; 🚌5, 6, 7, 21, 24) Shows earn street cred at the intimate Independent, featuring indie dreamers (Magnetic Fields, Death Cab for Cutie), rock legends (Meat Puppets, Luscious Jackson), alterna-pop (The Killers, Imagine Dragons) and comedians (Dave Chapelle, Comedians of Comedy). Ventilation is poor, but drinks are cheap – and movie nights offer free shows with a two-drink minimum.

BOOKSMITH BOOK READINGS

Map p322 (☎415-863-8688; www.booksmith.com; 1644 Haight St; ⏲10am-10pm Mon-Sat, to 8pm Sun; 👪; Ⓜ Haight St) SF is one of America's top three book markets, and visiting authors make the Booksmith a literary destination. Recent readings have included Kazuo Ishiguro, *What If?* comic artist Randall Munroe and '60s icon Peter Coyote. Check the website for book swaps and open-bar Shipwreck events, where authors wreck great books with hastily written fan-fiction. Advance book purchases secure reserved seating.

CLUB DELUXE JAZZ

Map p322 (☎415-552-6949; www.clubdeluxe.co/; 1511 Haight St; admission free-$5; ⏲4pm-2am Mon-Fri, 2pm-2am Sat & Sun; 🚌6, 7, 33, 37, 43) Blame it on the bossa nova or the Deluxe Spa Collins (gin, cucumber, ginger, mint, lemon and soda). Admission is either free or $5 for swinging jazz bands, comedy acts and monthly burlesque shows. Expect mood lighting, cats who wear hats well and dames who can swill highballs without losing their matte red lipstick.

SF LESBIAN GAY BISEXUAL TRANSGENDER COMMUNITY CENTER LGBT

Map p324 (☎415-865-5555; www.sfcenter.org; 1800 Market St; ⏲noon-10pm Mon-Thu, to 6pm Fri, 9am-6pm Sat; 👪; 🚌6, 7, Ⓜ F) The glass-walled teal Victorian is a gorgeous place to see and be seen, but because of poor endowment, too-high rental rates and weak programming, it hasn't panned out as a LGBT community hangout. Still, it's worth a look to see if something's on during Pride month (June).

SHOPPING

The Haight

AMOEBA MUSIC MUSIC

Map p322 (☎415-831-1200; www.amoeba.com; 1855 Haight St; ⏲11am-8pm; 🚌7, 33, 43, Ⓜ N) Enticements are hardly necessary to lure the masses to the West Coast's most eclectic collection of new and used music and video, but Amoeba offers listening stations, a free 'zine with uncannily accurate staff reviews, and a free concert series that recently starred Shabazz Palaces, Billy Bragg and Polyphonic Spree – plus a foundation that's saved one million acres of rainforest.

BOUND TOGETHER ANARCHIST BOOK COLLECTIVE BOOKS

Map p322 (☎415-431-8355; http://boundtogetherbooks.wordpress.com; 1369 Haight St; ⏲11:30am-7:30pm; 🚌6, 7, 33, 37, 43) Since 1976 this volunteer-run, nonprofit anarchist bookstore has kept free thinkers supplied with organic permaculture manuals, prison literature and radical comics, while coordinating the annual spring Anarchist Book Fair and restoring its 'Anarchists of the Americas' storefront mural – makes us tools of the state look like slackers. Hours are impressively regular, but call ahead to be sure.

TANTRUM TOYS, GIFTS

(☎415-504-6980; www.shoptantrum.com; 858 Cole St; ⏲11am-7pm; 👪; 🚌6, 7, 33, 37, 43, Ⓜ N) Overbooked kids and overworked adults deserve a time out for Tantrum, delightfully stocked with musical otters, light-up ducks, and a mechanical seal you can ride for a quarter. Midcentury modern circus is the design aesthetic in new and vintage items, including circus shadow puppets, candy-striped hula-hoops and vintage pinafores worthy of *Alice in Wonderland.*

DISTRACTIONS ACCESSORIES, CLOTHING

Map p322 (☎415-252-8751; http://distractionsonhaight.tumblr.com/; 1552 Haight St; ⊙11am-8pm; 🚌6, 7, 33, 37, 43) Strap on your goggles and hang onto your top hat: with steam-punk-style assists from Distractions, to-night you're gonna party like it's 1899. This Gold Rush mad-inventor look is SF's go-to alt-party style, from historically correct Edwardian Ball ensembles to post-apocalyptic Burning Man get-ups. So hang a compass from your corset, and rock that whaler's mask – you're among friends here.

PIEDMONT BOUTIQUE CLOTHING, ACCESSORIES

Map p322 (☎415-864-8075; www.piedmontboutique.com/; 1452 Haight St; ⊙11am-7pm; 🚌6, 7, 33, 37, 43) 'No food, no cell phones, no playing in the boas,' says the sign at the door – but inside, that last rule is gleefully ignored by drag stars, pageant drop-outs, strippers and people who take Halloween dead seriously (read: all SF). Since 1972 Piedmont's signature get-ups have been designed and sewed in SF, so they're not cheap – but those airplane earrings are priceless.

LOVED TO DEATH GIFTS, TAXIDERMY

Map p322 (☎415-551-1036; www.lovedtodeath.net; 1681 Haight St; ⊙11:30am-7pm Mon-Thu, to 8pm Fri & Sat, noon-7pm Sun; 🚌6, 7, 33, 37, 43, ⓂN) Stuffed deer exchange glassy stares with caged baby dolls over rusty dental tools: the signs are ominous, and for sale. Head upstairs for Goth gifts, including Victorian hair lockets and portable last rites kits. Not for the faint of heart, vegans or shutterbugs – no photos allowed, though you might recognize staff from Discovery Channel's *Oddities San Francisco* reality TV show.

WASTELAND VINTAGE, CLOTHING

Map p322 (☎415-863-3150; www.shopwasteland.com; 1660 Haight St; ⊙11am-8pm Mon-Sat, noon-7pm Sun; 🚌6, 7, 33, 37, 43, ⓂN) 🍃 The catwalk of thrift, this vintage superstore adds instant style with barely worn Marc Jacobs smock frocks, '70s Missoni sweaters and a steady supply of go-go boots. Hip occasionally verges on hideous with sequined sweaters and '80s power suits, but at reasonable (not necessarily bargain) prices anyone can afford fashion risks. If you've got excess baggage, Wasteland buys clothes noon to 6pm daily.

BRAINDROPS PIERCING STUDIO BODY ART

Map p322 (☎415-621-4162; www.braindrops.net; 1324 Haight St; ⊙noon-7pm Sun-Mon & Wed-Thu, to 8pm Fri & Sat; 🚌6, 7, 33, 37, 43) Sparkle here, there and where the sun doesn't shine with gentle assistance from SF's legendary piercing parlor. Braindrops' experienced professionals use laser-like precision instead of wobbly piercing guns, and the vast selection of body jewelry ranges from subtle nose studs to mammoth-bone ear spools. ID is required for all clients, plus accompaniment by legal guardian for minors.

GOORIN BROTHERS HATS ACCESSORIES

Map p322 (☎415-436-9450; www.goorin.com; 1446 Haight St; ⊙10am-7pm Sun-Thu, to 8pm Fri & Sat; 🚌6, 7, 33, 37, 43) High crowns, retro designs and California quail feathers make it easy for SF hipsters to withstand the fog while standing out in a crowd. Live your California dream in historically correct style: solve Dashiell Hammet mysteries in wide-brimmed '40s fedoras, headline the Fillmore in '60s White Rabbit top hats, and stop Friday-night SoMa traffic in funkadelic '70s suede cabbie caps.

FTC SKATEBOARDING SPORTS, CLOTHING

Map p322 (☎415-626-0663; www.ftcsf.com; 1632 Haight St; ⊙11am-7pm; 🚌6, 7, 33, 37, 43, ⓂN) Big air and big style are the tip at this local skateboard outfitter, featuring artist-designed decks by Keith Haring, Yoshitomo Nara and SF's own Jeremy Fish. Show local flair as you grab air on Raul Navarro's cable-car-design deck, or just look the part with signature fashion (mostly for dudes, some unisex). Ask staff about upcoming SF street games and pro expos.

COVE GIFTS, ACCESSORIES

Map p322 (☎415-863-8199; www.covertcove.com; 683 Haight St; ⊙11am-7pm Tue-Thu & Sun, 10am-9pm Fri & Sat; 🚌6, 7, 22, ⓂN) Antique typewriter ribbon tins, sea-breezy soaps for scrubbing sailors, succulents dripping from medicine bottles: such unusual gifts lead grateful recipients to believe you've spent weeks and small fortunes in San Francisco curiosity shops. But Cove regularly stocks rare finds at reasonable prices and will wrap them for you, too. Call ahead; hours are erratic.

UPPER PLAYGROUND CLOTHING, ACCESSORIES

Map p322 (☎415-861-1960; www.upperplayground.com; 220 Fillmore St; ⊙noon-7pm; 🚌6, 7, 22, ⓂN) Blend into the SF scenery with locally designed 'Left Coast' hoodie, bragadocious 'World Champion Internetter' tee, handy BART map smartphone case, and for special occasions, a cable-car bowtie. Men's gear dominates, but there are women's tees on side racks, kids' tees in the back room and slick graffiti art in UP's Fifty24SF Gallery next door.

REVOLVER CLOTHING, ACCESSORIES
Map p322 (☎415-583-3363; www.revolversf.com; 136 Fillmore St; ⊙noon-8pm; 🚌6, 7, 22, Ⓜ N) Entering this boutique is like wandering into the wardrobe of an SF barista commune, with easy pieces in soft natural fabrics for men and women strewn across wooden crates. Filmmakers meet surfers here on the hunt for SF's Copin indigo jeans, Californian-made Yukketen Chukka boots, and Hackwith's minimalist fog-hued dresses made just for Revolver.

URBAN MERCANTILE HOMEWARES, GIFTS
(☎415-643-6372; http://urbanmercantile.com; 85 Carl St; ⊙11am-6pm Tue-Sat, noon-5pm Sun; 🚌6, 7, 33, 37, 43, Ⓜ N) A design sourcebook come to life, this little storefront could be the start of a major home-decor overhaul. Start with indigo table linen or a hand-thrown celadon cup, and suddenly you're snapping up plush Missoni bathmats and graphite porcelain dinnerware. For gifts, there's a vast selection of letterpress cards and tiny, delicate modern jewelry.

PAST PERFECT ANTIQUES, VINTAGE
(☎415-418-6754; www.pastperfectsf.com; 854 Stanyan St; ⊙11am-6pm; 🚌6, 7, 33, Ⓜ N) When Victorian attics overflow, San Francisco eccentrics sell their excess antique seltzer bottles, hippie breastplate necklaces and elephant bookends at Past Perfect. This store is a collective, so prices vary wildly – some sellers apparently believe their cast-offs owe them back rent, while others are just happy to unload their exes' prized tiki barware.

NoPa

RARE DEVICE GIFTS
Map p322 (☎415-863-3969; www.raredevice.net; 600 Divisadero St; ⊙noon-8pm Mon-Fri, 11am-7pm Sat, 11am-6pm Sun; 🚌5, 6, 7, 21, 24) Sly SF wit is the rare device that makes this well-curated selection of gifts for all ages so irresistible. San Francisco map playmats let babies drool all over the Golden Gate Bridge, Metaphor organic coffee soap revives Mission barflies, Gamma Folk stoneware necklaces bring uptown fashion down to earth, and Little Otsu's un-planner finds time for joy in start-up schedules.

Hayes Valley

★NANCY BOY BEAUTY
Map p324 (☎415-552-3636; www.nancyboy.com; 347 Hayes St; ⊙11am-7pm Mon-Sat, to 6pm Sun; 🚌5, 21, 47, 49) All you closet pomaders and after-sun balmers: wear those products with pride, without feeling like the dupe of some cosmetics conglomerate. Clever Nancy Boy knows you'd rather pay for the product than for advertising campaigns featuring the starlet du jour, and delivers locally made products with effective plant oils that are tested on boyfriends, never animals.

★ISOTOPE COMICS
Map p324 (☎415-621-6543; www.isotopecomics.com; 326 Fell St; ⊙11am-7pm Tue-Fri, to 6pm Sat & Sun; 👪; 🚌5, 21, 47, 49) Toilet seats signed by famous cartoonists over the front counter show just how seriously Isotope takes comics. Newbies tentatively flip through superhero serials, while fanboys eye new graphic novels from SF's Last Gasp Publishing and head upstairs to lounge with local cartoonists – some of whom teach at Isotope's Comics University. Don't miss signings and epic over-21 after parties.

★PALOMA ACCESSORIES, GIFTS
Map p324 (https://instagram.com/palomahayesvalley; 112 Gough St; ⊙noon-7pm Tue-Sat; 🚌5, 6, 7, 21, 47, 49, Ⓜ Van Ness) Like raiding a surrealist's attic, this SF maker collective is a bonanza of unlikely and imaginatively reinvented finds. Don't be surprised to find billiard-ball cocktail rings, or real buffalo nickels on handbags made on-site by artisan Laureano Faedi. For his line of SF-history T-shirts, Laureano unearths insignia for SF's bizarre bygone businesses, from Playland at the Beach to Topsy's Roost, SF's chicken-coop-themed nightclub.

MAC CLOTHING, ACCESSORIES
Map p324 (☎415-863-3011; www.modernappealingclothing.com; 387 Grove St; ⊙11am-7pm Mon-Sat, noon-6pm Sun; 🚌5, 21, 47, 49) 'Modern Appealing Clothing' is what it promises and what it delivers for men and women, with streamlined chic from Maison Martin

Margiela, splashy graphic Minä Perhonen shifts and gallery-ready limited-edition tees by developmentally disabled artists at Oakland's Creative Growth. Fashion-savant staff are on your side, finding perfect fits and scores from the 40%-to-75%-off sales rack.

MARINE LAYER CLOTHING

Map p324 (☎415-829-7519; www.marinelayer.com/; 498 Octavia St; ⊙10am-7pm; 🚌5, 21, 47, 49, Ⓜ Van Ness) Get instant California cool without getting the shivers in Marine Layer's 'absurdly soft' tees, which this clever SF company makes from blending cotton and recycled beechwood yarn. That limited-edition 'good vibes' graphic tee designed and manufactured in California makes a feel-good, beach-ready statement – but for Ocean Beach, better add a Marine Layer 'shacket' (heavyweight flannel overshirt) or canvas chore coat.

GREEN ARCADE BOOKS

Map p324 (☎415-431-6800; www.thegreenarcade.com; 1680 Market St; ⊙noon-8pm Mon-Sat, to 7pm Sun; 🚌6, 7, 47, 49, Ⓜ Van Ness) Everything you always wanted to know about mushroom foraging, worm composting and running for office on an environmental platform – plus poetry and noir novels by SF authors. This bookstore emphasizes visionary possibility over eco-apocalypse doom, so you'll leave with a rosier outlook on making the world a greener place. Check the website for author events, covering invasive species to electronic art.

RELIQUARY CLOTHING, ACCESSORIES

Map p324 (☎415-431-4000; www.reliquarysf.com; 544 Hayes St; ⊙11am-7pm Mon-Sat, noon-6pm Sun; 🚌5, 21, 47, 49) Enter the well-traveled wardrobe of Leah Bershad, a former Gap designer whose folksy jet-set aesthetic is SF's antidote to khaki-and-fleece global domination. Hand-crafted and vintage items – embroidered peasant blouses, handknit ponchos, silver jewelry banged together by Humboldt hippies – share the spotlight with cult-brand finds like Raleigh denim, Fog Linen shifts and DS Durga's sexy unisex scents (Cowboy Grass, mmm).

FATTED CALF FOOD & DRINK

Map p324 (☎414-400-5614; www.fattedcalf.com; 320 Fell St; ⊙10am-8pm; 🚌5, 21, 47, 49, Ⓜ Van Ness) Hostess gifts that win you return invitations to SF dinner parties come from Fatted Calf. This Bay Area salumi maker's showcase is a one-stop shop for California artisan foods, including goat cheeses, jams and heirloom beans – plus meaty house specialties, from mortadella to duck confit. Don't miss Wednesday Butcher's Happy Hour (5:30pm to 7pm) for free bites, drinks and butchery demos.

GATHER GIFTS, ACCESSORIES

Map p324 (☎415-799-7130; www.gathersf.com/; 541 Octavia St; ⊙11am-7pm Mon-Sat, to 6pm Sun; 🚌5, 21, 47, 49, Ⓜ Van Ness) For elusive only-in-SF souvenirs to remind you of this singular city, duck into this hidden trove of locally designed and handcrafted finds. Lower Haight drinkers require wooden West Coasters, Zen Center meditators can moisturize thoughtfully with Perfect Harmony lotion, and SF converts scandalize folks back home with Californian-perspective geography tees (Florida's stubby, Seattle's forgotten). Check online for upcoming maker workshops.

SPORTS & ACTIVITIES

WORKSHOP WORKSHOPS

Map p322 (☎415-874-9186; www.workshopsf.org; 1798 McAllister St; workshops $45-98; ⊙class times vary; 🚌5, 21, 24, 43) Silicon Valley tech titans go low-tech in their downtime at Workshop, with hands-on courses in the not-quite-lost arts of pizza-throwing, belt-tooling, metalsmithing and hand-sewing. Instructors are patient and enthusiastic, and several classes cost under $50 – the organic-lip-tint-blending class costs less than a designer lipstick, and the kimchi cocktail course less than a round at the bar.

MAKESHIFT SOCIETY WORKSHOPS, CO-WORKING

Map p324 (☎415-625-3220; http://makeshiftsociety.com/sanfrancisco; 235 Gough St; workshops $25-75, day pass $30; ⊙9am-6pm Mon-Fri, plus after-hours workshops; 🚌5, 6, 21, 47, 49, Ⓑ Civic Center, Ⓜ Van Ness) Learn something new every day at this creative clubhouse for adults, where brown-bag socializing sessions spark ideas over lunch, and evening workshops range from gold-leafing to iPhonography (using your phone for artistic purposes). Hangout for productive co-working, space permitting (day passes available).

Golden Gate Park & the Avenues

THE RICHMOND | THE SUNSET

Neighborhood Top Five

1. Doing what comes naturally in **Golden Gate Park** (p199): skipping, lolling or lindy-hopping through America's most outlandish stretch of urban wilderness, and racing the buffalo toward the Pacific Ocean.

2. Following Andy Goldsworthy's sidewalk fault lines to groundbreaking art inside the **de Young Museum** (p200).

3. Enjoying sunsets on the wildflower-topped roof and wild nights at **California Academy of Sciences** (p200).

4. Numbing toes in the Pacific and expanding horizons to Asia at **Ocean Beach** (p203).

5. Watching timeless Pacific sunsets over the Victorian ruins of **Sutro Baths** (p202).

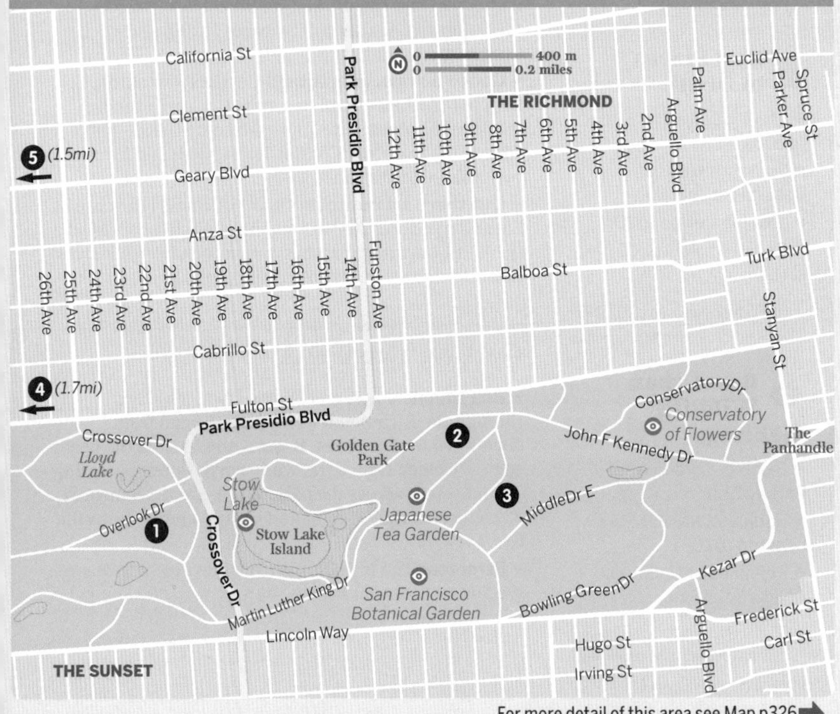

For more detail of this area see Map p326

Lonely Planet's Top Tip

Hear that echo across Golden Gate Park? It's probably a concert – and quite possibly a free one. Opera divas, indie acts, bluegrass greats and hip-hop heavies take turns rocking SF gratis. Most concerts are held in Sharon Meadow or Polo Fields on weekends; for upcoming events, consult the park calendar at www.golden-gate-park.com.

Best Places to Eat

- Aziza (p205)
- Dragon Beaux (p205)
- Outerlands (p207)
- Spruce (p206)
- Cinderella Russian Bakery (p204)

For reviews, see p204

Best Places to Drink

- The Plough & the Stars (p208)
- Tommy's Mexican Restaurant (p207)
- Trouble Coffee (p207)
- Beach Chalet (p207)
- Hollow (p207)

For reviews, see p207

Best Urban Wildlife Sightings

- Bison in Golden Gate Park (p199)
- Bank swallows at Fort Funston (p203)
- Penguins at California Academy of Sciences (p200)

For reviews, see p199

Explore Golden Gate Park & the Avenues

Civilization is overrated, with its traffic jams and office blocks – but once you reach the Conservatory of Flowers in Golden Gate Park, that's all behind you. Hang out with blue butterflies in the rainforest dome at the California Academy of Sciences, or globe-trot from Oceanic masks to James Turrell light installations in the worldly arts exhibits of the de Young Museum. Enjoy a moment of Zen and green tea in the Japanese Tea Garden, then summit Strawberry Hill for views past Stow Lake to the Pacific as red-tailed hawks swoop past.

Wander to San Francisco Botanical Garden for respite in the redwood grove before hopping the N streetcar all the way to Ocean Beach. Stroll the 4-mile stretch of sand to the Richmond for dinner at Aziza and tequila school at Tommy's Mexican Restaurant, or stay put in the Sunset for surf-shopping at Mollusk and dinner at Outerlands. With food and fog like this, you must be in heaven.

Local Life

- **Foggy days** Stay warm with Trouble Coffee (p207), hoodies from Mollusk (p209), matinees at Balboa Theatre (p208), and rainforest strolls inside the California Academy of Sciences (p200) and Conservatory of Flowers (p201).
- **Goose bumps, guaranteed** Get delicious chills with bare feet on Ocean Beach (p203), eerily lifelike ceremonial masks at de Young Museum (p200), cliff's-edge views along the Coastal Trail (p202) and ice-cream cocktails at Trad'r Sam (p207).
- **Out-there art outposts** Outlandishness is a way of life at Park Life (p209) art openings, Frankenart Mart (p203) DIY art installations, and immersive We Players theater productions at Sutro Baths (p202).

Getting There & Away

- **Bus** Numbers 1, 31 and 38 run from downtown through the Richmond, while 7 and 6 head from downtown to the Sunset. Buses 5 and 21 skirt the north edge of Golden Gate Park, while north–south buses 28, 29 and 44 cut across the park. Bus 2 covers Clement St, 33 connects to the Haight and Castro, and 18 spans the Great Hwy.
- **Streetcar** The N line runs from downtown through the Sunset to Ocean Beach.

TOP SIGHT
GOLDEN GATE PARK

When San Franciscans refer to 'the park,' there's only one that gets the definite article: Golden Gate Park. Everything San Franciscans hold dear is here: free spirits, free music, redwoods, Frisbee, protests, fine art, bonsai and buffalo.

Former mayor Frank McCoppin's green scheme seemed impossible in 1866 to Manhattan's Central Park architect Frederick Law Olmsted – but civil engineer William Hammond Hall was undaunted by 1013 acres of dunes. Instead of casinos, resorts and racetracks, he insisted on natural features, including botanical gardens, scenic Stow Lake and the Japanese Tea Garden.

Today, elegant Victorian Conservatory of Flowers overshadows the **Dahlia Garden's** spiky floral mosh-pit. Across Sharon Meadow past Hippie Hill drum circles, SF's biggest children's playground awaits. Nearby are the quietly quaint Lawn Bowling Club and contemplative National AIDS Memorial Grove.

The scenery turns surreal at **California Academy of Sciences**, featuring 40,000 weird, wonderful animals under a wildflower-covered roof. Across the **Music Concourse**, global masterpieces line copper-clad de Young Museum. Heading south, spot Druid altars in **Monarch Bear Grove** behind the baseball diamond and 150 poetry-inspiring plants in the **Shakespeare Garden** (Garden of Shakespeare's Flowers; www.golden-gate-park.com/garden-of-shakespeares-flowers.html; Martin Luther King Jr Dr at Middle Dr East; sunrise-sunset; 7, 44, M N) FREE.

On the park's wild western side are the **Polo Fields**, site of 1967's Human Be-In and Hardly Strictly Bluegrass, and the **Buffalo Paddock** (www.golden-gate-park.com/buffalo-paddock.html; off John F Kennedy Dr, near 39th Ave; sunrise-sunset; 5, 21) FREE, where bison stampede toward windmills and **Ocean Beach** (p203) sunsets.

DON'T MISS...

- de Young Museum
- California Academy of Sciences
- San Francisco Botanical Garden
- Japanese Tea Garden
- Conservatory of Flowers

PRACTICALITIES

- Map p326, E4
- www.golden-gate-park.com/
- Stanyan St to Great Hwy
- 5, 7, 18, 21, 28, 29, 33, 44, M N

WILD NIGHTS AT THE ACADEMY

The penguins nod off to sleep, but night owls party on at the California Academy of Sciences' after-hours events. At the over-21 **NightLife**, nature-themed cocktails are served and strange mating rituals observed among shy internet daters (ID required; $12 entry; events 6pm to 10pm Thursdays). Kids may not technically sleep during Academy Sleepovers, but they might kick off promising careers as research scientists (ages five to 17, plus adult chaperones; $109 per person includes snack and breakfast; events 6pm to 8am). Book ahead online.

HUNGRY?

For sit-down meals, Academy Café, Golden Gate Golf Clubhouse (p211) and Beach Chalet (p207) are the most reliable, reasonable options inside the park. Inexpensive, tasty alternatives near the park include Cinderella Russian Bakery (p204), Underdog (p206), Manna (p206) and Velo Rouge Café (p208). Or look for hot-dog carts along John F Kennedy Dr and street-food trucks near the Music Concourse (between de Young Museum and California Academy of Sciences).

de Young Museum

The oxidized copper building keeps a low profile, but there's no denying the park's all-star attraction: the **de Young Museum** (☎415-750-3600; http://deyoung.famsf.org/; 50 Hagiwara Tea Garden Dr; adult/child $10/6, discount with Muni ticket $2, 1st Tue of month free, online booking fee $1 per ticket; ⏲9:30am-5:15pm Tue-Sun, to 8:45pm Fri Apr-Nov; 🚌5, 7, 44, ⓂN). The cross-cultural collection featuring African masks and Turkish kilims alongside California crafts and avant-garde American art has been broadening artistic horizons for a century, and its acclaimed building by Swiss architects Herzog & de Meuron (of Tate Modern fame) is equally daring.

The 144ft twisting sci-fi medieval armored **tower** is one architectural feature that seems incongruous with the park setting, but access to the tower viewing room is free and the elevator by Ruth Asawa's mesmerizing filigreed pods is worth the wait.

Upstairs, don't miss 19th-century **Oceanic collection** ceremonial oars and stunning Afghani rugs from the 11,000-plus **textile collection**. **Blockbuster basement shows** range from Oscar de la Renta gowns to Keith Haring graffiti art, but rotating **main floor installations** are just as riveting and diverse, from early Inuit carvings to disco-era SF photography.

Access to the **garden café** is free, as is entry to the **Osher Sculpture Garden** and its low-profile star attraction built into a hill: James Turrell's **Skyspace**.

California Academy of Sciences

Leave it to San Francisco to dedicate a glorious four-story monument entirely to freaks of nature: the **California Academy of Sciences** (☎415-379-8000; www.calacademy.org; 55 Music Concourse Dr; adult/child $34.95/24.95; ⏲9:30am-5pm Mon-Sat, 11am-5pm Sun; Ⓟ👪; 🚌5, 6, 7, 21, 31, 33, 44, ⓂN) 🍃. The Academy's tradition of weird science dates from 1853, with thousands of live animals and 60 research scientists now under a 2.5-acre wildflower-covered roof. Butterflies alight on visitors in the glass **Osher Rainforest Dome**, a rare white alligator stalks a **mezzanine swamp** and penguins paddle the tank in the **African Hall**.

In the basement **Steinhart Aquarium**, kids duck inside a glass bubble to enter an **Eel Forest**, find Nemos in the tropical-fish tanks and pet starfish in the hands-on **Discovery Tidepool**. Glimpse into infinity in **Morrison Planetarium** and ride the elevator to the blooming **Living Roof** for park panoramas.

San Francisco Botanical Garden

Sniff your way around the world inside the 55-acre **San Francisco Botanical Garden** (Strybing Arboretum; ☎415-661-1316; www.strybing.org; 1199 9th Ave;

adult/child $7/5, 2nd Tue of month free; 7:30am-7pm Mar-Sep, to 6pm Oct–mid-Nov & Mar, to 5pm mid-Nov–Jan, last entry 1hr before closing, bookstore 10am-4pm; ; 6, 7, 44, N) , from South African savannah grasses to Japanese magnolias. Don't miss the California native-plant meadow, redwood grove and **Ancient Planet Garden** with plants dating back to California's dinosaur days. **Free tours** take place daily; for details, stop by the bookstore inside the entrance. Last entrance is one hour before closing.

Japanese Tea Garden

Since 1894 this 5-acre **garden** (tea ceremony reservations 415-752-1171; www.japaneseteagardensf.com; 75 Hagiwara Tea Garden Dr; adult/child $8/2, before 10am Mon, Wed & Fri free; 9am-6pm Mar-Oct, to 4:45pm Nov-Feb; ; 5, 7, 44, N) has blushed pink with cherry blossoms in spring, turned flaming red with maple leaves in fall and lost all track of time in the meditative **Zen Garden**. The century-old **bonsai grove** was cultivated by the Hagiwara family, who returned from WWII Japanese American internment camps to discover many of their prized miniature evergreens had been sold – and spent decades recovering these precious trees.

Free tours cover the garden's history Mondays and Wednesdays at 9:30am. Stop by the **Tea House** for traditional green tea and fortune cookies – first introduced to the US right here, over 120 years ago.

Conservatory of Flowers

Flower power is alive and well at SF's **Conservatory of Flowers** (info 415-831-2090; www.conservatoryofflowers.org; 100 John F Kennedy Dr; adult/child $8/2, 1st Tue of month free; 10am-4:30pm Tue-Sun; ; 5, 7, 21, 33, N). Inside this recently restored 1878 Victorian greenhouse, orchids command center stage like opera divas, lilies float contemplatively in ponds and gluttonous carnivorous plants gulp insects.

Stow Lake

A park within the park, **Stow Lake** (www.sfrecpark.org; sunrise-sunset; ; 7, 44, N) offers waterfall views, picnics in the **Taiwanese pagoda** and bird-watching on a picturesque island called **Strawberry Hill**. Pedal boats, rowboats and electric boats are available daily in good weather at the 1946 boathouse (p210). Ghost-hunters come at night seeking the **White Lady** – legend has it she has haunted Stow Lake for a century, searching these shores for her lost child.

National AIDS Memorial Grove

This tranquil 10-acre living **memorial grove** (volunteer & tours 415-765-0497; www.aidsmemorial.org/; Bowling Green Dr; sunrise-sunset; ; 7, 33, 44, N) FREE was founded in 1991 to remember millions of individual lives lost to the AIDS epidemic, comfort heartbroken families and communities, and strengthen national resolve for compassionate care and a lasting cure. Volunteer workdays (8:30am to 12:30pm) and free tours (9am to noon) held the third Saturday of each month, March to October.

Children's Playground

Kids have had the run of the park's southeast end since 1887. Highlights of this historic **children's playground** (Koret Children's Quarter; 415-831-2700; www.golden-gate-park.com/childrens-playground.html; off Kezar Dr at Bowling Green Dr; sunrise-sunset; ; 7, 33, N) include 1970s concrete slides, a new climbing wall and a vintage 1912 carousel (per ride adult/child $2/1; open daily 10am to 4:15pm).

SIGHTS

The Richmond

GOLDEN GATE PARK PARK

See p199.

★COASTAL TRAIL TRAIL

Map p326 (www.californiacoastaltrail.info; Fort Funston to Golden Gate Bridge; sunrise-sunset; 1, 18, 38) Hit your stride on the 10.5-mile stretch of Coastal Trail starting at Fort Funston, crossing 4 miles of sandy Ocean Beach, wrapping around the Presidio to the Golden Gate Bridge. Casual strollers can pick up the trail near Sutro Baths, and head around Land's End for end-of-the-world views and glimpses of shipwrecks at low tide. At Lincoln Park, duck into the Legion of Honor or descend gloriously tiled Lincoln Park Steps (near 32nd Ave).

LEGION OF HONOR MUSEUM

Map p326 (415-750-3600; http://legionofhonor.famsf.org; 100 34th Ave; adult/child $10/6, discount with Muni ticket $2, 1st Tue of month free; 9:30am-5:15pm Tue-Sun; ; 1, 2, 18, 38) A museum as eccentric and illuminating as San Francisco itself, the Legion showcases a wildly eclectic collection ranging from Monet water lilies to John Cage soundscapes, ancient Iraqi ivories to R Crumb comics. Upstairs are blockbuster shows of Old Masters and Impressionists, but don't miss selections from the Legion's Achenbach Foundation of Graphic Arts collection of 90,0000 works on paper, ranging from Rembrandt to Ed Ruscha.

A marble-clad replica of Paris' Légion d'Honneur, the Legion is a monumental tribute to Californians killed in France in WWI. It was built by Alma de Bretteville Spreckels, a larger-than-life sculptor's model who donated her fortune to gift this museum to San Francisco. The centerpiece of 'Big Alma's' legacy is Rodin's *The Kiss* – but at 4pm on weekends, pipe organ recitals steal the show in the Rodin gallery.

SUTRO BATHS PARK

Map p326 (www.nps.gov/goga/historyculture/sutro-baths.htm; 680 Point Lobos Ave; sunrise-sunset, visitor center 9am-5pm; P; 5, 31, 38) FREE Hard to imagine from these ruins, but Victorian dandies and working stiffs once converged here for bracing baths in itchy wool rental swimsuits. Millionaire Adolph Sutro built hot and cold indoor pools to accommodate 10,000 unwashed masses in 1896, but the masses apparently preferred dirt – despite added attractions including trapezes and Egyptian mummies,

LOCAL KNOWLEDGE

THE INTERNET ARCHIVE

Ever wonder where blogs go when they die, or where embarrassing photos end up once they're taken offline? Your answer is right here in SF's Richmond district, in a 1923 Greek Revival landmark that was once a Christian Science church. The nonprofit **Internet Archive** (Map p326; 415-561-6767; https://archive.org/index.php; 300 Funston Ave; open for events only) is a sanctuary for more than 20 petabytes (that's 200 million gigabytes) worth of bygone media, and counting.

The Archive was founded in 1996 by Brewster Kahle, the San Franciscan web pioneer who developed an internet prototype in the 1980s and made his fortune with search technologies sold to AOL and Amazon. More than 430 billion websites are now stored and accessible online through the Internet Archive's Wayback Machine (https://archive.org/web/). The Archive has also preserved for posterity two million books and three million hours of TV – plus 9000 hours of Grateful Dead shows, with the band's permission.

This has been accomplished by global volunteers led by 100-plus dedicated local archivists, who have each committed three years or more to the effort. Artist Nuala Creed has archived the archivists, capturing their likenesses in **100 ceramic figures** clustered sociably around the old church pews on the main floor of the Archive. The most recognizable figure is Aaron Swartz, the Reddit co-founder who served as a volunteer archivist from 2007 to 2009, and whose federal indictment in 2013 for downloading MIT's JSTOR archive ended with his suicide. Visitors can enter the Archive to see the figures most Fridays from 1pm to 2pm; call to confirm.

the baths went bust in 1952. At low tide, follow the steep path past the now-ruined baths and through the sea-cave tunnel to find sublime Pacific panoramas.

These splendid ruins made a fitting backdrop for 1971's May–December comedy classic *Harold and Maude,* and recently set the scene for theatrical performances by the Bay Area's **We Players** (www.weplayers.org). Above the baths are the new **Land's End Lookout** visitor center and café plus the **Sutro Heights Park** public gardens, built in 1885 and restored with native plants.

LINCOLN PARK — PARK

Map p326 (http://sfrecpark.org/; Clement St; sunrise-sunset; 1, 18, 38) America's legendary coast-to-coast Lincoln Hwy officially ends at 100-acre Lincoln Park, which served as San Francisco's cemetery until 1909. The city's best urban hike leads through Lincoln Park around **Land's End**, following a partially paved coastline trail with glorious Golden Gate views and low-tide sightings of coastal shipwrecks. Pick up the trailhead north of the Legion of Honor (p202), or head up newly tiled **Lincoln Park Steps** near 32nd Ave. Book ahead for scenic Lincoln Park Golf Course (p210).

FRANKENART MART — ART GALLERY

Map p326 (415-221-2394; www.frankenartmart.com; 515 Balboa St; 4-9pm Thu-Fri, 1-8pm Sat, 1-6pm Sun; 5, 31, 44) FREE Art is what you make of it at this participatory art gallery, where you're invited to interpret themes such as Butcher Shop, Startup and Silent Movie Gym and contribute haiku for Poetry in a Can. Art is available for sale or barter with Mart representatives, though the cats drive a hard bargain. Kids are welcome with adult companions, but not all art may be suitable for all ages. See online calendar for free-hot-dog Sundays and other special events.

COLUMBARIUM — NOTABLE BUILDING

Map p326 (415-771-0717; www.neptune-society.com/columbarium; 1 Loraine Ct; 8am-5pm Mon-Fri, 10am-3pm Sat & Sun; 5, 31, 33, 38) FREE Art nouveau stained-glass windows and a dome skylight illuminate more than 8000 niches honoring dearly departed San Franciscans and their beloved pets. San Francisco's Columbarium revived the ancient Roman custom of sheltering cremated remains in 1898, when burial grounds crowded the Richmond district. The Columbarium was neglected from 1934 until its 1979 restoration by the Neptune Society, a cremation advocacy group. Today visitors admire the neoclassical architecture, and pay respects to the niche of pioneering gay city supervisor Harvey Milk.

LOCAL KNOWLEDGE

FORT FUNSTON'S PLUCKY LITTLE CLIFF-DWELLERS

Fort Funston is a refuge for the smallest birds in North America: bank swallows. They may be little, but they throw all 10g to 20g of themselves into their work each April, burrowing tunnels up to 4ft deep into Fort Funston's sandstone cliffs to provide safe havens for their tiny chicks. Heftier females are sought-after mates, since they can handle more of the heavy lifting of nest-building and hauling insects to feed chicks. These plucky little 5in birds are endangered in California, but as many as 250 bank swallows have been spotted recently in Fort Funston's cliffs, alongside starlings that squat in old nests. Bring binoculars and you may spot dust streams from tunneling swallows in April, adults hunting for insects after spring storms, and chicks finding their wings June to August.

The Sunset

OCEAN BEACH — BEACH

Map p326 (415-561-4323; www.parksconservancy.org; Great Hwy; sunrise-sunset; P; 5, 18, 31, MN) The sun sets over the Pacific just beyond the fog at this blustery beach. Most days here are too chilly for bikini-clad clambakes, but fine for hardy beachcombers and hardcore surfers braving riptides (casual swimmers beware). Bonfire policies are under review, but fires are currently permitted in artist-designed fire pits only; no alcohol allowed. On Ocean Beach's south end, beachcombers spot sand dollars and 19th-century shipwrecks. Stick to paths in fragile southern dunes, where skittish snowy plover shorebirds shelter in winter.

FORT FUNSTON — PARK

(415-561-4323; www.parksconservancy.org; Fort Funston Rd, off Skyline Blvd; sunrise-sunset; P; ML) Grassy dunes up to 200ft high at Fort Funston give an idea what the Sunset looked like until the 20th century. A defunct military installation, Fort Funston still has 146-ton WWII guns aimed seaward and abandoned Nike missile silos near the parking lot. Nuclear missiles were never launched from Fort Funston, but flocks of hang gliders launch and land here. Butterflies and shorebirds flock to Fort Funston, which is now part of the Golden Gate National Recreation Area.

Loop trails and hang-glider launch areas are wheelchair- and stroller-accessible, and dogs are allowed off-leash in many areas. The National Park Service is gradually replacing invasive ice plants with native vegetation, and volunteers are welcome to join the effort at **Fort Funston Native Plant Nursery** (see website for details). Park entrance is on your right off Skyline Blvd, past Lake Merced.

SAN FRANCISCO ZOO ZOO

(415-753-7080; www.sfzoo.org; 1 Zoo Rd, off Sloat Blvd; adult/child 4-14/0-3yr $17/11/free, $1 discount with Muni ticket; 10am-5pm incl holidays; P; 18, 23, ML) Even parents who object to zoos on principle sometimes cave in to kids' demands for SF Zoo excursions – and end up enjoying well-kept habitats, including the Lemur Forest and the Savannah (featuring giraffes, zebras and ostrich). Star attractions include Bear Country, the Gorilla Preserve, barnyard-style petting zoo, Dentzel carousel (per ride $3) and miniature steam train (per ride $5). Interactive storybook features are activated with a Zoo Key ($3) and rental strollers and wheelchairs are available ($10 to $12 and $15, respectively).

EATING

The Richmond

★CINDERELLA RUSSIAN BAKERY RUSSIAN $

Map p326 (415-751-6723; www.cinderellabakery.com/; 436 Balboa St; pastries $1.50-3.50, mains $7-13; 7am-7pm; ; 5, 21, 31, 33) Fog banks and cold wars are no match for the heartwarming powers of the Cinderella, serving treats like your babushka used to make since 1953. Join SF's Russian community in Cinderella's new parklet near Golden Gate Park for scrumptious, just-baked egg and green onion piroshki pastry, hearty borscht and decadent dumplings – all at neighborly prices.

PRETTY PLEASE BAKESHOP BAKERY $

Map p326 (415-347-3733; www.prettypleasesf.com; 291 3rd Ave; baked goods $2-5.50; 11am-7pm Tue-Fri, to 6pm Sat, to 5pm Sun; ; 1, 2, 33, 38, 44) Since you asked nicely, pastry chef Alison Okabayashi will hand over your choice of all-American treats: mini-cheesecakes, whoopie pies and PB&J cake. Best of all are her upscale, preservative-free versions of Hostess cakes: Ding Dongs are buttercream-filled chocolate cakes dipped in Guittard ganache, and Twinks are cream-filled sponge cakes in original vanilla, pumpkin spice or red velvet.

SPICES SICHUAN $

Map p326 (415-752-8884; http://spicessf.com/; 294 8th Ave; mains $7-19; 11am-11pm; 1, 2, 38, 44) The menu reads like an oddly dubbed Hong Kong action flick, with dishes labeled 'fire-burst!!' and 'spicy gangsta' – but peppercorn-infused 'numbing spicy' cucumber, silken 'stinky!' *ma-po* tofu and brain-curdling 'flaming pot' chicken are worthy of exclamation. When you head toward the kitchen for the bathroom, the chili aroma will make your eyes water…or maybe that's just gratitude. Cash only.

GENKI DESSERT, GROCERIES $

Map p326 (415-379-6414; www.genkicrepes.com; 330 Clement St; crepes $5-7; 11am-11:30pm Mon, 10:30am-11:30pm Tue-Thu & Sun, 10:30am-12:30am Fri & Sat; ; 1, 2, 33, 38) Life is always sweet at Genki, with aisles of packaged Japanese gummy candies nonsensically boasting pineapple flavors 'imposing as a southern island king,' a dozen variations on tapioca bubble tea, and French crepes by way of Tokyo with green-tea ice cream and Nutella. Stock up in the beauty supply and Pocky aisle to satisfy sudden hair-dye or snack whims.

WING LEE DIM SUM $

Map p326 (415-668-9481; 503 Clement St; dim sum $1.60-3.50; 10am-6pm; 1, 2, 38, 44) To feed two famished surfers for $10, just Wing Lee it. Line up with small bills and walk away loaded with shrimp-and-leek dumplings, BBQ pork buns (baked or steamed), chicken *shu mai* (open-topped dumplings), potstickers, and crispy sesame balls with chewy red-bean centers. Fluorescent-lit lunch tables aren't made for dates, but these dumplings won't last long anyway.

★DRAGON BEAUX DIM SUM **$$**

Map p326 (☎415-333-8899; www.dragonbeaux.com; 5700 Geary Blvd; dumplings $4-9; ⊙11:30am-2:30pm & 5:30-10pm Mon-Thu, to 10:30pm Fri, 10am-3pm & 5:30-10pm Sat & Sun; 👪; 🚌2, 38) Hong Kong meets Vegas at SF's most glamorous, decadent Cantonese restaurant. Say yes to cartloads of succulent roast meats – hello, roast duck and pork belly – and creative dumplings, especially XO dumplings with plump, brandy-laced shrimp in spinach wrappers. Expect premium teas, sharp service and impeccable Cantonese standards, like Chinese doughnuts, *har gow* (shrimp dumplings) and Chinese broccoli in oyster sauce.

KABUTO SUSHI **$$**

Map p326 (☎415-752-5652; www.kabutosushi.com; 5121 Geary Blvd; sushi $6-12; ⊙11:30am-2:30pm & 5:30-10:30pm Tue-Sat, 5-9:30pm Sun; 🚌1, 2, 28, 31, 38) Even Tokyo traditionalists and seafood agnostics squeal over innovative sushi served in this converted hot-dog drive-in. Sushi chefs top nori-wrapped rice with *hamachi* (yellowtail) and pear, *foie gras* with raspberries and chive, and – eureka! – the '49er oyster with sea urchin, caviar, a quail's egg and gold leaf, chased with rare sake. Reserve ahead; maximum party of four.

BURMA SUPERSTAR BURMESE **$$**

Map p326 (☎415-387-2147; www.burmasuperstar.com; 309 Clement St; mains $11-28; ⊙11:30am-3:30pm & 5-9:30pm Sun-Thu, to 10pm Fri & Sat; 🚌1, 2, 33, 38, 44) Yes, there's a wait, but do you see anyone walking away? Blame it on fragrant *moh hinga* (catfish curry) and traditional Burmese green-tea salads tarted up with lime and dried shrimp. Reservations aren't accepted – ask the host to call you so you can browse Burmese cookbooks at Green Apple Books while you wait.

HALU JAPANESE **$$**

Map p326 (☎415-221-9165; 312 8th Ave; yakitori $2.50-6.50, ramen $12-15; ⊙5-10pm Tue-Thu, to 11pm Fri & Sat; 🚌1, 2, 38, 44) Nibbling creative *yakitori* (skewers) at this snug five-table joint plastered with Beatles memorabilia is like dining aboard the Yellow Submarine. Chef/owner Shig was a drummer with John Lennon's Plastic Ono Band, and though he rocks ramen, sticks are still his specialty. Get anything skewered and wrapped in bacon – scallops, quail eggs, *mochi* (rice cake) – and if you're up for offal, have a heart.

THE FOG BELT

Not sure what to wear for a day in Golden Gate Park or dinner in the Avenues? Join the club. Downtown may be sunny and hot, while the Avenues are blanketed in coastal fog that lowers temperatures by as much as 20°F (10°C).

The fog bank usually begins around Stanyan St, so the area to the west is known as the fog belt. For a more exact assessment of the fog situation, view satellite imagery on the **National Oceanic and Atmospheric Administration** (NOAA; www.wrh.noaa.gov/mtr) website. When the fog wears out its welcome, take a bus to the Castro or the Mission on the sunnier side of town – and when the fog reaches the Mission, hop BART to sunny Berkeley across the bay.

CASSAVA BAKERY, CALIFORNIAN **$$**

Map p326 (☎415-640-8990; www.cassavasf.com; 3519 Balboa St; breakfast & lunch mains $7-12, dinner mains $13-21; ⊙8:30am-2:30pm Mon, 8:30am-2:30pm & 5:30-9pm Wed-Fri, 10am-2:30pm & 5:30-9pm Sat, 10am-2:30pm Sun; 🖉; 🚌5, 18, 31, 38) Early risers and park joggers are rewarded with SF-roasted Ritual coffee and Cassava's housemade, multilingual breakfasts – choose from Japanese miso-rice with poached egg, maple-ricotta Belgian waffles, or Californian farm egg with avocado and Meyer lemon aoili on toast. Grab creative panini before a Balboa Theatre double feature, and return to debrief over wine and bargain three-course dinners ($42). Communal seating.

★AZIZA MOROCCAN, CALIFORNIAN **$$$**

Map p326 (☎415-752-2222; www.aziza-sf.com; 5800 Geary Blvd; mains $19-29; ⊙5:30-10:30pm Wed-Mon; 🚌1, 2, 29, 31, 38) Chef Mourad Lahlou's inspiration is Moroccan and his ingredients organic Californian, but the flavors are out of this world: Sonoma duck confit melts into caramelized onion inside flaky pastry *basteeya,* while saffron infuses slow-cooked Sonoma lamb atop barley. Chef

LOCAL KNOWLEDGE

SEA FORAGING WITH KIRK LOMBARD

If restaurant menus aren't adventurous enough for you, try something off the menu and on the beaches. Sea-life expert Kirk Lombard was nominated for a James Beard Award for introducing urbanites to the bounty of San Francisco Bay on his Sea Foraging Adventures (p278).

While working for US Fish & Game, Lombard noticed that many anglers were ignoring meals in San Francisco's midst: bullwhip kelp perfect for pickling on Ocean Beach, smelt netted on Baker Beach ideal for panko-crusting and pan-frying, and barbecue-ready monkeyface prickleback eels sniggled right under the Golden Gate Bridge.

'People can't believe we have so much edible food in the Bay,' he says. 'They know big, deep-water ocean fish are endangered, but don't realize it can be healthier and more sustainable to eat lower down the food chain.'

Lombard is a transplant from New York, where his grandfather took him fishing on the Hudson River. 'Back when I was a kid, the Hudson was so polluted, it caught fire a couple times – now that's a clear sign you don't want to eat the fish,' he jokes. 'Foraging around the Bay makes people more aware of what a healthy, diverse aquaculture looks and tastes like, and it's the best motivation I can think of to keep it that way.'

Mourad's crossroads cuisine wins Michelin stars and *Iron Chef* battles, but pastry chef Melissa Chou's strawberry-fennel pavlova is the perfect goodnight kiss.

SPRUCE CALIFORNIAN **$$$**

(415-931-5100; www.sprucesf.com; 3640 Sacramento St; mains $18-42; 11:30am-2:30pm & 5-10pm Mon-Fri, 5-11pm Sat, 5-10pm Sun; 1, 2, 33, 43) VIP all the way: chandeliers, tawny leather chairs, 2500 wines and dinners with Obama. Ladies who lunch dispense with polite conversation, tearing into grass-fed burgers on house-baked English muffins loaded with pickled onions, heirloom tomato grown on the restaurant's own organic farm and optional *foie gras*. Want fries with that? Oh yes, you do: Spruce's are cooked in duck fat.

The Sunset

MASALA DOSA INDIAN **$**

Map p326 (415-566-6976; www.masaladosasf.com; 1375 9th Ave; dishes $6-14; 11am-11pm; 6, 7, 33, 43, 44, N) Warm up on Golden Gate Park's south side with South Indian fare in a mood-lit storefront bistro. The house specialty is paper *dosa*, a massive crispy lentil-flour pancake served with *sambar* (spicy soup) and chutney – but onion and pea *uthappam* is heartier and equally gluten-free. Standout mains include chicken Madras rich with coconut milk and fragrant wild-salmon masala.

UNDERDOG HOT DOGS **$**

Map p326 (415-665-8881; www.underdogorganic.com; 1634 Irving St; hot dogs $4-5; 11am-9pm Sun-Wed, to 10pm Thu-Sat; 7, 28, 29, N) For bargain organic meals on the run in a bun, Underdog is the surprise winner. Meats are USDA-certified organic, and smoky veggie chipotle hot dogs could make carnivores into fans of fake meat. Organic condiment options can be overwhelming, but the off-the-menu staff favorite combo is no-fail: any hot dog with barbecue sauce and housemade coleslaw. Gluten-free and vegan options available.

MANNA KOREAN **$**

Map p326 (415-665-5969; http://mannasf.com/; 845 Irving St; mains $10-15; 11am-9:30pm Tue-Sun; 6, 7, 43, 44, N) As Korean grandmothers and everyone else who lives in SF's Sunset district will tell you, nothing cures fog chills like home-style Korean cooking. Manna's *kalbi* (barbecue short ribs) and *dol-sot bibimbap* (rice, vegetables, steak and egg in a sizzling stone pot) are surefire toe-warmers, especially with addictive *gojujang* (sweetly spicy Korean chili sauce). Parties of four maximum; expect a wait.

SAN TUNG DIM SUM **$**

Map p326 (415-242-0828; http://santungchineserestaurant.com/; 1031 Irving St; mains $8-17; 11am-3pm & 5-9:30pm Thu-Tue; 6, 43, 44, 71, N) Arrive at 5:30pm on a Sunday and already the place is packed – it's this crowded for a reason. Actually four reasons:

first is the dry braised chicken wings (tender, moist morsels that defy the very name), followed by housemade dumplings and noodles. But the kicker is the bill: a three-course meal for two for $25, plus $8 weekday lunch specials.

★OUTERLANDS CALIFORNIAN $$

Map p326 (☎415-661-6140; www.outerlandssf.com; 4001 Judah St; sandwiches & small plates $7-14, mains $18-22; ⏰10am-3pm Tue-Fri, from 9am Sat & Sun, 5:30-10pm Tue-Sun; ⓥ; 🚌18, ⓂN) When windy Ocean Beach leaves you feeling shipwrecked, drift into this beach-shack bistro for organic, California coastal comfort food. Brunch demands Dutch pancakes in iron skillets with housemade ricotta, lunch brings $12 grilled artisan cheese combos with surfer-warming soup, and dinner means light, creative coastal fare like clam stew with mezcal broth (hungry surfers: order housebaked levain bread). Reserve ahead.

NOPALITO MEXICAN $$

Map p326 (☎415-233-9966; www.nopalitosf.com; 1224 9th Ave; mains $11-21; ⏰11:30am-10pm; ⓥ; 🚌6, 7, 43, 44, ⓂN) Head south of Golden Gate Park's border for upscale, sustainably sourced Cal-Mex, including cheesy squash blossom *quesadillas* with heritage corn tortillas, melt-in-your-mouth *carnitas* (beer-braised pork) and cinnamon-laced Mexican hot chocolate. Reservations aren't accepted, but on sunny weekends when every park-goer craves margaritas and ceviche, call to join the wait list an hour ahead or pre-order online.

DRINKING & NIGHTLIFE

TOMMY'S MEXICAN RESTAURANT BAR

Map p326 (☎415-387-4747; http://tommysmexican.com/; 5929 Geary Blvd; ⏰noon-11pm Wed-Mon; 🚌1, 29, 31, 38) Welcome to SF's temple of tequila since 1965. Tommy's serves enchiladas as a cover for day-drinking until 7pm, when margarita pitchers with *blanco, reposado or añejo* tequila rule. Cuervo Gold is displayed 'for educational purposes only' – it doesn't meet Tommy's strict criteria of unadulterated 100% agave, preferably aged in small barrels. Luckily for connoisseurs, 311 tasty tequilas do.

TROUBLE COFFEE & COCONUT CLUB CAFÉ

Map p326 (4033 Judah St; ⏰7am-7pm; 🚌18, ⓂN) Coconuts are unlikely near blustery Ocean Beach, but here comes Trouble with the 'Build Your Own Damn House' breakfast special: coffee, thick-cut cinnamon-laced toast and an entire young coconut. Join surfers sipping house roasts on driftwood benches outside, or toss back espresso in stoneware cups at the reclaimed wood counter. Featured on NPR, but not Instagram – sorry, no indoor photos.

BEACH CHALET BREWERY, BAR

Map p326 (☎415-386-8439; www.beachchalet.com; 1000 Great Hwy; ⏰9am-10pm Mon-Thu, to 11pm Fri, 8am-11pm Sat & Sun; 🚌5, 18, 31) Microbrews with views: watch Pacific sunsets through pint glasses of the Beach Chalet's house beer, with live music most Fridays and Saturdays. Downstairs, splendid 1930s Works Project Administration (WPA) frescoes celebrate the building of Golden Gate Park. The backyard Park Chalet hosts raucous Taco Tuesdays (tacos $3.50), mimosa-fueled Sunday Recovery Brunch Buffets, and Wednesday-to-Friday happy hours (3pm to 6pm).

HOLLOW CAFÉ

Map p326 (☎415-242-4119; www.hollowsf.com; 1435 Irving St; ⏰8am-6pm Mon-Fri, from 9am Sat & Sun; 🚌7, 28, 29, ⓂN) An enigma wrapped in a mystery inside a garage espresso bar, Hollow serves cultish Ritual coffee and Guinness cupcakes alongside beard conditioner and arsenic-scented perfume. The ideal retreat on foggy Golden Gate Park days, Hollow packs surprisingly ample seating into its snug single-car-garage space – plus arty shopping in the next-door annex that rivals the de Young Museum store.

TRAD'R SAM BAR

Map p326 (☎415-221-0773; 6150 Geary Blvd; ⏰9am-2am; 🚌1, 29, 31, 38) Island getaways at this vintage tiki dive will make you forget that Ocean Beach chill. Sailor-strength hot buttered rum will leave you three sheets to the wind, and five-rum Zombies will leave you wondering what happened to your brain. Kitsch lovers order the Hurricane, which comes with two straws for a reason: drink it solo and it'll blow you away.

540 CLUB BAR

Map p326 (415-752-7276; www.540-club.com; 540 Clement St; 11am-2am; ; 1, 2, 38, 44) Bank on bargain booze in this converted savings and loan office – just look for the neon-pink elephant over the archway. Come for weekday happy hours (4pm to 7pm), Tuesday tiki drinks featuring Californian spirits, and infamous punk Catholic School Karaoke (see website). Loosen up for darts and pool with a dozen beers on tap. Free wi-fi; dog-friendly; cash only.

VELO ROUGE CAFÉ CAFÉ

Map p326 (415-752-7799; 798 Arguello Blvd; 6:30am-5pm Mon & Tue, 6:30am-10pm Wed-Fri, 8am-10pm Sat, 8am-5pm Sun; 5, 21, 31, 33, 38) Bike one block from Golden Gate Park and you've earned a Blue Bottle coffee break or a frosty Chimay beer surrounded by charming pre-doping-scandal Tour de France memorabilia. Grilled panini, Jack Johnson banana pancakes and mega-salads prepare you to bike the Golden Gate Bridge – return by 6pm for $5 wine at happy hour and pizza specials.

SOCIAL BREWERY

Map p326 (415-681-0330; www.socialkitchenandbrewery.com; 1326 9th Ave; 4pm-midnight Mon-Thu, to 1am Fri, 11:30am-2am Sat, 11:30am-midnight Sun; 6, 7, 43, 44, MN) In every Social situation, there are a couple of troublemakers – specifically the bitter Belgian Rapscallion, and the bewitching Black Moon Spell house brews. This snazzy, sky-lit loft building looks like an architect's office but tastes like a neighborhood brewpub, and before 10:30pm serves addictive sweet potato tempura fries and lime-laced Brussels sprout chips – but hey, hogging the bowl is anti-Social.

ENTERTAINMENT

THE PLOUGH & THE STARS LIVE MUSIC

Map p326 (415-751-1122; www.theploughandstars.com; 116 Clement St; 3pm-2am Mon-Thu, from 2pm Fri-Sun, showtime 9pm; 1, 2, 33, 38, 44) Bands who sell out shows from Ireland to Appalachia and headline SF's Hardly Strictly Bluegrass festival jam here on weeknights, taking breaks to clink pint glasses of Guinness at long union-hall tables. Mondays compensate for no live music with an all-day happy hour, plus free pool and blarney from regulars; expect modest cover charges ($6 to $14) for barnstorming weekend shows.

BALBOA THEATRE CINEMA

Map p326 (415-221-8184; www.balboamovies.com; 3630 Balboa St; adult/child $10/7.50; showtimes vary; ; 5, 18, 31, 38) First stop, Cannes; next stop, Balboa and 37th, where film-fest favorites split the bill with Chaplin classics, family-friendly Saturday matinees and special screenings with expert commentary – like Spike Jonze's *Her* with Google's artificial intelligence expert. Filmmakers vie for marquee spots at this 1926 movie palace run by nonprofit San Francisco Neighborhood Theater Foundation, which keeps tickets affordable and programming exciting.

NECK OF THE WOODS CLUB

Map p326 (415-387-6343; http://neckofthewoodssf.com; 406 Clement St; 6pm-2am; 1, 2, 33, 38, 44) A vast yet intimate two-story venue with all the right moves, including Salsa Mondays ($20 per class), Burlesque Thursdays, occasional Russian Karaoke (no language skills required) and weekend indie rock acts pounding the upstairs stage (listen to the lineup online). Downstairs the sleek yet cozy lounge serves happy hour $4 well drinks and beer, and hosts wholly unpredictable open mic nights.

FOUR STAR THEATER CINEMA

Map p326 (415-666-3488; www.lntsf.com/; 2200 Clement St; adult/child & matinee $10.50/8.50; showtimes vary; 1, 2, 29, 38) Before John Woo, Ang Lee and Wong Kar-wai hit multiplex marquees, they brought down the house in the Four Star's postage-stamp-sized screening rooms. Running since 1964, this international neighborhood cinema still shows Jackie Chan action flicks alongside international film-festival favorites – see website for showtimes and tickets.

SHOPPING

★**FOGGY NOTION** GIFTS, ACCESSORIES

Map p326 (415-683-5654; www.foggy-notion.com; 275 6th Ave; 11am-7pm Mon-Sat, to 6pm Sun; 1, 2, 38, 49) You can't take Golden Gate Park home with you – the city would seem naked without it – but Foggy Notion specializes in sense memories of SF's

WHERE TO GEAR UP FOR OCEAN BEACH

Mollusk (Map p326; ☎415-564-6300; www.mollusksurfshop.com; 4500 Irving St; ⏰10am-6:30pm Mon-Sat, to 6pm Sun; 🚌18, Ⓜ N) The geodesic-dome tugboat marks the spot where ocean meets art in this surf gallery. Legendary shapers (surfboard makers) create limited-edition boards for Mollusk, and signature big wave T-shirts and hoodies win nods of recognition on Ocean Beach. Kooks (newbies) get vicarious big-wave thrills from coffee-table books on California surf culture, Thomas Campbell ocean collages and other works by SF surfer-artists.

Aqua Surf Shop (Map p326; ☎415-242-9283; www.aquasurfshop.com/; 3847 Judah St; rental per day board/wetsuit $25/15; ⏰10am-5:30pm Sun-Tue, to 7pm Wed-Sat; 🚌18, Ⓜ N) Earn Sunset street cred the hardcore way, with Aqua's wetsuit/surfboard/bodyboard rentals ($15/25/10) plus referrals for surf instructors who can show you how to handle Ocean Beach riptides. For instant cool factor without getting wet, hit Aqua pop-up events and be the first to score new Aqua tees designed by SF artist Jeremy Fish.

On the Run (Map p326; ☎415-682-2043; www.ontherunshoes.com; 1310 9th Ave; ⏰10am-7pm Mon-Fri, to 6pm Sat, 11am-6pm Sun; 🚌6, 7, 43, 44, Ⓜ N) If your morning jog leaves your feet or shins hurting, get your gait checked here before you hit Golden Gate Park trails or Ocean Beach. The pros will recommend the right orthopedic inserts or shoes to relieve the pressure for free – and if you choose to buy inserts here, they'll mold them to fit while you wait.

urban wilderness. SF's finest all-natural, all-artisan gift selection includes Juniper Ridge's hiking-trail scents, Golden Gate Park honey, SF artist Julia Canwright's handprinted canvas backpacks, and Wildman beard conditioner for scruff soft as fog.

★JADE CHOCOLATES — FOOD

Map p326 (☎415-350-3878; www.jadechocolates.com; 4207 Geary Blvd; ⏰11am-6pm Mon-Sat, 3-6pm Sun; 🚌2, 31, 38, 44) SF-born chocolatier Mindy Fong hits the sweet spot between East and West with only-in-SF treats like passion fruit caramels, jasmine-pearl tea truffles and the legendary peanut Buddha with mango jam. Fusion flavors originally inspired by Fong's pregnancy cravings have won national acclaim, but Jade Chocolates keeps its SF edge with experimental chocolates featuring sriracha, California's homegrown, Asian-inspired chili sauce.

★PARK LIFE — ART, GIFTS

Map p326 (☎415-386-7275; www.parklifestore.com; 220 Clement St; ⏰11am-8pm Mon-Sat, to 6pm Sun; 🚌1, 2, 33, 38, 44) The Swiss Army knife of hip SF stores: design store, indie publisher and art gallery all in one. It's exceptionally gifted with presents too good to give away, including Golden State pendants, T-shirts for SF's imaginary Aesthetics team, Park Life's catalog of Andrew Schoultz street murals and Anthony Discenza's cryptically cautionary road sign: 'This could be about anything at all.'

★THE GREAT OVERLAND BOOK COMPANY — BOOKS

Map p326 (☎415-664-0126; 345 Judah St; ⏰11am-7pm; 🚌6, 7, 44, Ⓜ N) SF obsessions go deep at Great Overland, purveyor of rare and obscure books on SF's pet subjects. DIY dandies find inspiration in 1891 *World's Fair Household Companion* recipes for bone-marrow pomade, while bartenders pore over Prohibition pamphlets on making the best of bathtub brandy. For spine-chilling SF history, check out original 1860s Vigilance Committee records and 1949 House Un-American Activities reports.

LAST STRAW — GIFTS, ACCESSORIES

Map p326 (☎415-566-4692; 4540 Irving St; ⏰noon-6pm Tue-Sat; 🚌7, 18, Ⓜ N) Gifts come from the heart inside this front-parlor gift shop, packed with outer-avenues necessities: *haori* jackets, indigo beach totes, and fisherman's scarves knitted on a nearby houseboat. Open jewelry chests to find hidden treasures under $50, including Amano's Sonoma-made chiseled silver *señorita* hoops. No credit cards, but owner Marge accepts cash, checks and – proof that SF idealism lives – IOUs.

SPACE TO CONGREGATE

John F Kennedy Dr is closed to motor vehicles east of Crossover Dr (around 8th Ave) all day Sunday and Saturday mornings to accommodate runners, skateboarders, unicyclists and meandering dreamers. To plan a picnic, concert or protest in the park and get detailed park maps, check in at **McLaren Lodge** (Map p326; ☎415-831-2700; www.golden-gate-park.com; 501 Stanyan St, cnr Fell & Stanyan Sts; ⏰8am-5pm Mon-Fri; 🚌5, 7, 21, 33) at the eastern entrance of the park, under the splendid cypress that's the city's official tree.

GREEN APPLE BOOKS BOOKS

Map p326 (☎415-387-2272; www.greenapplebooks.com; 506 Clement St; ⏰10am-10:30pm; 🚌1, 2, 33, 38, 44) Blissed-out book lovers emerge blinking at sunset after days browsing three floors of new releases, used titles and staff picks more reliable than *New York Times* reviews. Find out what's on SF's mind in the local interest section, and stick around for author events.

But wait, there's more in the fiction/music annex two doors down, plus a new **parkside location** (Map p326; ☎415-742-5833; 1231 9th Ave; 🚌44, 71, Ⓜ N).

GENERAL STORE GIFTS, ACCESSORIES

Map p326 (☎415-682-0600; http://shop-generalstore.com; 4035 Judah St; ⏰11am-7pm Mon-Fri, from 10am Sat & Sun; 🚌18, Ⓜ N) Anyone born in the wrong place or time to be a NorCal hippie architect can still look the part, thanks to a) beards and b) General Store. Pine-lined walls showcase handcrafted indigo scarves, slingshots, lap looms, surfer salve and beach checker sets. To impress sustainability-minded SF hosts, gift them with succulents from the backyard greenhouse instead of cut flowers.

URBAN BAZAAR GIFTS

Map p326 (☎415-664-4422; http://urbanbazaarsf.com; 1371 9th Ave; ⏰11am-5:30pm Sun-Mon, to 7pm Tue-Sat; 👪; 🚌6, 7, 43, 44, Ⓜ N) 🍃 Show some SF love with gifts for adults and kids made by local artisans and fair-trade collectives, including Ocean Beach–scented soap, Victorian Painted Lady stamp sets and Muni temporary tattoos. Check the website for workshops with SF artisans ($3 to $55, including materials), and hang out with the entire neighborhood at backyard pop-up events and holiday fairs.

SPORTS & ACTIVITIES

GOLDEN GATE PARK BIKE & SKATE BICYCLING

Map p326 (☎415-668-1117; www.goldengateparkbikeandskate.com; 3038 Fulton St; skates per hr $5-6, per day $20-24, bikes per hr $3-5, per day $15-25, tandem bikes per hr/day $15/75, discs $6/25; ⏰10am-6pm summer, to 7pm winter; 👪; 🚌5, 21, 31, 44) Besides bikes and skates (four-wheeled and in-line, helmets included in rentals), this rental shop just outside Golden Gate Park rents disc putters and drivers for the park's free Frisbee golf course. Call ahead to confirm it's open if the weather looks iffy.

SAN FRAN CYCLO BICYCLING

Map p326 (☎415-831-8031; http://sanfrancyclo.com; 746 Arguello Blvd; rental bicycle per hr $10-35, kid's bicycle/bike seat per day $20, helmet per day $10; ⏰11am-7pm Mon-Fri, 10am-5pm Sat & Sun; 👪; 🚌5, 21, 31, 33, 38) Glide around Golden Gate Park and zip across the Bridge on sleek new bikes, including hybrid options and electric bikes. Storefront for pickup/drop off is just north of Golden Gate Park near the Velo Rouge Café (p208), a handy pit stop and SF cycling-scene hub. Customized city bike tours are available in good weather (two/three/five hours $50/75/125).

LINCOLN PARK GOLF COURSE GOLF

Map p326 (☎415-221-9911, reservations 415-750-4653; http://sfrecpark.org/parks-open-spaces/golf-courses; 34th Ave & Clement St, Lincoln Park; adult/child Mon-Thu $39/20, Fri-Sun $43/22, cart $28; ⏰sunrise-sunset; 👪; 🚌1, 18, 38) For game-sabotaging views, the hilly, 18-hole Lincoln Park course wraps around Land's End and the Legion of Honor to face Golden Gate Bridge. This 1928 course has the most iconic SF vistas, so watch out for daydreaming hikers and brides posing for wedding pictures – fore!

STOW LAKE BOATHOUSE BOATING

Map p326 (http://stowlakeboathouse.com; 50 Stow Lake Dr; boats per hr $20-34; ⏰10am-5pm Mon-Fri, to 6pm Sat & Sun; 🚌5, 7, 29, 44) 🍃 Push off from the dock of this vintage 1948 boathouse in a pedal-powered, electric or row boat to glide across Stow Lake (p201), and return for organic Three Twins ice cream at the renovated boathouse café (11am to 5:30pm).

LINDY IN THE PARK DANCE

Map p326 (www.lindyinthepark.com; John F Kennedy Dr, btwn 8th & 10th Aves; ⌚11am-2pm Sun; 👪; Ⓜ Fulton St) FREE Sundays swing at the free Lindy-hopping dance party in Golden Gate Park, on the south sidewalk near the de Young Museum (p200), weather permitting. All are welcome; dancers range from first-timers to semiprofessionals, hipsters to groovy grandparents. Free half-hour lessons begin at noon, but you can always just watch or wing it.

LAWN BOWLING CLUB BOWLING

Map p326 (☎415-487-8787; www.golden-gate-park.com; Bowling Green Dr, Golden Gate Park; ⌚11am-4pm Apr-Oct, from 11am Nov-Mar, weather permitting; 🚌5, 7, 21, 33, Ⓜ N) Pins seem ungainly and bowling shirts unthinkable once you've joined sweater-clad enthusiasts on America's first public lawn-bowling green. Free lessons are available from volunteers on Wednesdays at noon. Flat-soled shoes are mandatory, but otherwise bowlers dress for comfort and the weather – though all-white clothing has been customary at club social events since 1901.

SAN FRANCISCO DISC GOLF SPORTS

Map p326 (www.sfdiscgolf.org; Marx Meadow Dr, off Fulton St btwn 25th & 30th Aves; ⌚sunrise-sunset; 🚌5, 28, 29, 31, 38) FREE Wander the tranquil fairy-tale woods of outer Golden Gate Park, and you'll find fierce Frisbee golf games in progress at a permanent 18-hole disc-golf course. Rent tournament discs at Golden Gate Park Bike & Skate to mingle with disc-tossing singles on Sundays (8:30am to 10am; $5) or join Tuesday twilight doubles tournaments (5pm; $5) – winners take home cash.

SAN FRANCISCO MODEL YACHT CLUB BOATING

Map p326 (☎415-386-1037; www.sfmyc.org; Spreckels Lake, Golden Gate Park; ⌚sunrise-sunset; 👪; 🚌5, 18, 31) America's Cup races can't compare to these remote-controlled miniature regattas for excitement. Kids cheer for scale-model yachts built and operated by local collectors 1pm to 4pm Saturday and Sunday, plus occasional weekdays in fine weather. Spreckels Lake is also a refuge for turtles, who snooze on the shore, unphased by regattas. When members are around, check out vintage boats in the clubhouse.

GOLDEN GATE JOAD ARCHERY

Map p326 (www.goldengatejoad.com; Golden Gate Park Archery Range, Fulton St & 47th Ave; 2hr lesson incl archery gear rental $20; ⌚classes Sat mornings; 👪; 🚌5, 18, 31) Blockbusters like *The Avengers, The Hunger Games* and *Brave* have revived San Francisco's Victorian-era archery craze, and you can take aim Saturday mornings in Golden Gate Park with SF's nonprofit Junior Olympic Archery Division (JOAD). Patient, certified coaches offer traditional bow archery classes for adults and kids ages eight and up (with guardian consent). Book online; beginner classes fill quickly.

GOLDEN GATE MUNICIPAL GOLF COURSE GOLF

Map p326 (☎415-751-8987; www.goldengateparkgolf.com; 970 47th Ave, off Fulton St, Golden Gate Park; adult/child Mon-Thu $17/9, Fri-Sun $21/11; ⌚7am-5pm; 👪; 🚌5, 18, 31) This challenging nine-hole, par-27 course is built on sand dunes, with 100yd drop-offs and 180yd elevated greens. No reservations are taken, but it's busiest before 9am weekdays and after school. On weekend afternoons, bide your time waiting with excellent clubhouse wood-fired BBQ sandwiches (its sauce secret: Anchor Steam beer). Equipment rentals (adult/child $15/6) and practice range available; kids welcome.

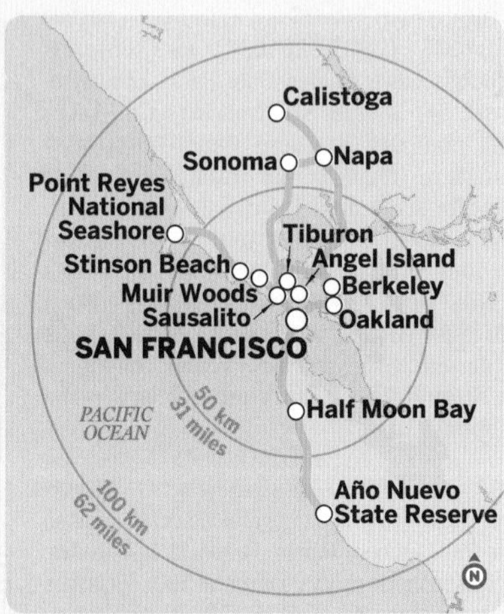

Day Trips from San Francisco

Berkeley p213

Home to a cutting-edge university, socially progressive activists and a 'Gourmet Ghetto,' here summer weather is up to 20°F (7°C) warmer than in San Francisco.

Muir Woods to Stinson Beach p216

Some of the world's tallest trees reach skyward in primordial forests near windblown beaches, just across the Golden Gate Bridge.

Sausalito & Tiburon p220

Picturesque bayside towns, perfect for strolling, are a fast ferry ride away in Marin County. Meet for sunset drinks and seafood by the water.

Napa Valley p222

Fancy-pants Napa vineyards first put California on the world's viticulture map. Cycle through rolling countryside, tipple top-tier wines and nab seats at star chefs' tables.

Sonoma Valley p228

With its 19th-century California mission town, farm-to-table kitchens and pastoral wineries that welcome picnicking, Sonoma retains its folksy ways.

Berkeley

Explore

As the birthplace of the 1960s Free Speech Movement, and the home of the hallowed halls of the University of California, Berkeley is no bashful wallflower. You can't legally walk around nude anymore, but 'Berserkeley' remains the Bay Area's radical hub, crawling with university students. 'Nuclear Free Zone' street signs mark the city limits.

The main destinations of day-trippers are downtown Berkeley and the university campus. Just north of campus along Shattuck Ave lies North Berkeley's 'Gourmet Ghetto.' The hills above Berkeley are crisscrossed by hiking trails through Tilden Regional Park, which has bird's-eye views over the bay.

The Best...

- **Sight** University of California, Berkeley
- **Place to Eat** Chez Panisse (p215)
- **Entertainment** Freight & Salvage Coffeehouse (p215)

Top Tip

During weekday commuter rush hours, avoid driving over the Bay Bridge or along the I-80 Fwy. Try taking public transportation instead.

Getting There & Away

- **Car** Bay Bridge to I-80 Fwy East; exit University Ave.
- **Train** Downtown Berkeley's **BART** (☎511, 510-465-2278; www.bart.gov) station is convenient ($3.90, 25 minutes, every 10 to 20 minutes).
- **Bus AC Transit** (☎511; www.actransit.org) runs frequent buses from San Francisco's Transbay Temporary Terminal (Howard, Main and Beale Sts) to Berkeley ($4.20, 45 minutes), with connecting buses around town ($2.10).

Need to Know

- **Area Code** ☎510
- **Location** 11 miles northeast of San Francisco.
- **Tourist office** (☎800-847-4823, 510-549-7040; www.visitberkeley.com; 2030 Addison St; ⏰9am-1pm & 2-5pm Mon-Fri, 10am-1pm & 2-4pm Sat)

SIGHTS

★UNIVERSITY OF CALIFORNIA, BERKELEY — UNIVERSITY

(www.berkeley.edu) The campus of UC Berkeley – aka 'Cal' – is one of California's oldest, founded in 1868. From Telegraph Ave, enter **Sproul Plaza**, ground zero for people-watching, soapbox oration and drum circles. The adjacent **Visitor Services Center** (☎510-642-5215; http://visitors.berkeley.edu; 101 Sproul Hall; ⏰tours usually 10am Mon-Sat & 1pm Sun) offers free guided campus tours (reservations required). Alternatively, enter campus off Oxford St, a short walk east of the Downtown Berkeley BART station.

The **Campanile** (Sather Tower; http://visitors.berkeley.edu/camp/; adult/child $3/2; ⏰10am-3:45pm Mon-Fri, to 4:45pm Sat, 10am-1:30pm & 3-4:45pm Sun; 👪) was modeled on St Mark's Basilica in Venice. The 307ft spire has knockout views, and some of the carillon's 61 bells are as big as a Volkswagen. Recitals take place daily at 7:50am, noon and 6pm, with a longer piece on Sundays at 2pm.

Reopening just west of campus in 2016, the **UC Berkeley Art Museum** (☎510-642-0808; www.bampfa.berkeley.edu; 2155 Center St) showcases works from ancient Chinese to cutting-edge contemporary. The new downtown location will also house the wide-ranging Pacific Film Archive (p215).

The recently renovated **Phoebe A Hearst Museum of Anthropology** (☎510-642-3682; http://hearstmuseum.berkeley.edu; Kroeber Hall, Bancroft Way at College Ave; ⏰call for hours & prices) showcases the diversity of indigenous cultures, with artifacts from ancient Peru, Africa and Oceania. The Native Californian woven basketry is a highlight.

Uphill east of the main campus, **UC Botanical Garden at Berkeley** (☎510-643-2755; www.botanicalgarden.berkeley.edu; 200 Centennial Dr; adult/child $10/2; ⏰9am-5pm, last entry 4:30pm, closed 1st Tue each month) protects more than 13,000 species of plants. It's one of the USA's most varied floral collections.

TELEGRAPH AVENUE — STREET

Running south of campus, Telegraph Ave is the heart of Berkeley's student village, a constant flow of shoppers, buskers and street vendors. Graying Birkenstock-clad hippies shuffle by street hawkers, musical buskers and ponytailed panhandlers. If you're on the hunt for books, vinyl records, new-age crystals or political bumper stickers, this is the place.

East Bay

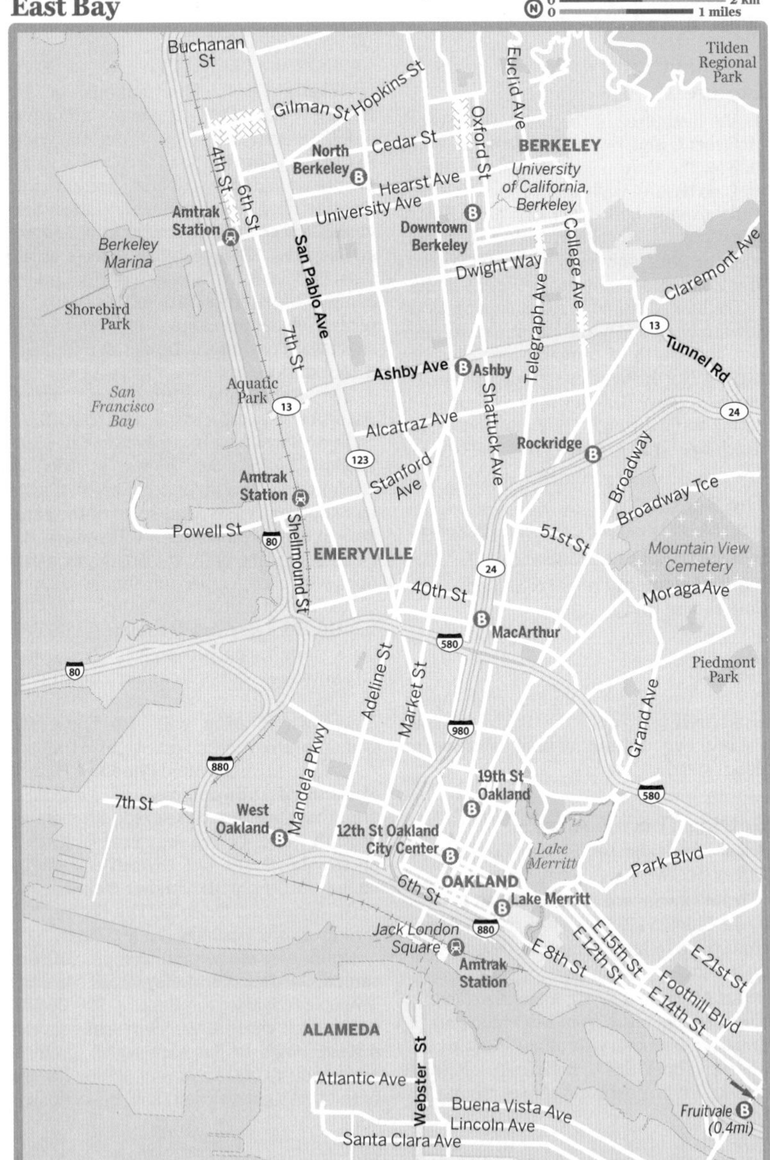

TILDEN REGIONAL PARK PARK
(www.ebparks.org/parks/tilden; ⌚5am-10pm) Escape to Berkeley's hills and revel in nearly 40 miles of hiking and biking trails, a botanical garden, a public golf course, seasonal swimming at Lake Anza (adult/child $3.50/2.50) and plenty of kids' stuff, including a merry-go-round (per ride $2) and mini steam train (per ride $3).

From the Downtown Berkeley BART station, AC Transit bus 67 runs into and around the park on weekends and holidays, but on weekdays it only stops at the park entrance ($2.10, 20 minutes).

TAKARA SAKE MUSEUM

(☎510-540-8250; www.takarasake.com; 708 Addison St; admission free, tasting fee $5-10; ⏰noon-6pm, last tasting 5:30pm) Stop by to view traditional wooden tools used for making sake and a short video of the brewing process. Factory tours aren't offered, but sake flights are poured in a spacious tasting room inlaid with glass floor tiles made from recycling sake, whiskey and beer bottles.

EATING & DRINKING

CHEESE BOARD PIZZA PIZZA $

(☎510-549-3055; www.cheeseboardcollective.coop; 1512 Shattuck Ave; slice/half-pizza $2.50/10; ⏰11:30am-3pm & 4:30-8pm Tue-Sat; 🖉) A Gourmet Ghetto mainstay, this worker-owned collective crafts only one wildly creative flavor of crispy vegetarian pizza each day. Live music jams at lunch and dinner. Cheese Board's next-door bakery vends oven-fresh bread, baked goods and gourmet cheeses.

VIK'S CHAAT CORNER INDIAN $

(☎510-644-4432; www.vikschaatcorner.com; 2390 4th St; items $5-10; ⏰11am-6pm Mon-Thu, to 8pm Fri-Sun; 🖉) 🍃 At the back of a South Asian grocery store, this high-ceilinged cafeteria serves hot, authentic Indian street food, curries, *dosa* (filled crepes) and more. Daily specials are plated with all the trimmings. Expect a wait.

IPPUKU JAPANESE $$

(☎510-665-1969; www.ippukuberkeley.com; 2130 Center St; shared plates $5-20; ⏰5-10pm Sun-Thu, to 11pm Fri & Sat) Specializing in *shōchū* liquor, Ippuku is sweetly reminiscent of *izakaya* (Japanese pubs serving food) back in Tokyo. Choose from a menu of skewered meats and vegetables, side dishes and handmade noodles after settling in at a low-slung *tatami* table (no shoes, please) or wooden booth. Reservations essential.

★**CHEZ PANISSE** CALIFORNIAN $$$

(☎café 510-548-5049, restaurant 510-548-5525; www.chezpanisse.com; 1517 Shattuck Ave; café dinner mains $19-32, restaurant prix-fixe dinner $75-125; ⏰café 11:30am-2:45pm & 5-10:30pm Mon-Thu, 11:30am-3pm & 5-11:30pm Fri & Sat, restaurant seatings 5:30pm & 8pm Mon-Sat) 🍃 The temple of Alice Waters – doyenne of California cuisine – remains at the pinnacle of Bay Area dining. Reserve 28 days in advance for legendary dinners in the cozy Craftsman-style dining room, where no substitutions are allowed on the daily-changing restaurant menu. If you'd prefer to order à la carte, book the less expensive but equally lovely upstairs café.

JUPITER PUB

(www.jupiterbeer.com; 2181 Shattuck Ave; ⏰11:30am-1am Mon-Thu, to 1:30am Fri, noon-1:30am Sat, to midnight Sun) Packed with students, this downtown brewpub pours loads of regional craft beers and has an outdoor beer garden, decent pizza and live bands most nights. Sit upstairs for a bird's-eye view of buzzing Shattuck Ave.

ASHA TEA HOUSE CAFÉ

(www.ashateahouse.com; 2086 University Ave; ⏰11am-10pm Mon-Sat, to 8pm Sun; 📶) Find your bliss at this industrial-modern tea shop, where acrylic prints of verdant tea plantations overhang the bar. Hand-crafted Indian chai, Japanese *matcha* (powdered green tea) and Hong Kong–style milk tea star on a connoisseur's drinks menu.

TORPEDO ROOM BREWERY

(www.sierranevada.com/brewery/california/torpedoroom; 2031 4th St; ⏰11:30am-8pm Tue-Fri, 11am-8pm Sat, noon-5pm Sun) Sample a flight of 4oz pours (no pints) from rotating drafts and guest taps at Sierra Nevada brewery's tasting room. It's in West Berkeley, a block south of University Ave.

ENTERTAINMENT

★**FREIGHT & SALVAGE COFFEEHOUSE** LIVE MUSIC

(☎510-644-2020; www.thefreight.org; 2020 Addison St; 👪) All-ages, alcohol-free coffeehouse dating from the radical '60s hosts traditional folk, bluegrass, jazz, blues and world music shows – come to hear the fiddle, guitars, strings and soul.

PACIFIC FILM ARCHIVE THEATER CINEMA

(PFA; ☎510-642-5249; www.bampfa.berkeley.edu; 2575 Bancroft Way; adult/child $9.50/6.50) Renowned movie theater that explores the art of filmmaking, including rare, new and historic prints from around the globe. It's moving downtown in 2016.

EAST BAY BY BART

To escape San Francisco's famous fog, chase some California sunshine over in the East Bay by hopping a BART train to:

Downtown Berkeley Station It's close to the UC Berkeley campus, the downtown arts district and Telegraph Ave's funky shops and student cafés.

Rockridge Station Straddling the Berkeley/Oakland border, College Ave encourages lazy-day strolling with a bevy of local shops and eateries.

19th Street Oakland Station After dark, Oakland's Uptown district buzzes with hip cocktail bars, break-out restaurants and two glittering art-deco landmarks, the **Fox Theater** (510-302-2250; www.thefoxoakland.com; 1807 Telegraph Ave) and the **Paramount Theatre** (510-465-6400; www.paramounttheatre.com; 2025 Broadway). By day, amble east to Lake Merritt and follow the scenic lakeshore recreational path around to the 1950s storybook **Children's Fairyland** (510-238-6876; http://fairyland.org; 699 Bellevue Ave; admission $8; 10am-4pm Mon-Fri, to 5pm Sat & Sun Jun-Aug, off-season hours vary;), the botanical gardens or the **boating center** (510-238-2196; www2.oaklandnet.com; 568 Bellevue Ave; boat rentals per hr $12-24, cash only; daily Mar-Oct, Sat & Sun only Nov-Feb).

Lake Merritt Station Walk two blocks north to the fascinating **Oakland Museum of California** (OMCA; 510-318-8400, 888-625-6873; www.museumca.org; 1000 Oak St; adult/child $15/6, 1st Sun each month free; 11am-5pm Wed-Thu, to 9pm Fri, 10am-6pm Sat & Sun;). Afterward, head west for a bowl of savory noodles in Chinatown. Alternatively, keep going north for happy-hour drinks at the **Lake Chalet** (510-208-5253; www.thelakechalet.com; 1520 Lakeside Dr; mains $15-36; 11am-10pm Mon-Thu, to 11pm Fri, 10am-11pm Sat, to 10pm Sun), where you can book ahead for a **gondola cruise** (510-663-6603; http://gondolaservizio.com; 1520 Lakeside Dr; 30/50min cruise $60/85) at sunset.

12th Street Oakland City Center Station Wander south into the Old Oakland historic district, where local restaurants hover around Washington and 9th Sts. Keep going down Broadway to waterfront Jack London Square, where a replica of the writer's Klondike Gold Rush–era log cabin stands by **Heinhold's First & Last Chance** (www.heinolds.com; 48 Webster St; 3-11pm Mon, noon-11pm Tue-Sun, to 1am Fri & Sat) saloon. FDR's presidential yacht, the **USS Potomac** (510-627-1215; www.usspotomac.org; 540 Water St; adult/child $10/free; 11am-3pm Wed, Fri & Sun), is docked nearby.

Coliseum Station Check out big-name musical acts and touring shows or **Golden State Warriors** (888-479-4667; www.nba.com/warriors; B Coliseum) basketball at Oracle Arena, or watch **Oakland A's** (877-493-2255; http://oakland.athletics.mlb.com; B Coliseum) baseball or **Oakland Raiders** (510-864-5020; www.raiders.com; B Coliseum) football at O.co Coliseum.

BERKELEY REPERTORY THEATRE THEATER

(510-647-2949; www.berkeleyrep.org; 2025 Addison St; tickets $40-100) Some San Franciscans cross the bay just to see Berkeley Rep's bold versions of classics and thought-provoking contemporary plays that spotlight social issues.

ZELLERBACH HALL PERFORMING ARTS

(510-642-9988; http://tickets.berkeley.edu) UC's premier stage showcases top-flight musical ensembles, dance troupes and famous performers from the US and abroad.

Muir Woods to Stinson Beach

Explore

Coast redwoods, the tallest living things on the planet, exist only on the West Coast, extending north from California's Big Sur into southern Oregon. Today you can amble around a glorious old-growth stand of redwoods just 10 miles from the Golden Gate Bridge. You could spend as little as an hour in Muir Woods, following crowds along the main paths, but for perspective on the ancient forest, hike the park's longer trails, which lift you above the big trees onto rugged ridgelines where ocean panoramas unfurl. Afterward, continue to the coast and along Hwy 1 to pebbly Muir Beach and crescent-shaped Stinson Beach – but you'd do well to bring a sweater, not a bikini: chances are it'll be chilly.

The Best...

- **Sight** Cathedral Grove (p218)
- **Hike** Dipsea Trail (p218)
- **Place to Eat** Parkside Café (p220)

Top Tip

To beat the crowds, come early in the day, before sunset or midweek; otherwise the parking lots fill up. Consider riding the seasonal shuttle bus to Muir Woods.

Getting There & Away

- **Car** Take Hwy 101 north across the Golden Gate Bridge, exiting at Hwy 1. Continue north along Hwy 1/Shoreline Hwy to Panoramic Hwy (a right-hand fork). Follow Panoramic Hwy almost a mile, turning left onto Muir Woods Rd.
- **Ferry & Bus** On weekends and holidays from April through October (daily between late June and mid-August), **Marin Transit** (☎415-455-2000, 511; www.marintransit.org) bus 66 ('Muir Woods Shuttle') departs Sausalito (round-trip adult/child $5/free, 50 minutes), connecting with Golden Gate Ferry (p56) service from San Francisco ($10.75, 30 minutes). On weekends and holidays, **West Marin Stagecoach** (☎415-526-3239; www.marintransit.org/stage.html) bus 61 links Stinson Beach with Sausalito ($2, 1½ hours).

Need to Know

- **Area Code** ☎415
- **Location** 12 miles northwest of San Francisco

SIGHTS

★**MUIR WOODS NATIONAL MONUMENT** FOREST

(☎415-388-2595; www.nps.gov/muwo; 1 Muir Woods Rd, Mill Valley; adult/child $10/free; ⏲8am-sunset) The closest stand of coastal

MARIN HEADLANDS

Jaggedly rising on the north side of the Golden Gate Bridge, the rugged beauty of these windswept headlands is all the more striking given that they're only a few miles from San Francisco's urban core. A few forts and bunkers are left over from more than a century of use by the US military.

Today this development-free open space is protected by **Golden Gate National Recreation Area** (www.nps.gov/goga). Rugged hiking and mountain-biking trails wind through the headlands, affording panoramic cliff-edge views of the sea, the bridge and the city. Some trails lead to isolated beaches and secluded picnic spots.

Uphill and across the road from the **Marin Headlands Visitor Center** (☎415-331-1540; www.nps.gov/goga/marin-headlands.htm; Fort Barry; ⏲9:30am-4:30pm), peek into the open studios of the **Headlands Center for the Arts** (☎415-331-2787; www.headlands.org; 944 Simmonds Rd; ⏲noon-5pm Sun-Thu) FREE. Then visit the playful 'patients' in the wildlife hospital at the eco-conscious, educational and child-friendly **Marine Mammal Center** (☎415-289-7325; www.marinemammalcenter.org; 2000 Bunker Rd; ⏲10am-5pm; 👪) FREE.

It's a steep half-mile hike down from the end of Conzelman Rd to 19th-century **Point Bonita Lighthouse** (www.nps.gov/goga/pobo.htm; off Field Rd; ⏲12:30-3:30pm Sat-Mon) FREE, reached via a tunnel and suspension bridges. History hounds will want to poke around **Nike Missile Site SF-88** (☎415-331-1453; www.nps.gov/goga/nike-missile-site.htm; off Field Rd; ⏲12:30-3:30pm Thu-Sat) FREE, a genuine Cold War–era relic.

If you're driving, take the Alexander Ave exit off Hwy 101 northbound immediately after crossing the Golden Gate Bridge, then turn left under the freeway and follow the signs. On weekends and holidays, Muni (p274) bus 76X runs hourly from downtown San Francisco to the Marin Headlands Visitor Center ($2.25, 45 minutes).

Marin County

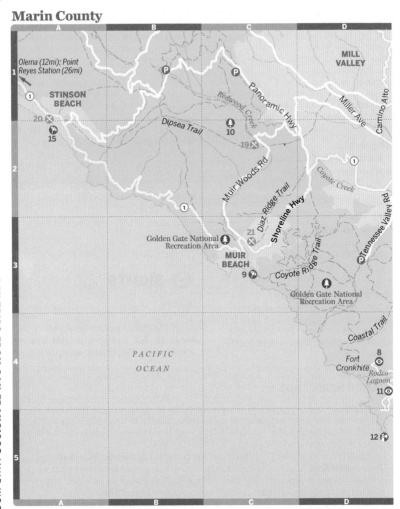

redwoods to San Francisco, this old-growth forest dates back to time immemorial. Even during peak periods, when the park is jam-packed with local families and tourists all gaping up at the giant trees, a short hike will get you out of the densest crowds and onto trails with unforgettable vistas.

These trees were initially eyed by loggers, and Redwood Creek, as the area was known, seemed ideal for a dam. President Theodore Roosevelt declared the site a national monument in 1908, its name honoring John Muir, naturalist and founder of the Sierra Club environmental group.

The 1-mile **Main Loop Trail** is easy, leading alongside Redwood Creek to 1000-year-old trees at **Cathedral Grove**. The **Dipsea Trail** is a steep 2-mile (one-way) hike to the top of aptly named Cardiac Hill, leading up from the canyon through fern-fringed forest to an exposed ridge, from where you can see Mt Tamalpais, the Pacific and San Francisco. If you're up for a longer trek, keep hiking all the way down to the tiny coastal town of **Stinson Beach** (9.5 miles round-trip).

You can also walk down into Muir Woods via trails from the Panoramic Hwy (such as the Bootjack Trail from Bootjack picnic area) or nearby Mt Tamalpais State

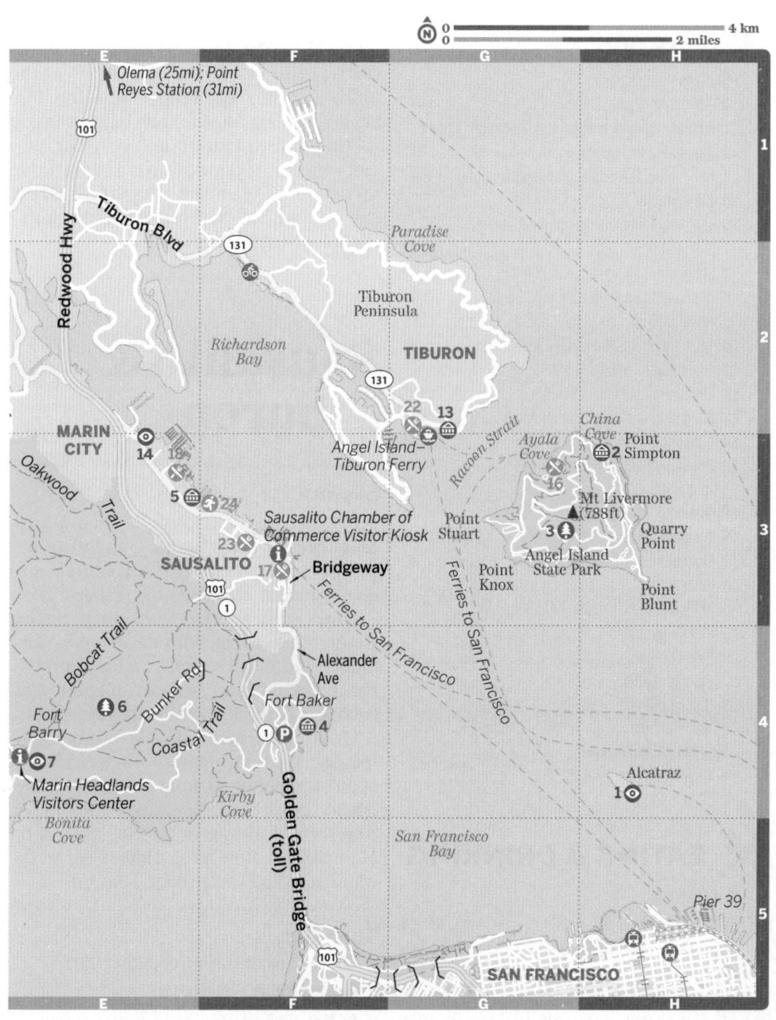

Park's Pantoll Station (via the Stapleveldt and Ben Johnson Trails).

MUIR BEACH BEACH

(www.nps.gov/goga; off Pacific Way) FREE The turnoff to Muir Beach from Hwy 1 is marked by the coast's longest row of mailboxes near mile marker 5.7, just before the Pelican Inn.

Further north along Hwy 1 there are stunning coastal views from **Muir Beach Overlook**. During WWII, watch for invading Japanese ships was kept from the surrounding concrete lookouts.

STINSON BEACH BEACH

(www.nps.gov/goga; off Hwy 1) Positively buzzing on warm weekends, the town of Stinson Beach is just over six curving, cliff-hugging miles north of Muir Beach. When it's not blanketed with fog, the beach affords looks at Point Reyes and San Francisco on clear days.

The three-mile-long strand is a popular surf spot, but swimming is advised only from late May to mid-September. For updated weather and surf conditions, call ☎415-868-1922.

Marin County

Sights

1	Alcatraz	H4
2	Angel Island Immigration Station	H3
3	Angel Island State Park	G3
4	Bay Area Discovery Museum	F4
5	Bay Model Visitors Center	E3
6	Golden Gate National Recreation Area	E4
7	Headlands Center for the Arts	E4
8	Marine Mammal Center	D4
9	Muir Beach	C3
10	Muir Woods National Monument	C2
11	Nike Missile Site SF-88	D4
12	Point Bonita Lighthouse	D5
13	Railroad & Ferry Depot Museum	G2
14	Sausalito Houseboats	E3
15	Stinson Beach	A2

Eating

16	Angel Island Café	G3
17	Barrel House Tavern	F3
18	Fish	E3
19	Muir Woods Trading Company	C2
20	Parkside Café	A1
21	Pelican Inn	C3
22	Sam's Anchor Cafe	G2
23	Sushi Ran	F3

Sports & Activities

24	Sea Trek Kayak & SUP	F3

EATING & DRINKING

MUIR WOODS TRADING COMPANY CAFÉ **$**

(☎415-388-7059; www.muirwoodstradingcompany.com; 1 Muir Woods Rd, Mill Valley; items $3-11; ⏰from 9am daily, closing varies 4pm to 7pm; 👪) It's pricey, but this little café near the park entrance serves melty-good grilled cheese sandwiches, savory soups and hot drinks that hit the spot on foggy days.

★**PARKSIDE CAFÉ** AMERICAN **$$**

(☎415-868-1272; www.parksidecafe.com; 43 Arenal Ave; mains $8-28; ⏰7:30am-9pm, coffee from 6am; 👪) Next to Stinson Beach, this old-fashioned eatery is beloved for hearty Californian breakfasts, wood-fired pizzas and coastal cuisine like Tomales Bay oysters and BBQ king salmon. Beachgoers scarf down ice cream and fresh-baked goods at the snack bar.

PELICAN INN PUB FOOD **$$$**

(☎415-383-6000; www.pelicaninn.com; 10 Pacific Way, Muir Beach; mains $11-34; 👪) At the oh-so-English Tudor-style Pelican Inn, hikers and cyclists come for pub lunches inside its timbered restaurant and cozy bar, perfect for a pint, a game of darts and warming up beside the open fire. The British fare is respectable, but nothing mind-blowing – it's the setting that's magical.

Sausalito & Tiburon

Explore

Perched above Richardson Bay, Sausalito is cosseted with art galleries, houseboats and picture-postcard bay vistas. It's often sunnier than San Francisco too. Especially on summer weekends, the town can become a victim of its charm, with day-trippers jamming the sidewalks, shops and restaurants. For the locals' scene, wander inland to Caledonia St or stroll down by the houseboats.

On a small peninsula jutting out into the bay, Tiburon (Spanish for 'shark') is a popular jumping-off point for trips to Angel Island. Browse the boutique shops inside transformed 19th-century houseboats on Main St's 'Ark Row,' grab a bite to eat on the waterfront and you've done Tiburon.

The Best...

- **Sight** Sausalito Houseboats (p221)
- **Place to Eat** Fish (p222)
- **Activity** Sea Trek Kayak & SUP (p222)

Top Tip

Rent a bicycle in San Francisco, cycle over the Golden Gate Bridge, then ride the ferry back from Sausalito. If you drive, expect weekend traffic jams in town.

Getting There & Away

- **Ferry** Golden Gate Ferry (p56) sails from San Francisco's Ferry Building to Sausalito ($10.75, 30 minutes). **Blue & Gold Fleet** (☎415-705-8200; www.blueandgoldfleet.com) sails to Sausalito from Fisherman's Wharf ($11.50, 30 minutes) and to Tiburon from

Fisherman's Wharf or the Ferry Building ($11.50, 25 minutes).

➡ **Car** Drive Hwy 101 north across the Golden Gate Bridge. For Sausalito, take the immediate Alexander Ave or main Sausalito exit; for Tiburon, exit at Tiburon Blvd/E Blithedale Ave.

➡ **Bus Golden Gate Transit** (☎415-455-2000, 511; www.goldengatetransit.org) Bus 10 runs hourly to Sausalito from downtown San Francisco ($5, 50 minutes).

Need to Know

➡ **Area Code** ☎415

➡ **Location** Sausalito is 5 miles north of San Francisco; Tiburon is 12 miles north-northeast.

➡ **Tourist office** (☎415-331-1093; www.sausalito.org; foot of El Portal St; ⏲10am-4pm)

SIGHTS

Sausalito's main strip is Bridgeway Blvd, leading along the bay to downtown and the ferry terminal.

★SAUSALITO HOUSEBOATS ARCHITECTURE

Bohemia still thrives along the shoreline of Richardson Bay, where free spirits inhabit quirky homes that bobble in the waves among the seabirds and seals. Structures range from psychedelic mural-splashed castles to dilapidated salt-sprayed shacks and immaculate three-story floating mansions. It's a tight-knit community, where residents tend dockside gardens and stop to chat on the creaky wooden boardwalks.

Find some of the houseboat docks located off Bridgeway between Gate 5 and Gate 6½ Rds.

BAY MODEL VISITORS CENTER MUSEUM

(☎415-332-3871; www.spn.usace.army.mil/Missions/Recreation/BayModelVisitorCenter.aspx; 2100 Bridgeway Blvd; ⏲9am-4pm Tue-Sat, plus 10am-5pm Sat & Sun in summer; 👪) FREE Until computers rendered it obsolete, this enormous 1.5-acre hydraulic scale model of the entire San Francisco Bay and delta helped scientists understand the effects of tides and currents on the land. A 24-hour period is represented in only 15 minutes. Bring a jacket – the converted shipyard warehouse is chilly.

BAY AREA DISCOVERY MUSEUM MUSEUM

(☎415-339-3900; www.baykidsmuseum.org; 557 McReynolds Rd; admission $14, free 1st Wed each month; ⏲9am-5pm Tue-Sun; 👪) At Fort Baker, this hands-on activity museum is fun for kids up to eight years old. Multilingual exhibits include a wave workshop, small underwater tunnel and outdoor play area with a faux-shipwreck to romp around. The café sells healthful nibbles.

ANGEL ISLAND

Rising from the middle of San Francisco Bay, Angel Island has served as a Miwok camp, cattle ranch, US military base, immigration station, WWII Japanese internment camp and Nike missile site. Today the island is a **state park** (☎415-435-5390; www.parks.ca.gov) FREE with interesting and thought-provoking forts, interpretive exhibits and bunkers to explore.

Families spread out picnics in protected coves near the ferry dock. Escape the crowds and get back to nature on 13 miles of hiking trails – including up **Mt Livermore** (788ft) for panoramic views when it's not foggy – or by cycling the mostly paved 6-mile perimeter loop road.

Nicknamed the 'Ellis Island of the West,' Angel Island's early-20th-century **US Immigration Station** (☎415-435-5537; www.aiisf.org/visit; adult/child $5/3, incl tour $7/5, cash only; ⏲11am-3pm) is a 1.5-mile walk or bike ride from the ferry dock at Ayala Cove (round-trip shuttle $6). Guided tours are usually given three times daily; show up early, before tickets sell out.

The best times to visit the island are summer weekends, when more historic buildings are open, or during spring wildflower season. Take the **Angel Island–Tiburon Ferry** (☎415-435-2131; www.angelislandferry.com) from Tiburon (round-trip adult/child $15/13) or **Blue & Gold Fleet** (Map p298; ☎415-705-8200; www.blueandgoldfleet.com) ferries from San Francisco (round-trip adult/child $18/9). Rent bicycles (per hour/day $13.50/50) near the island's ferry dock and casual **café** (www.angelisland.com; mains $7-14; ⏲10am-3pm Mon-Fri, to 4pm Sat & Sun, weather permitting; 📶👪).

RAILROAD & FERRY DEPOT MUSEUM MUSEUM

(☎415-435-1853; www.landmarkssociety.com; 1920 Paradise Dr; suggested donation $5; ⏲1-4pm Wed-Sun Apr-Oct) Formerly the terminus of a ferry to San Francisco and a railroad that reached north to Ukiah, this late-19th-century building showcases a scale model of Tiburon's commercial hub circa 1910. Peek at the restored stationmaster's quarters upstairs.

EATING & DRINKING

★**FISH** SEAFOOD $$

(☎415-331-3474; www.331fish.com; 350 Harbor Dr; mains $12-28; ⏲11:30am-8:30pm;) At this dockside joint, chow down on fish sandwiches, BBQ oysters and Dungeness crab rolls at breezy waterfront picnic tables. A local leader in promoting fresh and sustainably caught fish, this place has wonderful wild salmon in season. Cash only.

SAM'S ANCHOR CAFE SEAFOOD $$

(☎415-435-4527; www.samscafe.com; 27 Main St; mains $12-24; ⏲11am-10pm Mon-Fri, from 9:30am Sat & Sun;) Sam's has been slinging seafood and burgers since 1920, and though the entrance looks like a shambling little shack, the area out back has unbeatable waterfront views. On a warm afternoon, you can't beat a cocktail on the deck, but the food's just so-so.

SUSHI RAN JAPANESE $$$

(☎415-332-3620; http://sushiran.com; 107 Caledonia St; shared dishes $4-38; ⏲11:45am-2:30pm Mon-Fri, 5-10pm Sun-Thu, 5-11pm Fri & Sat) One of the Bay Area's top sushi spots melds East-West tastes of land and sea, like grilled squid topped with chrysanthemum flowers, fiddlehead-fern tempura and hand rolls of soft-shell crab or creamy scallops. A wine and sake bar eases the pain of long waits – better yet, reserve ahead.

BARREL HOUSE TAVERN CALIFORNIAN $$$

(☎415-729-9593; http://barrelhousetavern.com; 660 Bridgeway; shared dishes $4-19, mains $18-28; ⏲11:30am-9pm Mon-Fri, 11am-10pm Sat & Sun) You can practically dangle your legs out over the water on the sunny upstairs deck, a short dash from the ferry terminal. California craft beer and wine complement the raw seafood bar, flatbreads and charcuterie platters.

SPORTS & ACTIVITIES

★**SEA TREK KAYAK & SUP** WATER SPORTS

(☎415-332-8494; www.seatrek.com; 2100 Marinship Way; single kayaks or SUP sets per hr $20; ⏲9am-5pm Mon-Fri, from 8:30am Sat & Sun Apr-Oct, 9am-4pm daily Nov-Mar) On a sunny day, Richardson Bay is irresistible. Kayaks and stand-up paddle boarding (SUP) sets can be rented here, near the Bay Model Visitor Center. No experience or reservations are necessary. Lessons and tours – you can paddle underneath the Golden Gate Bridge or over to Angel Island – require advance booking.

Napa Valley

Explore

California's most glamorous farmland, the 30-mile-long Napa Valley is renowned for Cabernet Sauvignon and Chardonnay, winery art collections, top-drawer chefs, volcanic mud baths and architect-designed monuments to ego. It's the most-visited part of Wine Country – Hwy 29 slows to a standstill on summer weekends, so come midweek if possible. Napa can be done as a day trip, but you'd be smart to stay one night if only for the sake of romance.

The riverside city of Napa, furthest south, surprisingly lacks much charm. Calistoga, in the north, is the least-gentrified town, freckled with historic hot-springs resorts. Posh mid-valley destinations include the hamlets of St Helena, where traffic snarls, and Yountville, a 19th-century stagecoach stop that has more Michelin-starred eateries per capita than San Francisco.

The Best...

- **Sight** di Rosa Art + Nature Preserve (p224)
- **Place to Eat** French Laundry (p227)
- **Place to Drink** Hess Collection (p224)

Top Tip

Many Napa Valley wineries legally cannot receive drop-in visitors (or allow picnicking). Book well ahead for tastings at famous-name winemakers. Carry your cellphone for making last-minute reservations.

Getting There & Away

➡ **Car** From SF (at least 70 minutes), take Hwy 101 to Hwy 37 east. At the Hwy 121/37 split, take Hwy 121 north; at Hwy 29, turn north. The Bay Bridge is quicker but less scenic: take I-80E to Hwy 37 west, then Hwy 29 north.

➡ **Train, Ferry & Bus** From SF on weekdays, take **BART** (www.bart.gov) to El Cerrito del Norte station ($6.55, 30 minutes), then catch **Vine Transit** (☎800-696-6443, 707-251-2800; www.ridethevine.com) bus 29 to Napa ($3.25, 50 minutes). Departing several times daily from SF's Pier 41 and the Ferry Building, **Vallejo Baylink Ferry** (☎877-643-3779; sanfranciscobayferry.com) ($14.20, 60 to 80 minutes) connects with Vine Transit bus 11 to Napa ($1.50, 1¼ hours).

Need to Know

➡ **Area Code** ☎707

➡ **Location** 50 miles northeast of San Francisco

➡ **Tourist office** (☎855-847-6272, 707-251-5895; www.visitnapavalley.com; 600 Main St; ⏲9am-5pm; 🚻)

SIGHTS

Many wineries require advance reservations. Don't try to visit more than a few wineries in one day. Hwy 29 heads north from Napa via the valley towns of Yountville and St Helena to Calistoga. Often less-trafficked, the scenic Silverado Trail runs parallel through the valley. Drive up one way, down the other.

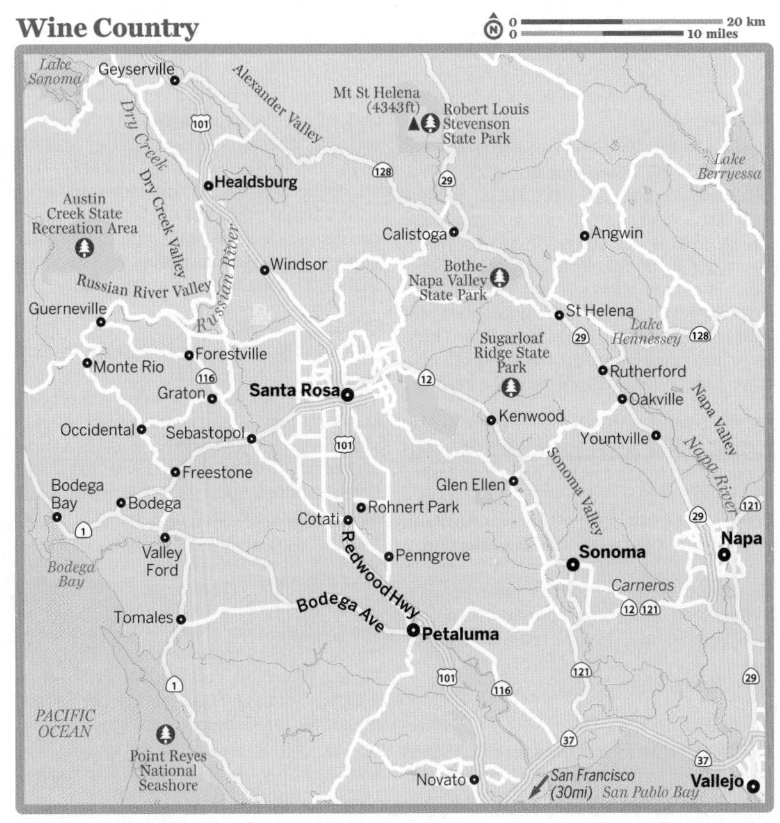

WINE COUNTRY WITHOUT A CAR

Getaway Adventures (☎707-568-3040, 800-499-2453; http://getawayadventures.com; 5½hr tour $149-175) Offers 'Sip-n-Cycle' and 'Pedal-n-Paddle' cycling tours around Calistoga and Carneros outside Napa, including a picnic lunch at a winery. Reservations required.

Calistoga Bike Shop (☎707-942-9687, 866-942-2453; http://calistogabikeshop.com; 1318 Lincoln Ave; bicycle rental per day $39-120, tours from $149; ⏲10am-6pm) Reserve ahead for an extensive selection of rental bikes and guided tours. DIY touring packages cover free tastings and wine pickup.

Napa Valley Bike Tours (☎707-251-8687; www.napavalleybiketours.com; 6500 Washington St, Yountville; bicycle rental per day $45-90, tours from $109; ⏲8:30am-5pm) Rent your own wheels or take a guided wine-tasting or an off-road vineyard tour. Self-guided cycling packages include lunch and wine pickup. Reservations essential.

Wine Country Cyclery (☎707-966-6800; www.winecountrycyclery.com; 262 W Napa St, Sonoma; bicycle rental per day $30-65; ⏲10am-6pm) Quality bike rentals conveniently in downtown Sonoma. Reservations recommended, especially for weekends and holidays.

Goodtime Touring Co (☎707-938-2080; www.goodtimetouring.com; bicycle rental per day $30-65, tours $129-189) Personalized, small-group bicycle tours of Sonoma town and valley, including a picnic lunch and sometimes cheese-tasting.

Napa Valley Wine Train (☎707-253-2111, 800-427-4124; http://winetrain.com; 1275 McKinstry St, Napa; 3hr tour from $124) Cushy, touristy train trips on a historical rail line between Napa and St Helena. Book in advance.

★DI ROSA ART + NATURE PRESERVE — GALLERY, GARDENS

(☎707-226-5991; www.dirosaart.org; 5200 Hwy 121, Napa; admission $5, tours $12-15; ⏲10am-4pm Wed-Sun) When you notice scrap-metal sheep grazing Carneros vineyards, you've spotted one of the best-anywhere collections of contemporary Northern California art. Reservations are recommended for tours covering everything from Tony Oursler's video projections in the wine cellar to towering outdoor sculptures in the gardens.

★HESS COLLECTION — WINERY, GALLERY

(☎707-255-1144; www.hesscollection.com; 4411 Redwood Rd, Napa; museum entry free, tasting $20, tours free-$65; ⏲10am-5:30pm, last tasting 5pm, tours 10:30am-3pm) Blue-chip art and big reds are the pride of Hess Collection, a winery and art gallery reached via a winding mountain road. Monster Cabernet Sauvignon and oaky Chardonnay are paired with large canvas and mixed-media art by modernists like Robert Motherwell. Reservations recommended.

FROG'S LEAP — WINERY

(☎707-963-4704; www.frogsleap.com; 8815 Conn Creek Rd, Rutherford; tasting $20, incl tour $25; ⏲10am-4pm by appointment only;) Meandering paths wind through fruit-bearing orchards and gardens surrounding an 1884 barn and farmstead with chickens. The atmosphere is casual and down-to-earth, with a major emphasis on *fun*. The LEED-certified, solar-powered and all-organic winery makes meritorious Sauvignon Blanc, Cabernet Sauvignon and Merlot.

ROBERT SINSKEY — WINERY

(☎707-944-9090; www.robertsinskey.com; 6320 Silverado Trail, Napa; tasting $25, incl tour $75; ⏲10am-4:30pm) Chef-owned Robert Sinskey's hilltop tasting room, constructed of stone, redwood and teak, resembles a small cathedral – fitting, given the sacred status here bestowed upon food and wine. Small bites accompany tastings. Reserve ahead for wine-cave and culinary tours.

PRIDE MOUNTAIN — WINERY

(☎707-963-4949; www.pridewines.com; 4026 Spring Mountain Rd, St Helena; tasting $20, incl tour $25-75; ⏲by appointment only) High atop Spring Mountain, cult-favorite Pride straddles the Sonoma–Napa county border and makes stellar Cabernet Sauvignon, heavy-hitting Merlot and elegant Viognier. Picnicking at the hilltop estate is spectacular, but you must first reserve a tasting.

MUMM NAPA WINERY, GALLERY

(707-967-7700, 800-686-6272; www.mummnapa.com; 8445 Silverado Trail, Rutherford; tasting $18-40, tour $30; 10am-6pm, last seating 5:45pm) Valley views are as spectacular as the fine-art photography exhibits at Mumm. Reservations are only needed if you want to sample sparkling wines while seated on a terrace overlooking the vineyards – ideal for impressing your date.

REGUSCI WINERY

(707-254-0403; www.regusciwinery.com; 5584 Silverado Trail, Napa; tasting $25-35, incl tour $60; 10am-4pm) At one of Napa's oldest wineries, vineyards in the premier Stag's Leap District wrap around a century-old stone building on the valley's quieter eastern side. Enjoy estate-grown Cabernet Sauvignon and other rich reds. Reservations required for tours and some tastings.

CASTELLO DI AMOROSA WINERY, CASTLE

(707-967-6272; www.castellodiamorosa.com; 4045 Hwy 29, Calistoga; admission & tasting $20-45, incl guided tour $35-75; 9:30am-6pm Mar-Oct, to 5pm Nov-Feb) It's a near-perfect recreation of a 13th-century Tuscan castle, complete with moat, frescoes hand-painted by Italian artisans and a torture chamber filled with period equipment. Trust us, take the tour (book ahead and bring a sweater). Oh, the wine? Some respectable Italian varietals and blends.

CASA NUESTRA WINERY

(707-963-5783, 866-844-9463; www.casanuestra.com; 3451 Silverado Trail N, St Helena; tasting $10; 10am-4:30pm by appointment only) A peace flag and portrait of Elvis greet you in the tasting barn at this old-school, '70s-vintage, mom-and-pop winery with playful goats beside a little picnic area. Diverse blends and varietals bottled here include Chenin Blanc from 55-year-old organic vines. Call ahead.

CADE WINERY

(707-965-2746; www.cadewinery.com; 360 Howell Mountain Rd S, Angwin; tasting $40, incl tour $70; by appointment only) Ascend Howell Mountain for drop-dead vistas and hawks riding thermals at Napa's oh-so-swank, first-ever all organically farmed and LEED gold-certified winery, partly owned by ex-SF mayor Gavin Newsom. Reservations required.

ROBERT MONDAVI WINERY

(888-766-6328; www.robertmondaviwinery.com; 7801 Hwy 29, Oakville; tasting & tour $20-55; 10am-5pm) Founded by a pioneering Napa vintner in 1965, today this corporate-owned winery is swarming with tour buses. Yet introductory winemaking tours with guided tastings are worthwhile for novices – make reservations.

TOP FIVE PLACES TO SLEEP IN NAPA & SONOMA

You can easily visit Napa and Sonoma on a day trip from San Francisco, but after a day of wine-tasting and a big dinner feast, you may not feel like driving back to the city. Excellent options for overnight stays in Wine Country include:

Carneros Inn (888-400-9000, 707-299-4900; www.thecarnerosinn.com; 4048 Sonoma Hwy; r from $500) At this luxury resort, prettily set beside vineyards only 5 miles west of Napa, chic cottages for couples are designed with romance in mind.

Indian Springs Resort (707-942-4913; www.indianspringscalistoga.com; 1712 Lincoln Ave, Calistoga; r/cottage from $239/359) Historic bungalows, a restored 1930s Spanish-style lodge and a hot-springs spa (p226) await in Calistoga, in northern Napa Valley.

Maison Fleurie (800-788-0369, 707-944-2056; www.maisonfleurienapa.com; 6529 Yount St, Yountville; r incl breakfast $170-395) In Yountville, under 10 miles north of Napa, B&B rooms at this ivy-covered country inn are all done up in French-provincial style.

Beltane Ranch (707-833-4233; www.beltaneranch.com; 11775 Hwy 12, Glen Ellen; d incl breakfast $205-295) Surrounded by horse pastures in the middle of Sonoma Valley, this lemon-yellow 1890 ranch house harbors five peaceful B&B rooms.

Sonoma Hotel (707-996-2996, 800-468-6016; www.sonomahotel.com; 110 W Spain St; r incl breakfast from $160) Old-fashioned rooms squeeze together inside this 19th-century landmark on bustling Sonoma Plaza in downtown Sonoma.

CALISTOGA'S MUD BATHS

Calistoga is synonymous with the sparkling mineral water bearing its name, bottled here since 1924. Even earlier in the mid-19th century, its springs and geysers earned it the nickname the 'hot springs of the West.'

The town is still famous for its spas and mud-bath emporiums, where you're buried like a tree root in warm mud, made with ancient volcanic ash from nearby Mt St Helena, an extinct volcano. Afterward you'll soak in a tub filled with clear, hot mineral water, then step into a steam room and later take a catnap while wrapped in blankets.

Serene **Indian Springs Spa** (707-942-4913; www.indianspringscalistoga.com; 1712 Lincoln Ave; by appointment 9am-8pm) mines its own volcanic ash. Mud baths ($85) include access to a giant spring-fed swimming pool (pack a swimsuit) and meditative gardens surrounding the Buddha pond.

Vintage 1950s **Dr Wilkinson's Hot Springs Resort** (707-942-4102; www.drwilkinson.com; 1507 Lincoln Ave; by appointment 8:30am-3:45pm) uses more peat moss for lighter mud baths ($89).

Contempo **Spa Solage** (855-790-6023; www.solagecalistoga.com/spa; 755 Silverado Trail; by appointment 8am-8pm) is the chic choice for DIY paint-on mud treatments ($110). Bring your own swimwear to soak in the co-ed mineral-springs pool.

ARTESA — WINERY

(707-254-2126; www.artesawinery.com; 1345 Henry Rd, Napa; tasting $20-25, incl tour $30; 10am-5pm, last pour 4:30pm) Begin or end the day with a tipple of Brut Rosé, Chardonnay or Pinot Noir at this Carneros winery, southwest of Napa. Built into a mountainside, the ultramodern Barcelona-style architecture is stunning, and you can't beat the top-of-the-world vistas. Tours are first-come, first-served.

ROBERT LOUIS STEVENSON STATE PARK — STATE PARK

(707-942-4575; www.parks.ca.gov; 3801 Hwy 29; sunrise-sunset) FREE A long-extinct volcanic cone, Mt St Helena marks Napa Valley's northern end at this undeveloped state park near Calistoga. It's a strenuous 5-mile climb to the summit (4343ft), but what a view – almost 200 miles all the way to Mt Shasta on a clear day. The much easier Table Rock Trail ends at drop-dead valley panoramas; it's a 4.4-mile round-trip.

EATING

Napa Valley is an outpost of San Francisco's food scene – make table reservations in advance and plan to have a lingering lunch or dinner mid-valley. Most restaurants don't serve late – average Napa visitors get too drunk during the daytime to stay up for a 9pm table.

★OXBOW PUBLIC MARKET — MARKET $

(707-226-6529; http://oxbowpublicmarket.com; 610 & 644 1st St, Napa; items from $3; 9am-7pm Wed-Mon, to 8pm Tue, some restaurants open later) Napa's gourmet marketplace showcases local, sustainably produced artisanal food, such as Hog Island oysters, wild mushroom soup and pizza from celeb chef Todd Humphries' Kitchen Door, crab and duck tacos at C Casa, Model Bakery's baked goods, Three Twins certified-organic ice cream and Ritual coffee. Come hungry and plan to graze.

Tuesday is locals' night, with many discounts. Tuesday and Saturday mornings, there's a farmers market.

GOTT'S ROADSIDE — AMERICAN $$

(707-963-3486; http://gotts.com; 933 Main St, St Helena; mains $8-16; 10am-10pm May-Sep, 8am-9pm Oct-Apr;) Wiggle your toes in the grass at this 1950s drive-in diner with modern 21st-century sensibilities: burgers are all-natural beef or sushi-grade ahi tuna, with chili-dusted sweet-potato fries and thick handmade milkshakes. Avoid weekend waits by phoning ahead or ordering online. There's another branch at Napa's Oxbow Public Market.

REDD WOOD — ITALIAN $$

(707-299-5030; www.redd-wood.com; 6755 Washington St, Yountville; pizzas $14-17, most mains $17-27; 8am-10pm Sun-Thu, to 11pm Fri & Sat) In a mini empire of Yountville restaurants, chef Richard Reddington's casual

Italian trattoria serves outstanding homemade pastas and tender-to-the-tooth pizzas from a wood-fired oven. On the midday menu are charcuterie platters, sweets and more for late-afternoon noshing.

BOUNTY HUNTER WINE BAR & SMOKIN' BBQ BARBECUE $$

(☎707-226-3976; www.bountyhunterwinebar.com; 975 1st St, Napa; mains $14-28; ⏱11am-10pm Sun-Thu, to midnight Fri & Sat; 👪) With pressed-tin ceilings and trophy heads on the walls, this downtown Napa hangout has an Old West vibe. That's a fitting backdrop for BBQ, made with house-smoked meats and whole chickens roasted over cans of beer. Dozens of wines and whiskeys by the glass.

★FRENCH LAUNDRY CALIFORNIAN $$$

(☎707-944-2380; www.frenchlaundry.com; 6640 Washington St, Yountville; prix-fixe dinner $295; ⏱seatings 11am-1pm Fri-Sun, 5:30-9:15pm daily) A high-wattage culinary experience on par with the world's best, Thomas Keller's French Laundry is at the pinnacle of California dining, offering nine-course tasting menus of culinary derring-do. Book exactly two months (to the day) ahead: call at 10am sharp, or log onto www.opentable.com at precisely midnight. Avoid tables before 7pm; first-service seating moves a touch quickly.

If you can't score a reservation, console yourself at Keller's nearby note-perfect French bistro, **Bouchon** (☎707-944-8037; www.thomaskeller.com; 6354 Washington St, Yountville; mains $19-59; ⏱11am-midnight Mon-Fri,

WORTH A DETOUR

POINT REYES NATIONAL SEASHORE

On an entirely different tectonic plate from California's mainland, the Point Reyes peninsula is a rough-hewn beauty. Jutting 10 miles out to sea, it lures marine mammals, migratory birds and whale-watching tourists with over 100 sq miles of wild ocean beaches, scalloped sand dunes, peaceful lagoons and wind-battered ridges. Bring warm clothing, as even the sunniest days can quickly turn cold and foggy.

Though it may seem counter-intuitive, winter is the best season to visit for wildlife-spotting – whales breaching offshore, elephant seals giving birth and birds alighting everywhere. Around 150 miles of hiking trails crisscross the peninsula, some leading to hidden beaches. The beaches on the peninsula's western side get hammered by powerful surf and aren't safe for swimming.

A mile west of Olema, orient yourself at **Bear Valley Visitor Center** (☎415-464-5100; www.nps.gov/pore; ⏱10am-5pm Mon-Fri, from 9am Sat & Sun), then traipse the nearby 0.6-mile **Earthquake Trail** or the 0.8-mile **Kule Loklo Trail** leading to a reproduction Miwok village. Off Limantour Rd, you can trek atop ocean bluffs past grazing herds of tule elk for nearly 5 miles each way to **Tomales Point**, separating Tomales Bay from the Pacific. To paddle a kayak out into the bay, reserve with **Blue Waters Kayaking** (☎415-669-2600; www.bluewaterskayaking.com; rentals/tours from $50/68; 👪).

At the peninsula's westernmost tip, **Point Reyes Lighthouse** (☎415-669-1534; ⏱lighthouse 10am-4:30pm Fri-Mon, lens room 2:30-4pm Fri-Mon) FREE is buffeted by ferocious winds. It sits 600ft below the headlands, down some 300-odd steps, so that its light can shine below the fog that usually blankets the point. On weekends and holidays between late December and late March or early April, all visitors must ride the shuttle bus (adult/child $7/free) from Drakes Beach to the lighthouse and **Chimney Rock**, where you can spy on an elephant-seal colony and migratory gray whales. Buy shuttle tickets at the **Kenneth C Patrick Visitor Center** (☎415-669-1250; ⏱9:30am-4:30pm Sat, Sun & holidays late Dec-late Mar or early Apr).

Two miles north of Olema, the tiny town of **Point Reyes Station** has cozy cafés and upscale restaurants. Step inside **Bovine Bakery** (www.thebovinebakery.com; 11315 Hwy 1; most items $2-6; ⏱6:30am-5pm Mon-Fri, 7am-5pm Sat & Sun) 🍃 for morning buns and hot coffee. Gather a picnic lunch at **Tomales Bay Foods & Cowgirl Creamery** (www.cowgirlcreamery.com; 80 4th St; sandwiches $6-12; ⏱10am-6pm Wed-Sun; 🌶) 🍃 or at **Perry's Deli** (http://perrysinvernessparkgrocery.com; 12301 Sir Francis Drake Blvd, Inverness Park; sandwiches $5-11; ⏱7am-8pm Mon-Thu, to 9pm Fri & Sat, 8am-8pm Sun), 2 miles west of town.

The entrance to Point Reyes National Seashore is over 40 miles northwest of San Francisco (at least an hour's drive).

from 10am Sat & Sun), which is (much) easier to book, or with phenomenal pastries from **Bouchon Bakery** (☎707-944-2253; www.thomaskeller.com; 6528 Washington St, Yountville; items from $3; ⏰7am-7pm).

ARCHETYPE FUSION **$$$**

(☎707-968-9200; http://archetypenapa.com; 1429 Main St; dinner mains $19-36; ⏰11:30am-2:30pm & 5:30-9pm Wed-Fri, 9am-2:30pm & 5:30-9pm Sat & Sun) In an architect-designed dining room that breaks the Wine Country mold, Archetype effortlessly melds Asian and Mediterranean techniques with the best of Northern California farms and foraging. Savor anything from the oak wood-burning oven and grill, or show up for weekend brunches on the sunny back patio. Happy-hour drinks and bites are a steal (from $5).

SOLBAR CALIFORNIAN **$$$**

(☎707-226-0850; www.solagecalistoga.com; 755 Silverado Trail N, Calistoga; lounge menu dishes $4-16, dinner mains $26-38; ⏰7am-3pm & 5:30-9pm, to 9:30pm Fri & Sat) Farm life goes way upscale at this Michelin-starred resort restaurant, whose menu maximizes seasonal produce in elegant dishes, playfully composed like rainbow carrot salad with coffee-date sauce or duck breast with blood-orange sauce. This being a spa (p226) resort, too, the menu is split for calorie-counters into light and hearty dishes. Reservations essential.

Sonoma Valley

Explore

There are three Sonomas: the town, valley and county. Think of them as nested Russian dolls.

Anchoring the bucolic 17-mile-long Sonoma Valley, the town of Sonoma makes a great jumping-off point for exploring Wine Country. Its 19th-century historical buildings surround Sonoma Plaza, California's largest town square. Halfway up the valley, the tiny village of Glen Ellen is like a Norman Rockwell painting come to life – quite a contrast to the suburban sprawl around Santa Rosa, the valley's northernmost town.

The Sonoma Hwy (Hwy 12) runs all the way through Sonoma Valley, passing wineries especially revered for Zinfandel and Syrah, before turning west at Santa Rosa toward Hwy 101. Running parallel up Sonoma Valley's west side to Glen Ellen, Arnold Dr sees less traffic than Hwy 12, but has fewer wineries.

The Best...

- **Sight** Sonoma Plaza (p229)
- **Place to Eat** Cafe La Haye (p231)
- **Place to Drink** Bartholomew Park Winery (p229)

Top Tip

If you're not up for driving, hit downtown Sonoma's tasting rooms around shady Sonoma Plaza, where it's legal to drink wine on the grass from after 11am until dark.

Getting There & Away

- **Car** From San Francisco to downtown Sonoma (at least one hour), take Hwy 101 north to Hwy 37 east. At the Hwy 37/121 split, take Hwy 121 north, then Hwy 12 north.
- **Bus** Service is infrequent and slow. From San Francisco, **Golden Gate Transit** (☎415-455-2000, 511; www.goldengate.org) buses connect twice hourly to Santa Rosa ($11.75, 2¼ hours), from where limited **Sonoma County Transit** (☎707-576-7433, 800-345-7433; http://sctransit.com) buses run to downtown Sonoma ($3.05, 70 minutes) via Sonoma Valley towns.

Need to Know

- **Area Code** ☎707
- **Location** 45 miles north-northeast of San Francisco
- **Tourist office** (☎866-966-1090, 707-996-1090; www.sonomavalley.com; 453 1st St E; ⏰9am-5pm Mon-Sat, 10am-5pm Sun)

SIGHTS

Less pretentious and more laid-back than Napa, Sonoma Valley shelters more than 40 wineries alongside Hwy 12. You usually don't need tasting appointments, but call ahead to book vineyard tours. For picnicking, some wineries now charge fees and require reservations for picnic tables; otherwise, buy a bottle of your host's wine – it's only polite.

★SONOMA PLAZA SQUARE
(btwn Napa, Spain & 1st Sts) Century-old trees cast sun-dappled shade on the plaza, a great spot for a picnic with a bottle of wine. Smack in the center of the plaza, **City Hall** (1908) has identical facades on four sides, reportedly because plaza businesses all demanded it face their direction. At the plaza's northeast corner, the **Bear Flag Monument** marks Sonoma's moment of revolutionary glory.

SONOMA STATE HISTORIC PARK HISTORIC SITE
(☎707-938-9560; www.parks.ca.gov; adult/child $3/2; ⌚10am-5pm) The park comprises multiple sites, most side-by-side. The 1823 **Mission San Francisco Solano de Sonoma** (☎707-938-9560; www.parks.ca.gov; 114 E Spain St; adult/child $3/2; ⌚10am-5pm) anchors the plaza, and was the final California mission. **Sonoma Barracks** (☎707-939-9420; parks.ca.gov; 20 E Spain St; adult/child $3/2; ⌚10am-5pm) houses exhibits on 19th-century life. The 1886 **Toscano Hotel** (☎707-938-9560; parks.ca.gov; 20 E Spain St) FREE lobby is beautifully preserved – peek inside. The 1852 **General Vallejo Home** (☎707-938-9559; 363 3rd St W; adult/child $3/2; ⌚10am-5pm) lies a half-mile northwest. One ticket allows admission to all.

Check the website for weekend guided tour schedules.

★BARTHOLOMEW PARK WINERY WINERY
(☎707-939-3026; www.bartpark.com; 1000 Vineyard Lane, Sonoma; tasting $10-30; ⌚11am-4:30pm) Inside a 400-acre nature preserve ideal for picnicking, these family-owned vineyards were first cultivated in 1857. Now organic-certified, they yield citrusy Sauvignon Blanc, lush Zinfandel and a softer style of Cabernet Sauvignon. After tasting, peruse the tiny historical museum or go for a hike on 3 miles of marked trails. 'Bart Park' is a great bike-to destination.

GUNDLACH-BUNDSCHU WINERY WINERY
(☎707-939-3015; www.gunbun.com; 2000 Denmark St, Sonoma; tasting $10-25, incl tour $30-50; ⌚11am-4:30pm, to 5:30pm Jun–mid-Oct) California's oldest family-run winery looks like a castle, but has an unfancy vibe. Founded in 1858 by a Bavarian immigrant, its signatures are Gewürztraminer and Pinot Noir, but 'Gun-Bun' was the first US winery to produce 100% Merlot. Down a winding lane, this terrific bike-to winery offers picnicking and a lake-view patio. Tour the 1800-barrel cave by reservation only.

TRAFFIC ALERT

Hwys 121 and 37 pass by Sonoma Raceway, which on major auto-racing event days causes huge traffic backups lasting for miles. Check the calendar at www.racesonoma.com. If there's a race, take Hwy 101 north to Santa Rosa instead, then drop back down Hwy 12 south into Sonoma Valley.

JACK LONDON STATE HISTORIC PARK STATE PARK
(☎707-938-5216; www.jacklondonpark.com; 2400 London Ranch Rd, Glen Ellen; per car $10, cottage entry adult/child $4/2; ⌚park 9:30am-5pm, museum 10am-5pm, cottage noon-4pm) Napa has Robert Louis Stevenson, but Sonoma's got Jack London. This 1400-acre park frames that author's last years; inspect the original writer's cottage or browse memorabilia inside the small **museum** standing in a redwood grove. Miles of hiking and mountain-biking trails weave through oak-dotted woodlands and meander by a small lake. Watch out for poison oak!

KUNDE WINERY
(☎707-833-5501; www.kunde.com; 9825 Hwy 12, Kenwood; tasting $10-25, incl tour $30-40; ⌚10:30am-5pm) Let your spirit be uplifted at this hillside estate winery, where more than 20 varietals of sustainably grown grapes are harvested in small batches, then transformed into premium wines aged in lava-rock caves. Lemon-zest Sauvignon Blanc, berry Zinfandel and chocolate-noted Cabernet Sauvignon are winners. Book ahead for mountaintop tastings and guided estate hiking tours.

CORNERSTONE SONOMA GARDENS
(☎707-933-3010; www.cornerstonesonoma.com; 23570 Arnold Dr, Sonoma; ⌚10am-5pm, gardens until 4pm;) FREE There's nothing traditional about Cornerstone Gardens, which showcases over a dozen walk-through gardens by avant-garde landscape designers who explore the intersection of art and nature. Let the kids run free while you explore, shop, taste wine or grab a bite to eat.

BENZIGER WINERY
(☎707-935-3000, 888-490-2739; www.benziger.com; 1883 London Ranch Rd, Glen Ellen; tasting $15-40, tours $25-50; ⌚10am-5pm, tram tours 11am-3:30pm;) Pastoral Benziger is

Sonoma's best crash course in winemaking with an open-air tram ride (weather permitting) through biodynamic vineyards. Great picnicking, plus a playground, make it tops for families. The large-production wine's just OK; the tour's the thing.

BR COHN WINERY
(☎707-938-4064, 800-330-4064; www.brcohn.com; 15000 Sonoma Hwy, Glen Ellen; tasting $15, incl tour $20; ⊙10am-5pm) Picnic like a rock star at always-busy BR Cohn, whose founder managed '70s superband the Doobie Brothers before moving on to make organic olive oils and crowd-pleasing, if high-priced, wines – including gold-medal Cabernet Sauvignon and Chardonnay.

CLINE CELLARS WINERY
(☎800-546-2070, 707-940-4030; www.clinecellars.com; 24737 Arnold Dr, Sonoma; tasting free-$20; ⊙tasting room 10am-6pm, museum 10am-4pm) Rainy days are made for fireside tastings of value-priced, old-vine Zinfandel and Mourvedre inside an 1850s farmhouse. Free, short winery tours depart at 11am, 1pm and 3pm daily.

Stroll out back to the **museum**, housing 1930s miniature-scale replicas of California's original 21 Spanish colonial missions.

RAVENSWOOD WINERY WINERY
(☎888-669-4679, 707-933-2332; www.ravenswoodwinery.com; 18701 Gehricke Rd, Sonoma; tasting $18, incl tour $25; ⊙10am-4:30pm) With the slogan 'no wimpy wines,' this hilltop tasting room that's always hectic pours a full slate of estate-grown, single-vineyard Zinfandel and Bordeaux blends. Wine newbies welcome. Tour reservations requested.

VINEYARDS BEYOND SONOMA VALLEY

Even more stand-out wineries await in other corners of Sonoma County. West of Hwy 101 and Santa Rosa, the woodsy **Russian River Valley** (http://rrvw.org) is home to prized Pinot Noir grapes. Further north on Hwy 101, well-heeled Healdsburg is the gateway to the rural **Dry Creek Valley** (www.drycreekvalley.org) and **Alexander Valley** (http://alexandervalley.org) vineyards, which craft earthy Zinfandel and Cabernet Sauvignon, respectively.

LOXTON WINERY
(☎707-935-7221; www.loxtonwines.com; 11466 Dunbar Rd, Glen Ellen; tasting $5, tour $20; ⊙11am-5pm) Say g'day to the Aussie winemaker at this no-frills winery where the 'tasting room' is a small warehouse. Drop by to taste Syrah (aka Shiraz), Zinfandel and tawny port. Book ahead for weekend 'walkabout' vineyard tours.

HOMEWOOD WINERY
(☎707-996-6353; www.homewoodwinery.com; 23120 Burndale Rd, Sonoma; tasting $5; ⊙10am-4pm; 🐾) Barn cats dart about at this rustic winery, where the tiny tasting room pours standout ports and affordable Rhône-style blends – 'Da redder, da better' – plus some late-harvest dessert wines.

EATING

GLEN ELLEN VILLAGE MARKET DELI, MARKET $
(www.sonoma-glenellenmkt.com; 13751 Arnold Dr, Glen Ellen; ⊙5am-9pm) Fantastic market has a huge deli, salad bar and local bakery selection, ideal for picnickers.

FREMONT DINER AMERICAN, SOUTHERN $$
(☎707-938-7370; www.thefremontdiner.com; 2698 Fremont Dr, Sonoma; mains $9-22; ⊙8am-3pm Mon-Wed, to 9pm Thu-Sun; 👪) Lines snake out the door at this farm-to-table roadside diner with Southern flavor. When the sun shines, nab an outdoor picnic table and wolf down biscuits with gravy, black-pepper brisket hash and fresh pie. Arrive early to avoid waiting (no reservations).

HOPMONK TAVERN PUB FOOD $$
(☎707-935-9100; www.hopmonk.com; 691 Broadway, Sonoma; mains $11-23; ⊙11:30am-9pm Sun-Thu, to 9:30pm Fri & Sat) South of Sonoma Plaza, this happening gastropub and outdoor beer garden takes its brews seriously, with over a dozen of its own and guest beers on tap. Burgers, sandwiches, salads and shared bites are all appetizingly priced. Live music on weekends.

FIG CAFE & WINEBAR FRENCH, CALIFORNIAN $$
(☎707-938-2130; www.thefigcafe.com; 13690 Arnold Dr, Glen Ellen; mains $14-26, 3-course prix-fixe dinner $36; ⊙brunch 10am-2:30pm Sat & Sun, dinner 5-9pm Sun-Thu, to 9:30pm Fri & Sat) For Californian twists on country French comfort food – imagine organic stone-fruit salad, steamed mussels, fried olives and

WORTH A DETOUR

HIGHWAY 1 SOUTH OF SAN FRANCISCO

Unspooling south of San Francisco toward the surf mecca of Santa Cruz, coastal Hwy 1 is bordered by craggy beaches, sea-salted lighthouses, organic farms and tiny towns. At beckoning vista points, spot migratory whales breaching offshore in winter or kitesurfers skimming waves like giant mosquitoes.

The beauty prize–winning beaches begin less than 10 miles south of San Francisco in **Pacifica**. After driving through the tunnels, pull over for **Devil's Slide Trail**, a paved 1.3-mile section of old Hwy 1. Five miles south of town, **Montara State Beach** (www.parks.ca.gov; Hwy 1; ⌚8am-sunset) FREE is a local favorite for its pristine sand. Further south by Moss Beach, **Fitzgerald Marine Reserve** (☎650-728-3584; www.fitzgeraldreserve.org; 200 Nevada Ave; ⌚8am-sunset; 👪) FREE protects tide pools teeming with sea life, best viewed at low tide.

Next up is 4-mile-long, crescent-shaped **Half Moon Bay State Beach** (www.parks.ca.gov; off Hwy 1; per car $10; ⌚8am-sunset; 👪). Turn off at **Pillar Point Harbor**, packed with seafood shacks, and climb the sand dunes above **Mavericks** surf break, where in winter death-defying surfers ride 40ft-plus swells past rocky cliffs. When the bay is calm, paddle out with **Half Moon Bay Kayak Co** (☎650-773-6101; www.hmbkayak.com; 2 Johnson Pier; kayak/SUP rental per hr from $25; ⌚9am-5pm Wed-Mon, last rental 3:30pm). Off Hwy 92, poke around downtown's quaint Main St shops.

Fifteen miles further south, **Pescadero State Beach & Marsh Nature Preserve** (www.parks.ca.gov; off Hwy 1; per car $8; ⌚8am-sunset) attracts beachcombers and birders. Detour a few miles inland to Pescadero village for **Arcangeli Grocery Co** (Norm's Market; www.normsmarket.com; 287 Stage Rd; ⌚10am-6pm) bakery-deli and the cheese shop at family-owned **Harley Farms** (☎650-879-0480; http://harleyfarms.com; 250 North St; 2hr tour adult/child $20/10; ⌚10am-5pm; 👪), which offers goat-dairy farm tours by reservation.

Three miles south of the Pescadero turnoff, **Bean Hollow State Beach** (www.parks.ca.gov; off Hwy 1; ⌚8am-sunset) FREE is awash in gemstone pebbles. **Pigeon Point Light Station** (☎650-879-2120; www.parks.ca.gov; Pigeon Point Rd; ⌚8am-sunset, visitor center 10am-4pm Thu-Mon), one of coastal California's tallest lighthouses, stands on a windswept coastal perch off Hwy 1. Another 5 miles south, **Año Nuevo State Reserve** (☎information 650-879-0227, tour reservations 800-444-4445; www.parks.ca.gov; off Hwy 1; entry per car $10, 2½hr tour per person $7; ⌚8:30am-5pm, last entry 3:30pm Apr-Nov, tours only mid-Dec–Mar) is home to an enormous colony of elephant seals. Book well ahead for a guided walking tour during the cacophonous winter birthing and mating season.

house-made sausage – visit this convivial brasserie in Glen Ellen village. No reservations or corkage fee on BYOB wine.

RED GRAPE ITALIAN $$

(☎707-996-4103; http://theredgrape.com; 529 1st St W, Sonoma; mains $11-19; ⌚11:30am-9pm; 👪) Step inside a sunlight-filled pizzeria at the corner of Sonoma Plaza for thin-crust pies topped with local cheeses and cured meats, market-fresh salads or fresh, handmade pastas. Order Sonoma County wines by the glass or bottle.

★CAFE LA HAYE CALIFORNIAN $$$

(☎707-935-5994; www.cafelahaye.com; 140 E Napa St, Sonoma; mains $18-30; ⌚5:30-9pm Tue-Sat; 🐾) It's downtown Sonoma's top picks for earthy New American cooking, made with produce sourced from within 60 miles. Its tiny dining room is packed cheek-by-jowl and service borders on perfunctory, but the clean simplicity and flavor-packed cooking make it many foodies' first choice. Reserve well ahead.

GLEN ELLEN STAR CALIFORNIAN, ITALIAN $$$

(☎707-343-1384; http://glenellenstar.com; 13648 Arnold Dr, Glen Ellen; pizza $14-20, mains $24-38; ⌚5:30-9pm Sun-Thu, to 9:30pm Fri & Sat) Helmed by chef Ari Weiswasser, formerly of Thomas Keller's French Laundry, this petite bistro shines a light on Sonoma farms and ranches. Local, organic and seasonal ingredients star in dishes like spring lamb ragu, brick-baked chicken or cauliflower agnolotti with wild mushrooms and carrot butter. Reservations recommended.

Sleeping

San Francisco hotel rates are among the world's highest. Plan ahead – well ahead – and grab bargains when you see them. Given the choice, we favor boutique properties over chains, for they provide the greatest sense of place, but take what you can get at a price you can afford.

When to Book

Travelers often only consider the cost of an airline ticket when booking dates, but we highly recommend you first confirm the availability of good hotel rates before booking flights. 'City-wide sellouts' happen several times a year when there's a big convention or event in town. Check the **SF Convention & Visitors Bureau convention calendar** (www.sanfrancisco.travel/article/hotel-availability), which shows the availability 'opportunity' for meeting planners. Look for times that list 'high opportunity' – this means many rooms are available in convention hotels, and by extension, smaller hotels. But if the calendar lists a specific convention, choose other dates or pay a premium – sometimes double or triple base rates.

Room Rates & Fees

San Francisco is in a boom cycle – this is the epicenter of tech and the whole world wants to be here. There simply aren't enough beds. Between 2012 and 2015, rates at many downtown hotels jumped 100%. Day-to-day rates fluctuate wildly. Brace yourself. Prices in this chapter reflect average costs of a basic double room, April to October, excluding city-wide sellouts, when hotels charge 'compression rates' – a handy term when negotiating with hotels.

To get the best prices at chains, where rates change daily, call the hotel during business hours and speak with in-house reservations, rather than toll-free central reservations, for up-to-date information about inventories and specials. Some hotels have internet-only deals, but when booking online, know that 'best rate' does not necessarily mean lowest-available rate. When in doubt, call the hotel directly. Online booking engines (eg Priceline) offer lower rates but have many restrictions and may be nonrefundable.

Although hostels and budget hotels are cheapest, rooms are never truly cheap in SF: expect $100 for a private hostel room, $200 for a budget motel and over $300 for midrange hotels. Note the hefty 14% room tax on top of quoted rates. Most hotels offer free wifi (only luxury hotels charge, claiming it's for secured lines). Prices run higher June to August and plummet from November to April. Ask about weekly rates. On weekends and holidays, rates for business and luxury hotels decrease but increase for tourist hotels; weekdays the opposite is true.

Hotels vs Home Rentals

Significant housing stock in San Francisco has been pulled off the market, as owners decide instead to rent their rooms and apartments to short-term vacationers instead of long-term tenants, via Airbnb and other home-rental sites. The downside for travelers is you don't necessarily know what you're getting into, and if you get a bad room, you can't simply call the front desk and switch rooms. The upside: you may get a glorious garden apartment at a great rate. *Caveat emptor.* At this writing, there were big fights in City Hall about regulating these sites. Stay tuned.

Lonely Planet's Top Choices

Hotel Drisco (p241) Stately boutique hotel in civilized Pacific Heights.

Argonaut Hotel (p235) Nautical-themed hotel at Fisherman's Wharf.

Hotel Vitale (p239) Contemporary downtowner with knockout waterfront vistas.

Inn at the Presidio (p235) National-park lodge in historic building, surrounded by nature.

Hotel Bohème (p240) Artsy mid-budget boutique charmer in the heart of North Beach.

Best by Budget

$

HI San Francisco Fisherman's Wharf (p235) Waterfront hostel with million-dollar views.

San Remo Hotel (p239) Spartan furnishings, shared bathrooms, great rates.

Pacific Tradewinds Hostel (p240) Downtown hostel with snappy design.

$$

Inn at the Presidio (p235) Small luxury inn surrounded by national-park land.

Kensington Park Hotel (p237) Spiffy Union Square boutique hotel.

Hotel Carlton (p237) Freshly redesigned with good-value rooms.

Golden Gate Hotel (p240) Old-fashioned small hotel with resident cat.

Coventry Motor Inn (p235) Value-priced plain-Jane motel with big rooms.

$$$

Hotel Drisco (p241) Luxury inn atop Pacific Heights.

Loews Regency (p238) Five-star service; knockout views.

Palace Hotel (p239) Stately classical hotel, century-old landmark.

Marker (p236) Snazzy design, useful amenities, central location.

Hotel Zetta (p238) Tech-centric downtowner, filled with art.

Argonaut Hotel (p235) Nautically themed hotel at Fisherman's Wharf.

Best for Kids

Hotel Zephyr (p235) Games everywhere in a vast outdoor courtyard.

Hotel del Sol (p236) Colorful theme rooms, plus a heated outdoor pool.

Argonaut Hotel (p235) The Wharf's best hotel, with a giant lobby to explore.

Americania Hotel (p238) Better-than-average motel with pool.

Seal Rock Inn (p242) Ocean-front family motel, far from the city center.

Best for Views

Loews Regency (p238) Bridge-to-bridge views from a five-star skyscraper.

Sir Francis Drake Hotel (p239) Playful 1920s tower hotel above Union Square.

Fairmont San Francisco (p241) Hilltop vistas plus SF's grandest lobby.

Mark Hopkins Intercontinental (p241) Nob Hill address for stately charm.

Hotel Vitale (p239) Shagadelic chic with a Bay Bridge view.

Argonaut Hotel (p235) The Wharf's best, with fab bayfront vistas.

NEED TO KNOW

Prices

The following price ranges refer to double rooms, with bath, in high season (summer); you can sometimes do better, except when there's a convention.

$	under $150
$$	$150 to $350
$$$	over $350

Parking

Hotel parking costs $40 to $60 per night extra. When there's a *free* self-service lot, we've included the parking symbol. Hotels without parking often have valet parking or an agreement with a nearby garage; call ahead.

Reconfirming

If you're arriving after 4pm, guarantee with a credit card or your reservation may be cancelled.

Tipping

Tipping housekeepers in US hotels is standard practice; leave a few dollars on your pillow each morning and be guaranteed excellent housekeeping.

Breakfast

Breakfast is not included in rates unless specified.

What's a Double?

In the US, a double room means accommodations for two people in one bed. If you want two beds in one room, specify this.

Where to Stay

Neighborhood	For	Against
The Marina, Fisherman's Wharf & the Piers	Near the northern waterfront; good for kids; lots of restaurants and nightlife at the Marina; many motels on Lombard St – with parking.	Fisherman's Wharf is all tourists; parking at the Marina and Wharf is a nightmare.
Downtown, Civic Center & SoMa	Biggest selection of hotels; near all public transportation, including cable cars; walkable to many sights, restaurants, shopping and theaters. Parts of SoMa are close to major downtown sights; great nightlife.	Downtown quiet at night; Civic Center feels rough – the worst area extends three blocks in all directions from Eddy and Jones Sts; parking expensive. SoMa: few restaurants, gritty streets at nighttime.
North Beach & Chinatown	Culturally colorful; great strolling; lots of cafés and restaurants; terrific sense of place.	Street noise; limited choices and transport; next-to-impossible parking.
Nob Hill, Russian Hill & Fillmore	Stately, classic hotels atop Nob Hill; good restaurants and shopping in Pacific Heights and Japantown.	The Hills are steep, hard on the out-of-shape; parking difficult; slightly removed from major sights.
The Mission & Potrero Hill	Mission's flat terrain makes walking easier; good for biking; easy access to BART.	Limited choice; distance from sights; gritty street scene on main thoroughfares.
The Castro & Noe Valley	Great nightlife, especially for GLBT travelers; provides a good taste of local life; easy access to Market St transit.	Distance from major tourist sights; few choices; limited parking.
The Haight & Hayes Valley	Lots of bars and restaurants; Hayes Valley near cultural sights; the Haight near Golden Gate Park.	Limited public transportation in the Haight; gritty street scene at night on major thoroughfares; parking difficult.
Golden Gate Park & the Avenues	Quiet nights; good for outdoor recreation; easier parking.	Very far from major sights; foggy and cold in summer; limited transportation and restaurants.

The Marina, Fisherman's Wharf & the Piers

★HI SAN FRANCISCO FISHERMAN'S WHARF HOSTEL $

Map p300 (415-771-7277; www.sfhostels.com; Bldg 240, Fort Mason; dm incl breakfast $30-42, r $75-109; 28, 30, 47, 49) Trading downtown convenience for a glorious park-like setting with million-dollar waterfront views, this hostel occupies a former army hospital building, with bargain-priced private rooms and dorms (some co-ed) with four to 22 beds (avoid bunks one and two – they're by doorways). Huge kitchen. No curfew but no heat during daytime: bring warm clothes. Limited free parking.

COVENTRY MOTOR INN MOTEL $$

Map p300 (415-567-1200; www.coventrymotorinn.com; 1901 Lombard St; r $160-225; 22, 28, 30, 43) Of the many motels lining Lombard St (Hwy 101), the generic Coventry has the highest quality-to-value ratio with spacious, well-maintained (if plain) rooms and extras like air-con (good for quiet sleeps) and covered parking. Parents: there's plenty of floor space to unpack kids' toys, but no pool.

MARINA INN HOTEL $$

Map p300 (415-928-1000; www.marinainn.com; 3110 Octavia St; r $150-180; 28, 30, 47, 49) An excellent value in the Marina, this vintage 1920s hotel has small, clean rooms with cabbage-rose decor, offering a cozier alternative to a motel. Single-pane glass means street noise; bring earplugs. Close to Union St shopping and bars.

HOTEL ZEPHYR DESIGN HOTEL $$

Map p298 (844-617-6555, 415-617-6565; www.hotelzephyrsf.com; 250 Beach St; r $250-400; 8, 39, 47, Powell-Mason, MF) Completely redone in 2015, this vintage-1960s hotel surrounds a vast courtyard with fire pits and lounge chairs, modern art from nautical junk, and games like ping-pong in a tube – reminders you're here to play, not work. Rooms are fresh and spiffy, with up-to-date amenities, including smart TVs that link with your devices. Best rooms face the water.

THE TUSCAN BOUTIQUE HOTEL $$

Map p298 (415-561-1100, 800-648-4626; www.tuscanhotel.com; 425 North Point St; r from $289; 47, Powell-Mason, MF) Staying at touristy Fisherman's Wharf doesn't mean you have to settle for plain-Jane chains like Sheraton. The Tuscan is as comfortable, but has more character, with spacious rooms styled with white-on-white linens and colorful accent fabrics. Kids love the in-room Nintendo; parents love the afternoon wine hour.

WHARF INN MOTEL $$

Map p298 (415-673-7411, 800-548-9918; www.wharfinn.com; 2601 Mason St; r $215-300; 47, Powell-Mason, MF) This standard-issue, two-story motor lodge at the Wharf has clean, nothing-special rooms, ideal for kids who make messes. Some rooms are loud; bring earplugs. Rates fluctuate wildly with the tourist tide.

MARINA MOTEL MOTEL $$

Map p300 (415-921-9406, 800-346-6118; www.marinamotel.com; 2576 Lombard St; r $189-269; 28, 30, 41, 43, 45) Established in 1939 to accommodate visitors arriving via the new Golden Gate Bridge, the Marina has an inviting Spanish-Mediterranean look, with a quiet bougainvillea-lined courtyard. Rooms are homey, simple and well maintained (never mind occasional scuffs); some have full kitchens (extra $10 to $20). Rooms on Lombard St are loud; request one in back.

★INN AT THE PRESIDIO HOTEL $$$

Map p302 (415-800-7356; www.innatthepresidio.com; 42 Moraga Ave; r incl breakfast $270-360; 43, PresidiGo Shuttle) Built in 1903 as bachelor quarters for army officers, this three-story red-brick building in the Presidio was transformed in 2012 into a spiffy national-park lodge, styled with leather, linen and wood. Oversized rooms are plush, including feather beds with Egyptian-cotton sheets. Suites have fireplaces. Nature surrounds you, with hiking trailheads out back, but taxis downtown cost $25.

★ARGONAUT HOTEL BOUTIQUE HOTEL $$$

Map p298 (415-563-0800, 800-790-1415; www.argonauthotel.com; 495 Jefferson St; r from $439, with view from $489; 19, 47, 49, Powell-Hyde) Fisherman's Wharf's top hotel was built as a cannery in 1908 and has century-old wooden beams and exposed brick walls. Rooms sport an over-the-top nautical theme, with porthole-shaped mirrors and plush, deep-blue carpets.

WEBSITES

B&B San Francisco (www.bbsf.com) Personable, privately owned B&Bs and neighborhood inns.

Hotel Tonight (www.hoteltonight.com) SF-based hotel search app offering discount last-minute bookings.

Airbnb (www.airbnb.com) SF-based app offering short-term home-sharing and vacation rentals.

Lonely Planet (www.lonelyplanet.com/usa/san-francisco/hotels) Expert author reviews, user feedback, booking engine.

Though all have the amenities of an upper-end hotel – ultra-comfy beds, iPod docks – some rooms are tiny with limited sunlight. Pay extra for a mesmerizing bay view. Kids meet other kids in the big lobby.

HOTEL DEL SOL MOTEL **$$$**
Map p300 (415-921-5520, 877-433-5765; www.thehoteldelsol.com; 3100 Webster St; d $349-500; ; 22, 28, 30, 43) The spiffy, kid-friendly Marina District del Sol is a riot of color, with tropical-themed decor. A quiet, revamped 1950s motor lodge with palm-lined central courtyard, it's one of the few San Francisco hotels with a heated outdoor pool. Family suites have trundle beds and board games. Free parking.

Downtown, Civic Center & SoMa

HI SAN FRANCISCO DOWNTOWN HOSTEL **$**
Map p304 (415-788-5604; www.sfhostels.com; 312 Mason St; dm $39-50, r incl breakfast $90-145; ; Powell, Powell) Location, location – a block from Union Square, this well-managed hostel has contemporary furnishings and looks fresh, clean and colorful. Dorms have four beds; private rooms sport low-slung platform beds (beware sharp corners) and some even have down pillows (by request). Extras include free breakfast, quiet area, social lounge, clean kitchen and full activities calendar.

ADELAIDE HOSTEL HOSTEL **$**
Map p306 (415-359-1915, 877-359-1915; www.adelaidehostel.com; 5 Isadora Duncan Lane; dm $37-50, r $120-220, incl breakfast; ; 38) Down a hidden alley, the 22-room Adelaide has up-to-date furnishings and marble-tiled baths – also the occasional rust stain and dust bunny. Extras include breakfast, group activities and two common areas (one quiet). Good service; friendly crowd. Note: your private room may wind up being in the nearby Dakota or Fitzgerald Hotels; of the two, Fitzgerald is the better.

HI SAN FRANCISCO CITY CENTER HOSTEL **$**
Map p306 (415-474-5721; www.sfhostels.org; 685 Ellis St; dm incl breakfast $40-52, r $124-140, incl breakfast; ; 19, 38, 47, 49) A converted seven-story, 1920s apartment building, this better-than-average hostel has private baths in all rooms, including dorms. All-you-can-eat pancakes or eggs cost $1. The neighborhood, on the edge of the gritty Tenderloin, is sketchy, but nearby are good bars and cheap eats.

USA HOSTELS HOSTEL **$**
Map p306 (415-440-5600, 877-483-2950; www.usahostels.com; 711 Post St; dm $58-73, r $134-179; ; 2, 3, 27, 38) This former 1909 hotel is now a good-looking hostel resembling a college dormitory, bustling with international students. Private rooms have fridge, microwave and TV. Dorms have built-in privacy screens with reading light and electrical outlet, and lockers contain outlets to charge electronics. Common areas include a big kitchen, laundry and games space.

★MARKER BOUTIQUE HOTEL **$$**
Map p306 (844-736-2753, 415-292-0100; http://themarkersanfrancisco.com; 501 Geary St; r from $209; ; 38, Powell-Hyde, Powell-Mason) Snazzy Marker gets details right, with guest rooms a riot of color – lipstick-red lacquer, navy-blue velvet and shiny-purple silk – plus substantive amenities like high-thread-count sheets, ergonomic workspaces, multiple electrical outlets, and ample drawer, closet and bathroom-vanity space. Extras include a spa with a Jacuzzi, small gym, evening wine reception and bragging rights to a stylin' address.

KENSINGTON PARK HOTEL BOUTIQUE HOTEL $$

Map p304 (☎415-788-6400; www.kensingtonpark hotel.com; 450 Post St; r $234-337; ; Powell-Hyde, Powell-Mason, M Powell, B Powell) The dramatic 1925 Spanish-Moorish lobby plays a moody counterpoint to the guest rooms' sophisticated mash-up of Queen Anne and contemporary furnishings. Some rooms are small but have extras like down pillows. Downstairs is the top-flight seafood restaurant Farallon. Central location, just off Union Square, apart from the sketchy Tenderloin.

HOTEL TRITON BOUTIQUE HOTEL $$

Map p304 (☎415-394-0500, 800-800-1299; www.hoteltriton.com; 342 Grant Ave; r $269-389; ; M Montgomery, B Montgomery) The Triton's lobby thumps with high-energy music and pops with color like the pages of a comic book. Self-consciously hip rooms sport SF-centric details, like wallpaper repeating two random columns of Kerouac's *On the Road,* redeemed by snappy colors, ecofriendly amenities and shag-worthy beds. Baths have limited space but there's unlimited Häagen-Dazs ice cream on request. Don't miss tarot-card readings and chair massages during nightly wine hour. Kids get special amenities.

HOTEL DIVA BOUTIQUE HOTEL $$

Map p304 (☎844-592-4559, 415-885-0200; www.hoteldiva.com; 440 Geary St; r $279-350; ; 38, Powell-Hyde, Powell-Mason) Favored by mid-budget fashionistas and traveling club kids, industrial-chic Diva's stainless-steel and black-granite aesthetic conveys a sexy urban look. Beds are comfy, with good sheets, feather pillows and down comforters adding much-needed softness to the hard-edged design. Best for a party but if you're here on business, escape your room to work in the artist-designed lounges.

HOTEL CARLTON DESIGN HOTEL $$

Map p306 (☎415-673-0242, 800-922-7586; www.hotelcarltonsf.com; 1075 Sutter St; r $269-309; ; 2, 3, 19, 38, 47, 49) Renovated in 2013, this fresh-looking mid-budget hotel trades convenience for value – it's a 10-minute walk to Union Square – but feels inviting for its playful design that nods to North Africa, and its spotlessly clean rooms with colorful accents. Downstairs there's a terrific Middle Eastern restaurant. Quietest rooms are those with suffix -08 to -19.

Rooftop solar panels provide power and the hotel claims carbon-neutral status.

PHOENIX HOTEL MOTEL $$

Map p306 (☎415-776-1380, 800-248-9466; www.thephoenixhotel.com; 601 Eddy St; r $249-359; P; 19, 31, 47, 49) The city's rocker crash pad draws minor celebs and Dionysian revelers to a 1950s motor lodge with basic rooms dolled up with tropical decor. The former coffee shop is now the happening gastro-lounge Chambers. Parking is free, as is admission to Kabuki Springs & Spa (p145). One complaint: noise – bring earplugs. Check out the cool shrine to actor-director Vincent Gallo opposite room 43.

HOTEL ABRI HOTEL $$

Map p304 (☎888-229-0677, 415-392-8800; www.hotelabrisf.com; 127 Ellis St; r $245-359; ; M Powell, B Powell) Inside a remodeled early-20th-century building, the Abri has a contemporary sensibility, with bold black-and-tan motifs, pillow-top beds with feather pillows, iPod docks, flat-screen TVs and big workstations. Few bathrooms have tubs but rainfall showerheads compensate. The hotel's popularity has meant wear-and-tear on the once-fresh furnishings, but rooms remain comfy, the staff friendly and accommodating. Request a quiet room, *not* above the Subway sandwich shop, to avoid the pervasive smell of baking bread.

GOOD HOTEL MOTEL $$

Map p308 (☎415-621-7001, 800-444-5819; www.thegoodhotel.com; 112 7th St; r $199-279; ; M Civic Center, B Civic Center) A revamped motel attached to a restyled apartment hotel, Good Hotel places a premium on green with reclaimed-wood headboards, light fixtures of repurposed bottles, and fleece bedspreads made from recycled soda bottles and cast-off fabrics. It's like a smartly decorated college dorm – youthful and fun. Drawbacks are a sometimes-sketchy neighborhood and street noise; book in back.

The front desk rents bikes. For air-con – or if you have lots of luggage to unload – book the motel side. Self-parking costs $35. The pool is across the street at the Americania Hotel.

BEST WESTERN CARRIAGE INN MOTEL $$

Map p308 (☎415-552-8600, 800-780-7234; www.carriageinnsf.com; 140 7th St; r $229-349; ; M Civic Center, B Civic Center) An upmarket motor lodge with bigger-than-average rooms, styled with colorful textiles, the Carriage Inn gives good bang for your buck, but it's on a sometimes-sketchy street. Self-parking costs $35. The pool is across the street at the Americania Hotel.

HOTEL UNION SQUARE HOTEL $$

Map p304 (415-397-3000, 800-553-1900; www.hotelunionsquare.com; 114 Powell St; r $196-299; ; MPowell, BPowell) Hotel Union Square looks sharp, with smart design touches complementing the original brick walls. The main drawbacks are lack of sunlight and very small rooms, but designers have compensated with cleverly concealed lighting, mirrored walls and plush fabrics. Convenient location near major transport – never mind the panhandlers outside. Not all rooms have air-con.

BERESFORD ARMS HOTEL HOTEL $$

Map p306 (415-673-2600, 800-533-5633; www.beresford.com; 701 Post St; r $159-279; ; 2, 3, 27, 38) Because its 1912 building originally housed apartments, the Beresford has bigger-than-average rooms, some with kitchens. We appreciate the fancy-looking lobby, large well-kept (if conservatively decorated) rooms, reasonable minibar prices and respectable location just beyond the riffraff of the Tenderloin, but service is decidedly perfunctory. Best rooms are the junior and parlor suites, which have fridges and/or kitchens.

ANDREWS HOTEL HOTEL $$

Map p306 (415-563-6877, 800-926-3739; www.andrewshotel.com; 624 Post St; r incl breakfast $189-299; ; 2, 3, 27, 38, Powell-Mason, Powell-Hyde) Two blocks west of Union Square, this 1905 hotel has personable staff, small but comfortable rooms (the quietest are in back) and a good Italian restaurant downstairs. Though it's nothing fancy, we love the Andrews' homey feel – it's like staying at your aunt's house, without having to pet the cat. Only suites and queens have bathtubs; otherwise expect tiny stand-up showers.

AMERICANIA HOTEL MOTEL $$

Map p308 (415-626-0200; www.americaniahotel.com; 121 7th St; r $229-289; ; MCivic Center, BCivic Center) Rooms at this restyled motor lodge face a central courtyard and look sharp, with a retro-'70s aesthetic incorporating black-and-teal-checked carpeting, white-vinyl headboards, pop art and playful extras. Kids love the small outdoor heated pool. Parents love the microbrews at the excellent downstairs burger joint – but may dislike the sometimes-gritty neighborhood and $25 charge for self-parking.

STRATFORD HOTEL HOTEL $$

Map p304 (888-504-6835, 415-397-7080; www.hotelstratford.com; 242 Powell St; r incl breakfast $189-249; ; MPowell, BPowell) A good-value hotel at Union Square, the eight-story Stratford has simple white-walled rooms with plain furnishing and occasional scuff marks – but they're clean, as are the baths which have rainfall showerheads but no bathtubs. Rooms on Powell St are loud. The elevator is s-l-o-w.

FITZGERALD HOTEL HOTEL $$

Map p306 (415-775-8100; www.fitzgeraldhotel.com; 620 Post St; r $140-230; ; 2, 3, 27, 38) Upgrade from hostel to hotel at the good-value Fitzgerald decorated with mismatched furniture liquidated from fancier hotels. The old-fashioned building (built in 1910) needs upgrades (note the temperamental elevator), rooms are tiny and have occasional scuff marks and torn curtains, but bathrooms are clean, rooms have fridges and microwaves, and there's a little fireplace lounge downstairs.

MOSSER HOTEL HOTEL $$

Map p308 (415-986-4400, 800-227-3804; www.themosser.com; 54 4th St; r $259-289, without bathroom $129-159; ; MPowell, BPowell) A tourist-class hotel with semi-stylish details, the Mosser has tiny rooms and tinier bathrooms, but rates for rooms with shared bathroom are (sometimes) a bargain. Service can be lackluster and the building is old, but it's centrally located and rooms are a fraction of the price of the neighboring Marriott, a boon for conventioneers on a budget.

HOTEL ZETTA HOTEL $$$

Map p304 (415-543-8555, 855-212-4187; www.hotelzetta.com; 55 5th St; r from $324; ; BPowell St, MPowell St) Opened 2013, this snappy eco-conscious downtowner by the Viceroy group plays to techies who work too much, with a mezzanine-level 'play room' with billiards, shuffleboard and two-story-high Plinko wall rising above the art-filled lobby. Upstairs, bigger-than-average rooms look sharp with padded black-leather headboards and low-slung platform beds; web-enabled flat-screen TVs link with your devices.

LOEWS REGENCY LUXURY HOTEL $$$

Map p303 (844-271-6289, 415-276-9888; www.loewshotels.com/regency-san-francisco; 222 Sansome St; r from $600; ; California, MMontgomery, BMontgomery) On the top 11 floors of SF's third-tallest building, Loews offers sweeping, bird's-eye views from every room. There's nothing risky about the classical decor but details are sumptuous. For a splurge, book a 'Luxury Golden Gate King' (from $769), with bathtub surrounded by floor-to-ceiling windows overlooking the Golden Gate. Alas, no pool – hence the four stars – but there's a spa; and service equals, sometimes beats, the city's five-stars.

TAJ CAMPTON PLACE LUXURY HOTEL $$$

Map p304 (415-781-5555, 866-969-1825; www.tajhotels.com; 340 Stockton St; r from $425; 30, 45, Montgomery) Impeccable service sets Campton Place apart – this is where to put your fur-clad rich aunt when she wants discretion above all. Details are lavish, if beige. Cheapest rooms are tiny; pay to upgrade or be imprisoned in a jewelry box. Excellent on-site formal restaurant.

PALACE HOTEL HOTEL $$$

Map p304 (415-512-1111; www.sfpalace.com; 2 New Montgomery St; r from $300; Montgomery, Montgomery) The 1906 landmark Palace stands as a monument to turn-of-the-century grandeur, aglow with 100-year-old Austrian crystal chandeliers. Cushy (if staid) accommodations cater to expense-account travelers but prices drop on weekends. Even if you're not staying here, see the opulent Garden Court, one of Northern California's most beautiful rooms, and sip tea beneath a translucent glass ceiling. There's also a spa; kids love the big pool.

HOTEL VITALE BOUTIQUE HOTEL $$$

Map p308 (415-278-3700, 888-890-8688; www.hotelvitale.com; 8 Mission St; r $385-675; Embarcadero, Embarcadero) The ugly exterior disguises a fashion-forward hotel, with echoes of mid-century-modern design, enhanced by up-to-the-minute luxuries. Beds are dressed with 450-thread-count sheets. There is an excellent on-site spa with two rooftop hot tubs. Best rooms face the bay and have spectacular bridge views.

INN AT UNION SQUARE BOUTIQUE HOTEL $$$

Map p304 (415-397-3510, 800-288-4346; www.unionsquare.com; 440 Post St; r $243-429; Powell-Hyde, Powell-Mason, Powell, Powell) Traditionalists love the conservative chintz decor and personalized service of this understated boutique charmer, best for older travelers who want both quiet and central location. Extras include twice-daily maid service and breakfast served fireside. Great for shopping and theaters.

HARBOR COURT HOTEL BOUTIQUE HOTEL $$$

Map p308 (415-882-1300, 866-792-6283; www.harborcourthotel.com; 165 Steuart St; r from $299; Embarcadero, Embarcadero) Rooms are tiny at this repurposed, vintage-1928 YMCA hotel, but designers compensated with pull-out drawers under platform beds and attractive textures and colors. Book a bay-view room (trust us). Downstairs, guests gather fireside in the handsome bayside common area. Lively bars and restaurants line the street outside. The adjoining YMCA (extra charge) has an excellent gym and pool.

WESTIN ST FRANCIS HOTEL HOTEL $$$

Map p304 (415-397-7000, 800-228-3000; www.westinstfrancis.com; 335 Powell St; r from $289; Powell-Mason, Powell-Hyde, Powell, Powell) This is one of SF's most storied hotels – Gerald Ford was shot right outside. Tower rooms have stellar views but feel architecturally generic. We prefer the original building's old-fashioned charm, with its high ceilings and crown moldings. Westin beds set the industry standard for comfort but service is decidedly business class, not first.

SIR FRANCIS DRAKE HOTEL HOTEL $$$

Map p304 (415-392-7755, 800-795-7129; www.sirfrancisdrake.com; 450 Powell St; r $279-449; Powell-Mason, Powell-Hyde, Powell, Powell) The city's most famous doormen, clad like cartoon Beefeaters, stand sentinel at this 1920s tower with magnificent Spanish-Moorish lobby that gets defaced with tacky posters when a convention's in town. Rooms are styled in bold prints on neutral greige and have business-class amenities. Book 16th- to 20th-floor rooms for expansive views. Alas, service is lackluster. If you can get someone's attention, ask about the secret room between elevator platforms, where during Prohibition the hotel operated a speakeasy.

North Beach & Chinatown

SAN REMO HOTEL HOTEL $

Map p318 (415-776-8688, 800-352-7366; www.sanremohotel.com; 2237 Mason St; r without bathroom $119-159; 30, 47, Powell-Mason) One of the city's best-value stays, the San Remo dates to 1906 and is long on old-fashioned charm. Rooms are simply done with mismatched turn-of-the-century furnishings and all rooms share bathrooms. Think reputable, vintage boardinghouse. Note: least-expensive rooms have windows onto the corridor, not the outdoors. Family suites accommodate up to five. No elevator.

PACIFIC TRADEWINDS HOSTEL HOSTEL $

Map p318 (☎415-433-7970, 888-734-6783; san-francisco-hostel.com; 680 Sacramento St; dm $38; ⊙front desk 8am-midnight; @📶; 🚌1, 🚋California St, Ⓑ Montgomery) San Francisco's smartest-looking all-dorm hostel has a blue-and-white nautical theme, fully equipped kitchen, spotless glass-brick showers and no lockout time. Bunks are bolted to the wall so there's no bed-shaking when your bunkmate shifts. Alas, no elevator means hauling bags up three flights but it's worth it. Great service, fun staff.

★**ORCHARD GARDEN HOTEL** BOUTIQUE HOTEL $$

Map p318 (☎415-399-9807, 888-717-2881; www.theorchardgardenhotel.com; 466 Bush St; r $275-400; ❄@📶; 🚌2, 3, 30, 45, Ⓑ Montgomery) 🍃 San Francisco's first all-green-practices hotel uses sustainably grown wood, chemical-free cleaning products and recycled fabrics in its soothingly quiet rooms. Don't think you'll be trading comfort for conscience: rooms have a few unexpectedly luxe touches like high-end down pillows and Egyptian-cotton sheets. Don't miss the sunny rooftop terrace – a lovely spot at day's end.

★**HOTEL BOHÈME** BOUTIQUE HOTEL $$

Map p318 (☎415-433-9111; www.hotelboheme.com; 444 Columbus Ave; r $225–295; @📶; 🚌10, 12, 30, 41, 45) Our favorite boutique hotel is a love letter to the Beat era, with moody color schemes, Chinese umbrellas as light fixtures and photos from the Beat years on the walls. Rooms are smallish, some front on noisy Columbus Ave (quieter rooms are in back) and bathrooms are teensy, but it's smack in North Beach's vibrant scene. No elevator.

WASHINGTON SQUARE INN B&B $$

Map p318 (☎415-981-4220, 800-388-0220; www.wsisf.com; 1660 Stockton St; r incl breakfast $209-359; @📶; 🚌30, 41, 45, 🚋Powell-Mason) On leafy, sun-dappled Washington Sq, this inn looks decidedly European and caters to the over-40 set, with tasteful rooms styled with a few choice antiques, including carved, wooden armoires. Least-expensive rooms are tiny, but what a stellar address. Wine and cheese each evening and breakfast in bed are lovely extras. No elevator.

SW HOTEL HOTEL $$

Map p318 (☎415-362-2999, 888-595-9188; www.swhotel.com; 615 Broadway; s $139, d $189-325; ❄📶; 🚌10, 12, 30, 45) The notorious Sam Wong has been totally overhauled, and now it's a respectable, good-value hotel, heavy on the pastels and air freshener. Its number-one selling point is location – on the Broadway axis dividing North Beach and Chinatown – but some rooms are incredibly loud: bring earplugs or use air-con (not available in cheaper rooms). Parking not always available.

🛏 Nob Hill, Russian Hill & Fillmore

HOTEL REX BOUTIQUE HOTEL $$

Map p316 (☎415-433-4434, 800-433-4434; www.thehotelrex.com; 562 Sutter St; r $309–369; ❄@📶🐾; 🚋Powell-Hyde, Powell-Mason, Ⓜ Powell, Ⓑ Powell) 🍃 The Rex draws aesthetic inspiration from early-20th-century literary salons, and sometimes hosts author readings in its cozy lobby bar. Rooms feel inviting (if small) for their traditional masculine color palettes. Beds are particularly great, with crisp linens and down pillows. Caveats: rear-facing rooms lack sunlight but are quiet; street-facing rooms are bright, but noisy. Request air-con.

WHITE SWAN INN BOUTIQUE HOTEL $$

Map p316 (☎415-775-1755, 800-999-9570; www.whiteswaninnsf.com; 845 Bush St; r incl breakfast $260-335; Ⓟ@📶; 🚌2, 3, 27) Like an English country inn, the romantic White Swan is styled with cabbage-rose wallpaper, red-plaid flannel bedspreads and Colonial-style furniture. Each oversized room has a gas fireplace – cozy on a foggy night – and there's wine and cheese in the library.

PETITE AUBERGE BOUTIQUE HOTEL $$

Map p316 (☎415-928-6000, 800-365-3004; www.petiteaubergesf.com; 863 Bush St; r incl breakfast $250-380; 📶; 🚌2, 3, 27) Petite Auberge feels like a French country inn, with floral-print fabrics, sunny-yellow colors and in-room gas fireplaces – among downtown's most charming midprice stays. Alas, several rooms are dark (especially tiny 22) and face an alley where rubbish collectors rattle cans early (request a quiet room). Breakfast and afternoon wine served fireside in the cozy salon.

GOLDEN GATE HOTEL HOTEL $$

Map p316 (☎415-392-3702, 800-835-1118; www.goldengatehotel.com; 775 Bush St; r $215, without bathroom $145; @📶; 🚌2, 3, 🚋Powell-Hyde, Powell-Mason) Like an old-fashioned *pension*, the Golden Gate has kindly owners and simple rooms with mismatched furniture, inside a 1913 Edwardian hotel safely up the hill from the Tenderloin. Rooms are small, clean and comfortable and most have private bathrooms (some with antique claw-foot bathtubs). Enormous croissants, homemade cookies and a resident cat provide TLC after long days of sightseeing.

QUEEN ANNE HOTEL B&B $$

Map p315 (415-441-2828, 800-227-3970; www.queenanne.com; 1590 Sutter St; r incl breakfast $275-350; 2, 3) The Queen Anne occupies a lovely 1890 Victorian mansion, formerly a girls' boarding school. Though the chintz decor borders on twee, it matches the stately house. Rooms are comfy (some are tiny) and have a mishmash of antiques; some have romantic wood-burning fireplaces.

★**HOTEL DRISCO** BOUTIQUE HOTEL $$$

Map p300 (415-346-2880, 800-634-7277; www.hoteldrisco.com; 2901 Pacific Ave; r incl breakfast $338-475; 3, 24) The only hotel in Pacific Heights, a stately 1903 apartment-hotel tucked between mansions, stands high on the ridgeline. We love the architecture, attentive service and chic rooms, with their elegantly austere decor, but the high-on-a-hill location is convenient only to the Marina; anywhere else requires bus or taxi. Still, for a real boutique hotel, it's tops.

FAIRMONT SAN FRANCISCO LUXURY HOTEL $$$

Map p316 (415-772-5000, 800-441-1414; www.fairmont.com; 950 Mason St; r from $329; California St) Heads of state choose the Fairmont, whose magnificent lobby is decked out with crystal chandeliers, marble floors and towering yellow-marble columns. Notwithstanding the opulent Presidential suite, rooms have traditional business-class furnishings and lack finer details of top-end luxury hotels. Still, few addresses compare. For old-fashioned character, reserve the original 1906 building; for jaw-dropping views, the tower.

MARK HOPKINS INTERCONTINENTAL HOTEL $$$

Map p316 (415-392-3434, 800-327-0200; www.intercontinentalmarkhopkins.com; 999 California St; r from $300; California St) Glistening marble floors reflect glowing crystal chandeliers in the lobby of the 1926 Mark Hopkins, a San Francisco landmark. Detractors call it staid, but its timelessness is precisely why others (including Michelle Obama) love it. Rooms are done in business-classy style, with Frette linens, and most have knockout hilltop views, but some details miss: anticipate four-, not five-star, service.

HOTEL KABUKI HOTEL $$$

Map p315 (415-922-3200, 800-533-4567; www.hotelkabuki.com; 1625 Post St; r $309-469; 2, 3, 38) The Kabuki nods to Japan, with *shoji* (rice-paper screens) on windows and orange-silk dust ruffles beneath platform beds. The boxy 1960s architecture is plain, but rooms are spacious (upgrades slated for 2016). Best details: deep Japanese soaking tubs with adjoining showers and free passes to Kabuki Springs & Spa (p145) when you book directly through JDV hotels).

The Mission & Potrero Hill

INN SAN FRANCISCO B&B $$

Map p312 (800-359-0913, 415-641-0188; www.innsf.com; 943 S Van Ness Ave; r incl breakfast $215-255, without bathroom $165-225, cottage $385-475; 14, 49) This stately Mission-district inn occupies an elegant 1872 Italianate-Victorian mansion, impeccably maintained, and packed with antiques. All rooms have fresh-cut flowers and sumptuous mattresses with featherbeds; some have a Jacuzzi. There's also a free-standing garden cottage that sleeps up to six. Outside there's an English garden and redwood hot tub open 24 hours (a rarity). Limited parking: reserve ahead. No elevator.

The Castro & Noe Valley

WILLOWS INN GLBT, B&B $

Map p320 (415-431-4770; www.willowssf.com; 710 14th St; s $120-160, d $130-175, tr $170-190, q $180-205, all without bathroom; Church) Willows has the homey comforts of a B&B, without any fuss. None of the 12 rooms has private bathroom but all have sinks. Shared kitchenette. Rooms on 14th St are sunnier and have good street views, and though they have double-pane glass, they're noisier; ask when you book. No elevator.

INN ON CASTRO GLBT, B&B $$

Map p320 (415-861-0321; www.innoncastro.com; 321 Castro St; r incl breakfast $235-275, without bathroom $165-185, self-catering apt $235-290; Castro) A portal to the Castro's disco heyday, this Edwardian town house is decked out with top-end '70s-mod furnishings. Rooms are retro-cool and spotlessly kept. Exceptional breakfasts – the owner is a chef. Several nearby, great-value apartments are also available for rental. No elevator.

BECK'S MOTOR LODGE MOTEL $$

Map p320 (☎415-621-8212, 800-227-4360; www.becksmotorlodge.com; 2222 Market St; r $189-279; P ❄ 📶; M Castro St) This three-story motor-lodge motel got a makeover in 2015, and rooms look colorful, sharp and clean. (Request one that's been renovated.) Though technically not gay, its placement at the center of the Castro makes it the de facto gay favorite. We don't recommend bringing kids, especially during big gay events, when rooms are reserved months ahead. Book a rear-facing unit for quiet, a room in front to cruise with your blinds open.

★ **PARKER GUEST HOUSE** B&B $$$

Map p320 (☎888-520-7275, 415-621-3222; www.parkerguesthouse.com; 520 Church St; r incl breakfast $209-279; @ 📶; 🚌33, M J) The Castro's stateliest gay digs occupy two side-by-side Edwardian mansions. Details are elegant and formal, never froufrou. Rooms feel more like a swanky hotel than a B&B, with super-comfortable beds and down duvets. Bath fixtures gleam. The garden is ideal for a lovers' tryst – as is the steam room. No elevator.

The Haight & Hayes Valley

HAYES VALLEY INN HOTEL $

Map p324 (☎415-431-9131, 800-930-7999; www.hayesvalleyinn.com; 417 Gough St; d incl breakfast without bathroom $100-175; @ 📶 👪 🐾; 🚌21, M Van Ness) Like a European *pension*, this amazingly reasonable find has simple, small rooms with shared bathrooms, a border collie in the parlor, and staff eager to mother you. Two rooms have bunks, two others have single beds – ideal for families. Our only complaints are street noise and too-few bathrooms. Good shopping nearby. No elevator.

METRO HOTEL HOTEL $

Map p322 (☎415-861-5364; www.metrohotelsf.com; 319 Divisadero St; r $88-100; @ 📶; 🚌6, 24, 71) On a thoroughfare bisecting the Upper and Lower Haight districts, this straightforward, zero-frills hotel provides cheap, clean rooms with private bathroom, an outdoor garden patio and 24-hour reception. Some rooms have two double beds; one room sleeps six ($150). The location is largely residential but you can walk to the Haight's bars and restaurants. No elevator.

CHATEAU TIVOLI B&B $$

(☎415-776-5462, 800-228-1647; www.chateautivoli.com; 1057 Steiner St; r incl breakfast $175-300, without bathroom $130-200; 📶 👪; 🚌5, 22) This imposing, glorious chateau on a secondary thoroughfare near Alamo Sq once hosted Isadora Duncan and Mark Twain, and though its two-toned gabled roofs have faded, its grand domed turrets, cornices and gorgeous carved woodwork retain their luster. Guest rooms are full of soul, character and, rumor has it, the ghost of a Victorian opera diva. No elevator, no TVs.

PARSONAGE B&B $$

Map p324 (☎415-863-3699; www.theparsonage.com; 198 Haight St; r $220-280; @ 📶; 🚌6, 71, M F) A 23-room Italianate-Victorian convenient to Market St transit, the Parsonage retains gorgeous original details, including rose-brass chandeliers and Carrera-marble fireplaces. The spacious, airy rooms are lovely with oriental rugs, period antiques and, in some, wood-burning fireplaces. Take breakfast in the formal dining room, from 8am to 10am, then brandy and chocolates before bed. Charming owners. There's even an elevator.

SLEEP OVER SAUCE B&B $$

Map p324 (☎415-252-1423; www.sleepsf.com; 135 Gough St; d $165-195, q $260-295; @ 📶; M Van Ness) We like the homey vibe of this eight-room inn, set above a pretty good dinner house and bar. Rooms are simple, with dark-wood furniture and nothing froufrou; guests share a big common area with fireplace. Bathrooms are sparkling clean, but some are across the hall. No elevator, no front desk – check in at the restaurant downstairs.

Golden Gate Park & the Avenues

SEAL ROCK INN MOTEL $$

Map p326 (☎415-752-8000, 888-732-5762; www.sealrockinn.com; 545 Point Lobos Ave; s $140-187, d $150-197; P 📶 👪; 🚌38) Far from downtown, this vintage-1950s ocean-side motel has big rooms (many sleep four); all have refrigerator and microwave. It's best for families wanting to linger near the beach or hike the coast. Ping-pong keeps kids from getting antsy; ask if the pool has reopened. Reserve way ahead for 3rd-floor rooms, which have gas fireplaces. Plan ahead for meal times: the on-site restaurant keeps erratic hours and there's little else nearby.

Understand San Francisco

San Francisco Today

Congratulations: you're right on time for SF's latest tech boom, art show, green initiative, water-saving idea and (fair warning) marriage proposal. SF has its ups and downs, but as anyone who's clung on to the side of a cable car will tell you, this town gives one hell of a ride.

Best on Film

Milk (2008) Sean Penn won an Oscar for his portrayal of America's first openly gay elected official.

Tales of the City (1993) Laura Linney unravels a mystery in SF's swinging '70s disco scene.

Harold and Maude (1971) Conservatory of Flowers and Sutro Baths make metaphorically apt backdrops for May-to-December romance.

Chan Is Missing (1982) When Chan disappears, two cabbies realize they don't know Chan, Chinatown or themselves.

Best in Print

Howl and Other Poems (Allen Ginsberg; 1956) Mind-altering, law-changing words defined a generation of 'angel-headed hipsters.'

Time and Materials (Robert Hass; 2007) Every Pulitzer Prize–winning syllable is as essential as a rivet in the Golden Gate Bridge.

On the Road (Jack Kerouac; 1957) Banged out in a San Francisco attic, Kerouac's travelogue set postwar America free.

Slouching Towards Bethlehem (Joan Didion; 1968) Scorching truth burns through San Francisco fog during the Summer of Love.

SF Goes Boom

The Bay Area currently leads the nation in job creation: mobile apps and social media are booming SF industries, with restaurants, bars, clubs and performance spaces flourishing as the tech money flows in.

But the economic upturn does have downsides. Longtime San Franciscans struggle to keep pace with rising house and food prices. Luxury buses whisking SF-based tech workers to Silicon Valley jobs have come to symbolize a growing income divide, as service workers commute long distances into SF via floundering public transit.

Arts Stage a Comeback

Through tech booms and busts, San Francisco prides itself on creativity. So when Mayor Ed Lee offered Twitter tax incentives in 2013 to keep its headquarters in San Francisco, artists demanded to know: what would the city do to keep arts in SF?

Good question. The city's top real estate owner is Academy of Art College – but warehouses that formerly housed galleries, rehearsal spaces and performance venues are increasingly occupied by start-ups. The city has more art-school grads than ever, but fewer places for them to make and show work.

San Franciso's arts community is rallying though. Nonprofits cut a deal with the city enabling them to buy buildings on a blighted stretch of Market St at subsidized rates. A gallery district has taken root in Potrero Flats, and performance venues have sprouted up in SoMa. Techie arts patrons bought a Dogpatch warehouse to create the Minnestoa Street Project arts center. Now no matter when you arrive in SF, it's showtime.

Here Comes the Bride ... Again

San Francisco was the first city to authorize same-sex marriages back in 2004 – but some 4036 honeymoons ended abruptly when their marriages were legally invalidated by the state. Court battles ensued, and California voters narrowly passed a measure to legally define marriage as between a man and a woman.

But for star-crossed San Francisco couples, there is a happy ending. Countersuits were initiated and in 2013, the US Supreme Court upheld California courts' ruling in favor of state civil rights protections, setting a nationwide precedent. Upon further appeal, the Supreme Court declared laws prohibiting same-sex marriage unconstutitional nationwide in 2015. The day of the decision, many longtime partners got hitched at City Hall – some for the second or third time, to the same person.

Green City, USA

According to the North American Green Cities Index, San Francisco is the greenest of them all. Anything you might want to do here, you can do with a clean, green conscience. In fact, San Francisco is on track to become a zero-waste city by 2020, and to that end mandates citywide composting and bans plastic bags. Practices that are standard-setting elsewhere are mainstream here, including LEED-certified green public buildings, electric buses, organic cocktail bars and dozens of car parking spaces that have been converted into public green oases.

In a Drought, Surrounded by Water

California is experiencing the worst drought in 1200 years, which leaves San Francisco in a peculiar position: surrounded by water on three sides, the city must curb its water consumption. Although SF is a conservation leader, the drought is bringing water issues to the fore. San Franciscans love their local produce and technology, but together crop irrigation and electricity production account for 78% of local water usage. Desalination would seem an obvious solution, except that it requires too much electricity.

Instead of waiting to get really thirsty, San Franciscans are taking action now. Chefs are featuring dry-farmed ingredients, and savvy SF foodies are minimizing intake of water-intensive produce like avocados and almonds. Recycled water is already widely used for public parks and private yards, and locals are using shower runoff for houseplants. You'll notice SF smokers being extra mindful of fire hazards, since water scarcity makes it harder to fight fires. As a visitor, limiting showers and unplugging devices may seem like small gestures, but that's a start – and California will owe you a big, wet smooch.

if San Francisco were 100 people

42 would be Caucasian
33 would be Asian
15 would be Hispanic/Latino
6 would be African American
4 would be other

politics

(% of population)

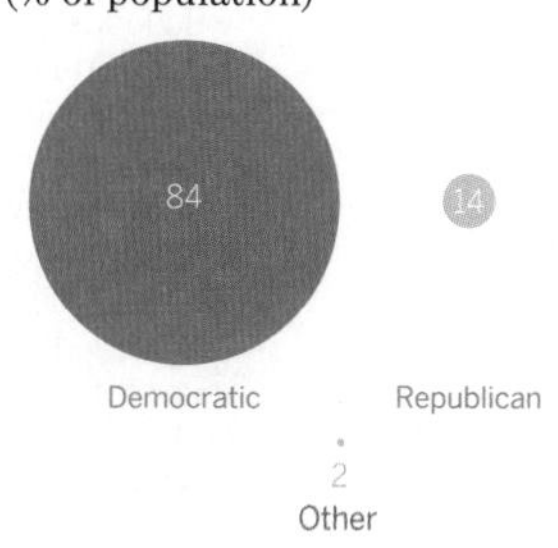

population per sq mile

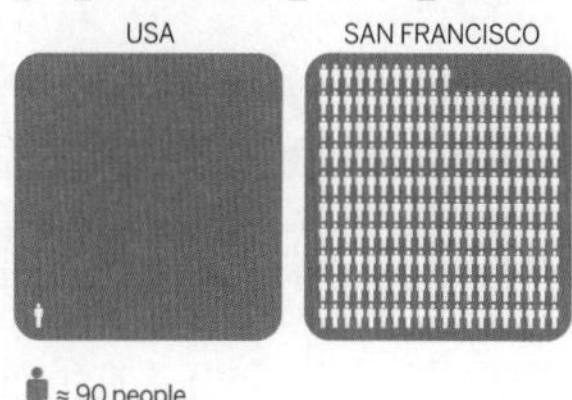

History

Native Californians had found gold in California long before 1849 – but it hardly seemed worth mentioning, as long as there were oysters for lunch and venison for dinner. Once word circulated, San Francisco was transformed almost overnight from bucolic trading backwater to Gold Rush metropolis. One hundred and sixty-odd (make that very odd) years of booms, busts, history-making hijinks and lowdown dirty dealings later, San Francisco remains the wildest city in the west – and still dreams of oysters for lunch, and venison for dinner.

Top 5 Sites for Native History

- *Mission Dolores (the Mission)*
- *Alcatraz*
- *The Presidio*
- *Rincon Center Murals (Financial District)*
- *San Francisco Historical Society (Downtown)*

Cowboys on a Mission

When Spanish cowboys brought 340 horses, 302 head of cattle and 160 mules to settle Misión San Francisco de Asís (Mission San Francisco) in 1776, there was a slight hitch: the area had already been settled by Native Americans for over 14,300 years. Since there were enough shellfish and wild foodstuffs to go around, the arrival of Captain Juan Bautista de Anza, Father Francisco Palou and their livestock initially met with no apparent resistance – until the Spaniards began to demand more than dinner.

The new arrivals expected the local Ohlone to build them a mission and to take over its management within 10 years. In exchange, the Ohlone were allowed one meal a day, if any, and a place in God's kingdom – which came much sooner than expected for many. Smallpox and other introduced diseases decimated the Ohlone population by almost three-quarters during the 50 years of Spanish rule in California. While some Ohlone managed to escape the life of obligatory construction work and prayer, others were caught, returned to the adobe barracks and punished.

As the name suggests, Mission Dolores ('mission of the sorrows') settlement never really prospered. The sandy, scrubby fields were difficult to farm, fleas were a constant irritation and the 20 soldiers who manned the local Presidio army encampment stole to supplement their single scanty shipment of provisions per year. Spain wasn't especially sorry to hand over the troublesome settlement to the newly independent nation of Mexico, but Mexico soon made the colony a profitable venture with a bustling hide and tallow trade at Yerba Buena Cove, where the Financial District now stands.

TIMELINE

June 1776

Captain Juan Bautista de Anza and Father Francisco Palou arrive in SF with cattle and settlers. With Ohlone conscripts, they build the Misión San Francisco de Asís (now Mission Dolores).

1835

President Andrew Jackson's emissary makes an offer of $500,000 to buy Northern California. Mexico testily refuses and tries to sell California to Britain.

1846

The Mexican–American War breaks out and drags on for two years, with much posturing but little actual bloodshed in California.

Meanwhile, US–Mexico relations steadily deteriorated, made worse by rumors that Mexico was entertaining a British buy-out offer for California. The Mexican–American War broke out in 1846 and dragged on for two years before ending with the Treaty of Guadalupe Hidalgo. This treaty formally ceded California and the present-day southwestern states to the USA – a loss that was initially reckoned by missionizing Church fathers in souls, but within months could be counted in ingots.

'Gold! Gold! Gold!'

Say what you will about Sam Brannan, but the man knew how to sell a story. In 1848, the San Francisco real-estate speculator and tabloid founder published rumors of a find 120 miles away near Sutter's Mill, where sawmill employees had found gold flakes in the water. Hoping to scoop other newspapers and maybe sell swampland to rubes back east, Brannan published golden gossip as solid fact. When San Franciscans proved skeptical, Brannan traveled to Sutter's Fort and convinced fellow Mormons to entrust him with a vial of gold for the church, swearing to keep their secret. Brannan kept his word for about a day. Upon his arrival, he ran through Portsmouth Square, brandishing the vial and shouting, 'Gold! Gold! Gold on the American River!'

But Brannan's plan backfired. Within weeks San Francisco's population shrank to 200, as every able-bodied individual headed to the hills to pan for gold. Brannan's newspaper folded; there was no one around to read, write or print it. Good thing Brannan had a backup plan: he'd bought every available shovel, pick and pan, and opened a general store near Sutter's Fort. Within its first 70 days, Brannan & Co sold $36,000 in equipment – almost a million bucks in today's terms.

Luckily for Brannan's profit margins, other newspapers around the world weren't that scrupulous about getting their facts straight either, hastily publishing stories of 'gold mountains' near San Francisco. Boatloads of prospectors arrived from Australia, China, South America and Europe while another 40,000 prospectors trudged overland, eager to scoop up their fortunes on the hillsides. Prices for mining supplies shot up tenfold and Brannan began raking in $150,000 a month, almost $4 million in today's terms. Food wasn't cheap, either: a dozen eggs could cost as much as $10 in San Francisco in 1849, the equivalent of $272 today.

After bawdy Jenny Lind Theater became SF's first city hall in 1852, competitor Bella Union seized the competitive advantage with this advertising campaign: 'As sweet and charming creatures as ever escaped a female seminary. Lovely tresses! Lovely lips! Buxom forms! at the BELLA UNION. And such fun! If you don't want to risk both optics, SHUT ONE EYE.'

Lawless, Loose & Lowdown

By 1850, the year California was fast-tracked for admission as the 31st state in the Union, San Francisco's population had skyrocketed from 800 a year earlier to an estimated 25,000. But for all the new money in town, it wasn't exactly easy living. The fleas were still a problem, and the rats were getting worse – but at least there were plenty of distractions.

1848

Gold is discovered near present-day Placerville. San Francisco's newspaper publisher Sam Brannan spills the secret, and the Gold Rush is on.

1850

With hopes of solid-gold tax revenues, the US hastily dubs California the 31st state.

1851

Gold discovery in Australia leads to cheering in the streets of Melbourne – and panic in the streets of San Francisco as the price for California gold plummets.

1861–65

While the US Civil War divides North from South, back east SF perversely profits in the west as industry diverted from factories burdened by the war effort heads to San Francisco.

Most of the early prospectors (called forty-niners, after their arrival date) were men under the age of 40, and to keep them entertained – and fleece the gullible – some 500 saloons, 20 theaters and numerous venues of ill repute opened within five years. A buck might procure whiskey, opium or one of the women frolicking on swings over the bar on San Francisco's 'Barbary Coast.' At gaming tables, luck literally was a lady: women card dealers dealt winning hands to those who engaged their back-room services. In 1851, visiting French journalist (and noted brothel expert) Albert Bernard de Russailh noted, 'There are also some honest women in San Francisco, but not very many.'

Wise prospectors arrived early and got out quick – but there weren't very many of those, either. As gold became harder to find, backstabbing became more common, sometimes literally. Successful Peruvians and Chileans were harassed and denied renewals to their mining claims, and most left California by 1855. Native Californian laborers who had helped the forty-niners strike it rich were also denied the right to hold claims. Despite San Francisco's well-earned reputation for freewheeling lawlessness, crime was swiftly and conveniently blamed on Australian newcomers. From 1851 to 1856, San Francisco's self-appointed Vigilance Committee tried, convicted and hanged suspect 'Sydney Ducks' in hour-long proceedings that came to be known as 'kangaroo trials.' Along with Australians, Chinese – the most populous group in California by 1860 – were at the receiving end of misplaced resentment.

Joshua Norton arrived in San Francisco from South Africa with $40,000 in 1849, quickly made and lost a fortune in Peruvian rice, and disappeared. He returned a decade later in theatrical military attire, proclaiming himself 'Emperor of the United States and Protector of Mexico.' For historical walking tours, see www.emperornortontour.com.

Chinatown's Gold Mountain

Within a year of the 1849 Gold Rush, Chinatown was already established in San Francisco – better known in Cantonese as 'Gold Mountain.' At first Chinatown wasn't exclusively Chinese at all, but a bachelor community of Mexican, American, European, African American and Chinese miners who bunked, prospected and caroused side by side. But when gold prices came crashing down with the discovery of gold in Australia, miners turned irrational resentments on resident Australians and Chinese. Australian lodging houses were burned to the ground, anti-Chinese riots broke out and Chinese land claims were rendered null and void. In 1870, San Francisco officially restricted housing and employment for anyone born in China.

The 1882 US Chinese Exclusion Act prevented new immigration from China, barred Chinese from citizenship until 1943 and spurred the passage of 100 parallel ordinances limiting rights for Japanese San Franciscans. Not coincidentally, anti-Chinese laws served the needs of local magnates looking for cheap labor to build the first cross-country railroad. With little other choice of legitimate employment, an estimated 12,000 Chinese laborers did the dangerous work of dynamiting rail tunnels through the Sierra Nevada.

May 1869

The Golden Spike completes the first transcontinental railroad. The news travels via San Franciscan David Brooks' invention, the telegraph.

1870

William Hammond Hall sees the development of Golden Gate Park through to completion from 1870 to 1887.

1882

The US Chinese Exclusion Act suspends new immigration from China; these racially targeted laws remain until 1943.

April 18, 1906

A massive earthquake levels entire blocks of SF in 47 seconds, setting off fires that rage for three days. Survivors start rebuilding while the town is still smoldering.

After the 1906 fire, city officials planned to oust Chinese residents altogether and develop the prime property of Chinatown, but the Chinese consulate and rifle-toting Chinatown merchants persuaded the city otherwise. Today Chinatown is a major economic boon to the city as one of its top tourist attractions, yet many residents scrape by on less than $10,000 a year – not exactly a Gold Mountain. Upwardly mobile residents tend to leave Chinatown, new arrivals move in, and the cycle begins anew.

Keeping the West Wild

As gold, silver and railroad money flowed into San Francisco, the city grew. It didn't exactly blossom at first, though – public works were completely neglected, and heavily populated sections of the city were mired in muck. Eventually the debris-choked waterfront filled in and streets were graded and paved. As soon as Andrew Hallidie's invention of the cable car made the formidable crag accessible in 1873, Nob Hill sprouted mansions for millionaires, including the 'Big Four' railroad barons: Leland Stanford, Collis P Huntington, Mark Hopkins and Charles Crocker. Wherever there was green in the city, real-estate speculators saw greenbacks, cleverly repackaging even flea-plagued cattle pastures of the Mission District and Cow Hollow as desirable residential districts. The Gold Rush was officially over; the land rush was on.

Naturalist John Muir came through San Francisco in 1868, but quickly left with a shudder for Yosemite. The early environmentalist organization he founded, the Sierra Club, would eventually find its major backers in San Francisco. The unspoiled wilderness that Muir and his organization successfully lobbied to protect includes one of San Francisco's most popular escapes: Muir Woods.

San Franciscans determined to preserve the city's natural splendors pushed to establish the city's first park in 1867, when squatters were paid to vacate the area now known as Buena Vista Park. With a mandate from San Francisco voters to transform sand dunes into a vast city park, tenacious engineer William Hammond Hall saw the development of Golden Gate Park through to completion from 1870 to 1887 – despite developers' best attempts to scuttle park plans in favor of casinos, amusement parks, resorts, racetracks and an igloo village. Populist millionaire Adolph Sutro decided that every working stiff should be able to escape Downtown tenements for the sand dunes and sunsets of Ocean Beach, accessible for a nickel on his public railway. Sutro's idea proved wildly popular, and by way of thanks, he was elected mayor in 1894.

GOLDEN GATE PARK

William Hammond Hall briefly quit his job building Golden Gate Park in 1886 over proposals to convert the park into a racetrack lined with tract homes. When a casino and carnival were established in the park for the 1893 Midwinter's Fair, Hammond Hall fought to get the park returned to its intended purpose.

Double Disaster

By the 20th century, San Francisco had earned a reputation for scandal, corruption, earthquakes and other calamities – none of it good for

1910

Angel Island opens as the West Coast immigration station. Over 30 years, 175,000 arrivals from Asia are subjected to months or years of interrogation and prison-like conditions.

1913

California's Alien Land Law prohibits property ownership by Asians, including Japanese, Koreans and Indians. Lawyer Juichi Soyeda immediately files suit; he wins in 1952, 23 years after his death.

1915

Postquake San Francisco hosts the Panama–Pacific International Exposition. The city cements its reputation as a showplace for new technology, outlandish ideas and the arts.

1927

After a year of tinkering, 21-year-old Philo Farnsworth transmits the first successful TV broadcast of...a straight line.

business. To redirect attention from its notorious waterfront fleshpots to its comparatively underexposed urban assets, the city commissioned Chicago architect Daniel Burnham to give San Francisco a beaux arts Civic Center to rival Baron Haussmann's Paris. This elaborate plan had just been finalized when disaster struck ... twice.

On April 18, 1906, a quake estimated at a terrifying 7.8 to 8.3 on today's Richter scale struck the city. In 47 seconds, San Franciscans discovered just how many corners had been cut on government contracts. Unreinforced buildings collapsed, including City Hall. The sole functioning downtown water source was a fountain donated to the city by opera prodigy Lotta Crabtree. Assembly lines were formed to haul buckets of water from Lotta's Fountain, but the water couldn't reach the crest of steep hills fast enough. Nob Hill mansions with priceless Old Master and impressionist art collections were reduced to ashes; inhabitants were lucky to escape with their lives. Survivors fled to Potrero Hill and Buena Vista Park, and for three days watched their city and its dreams of grandeur go up in smoke.

Built soon after the earthquake in 1907, the Great American Music Hall shows the unabashed flamboyance of post-earthquake San Francisco. Carved gilt decor recalls the city's Gold Rush heyday, and scantily clad frescoed figures hint at other possible backstage entertainments – this music hall was also a bordello.

The Show Must Go On

Yet San Francisco had learned one thing through 50 years of booms and busts: how to stage a comeback. All but one of the city's 20 historic theaters had been completely destroyed by the earthquake and fire, but theater tents were soon set up amid the rubble. The smoke wafting across makeshift stages wasn't a special effect when surviving entertainers began marathon performances to lift the city's spirits. Opera divas sang their hearts out to San Francisco gratis – though the world's most famous tenor, Enrico Caruso, vowed never to return to the city after the quake jolted him out of bed at the Palace Hotel. Soprano Luisa Tetrazzini ditched New York's Metropolitan Opera to return to San Francisco and sang on Market St to an audience of 250,000 – virtually every surviving San Franciscan.

San Franciscans rose to the occasion, and rebuilt their city at an astounding rate of 15 buildings a day. In a show of popular priorities, San Francisco's theaters were rebuilt long before City Hall's grandiose Civic Center was completed. Most of the Barbary Coast had gone down in flames, so the theater scene and most red-light entertainments decamped to the Tenderloin, where they remain.

But San Francisco's greatest comeback performance was the 1915 Panama–Pacific International Exposition, held in celebration of the completion of the Panama Canal. Earthquake rubble was used to fill 635 marshy acres of the Marina, where famous architects built elaborate pavilions showcasing San Francisco's Pacific Rim connections, exotic foods and forward thinking. Crowds gasped at displays of the latest, greatest inventions, including the world's first steam locomotive,

1934

A West Coast longshoremen's strike ends with 34 strikers and sympathizers shot by police. A mass funeral and citywide strike follow; longshoremen win historic concessions.

1937

After four years of dangerous labor in treacherous riptides, the Golden Gate Bridge is complete.

February 1942

Executive Order 9066 mandates internment of 120,000 Japanese Americans. The Japanese American Citizens League files civil rights claims.

1957

City Lights wins a landmark ruling against book banning over the publication of Allen Ginsberg's *Howl*, and free speech and free spirits enjoy a reprieve from McCarthyism.

a color printing press and early typewriter (at 14 tons, not exactly a laptop). When the party ended, Bernard Maybeck's Palace of Fine Arts plaster folly was the one temporary exhibit San Franciscans couldn't bear to see torn down, so the structure was recast in concrete.

The Left Coast

San Francisco's port thrived in 1934, but local longshoremen pulling long hours unloading heavy cargo for scant pay didn't see the upside of the shipping boom. When they protested dangerous working conditions, shipping tycoons sought dockworkers elsewhere – only to discover San Francisco's longshoremen had coordinated their strike with 35,000 workers along the West Coast. After 83 days, police and the National Guard broke the strike, killing 34 strikers and wounding 40 sympathizers. Public sympathy forced concessions from shipping magnates. Coit Tower frescoes completed in 1934 capture the pro-worker sentiment that swept the city – known henceforth as America's 'Left Coast.'

When WWII brought a shipbuilding boom to town, women and 40,000 African American arrivals claimed key roles in San Francisco's workforce. But with misplaced anxiety about possible attacks from the Pacific, Japanese San Franciscans and Japantown became convenient targets for public animosity. Two months after the attack on Pearl Harbor, President Franklin D Roosevelt signed Executive Order 9066, ordering the relocation of 120,000 Japanese Americans to internment camps. The San Francisco–based Japanese American Citizens League (JACL) immediately challenged the grounds for internment and lobbied tirelessly for more than 40 years to overturn the executive order, gain symbolic reparations for internees, and restore the community's standing with a formal letter of apology signed by President George HW Bush in 1988. By setting key legal precedents from the 1940s onward, JACL paved the way for the 1964 Civil Rights Act.

Beats: Free Speech, Free Spirits

Members of the armed services dismissed from service for homosexuality and other 'subversive' behavior during WWII were discharged onto the streets of San Francisco, as if that would teach them a lesson. Instead, the new arrivals found themselves at home in the low-rent, laissez-faire neighborhoods of North Beach and the Haight. So when the rest of the country took a sharp right turn with McCarthyism in the 1950s, rebels and romantics headed for San Francisco – including Jack Kerouac. By the time *On the Road* was published in 1957 chronicling his westward journey, the motley crowd of writers, artists, dreamers and unclassifiable characters Kerouac called 'the mad ones' had found their way to like-minded San Francisco.

Top 5 for Beats

- *City Lights (North Beach)*
- *Beat Museum (North Beach)*
- *Vesuvio (North Beach)*
- *Li Po (Chinatown)*
- *Bob Kaufman Alley (North Beach)*

1959

Mayor George Christopher authorizes measures against gay citizens. WWII veteran José Sarria responds by becoming America's first openly gay man to run for public office – in drag.

January 1966

The Trips Festival is organized by techno-futurist Stewart Brand and features author Ken Kesey, the Grateful Dead, Janis Joplin, Native American activists and Hells Angels.

October 1966

In Oakland, Huey Newton and Bobby Seale found the Black Panther Party for Self-Defense, demanding 'Land, Bread, Housing, Education, Clothing, Justice and Peace.'

January 1967

The Summer of Love kicks off with the Human Be-In, with draft cards used as rolling papers, free Grateful Dead gigs and Allen Ginsberg naked, as usual.

San Francisco didn't always take kindly to the nonconformists derisively referred to in the press as 'beatniks,' and police and poets were increasingly at odds on the streets of North Beach. Officers tried to fine 'beatnik chicks' for wearing sandals, only to be mercilessly taunted in verse by self-described African American Jewish voodoo anarchist and legendary street-corner Beat poet Bob Kaufman. Poet Lawrence Ferlinghetti and bookstore manager Shigeyoshi Murao of City Lights were arrested for 'willfully and lewdly' printing Allen Ginsberg's magnificent, incendiary epic poem *Howl*. But artistic freedom prevailed in 1957, when City Lights won its landmark ruling against book banning.

The kindred Beat spirits Ginsberg described in *Howl* as 'angelheaded hipsters burning for the ancient heavenly connection' experimented with art, radical politics, marijuana and one another, defying 1950s social-climbing conventions and Senator Joe McCarthy's alarmist call to weed out 'communists in our midst.' When McCarthy's House Un-American Activities Committee (HUAC) convened in San Francisco in 1960 to expose alleged communists, UC Berkeley students organized a disruptive, sing-along sit-in at City Hall. After police turned fire hoses on the protesters, thousands of San Franciscans rallied and HUAC split town, never to return. It was official: the '60s had begun.

Best Ways to Revive the Summer of Love

Give a free concert on Haight St or give freely to any local nonprofit

Commune with nature in Golden Gate Park

Walk on the wild side of hippie history on the Haight Flashback walking tour

Read '60s manifestos at Bound Together Anarchist Book Collective

Write your own manifesto, fueled by hemp-milk lattes at Coffee to the People

Flower Power

San Francisco was a testing ground for freedom of expression in the 1960s, as comedian Lenny Bruce uttered the F-word on stage and burlesque dancer Carol Doda bared it all for titillated audiences in North Beach clubs. But neither jokes nor striptease would pop the last button of rigid 1950s social norms – no, that was a job for the CIA. In a pronounced lapse in screening judgment, the CIA hired local writer Ken Kesey to test psychoactive drugs intended to create the ultimate soldier. Instead, they inspired Kesey to write the novel *One Flew Over the Cuckoo's Nest,* drive psychedelic busloads of Merry Pranksters across country, and introduce San Francisco to LSD and the Grateful Dead at the legendary Acid Tests.

After the Civil Rights movement anything seemed possible, and for a while it seemed that the freaky force of free thinking would stop the unpopular Vietnam War. At the January 14, 1967 Human Be-In in Golden Gate Park, trip-master Timothy Leary urged a crowd of 20,000 to dream a new American dream and 'turn on, tune in, drop out.' Free music rang out in the streets, free food was provided by the Diggers, free LSD was circulated by Owsley Stanley, free crash pads were all over the Haight and free love transpired on some very dubious free mattresses. For the duration of the Summer of Love – weeks, months, even a year, depending who you talk to and how stoned they were at the time – it seemed possible to make love, not war.

1969

The first computer link is established between Stanford Research Institute and UCLA via ARPANET and an unsolicited group message is sent across the network: email and spam are born.

November 1969

Native American activists reclaim the abandoned island of Alcatraz as reparation for broken treaties. The occupation lasts 19 months, until FBI agents forcibly oust the activists.

April 1977

The Apple II is introduced in SF at the first West Coast Computer Faire and stuns the crowd with its computing speed (1MHz).

1977

Harvey Milk becomes the first openly gay man elected to US public office. Milk sponsors a gay-rights bill and trend-setting 'pooper-scooper' ordinance before his murder by opponent Dan White.

But a chill soon settled over San Francisco, and for once it wasn't the afternoon fog. Civil rights hero Martin Luther King Jr was assassinated on April 8, 1968, followed by the fatal shooting of Robert Kennedy on June 5 after he'd won California's presidential primary. Radicals worldwide called for revolution, and separatist groups like Oakland's Black Panther Party for Self-Defense took up arms. Meanwhile, recreational drug-taking was turning into a thankless career for many, a distinct itch in the nether regions was making the rounds of Haight squats, and still more busloads of teenage runaways were arriving in the ill-equipped, wigged-out Haight. Haight Ashbury Free Clinic helped with the rehabbing and the itching, but disillusionment seemed incurable when Hell's Angels beat protestors in Berkeley and turned on the crowd at a free Rolling Stones concert at Altamont.

Many idealists headed 'back to the land' in the bucolic North Bay, jumpstarting California's organic farm movement. A dark streak emerged among those who remained, including young Charles Manson, the Symbionese Liberation Army (better known post-1974 as Patty Hearst's kidnappers) and an evangelical egomaniac named Jim Jones, who would oblige 900 followers to commit mass suicide in 1978. By the time Be-In LSD supplier Stanley was released from a three-year jail term in 1970, the party seemed to be over. But in the Castro, it was just getting started.

Pride

By the 1970s, San Francisco's gay community was fed up with police raids, done with hetero Haight squats and ready for music with an actual beat. In 1959, after an opponent accused then-mayor George Christopher of allowing San Francisco to become 'the national headquarters of the organized homosexuals,' Christopher authorized crackdowns on gay bars and started a blacklist of gay citizens.

Never one to be harassed or upstaged, WWII veteran and drag star José Sarria became the first openly gay man to run for public office in 1962, on a platform to end police harassment of gay San Franciscans. He won 5600 votes. Undaunted, he declared himself Absolute Empress of San Francisco, the widow and true heir of Emperor Norton. When local media echoed the Empress' criticism of the continuing raids, police crackdowns stopped – a feat not achieved for years elsewhere, until New York's 1969 Stonewall protests.

By the mid-1970s, the rainbow flag was flying high over gay businesses and homes in the out-and-proud Castro, and the sexual revolution was in full swing at gay clubs and bathhouses on Polk St and in SoMa. The Castro was triumphant when Castro camera-store owner Harvey Milk was elected city Supervisor, becoming the nation's first openly gay elected official – but as Milk himself eerily predicted, his time in office would be cut short by an act of extremist violence. Dan White,

PROTEST

On November 20, 1969, 79 Native American activists defied Coast Guard blockades to symbolically reclaim Alcatraz as native land. Hundreds of supporters joined the protest, until FBI raids ousted the protestors on June 11, 1971. Public support for the protesters strengthened self-rule for Native territories, signed into law by Richard Nixon.

November 1978

After moving his People's Temple from SF to Guyana, Jim Jones orders the murders of a congressman and four journalists, and mass suicide of 900 followers.

1981

The first cases of AIDS are identified. The disease has since taken 30 million lives, but early intervention in SF instituted key prevention measures and set global treatment standards.

1989

Hundreds of sea lions haul out on the yacht slips near Pier 39. State law and wildlife officials grant them squatters' rights, and the beach bums become San Francisco mascots.

October 17, 1989

The Loma Prieta earthquake hits 6.9 on the Richter scale; a freeway in SF and a Bay Bridge section collapse in 15 seconds, killing 41.

a washed-up politician hyped on Hostess Twinkies, fatally shot Milk and then-mayor George Moscone at City Hall in 1978. The charge was reduced to manslaughter due to the infamous 'Twinkie Defense' faulting the ultrasweet junk food, sparking an outpouring of public outrage dubbed the 'White Riot.' White was deeply disturbed, and committed suicide a year after his 1984 release.

By then San Francisco had another problem. A strange illness began to appear at local hospitals, and it seemed to be hitting the gay community especially hard. The first cases of AIDS reported in San Francisco were mistakenly referred to as GRID (Gay-Related Immune Deficiency), and a social stigma became attached to the virus. But San Francisco health providers and gay activists rallied to establish global standards for care and prevention, with vital early HIV/AIDS health initiatives funded not through federal agencies but with tireless local efforts – the Empress herself organized pioneering fundraisers. Yet unmarried same-sex partners had no legal standing to make lifesaving medical decisions.

Civil rights organizations, religious institutions and GLBT organizations increasingly popped the question: why couldn't same-sex couples get married too? Early backing came from the Japanese American Citizens League, which publicly endorsed marriage for same-sex couples as a civil right in 1994. Just 45 days after taking office in 2004, San Francisco mayor Gavin Newsom authorized same-sex weddings in San Francisco. The first couple to be married were Phyllis Lyon and Del Martin, a San Francisco couple who had spent 52 years together. California courts ultimately voided their and 4036 other San Francisco same-sex marriage contracts, but Lyon and Martin weren't dissuaded: they married again on June 18, 2008, with Mayor Newsom personally officiating. Martin passed away two months later at age 83, her wife by her side.

California courts struck down laws prohibiting same-sex marriage as law as unconstitutional in 2010. Upon appeal, the US Supreme Court upheld California's state ruling in July 2015, effectively legalizing same-sex marriage nationwide. In San Francisco, same-sex couples are once again getting hitched at City Hall – some for the second or third time to the same person, without ever getting divorced.

Best Ways to Show Gay Pride

- *Join the Pride Parade*
- *Get introduced to fabulous, fearless pioneers at GLBT Historical Society*
- *Peruse petitions at Human Rights Campaign*
- *Binge-watch movies from around the globe at San Francisco LGBTQ Film Festival*
- *Come out and play in the Mission, Castro and SoMa*

San Francisco 3.0

Industry dwindled steadily in San Francisco after WWII, as Oakland's port accommodated container ships and San Francisco's Presidio military base was deactivated. But onetime military tech contractors found work in a stretch of scrappy firms south of San Francisco, an area known today as Silicon Valley. When a company based in a South Bay garage called Hewlett-Packard introduced the 9100A 'computing genie' in 1968, a generation of unconventional thinkers and tinkerers took note.

March 2000

After the NASDAQ index peaks at double its value a year earlier, the dot-com bubble pops. Share prices drop dramatically, and the 'dot-bomb' closes businesses across SF within a month.

2003

Republican Arnold Schwarzenegger is elected governor of California. Schwarzenegger breaks party ranks on environmental issues and wins 2007 re-election.

2004

Google's IPO raises a historic $1.67 billion at $85 per share. By 2015, shares were worth more than seven times that amount and the company's worth had reached $368 billion.

February 2004

Defying a Californian ban, SF mayor Gavin Newsom licenses 4037 same-sex marriages. Courts declare the marriages void but the civil rights challenge stands.

Ads breathlessly gushed that Hewlett-Packard's 'light' (40lb) machine could 'take on roots of a fifth-degree polynomial, Bessel functions, elliptic integrals and regression analysis' – all for the low, low price of $4900 (about $29,000 today). Consumers didn't know what to do with such a computer, until its potential was explained in simple terms by Stewart Brand, an LSD tester for the CIA with Ken Kesey and organizer of the first Trips Festival in 1966. In his 1969 *Whole Earth Catalog*, Brand reasoned that the technology governments used to run countries could empower ordinary people. That same year, University of California, Los Angeles, professor Len Kleinrock sent the first rudimentary email from his computer to another at Stanford. The message he typed was 'L,' then 'O,' then 'G' – at which point the computer crashed.

The next wave of California techies was determined to create a personal computer that could compute and communicate without crashing. When 21-year-old Steve Jobs and Steve Wozniak introduced the Apple II at San Francisco's West Coast Computer Faire in 1977, techies were awed by the memory (4KB of RAM!) and the microprocessor speed (1MHz!). The Mac II originally retailed for the equivalent today of $4300 (or for 48KB of RAM, more than twice that amount) – a staggering investment for what seemed like a glorified calculator/typewriter. Even if machines could talk to one another, pundits reasoned, what would they talk about?

A trillion web pages and a couple of million mobile apps later, it turns out machines have plenty to communicate. By the mid-1990s, the dot-com industry boomed in SoMa warehouses, as start-up ventures rushed to put news, politics, fashion, and yes, sex online. But when venture capital funding dried up, multimillion-dollar sites shriveled into online oblivion. The paper fortunes of the dot-com boom disappeared on one NASDAQ-plummeting day, March 10, 2000, leaving San Francisco service-sector employees and 26-year-old vice-presidents alike without any immediate job prospects. City dot-com revenues vanished; a 1999 FBI probe revealed that a windfall ended up in the pockets of real-estate developers. Today San Francisco is again booming with start-ups aiming to succeed just like San Francisco–based Twitter, Pinterest and Instagram – and just south of the city, Facebook, LinkedIn, YouTube, Apple, Google, Yahoo! and more.

Meanwhile, inside shiny new glass towers at SoMa's Mission Bay, biotech start-ups are putting down roots and yielding research. Biotech is nothing new here: since Genentech was founded over beer at a San Francisco bar in 1976, the company has cloned human insulin and introduced the hepatitis B vaccine. California voters approved a $3 billion bond measure in 2004 for stem cell research, and by 2008 California had become the nation's biggest funder of stem cell research. With so many global health crises demanding researchers' attention and funding, many cures still seem a distant, if not impossible, dream – but if history is any indication, the impossible is almost certain to happen in San Francisco.

Top 5 for Trippy Technology

- *Exploratorium (Fisherman's Wharf)*
- *SFMOMA (SoMa)*
- *Audium (Japantown)*
- *The Interval (Fort Mason)*
- *Internet Archive (Richmond)*

2010

After SF couples file suit, California courts declare laws prohibiting same-sex marriage unconstitutional.

2014

The San Francisco Giants win their third World Series title in five years. 'Fear the Beard' and 'Rally Thong' become SF cheers.

2015

The US Supreme Court upholds the same-sex marriage ruling of 2010, making same-sex marriage legal nationwide.

2016

San Francisco aims to become a zero-waste city by 2020, and to that end mandates citywide composting and bans plastic bags.

Local Cuisine & Drinks

Two secret ingredients have transformed this small city into a global culinary capital: dirt and competition. Almost anything grows in the fertile farmland around San Francisco, and rocky hillsides yield fine wines in nearby Sonoma and Napa. Add Pacific seafood and coastal pasture-raised meats, and it seems like a no-fail recipe for a feast. But chefs need to work even harder to stand out in San Francisco, where everyone has access to top-notch ingredients, and there's about one restaurant for every 227 people – more than anywhere else in North America, and twice as many as in New York. San Franciscans grow their own food in 38 official community gardens (with dozens more proposed) and renegade rooftop farms across town. Mock if you must, but people have been known to move to SF for the food (ahem).

History

San Francisco is famous for its sourdough bread. The most famous 'mother dough' in town dates back to 1849, when baker Isidore Boudin hit on a combination of wild yeast and bacteria dubbed *Lactobacillus sanfranciscensis* – and it's been kept alive ever since.

Before San Francisco joined the United States, it belonged to Mexico, which established NorCal ranching and farming traditions. Early arrivals to California's Gold Rush came from around the Pacific Rim, and since most were men not accustomed to cooking for themselves, they relied on makeshift restaurants. SF's cross-cultural cravings began with forty-niner favorites: Mexican tamales, Chinese chow mein, local oysters and French wines.

Immigrant ingenuity is the hallmark of San Francisco food. Between hot meals, miners survived on chocolate bars, invented in San Francisco by Domingo Ghirardelli. Before the first Italian restaurant in the USA opened in 1886 at North Beach, Italian fishermen cooked up vats of *cioppino* (seafood stew) dockside. The 1942–64 US Bracero Program importing Mexican agricultural labor brought local variations on Mexican staples – including megameals wrapped in flour tortillas called burritos.

After the 1960s, many disillusioned idealists concluded that the revolution was not about to be served on a platter – but chef Alice Waters

UNCONVENTIONAL DINING

Pickled wildflowers, crispy trout cheeks, beer ice cream: San Francisco restaurant menus are plenty unconventional by US standards. But in the interests of fair pay and public health – not to mention SF's restaurant lobby – San Francisco strictly limits off-license food businesses. Underground dining clubs in private homes are rare, street food vendors must post city health ratings, and pop-ups are held in licensed facilities and/or hosted by licensed caterers.

But that doesn't mean you have to leave the cooking to the professionals – DIY opportunities abound here. To satisfy adventurous appetites, try collecting your own dinner on SF beaches with Sea Foraging Adventures (p278), sharpen your knife skills at 18 Reasons (p168), learn to blow sugar from chocolatier Michael Recchiuti at theLab (p154), and harvest ingredients for Outstanding in the Field (p26) feasts in secret sea caves.

EVAN RICH: CHEF & RESTAURATEUR

East Coast v West Coast

I was born and raised in Queens and I thought the New York restaurant scene had it all. San Francisco proved me wrong...but I had to eat at Chez Panisse twice to really understand Californian cuisine. The first time I thought, right, it's basically a classic rustic French approach to food. Then after being here a year, I went back to Chez Panisse and I recognized all the subtleties I'd missed, the way each preparation highlighted the varietal characteristics of a particular ingredient. That takes finesse.

Getting Fresh in SF

Working with Daniel [Patterson, at Coi] I learned there's a life force, an energy to produce when it's freshly picked, so you have to think fast to maximize that flavor. Ideally I'd like to serve a dish made with ingredients harvested within a couple hours – we're working on planting a kitchen garden down the block.

Innovation Served Nightly

We're around the corner from SFJazz Center, so yeah, the pressure is on to improvise with the best. Our neighborhood regulars are from Apple and Google, technology leaders who trust us to innovate but also execute at a certain level. We can't afford to have an off-night here or we'll hear about it from our customers all over Twitter and Yelp – because they invented that stuff.

Evan Rich is co-chef/owner with spouse and fellow chef Sarah Rich of Rich Table (p187), 2013 James Beard nominee for Best New Restaurant in America.

thought otherwise. In 1971 she opened Chez Panisse (p215) in a converted house in Berkeley, with the then-radical notion of highlighting the ultrafresh flavors of the Bay Area's seasonal, sustainably produced bounty – and diners tasted the difference for themselves. Today, Waters' call for good, clean, fair food has become a worldwide Slow Food manifesto – and a rallying call for Bay Area chefs like Evan and Sarah Rich.

SF's Top 3 Food Trends

Dim Sum

Since one out of three San Franciscans has Asian roots, SF's go-to comfort foods aren't just burgers and pizza – though you'll find plenty of those – but also kimchi, tandoori, and above all, dim sum. Dim sum is Cantonese for what's known in Mandarin as *xiao che* (small eats); some also call it yum cha (drink tea).

Traditionally, waitstaff roll carts past your table with steaming baskets of dumplings, platters of garlicky greens and, finally, crispy sweet sesame balls. But in SF's new upscale dim sum eateries like Dragon Beaux (p205) and Hakkasan (p90), you'll find succulent duck dumplings worthy of fine-dining tasting menus. Expect a queue for dim sum brunches along Geary St and in Chinatown, and for gourmet *bao* (buns) at the Chairman food truck.

Top 5 Dim Sum

Chairman food truck (Off the Grid; Marina)

Dragon Beaux (the Richmond)

City View (Chinatown)

Hakkasan (Downtown)

Lai Hong Lounge (Chinatown)

Vegetable-Centric Dining

To all you beleaguered vegetarians, accustomed to eating out at places where the only non-animal dish is some unspeakable vegetarian lasagne: you're in San Francisco now. With the most farmers markets of any metropolitan area in the US (30 and counting), you're not about to run out of veggie options anytime soon.

While fine dining chefs elsewhere stake their reputations on steak, California-grown fruits and vegetables are not side dishes to Bay Area

MARTINI OR MARTINEZ?

Legend has it that the martini was invented in the 1880s when a boozehound walked into an SF bar and demanded something to tide him on the bay crossing to Martinez. The original was made with vermouth, gin, bitters, lemon, maraschino cherry and ice, though by the 1950s the recipe was reduced to gin with vermouth vapors and an olive or a twist. Today Comstock Saloon (p125) offers the original Martinez, and Aub Zam Zam (p191) the Sinatra Rat Pack version.

chefs, but tasting-menu highlights. Even nonvegetarians opt for fine-dining at all-vegetarian Greens (p64) and the vegetarian prix fixe at French Laundry, Chez Panisse and Coi (p121) – and meat is merely a side dish at Al's Place (p158). Salad isn't just for diet lunches anymore – it's a main gourmet attraction at Al's, Blue Barn Gourmet (p65), Souvla (p187) and Burma Superstar (p205).

Top 5 for Local & Sustainable Seafood

- *Benu (SoMa)*
- *Hog Island Oyster Company (Ferry Building)*
- *Ichi Sushi (Mission)*
- *Al's Place (Mission)*
- *Tataki (Noe Valley)*

Sustainable Seafood

The Pacific offers a haul of seafood to San Francisco diners, but there's trouble in these waters: some species are nearing extinction, throwing the local aquaculture off balance. SF's top seafood chefs are taking action to avoid overfishing, opting for line-caught fish and locally farmed oysters and caviar. To help diners identify sustainable options, Monterey Bay Aquarium has produced a free Seafood Watch app (www.montereybayaquarium.org/cr/seafoodwatch.aspx).

Drink Specialties

Wine

Wine has been the local drink ever since Mission Solano was established in Sonoma with acres of vineyards – more than strictly necessary for communion wine. Some local vines survived federal scrutiny during Prohibition, on the grounds that the grapes were needed for sacramental wines back east – a bootlegging bonanza. Today many of the USA's best wines are produced within two hours of the city, including excellent Cabernet, Zinfandel, Syrah, Pinot Noir, Viognier, Chardonnay, Sauvignon Blanc and sparkling wines.

Top 5 Tasting Room Experiences

- *Bartholomew Park Winery (Day Trips)*
- *Frog's Leap (Day Trips)*
- *Hess Collection (Day Trips)*
- *Robert Sinskey (Day Trips)*
- *Sutton Cellars (Dogpatch)*

Beer

Blowing off steam took on new meaning during the Gold Rush, when entrepreneurs trying to keep up with the demand for drink started brewing beer at higher temperatures. The result was a full, rich flavor and such powerful effervescence that when a keg was tapped, a mist would rise like steam. San Francisco's Anchor Brewing Company has made its signature amber ale this way since 1896. Other favorite local brews include Trumer Pils, Sierra Nevada Pale Ale, Boont Amber Ale and 21st Amendment's Hell or High Watermelon Wheat.

Historic Cocktails

Cocktails have appeared on San Francisco happy-hour menus since its Barbary Coast days, when they were used to sedate sailors and drag them onto outbound ships. Today SF bartenders are reviving time-honored traditions: ladling rum punch from crystal bowls, topping Pisco sours with traditional foamy egg whites as though no one had ever heard of veganism or salmonella, and apparently still trying to knock sailors cold with Old Fashioneds made with bourbon, bitters, zest and vengeance.

Literary San Francisco

San Francisco has more writers than any other US city, and hoards three times as many library books as the national average. But the truth of San Francisco is even stranger than its fiction: where else could poetry fight the law and win? Yet that's exactly what happened in the 1957 landmark anti-censorship ruling for People v Ferlinghetti. Though it may seem anachronistic here in the capital of new technology, San Franciscans continue to buy more books per capita than other US cities. Fellow bibliophiles aren't hard to find here – they're trolling member-supported book collectives along 24th Street's Paper Trail.

Required Reading

Any self-respecting SF bookshelf hosts plenty of poetry (Beat authors obligatory), a graphic novel, nonfiction essays about the San Francisco scene and at least one novel by a Bay Area author.

Poetry

San Francisco's Kenneth Rexroth popularized haiku here back in the 1950s, and San Franciscans still enjoy nothing more than a few well-chosen words. When the city has you waxing poetic, hit an open mic in the Mission. Key titles:

➡ *Howl and Other Poems* (Allen Ginsberg) Each line of Ginsberg's epic title poem is an ecstatic improvised mantra, chronicling the waking dreams of the Beat generation and taking a stand against postwar conformity. Publisher Lawrence Ferlinghetti was taken to court for 'willfully and lewdly' publishing *Howl* – resulting in a landmark free-speech triumph.

➡ *Time and Materials* (Robert Hass) Each word in these Pulitzer Prize–winning poems by the Berkeley-based US poet laureate is as essential and uplifting as a rivet in the Golden Gate Bridge.

➡ *A Coney Island of the Mind* (Lawrence Ferlinghetti) This slim 1958 collection by San Francisco's Beat poet laureate is an indispensable doorstop for the imagination.

➡ *Native Tongue* (Alejandro Murguía) San Francisco's newest poet laureate is a master interpreter of San Franciscan behavior, rhythmic performance poet and charismatic co-founder of Mission Cultural Center.

Fiction

Many San Franciscans seem like characters in a novel – and after a few days here, you'll swear you've seen Armistead Maupin's corn-fed Castro newbies, Dashiell Hammett's dangerous redheads, Philip K Dick's sci-fi subversives and Amy Tan's American-born daughters explaining slang to Chinese-speaking moms. Key titles:

➡ *Tales of the City* (Armistead Maupin) The 1976 *San Francisco Chronicle* serial follows classic San Francisco characters. See also the miniseries version.

➡ *The Joy Luck Club* (Amy Tan) The stories of four Chinese-born women and their American-born daughters are woven into a textured tale of immigration and aspiration in San Francisco's Chinatown.

Best for Readings

- *City Lights (North Beach)*
- *Booksmith (the Haight)*
- *San Francisco Main Library (Civic Center)*
- *Adobe Books (Mission)*
- *Verdi Club (Mission)*

Best for Spoken Word

- *Yerba Buena Center for the Arts (SoMa)*
- *Public Works (Downtown)*
- *Make-Out Room (the Mission)*
- *Amnesia (the Mission)*
- *Marsh (the Mission)*

➡ *The Man in the High Castle* (Philip K Dick) The Berkeley sci-fi author presents a trippy parallel-universe scenario: imagine San Francisco c 1962, if the US had lost WWII to the Axis powers and California became a Japanese-German Colony. But there's a twist: an underground novel begins circulating, describing a world where California is free.

Nonfiction & Memoir

People-watching rivals reading as a preferred San Francisco pastime, and close observation of antics that would seem bizarre anywhere but here pays off in stranger-than-fiction nonfiction – hence Hunter S Thompson's gonzo journalism and Joan Didion's core-shaking truth-telling. Key titles:

➡ *Slouching Towards Bethlehem* (Joan Didion) Like hot sun through San Francisco summer fog, Didion's 1968 essays burn through the hippie haze to reveal glassy-eyed teenagers adrift in the Summer of Love.

➡ *On the Road* (Jack Kerouac) The book Kerouac banged out on one long scroll of paper in a San Francisco attic over a couple of sleepless months of 1951 shook America awake.

➡ *Hell's Angels: A Strange and Terrible Saga* (Hunter S Thompson) This spare-no-details account of the outlaw Bay Area motorcycle club invented gonzo journalism and scandalized the nation when it was published in 1966.

➡ *The Electric Kool-Aid Acid Test* (Tom Wolfe) His groovy style may seem dated, but Wolfe had extraordinary presence of mind to capture SF in the '60s with Ken Kesey, the Merry Pranksters, the Grateful Dead and Hell's Angels.

➡ *Cool Gray City* (Gary Kamiya) Longtime SF taxi driver Kamiya explores his 7x7-mile city block by block in this 2015 book, capturing 49 poetically true tales of San Francisco – an outlandish city 'only borrowed from the sea,' and audaciously reimagined each time the fog rolls back.

Best for Comics & Graphic Novels

- *Cartoon Art Museum gift shop (SoMa)*
- *Isotope (Hayes Valley)*
- *Kinokuniya Books & Stationery (Japantown)*
- *Alternative Press Expo (Month by Month)*
- *Bound Together Anarchist Book Collective (the Haight)*

Graphic Novels

Ambrose Bierce and Mark Twain set the San Francisco standard for sardonic wit, but recently Bay Area graphic novelists like R Crumb and Daniel Clowes have added a twist to this tradition with finely drawn, deadpan behavioral studies. Key titles:

➡ *Ghost World* (Daniel Clowes) The Oakland-based graphic novelist's sleeper hit follows recent high-school grads Enid and Rebecca as they make plans, make do, grow up and grow apart.

➡ *American Born Chinese* (Gene Yang) Chinese Monkey King fables are intricately interwoven with teenage tales of assimilation – no wonder this won the Eisner Award for best graphic novel, plus the Harvey comic-art award for SF cartoonist Lark Pien.

➡ *All Over Coffee* (Paul Madonna) The San Francisco–based artist combines watercolor landscapes of the city with stories that could only happen in these peculiar urban microclimates.

Best for 'Zines

- *Needles & Pens (the Mission)*
- *826 Valencia (the Mission)*
- *Adobe Books (the Mission)*
- *Bound Together Anarchist Book Collective (the Haight)*
- *The Magazine (Tenderloin)*

'Zines

The local 'zine scene has been the underground mother lode of riveting reading since the '70s brought punk, DIY spirit and V Vale's groundbreaking *RE/Search* to San Francisco. The most successful local 'zine of all, McSweeney's, is the initiative of Dave Eggers, who achieved first-person fame with *A Heartbreaking Work of Staggering Genius* and generously used the proceeds to found 826 Valencia, a nonprofit writing program for teens. McSweeney's also publishes an excellent map of literary San Francisco, so you can walk the talk.

Spoken Word

San Francisco's literary tradition doesn't just hang out on bookshelves. Beat authors like Kerouac freed up generations of open-mic monologuists from the tyranny of tales with morals and punctuation. Allen Ginsberg's ecstatic readings of *Howl* continue to inspire slam poets at Litquake (p22), and at open mics in the Mission, Tenderloin and North Beach.

Visual Arts

Art explodes from frames and jumps off the pedestal in San Francisco, where murals, street performances and impromptu sidewalk altars flow from alleyways right into galleries. Velvet ropes would only get in the way of SF's enveloping installations and interactive new-media art – often provocative, sometimes overwhelming, but never standoffish.

Media & Methods

San Francisco has some unfair artistic advantages: it's a photogenic city with a colorful past, with 150-year-old photography and painting traditions to prove it. Homegrown traditions of '50s Beat collage, '60s psychedelia, '70s punk, '80s graffiti, '90s skater graphics and 2000s new-media art keep San Francisco's art scene vibrant.

Photography

Pioneering 19th-century photographer Pirkle Jones saw expressive potential in California landscape photography, but it was SF native Ansel Adams' photos of Northern California's sublime wilds and his accounts of photography in Yosemite in the 1940s that would draw generations of camera-clutching visitors to San Francisco. Adams founded Group f/64 with pioneering street photographer Imogen Cunningham and still life master Edward Weston, who kept a studio in SF and made frequent visits from his permanent base in nearby Carmel.

Adams and Cunningham taught at San Francisco Art Institute alongside the definitive documentarian of the Great Depression, Dorothea Lange. Among her many poignant photographs are portraits of Californian migrant farm laborers and Japanese Americans forced to leave their San Francisco homes for WWII internment camps. Many of Lange's internment photographs conflicted with official propaganda and were impounded by the Army, not to be shown for 50 years.

After the censorship of her photographs, Lange co-founded the groundbreaking art photography magazine *Aperture* with Adams and fellow photographers in San Francisco. Today her legacy of cultural critique continues with the colorful Californian suburban dystopias of Larry Sultan and Todd Hido. *Aperture* still publishes, and SF Camerawork continues the proud San Franciscan tradition of boundary-pushing photography shows and publications.

Best for Photography

- *SFMOMA (Downtown)*
- *SF Camerawork (Civic Center)*
- *de Young Museum (Golden Gate Park)*
- *Fraenkel Gallery at 49 Geary (Union Square)*
- *Chinese Historical Society of America (Chinatown)*

Social Commentary

The 1930s social realist movement brought Mexican muralist Diego Rivera and vivid surrealist painter Frida Kahlo to San Francisco, where Rivera was invited to paint a cautionary fresco of California on the San Francisco Stock Exchange Lunch Club. In over a decade spent working on projects in the city, the modern art power couple inspired bold new approaches to public art in San Francisco. Starting in the 1970s, their larger-than-life figures and leftist leanings have been reprised in works by Mission muralistas, as seen on the Women's Building and along Balmy Alley.

The Depression-era Work Projects Administration (WPA) sponsored several SF muralists to create original works for the Rincon Annex Post Office, Coit Tower, Aquatic Park Bathhouse and Beach Chalet. When the

Best for Provocation

- *Catharine Clark Gallery (Potrero Hill)*
- *Luggage Store Gallery (Civic Center)*
- *Galería de la Raza (the Mission)*
- *Yerba Buena Center for the Arts (SoMa)*
- *Frankenart Mart (Golden Gate Park & the Avenues)*

murals at Rincon Post Office and Coit Tower turned out to be more radical than the government-sponsored arts program had anticipated, censors demanded changes before the murals could be unveiled. But the artworks outlasted the censors, and today are celebrated national landmarks.

Offsetting high-minded revolutionary art is gutsy, irreverent SF satire. Tony Labatt's 1970s video of disco balls dangling from his nether regions sums up SF's disco-era narcissism, while Lynn Hershman Leeson's performances as alter-ego Roberta Breitmore chronicled 1970s encounters with feminism, self-help and diet fads. San Francisco provocateur Enrique Chagoya serves comic relief for the banking-crisis era with his Warhol-esque 'Mergers, Acquisitions and Lentils' soup-cans at Electric Works.

Best for Inspired Abstraction

- *Haines Gallery at 49 Geary (Union Square)*
- *Hosfelt Gallery (Potrero)*
- *Gregory Lind Gallery at 49 Geary (Union Square)*
- *Eleanor Harwood Gallery (the Mission)*
- *Ratio 3 (the Mission)*

Abstract Thinking

Local art schools attracted major abstract expressionists during SF's vibrant postwar period, when Clyfford Still, David Park and Elmer Bischoff taught at the San Francisco Art Institute. Still and Park founded the misleadingly named Bay Area Figurative Art movement, an elemental style often associated with San Francisco painter Richard Diebenkorn's fractured, color-blocked landscapes. Diebenkorn influenced San Francisco pop artist Wayne Thiebaud, who tilted Sunset street grids into giddy abstract cityscapes.

High Concept, High Craft

San Francisco's peculiar dedication to craft and personal vision can get obsessive. Consider *The Rose,* the painting Jay DeFeo began in the 1950s and worked on for eight years, layering it with 2000lb of paint until a hole had to be cut in the wall of her apartment to forklift it out. Sculptor Ruth Asawa started weaving not with wool but metal in the 1950s, following a childhood behind barbed wire in Japanese American internment camps. Her legacy includes sculptures that look like jellyfish within onion domes within mushrooms, and Union Sq's beloved bronze San Francisco fountain. SF's most famous obsessive is Matthew Barney, who made his definitive debut at SFMOMA with *Cremaster Cycle* videos involving vats of Vaseline.

Best for Murals

- *San Francisco Art Institute's Diego Rivera Gallery (Russian Hill)*
- *Coit Tower (North Beach)*
- *WPA Murals at Rincon Annex (SoMa)*
- *Balmy Alley (the Mission)*
- *Clarion Alley (the Mission)*
- *Luggage Store Gallery (the Tenderloin)*

Street Smarts

With Balmy Alley murals as inspiration, SF skateboard decks and Clarion Alley garage doors were transformed in the 1990s with boldly outlined, oddly poignant graphics, dubbed 'Mission School' for their storytelling *muralista* sensibilities and graffiti-tag urgency. The Mission School's professor emeritus was the late Margaret Kilgallen, whose closely observed character studies blended hand-painted street signage, comic-book pathos and a miniaturist's attention to detail.

Clare Rojas expanded on these principles with urban folk-art wall paintings, featuring looming, clueless California grizzly bears and tiny, fierce girls in hoodies. Street-art-star Barry McGee paints piles of found bottles with freckled, feckless characters, and still shows at the Luggage Store Gallery.

New Media

For 40 years, the Bay Area has been the global hub for technical breakthroughs – and local artists have been using technology creatively to pioneer new media art. Since the '80s, Silicon Valley artist Jim Campbell has been building motherboards to misbehave. In one famous Campbell artwork, a running figure freezes as soon as it senses viewers approaching, like a deer in the headlights – and resumes activity only if you stand still. Rebecca Bollinger's grouped sketches are inspired by images found through web keyword searches, while Kota Ezawa created special cartoon-image software to turn the OJ Simpson trial into the multichannel cartoon animation.

San Francisco's interactive artists invite you to burp the art and change its DNA. John Slepian programmed a hairy rubber nub swaddled in blankets to sob disconsolately, until you pick it up and pat its posterior. New media artist Scott Snibbe created an app that allows users to not only

Diego Rivera's mural *The Making of a Fresco Showing the Building of a City* in the Diego Rivera Gallery (p132)

remix but alter the musical DNA of Bjork's *Biophilia* compositions, attacking songs with visual viruses and splicing new riffs into the melodies.

Public Sculpture

San Francisco owes its sculpture tradition to a nude sculptor's model: Big Alma Spreckels. Her 'sugar daddy' Adolph Spreckels left her sugar-plantation fortunes, which she donated to build the Legion of Honor and its Rodin sculpture court. The next benefactor was the WPA, whose government-funded Aquatic Park Bathhouse commissions included the totemic seal by Beniamino Bufano and green-slate nautical frieze by pioneering African American artist Sargent Johnson.

Bufano also sculpted Chinese revolutionary Sun Yat-sen's statue in Chinatown and San Francisco City College's 1968 *St Francis of the Guns,* made of 1968 guns collected in a San Francisco gun-buyback scheme. St Francis' mosaic robe features four assassinated leaders: Abraham Lincoln, Dr Martin Luther King Jr, John Fitzgerald and Robert Kennedy.

But the sculptor who has made the biggest impact on the San Francisco landscape in sheer scale is Richard Serra, from the rooftop sculpture garden at SFMOMA to University of California San Francisco's Mission Bay campus. Serra's massive rusted-metal minimalist shapes have been favorably compared to ship's prows – and less generously, Soviet factory seconds.

Public sculptures have been favorite San Franciscan subjects of debate since 1894, when vigilante art critics pulled down the statue of Henry D Cogswell over a drinking fountain he'd donated. Claes Oldenburg and Coosje van Bruggen's 2002 *Cupid's Span* represents the city's reputation for romance with a bow and arrow sunk into the Embarcadero. But the city wasn't smitten: a recent poll ranks it among SF's most despised public artworks. Tony Bennett's musical anthem 'I Left My Heart in San Francisco' inspired SF General's Hearts in San Francisco fundraising project, but the cartoon hearts are regularly graffitied and marked by territorial canine critics.

Best for New Media

- *di Rosa Art + Nature Preserve (Napa Valley)*
- *SFMOMA (SoMa)*
- *Catharine Clark Gallery (SoMa)*
- *Southern Exposure (the Mission)*
- *de Young Museum (Golden Gate Park)*

San Francisco Music

Only an extremely eclectic DJ can cover SF's varied musical tastes. Classical, bluegrass, Latin music and Chinese and Italian opera have lifted San Franciscan spirits through earthquakes and fires, booms and busts. Music trends that started around the Bay never really went away: '50s free-form jazz and folk; '60s psychedelic rock; '70s disco bathhouse anthems; and '90s west-coast rap and Berkeley's pop-punk revival. Today DJ mash-ups put SF's entire back catalog to work.

Best for Classical & Opera

San Francisco Symphony (Civic Center)

San Francisco Opera (Civic Center)

Stern Grove Festival (Golden Gate Park)

Zellerbach Hall (Berkeley)

Classical Music & Opera

Since conductor Michael Tilson Thomas was wooed away from London Symphony Orchestra to take the baton here in 1995, San Francisco Symphony has stacked up international accolades. Under MTT, SF Symphony has won more Grammys than the Beatles – 16 and counting. You can see why: Thomas conducts on the tips of his toes, enthralling audiences with full-throttle Mahler and Beethoven and some genuinely odd experimental music. San Francisco Opera is the USA's second-largest opera company after New York's Metropolitan Opera, but it's second to none with risk-taking. You'd never guess San Francisco's opera roots go back to the 19th century from avant-garde productions like *Harvey Milk,* Stephen King's *Dolores Claiborne* and the Chinese courtesan epic *Dream of the Red Chamber*.

Rock

San Francisco's rock of choice lately is preceded by the prefix alt- or indie- at music extravaganzas like Outside Lands, Noise Pop and Napa's **Bottle Rock** (www.bottlerocknapavalley.com). SF acts like Rogue Wave, Peggy Honeywell and Joanna Newsom add acoustic roots stylings even when they're not playing Berkeley's twangy Freight & Salvage or Hardly Strictly Bluegrass Festival. Vintage SF sounds become new again in the surf-pop of Union Pacific, the trippy lo-fi tunes of Paint the Trees White, and the sunny '60s sounds of Panic Is Perfect.

Classical music is accessible and often free in San Francisco – a local tradition started when opera divas performed gratis to raise SF's spirits after the 1906 earthquake and fire. For listings of free concerts around town, see www.sfcv.org.

But San Francisco rock isn't all California sunshine and acoustic twang. Black Rebel Motorcycle Club and Deerhoof throw Mission grit into their walls of sound. Metalheads need no introduction to SF's mighty Metallica, the triumphant survivors of a genre nearly smothered in the '80s by its own hair.

Before you arrived, you may have had the impression San Francisco's rock scene had OD'ed long ago. Fair enough. San Francisco has the ignominious distinction of being a world capital of rocker drug overdoses. In the Haight, you can pass places Janis Joplin nearly met her maker; 32 Delmar St, where Sid Vicious went on the heroin bender that finally broke up the Sex Pistols; and the Grateful Dead flophouse where the band was drug-raided. Grateful Dead guitarist Jerry Garcia eluded the bust and survived for decades, until his death in rehab in 1995.

But baby boomers keep the sound of San Francisco in the '60s alive, and much of it stands the tests of time and sobriety. After Joan Baez and Bob Dylan had their Northern California fling, folk turned into folk rock, and Jimi Hendrix turned the American anthem into a jam suitable for an acid trip. When Janis Joplin and Big Brother & the Holding Company applied their rough musical stylings to 'Me and Bobby McGee,' it was like applying that last necessary pass of sandpaper to the sometimes clunky, wooden verses of traditional folk songs. Jefferson Airplane held court at the Fillmore, turning Lewis Carroll's children's classic into the psychedelic anthem 'White Rabbit,' with singer Grace Slick's piercing wail.

The '60s were quite a trip, but the '70s rocked around the Bay. Crosby, Stills, Nash & Young splintered, but Neil Young keeps 'rockin' in the free world' from his ranch south of SF with his earnest, bluesy whine. Since the 1970s, California-born, longtime Sonoma resident Tom Waits has been singing in an after-hours honky-tonk voice with a permanent catch in the throat. SF's own Steve Miller Band turned out stoner hits like 'The Joker,' Van Morrison lived in Marin and regularly played SF clubs in the '70s, and the Doobie Brothers have played bluesy stoner rock around the Bay since the 1970s. But SF's most iconic '70s rocker is Mission-born Carlos Santana, who combined a guitar moan and Latin backbeat in 'Black Magic Woman,' 'Evil Ways' and 'Oye Como Va.' Santana made a comeback with 1999's Grammy-winning *Supernatural* and 2005's *All That I Am,* featuring fellow San Franciscan Kirk Hammett of Metallica.

The ultimate SF rock anthem is an '80s power ballad by San Francisco supergroup Journey: 'Lights' (sing along now: 'When the lights go down in the city/and the sun shines on the bay…'). Giants fans also warm up for games air-guitar-rocking to Journey's 'Don't Stop Believing,' the unofficial theme song of the Giants' World Series championships.

Best for Rock & Punk

Fillmore Auditorium (Japantown)

Warfield (Union Square)

Bottom of the Hill (Potrero Hill)

Great American Music Hall (the Tenderloin)

Slim's (SoMa)

Hardly Strictly Bluegrass Festival (October; Golden Gate Park)

Funk & Hip-Hop

If there's anything San Francisco loves more than an anthem, it's an anthem with a funky groove. The '60s were embodied by freaky-funky, racially integrated San Francisco supergroup Sly and the Family Stone, whose number-one hits are funk manifestos: 'Everyday People,' 'Stand' and 'Thank You (Falettinme Be Mice Elf Agin).' The '70s sexual revolution is summed up in the disco anthem 'You Make Me Feel (Mighty Real)' by Sylvester – the Cockettes drag diva who was tragically lost to the HIV/AIDS epidemic, yet still brings SF crowds to the dance floor.

San Francisco's '70s funk was reverb from across the bay in Oakland, where Tower of Power worked a groove with taut horn arrangements. All this trippy funk worked its way into the DNA of the Bay Area hip-hop scene, spawning the jazz-inflected, free-form Charlie Hunter and the infectious wokka-wokka baseline of rapper Lyrics Born. Oakland's MC Hammer was an '80s crossover hip-hop hitmaker best known for

SF ECLECTIC HITS PLAYLIST

- 'Take Five' by Dave Brubeck Quartet (1959)
- 'Make You Feel That Way' by Blackalicious (2002)
- 'Everyday People' by Sly and the Family Stone (1968)
- 'Evil Ways' by Santana (1969)
- 'Restless Year' by Ezra Furman (2015)
- 'Uncle John's Band' by Grateful Dead (1970)
- 'Stay Human (All the Freaky People)' by Michael Franti & Spearhead (2007)
- 'San Francisco Anthem' by San Quinn (2008)
- 'The American in Me' by The Avengers (1979)
- 'Come Back from San Francisco' by Magnetic Fields (1999)
- 'California' by Rogue Wave (2005)
- 'Me and Bobby McGee' by Janis Joplin (1971)
- 'Lights' by Journey (1978)

Best for Funk, R&B and Hip-Hop

Mezzanine (SoMa)

Outside Lands (August; Golden Gate Park)

Independent (Haight/NoPa)

Boom Boom Room (Japantown)

Warfield (Union Square)

inflicting harem pants on the world, though his influence is heard in E-40's bouncing hyphy sound. Political commentary and pop hooks became East Bay hip-hop signatures with Michael Franti & Spearhead, Blackalicious and the Coup. But the Bay Area is still best known as the home of the world's most talented and notorious rapper: Tupac Shakur, killed in 1996 by an assailant out to settle an East Coast/West Coast gangsta rap rivalry. Today San Francisco rappers are less pugnacious and more tech-savvy, as you hear in SF MC San Quinn's 'San Francisco Anthem': 'We got the cable cars/but my car's got cable/I'm on demand like Comcast/with these squares I don't contrast.'

Punk

London may have been more political and Los Angeles more hardcore, but San Francisco's take on punk was weirder. Dead Kennedys frontman Jello Biafra ran for mayor in 1979 with a platform written on the back of a bar napkin: ban cars, set official rates for bribery and force businessmen to dress as clowns. He received 6000 votes and his political endorsement is still highly prized. But for oddity even Jello can't top The Residents, whose identities remain unknown after 60 records and three decades of performances wearing giant eyeballs over their heads.

Today punk's not dead in the Bay Area. The Avengers played with the Sex Pistols the night they broke up in San Francisco, and by all accounts, lead singer Penelope Houston upstaged Johnny Rotten for freakish intensity – and unlike the Pistols, the Avengers are still going strong. In the '90s, ska-inflected Rancid and pop-punk Green Day brought punk staggering out of Berkeley's 924 Gilman into the mass-media spotlight. Hardcore punks sneered at Green Day's chart-topping hits, but the group earned street cred (and Grammys) in 2004 with the dark social critique of *American Idiot* – at least until that album became a Broadway musical.

Landmark clubs like SUB-Mission, Hemlock Tavern and Slim's keep SF punk alive and pogoing. Following the early success of *Punk in Drublic,* SF-based NOFX recorded an impressively degenerate show at Slim's called *I Hear They've Gotten Worse Live!* Punk continues to evolve in San Francisco, with queercore Pansy Division, glam-punk songwriter Ezra Furman and the brass-ballsiness of Latin ska-punk La Plebe.

Search & Destroy was San Francisco's poorly photocopied and totally riveting chronicle of the '70s punk scene as it happened from 1977 to 1979, starting with an initial run financed with $100 from Allen Ginsberg and Lawrence Ferlinghetti, and morphing into V Vale's seminal 'zine *RE/Search* in the 1980s.

Jazz

Ever since house bands pounded out ragtime hits to distract Barbary Coast audiences from bar-room brawls, San Francisco has echoed with jazz. The new SFJAZZ Center is the nation's second jazz center and a magnet for global talents as artists-in-residence. But jazz will find you all around town, from the Mission's stalwart Revolution Cafe, to North Beach's experimental Doc's Lab and the Haight's swinging Club Deluxe.

SF played it cool in the 1950s with West Coast jazz innovated by the legendary Dave Brubeck Quartet, whose *Time Out* is among the best-selling jazz albums of all time. Bebop had disciples among the Beats, and the SF scene is memorably chronicled in Kerouac's *On the Road.* Billie Holiday and Miles Davis recorded here, and today John Coltrane is revered as a saint at the African Orthodox Church of St John Coltrane.

During the '60s, the SF jazz scene exploded into a kaleidoscope of styles. Trumpeter Don Cherry blew minds with Ornette Coleman's avant-garde ensemble, while Dixieland band Turk Murphy kept roots jazz relevant.

Today jazz takes many turns in SF, and pops up where you least expect to find it. At new venues like SFJAZZ and The Chapel, tempos shift from Latin jazz to klezmer, acid jazz to swing. So where are the jazz traditionalists? Playing the Hardly Strictly Bluegrass Festival, and mixing with Afrofunk at Bissap Baobab. But you can't miss SF jazz at Christmas: San Franciscan Vince Guaraldi wrote the jazzy score for *A Charlie Brown Christmas,* the beloved antidote to standard Christmas carols.

San Francisco Architecture

Superman wouldn't be so impressive in San Francisco, where most buildings are low enough for even a middling superhero to leap in a single bound. The Transamerica Pyramid and Ferry Building clock tower are helpful pointers to orient newcomers, and Coit Tower adds emphatic punctuation to the city skyline – but San Francisco's low-profile buildings are its highlights, from Mission adobe and Haight Victorians to wildflower-covered roofs in Golden Gate Park. Keeping a low profile in the midst of it all are Western storefronts, their squared-off rooflines as iconic as a cowboy's hat.

The Mission & Early SF

Not much is left of San Francisco's original Ohlone-style architecture, beyond the grass memorial hut you'll see in the graveyard of Spanish Mission Dolores and the wall of the original Presidio (military post), both built in adobe with conscripted Ohlone labor. When the Gold Rush began, buildings were slapped together from ready-made sawn timber components, sometimes shipped from the East Coast or Australia – an early precursor to postwar prefab.

In SF's Barbary Coast days, City Hall wasn't much to look at, at least from outside: it was housed in the burlesque Jenny Lind Theater at Portsmouth Square. Most waterfront buildings from SF's hot-headed Wild West days were lost to arson, including San Francisco's long-lost waterfront neighborhoods of Sydneytown and Chiletown, named for early Gold Rush arrivals. Eventually, builders of Jackson Square got wise and switched to brick.

But masonry was no match for the 1906 earthquake and fire. The waterfront was almost completely leveled, with the mysterious, highly explosive exception of the Italianate 1866 AP Hotaling's Warehouse – which at the time housed SF's largest whiskey stash. The snappiest comeback in SF history is now commemorated in a bronze plaque on the building: 'If, as they say, God spanked the town/For being over-frisky/Why did He burn His churches down/And spare Hotaling's whiskey?'

Uphill toward North Beach, you'll spot a few other original 1860s to 1880s Italianate brick storefronts wisely built on bedrock. Elevated false facades are capped with jutting cornices, a straight roofline and graceful arches over tall windows.

Best for Early Architecture

- *Mission Dolores (Mission)*
- *Presidio (Marina & Presidio)*
- *Cottage Row (Fillmore)*
- *Jackson Square (Downtown)*
- *Old St Mary's Cathedral & Square (Chinatown)*
- *Octagon House (Cow Hollow)*

Some Victorian mansions are now B&Bs, so you too can live large in swanky San Francisco digs of yore: we recommend B&Bs in the Haight, Pacific Heights, Mission and Castro.

Victoriana

To make room for new arrivals with the gold, railroad and shipping booms, San Francisco had to expand fast. Wooden Victorian row houses cropped up almost overnight with a similar underlying floor plan, but with eye-catching embellishments. Legend has it that inhabitants stumbling home after Barbary Coast nights needed these pointers to recognize their homes. Some of these 'Painted Ladies' proved surprisingly sturdy: several upstanding Victorian row houses remain in Pacific Heights, the Haight and the Mission.

The Victorian era was a time of colonial conquest and the culmination of the European Age of Discovery, and Victorians liked to imagine themselves as the true successors of great early civilizations. San Franciscans incorporated designs from ancient Rome, Egypt and the Italian Renaissance into grand mansions around Alamo Square, giving fresh-out-of-the-box San Francisco a hodge-podge instant culture.

Best for Victorian Architecture

- *Alamo Square (the Haight)*
- *Haas-Lilienthal House (Pacific Heights)*
- *Conservatory of Flowers (Golden Gate Park)*
- *Columbarium (Golden Gate Park & the Avenues)*
- *Palace Hotel (Downtown)*

Pacific Polyglot Architecture

A trip across town or even down the block will bring you face to facade with San Francisco's Spanish and Mexican heritage, Asian ancestry and California arts-and-crafts roots. Italianate bordello baroque was the look of choice for San Francisco dance halls like the 1907 Great American Music Hall, while Chinatown merchants designed their own streamlined, pagoda-topped Chinatown deco to attract tourists to Grant St. San Francisco's cinemas and theaters dispense with all geographical logic in favor of pure fantasy, from the scalloped Moorish arches of Thomas Patterson Ross' 1913 Exotic Revivalist Alcazar Theater at 650 Geary St to the Chinoiserie deco decor elements inside architect Timothy Pflueger's 1925 Pacific Telephone & Telegraph Company Building.

Mission & Meso-American Influences

Never mind that Mexico and Spain actually fought over California, and missionaries and Aztecs had fundamental religious and cultural differences: San Francisco's flights of architectural fancy paved over historical differences with cement, tile and stucco. Meso-American influences are obvious in the stone-carved Aztec motifs on Sansome St banks and 1929 Mayan deco gilt reliefs that add jaw-dropping grandeur to Pflueger's 450 Sutter St – surely the world's most mystical dental office building.

San Francisco's 1915 to 1935 Mission Revival paid tribute to California's Hispanic heritage, influenced by the 1915 Panama–Pacific International Exposition held in San Francisco. Spanish baroque fads flourished with the 1918 construction of a new churrigueresque (Mexican-style Spanish baroque) Mission Dolores basilica, replacing the earlier brick Gothic cathedral damaged in the 1906 earthquake.

The look proved popular for secular buildings, including Pflueger's Mexican baroque Castro Theatre marquee. Pflueger also invited the great Mexican muralist Diego Rivera to San Francisco to create the 1931 *Allegory of California* fresco for San Francisco's Stock Exchange Lunch Club – sparking a mural trend that continues in Mission streets today.

Rebuilding Chinatown

Chinatown was originally hastily constructed by non-Chinese landlords from brick, which promptly collapsed into rubble in the 1906 earthquake. Fire swept the neighborhood, warping bricks into seemingly useless clinker bricks. But facing City Hall plans for forced relocation, Chinatown residents ingeniously repurposed clinker bricks and rebuilt their neighborhood.

Clinker brickwork became a California arts-and-crafts signature, championed by Chinatown YWCA architect Julia Morgan. The first licensed female architect in California and the chief architect of over-the-top Spanish-Gothic-Greek Hearst Castle, Morgan showed tasteful restraint and finesse combining cultural traditions in her designs for the pagoda-topped brick Chinatown YWCA (now the Chinese Historical

Society of America) and graceful Italianate Emanu-El Sisterhood Residence (now home to San Francisco Zen Center).

To attract business to the devastated neighborhood, Chinatown mounted a redevelopment initiative. A forward-thinking group of Chinatown merchants led by Look Tin Eli consulted with a cross-section of architects and rudimentary focus groups to create a signature Chinatown art-deco architectural style. Using this approach, they reinvented brothel-lined Dupont St as tourist-friendly, pagoda-topped Grant Ave, with dragon lanterns and crowd-pleasing modern chinoiserie buildings.

California Arts & Crafts

California arts-and-crafts style combines Mission influences with English arts-and-crafts architecture, as seen in Bay Area Craftsman cottages and earthy ecclesiastical structures like San Francisco's Swedenborgian Church.

Berkeley-based architect Bernard Maybeck reinvented England's arts-and-crafts movement with the down-to-earth California bungalow, a small, simple single-story design derived from summer homes favored by British officers serving in India. Though Maybeck's Greco-Roman 1915 Palace of Fine Arts was intended as a temporary structure, the beloved but crumbling fake ruin was recast in concrete in the 1960s – and it continues to serve as San Franciscans' favorite wedding-photo backdrop.

Modern Skyline

Once steel-frame buildings stood the test of the 1906 earthquake, San Francisco began to think big with its buildings. The city aspired to rival the capitols of Europe and commissioned architect Daniel Burnham to build a grand City Hall in the neoclassical Parisian beaux arts, or 'city beautiful,' style. But City Hall was reduced to a mere shell by the 1906 earthquake, and it wasn't until 1924 that Timothy Pfleuger built San Francisco's first real skyscraper: the Gothic deco, 26-story 1924 Pacific Telephone Building on 140 New Montgomery St. Recently restored, the telecom megalith is now the headquarters of Yelp and home to Mourad restaurant.

Top 5 Low-Profile SF Landmarks

- *California Academy of Sciences (Golden Gate Park)*
- *de Young Museum (Golden Gate Park)*
- *Swedenborgian Church (Marina & the Presidio)*
- *Chinese Historical Society of America (Chinatown)*
- *Frank Lloyd Wright Building – VC Morris Store (Union Square)*

Flatirons

Chicago and New York started a trend raising skylines to new heights, and San Francisco borrowed their flatiron skyscraper style to maximize prime real estate along Market St. The street cuts a diagonal across San Francisco's tidy east–west grid, leaving both flanks of four attractive, triangular flatiron buildings exposed to view.

Among the head shops and XXX dives around 1020 Market St at Taylor, you'll find the lacy, white flatiron featured as broody Brad Pitt's apartment in the film *Interview with a Vampire*. On a less seedy block above the Powell St cable car turnaround is the stone-cold silver fox known as the James Flood Building, a flinty character that has seen it all: fire, earthquakes and the Gap's attempts to revive bell-bottoms at its ground-floor flagship store. Flood's opulent cousin is the 1908 Phelan Building at 760 Market St, while that charming slip of a building on the block at 540 Market St is the 1913 Flatiron Building.

Streamlined SF

San Francisco became a forward-thinking port city in the 1930s, introducing the ocean-liner look of 1939 Streamline Moderne Aquatic Park Bathhouse and SF's sleek signature art-deco Golden Gate Bridge. But

MISSION BAY

Debates are rising over SoMa's new high-rise Mission Bay development. Proponents describe it as a forward-thinking green scheme, with mixed-use space and high-density housing accessible to Silicon Valley via low-impact CalTrain. Critics argue that such costly real estate attracts only tech millionaires, chain stores and high-priced retailers, excluding affordable housing, mom-and-pop businesses and cultural institutions. A 2014 proposal to allow further waterfront development was squashed by San Francisco voters, still waiting for Mission Bay to make good on its promises to the community.

except for the exclamation point of Coit Tower, most new SF buildings kept a low, sleek profile. Until the '60s, San Francisco was called 'the white city' because of its vast, low swaths of white stucco.

Skyscrapers

SF's skyline scarcely changed until the early 1960s, when seismic retrofitting and innovations made upward mobility possible in this shaky city. The 1959 Crown Zellerbach Building at 1 Bush St became a prototype for downtown buildings: a minimalist, tinted-glass rectangle with open-plan offices. The Financial District morphed into a Manhattanized forest of glass boxes, with one pointed exception: the Transamerica Pyramid. High-rises are now springing up along Market St, with slots for 'urban village' shops, condos, restaurants and cafés. This latest attempt at instant culture is consistent with the city's original Victorian vision – only bigger and blander.

Have some thoughts on how to improve San Francisco? Join the crowds debating city architecture, zoning and public use at SPUR (SoMa), San Francisco's nonprofit center for urban planning. SPUR hosts events and gallery shows to explore future city visions, and produces a handy app to help identify privately owned public open spaces (POPOs) downtown where you can enjoy picnics.

Prefab Chic

Amid Victorian-prefab row houses in San Francisco neighborhoods, you might also spot some newcomers that seem to have popped right out of the box. Around Patricia's Green in Hayes Valley, shipping containers have been repurposed into stores, cafés and a beer garden. San Francisco's *Dwell* magazine championed architect-designed, eco-prefab homes innovated in the Bay Area, and you can spot some early adopters in Diamond Heights and Bernal Heights. The exteriors can seem starkly minimal, but interior spaces make the most of air and light.

Adaptive Reuse

Instead of starting from scratch, avant-garde architects are repurposing San Francisco's eclectic architecture to meet the needs of a modern city. Architect Daniel Libeskind's design for the 2008 Contemporary Jewish Museum turned a historic power station into the Hebrew word for life, with a blue-steel pavilion as an emphatic accent.

When the Embarcadero freeway collapsed in the 1989 earthquake, the sun shone on the Embarcadero at last – and the potential of the waterfront and Ferry Building was revealed. San Francisco's neglected, partially rotten Piers 15 and 17 sheds were recently retrofitted and connected with Fujiko Nakaya's Fog Bridge to form a stunning, solar-powered new home for the Exploratorium.

But raising the roof on standards for adaptive reuse is the 2008 LEED-certified green building for the California Academy of Sciences. Pritzker Prize–winning architect Renzo Piano incorporated the previous building's neoclassical colonnaded facade, gutted the interior to make way for a basement aquarium and four-story rainforest, and capped it with a domed 'living roof' of California wildflowers perforated with skylights to let air circulate.

Survival Guide

Transportation

ARRIVING IN SAN FRANCISCO

The Bay Area has three international airports: San Francisco (SFO), Oakland (OAK), and San Jose (SJC). Direct flights from LA take 60 minutes; Chicago, four hours; Atlanta five hours; New York six hours. Factor in additional transit time – and cost – to reach San Francisco proper from Oakland or San Jose; what you save in airfare, you may wind up spending on ground transportation.

If you've unlimited time, consider the train, instead of car or plane, to avoid traffic hassles and excess carbon emissions.

San Francisco International Airport

One of America's busiest, **San Francisco International Airport** (SFO; www.flysfo.com; S McDonnell Rd) is 14 miles south of downtown off Hwy 101 and accessible by BART.

BART

BART (Bay Area Rapid Transit; www.bart.gov; one way $8.65) Direct 30-minute ride to/from downtown San Francisco. The SFO BART station is connected to the International Terminal; buy tickets from machines inside stations.

Bus

SamTrans (www.samtrans.com; one way $5) Express bus KX takes 30 to 45 minutes to reach Temporary Transbay Terminal, in the South of Market (SoMa) area.

Shuttle Bus

Airport Shuttles (one way $15-17) Depart from *upper-level* ticketing areas (not lower-level baggage claim); anticipate 45 minutes to most SF locations. For service to the airport, call at least four hours before departure to reserve pick-ups from any San Francisco location. Companies include **SuperShuttle** (☎800-258-3826; www.supershuttle.com), Quake City (☎415-255-4899; www.quakecityshuttle.com), Lorrie's (☎415-334-9000; www.gosfovan.com) and American Airporter Shuttle. (☎415-202-0733; www.americanairporter.com).

Taxi

Taxis to downtown San Francisco cost $40 to $50, and depart from the lower-level baggage claim area of SFO.

Car

The drive between the airport and the city can take as little as 20 minutes with no traffic, but give yourself an hour during morning and evening rush hours. If you're headed to the airport via Hwy 101, take the San Francisco International Airport exit. Don't be misled by the Airport Rd exit, which leads to parking lots and warehouses.

Oakland International Airport

Travelers arriving at **Oakland International Airport** (OAK; www.oaklandairport.com; 1 Airport Dr; 📶), 15 miles east of Downtown, have a longer trip to reach San Francisco, but OAK has fewer weather-related flight delays than SFO.

BART

The cheapest way to reach San Francisco from the Oakland Airport. BART peoplemover shuttles run every 10 to 20 minutes from Terminal 1 to the Coliseum station, where you connect with BART trains to downtown SF ($10.05, 25 minutes). Service operates 5am to midnight Monday to Friday, 6am to midnight Saturday, and 8am to midnight Sunday.

Bus

SuperShuttle (☎800-258-3826; www.supershuttle.com) Offers shared van rides from SFO to downtown SF for $17 per person (no reservation required); however, from OAK it costs $57 for up to four people (reservation required).

CLIMATE CHANGE & TRAVEL

Every form of transport that relies on carbon-based fuel generates CO_2, the main cause of human-induced climate change. Modern travel is dependent on airplanes, which might use less fuel per mile per person than most cars but travel much greater distances. The altitude at which aircraft emit gases (including CO_2) and particles also contributes to their climate change impact. Many websites offer 'carbon calculators' that allow people to estimate the carbon emissions generated by their journey and, for those who wish to do so, to offset the impact of the greenhouse gases emitted with contributions to portfolios of climate-friendly initiatives throughout the world. Lonely Planet offsets the carbon footprint of all staff and author travel.

Shuttle Bus

Airport Express (☎800-327-2024; www.airportexpressinc.com; ⊙5:15am-9:15pm) Runs a scheduled shuttle every two hours (from 5:30am to 9:30pm) between Oakland Airport and Sonoma ($34) and Marin ($26) counties.

Taxi

Leave curbside from Oakland airport and average $35 to $50 to Oakland, and $60 to $90 to SF.

Mineta San Jose International Airport

Fifty miles south of downtown San Francisco, **Mineta San Jose International Airport** (www.flysanjose.com; 1701 Airport Blvd, San Jose) is the least convenient, but by car it's a straight shot to the city via Hwy 101. The **VTA** (Valley Transit Authority; ☎408-321-2300; www.vta.org) Airport Flyer (bus 10; free; from 5am to 11:30pm) makes a continuous run every 15 to 30 minutes between the Santa Clara Caltrain station (Railroad Ave and Franklin St) and the airport terminals. From Santa Clara station, Caltrain (one way $9.25; 90 minutes) runs northbound trains to the SF terminus at 4th and King Sts, weekdays from 5am to 10:30pm, Saturday 7am to 10:30pm, and Sunday 8am to 9pm.

Temporary Transbay Terminal

Until the new terminal is complete in 2017, SF's intercity hub remains the **Temporary Transbay Terminal** (Map p308; Howard & Main Sts). From here you can catch the following buses:

AC Transit (www.actransit.org) Buses to the East Bay.

Golden Gate Transit (www.goldengate.org) Northbound buses to Marin and Sonoma counties.

Greyhound (☎800-231-2222; www.greyhound.com) Buses leave daily for Los Angeles ($59, eight to 12 hours), Truckee near Lake Tahoe ($31, 5½ hours) and other major destinations.

Megabus (http://us.megabus.com) Low-cost bus service to San Francisco from Los Angeles, Sacramento and Reno.

SamTrans (www.samtrans.com) Southbound buses to Palo Alto and the Pacific coast.

Train

Easy on the eyes and carbon emissions too, train travel is a good way to visit the Bay Area and beyond.

Caltrain (www.caltrain.com; cnr 4th & King Sts) connects San Francisco with Silicon Valley hubs and San Jose.

Amtrak (☎800-872-7245; www.amtrakcalifornia.com) serves San Francisco via stations in Oakland and Emeryville (near Oakland), with free shuttle-bus connections to San Francisco's Ferry Building and Caltrain station, and Oakland's Jack London Square. Amtrak offers rail passes good for seven days of travel in California within a 21-day period (from $159).

Most departures from Oakland are short hops to Sacramento, but several daily departures are long-haul trains, with coach service, sleepers and private rooms. The **Coast Starlight** (LA to Emeryville from $59, Oakland to Portland from $105, Oakland to Seattle from $128, LA to Seattle from $114) makes its spectacular 35-hour run from Los Angeles to Seattle via Emeryville/Oakland.

The **California Zephyr** (Chicago to Oakland from $313) runs from Chicago, through the Rockies and snow-capped Sierra Nevada, to Oakland (51 hours); it's almost always late.

GETTING AROUND SAN FRANCISCO

When San Franciscans aren't pressed for time, most walk, bike or ride Muni, instead of taking a car or cab. Traffic is notoriously bad at rush hour, and parking is next to impossible in center-city neighborhoods. Avoid driving until it's time to leave town.

Bus, Streetcar & Cable Car

Muni (Municipal Transit Agency; ☎511; www.sfmta.com) Muni operates bus, streetcar and cable car lines. Buses and streetcars are referred to interchangeably as Muni, but when streetcars run underground beneath Market St, they're called the Muni Metro. Some areas are better connected than others, but Muni spares you the costly hassle of driving and parking – and it's often faster than driving, especially along metro-streetcar lines J, K/T, L, M and N.

Schedules

For route-planning and schedules, consult http://transit.511.org. For real-time departures, see www.nextmuni.com, which synchs with GPS on buses and streetcars to provide best estimates on arrival times. This is the system tied to digital displays posted inside bus shelters. It's accurate for most lines, but not always for the F-line vintage streetcars or cable cars. Nighttime and weekend service is less frequent than weekday. Owl service (half-hourly from 1am to 5am) operates only on a few principal lines.

System Maps

A detailed Muni Street & Transit Map is available free online (www.sfmta.com).

Tickets

Standard fare for buses or streetcars is $2.25; buy tickets onboard buses and streetcars from drivers (exact change required) or at underground Muni stations (where machines give change). Cable car tickets cost $6 per ride, and can be bought at cable car turnaround kiosks or onboard from the conductor. Hang onto your ticket even if you're not planning to use it again: if you're caught without one by the transit police, you're subject to a $100 fine (repeat offenders may be fined up to $500).

Transfers

At the start of your Muni journey, free transfer tickets are available for additional Muni trips within 90 minutes (not including cable cars or BART). After 8:30pm, buses issue a Late Night Transfer good for travel until 5:30am the following morning.

Discounts & Passes

MUNI PASSPORTS

A **Muni Passport** (1/3/7 days $17/26/35) allows unlimited travel on all Muni transport, including cable cars. It's sold at the Muni kiosk at the Powell St cable car turnaround on Market St, SF's Visitor Information Center, the TIX Bay Area kiosk at Union Square and shops around town – see www.sfmta.com for exact locations. One-day (but not multi-day) passports available from cable-car conductors.

CLIPPER CARDS

Downtown Muni/BART stations have machines that issue the Clipper Card, a reloadable transit card with a $3 minimum that can be used on Muni, BART, AC Transit, Caltrain, SamTrans, and Golden Gate Transit and Ferry (not cable cars). Clipper Cards automatically deduct fares and apply transfers – only one Muni fare is deducted per 90-minute period.

FAST PASS

Monthly Muni Fast Pass (adult/child $68/23) Offers unlimited Muni travel for the calendar month, including cable cars. Fast Passes are available at the Muni kiosk at the Powell St cable-car turnaround, and from many businesses around town; for exact locations, see www.sfmta.com.

Bus

Muni buses display their route number and final destination on the front and side. If the number is followed by the letter A, B, X or R, then it's a limited-stop or express service.

KEY ROUTES

22 Fillmore From Dogpatch (Potrero Hill), through the Mission on 16th St, along Fillmore St past Japantown to Pacific Heights and the Marina.

33 Stanyan From San Francisco General Hospital, through the Mission, Castro and Haight, past Golden Gate Park to Clement St.

38 Geary From the Temporary Transbay Terminal, along Market to Geary Blvd, north of Golden Gate Park through the Richmond district to Ocean Beach.

71 Noriega From the Temporary Transbay Terminal, along Market and Haight Sts, along the southeast side of Golden Gate Park through the Sunset and to the Great Hwy at the beach.

HOW TO FIND MUNI STOPS

Muni stops are indicated by a street sign and/or a yellow-painted stripe on the nearest lamp post, with route numbers stamped on the yellow stripe; if there is no street sign or lamp post, look on the pavement for a yellow bar with route number painted on it. Ignore yellow circles and X's on the pavement, or bars that do not also have a route number; these other markings tell electric-trolley drivers when to engage or disengage the throttle; they do not indicate bus stops.

Streetcar

Muni Metro streetcars run 5am to midnight on weekdays, with limited schedules weekends. The K, L, M, N and T lines operate 24 hours, but above-ground Owl buses replace streetcars between 12:30am and 5:30am. The F-Market line runs vintage streetcars above ground along Market St to the Embarcadero, where they turn north to Fisherman's Wharf. The T line heads south along the Embarcadero through SoMa and Mission Bay, then down 3rd St. Other streetcars run underground below Market St to Downtown.

KEY ROUTES

F Fisherman's Wharf and Embarcadero to the Castro.

J Downtown to the Mission, the Castro and Noe Valley.

K, L, M Downtown to the Castro.

N Caltrain and SBC Ballpark to the Haight, Golden Gate Park and Ocean Beach.

T The Embarcadero to Caltrain and Bayview.

Cable Car

In this age of seat belts and air bags, a rickety cable-car ride is an anachronistic thrill. There are seats for about 30 passengers, who are often outnumbered by passengers clinging to creaking leather straps.

KEY ROUTES

California Street Runs east-west along California St, from the Downtown terminus at Market and Davis Sts through Chinatown and Nob Hill to Van Ness Ave. It's the least-traveled route, with shortest queues.

Powell-Mason Runs from the Powell St cable car turnaround past Union Square, turns west along Jackson St, and then descends north down Mason St, Columbus Ave and Taylor St toward Fisherman's Wharf. On the return trip it takes Washington St instead of Jackson St.

Powell-Hyde The most picturesque route follows the same tracks as the Powell-Mason line, until Jackson St, where it turns down Hyde St to terminate at Aquatic Park; coming back it takes Washington St.

BUSES AROUND THE BAY

Three public bus systems connect San Francisco to the rest of the Bay Area. Most buses leave from clearly marked bus stops; for transit maps and schedules, see the bus system websites.

AC Transit (www.actransit.org) East Bay bus services from the Temporary Transbay Terminal. For public transport connections from BART in the East Bay, get an AC Transit transfer ticket before leaving the BART station and then pay an additional 75¢ to $1.

Golden Gate Transit (www.goldengate.org) Connects San Francisco to Marin (tickets $4.50 to $7.50) and Sonoma counties (tickets $10.75 to $11.75); check schedules online, as service is erratic.

SamTrans (☎800-660-4287; www.samtrans.com) FREE Connects San Francisco and the South Bay, including bus services to/from SFO. Buses pick up/drop off from the Temporary Transbay Terminal and other marked bus stops within the city.

BART

The fastest link between Downtown and the Mission District also offers transit to SF airport, Oakland ($3.30) and Berkeley ($3.90). Four of the system's five lines pass through SF before terminating at Daly City or SFO. Within SF, one-way fares start at $1.85.

Tickets

Buy tickets at BART stations: you need a ticket to enter and exit the system. If your ticket still has value after you exit turnstiles, it's returned to you, with the remaining balance for later use. If your ticket's value is less than needed to exit, use an Addfare machine to pay the appropriate amount. The Clipper Card can be used for BART.

Transfers

At San Francisco BART stations, a 25¢ discount is available for Muni buses and streetcars; look for transfer machines before you pass through the turnstiles.

Taxi

Fares start at $3.50 at the flag drop and run about $2.75 per mile. Add at least 10% to the taxi fare as a tip ($1 minimum). For quickest service in San Francisco, download the Flywheel app for smartphones, which dispatches the nearest taxi.

The following companies dispatch taxis 24 hours:

DeSoto Cab (☎415-970-1300; www.desotogo.com)

Green Cab (☎415-626-4733) Fuel-efficient hybrids; worker-owned collective.

Luxor (☎415-282-4141; www.luxorcab.com)

Yellow Cab (☎415-333-3333; www.yellowcabsf.com)

Car & Motorcycle

If you can, avoid driving in San Francisco: traffic is a

given, street parking is harder to find than true love, and meter readers are ruthless.

Traffic

San Francisco streets mostly follow a grid bisected by Market St, with signs pointing toward tourist zones such as North Beach, Fisherman's Wharf and Chinatown. Try to avoid driving during rush hours: 7:30am to 9:30am and 4:30pm to 6:30pm, Monday to Friday. Before heading to any bridge, airport or other traffic choke-point, call ☎511 for a traffic update.

Parking

Parking is tricky and often costly, especially Downtown – ask your hotel about parking, and inquire about validation at restaurants and entertainment venues.

GARAGES

Downtown parking garages charge from $2 to $8 per hour and $25 to $50 per day, depending on how long you park and whether you require in-and-out privileges. The most convenient Downtown parking lots are at the Embarcadero Center, at 5th and Mission Sts, under Union Square and at Sutter and Stockton Sts. For more public parking garages, see www.sfmta.com; for a map of garages and rates, see http://sfpark.org.

PARKING RESTRICTIONS

Parking restrictions are indicated by the following color-coded sidewalk curbs:

Blue Disabled parking only; placard required.

Green Ten-minute parking zone from 9am to 6pm.

Red No parking or stopping.

White For picking up or dropping off passengers only.

Yellow Loading zone during posted times.

TOWING VIOLATIONS

Desperate motorists often resort to double-parking or parking in red zones or on sidewalks, but parking authorities are quick to tow cars. If this should happen to you, you'll have to retrieve your car at **Autoreturn** (☎415-865-8200; www.autoreturn.com; 450 7th St, SoMa; 24hr; M27, 42). Besides at least $73 in fines for parking violations, you'll also have to fork out a towing and storage fee ($483.75 for the first four hours, $63.50 for the rest of the first day, $25.50 for every additional day, plus a $27 transfer fee if your car is moved to a long-term lot). Cars are usually stored at 450 7th St, corner of Harrison St.

Rental

Typically a small rental car might cost $55 to $70 a day or $175 to $300 a week, plus 8.75% sales tax. Unless your credit card covers car-rental insurance, you'll need to add $10 to $20 per day for a loss/damage waiver. Most rates include unlimited mileage; with cheap rates, there's often a per-mile charge above a certain mileage.

Booking ahead usually ensures the best rates. Airport rates are generally lower than city rates, but may carry a hefty facility charge. As part of SF's citywide green initiative, rentals of hybrid cars and low-emissions vehicles from rental agencies at SFO are available at a discount.

To rent a motorcycle, contact **Dubbelju** (☎415-495-2774, 866-495-2774; www.dubbelju.com; 689a Bryant St, San Francisco; 9am-6pm Mon-Sat); rates start at $99 per day. **Go Car** (www.gocartours.com/) rents mini-cars with audio GPS instructions to major attractions in multiple languages; rates start at $56 per hour.

To get around town techie-style, you can rent a Segway from **Segway SF Bay** (www.segwaysfbay.com) for use on bike lanes and trails (they're banned on sidewalks). Rates start at $45 per 90 minutes, including free lessons and map. Guided Segway tours (from $70 per two hours) are available from **City Segway Tours** (http://citysegwaytours.com).

Major car-rental agencies include the following:

Alamo Rent-a-Car (☎415-693-0191, 800-327-9633; www.alamo.com; 750 Bush St, Downtown; 7am-7pm; Powell-Mason, Powell-Hyde, M2, 3, 30, 45)

Avis (☎415-929-2555, 800-831-2847; www.avis.com; 675 Post St, Downtown; 6am-6pm; M2, 3, 27, 38)

FURTHER AFIELD: LOS ANGELES & LAS VEGAS

For muscle beaches, celebrity sightings and camera-ready wackiness, head south on coastal Hwy 1 to Los Angeles. It'll take 12 hours depending on traffic and how often you stop. A quicker jaunt is less-scenic Hwy 101 (nine hours); the fastest route is boring inland I-5, which takes about six hours.

Las Vegas, Nevada, is a nine-hour nonstop drive from San Francisco. Cross the Bay Bridge to 580 east, to I-5 south, veering off toward 99 south (at exit 278), to 58 east, then I-15 the last 160 miles. A slower, gloriously scenic option is to go east through Yosemite National Park on Hwy 120 (summer only; verify by calling ☎800-GAS-ROAD) and south on Hwy 395, east on Hwy 190 through Death Valley National Park then south on Hwy 95 straight into Sin City.

Budget (☎415-433-3717, 800-527-0700; www.budget.com; 675 Post St, Downtown; ⏲6am-6pm; Ⓜ2, 3, 27, 38)

Dollar (☎800-800-5252; www.dollarcar.com; 364 O'Farrell St, Downtown; ⏲7am-6pm; Ⓜ38, ⒷPowell)

Hertz (☎415-771-2200, 800-654-3131; www.hertz.com; 325 Mason St, Downtown; ⏲6am-6pm; Ⓜ38, ⒷPowell)

Thrifty (☎415-788-8111, 800-367-2277; www.thrifty.com; 350 O'Farrell St, Downtown; ⏲7am-6pm; Ⓜ38, ⒷPowell)

Car Share

Car sharing is a convenient alternative to rentals, and spares you pick-up/drop-off and parking hassles: reserve a car online for an hour or two, or all day, and you can usually pick up/drop off your car within blocks of where you're staying. It also does the environment a favor: fewer cars on the road means less congestion and pollution. Lyft and Uber are available in San Francisco, but licensed taxis have greater access.

Zipcar (☎866-494-7227; www.zipcar.com) Rents various car types by the hour, for flat rates starting at $8.25 per hour, including gas and insurance; or per day for $89; a $25 application fee and $50 prepaid usage are required in advance. Drivers without a US driver's license should follow instructions on the website. Once approved, cars can be reserved online or by phone, provided you have your member card in pocket. Check the website for pick-up/drop-off locations.

Roadside Assistance

Members of **American Automobile Association** (AAA; ☎800-222-4357, 415-773-1900; www.aaa.com; 160 Sutter St; ⏲8:30am-5:30pm Mon-Fri) can call the ☎800 number any time for emergency road service and towing. AAA also provides travel insurance and free road maps of the region.

Boat

With the revival of the Embarcadero and reinvention of the Ferry Building as a gourmet dining destination, commuters and tourists alike are taking the scenic ferry across the bay.

Alcatraz

Alcatraz Cruises (Map p299; ☎415-981-7625; www.alcatrazcruises.com; day tours adult/child/family $30/18/92, night adult/child $37/22) has ferries (reservations essential) departing Pier 33 for Alcatraz every half-hour from 9am to 3:55pm and at 5:55pm and 6:30pm for night tours.

East Bay

Blue & Gold Fleet Ferries (Map p303; ☎415-705-8200; www.blueandgoldfleet.com; $6.25 one-way) operates from the Ferry Building, Pier 39 and Pier 41 at Fisherman's Wharf to Jack London Square in Oakland (one way $6.25). During baseball season, a Giants ferry service runs directly from the landing at AT&T Park's Seals Plaza entrance to Oakland and Alameda. Ticket booths are located at the Ferry Building and Piers 39 and 41.

Marin County

Golden Gate Transit Ferries (Map p303; ☎415-455-2000; www.goldengateferry.org; ⏲6am-9:30pm Mon-Fri, 10am-6pm Sat & Sun) runs regular ferry services from the Ferry Building to Larkspur and Sausalito (one-way adult/child $10.75/5.25). Transfers are available to Muni bus services and bicycles are permitted. Blue & Gold Fleet Ferries also operate to Tiburon or Sausalito (one way $11.50) from Pier 41.

Napa Valley

Get to Napa car-free (weekdays only) via **Vallejo Ferry** (Map p303; ☎877-643-3779; www.baylinkferry.com; adult/child $13/6.50) with departures from Ferry Building docks about every hour from 6:30am to 7pm weekdays and roughly every 90 minutes from 10am to 9pm on weekends; bikes are permitted. However, the connecting bus from the Vallejo Ferry Terminal – Napa Valley Vine bus 29 to downtown Napa, Yountville, St Helena or Calistoga – operates only on weekdays.

Caltrain

From the depot at 4th and King Sts in San Francisco, **Caltrain** (www.caltrain.com; cnr 4th & King Sts) heads south to Millbrae (connecting to BART and SFO, 30 minutes), Palo Alto (one hour) and San Jose (1½ hours). This is primarily a commuter line, with frequent departures during weekday rush hours and less often between nonrush hours and on weekends.

Bicycle

Contact the **San Francisco Bicycle Coalition** (www.sfbike.org) for maps, information, and legal matters regarding bicyclists. Bike sharing is new in SF: racks for **Bay Area Bike Share** (☎855-480-2453; www.bayareabikeshare.com; 1-/3-day membership $9/22; first 30min of riding free) are located east of Van Ness Ave, and South of Market; however, these come without helmets, and biking Downtown without proper protection can be particularly dangerous. To rent a bike for more than half an hour, see specific neighborhood chapters under Sports

BIKING AROUND THE BAY AREA

Within San Francisco Muni has racks that can accommodate two bikes (only) on the front of most buses.

Marin County Bikes are allowed on the Golden Gate Bridge, so getting north to Marin County is no problem. You can transport bicycles on Golden Gate Transit buses, which usually have free racks (three bikes only; first-come, first-served). Ferries also allow bikes on board.

Wine Country To transport your bike to Wine Country, take Golden Gate Transit or the Vallejo Ferry. Within Sonoma Valley, take Arnold Dr instead of busy Hwy 12; through Napa Valley, take the Silverado Trail instead of busy Hwy 29. The most spectacular ride in Wine Country is sun-dappled, tree-lined West Dry Creek Rd, in Sonoma's Dry Creek Valley.

East Bay Cyclists can't use the Bay Bridge. Ride BART. Bikes are allowed on uncrowded BART trains, but during rush hours special limits apply: between 6:30am and 9am and 4pm to 6:30pm, bikes can't board the first three cars. During commute hours, you can also carry your bike across the bay via the **Caltrans Bay Bridge Bicycle Commuter Shuttle** (☎510-286-6945; www.dot.ca.gov/dist4/shuttle.htm; tickets $1; ⏰6:40-8:10am & 3:50-6:15pm Mon-Fri), which operates from the northwest corner of Main St and Bryant St in San Francisco, and MacArthur BART station in Oakland (on 40th St, between Market St and BART entrance); shuttles fill – arrive early.

& Activities headings. Bicycles can be taken on BART, but not aboard crowded trains, and never in the first car, nor in the first three cars during weekday rush hours. On Amtrak, bikes can be checked as baggage for $5.

TOURS

Precita Eyes Mission Mural Tours (Map p312; ☎415-285-2287; www.precitaeyes.org; adult $15-20, child $3; ⏰see website calendar for tour dates; 👪; 🚌12, 14, 48, 49, Ⓑ24th St Mission) Muralists lead weekend walking tours covering 60 to 70 Mission murals in a six- to 10-block radius of mural-bedecked Balmy Alley. Tours last 90 minutes to two hours and 15 minutes for the more in-depth Classic Mural Walk. Proceeds fund mural upkeep at this community arts nonprofit.

Sea Foraging Adventures (www.seaforager.com; per person from $42; ⏰calendar & reservations online) California sea-life expert Kirk Lombard leads guided adventures to secret foraging spots around San Francisco's waterfront, finding urban edibles ranging from bullwhip seaweed to eels under the Golden Gate Bridge.

Chinatown Alleyway Tours (☎415-984-1478; www.chinatownalleywaytours.org; adult/student $26/16; ⏰11am Sat; 👪; 🚌1, 8, 10, 41) Neighborhood teens lead two-hour community nonprofit tours for up-close-and-personal peeks into Chinatown's past (weather permitting).

Green Tortoise (☎800-867-8647, 415-956-7500; www.greentortoise.com) Quasi-organized, bargain travel on customized, biodiesel-fueled buses, with built-in berths, that run from San Francisco to points across California and beyond, including Bay Area day tours to Russian River and Santa Cruz (from $40); three-day round trips to Mendocino, Yosemite or Death Valley (from $244); and three- to seven-day coastal trips south to Monterey, Big Sur and LA (from $246).

Public Library City Guides (☎415-557-4266; www.sfcityguides.org; donations/tips welcome) Volunteer local historians lead nonprofit tours organized by neighborhood and theme: Art Deco Marina, Gold Rush Downtown, Secrets of Fisherman's Wharf, Telegraph Hill Stairway Hike and more.

Detour (www.detour.com) Location-aware smartphone tours ($5 each, $20 unlimited) that use your phone's GPS to trigger the audio – in-depth neighborhood stories, told by colorful local characters.

Tree Frog Treks (☎415-876-3764; www.treefrogtreks.com; play night $35, day camp $100; 👪) Meet red-footed tortoises and blue-tongued skinks at scientific play dates on Saturday nights, and occasional nature discovery day-camps (for kids age 5 and up) in Golden Gate Park, the Presidio and Fort Funston.

Fire Engine Tours (Map p298; ☎415-333-7077; www.fireenginetours.com; departs Beach St, at the Cannery; adult/child $50/30; ⏰tours 9am, 11am, 1pm, 3pm) Hot stuff: a 75-minute ride in an open-air vintage fire engine over Golden Gate Bridge. Dress warmly!

Directory A–Z

Customs Regulations

Each person over 21 years is allowed to bring 1L of liquor and 200 cigarettes duty-free into the USA. Non-US citizens are allowed to bring $100 worth of duty-free gifts. If you're carrying over $10,000 in US and foreign cash, traveler's checks or money orders, you must declare the excess amount – undeclared sums in excess of $10,000 may be subject to confiscation.

Discount Cards

Some green-minded venues, such as the de Young Museum, the California Academy of Sciences and the Legion of Honor, also offer discounts to ticket-bearing Muni riders.

City Pass (www.citypass.com; adult/child $94/69) Covers cable cars, Muni and entry to four attractions, including California Academy of Sciences, Blue & Gold Fleet Bay Cruise, Aquarium of the Bay and either the Exploratorium or the de Young Museum.

Go Card (www.smartdestinations.com; adult/child 1-day $60/45, 2-day $88/60, 3-day $109/80) Access to the city's major attractions, including California Academy of Sciences, de Young Museum, Aquarium of the Bay, Conservatory of Flowers, Beat Museum and Go Car tours, plus discounts on packaged tours and waterfront restaurants and cafés.

Electricity

Electric current in the USA is 110 to 115 volts, 60Hz AC. Outlets may be suited for flat two-prong or three-prong plugs. If your appliance is made for another electrical system, get a transformer or adapter at Walgreens.

Emergency

Call ☎911 in an emergency, or ☎311 for nonemergencies.

San Francisco General Hospital (☎emergency 415-206-8111, main hospital 415-206-8000; www.sfdph.org; 1001 Potrero Ave; ⏰24hr; 🚌9, 10, 33, 48) Best for serious trauma. Provides care to uninsured patients, including psychiatric care; no documentation required beyond ID.

Drug & Alcohol Emergency Info Line (☎415-362-3400)

Trauma Recovery & Rape Treatment Center (☎24hr hotline 415-206-8125, business hours 415-437-3000; www.traumarecoverycenter.org)

Internet Access

SF has free wi-fi hot spots citywide – locate one nearby with www.openwifispots.com. Connect for free at most cafés and hotel lobbies, as well as at the following locations:

Apple Store (☎415-392-0202; www.apple.com/retail/sanfrancisco; 1 Stockton St; ⊙9am-9pm Mon-Sat, 10am-8pm Sun; 📶; ⓂPowell St) Free wi-fi and internet terminal usage.

San Francisco Main Library (☎415-557-4400; www.sfpl.org; 100 Larkin St; ⊙10am-6pm Mon & Sat, 9am-8pm Tue-Thu, noon-6pm Fri, noon-5pm Sun; 📶; ⓂCivic Center) Free 30-minute internet terminal usage; spotty wi-fi access.

Legal Matters

San Francisco police usually have more urgent business than fining you for picking a protected orange California poppy on public land (up to $500), littering ($250 and up), loitering on sidewalks against the Sit/Lie law ($100-to-$500 ticket), jaywalking (ie crossing streets outside a pedestrian crosswalk, which can cost $75 to $125) or failing to clean up after your puppy ($50, plus shaming glares from fellow dog owners).

Drinking alcoholic beverages outdoors is not officially allowed, though beer and wine is often permissible at street fairs and other outdoor events. You may be let off with a warning for being caught taking a puff on a joint, but don't count on it – possessing marijuana for personal use is still a misdemeanor in this lenient city, but it's legal with a medical-marijuana prescription. In recent years the police have also cracked down on park squatters and illegal camping.

If you are arrested for any reason, it's your right to remain silent, but never walk away from an officer until given permission or you could be charged with resisting arrest. Anyone arrested gets the right to make one phone call. If you want to call your consulate, the police will give you the number on request.

Medical Services

Before traveling, contact your health-insurance provider to learn what medical care they will cover outside your hometown (or home country). Overseas visitors should acquire travel insurance that covers medical situations in the US, where nonemergency care for uninsured patients can be expensive.

For nonemergency appointments at hospitals, you'll need proof of insurance or cash. Even with insurance, you'll most likely have to pay up front for nonemergency care, and then wrangle afterward with your insurance company to get reimbursed. San Francisco has excellent medical facilities, plus alternative medical practices and herbal apothecaries.

Clinics

American College of Traditional Chinese Medicine (☎415-282-9603; www.actcm.edu; 450 Connecticut St; ⊙8:30am-9pm Mon-Thu, 9am-5:30pm Fri & Sat; 🚌10, 19, 22) Acupuncture, herbal remedies and other traditional Chinese medical treatments provided at low cost.

Haight-Ashbury Free Clinic (HealthRIGHT 360; ☎415-746-1950; www.healthright360.org; 558 Clayton St; ⊙by appointment 8:45am-noon & 1-5pm; 🚌6, 7, 33, 37, 43, ⓂN) San Francisco's legendary 'rock clinic' provides substance abuse counseling and mental health and women's health services by appointment.

Lyon-Martin Women's Health Services (☎415-565-7667; www.lyon-martin.org; 1748 Market St, Suite 201; ⊙11am-7:30pm Mon & Tue, 9am-5:30pm Wed-Fri; 🚌F, 6, 7, ⓂVan Ness) Women's clinic with affordable gynecological, recovery, HIV and mental health services, by appointment only; lesbian- and transgender-friendly.

San Francisco City Clinic (☎415-487-5500; www.sfcityclinic.org; 356 7th St; ⊙8am-4pm Mon, Wed & Fri, 1-6pm Tue, 1-4pm Thu) Low-cost treatment for sexually transmitted diseases (STDs), including emergency contraception and post-exposure prevention (PEP) for HIV.

Emergency Rooms

For San Francisco General Hospital, see p279.

Davies Medical Center (☎415-600-6000; www.cpmc.org; 45 Castro Bldg, cnr Noe St & Duboce Ave; ⊙24hr; 🚌6, 7, 22, 24, ⓂN) Emergency services for common injuries.

University of California San Francisco Medical Center (☎415-476-1000; www.ucsfhealth.org; 505 Parnassus Ave; ⊙24hr; 🚌6, 7, 43, ⓂN) ER at leading university hospital.

Pharmacies

Pharmaca (☎415-661-1216; www.pharmaca.com; 925 Cole St; ⊙store 8am-8pm Mon-Fri, 9am-8pm Sat & Sun, pharmacy 9am-8pm Mon-Fri, 9am-6pm Sat, 10am-6pm Sun; 🚌6, 37, 43, ⓂN) Pharmacy plus naturopathic and alternative remedies; weekend chair massage available.

PRACTICALITIES

Newspapers & Magazines *San Francisco Chronicle* (www.sfgate.com) is the main daily newspaper; *SF Weekly* (www.sfweekly.com) is a free weekly with local gossip and entertainment; and the *San Francisco Examiner* (www.sfexaminer.com) is a free daily newspaper, with news, events, opinions and culture.

Radio For local listening in San Francisco and online via podcasts and/or streaming audio, check out KQED (FM 88.5; kqed.org), National Public Radio (NPR) and Public Broadcasting (PBS) affiliate; KALW (FM91.7; kalw.org), local NPR affiliate, with news, talk, music,original programming; KPOO (FM 89.5, kpoo.com), community nonprofit radio with jazz, R&B, blues and reggae; and KPFA (FM 94.1, kpfa.org), for alternative news and music.

Volunteering Offer your services to **VolunteerMatch** (www.volunteermatch.org), which matches your interests, talents and availability with a local nonprofit where you could donate your time, if only for a few hours; while **Craigslist** (http://sfbay.craigslist.org/vol) lists opportunities to support the Bay Area community, from nonprofit fashion-show fundraisers to teaching English to new arrivals.

Walgreens (415-861-3136; www.walgreens.com; 498 Castro St, cnr 18th St; 24hr; 24, 33, 35, MF, K, L, M) Twenty-four-hour pharmacy and over-the-counter meds; dozens of locations citywide (see website).

Money

US dollars are the only currency accepted in San Francisco. Barter is sometimes possible on **Craigslist** (http://sfbay.craigslist.org). Debit/credit cards are widely accepted, but it's wise to bring a combination of cash, cards and traveler's checks.

ATMs

Most banks have 24-hour ATMs, except in areas where street crime is a problem (such as near the BART stop at 16th and Mission Sts). For a service charge, you can withdraw cash from an ATM using a credit card; check with your bank about fees and immediately applied interest.

Money Changers

Though there are exchange bureaus located at airports, the best rates are generally at banks in the city. For the latest exchange rates, visit currency converter website www.xe.com.

Bank of America (415-837-1394; www.bankamerica.com; 1 Powell St, downstairs; 9am-6pm Mon-Fri, to 2pm Sat; MPowell St, BPowell St) Few downtown banks exchange currency; this BofA branch does.

Currency Exchange International (415-974-6600; www.sanfranciscocurrencyexchange.com; Westfield Center, 865 Market St, Level 1; 10am-8:30pm Mon-Sat, 11am-7pm Sun; MPowell St, BPowell St) Good rates on exchange; centrally located near Union Square.

Traveler's Checks

In the US, traveler's checks in US dollars are virtually as good as cash; you don't necessarily have to go to a bank to cash them, as some establishments – particularly hotels – will accept them like cash. The major advantage of traveler's checks in US dollars over cash is that they can be replaced if lost or stolen.

Opening Hours

Typical opening hours in San Francisco are as follows:

Banks 9am to 4:30pm or 5pm Monday to Friday (occasionally 9am to noon Saturday).

Offices 8:30am to 5:30pm Monday to Friday.

Restaurants Breakfast 8am to 11am, lunch noon to 3pm, dinner 5:30pm with last service 9pm to 9:30pm weekdays or 10pm weekends; Saturday and Sunday brunch 10am to 2pm.

Shops 10am to 6pm or 7pm Monday to Saturday, though hours often run 11am to 8pm Saturday, and 11am to 6pm Sunday.

Pets

San Franciscans have more pets than kids. It's definitely pet-friendly – although dogs still have to stay on a leash in many parts of town, and you're required by law to clean up your dog's litter (fines run up to $50). San Francisco's pioneering 'poop scoop' ordinance was America's first, championed by Supervisor Harvey Milk.

Leash Laws

To check out the best locations for Rover to roam free, see **San Francisco Dog Parks** (www.sfdogparks.com) and bone up on local leash laws at **SF Dog** (www.sfdog.org).

Pet Housing

To find SF hotels that allow dogs, check out www.dog-friendly.com.

Wag Hotel (☎415-876-0700; www.waghotels.com; 25 14th St; 🚌12) If you need to go away for a few days, you may check your pet into the swanky Wag Hotel. Rates begin at $37 for a 'kitty condo,' $50 for a doggie room and $89 to $150 for a posh canine suite; luxury extras available.

Community

There are opportunities galore for pet lovers to connect in San Francisco, including two SF-based websites: www.catster.com and www.dogster.com.

Post

Check www.usps.com for post-office locations throughout San Francisco. These are the most conveniently located for visitors:

Civic Center Post Office (Map p306; ☎800-275-8777; 101 Hyde St; ⌚9am-5pm Mon-Fri, 10am-2pm Sat; Ⓜ Civic Center, Ⓑ Civic Center)

Rincon Center Post Office (Map p303; ☎800-275-8777; www.usps.gov; 180 Steuart St; ⌚7:30am-5pm Mon-Fri, 9am-2pm Sat; Ⓜ Embarcadero, Ⓑ Embarcadero) Postal services plus historic murals in historic wing.

US Post Office (Map p304; ☎800-275-8777; www.usps.gov; Macy's, 170 O'Farrell St; ⌚10am-5pm Mon-Sat; 🚋Powell-Mason & Powell-Hyde, Ⓜ Powell St, Ⓑ Powell St) Inside Macy's department store.

Public Holidays

Most shops remain open on public holidays (with the exception of Independence Day, Thanksgiving, Christmas and New Year's Day), while banks, schools and offices are usually closed. Holidays that may affect business hours and transit schedules include the following:

New Year's Day January 1

Martin Luther King Jr Day Third Monday in January

Presidents' Day Third Monday in February

Easter Sunday (and Good Friday and Easter Monday) in March or April

Memorial Day Last Monday in May

Independence Day July 4

Labor Day First Monday in September

Columbus Day Second Monday in October

Veterans Day November 11

Thanksgiving Fourth Thursday in November

Christmas Day December 25

Safe Travel

Keep your city smarts and wits about you, especially at night in the Tenderloin, South of Market (SoMa) and the Mission. The Bayview-Hunters Point neighborhood (south of Potrero Hill, along the water) is plagued by crime and violence, and isn't suitable for wandering tourists. After dark, Mission Dolores Park, Buena Vista Park and the entry to Golden Gate Park at Haight and Stanyan Sts are used for drug deals and casual sex hookups.

Taxes

SF's 8.75% sales tax is added to virtually everything, including meals, shopping and car rentals; hotel-room tax is 14%. Groceries are about the only items not taxed, and unlike European Value Added Tax, sales tax is not refundable.

In response to city laws mandating health-care benefits for restaurant workers, some restaurants pass those costs to diners by tacking an additional 3% to 4% 'Healthy SF' charge onto the bill – it's usually mentioned in the menu's fine print.

Telephone

The US country code is ☎1. San Francisco's city/area code is ☎415. To place an international call, dial ☎011 + country code + city code + number (make sure to drop the 0 that precedes foreign city codes, or your call won't go through).

When calling Canada, there's no need to dial the international access code ☎011. When dialing from a land line, you must precede any area code by ☎1 for direct dialing, ☎0 for collect calls and operator assistance (both expensive); from cell phones, dial only the area code and number. As of 2015 when calling local numbers in San Francisco, you must dial the area code; thus, all local numbers now begin with ☎1-415.

Area Codes in the Bay Area

East Bay ☎510

Marin County ☎415

Peninsula ☎650

San Francisco ☎415

San Jose ☎408

Santa Cruz ☎831

Wine Country ☎707

Local calls from public pay phones usually start at 50¢. Hotel-room telephones often carry heavy surcharges, but local calls may be free: ask before you dial. Toll-free numbers start with 800, 855, 866, 877 or 888; phone numbers beginning with 900 usually incur high fees.

Cell Phones

Most US cell phones besides the iPhone operate on CDMA, not the European standard GSM – check compatibility with your phone-service provider. North American travelers can use their cell phones in San Francisco and the Bay Area, but should check with their carriers about roaming charges.

Operator Services

International operator ☎00

Local directory ☎411

Long-distance directory information ☎1 + area code + 555-1212

Operator ☎0

Toll-free number information ☎800-555-1212

Phonecards

For international calls from a public pay phone, it's a good idea to use a phone card, available at most corner markets and drug stores. Otherwise, when you dial ☎0, you're at the mercy of whatever international carrier operates that pay phone.

Time

San Francisco is on Pacific Standard Time (PST), three hours behind the East Coast's Eastern Standard Time (EST) and eight hours behind Greenwich Mean Time (GMT/UTC). March through October is Daylight Saving Time in the US.

Toilets

Citywide Self-cleaning, coin-operated outdoor kiosk commodes cost 25¢; there are 25 citywide, mostly at North Beach, Fisherman's Wharf, the Financial District and the Tenderloin. Toilet paper isn't always available, and there's a 20-minute time limit. Public library branches and some city parks also have restrooms.

Downtown Clean toilets and baby-changing tables can be found at Westfield San Francisco Centre and Macy's. Most hotel lobbies also have bathrooms.

Civic Center San Francisco Main Library has restrooms.

Haight-Ashbury & Mission District Woefully lacking in public toilets; you may have to buy coffee, beer or food to gain access to locked customer-only bathrooms.

Tourist Information

San Francisco Visitor Information Center (Map p304; ☎415-391-2000; www.sanfrancisco.travel; Hallidie Plaza, Market & Powell Sts, lower level; ⏰9am-5pm Mon-Fri, to 3pm Sat & Sun; 🚋Powell-Mason, Powell-Hyde, Ⓜ Powell St, Ⓑ Powell St) Provides practical multilingual information, sells transportation passes, publishes glossy maps and booklets, and provides interactive touch screens.

Golden Gate National Recreation Area Headquarters (GGNRA; Map p298; ☎415-561-4700; www.nps.gov/goga; 495 Jefferson St; ⏰8:30am-4:30pm Mon-Fri; 🚌19, 30, 47, 🚋Powell-Hyde, Ⓜ F) Find everything hikers need to know about the GGNRA, plus maps and information on camping, hiking and programs at these and other national parks in the Pacific West region (including Yosemite).

For further tourist information, check out the following websites:

Lonely Planet (www.lonelyplanet.com)

SFGate.com (www.sfgate.com)

SFist (www.sfist.com)

Travelers with Disabilities

All Bay Area transit companies offer wheelchair-accessible service and travel discounts for travelers with disabilities. Major car-rental companies can usually supply hand-controlled vehicles with one or two days' notice. For people with visual impairment, major intersections emit a chirping signal to indicate once it is safe to cross the street. Check the following resources:

San Francisco Bay Area Regional Transit Guide (www.transit.511.org/disabled/index.aspx) Covers accessibility for people with disabilities.

Muni's Street & Transit (www.sfmta.com/getting-around/accessibility) Details wheelchair-friendly bus routes and streetcar stops.

Independent Living Resource Center of San Francisco (☎415-543-6222; www.ilrcsf.org; ⏰9am-4:30pm Mon-Thu, to 4pm Fri) Provides further information about wheelchair accessibility on Bay Area public transit and in hotels and other local facilities.

Visas

Canadians

Canadian citizens currently only need proof of identity and citizenship to enter the US – but check the US Department of State for updates, as requirements may change.

Visa Waiver Program

USA Visa Waiver Program (VWP) allows nationals from 38 countries to enter the US without a visa, provided they are carrying a machine-readable passport. For the updated list of countries included in the program and current requirements, see the **US Department of**

State (http://travel.state.gov) website.

Citizens of VWP countries need to register with the **US Department of Homeland Security** (https://esta.cbp.dhs.gov/esta/) three days before their visit. There is a $14 fee for registration application; when approved, the registration is valid for two years.

Visas Required

You must obtain a visa from a US embassy or consulate in your home country if you:

- Do not currently hold a passport from a VWP country.
- Are from a VWP country, but don't have a machine-readable passport.
- Are from a VWP country, but currently hold a passport issued between October 26, 2005, and October 25, 2006, that does not have a digital photo on the information page or an integrated chip from the data page. (After October 25, 2006, the integrated chip is required on all machine-readable passports.)
- Are planning to stay longer than 90 days.
- Are planning to work or study in the US.

Work Visas

Foreign visitors are not legally allowed to work in the USA without the appropriate working visa. The most common, the H visa, can be difficult to obtain. It usually requires a sponsoring organization, such as the company you will be working for in the US. The company will need to demonstrate why you, rather than a US citizen, are most qualified for the job.

The type of work visa you need depends on your work:

H visa For temporary workers.

L visa For employees in intra-company transfers.

O visa For workers with extraordinary abilities.

P visa For athletes and entertainers.

Q visa For international cultural-exchange visitors.

Women Travelers

SF is excellent for solo women travelers: you can eat, stay, dine and go out alone without anyone making presumptions about your availability, interests or sexual orientation. That said, women should apply their street smarts here as in any other US city, just to be on the safe side.

The **Women's Building** (Map p312; ☎415-431-1180; www.womensbuilding.org; 3543 18th St; 👪; 🚌14, 22, 33, 49, 🅑16th St Mission, Ⓜ J) has a Community Resource Room offering information on health care, domestic violence, childcare, harassment, legal issues, employment and housing.

Behind the Scenes

SEND US YOUR FEEDBACK

We love to hear from travelers – your comments keep us on our toes and help make our books better. Our well-traveled team reads every word on what you loved or loathed about this book. Although we cannot reply individually to your submissions, we always guarantee that your feedback goes straight to the appropriate authors, in time for the next edition. Each person who sends us information is thanked in the next edition – and the most useful submissions are rewarded with a selection of digital PDF chapters.

Visit **lonelyplanet.com/contact** to submit your updates and suggestions or to ask for help. Our award-winning website also features inspirational travel stories, news and discussions.

Note: We may edit, reproduce and incorporate your comments in Lonely Planet products such as guidebooks, websites and digital products, so let us know if you don't want your comments reproduced or your name acknowledged. For a copy of our privacy policy visit lonelyplanet.com/privacy.

OUR READERS

Many thanks to the travelers who used the last edition and wrote to us with helpful hints, useful advice and interesting anecdotes: Badong Abesamis, Alejandro Gomez

AUTHOR THANKS

Alison Bing

Thanks to Cliff Wilkinson, Alison Ridgway, Sarah Sung, Lisa Park, DeeAnn Budney, PT Tenenbaum and, above all, Marco Flavio Marinucci, for making a Muni bus ride into the adventure of a lifetime.

John A Vlahides

I owe great thanks to my editor Cliff Wilkinson for giving me free reign – I'm grateful. And to you, dear readers: please accept my most heartfelt gratitude for letting me be your guide to San Francisco. Have fun. I know you will!

ACKNOWLEDGMENTS

Cover photograph: Golden Gate Bridge, Alan Copson/AWL.

Illustration on pp50–1 by Michael Weldon.

THIS BOOK

This 10th edition of Lonely Planet's *San Francisco* guidebook was researched and written by Alison Bing, John A Vlahides and Sara Benson. They also wrote the previous edition. This guidebook was produced by the following:

Destination Editor Clifton Wilkinson
Product Editors Carolyn Boicos, Alison Ridgway
Senior Cartographer Alison Lyall
Book Designer Katherine Marsh
Assisting Editors Peter Cruttenden, Anne Mulvaney, Kristin Odijk, Jeanette Wall
Cover Researcher Campbell McKenzie
Thanks to Victoria Harrison, Andi Jones, Elizabeth Jones, Claire Naylor, Karyn Noble, Kirsten Rawlings, Ellie Simpson, Lauren Wellicome, Tony Wheeler

See also separate subindexes for:
- EATING P291
- DRINKING & NIGHTLIFE P292
- ENTERTAINMENT P293
- SHOPPING P294
- SPORTS & ACTIVITIES P295
- SLEEPING P295

Index

Sights 000
Map Pages **000**
Photo Pages **000**

Sights 000
Map Pages **000**
Photo Pages **000**

EATING

DRINKING & NIGHTLIFE

Sights 000
Map Pages **000**
Photo Pages **000**

☆ ENTERTAINMENT

SHOPPING

Sights 000
Map Pages **000**
Photo Pages **000**

San Francisco Maps

Sights
- Beach
- Bird Sanctuary
- Buddhist
- Castle/Palace
- Christian
- Confucian
- Hindu
- Islamic
- Jain
- Jewish
- Monument
- Museum/Gallery/Historic Building
- Ruin
- Shinto
- Sikh
- Taoist
- Winery/Vineyard
- Zoo/Wildlife Sanctuary
- Other Sight

Activities, Courses & Tours
- Bodysurfing
- Diving
- Canoeing/Kayaking
- Course/Tour
- Sento Hot Baths/Onsen
- Skiing
- Snorkeling
- Surfing
- Swimming/Pool
- Walking
- Windsurfing
- Other Activity

Sleeping
- Sleeping
- Camping

Eating
- Eating

Drinking & Nightlife
- Drinking & Nightlife
- Cafe

Entertainment
- Entertainment

Shopping
- Shopping

Information
- Bank
- Embassy/Consulate
- Hospital/Medical
- Internet
- Police
- Post Office
- Telephone
- Toilet
- Tourist Information
- Other Information

Geographic
- Beach
- Gate
- Hut/Shelter
- Lighthouse
- Lookout
- Mountain/Volcano
- Oasis
- Park
- Pass
- Picnic Area
- Waterfall

Population
- Capital (National)
- Capital (State/Province)
- City/Large Town
- Town/Village

Transport
- Airport
- BART station
- Border crossing
- Boston T station
- Bus
- Cable car/Funicular
- Cycling
- Ferry
- Metro/Muni station
- Monorail
- Parking
- Petrol station
- Subway/SkyTrain station
- Taxi
- Train station/Railway
- Tram
- Underground station
- Other Transport

Note: Not all symbols displayed above appear on the maps in this book

Routes
- Tollway
- Freeway
- Primary
- Secondary
- Tertiary
- Lane
- Unsealed road
- Road under construction
- Plaza/Mall
- Steps
- Tunnel
- Pedestrian overpass
- Walking Tour
- Walking Tour detour
- Path/Walking Trail

Boundaries
- International
- State/Province
- Disputed
- Regional/Suburb
- Marine Park
- Cliff
- Wall

Hydrography
- River, Creek
- Intermittent River
- Canal
- Water
- Dry/Salt/Intermittent Lake
- Reef

Areas
- Airport/Runway
- Beach/Desert
- Cemetery (Christian)
- Cemetery (Other)
- Glacier
- Mudflat
- Park/Forest
- Sight (Building)
- Sportsground
- Swamp/Mangrove

MAP INDEX

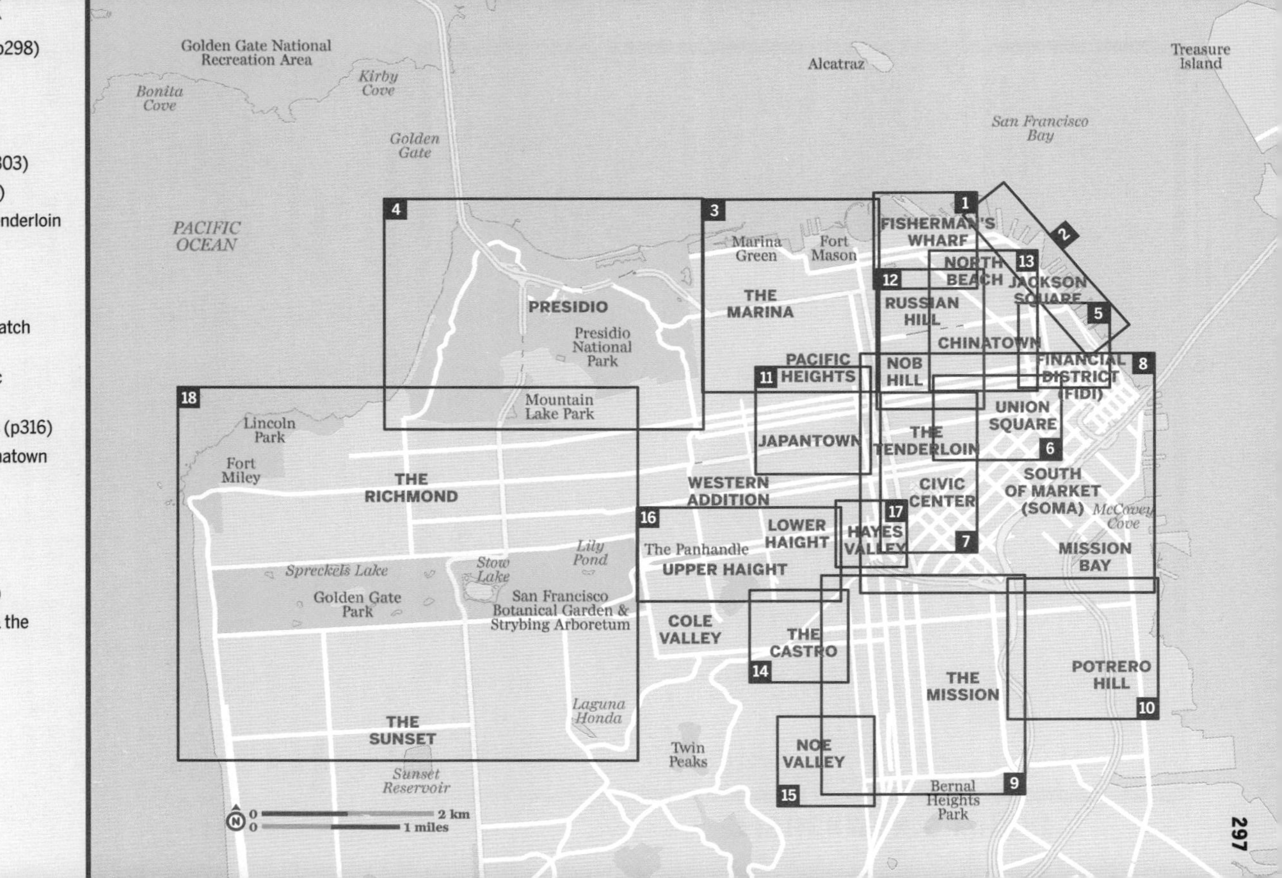

Golden Gate National Recreation Area
Bonita Cove
Kirby Cove
Golden Gate
PACIFIC OCEAN
Alcatraz
Treasure Island
San Francisco Bay
PRESIDIO
Presidio National Park
Mountain Lake Park
Lincoln Park
Fort Miley
THE RICHMOND
Spreckels Lake
Golden Gate Park
Stow Lake
Lily Pond
San Francisco Botanical Garden & Strybing Arboretum
THE SUNSET
Sunset Reservoir
Laguna Honda
Twin Peaks
Marina Green
Fort Mason
THE MARINA
PACIFIC HEIGHTS
JAPANTOWN
WESTERN ADDITION
The Panhandle
LOWER HAIGHT
UPPER HAIGHT
COLE VALLEY
THE CASTRO
NOE VALLEY
HAYES VALLEY
FISHERMAN'S WHARF
NORTH BEACH
JACKSON SQUARE
RUSSIAN HILL
CHINATOWN
NOB HILL
FINANCIAL DISTRICT (FIDI)
UNION SQUARE
THE TENDERLOIN
CIVIC CENTER
SOUTH OF MARKET (SOMA)
McCovey Cove
MISSION BAY
THE MISSION
POTRERO HILL
Bernal Heights Park
0 2 km
0 1 miles

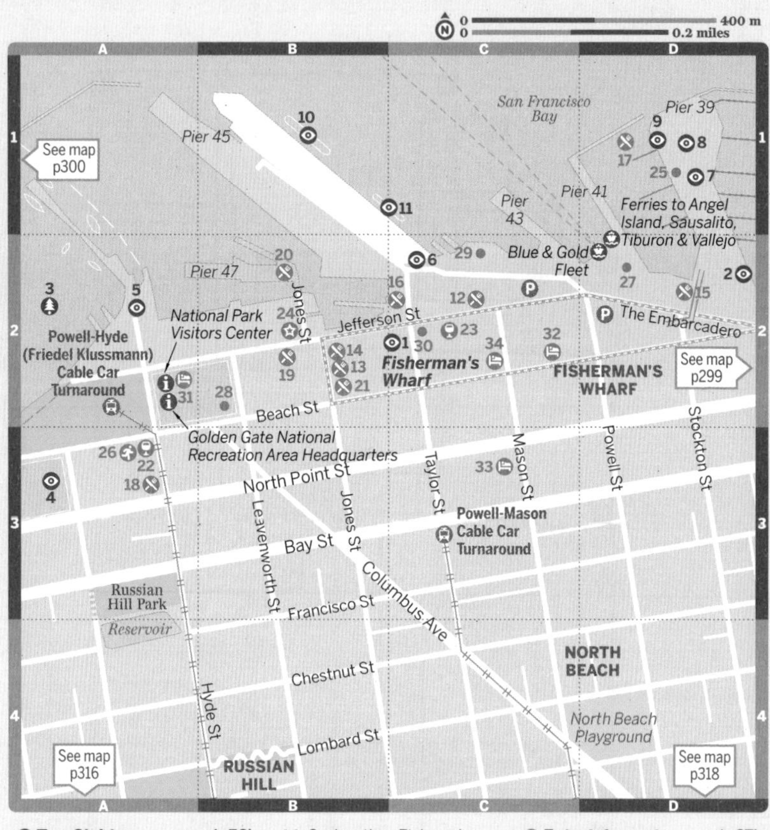

Top Sights (p52)
1 Fisherman's Wharf C2

Sights (p59)
2 Aquarium of the Bay D2
3 Aquatic Park A2
4 Ghirardelli Square A3
5 Maritime National Historical Park A2
6 Musée Mécanique C2
7 Pier 39 ....D1
8 San Francisco Carousel D1
9 Sea Lions at Pier 39 ......D1
10 SS Jeremiah O'Brien B1
11 USS Pampanito C1

Eating (p61)
12 Boudin Bakery C2
13 Carmel Pizza Co. B2
14 Codmother Fish and Chips.......................... B2
15 Eagle Cafe D2
16 Fisherman's Wharf Crab Stands C2
Fisherman's Wharf Food Trucks................ (see 21)
17 Forbes Island D1
18 Gary Danko A3
Ghirardelli Ice Cream.................(see 4)
19 In-N-Out Burger............ B2
Kara's Cupcakes.... (see 4)
20 Scoma's.......................... B2
21 Tanguito B2

Drinking & Nightlife (p66)
22 Buena Vista Cafe A3
23 Gold Dust Lounge......... C2

Entertainment (p67)
24 Lou's Fish Shack........... B2

Shopping (p67)
elizabethW ....(see 4)

Sports & Activities (p69)
25 Adventure Cat............... D1
26 Blazing Saddles A3
27 Blue & Gold Fleet D2
28 Fire Engine Tours.......... B2
29 Red & White Fleet C2
30 Ride the Ducks C2

Sleeping (p235)
31 Argonaut Hotel A2
32 Hotel Zephyr C2
33 The Tuscan.................... C3
34 Wharf Inn....................... C2

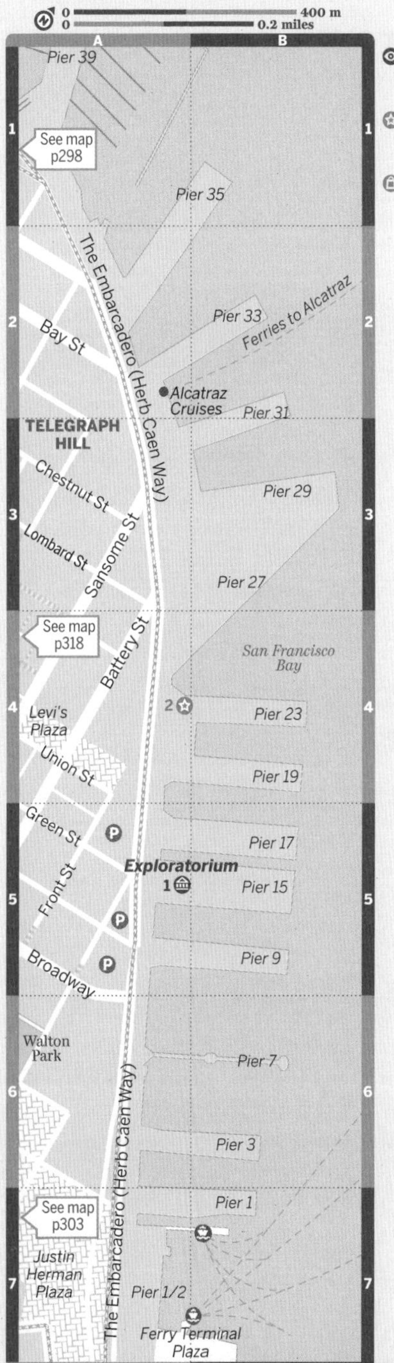

0 400 m
0 0.2 miles
A
B
Pier 39
See map p298
Pier 35
The Embarcadero (Herb Caen Way)
Pier 33
Ferries to Alcatraz
Bay St
Alcatraz Cruises
Pier 31
TELEGRAPH HILL
Chestnut St
Pier 29
Lombard St
Sansome St
Pier 27
See map p318
Battery St
San Francisco Bay
Levi's Plaza
Pier 23
Union St
Pier 19
Green St
Pier 17
Exploratorium
Front St
Pier 15
Broadway
Pier 9
Walton Park
Pier 7
Pier 3
Pier 1
See map p303
Justin Herman Plaza
Pier 1/2
Ferry Terminal Plaza

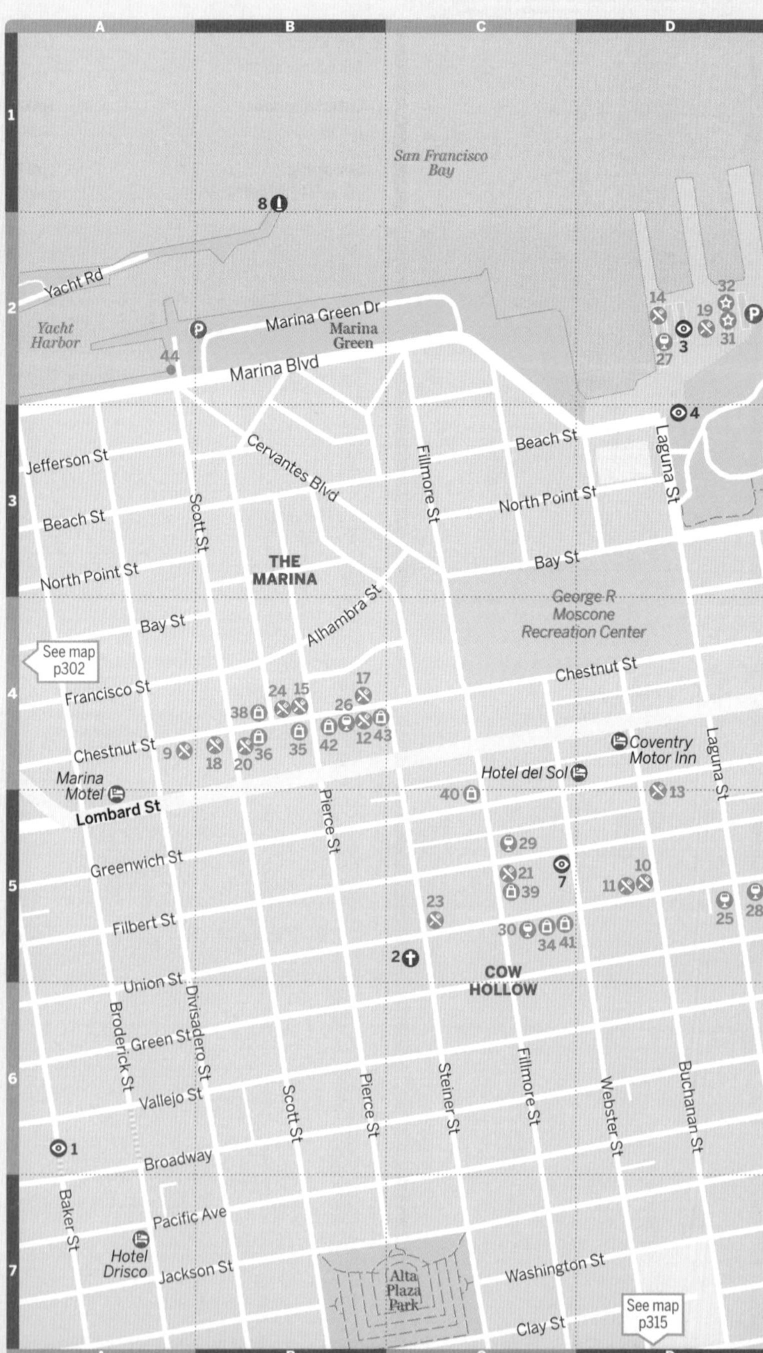

San Francisco Bay
Yacht Rd
Yacht Harbor
Marina Green Dr
Marina Green
Marina Blvd
Jefferson St
Beach St
North Point St
Bay St
Francisco St
Chestnut St
Lombard St
Greenwich St
Filbert St
Union St
Green St
Vallejo St
Broadway
Pacific Ave
Jackson St
Washington St
Clay St
Cervantes Blvd
Alhambra St
Scott St
Fillmore St
Laguna St
Pierce St
Steiner St
Webster St
Buchanan St
Broderick St
Divisadero St
Baker St
THE MARINA
COW HOLLOW
George R Moscone Recreation Center
Alta Plaza Park
Marina Motel
Hotel del Sol
Coventry Motor Inn
Hotel Drisco
See map p302
See map p315

Sights (p59)

1 Baker St Steps ... A6
2 Church of St Mary the Virgin ... C5
3 Fort Mason Center ... D2
4 Long Now Foundation ... D3
5 Maritime Museum ... F2
6 Octagon House ... E5
7 Vedanta Society ... C5
8 Wave Organ ... B1

Eating (p64)

9 A16 ... A4
10 Belga ... D5
11 Betelnut ... D5
12 Blue Barn Gourmet ... B4
13 Brazen Head ... D5
14 Greens ... D2
15 Grove ... B4
16 Lite Bite ... E5
17 Lucca Delicatessen ... B4
18 Mamacita ... B4
19 Off the Grid ... D2
20 Pluto's Fresh Food ... B4
21 Real Food ... C5
22 Roam Artisan Burger ... E5
23 Rose's Café ... C5
24 Seed and Salt ... B4

Drinking & Nightlife (p66)

25 Bus Stop ... D5
26 California Wine Merchant ... B4
27 Interval Bar & Cafe ... D2
28 Lightning Tavern ... D5
29 MatrixFillmore ... C5
30 West Coast Wine & Cheese ... C5

Entertainment (p67)

31 BATS Improv ... D2
32 Magic Theatre ... D2

Shopping (p68)

33 Ambiance ... E5
34 ATYS ... C5
35 Benefit ... B4
36 Dress ... B4
37 Itoya Top Drawer ... E5
38 Jack's ... B4
39 My Roommate's Closet ... C5
40 PlumpJack Wines ... C5
41 Sui Generis Illa ... C5
42 Toss Designs ... B4
43 Y and I Boutique ... B4

Sports & Activities (p70)

44 Oceanic Society Expeditions ... A2

THE PRESIDIO

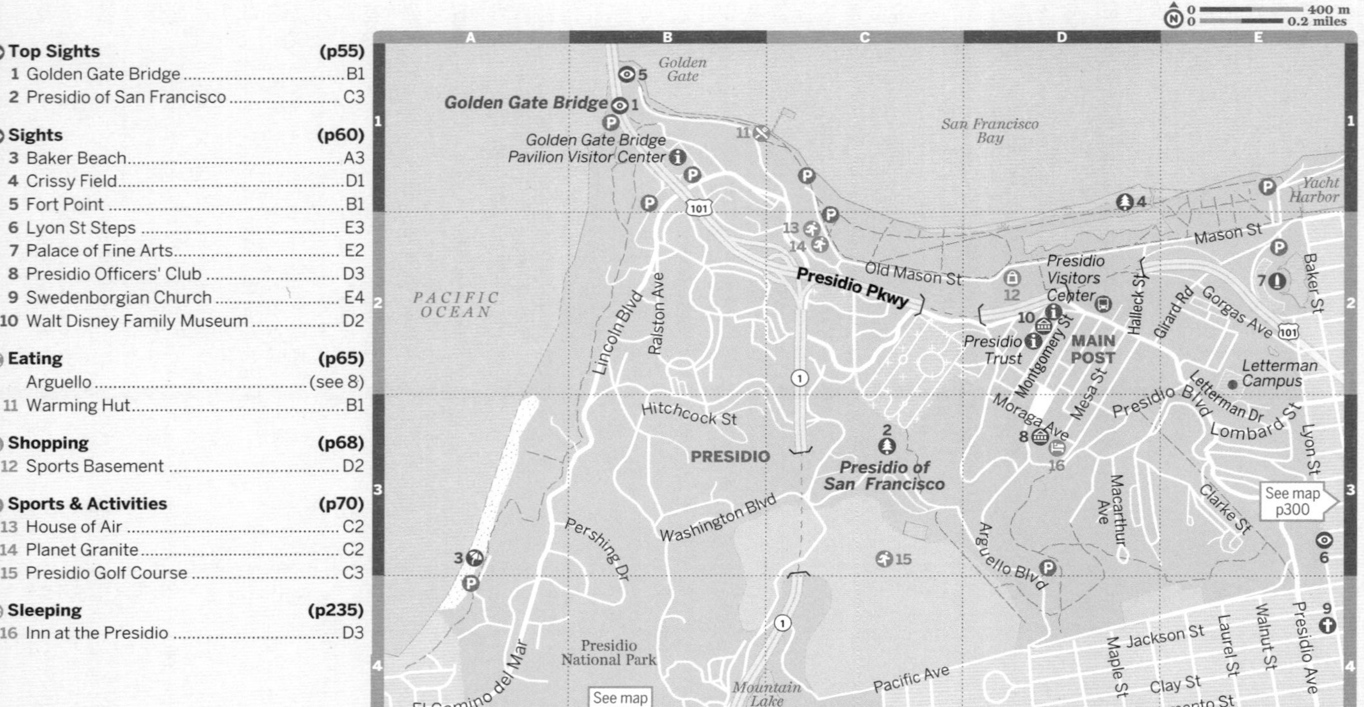

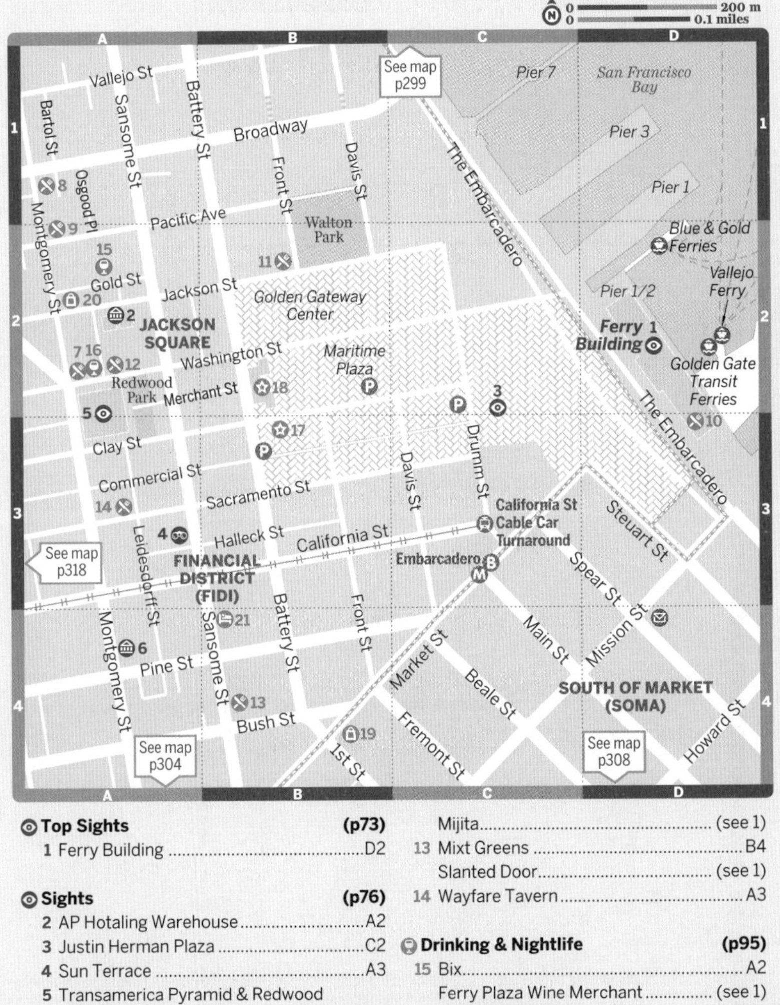

0 200 m
0 0.1 miles
See map p299
Pier 7
San Francisco Bay
Pier 3
Pier 1
Blue & Gold Ferries
Vallejo Ferry
Pier 1/2
Ferry Building
Golden Gate Transit Ferries
Vallejo St
Broadway
Pacific Ave
Jackson St
Gold St
Washington St
Merchant St
Clay St
Commercial St
Sacramento St
Halleck St
California St
Pine St
Bush St
Bartol St
Sansome St
Battery St
Front St
Davis St
Osgood Pl
Montgomery St
Walton Park
Golden Gateway Center
Maritime Plaza
JACKSON SQUARE
Redwood Park
The Embarcadero
Drumm St
California St Cable Car Turnaround
Embarcadero
Steuart St
Spear St
Main St
Mission St
Beale St
Fremont St
Market St
1st St
Howard St
Leidesdorff St
FINANCIAL DISTRICT (FIDI)
SOUTH OF MARKET (SOMA)
See map p318
See map p304
See map p308

UNION SQUARE

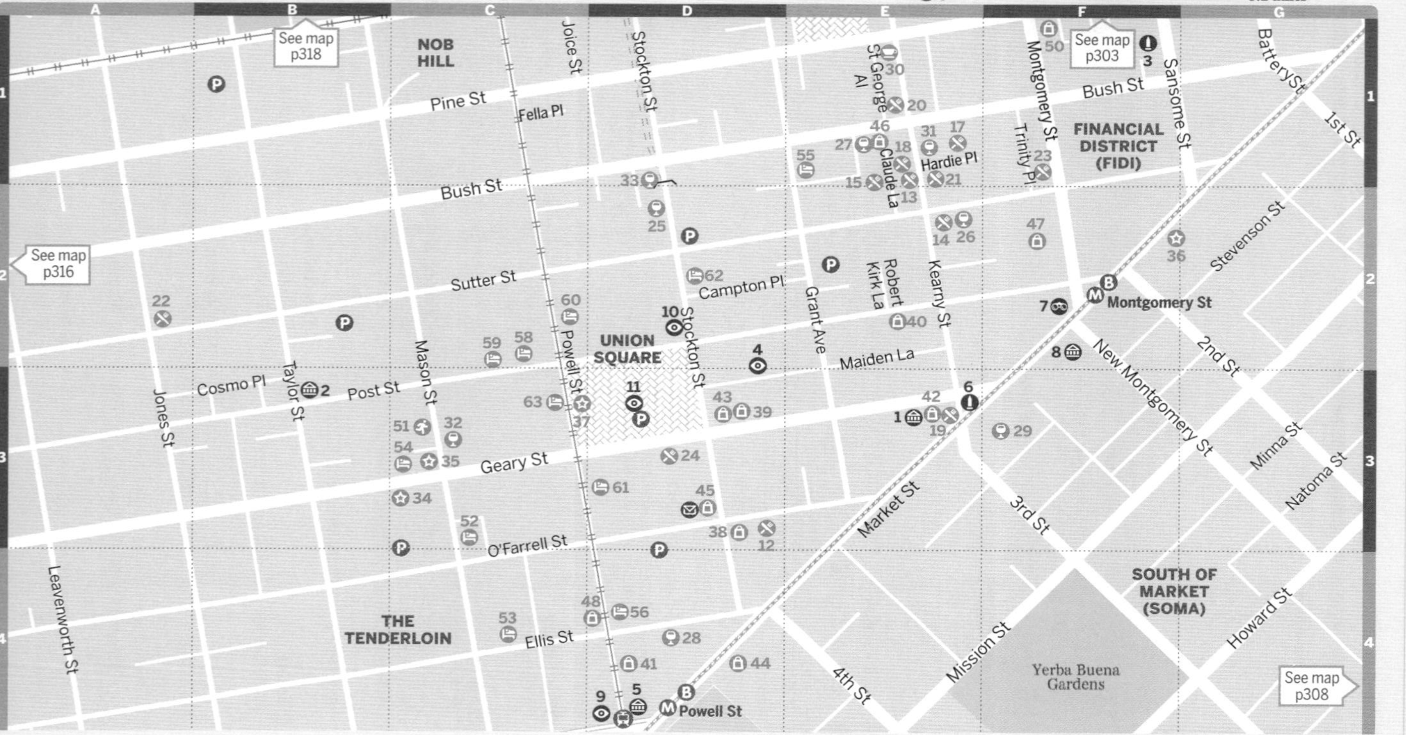

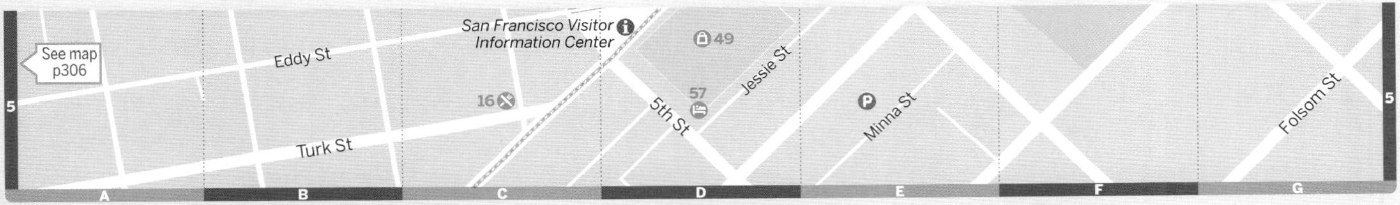

See map p306

San Francisco Visitor Information Center

Sights (p77)

1 49 Geary ... E3
2 Bohemian Club ... B3
3 Diego Rivera's Allegory of California Fresco ... F1
4 Frank Lloyd Wright Building ... D2
5 James Flood Building ... D4
6 Lotta's Fountain ... E3
7 One Montgomery Terrace ... F2
8 Palace Hotel ... F2
9 Powell St Cable Car Turnaround ... D4
10 Ruth Asawa's San Francisco Fountain ... D2
11 Union Square ... D3

Eating (p89)

12 Bio ... D3
13 Boxed Foods ... E1
14 Bread & Cocoa ... E2
15 Cafe Claude ... E1
16 Farmerbrown ... C5
17 Galette 88 ... E1
18 Gitane ... E1
19 Hakkasan ... E3
20 Muracci's Curry ... E1
21 Sushirrito ... E1
22 Sweet Woodruff ... A2
23 The Golden West ... F1
24 Tout Sweet ... D3

Drinking & Nightlife (p95)

25 Burritt Room ... D2
26 Gaspar Brasserie & Cognac Room ... E2
27 Irish Bank ... E1
28 John's Grill ... D4
29 Local Edition ... F3
30 PlenTea ... E1
31 Rickhouse ... E1
32 Ruby Skye ... C3
33 Tunnel Top ... D1

Entertainment (p101)

34 American Conservatory Theater ... C3
35 Biscuits & Blues ... C3
36 Commonwealth Club ... F2
Starlight Room ... (see 60)
37 TIX Bay Area ... C3

Shopping (p105)

38 Barneys ... D3
39 Britex Fabrics ... D3
40 Gump's ... E2
41 H&M ... D4
42 Harputs ... E3
43 John Varvatos ... D3
44 Levi's Flagship Store ... D4
45 Macy's ... D3
46 Margaret O'Leary ... E1
47 T-We Tea ... F2
48 Uniqlo ... D4
49 Westfield San Francisco Centre ... D5
50 Wingtip ... F1

Sports & Activities (p70)

51 Blazing Saddles ... C3

Sleeping (p236)

52 HI San Francisco Downtown ... C3
53 Hotel Abri ... C4
54 Hotel Diva ... C3
55 Hotel Triton ... E1
56 Hotel Union Square ... D4
57 Hotel Zetta ... D5
58 Inn at Union Square ... C2
59 Kensington Park Hotel ... C2
Palace Hotel ... (see 8)
60 Sir Francis Drake Hotel ... C2
61 Stratford Hotel ... D3
62 Taj Campton Place ... D2
63 Westin St Francis Hotel ... C3

CIVIC CENTER & THE TENDERLOIN

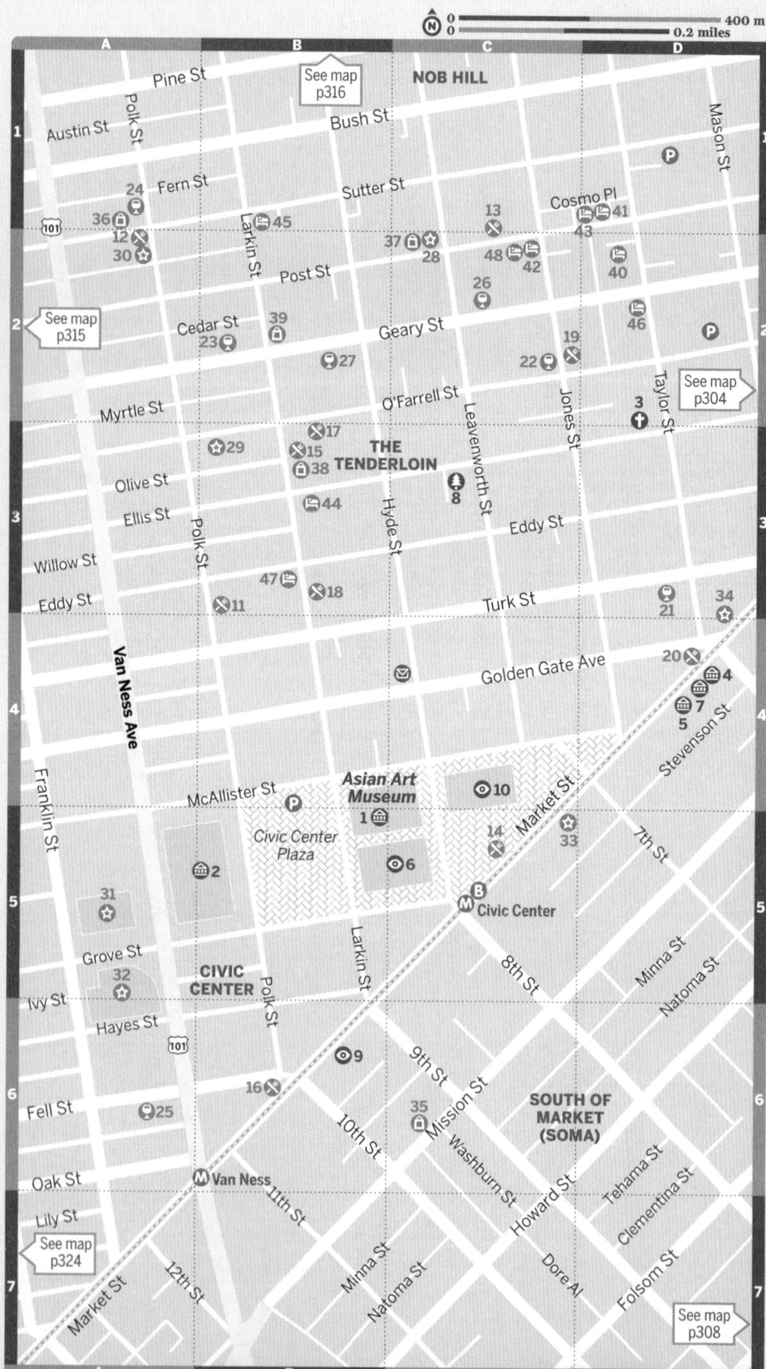

CIVIC CENTER & THE TENDERLOIN

Top Sights (p75)
1 Asian Art Museum B5

Sights (p84)
2 City Hall B5
3 Glide Memorial United Methodist Church D2
4 Luggage Store Gallery D4
5 Root Division D4
6 San Francisco Main Library C5
7 SF Camerawork D4
8 Tenderloin National Forest C3
9 Twitter Headquarters B6
10 United Nations Plaza C4

Eating (p91)
11 Brenda's French Soul Food B3
Cafe Asia ..... (see 1)
12 Cafe Zitouna A2
13 farm:table C1
14 Heart of the City Farmers Market C5
15 Lers Ros B3
16 Little Griddle B6
17 Sai Jai Thai B3
18 Saigon Sandwich Shop B3
19 Shalimar C2
20 The Hall D4

Drinking & Nightlife (p96)
21 Aunt Charlie's Lounge D3
22 Bourbon & Branch C2
23 Edinburgh Castle B2
24 Lush Lounge A1
25 Rickshaw Stop A6
26 Rye C2
27 Whiskey Thieves B2

Entertainment (p101)
28 Café Royale C2
29 Great American Music Hall B3
30 Hemlock Tavern A2
31 San Francisco Ballet A5
San Francisco Opera ..... (see 31)
32 San Francisco Symphony A5
33 Strand Theater C5
34 Warfield D3

Shopping (p107)
35 Electric Works C6
36 Gypsy Rosalie's A1
37 Kayo Books C2
38 San Francycle B3
39 The Magazine B2

Sleeping (p236)
40 Adelaide Hostel D2
41 Andrews Hotel D1
42 Beresford Arms Hotel C2
43 Fitzgerald Hotel D1
44 HI San Francisco City Center B3
45 Hotel Carlton B1
46 Marker D2
47 Phoenix Hotel B3
48 USA Hostels C2

Key on p310

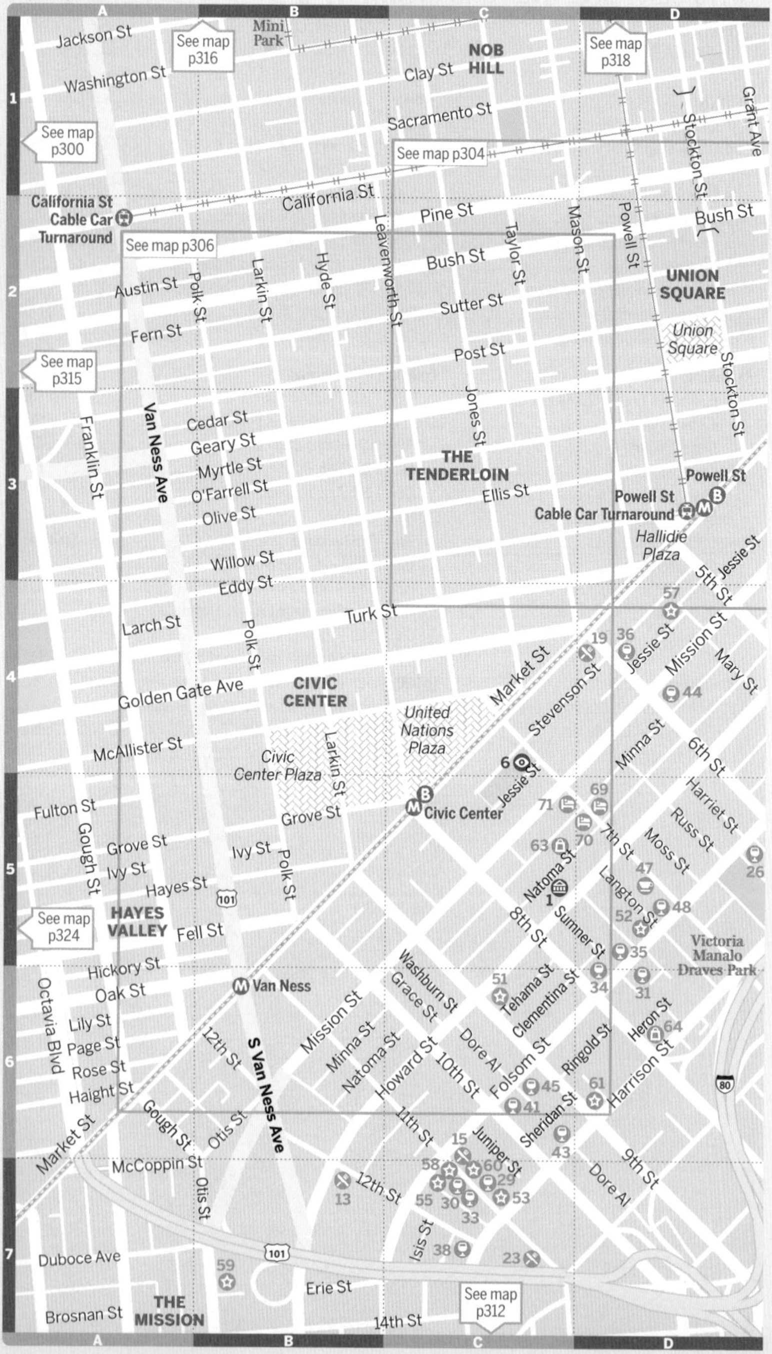

A B C D
1 2 3 4 5 6 7

See map p316
See map p318
See map p300
See map p304
See map p306
See map p315
See map p324
See map p312

NOB HILL
UNION SQUARE
THE TENDERLOIN
CIVIC CENTER
HAYES VALLEY
THE MISSION

Jackson St
Washington St
Mini Park
Clay St
Sacramento St
California St
Pine St
Bush St
Sutter St
Post St
Grant Ave
Stockton St
Powell St
Mason St
Taylor St
Jones St
Leavenworth St
Hyde St
Larkin St
Polk St
Van Ness Ave
Franklin St
Austin St
Fern St
Cedar St
Geary St
Myrtle St
O'Farrell St
Olive St
Ellis St
Willow St
Eddy St
Larch St
Turk St
Golden Gate Ave
McAllister St
Fulton St
Grove St
Ivy St
Hayes St
Fell St
Gough St
Hickory St
Oak St
Lily St
Page St
Rose St
Haight St
Octavia Blvd
Market St
12th St
S Van Ness Ave
Otis St
McCoppin St
Duboce Ave
Brosnan St
Erie St
14th St
California St Cable Car Turnaround
Powell St Cable Car Turnaround
Union Square
Hallidie Plaza
United Nations Plaza
Civic Center Plaza
Civic Center
Van Ness
Jessie St
5th St
Mission St
Mary St
Stevenson St
Minna St
6th St
Harriet St
Russ St
Moss St
7th St
Natoma St
Langton St
8th St
Sumner St
Victoria Manalo Draves Park
Washburn St
Grace St
Tehama St
Clementina St
Heron St
Ringold St
Harrison St
Howard St
10th St
Dore Al
Folsom St
Sheridan St
11th St
Juniper St
9th St
Isis St
101
80

1 6 13 15 19 23 26 29 30 31 33 34 35 36 38 41 43 44 45 47 48 51 52 53 55 57 58 59 60 61 63 64 69 70 71

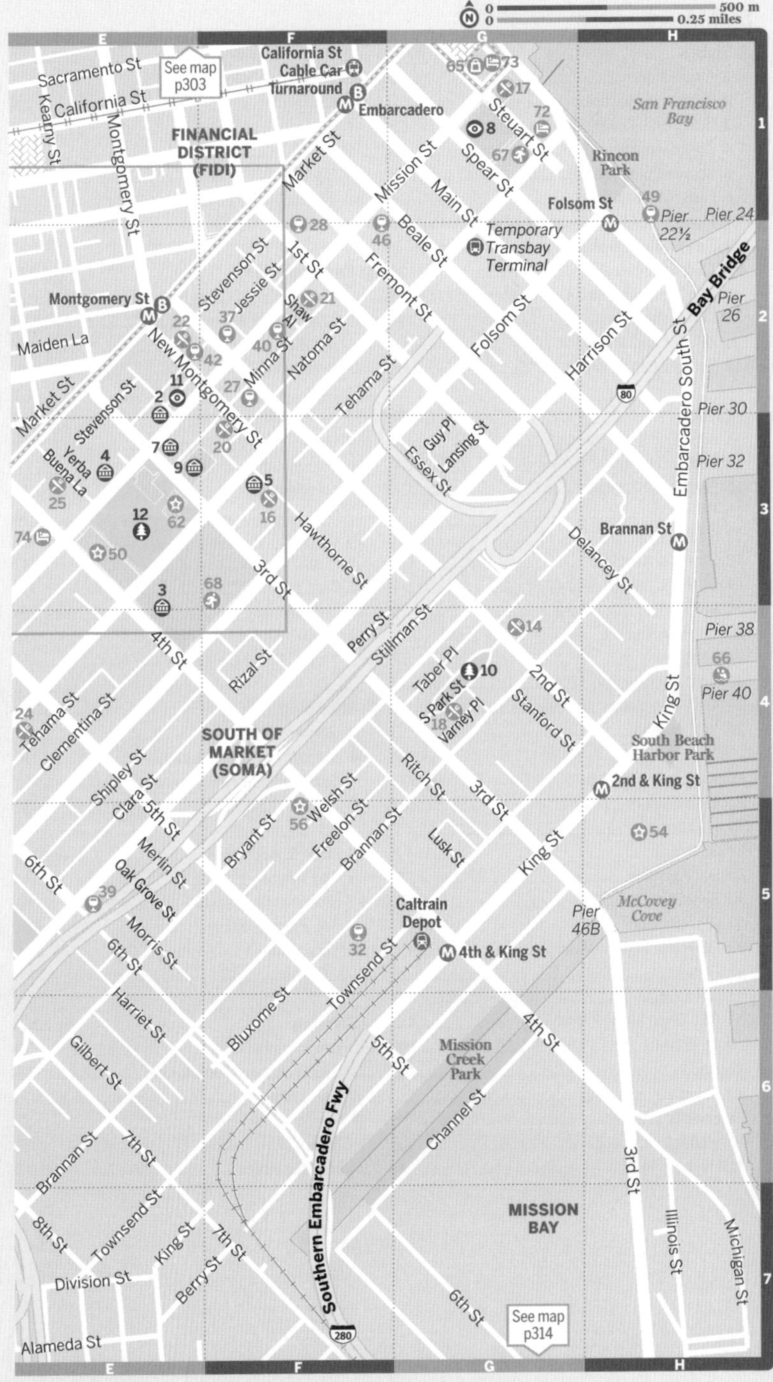

500 m
0.25 miles
SOMA
See map p303
See map p314
California St Cable Car Turnaround
Embarcadero
FINANCIAL DISTRICT (FIDI)
SOUTH OF MARKET (SOMA)
MISSION BAY
San Francisco Bay
Rincon Park
South Beach Harbor Park
McCovey Cove
Mission Creek Park
Temporary Transbay Terminal
Montgomery St
Folsom St
Brannan St
2nd & King St
4th & King St
Caltrain Depot
Bay Bridge
Southern Embarcadero Fwy
Pier 22½
Pier 24
Pier 26
Pier 30
Pier 32
Pier 38
Pier 40
Pier 46B
Sacramento St
California St
Kearny St
Montgomery St
Market St
Maiden La
Mission St
Steuart St
Spear St
Main St
Beale St
Fremont St
1st St
Stevenson St
Jessie St
Shaw Al
Minna St
Natoma St
New Montgomery St
Yerba Buena La
Tehama St
Folsom St
Harrison St
Embarcadero South St
Guy Pl
Lansing St
Essex St
Hawthorne St
3rd St
4th St
Rizal St
Perry St
Stillman St
Delancey St
Taber Pl
S Park St
Varney Pl
2nd St
Stanford St
King St
Clementina St
Shipley St
Clara St
5th St
Merlin St
Oak Grove St
Morris St
6th St
Harriet St
Gilbert St
Bryant St
Welsh St
Freelon St
Brannan St
Ritch St
Lusk St
Townsend St
Bluxome St
Channel St
7th St
8th St
Berry St
Division St
Alameda St
Illinois St
Michigan St

SOMA *Map on p308*

Sights (p79)

Eating (p93)

Drinking & Nightlife (p97)

Entertainment (p103)

Shopping (p108)

Sports & Activities (p109)

Sleeping (p236)

THE MISSION *Map on p312*

Sights (p148)

1 826 Valencia C4
2 Balmy Alley E7
3 Campfire Gallery C6
4 Catharine Clark Gallery G2
5 Clarion Alley C3
6 Creativity Explored B2
7 Dolores Park A4
8 Eleanor Harwood Gallery F7
9 Galería de la Raza F6
10 Hosfelt Gallery G2
11 Incline Gallery C4
12 Mission Dolores A3
13 Ratio 3 .... D7
14 Southern Exposure F4
15 Women's Building C4

Eating (p155)

16 Al's Place C8
17 Bi-Rite Creamery B3
18 Chino B2
19 Chow A2
20 Commonwealth C4
21 Craftsman & Wolves C4
22 El Techo de Lolinda C5
23 Foreign Cinema C5
24 Galajee C2
25 Humphry Slocombe E6
26 La Palma Mexicatessen F6
27 La Taqueria D7
28 Locanda C3
29 Lolo Cevicheria C5
30 Mission Cheese C4
31 Mission Chinese C4
32 Mission Community Market C5
33 Mission Pie D7
34 Namu Gaji B3
35 Old Jerusalem D7
36 Pancho Villa C2
37 Pizzeria Delfina B4
38 Radish C4
39 Rainbow Grocery D1
40 Tacolicious C4
41 Tartine B4
42 Tortas Los Picudos E6
43 Udupi Palace C5
44 Woodhouse Fish Co A1

Drinking & Nightlife (p160)

45 %ABV B2
46 20 Spot D5
47 Bissap Baobab D4
48 Borderlands C4
49 Dalva & Hideout C2
50 Doc's Clock D5
51 El Rio C8
52 Elixir C2
53 Four Barrel Coffee C2
54 Homestead E4
55 Latin American Club C5
56 Monk's Kettle B2
57 Phone Booth D6
58 Ritual Coffee Roasters C5
59 St. Vincent Tavern C6
60 Trick Dog E4
61 Zeitgeist C1

Entertainment (p162)

62 Amnesia C4
63 Brava Theater F6
64 Brick & Mortar C1
65 Joe Goode Performance Group E2
66 Make-Out Room C6
67 Marsh C5
68 Mighty G2
69 Mission Bowling Club D3
70 Oberlin Dance Collective D3
71 Revolution Cafe C5
72 Rite Spot Cafe E3
73 Roccapulco C8
74 Roxie Cinema C2
75 SUB-Mission C3
76 The Chapel C4
77 Verdi Club F3
78 Viracocha C5

Shopping (p164)

79 Accident & Artifact C1
80 Adobe Books & Backroom Gallery E6
81 Aggregate Supply C4
82 Alley Cat Books E6
83 Aquarius Records C5
84 Betabrand C4
85 Bi-Rite B4
86 Black & Blue Tattoo B2
87 Community Thrift C3
88 Dema C5
89 Dog-Eared Books C5
90 Good Vibrations C3
91 Gravel & Gold C5
92 Heath Ceramics E3
93 Little Paper Planes C4
94 Mission Skateboards E6
95 Modern Times Bookstore Collective F6
96 Needles & Pens B3
97 Nooworks C2
98 Paxton Gate C4
99 Press: Works on Paper E6
100 Tigerlily Perfumery C5
101 Voyager C2

Sports & Activities (p168)

102 18 Reasons B3
103 Dance Mission D6
104 Mission Cultural Center for Latino Arts D7
105 Potrero del Sol/La Raza Skatepark G7
106 Precita Eyes Mission Mural Tours E6

Sleeping (p241)

107 Inn San Francisco D5

THE MISSION

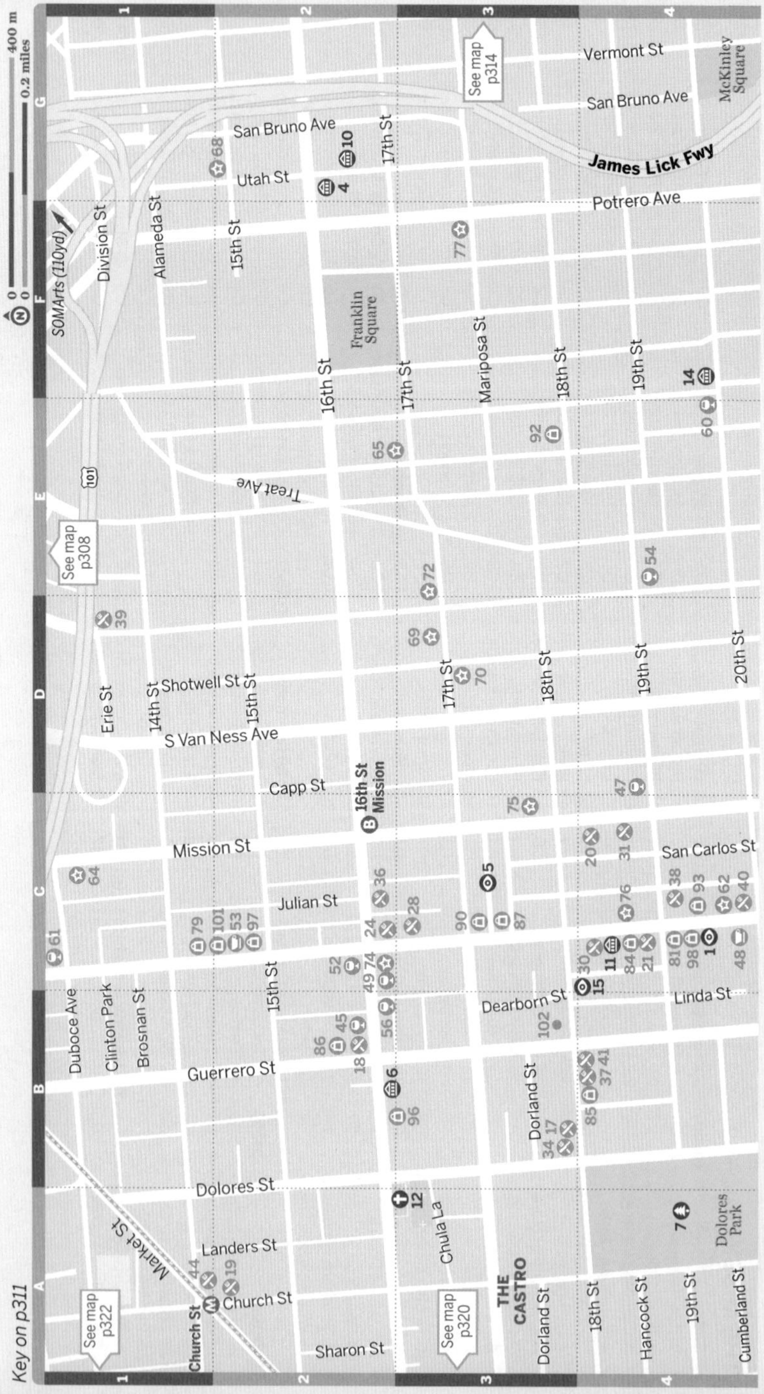

Key on p311

THE MISSION

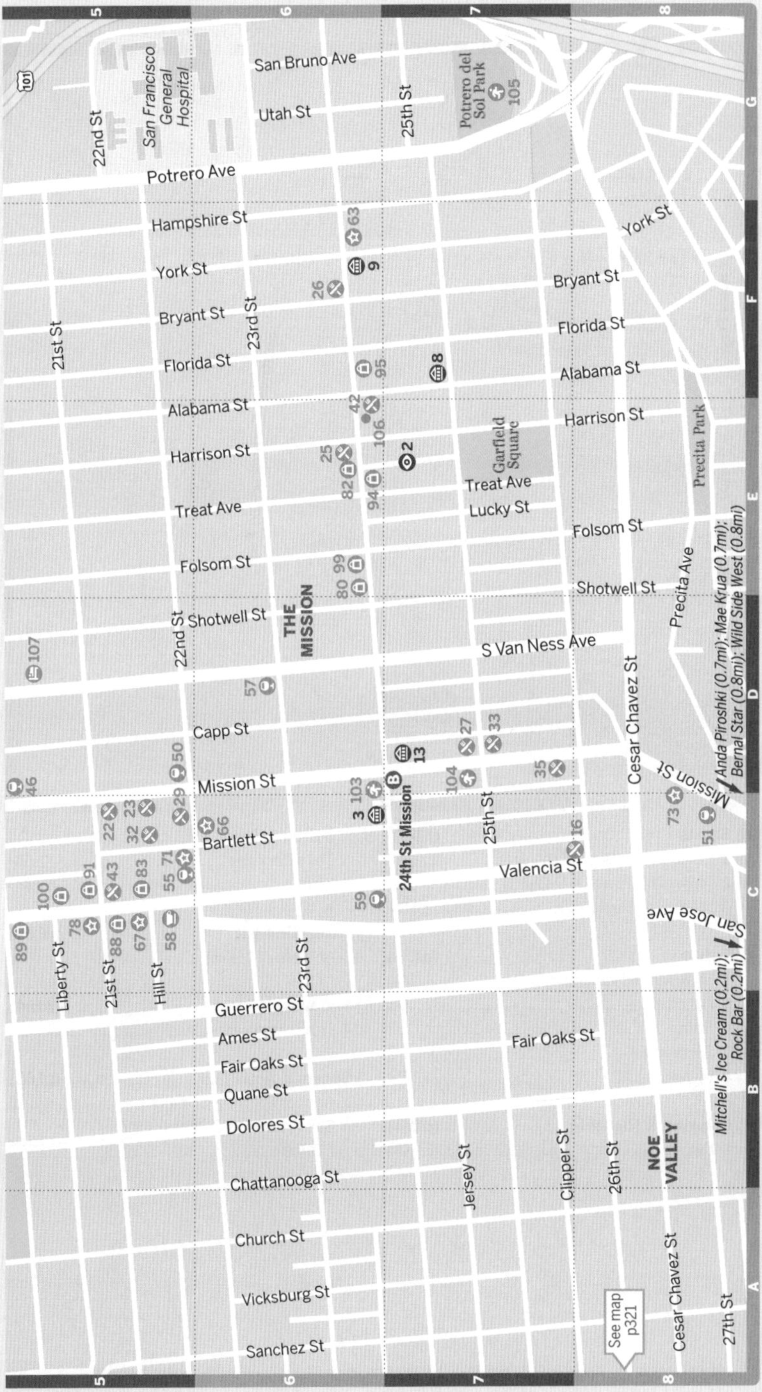
San Bruno Ave
Utah St
Potrero Ave
Hampshire St
York St
Bryant St
Florida St
Alabama St
Harrison St
Treat Ave
Folsom St
Shotwell St
S Van Ness Ave
Capp St
Mission St
Bartlett St
Valencia St
San Jose Ave
Guerrero St
Ames St
Fair Oaks St
Quane St
Dolores St
Chattanooga St
Church St
Vicksburg St
Sanchez St
21st St
22nd St
23rd St
24th St Mission
25th St
26th St
27th St
Liberty St
Hill St
Jersey St
Clipper St
Cesar Chavez St
Lucky St
Precita Ave
Precita Park
Garfield Square
Potrero del Sol Park
San Francisco General Hospital
THE MISSION
NOE VALLEY
101
Anda Piroshki (0.7mi); Mae Krua (0.7mi); Bernal Star (0.8mi); Wild Side West (0.8mi)
Mitchell's Ice Cream (0.2mi); Rock Bar (0.2mi)
See map p321
A
B
C
D
E
F
G
5
6
7
8
2
3
8
9
13
16
22
23
25
26
27
29
32
33
35
42
43
46
50
51
55
57
58
59
63
66
67
71
73
78
80
82
83
88
89
91
94
95
99
100
103
104
105
106
107

POTRERO HILL & DOGPATCH

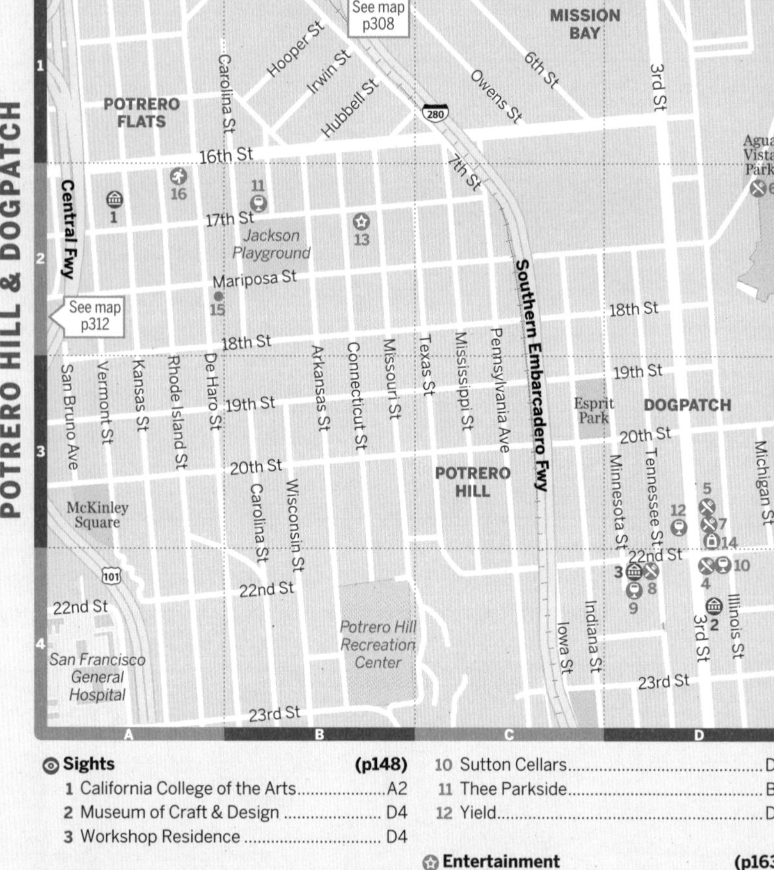

Sights **(p148)**
1 California College of the Arts ... A2
2 Museum of Craft & Design ... D4
3 Workshop Residence ... D4

Eating **(p154)**
4 Mr & Mrs Miscellaneous ... D4
5 Poco Dolce ... D3
6 Ramp ... D2
7 Serpentine ... D3
8 theLab & Little Nib ... D4

Drinking & Nightlife **(p154)**
9 Dig ... D4
10 Sutton Cellars ... D4
11 Thee Parkside ... B2
12 Yield ... D3

Entertainment **(p163)**
13 Bottom of the Hill ... B2

Shopping **(p154)**
14 Triple Aught Design ... D3

Sports & Activities **(p168)**
15 Anchor Brewing Company ... A2
16 San Francisco Center for the Book ... A2

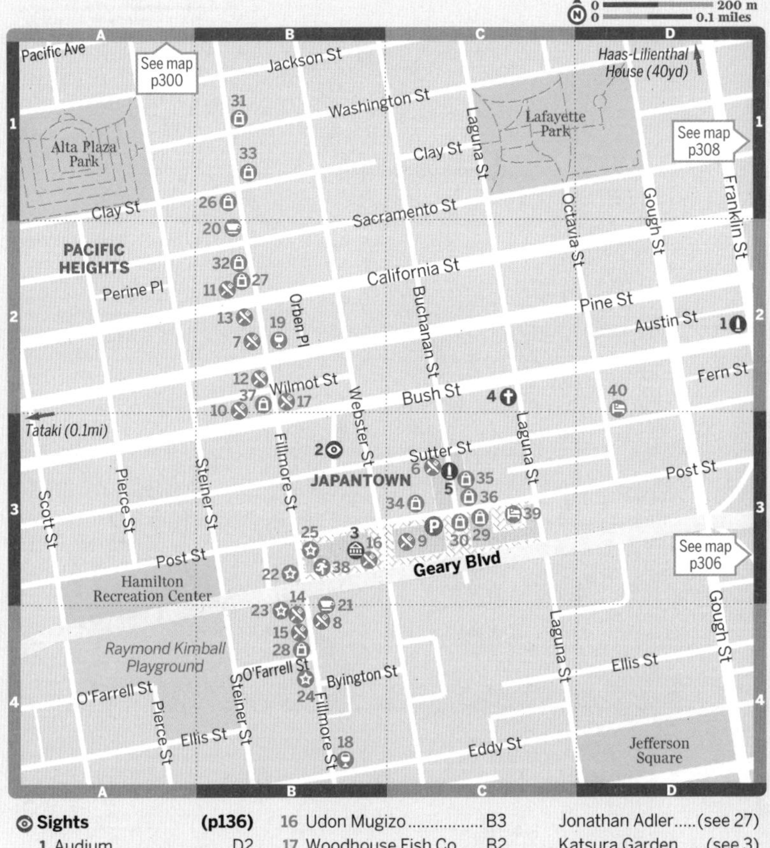

Sights (p136)

1 Audium D2
2 Cottage Row B3
3 Ikenobo Ikebana Society B3
4 Konko Church C2
Peace Pagoda (see 30)
5 Ruth Asawa Fountains C3

Eating (p139)

6 Benkyodo C3
7 Bun Mee B2
Crown & Crumpet (see 34)
Grove (see 19)
8 Izakaya Kou B4
9 Nijiya Supermarket C3
10 Out the Door B2
11 Pizzeria Delfina B2
12 Roam Artisan Burger B2
13 Sift Dessert Bar B2
14 State Bird Provisions B4
15 The Progress B4
16 Udon Mugizo B3
17 Woodhouse Fish Co B2

Drinking & Nightlife (p141)

18 1300 on Fillmore B4
19 Harry's Bar B2
20 Jane B2
21 Social Study B4

Entertainment (p141)

22 Boom Boom Room B3
23 Fillmore Auditorium B4
24 Sheba Piano Lounge B4
25 Sundance Kabuki Cinema B3

Shopping (p143)

26 Alice & Olivia B1
27 Benefit B2
28 Brooklyn Circus B4
Crossroads (see 37)
29 Ichiban Kan C3
30 Japan Center C3
Jonathan Adler (see 27)
Katsura Garden (see 3)
Kinokuniya Books & Stationery (see 3)
Kohshi (see 9)
31 Margaret O'Leary B1
32 Mudpie B2
33 Nest B1
34 New People C3
35 Sanko Cooking Supply C3
36 Soko Hardware C3
37 Zinc Details B2

Sports & Activities (p145)

38 Kabuki Springs & Spa B3
Real Escape Game (see 34)

Sleeping (p241)

39 Hotel Kabuki C3
40 Queen Anne Hotel D2

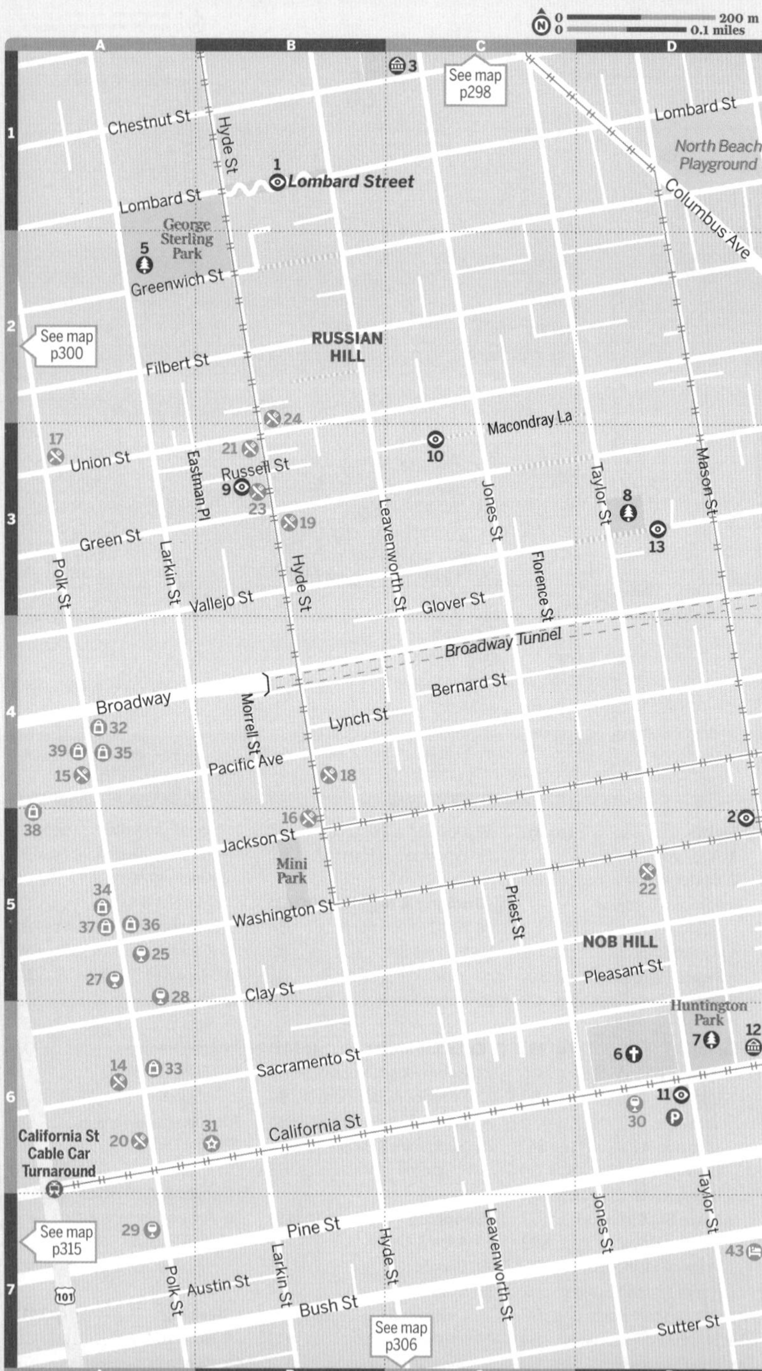

200 m
0.1 miles
See map p298
See map p300
See map p315
See map p306
Lombard Street
RUSSIAN HILL
NOB HILL
North Beach Playground
George Sterling Park
Mini Park
Huntington Park
California St Cable Car Turnaround
Broadway Tunnel
Chestnut St
Lombard St
Greenwich St
Filbert St
Union St
Green St
Vallejo St
Broadway
Pacific Ave
Jackson St
Washington St
Clay St
Sacramento St
California St
Pine St
Austin St
Bush St
Sutter St
Macondray La
Russell St
Glover St
Bernard St
Lynch St
Pleasant St
Columbus Ave
Hyde St
Larkin St
Polk St
Eastman Pl
Morrell St
Leavenworth St
Jones St
Florence St
Taylor St
Mason St
Priest St

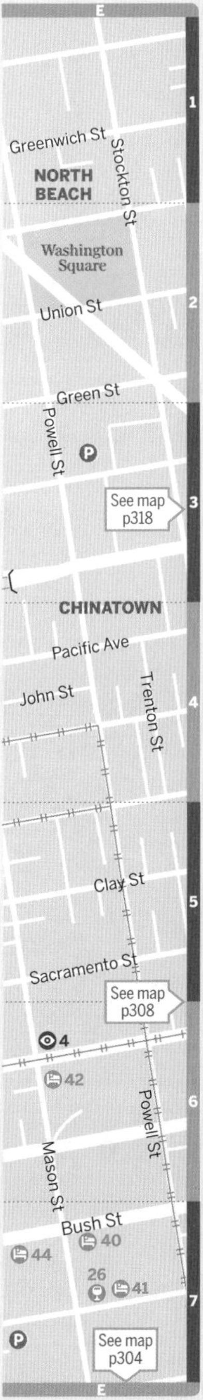

Top Sights (p131)
1 Lombard Street ... B1

Sights (p132)
2 Cable Car Museum ... D5
3 Diego Rivera Gallery ... C1
4 Fairmont San Francisco ... E6
5 George Sterling Park ... A2
6 Grace Cathedral ... D6
7 Huntington Park ... D6
8 Ina Coolbrith Park ... D3
9 Jack Kerouac's Love Shack ... B3
10 Macondray Lane ... C3
11 Masonic Auditorium and Temple ... D6
12 Pacific-Union Club ... D6
13 Vallejo St Steps ... D3

Eating (p137)
14 Acquerello ... A6
15 Cheese Plus ... A4
16 Cocotte ... B5
17 Leopold's ... A3
18 Seven Hills ... B4
19 Stone's Throw ... B3
20 Swan Oyster Depot ... A6
21 Swensen's ... B3
22 Venticello ... D5
23 Za ... B3
24 Zarzuela ... B2

Drinking & Nightlife (p140)
25 Amélie ... A5
26 Cantina ... E7
27 Cinch ... A5
28 Harper & Rye ... A5
29 Hi-Lo Club ... A7
30 The Big 4 ... D6
Tonga Room ... (see 4)
Top of the Mark ... (see 42)

Entertainment (p142)
31 Encore Karaoke Lounge ... B6

Shopping (p142)
32 Cris ... A4
33 Good Vibrations ... A6
34 Johnson Leathers ... A5
35 Molte Cose ... A4
36 Picnic ... A5
37 Relove ... A5
38 Studio ... A5
39 Velvet da Vinci ... A4

Sleeping (p240)
Fairmont San Francisco ... (see 4)
40 Golden Gate Hotel ... E7
41 Hotel Rex ... E7
42 Mark Hopkins Intercontinental ... E6
43 Petite Auberge ... D7
44 White Swan Inn ... E7

E
Greenwich St
Stockton St
NORTH BEACH
Washington Square
Union St
Green St
Powell St
See map p318
CHINATOWN
Pacific Ave
John St
Trenton St
Clay St
Sacramento St
See map p308
Powell St
Mason St
Bush St
See map p304
E

NORTH BEACH & CHINATOWN

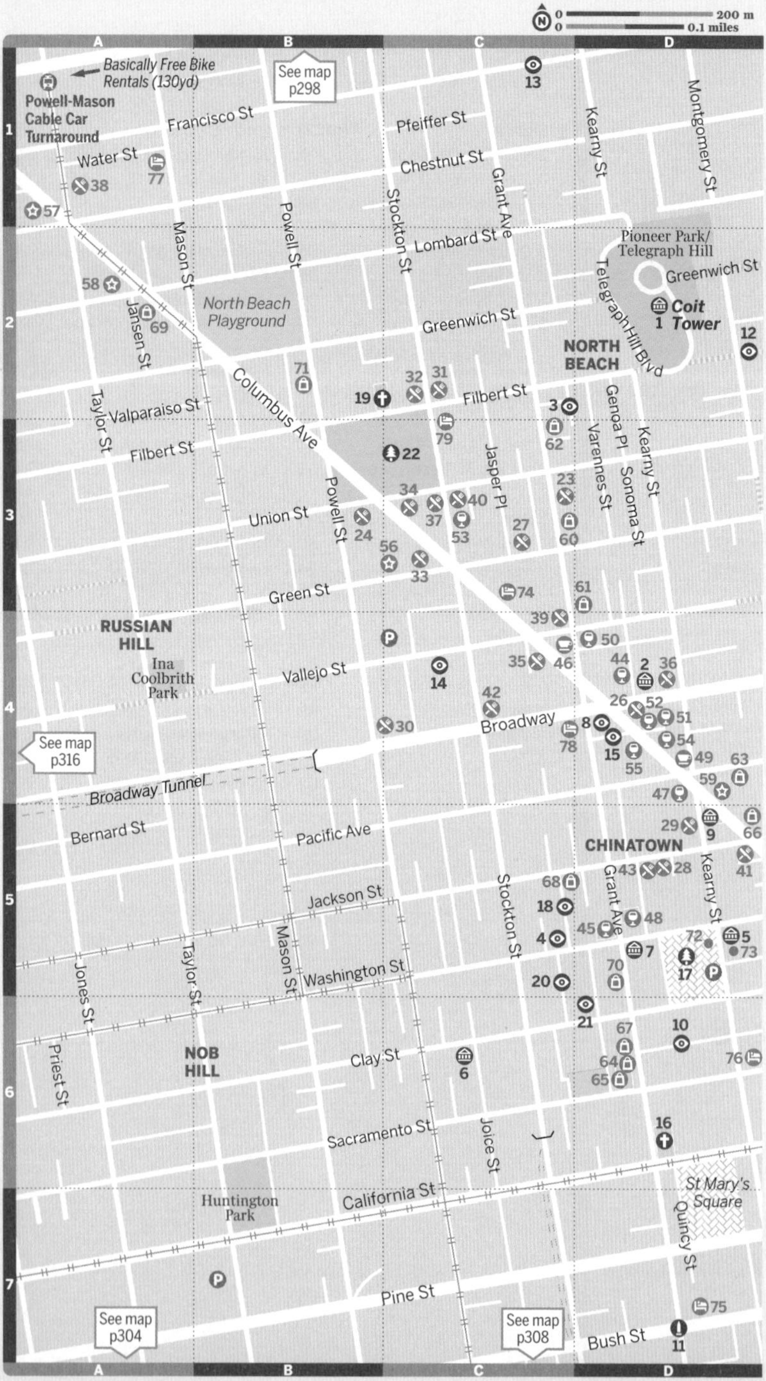

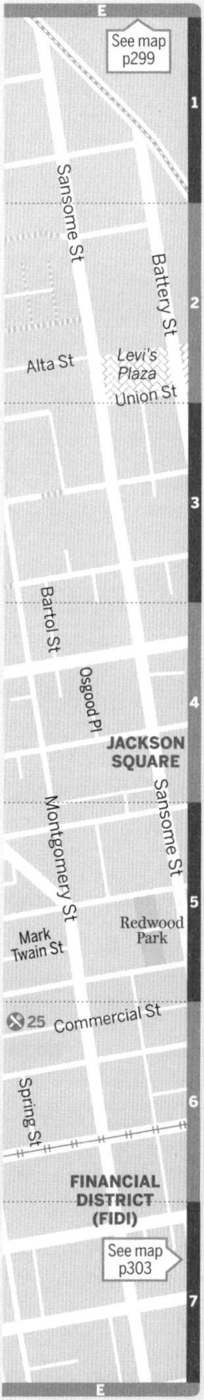
E
See map p299
1
Sansome St
Battery St
2
Alta St
Levi's Plaza
Union St
3
Bartol St
Osgood Pl
4
JACKSON SQUARE
Sansome St
Montgomery St
5
Redwood Park
Mark Twain St
25
Commercial St
6
Spring St
FINANCIAL DISTRICT (FIDI)
See map p303
7
E

Top Sights (p112)
1 Coit Tower D2

Sights (p113)
2 Beat Museum D4
3 Bob Kaufman Alley C2
4 Chinatown Alleyways C5
5 Chinese Culture Center D5
6 Chinese Historical Society of America C6
7 Chinese Telephone Exchange D5
8 City Lights D4
9 Columbus Tower D5
10 Commercial Street D6
11 Dragon's Gate D7
12 Filbert Street Steps D2
13 Francisco St Steps C1
14 Good Luck Parking Garage C4
15 Jack Kerouac Alley D4
16 Old St Mary's Cathedral & Square D6
17 Portsmouth Square D5
18 Ross Alley C5
19 Saints Peter & Paul Church B2
20 Spofford Alley C5
21 Tin How Temple D6
22 Washington Square C3

Eating (p119)
23 Cafe Jacqueline C3
24 Cinecittà B3
25 City View E6
26 E' Tutto Qua D4
27 Golden Boy C3
28 Great Eastern Restaurant D5
29 House of Nanking D5
30 Lai Hong Lounge C4
31 Liguria Bakery C2
32 Mama's C2
33 Mara's Italian Pastry C3
34 Mario's Bohemian Cigar Store Cafe C3
35 Molinari C4
36 Naked Lunch D4
37 Park Tavern C3
38 Pat's Cafe A1
39 Ristorante Ideale C4
40 Tony's Coal-Fired Pizza & Slice House C3
41 Trestle D5
42 Yuet Lee C4
43 Z & Y D5

Drinking & Nightlife (p125)
44 15 Romolo D4
45 Buddha Lounge D5
Cafe Zoetrope .... (see 9)
46 Caffe Trieste C4
47 Comstock Saloon D4
48 Li Po D5
49 Réveille D4
50 Saloon D4
51 Specs Museum Cafe D4
52 The Devil's Acre D4
53 Tony Nik's C3
54 Tosca Cafe D4
55 Vesuvio D4

Entertainment (p126)
56 Beach Blanket Babylon C3
57 Bimbo's 365 Club A1
58 Cobb's Comedy Club A2
59 Doc's Lab D4

Shopping (p127)
60 101 Music C3
61 Al's Attire D3
62 Aria C3
63 Artist & Craftsman Supply D4
64 Chinatown Kite Shop D6
65 Clarion Music Center D6
66 Eden & Eden D5
67 Far East Flea Market D6
68 Golden Gate Fortune Cookie Company C5
69 Lyle Tuttle Tattoo Art Museum & Shop A2
70 Red Blossom Tea Company D5
71 San Francisco Rock Posters & Collectibles B2

Sports & Activities (p118)
72 Chinatown Alleyway Tours D5
73 Chinatown Heritage Walking Tours D5
Drag Me Along Tours . (see 72)

Sleeping (p239)
74 Hotel Bohème C3
75 Orchard Garden Hotel D7
76 Pacific Tradewinds Hostel D6
77 San Remo Hotel A1
78 SW Hotel C4
79 Washington Square Inn C3

THE CASTRO

Sights (p172)
- Castro Theatre ....(see 36)
- 1 Corona Heights Park A2
- 2 GLBT History Museum B4
- Golden Gate Model Railroad Club .... (see 5)
- 3 Harvey Milk & Jane Warner Plazas B3
- 4 Nobby Clarke Mansion A4
- 5 Randall Junior Museum A2

Eating (p173)
- 6 Anchor Oyster Bar B4
- 7 Burgermeister D1
- 8 Chile Pies D2
- 9 Dinosaurs C2
- 10 Frances C3
- 11 Hecho C2
- 12 La Méditerranée B2
- 13 L'Ardoise C1
- 14 Mollie Stone's Market .. B4
- 15 Starbelly C2
- 16 Super Duper Burger B2
- 17 Taqueria Zapata B4

Drinking & Nightlife (p176)
- 18 440 Castro B3
- 19 Badlands B4
- 20 Beaux B3
- 21 Blackbird D1
- 22 Cafe B3
- 23 Cafe Flore C2
- 24 Edge B4
- 25 Hearth Coffee Roasters B3
- 26 HiTops C2
- 27 Lookout B2
- 28 Midnight Sun B4
- 29 Mix B4
- 30 Moby Dick B4
- 31 QBar B3
- 32 Samovar Tea Lounge ... C3
- 33 Toad Hall B4
- 34 Twin Peaks Tavern B3

Entertainment (p178)
- 35 Cafe du Nord/Swedish American Hall C1
- 36 Castro Theatre B3

Shopping (p179)
- 37 Alfio B4
- 38 Books Inc C2
- 39 Castro Farmers Market C2
- 40 Cliff's Variety B3
- 41 Human Rights Campaign Action Center & Store B4
- 42 Kenneth Wingard B3
- 43 Local Take B3
- 44 Sui Generis B3
- 45 Unionmade C3
- 46 Worn Out West B3

Sights (p173)

1 22nd St Hill C1

Eating (p176)

2 Barney's Burgers A2
3 Lovejoy's Tea Room C3
4 Noe Valley Bakery A2

Shopping (p179)

5 Ambiance B2
6 Isso C2
7 Omnivore C3
8 PlumpJack Wines B2
9 Rabat B2
10 The Podolls B2

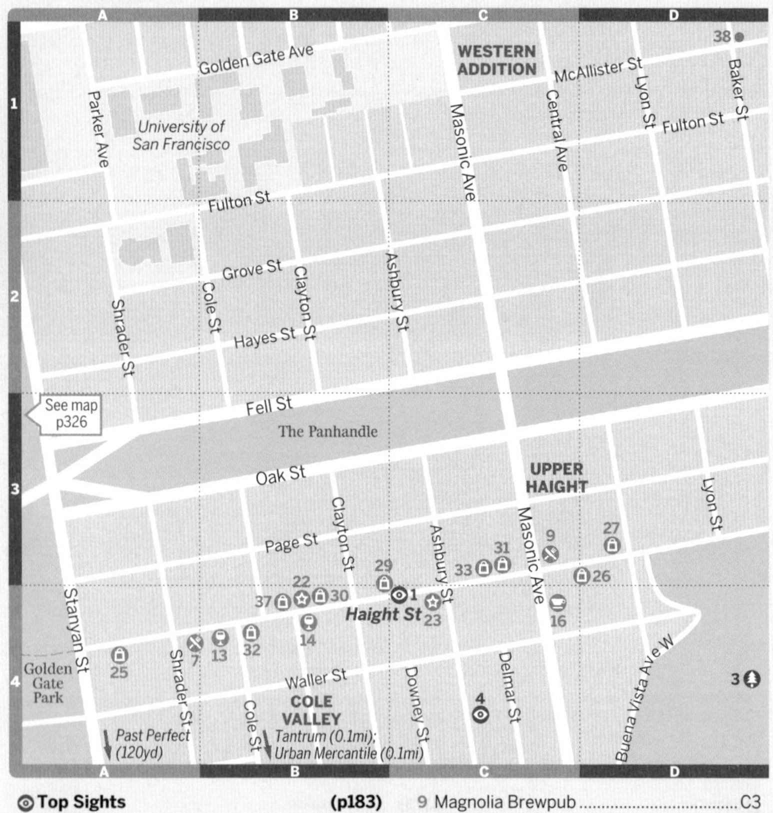

Top Sights (p183)

1 Haight St C4

Sights (p184)

2 Alamo Square Park F1
3 Buena Vista Park D4
4 Grateful Dead House C4

Eating (p184)

5 Axum Cafe G3
6 Bar Crudo E1
7 Escape from New York Pizza A4
8 Little Chihuahua F3
9 Magnolia Brewpub C3
10 Ragazza F3
11 Rosamunde Sausage Grill G3
12 Three Twins Ice Cream H2

Drinking & Nightlife (p190)

13 Alembic B4
14 Aub Zam Zam B4
15 Candybar E1
16 Coffee to the People C4
17 Madrone Art Bar F2
18 Noc Noc G3
19 Toronado G3
20 Uva Enoteca G3

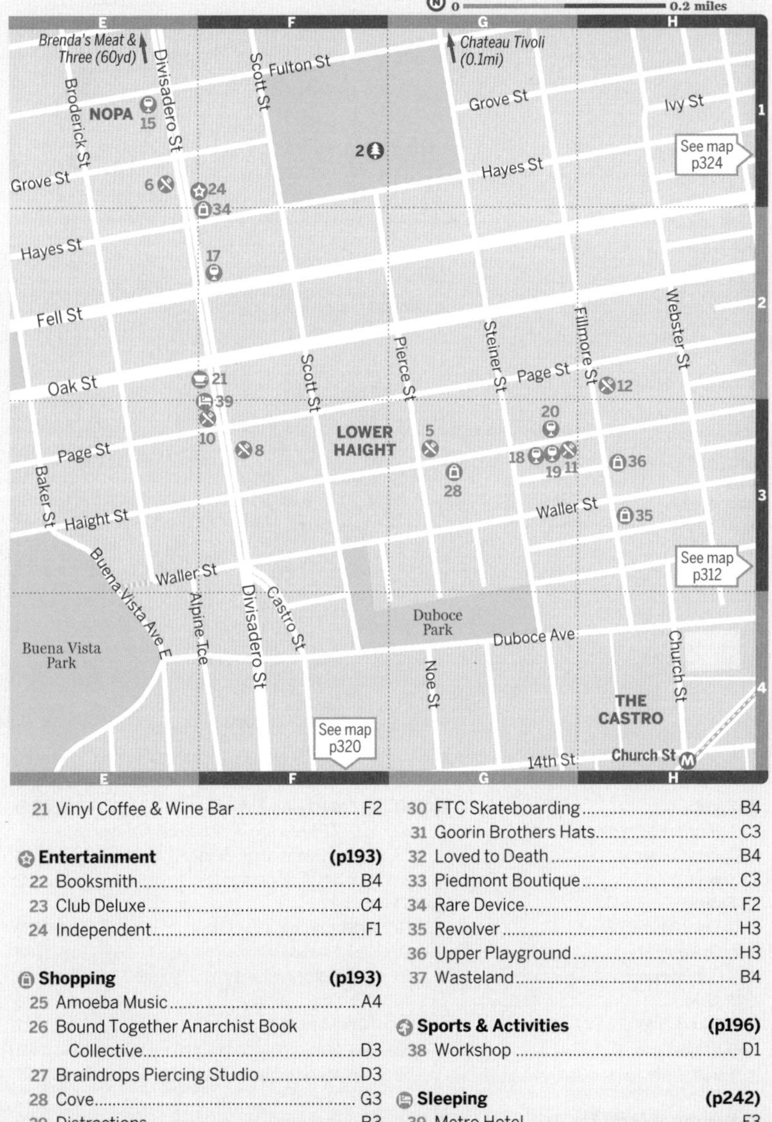

21 Vinyl Coffee & Wine Bar F2

Entertainment (p193)

22 Booksmith B4
23 Club Deluxe C4
24 Independent F1

Shopping (p193)

25 Amoeba Music A4
26 Bound Together Anarchist Book Collective D3
27 Braindrops Piercing Studio D3
28 Cove G3
29 Distractions B3
30 FTC Skateboarding B4
31 Goorin Brothers Hats C3
32 Loved to Death B4
33 Piedmont Boutique C3
34 Rare Device F2
35 Revolver H3
36 Upper Playground H3
37 Wasteland B4

Sports & Activities (p196)

38 Workshop D1

Sleeping (p242)

39 Metro Hotel F3

HAYES VALLEY

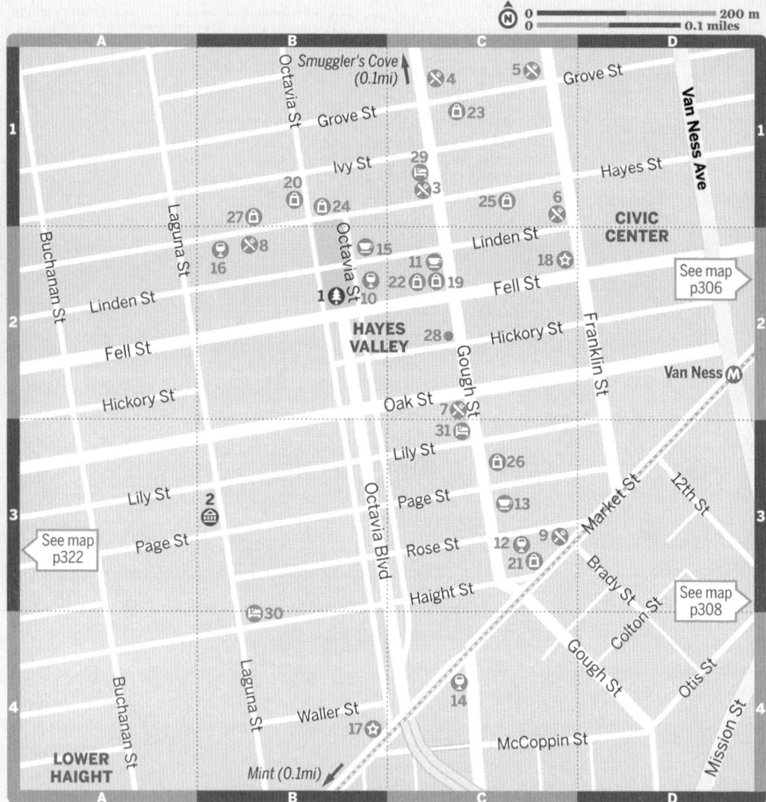

Sights (p184)
- 1 Patricia's Green B2
- 2 Zen Center B3

Eating (p187)
- 3 Chez Maman West C1
- 4 DragonEats C1
- 5 Jardinière C1
- 6 Nojo C1
- 7 Rich Table C2
- 8 Souvla B2
- 9 Zuni Cafe C3

Drinking & Nightlife (p192)
- 10 Biergarten B2
- 11 Blue Bottle Coffee Company C2
- 12 Hôtel Biron C3
- 13 KitTea C3
- 14 Martuni's C4
- 15 Ritual Coffee B2
- 16 Two Sisters Bar & Books B2

Entertainment (p192)
- 17 SF Lesbian Gay Bisexual Transgender Community Center B4
- 18 SFJAZZ Center C2

Shopping (p195)
- 19 Fatted Calf C2
- 20 Gather B1
- 21 Green Arcade C3
- 22 Isotope C2
- 23 MAC C1
- 24 Marine Layer B1
- 25 Nancy Boy C1
- 26 Paloma C3
- 27 Reliquary B1

Sports & Activities (p196)
- 28 Makeshift Society C2

Sleeping (p242)
- 29 Hayes Valley Inn C1
- 30 Parsonage B4
- 31 Sleep Over Sauce C3

GOLDEN GATE PARK & THE AVENUES *Map on p326*

Top Sights (p199)
1 California Academy of Sciences G4
2 Conservatory of Flowers H4
3 de Young Museum G4
4 Golden Gate Park E4
5 Japanese Tea Garden F4
6 San Francisco Botanical Garden F5

Sights (p202)
7 16th Ave Steps F6
8 Buffalo Paddock C4
9 Children's Playground H4
10 Coastal Trail B1
11 Columbarium H3
12 Dahlia Garden H4
13 Frankenart Mart G3
14 Hunter S Thompson Crash Pad H5
15 Internet Archive F2
16 Legion of Honor B2
17 Lincoln Park B1
18 National AIDS Memorial Grove H4
19 Ocean Beach A5
20 Shakespeare Garden G4
21 Stow Lake E4
22 Sutro Baths A2

Eating (p204)
23 Aziza E2
24 Burma Superstar G2
25 Cassava C3
26 Cinderella Russian Bakery G3
27 Dragon Beaux E2
28 Genki G2
29 Halu G2
30 Kabuto F2
31 Manna G5
32 Masala Dosa G5
33 Nopalito G5
34 Outerlands B6
35 Pretty Please Bakeshop G2
36 San Tung G5
37 Spices G2
38 Underdog F5
39 Wing Lee G2

Drinking & Nightlife (p207)
540 Club .... (see 39)
40 Beach Chalet A4
41 Hollow F5
42 Social G5
43 Tommy's Mexican Restaurant E2
44 Trad'r Sam D2
45 Trouble Coffee & Coconut Club B6
46 Velo Rouge Café H3

Entertainment (p208)
47 Balboa Theatre C3
48 Four Star Theater E2
49 Neck of the Woods G2
50 The Plough & the Stars H2

Shopping (p208)
51 Foggy Notion G2
General Store .... (see 34)
52 Green Apple Books G2
53 Green Apple Books on the Park G5
54 Helpers House of Couture H3
55 Jade Chocolates G2
56 Last Straw B5
57 Mollusk B5
Park Life .... (see 50)
58 The Great Overland Book Company G5
59 Urban Bazaar G5

Sports & Activities (p210)
60 Aqua Surf Shop B6
61 Golden Gate JOAD B4
62 Golden Gate Municipal Golf Course B4
63 Golden Gate Park Bike & Skate G3
64 Lawn Bowling Club H4
65 Lincoln Park Golf Course C2
66 Lindy in the Park G4
67 On the Run G5
68 San Fran Cyclo H3
69 San Francisco Disc Golf D4
70 San Francisco Model Yacht Club C4
71 Stow Lake Boathouse F4

Sleeping (p242)
72 Seal Rock Inn A3

Key on p325

GOLDEN GATE PARK & THE AVENUES

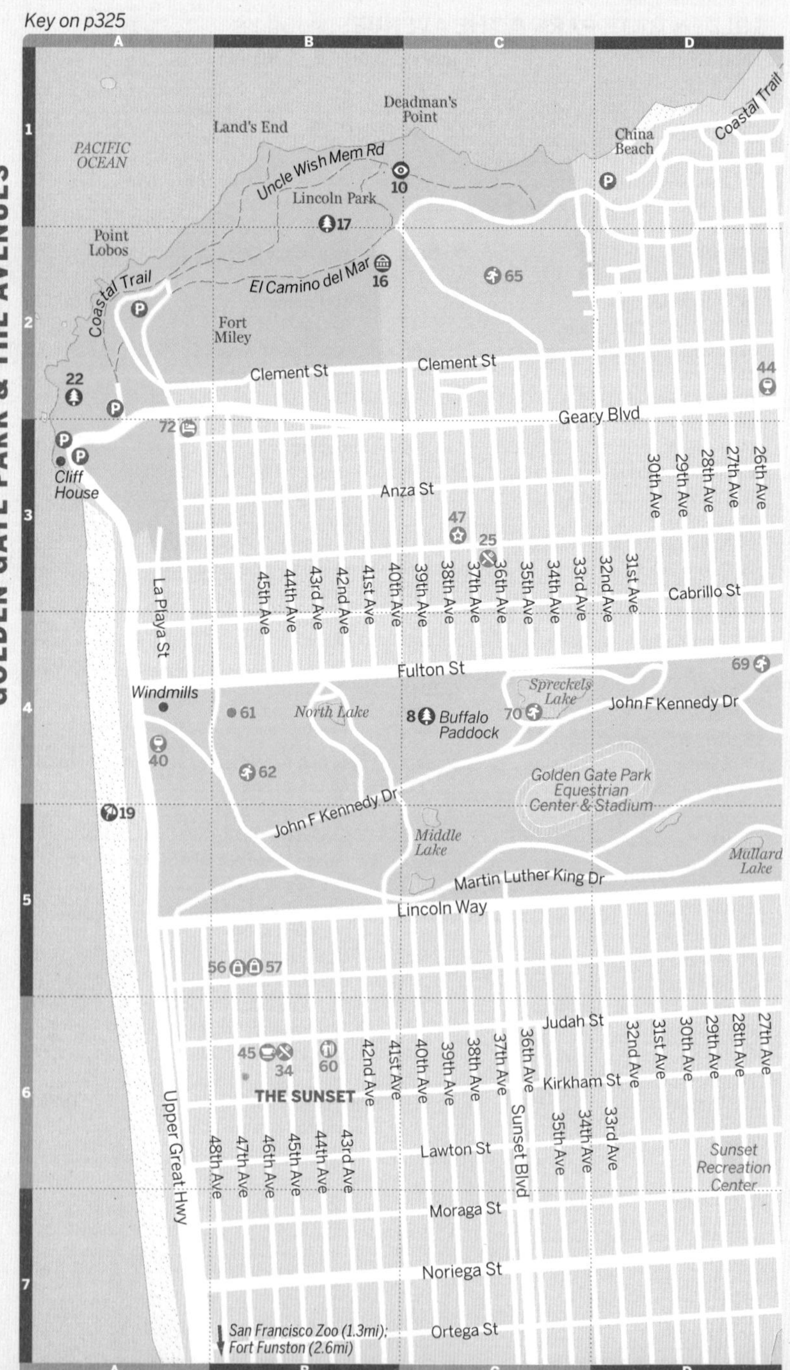